DICTIONARY OF

BUILDING

DICTIONARY OF
BUILDING

JOHN S. SCOTT

Third Edition

GRANADA
London Toronto Sydney New York

Granada Technical Books
Granada Publishing Ltd
8 Grafton Street, London W1X 3LA

First published in paperback
by Penguin Books 1964
Second edition 1974
Third edition 1984
This cased edition first published
in 1984 by Granada Publishing Limited
by arrangement with Penguin Books Limited

British Library Cataloguing in Publication Data
Scott, John S.
Dictionary of building.—3rd ed
1. Building—Dictionaries
I. Title
690'.03'21   TH9

ISBN 0–246–12264–1

Printed and bound in Great Britain by
Richard Clay (The Chaucer Press) Ltd,
Bungay, Suffolk

ABBREVIATIONS

(*1*) *Subjects*

carp. = carpentry
d.o. = drawing office practice
elec. = electrical
joi. = joinery
mech. = mechanical engineering

pai. = painting
pla. = plastering, floor, and wall tiling
plu. = plumbing
q.s. = quantity surveying
tim. = conversion and working of timber

The same sense of a term may be used in several of the subjects listed above. For the scope of each subject, see its definition in the text. Bricklaying, masonry, building drainage, and other general building terms are included but not classified under an abbreviation.

(*2*) *Dimensions*

For abbreviations of units, see the list of conversion factors on pages 8 and 9, also *The Penguin Dictionary of Civil Engineering*.

(*3*) *Authorities*

ASHVE = American Society of Heating and Ventilation Engineers
ASTM = American Society for Testing and Materials
BS (or BSS) = British Standard (Specification)
BSCP = British Standard Code of Practice
BSI = British Standards Institution

CROSS REFERENCES

Cross references are indicated by italic type, those to the *Dictionary of Civil Engineering* by the letter *C*.

Because this book cannot conveniently exceed 400 pages and because there are so many building terms, we have two volumes, a civil engineering and a building one.

The commonest building terms often have many names. To save space the explanation of each term is printed only once, with its alternative names, or at least some of them. At the alphabetical position of the alternative names, the entry is only 'See (main entry)'. But the main entry may be in the other volume. We are sorry about this unavoidable annoyance for the reader but at least half of the *Dictionary of Civil Engineering* is as useful to builders as it is to civil engineers.

No one can know everything. The author is always happy to correct mistakes and to learn of any improvements which might enable more information to be got into less space.

Dictionary of Civil Engineering
characteristic strength and limit state design, cranes, derricks, bridges, concrete, prestressed, reinforced, lightweight or plain, cast iron, steels
concrete formwork, timbering of excavations, space frames, tension structures, most scientific terms such as dewpoint, terotechnology, electro-osmosis for deep excavation in silt, sewerage, sewage disposal, hydrology, non-destructive testing, geophysics applied to civil engineering, welding

Dictionary of Building
air houses (inflatables)
building trades, their tools and materials, brazing, soldering, capillary joints, silver brazing, carpentry, timber houses, shoring of buildings, contracts, bills of quantities, quantity surveying, cracking in walls, dampness in buildings, house drainage, heating and ventilation, insulating materials and techniques, degree days, noise insulation, plastics, synthetic resins

ACKNOWLEDGEMENTS

Her Majesty's Stationery Office's free, well-indexed, sectional list (Building) lists the titles of Building Research Establishment publications, including the monthly digests (some 150 in all).

Useful annual publications include several building price books, also 'Specification' (five volumes in 1980) and, one of the most essential, the British Standards Institution Yearbook, the key to the encyclopaedia of information to be found in the 6000 or so British Standards (BS) and Codes of Practice (BSCP). It has over 1000 pages, lists all BSI publications and names the libraries where complete sets of standards and codes are kept and can be studied, in the UK and abroad. BSI Handbook No 3 summarizes 1500 British Standards concerned with building and is published in four loose-leaf binders. Other BSI special publications describe how to specify mortars, how to select smoke-reducing coal-fired stoves, etc. BS and BSCP describe only accepted practice; they cannot describe ultra-modern techniques because this might inhibit the development of these techniques.

Extracts from BS and BSCP are reproduced by permission of the British Standards Institution, 2 Park Street, London W1A 2BS.

Although the pronoun 'he' is used for convenience when referring to workers in the building trade, this should now read 'he' or 'she' as women are entering the field in increasing numbers.

The author has been grateful over many years for the conscientiousness and skill of the Reprints Department of Penguin Books, and of Michael Berdinner who was involved in editing the first edition.

IMPERIAL-TO-METRIC (MAINLY SI)
CONVERSION FACTORS AND ABBREVIATIONS OF UNITS

The 500 pages of BS 350 (*Conversion Factors and Tables*) are the best source of conversion factors, but those given below are the few that builders really need. Others are printed in the Penguin *Dictionary of Civil Engineering*.

LENGTH
: 39·37 inches (in.) = 3·281 feet (ft) = 1 metre (m)
25·4 millimetres (mm) = 1 in. = 2·54 centimetres (cm)
1 mile = 1760 yards = 5280 ft = 63,360 in.
= 1·6093 kilometre (km)

AREA
: 1 in^2 = 6·45 cm^2 = 645 mm^2
10·764 ft^2 = 1 m^2; 100 m^2 = 1 are = 119·6 $yard^2$
10,000 m^2 = 100 ares = 1 hectare (ha) = 2·47 acres
4840 $yard^2$ = 1 acre = 0·4047 ha; 1 $mile^2$ = 2·59 km^2

VOLUME
: 1 imperial gallon contains 4·546 litres = 10 lb of water
1 United States wet gallon contains 3·785 litres
1 m^3 = 1000 litres = 35·315 ft^3 = 1 tonne of water
1 ft^3 = 28·32 litres

TEMPERATURE
: 9 deg. Fahrenheit (F.) = 5 deg. Kelvin, Celsius or Centigrade (K. or C.). Also 0° C = 32° F and 100° C = 212° F.

WEIGHT or MASS
: 16 ounces (oz) = 1 pound (1b) = 454 grams (g)
2240 lb = 1 long ton = 1016 kilograms (kg)
1 kg = 2·2046 lb, so 1000 kg or 1 tonne = 2204·6 lb

FORCE
: 1 pound force (lb f) = 4·448 newton (N) and
1 N = 0·2248 lb f
1 kilogram force = 2·2046 lb f = 9·807 N

PRESSURE or STRESS
: 1 lb per $inch^2$ (psi) = 6894·8 $newton/m^2$ (N/m^2)
= 6·8948 $kilonewtons/m^2$ (kN/m^2)
1000 kN/m^2 = 1 $newton/millimetre^2$ (N/mm^2)
1 $meganewton/square metre$ (MN/m^2) = 1 N/mm^2 = 145 psi
1 standard atmosphere = 101·325 kN/m^2
= 0·101 325 N/mm^2
1 bar = 100 kN/m^2 = 100 Kilopascal (kPa)
NOTE The pascal (Pa) is an S I unit for pressure or force per unit area, adopted in 1971 by the Conférence Générale des Poids et Mesures. Thus
1 pascal (Pa) = 1 N/m^2 and 6·895 kPa = 1 psi
1 kilopascal (kPa) = 1 kN/m^2 = 0·001 N/mm^2
1 megapascal (MPa) = 1 MN/m^2 = 1 N/mm^2

HEAT
: 1 British thermal unit (Btu) = 1055 joule (J)
= 1·055 kilojoule (kJ)
= 252 gram-calories (c)
On the Continent the kilogram-calorie or large calorie of 1000 gram-calories has been used but as these are not SI

units they will probably drop out in favour of the joule (J) and kilojoule (kJ) so that the main conversion will be:

1 Btu = 1055 joule = 1·055 kJ

1000 Btu = 1·055 megajoule (MJ)

1 Btu/hour = 0·293 J/second = 0·293 watt (W)

3415 Btu/hour = 1 kilowatt (kW)

THERMAL CONDUCTIVITY or K-VALUE

1 Btu/in. ft^2 hour degree F. = 0·144 watt/metre deg. C.

THERMAL CONDUCTANCE
and AIR-TO-AIR TRANSMITTANCE or U-VALUE

1 Btu/ft^2 hour degree F. = 5·678 watt/m^2 degree C, U-value. Though nearly the same unit, the U-value and the conductance are different. The air-to-air transmittance or U-value gives a direct measure of the insulating usefulness of a wall, roof, etc. The conductance is numerically slightly larger (therefore less insulating) because it does not include the air resistance each side of the wall or roof and is therefore less immediately useful to the builder than the U-value.

A

abrasion resistance [pai.] The resistance of a *finish* to wear by the fingers or by even softer surfaces.

abrasives Hard materials (usually powders, grits, or stones) in various forms such as paste, *glasspaper*, emery wheels, or water-resisting emery cloth, used for rubbing down paint, wood, or other building materials, or for sharpening tools. The best known abrasives are quartz or flint sand, powdered glass, carborundum, emery (corundum), garnet, *diamond* (*C*).

ABS Acrylonitrile-butadiene-styrene, a *plastics* from which pipes and fittings are made, suitable for pressures up to 15 atmospheres (BS 5392). Because ABS softens at a temperature higher than *polyvinyl chloride*, it is often used for waste pipes, but is flammable, ignitable and releases the poisonous gas carbon monoxide when it burns.

absorption (1) The water absorbed by a brick, concrete, etc., as a percentage of its dry weight. *Engineering bricks* in Britain are boiled for five hours to measure their absorption. Absorption below 7% usually indicates good frost resistance but some bricks with 12% absorption resist frost well (BRE Digest 164). *Brick damp courses* are made from engineering bricks.

(2) In acoustics, absorptive materials reduce echoes (reverberation) within a room, but have little effect on the passing of sound through a wall or floor, except insofar as they reduce the sound within the room. Soft partition or wall surfaces, being more absorptive than hard, may or may not improve acoustics but they will reduce the *reverberation period*. So will the fitting of windows or other openings in the walls, and the presence of people. *See* **audiograph, sabin**.

(3) *See* **absorptive power**.

absorption rate, suction, initial of absorption The amount of water absorbed by a brick when it is partly immersed in water for one minute. This property is used in USA for describing bricks. *See* **water retentivity**, *and above*.

absorptive power, emissivity The relative rate of emission or absorption of heat from a body, compared with that from a similarly shaped black body in the same conditions.

abstracting [q.s.] The process, before drawing up a *bill of quantities*, of assembling and adding similar tasks in the *contract* which will be paid for at the same price under one *item*. The items are arranged in trades to make billing easier.

abutment An intersection between a roof and a wall. *See also C*.

abutment piece [carp.] (USA) A *sill* or *sole plate*.

abutting tenons [carp.] Two *tenons* entering from opposite sides and meeting in the centre of a *mortise*.

accelerated weathering, a. ageing Exposure in testing of a building material to more severe cycles of heat, frost, wetness and dryness than is natural.

accelerator (1) A substance such as *calcium chloride* formerly added to concrete or mortar (up to 1·5% by weight of the cement) to hasten its hardening rate; or an inorganic salt such as alum or K_2SO_4 or $ZnSO_4$ added to *anhydrous* calcium sulphate to make a useful wall plaster; or a hardener or *catalyst* added to a *synthetic resin* to harden it. BS 5075, which specifies concrete *admixtures*, advises that chlorides should not be used in any *prestressed concrete* (*C*) where the *tendons* (*C*) are in close contact with the concrete, nor in reinforced concrete, nor in concretes made with high-alumina, sulphate-resisting, nor supersulphated cements. Chlorides increase metallic corrosion. If aggregates are obtained from the sea, the 1·5% should be reduced because seawater contains 3·5% chloride. Since calcium chloride also increases the *shrinkage (C)* of concretes, many engineers are reluctant to specify calcium chloride in any reinforced or prestressed concrete. *See* **separate application**.

(2) A pump for circulating the water through a heating system. *Small-bore systems* include a pump, unlike the older systems which used larger pipes.

access An approach. A maintenance access is usually a removable panel in a duct, chase, or conduit.

access eye, inspection fitting (USA **cleanout**) [plu.] An opening in a *drain pipe*, duct, etc., closed by a plate bolted or wedged on, often provided at bends to enable the pipe to be rodded. *See* **rodding eye**.

acetal resins [plu.] Resins made by polymerizing formaldehyde. They can replace die-cast metal in e.g. *pillar taps*.

acetone [pai.] A highly flammable, powerful, organic *solvent* used for removing paint or finger-nail varnish. It was part of many aeroplane dopes and *lacquers*.

acoustical fibre building board Low density *fibre board*, sometimes perforated to increase its sound *absorption*.

acoustical reduction factor The reciprocal of the *acoustical transmission factor*.

acoustical transmission factor Of a surface, partition, or device, at a given frequency and under specified conditions, the ratio which the sound energy transmitted through and beyond the surface, partition, or device, bears to that incident upon it (BS 661). The *sound-reduction factor* is its reciprocal.

acoustic clip *See* **floor clip**.

acoustic construction Any building method aimed at reducing the sound entering or leaving a room, for example *discontinuous construction*.

acoustic plaster Wall plaster having a high sound *absorption*, often containing aluminium powder which evolves gas on contact with water. This gas remains in the set plaster, giving it a honeycombed structure, especially with a porous slag aggregate or *vermiculite*. Lime plaster, though its absorption is not high, has twice the absorption of gypsum plasters, which are *hard plasters* and poorly absorptive.

acoustics The science of sound. The sound *absorption* and transmission of walls, and their shape, control the acoustic properties of rooms.

acoustic screen, a. shed A lightweight structure, e.g. of timber frame and 6 mm (¼ in.) thick plywood, completely surrounding a man working with a concrete breaker or other noisy tool. Although the screen weighs only about 5 kg/m^2 (1 lb/ft^2) it reduces the noise by some 20 decibels. The workman has to wear ear muffs or ear plugs, possibly also goggles and dust mask.

acoustic tile Square blocks, often perforated, made of soft, sound-absorbent material such as *cork, insulating fibre board*, or plaster, instead of hard *ceramics* with low sound *absorption*.

acrylic resin paint [pai.] *Synthetic resin* paints, chemically similar to *Perspex*, which are very durable and hold colour well. Acrylics have many other uses in building.

adaptor [elec., plu.] A device for connecting a pipe or electrical supply point to another of different design. Electrical plug adaptors are widely used. In pipelaying, adaptors can join *pitch fibre* pipes to pipes of other materials – rainwater or soil pipes.

additive An *admixture*.

adds [q.s.] Overall quantities, before *deducts* such as window openings are subtracted from them.

adhesion (1) **bond** The sticking together of structural parts by mechanical or chemical bonding, using a *cement* or *glue*. Timber parts are stuck with glue, bricks are bonded in *mortar*, and steel is bonded to concrete by its adhesion with the cement. *See* **specific adhesion** (*C*), **suction**.

(2) [pai.] The attachment of a *paint* or *varnish* film to its *ground*.

adhesives (1) [tim.] *Glues*.

(2) *Bitumen* (*C*), *resins*, *mastics*, and so on for fixing *wall tiles*, floor blocks, etc.

admixture, additive In concrete, mortar or plaster, a substance other than *aggregate*, cement, plaster or water, added in small quantities to alter the properties of the mix or of the hardened substance. Admixtures, especially in plasters, require the written permission of the designer, though *masonry cement* (BS 5224) contains an *air-entraining agent* (*C*) and sometimes other substances, but chlorides are forbidden. *See* BS 5075, *also* **mortar plasticizers**.

adobe Unburnt, sunbaked *bricks* or *blocks* about 45 × 30 × 10 cm (18 × 12 × 4 in.), containing straw chopped to around 15 cm (6 in.) length as reinforcement, in Central America, southwest USA, Australia, and other semi-arid regions. Lima Cathedral is built of adobe blocks. *See* **cob**.

adze (USA **adz**) [carp.] A tool like an axe, used for roughly surfacing timber, the predecessor of the *plane*. The cutting blade of an adze is perpendicular to the shaft, that of an axe is in the same plane. The operator strikes the timber towards himself and he must take care not to hurt himself. This very ancient tool is coming into its own in the *cutter block* used in many modern joinery machines. *See* **railway tools** (*C* illus.).

adze-eye hammer [carp.] A *claw hammer* in which the head has a socket which extends farther up the handle than usual. The term is American; but these excellent hammers are used also by British carpenters.

aerated concrete, cellular c. A lightweight, weak, highly insulating material, sometimes containing sand, easy to nail and saw with carpenter's tools. It is much weaker and has more *moisture movement* than ordinary concrete. *See* **gas c., lightweight c.**

African mahogany [tim.] The best-known timbers of this name imported to Britain are from West Africa, generally Nigeria or Ghana, of the Khaya family. (Many different species are exported from East and South Africa as mahogany.) Khaya is generally similar to *Honduras mahogany* but is less uniform and sometimes spongy or with *shake*. Makore and gaboon are other West African mahoganies.

after-flush [plu.] The small quantity of water remaining in the *cistern* after a w.c. pan is *flushed*. It trickles slowly down and remakes the *seal*.

after-tack [pai.] The defect of a paint film which has been *tack* free and then becomes *tacky*.

ageing (USA **aging**) [pai.] Storing *varnishes* during or after manufacture to improve their *gloss* and reduce *pinholing, crawling*, and *lining*. *See also* *C*.

agent, contractor's a. A civil engineer or other person who legally represents the *contractor* at the site.

aggregate Broken stone, slag, gravel, sand, or similar inert material which forms a substantial part of such materials as *plaster*, *concrete*, asphalt, or tarmacadam. Aggregate is described as coarse if it stays on a screen with 5 mm ($\frac{3}{16}$ in.) square holes, and as sand or fine aggregate if it passes through them.

Agrément Board (Now the **British Board of Agrément**) Set up by the Government in 1966 to encourage innovation in building by issuing *appraisal* certificates for inventions and practices, based on an agrément board founded in France in 1958. Its scope has been widened to include traditional products with an export potential. It is a member of the European Union of Agrément (UEAtc) which exists to enable appraisals in one country to be used in another. *See* **National Building Agency**.

airborne noise All sound is airborne but this term excludes impact noise such as footsteps which pass through a wall or floor before they become airborne and are heard.

air brick A perforated block built into a wall to ventilate a room or the underside of a wooden floor.

air brush [pai.] A small *spray gun*.

air change A quantity of fresh air equal to the volume of the room being ventilated. The standard of ventilation is described by the number of air changes per hour. Hot underground kitchens may need up to 60 changes, boiler houses, laundries, and smoking-rooms 10 to 20, classrooms 6, teashops 4, library reading-rooms and typists' offices 2, storerooms 1½.

air conditioning Bringing the air in a building to a desired temperature, purity, and humidity, often by washing with cold water and then heating or cooling the air, which is blown or sucked in as required. *See* **air change, air washer, modulated control, plenum system, unit air conditioner.** *and* BS 5643.

air-cooled slag Dense *blast-furnace slag*, often suitable for concrete aggregate or roadstone.

air-dry [tim.] A description of *timber* which has a *moisture content* in equilibrium with the surrounding air. In Britain, air-dry timber varies from 19% to 23% in moisture content, according to species and season.

air grating A perforated metal plate across a duct by which air enters a room. *See* **register**.

air gun A *spray gun*.

air house, air dome, balloon structure, inflatable, pneumatic architecture, pressurized structure, radome, etc. Some 40 000 air houses were inflated between 1950 and 1980. They are quick and cheap to build, maintain and move, and cover large spans without internal supports, but their fire risk is high and their life is short. They need *air locks* at entrances and a constant power supply to drive the fan, though the electricity to support a 60 × 30 m (200 × 100 ft) air house cost only £100 per quarter, a fraction of the cost of heating a house for three winter months, in Britain in 1981.

There are two main types of air house. The cheaper (pressurized or air-supported) have a tent-roof (the membrane) anchored to the ground at the edges, usually to concrete beams, and held up in the middle by an internal air pressure of 15 to 30 mm (0·6 to 1·2 in.) of water gauge. The second, costlier, but more convenient (air-inflated), have inflated stiffening ribs rather like inner tubes to hold the membrane up. They need neither air locks nor *anchorage*, so are more quickly erected. One man can erect a 47 m² (510 ft²) Numex hut in 8 minutes. Even smaller ones are used for car camping.

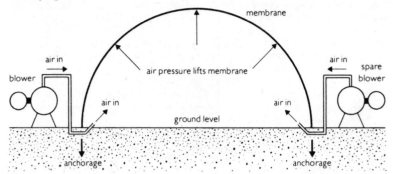

Air house – cross section.

A minimum of 100% spare fan and motor capacity is needed, plus stand-by generators in case of power cuts. The fan must provide one to four air changes per hour and in cold climates the air must be heated to melt the snow on the membrane. No solution has yet been found for *condensation* problems but insulation of the membrane is being tried. Nature has an infinite variety of structures that are inflated, mostly with water, from plant stalks to fruit and jellyfish. Structural engineers, however, have only recently had weldable strong membranes and trouble-free electric fans to work with. One fan in an air house had been running without trouble for 12 years by 1980, though in a cold winter the intake air might have to be heated to prevent icing up. (Institution of Structural Engineers; Air-supported structures symposium, 1980.)

Other inflated structures within our subject are *Fabridams* (*C*) and *Freyssinet's flat jack* (*C*). Air houses pay for themselves quickly when used to shelter urgent buildings being put up in winter, or on farms to protect early crops. (Illus. above and pp. 18, 115)

air lock (1) Any device for preventing flow of air, often merely two doors in series, one of which has to be closed before the other is opened, as in an *air house*. (Illus. p. 16) *See* **lobby, weather strip**.

(2) [plu.] A bubble of air, trapped in a pipe, that prevents the water flowing as it should. An air lock can sometimes be driven out without adding extra fittings, merely by connecting a high-pressure supply (the main) to the lowest point in the system – the drain valve. A hose is needed with good connections or the water may spray all over the cellar, but if the water is turned on gently the air bubble may be forced upwards. This should not, the first time at least, be attempted single-handed because the water is almost certain to overflow from the cistern at the roof, and this annoyance should be minimized by a helper announcing it to the person controlling the flow from the main, who can then close the valve. (Illus. p. 17)

(3) Yet another type of air lock, in a radiator which will not heat, is easily

cleared by 'bleeding' it. A tiny box spanner (*radiator key*), bought from a hardware shop, can be fitted into a valve at one of the two top corners of the radiator. When this valve is unscrewed, the air is bled off (released) and the radiator warms up. This may have to be done several days in succession at the beginning of the winter.

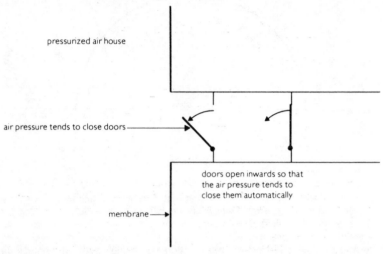

pressurized air house

air pressure tends to close doors

doors open inwards so that the air pressure tends to close them automatically

membrane →

Air lock. Preferably some mechanical or electrical device should prevent the two doors being opened at the same time, or there should be more than two doors (or both).

air shaft, light well An unroofed space within a large building, that provides some light and ventilation for windows facing it – often lined with *calcium silicate* bricks.

air slaking Chemical absorption, by *quicklime* or *cement*, of moisture from the air. Air slaking may in a few weeks so damage these *binders* as to make them useless.

air termination network Those parts of a lightning protective system at the roof, which collect the electrical discharges from the air, and lead them to the *lightning conductors*.

air test [plu.] Using a *screw plug* to block the top of a drain length (sometimes also a plug at its lower end) it is possible to pump air into a sound length of drain, and to test it by a *U-gauge* connected to the upper screw plug. This upper screw plug can be connected to the top of the *anti-siphonage pipe*, on the roof. The seals cannot withstand more than about 80 mm (3 in.) of water pressure, but a U-gauge is sensitive to small leaks. The test pressure is 4 cm (1·5 in.). The U-gauge is also used for testing the gas pipes fixed in a house, but the test pressure is then about 30 cm (12 in.). *See* **drain tests**.

air-to-air heat-transmission coefficient The *U-value*.

air-to-air resistance The resistance (R) to the passage of heat provided by a wall, the reciprocal of the *air-to-air heat-transmission coefficient*. $R = \frac{1}{U}$.

Compression joint fitted at a high point in a pipe circuit, so as to leak out possible air-locks. When flow ceases (evidence of a bubble), the fitting is unscrewed until the air is heard to escape. When the noise ceases, drops of water flow out and the joint is screwed up again. The flow should then start again.

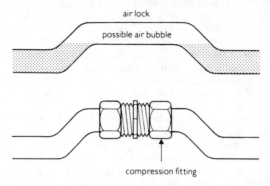

air lock

possible air bubble

compression fitting

air washer In *air conditioning*, a chamber through which air passes into water sprays or over wet plates. The water cleans the air of dust and smells, and brings it to nearly its own temperature. If heated later, the air can have a very low *relative humidity* (C).

alburnum [tim.] *Sapwood.*

alder [tim.] (Alnus glutinosa (British), Alnus rubra (American, Pacific coast)) A hardwood which fades to pale brown when seasoned. Very high *shrinkage* and suitable for permanently dry or permanently wet conditions, e.g. piling, *joinery*, and *plywood*.

alkali-resistant glass fibre *See* **glass-reinforced cement**.

alkali-resistant paint Few paints are alkali-resistant. *Cement paints, masonry paints*, bitumens and *epoxy resins* are the main ones but *pigments* also need to be alkali resistant. Alkali-resistant *primers* are available but they are not effective unless they are dry. On a plastered brick wall this means waiting a year or two after it is built. *See* **saponification**, B R E Digests 197, 198.

alkathene *Polythene.*

alkyd resin [pai.] *Synthetic resins* made from an alcohol combined with an acid, weather-resistant and used in many modern paints and varnishes. *See* **oil-modified alkyd**.

alligatoring [pai.] *Crocodiling.*

alligator wrench [plu.] A *pipe wrench*.

all-in contract [q.s.] A *package deal*.

all-rowlock wall A wall built in *rat-trap bond*.

aluminium foil Aluminium *sheet* which is thinner than 0·15 mm (0·006 in.). It reflects both visible light and infra-red (heat) rays. It is therefore used as an *insulator*. It is also used as an insulator on *sarking felt* and *insulating plasterboard*.

aluminium powder Flakes of aluminium obtained by putting *aluminium foil* through a stamp battery or *ball mill* (C). The highest metallic lustre is obtained in paints made with *leafing* aluminium powder.

aluminium primer [pai.] *Primer* made from *leafing* aluminium powder which gives high water resistance but may lead to poor adhesion of later coats, though it makes a useful *knotting*. With different *vehicles*, aluminium paint has been used on *asbestos-cement*, on metals and as a *sealer* over tar, etc. (BS 4756).

aluminous cement, high-alumina cement, Fondu Although for structural purposes this cement has not been accepted by BSCP 114 since August 1974, it has many completely safe non-structural uses, e.g. garden paths. It acquires its full strength in 24 hours, compared with a month for Portland cement, but is more costly. If mixed with Portland cement it sets within a few seconds of the addition of water. *See* **high-alumina cement** (*C*).

American bond, English garden wall b., Scotch b. (USA **common b.**) Brickwork with all the bricks laid as *stretchers* except for a *header* course every fifth, sixth or seventh course.

American Society for Testing and Materials A US organization that corresponds to the *British Standards Institution*.

amyl acetate, banana oil [pai.] A solvent with a strong banana-like smell used in cellulose lacquers, *bronzing fluids*, and metallic paints.

anchor (1) Any means whereby a building part is held. It may be some sort of bolt, or other metal part, *grouted* (*C*) into the masonry or held into it by expansion within a hole. *See* **Rawlplug**, *also C*.

(2) **clip** An L-shaped piece of metal that holds glass into a rebate. One of its legs is drilled for nailing it in. *See also* (illus. p. 36) **bench hook**.

anchorage For a pressurized *air house*, the means of holding down the *membrane* against the uplift resulting from the air pressure inside it. (Illus. below) *See also C*.

anchor block (USA) A wood *fixing brick*.

anchor plate A cast-iron plate, about 300 × 300 × 3 mm (12 × 12 × ¼ in.), used as a *flooring tile* in factories. It is bedded in a plastic mortar *screed* and held by downward-projecting *lugs*.

anchor strip A *lining plate* of thermoplastic laminated sheet.

Ancient Monuments Acts Owners of buildings listed under these Acts must

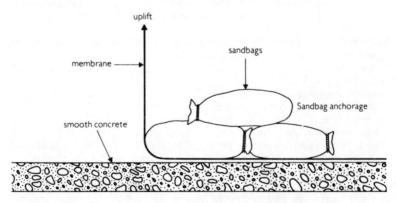

Anchorage for an air house. Many other types of anchorage have been used. Compare p. 115.

Galvanized steel angle beads to protect plaster corners. (Courtesy Expamet.)

notify the Department of the Environment, Directory of Ancient Monuments and Historic Buildings, at the planning stage if they intend to repair or even clean them. Local planning officers can usually advise.

angiosperms [tim.] A large group of flowering plants that includes *deciduous* trees, therefore all *hardwoods*, but not pine trees.

angle bead, a. staff, corner b. [pla.] A moulding, originally of hard plaster but now of galvanized steel, made for plasterers to work to at salient corners, as a permanent *screed*. (Illus. above)

angle block, glue b., blocking [carp.] A small block, usually shaped like a right-angled triangle. It is glued and tacked into the corner of a frame to stiffen it, particularly under stairs.

angle brace [carp.], **a. tie** A bar fixed across an angle in a frame to stiffen it.

angle bracket [carp.] A *bracket*, particularly one projecting from a wall to hold up a shelf.

angle closer A brick cut specially to complete, i.e. close, the bond at the corner of a wall.

angle divider [carp.] A *bevel* which bisects angles and can also be used as a try *square*.

angle-drafted margin A *drafted margin* round two faces of a stone at a corner.

angle float [pla.] A plasterer's tool for shaping an internal corner.

angle gauge A *template* made for setting out or checking angles on a building site.

angle grinder [mech.] A power-operated, hand-held tool resembling an electric drill but carrying a rigid abrasive disc for grinding or cutting metal or masonry. Different abrasives are used for cutting different materials. *Disc sanders* carry a flexible disc.

angle joint [carp.] A joint between two pieces of timber at a corner. *See* **bridle, cocking, dovetail, end-lap joint, halving, housing, joggle, mitre, mortise and tenon.**

19

angle of saw-tooth [carp.] The angle between the *face* and the *back* of a *sawtooth*. It varies between 40° and 70°.

angle rafter, a. ridge [carp.] A *hip rafter*.

angle staff, a. shaft An *angle bead*.

angle tie [carp.] (1) **dragon tie** A horizontal timber which carries one end of the *dragon beam* and ties the *wall plates* together at a corner of the building. (2) An *angle brace*.

angle tile, arris t., angular hip t. A *plain tile* moulded to a right angle for covering a *hip* or *ridge*, or, in *tile-hanging*, a corner of a building.

angle trowel, twitcher [pla.] A small rectangular *trowel* with upturned edges for working internal angles, or a vee-shaped trowel for working external angles (B S 4049). *See* **plasterer** (illus. p. 246).

angling, angled A description of a part which is set at an angle, usually not a right angle.

anhydrite ($CaSO_4$) A mineral from which anhydrite plaster is made by mixing the ground mineral with *accelerators* of set. It differs from anhydrous *gypsum plaster*.

anhydrous Matter containing no water. Anhydrous *gypsum plasters* have been heated more strongly than *plaster of Paris*. They do not react quickly with water and an *accelerator* of set is added to make them usable in building. *Keene's* and Sirapite are examples, respectively of class D and C to B S 1191. Both are suitable as a final coat on a sanded undercoat but should not be applied to *building board*.

animal black [pai.] Black *pigments* made by calcining such animal products as bone or ivory chippings, e.g. drop black, bone black, and ivory black. *Compare* **mineral black**.

animal glue, Scotch g. [carp.] *Glue* from the bones, sinews, hides, horn, or skin of animals, sold in cake or grain form, prepared by soaking the glue overnight and then heating to 60° C. (140° F.) (boiling spoils the glue) and applying to the warm joint. The glue is strong but has no resistance to water. *Fish glue* has similar properties.

annual ring, growth r., year r. [tim.] One ring of *springwood* with *summerwood*, added to the growing tree each year. Since the ring thickness is affected by rainfall and evaporation, it is possible to date an old timber in a house by comparing the sequences of its rings with other timbers grown in the same district which (if of the same date) will have rings in similar sequence.

annular bit [carp.] A *hole saw*.

annunciator A signal board to show which of a number of bell buttons was pushed to operate the signal bell. It is also used in electrical fire-alarms. *See* **drop annunciator**.

anodizing *See* C.

anti-actinic glass *Anti-sun glass*.

anti-bandit glazing *Security glazing* that delays access through glass for a short time.

anti-condensation paint [pai.] Absorbs moisture but has little effect on really heavy *condensation*. Such paints are expensive and get dirty easily, so it is better to eliminate the condensation than to rely on them.

anti-corrosive paints Paints which contain *inhibiting pigments* to delay corrosion of metal surfaces. Most *priming coats* for steel are anti-corrosive.

anti-graffiti treatment [pai.] *Textured finishes* can easily be arranged to contain enough small stones to discourage markings with felt pens, lipstick, etc. Other treatments exist, e.g. *cement-rubber latex*.

antimony oxide [pai.] (Sb_2O_3) A brilliant *white pigment* with a faint pink undertone and a *hiding power* second only to *titanium dioxide*. It will not *feed*.

anti-noise paint A rough-surfaced paint like *anti-condensation paint*, therefore with high sound *absorption*.

anti-siphon pipe [plu.] A pipe which admits air to the downstream side of the water *seal* of all the *traps* to which it is connected, and thus helps to ventilate the drains through its top end, the *ventilation pipe*. Its main function is to prevent the water seals being sucked away by water passing down the *soil stack*. *See* **single-stack system**.

anti-siphon trap, deep-seal t. [plu.] A *waste* trap which can lose its *seal* with difficulty or not at all, because of the large volume of water in it, achieved by an enlargement of the lower part of the U. In the *single-stack system* of plumbing, these traps may save the expense of *anti-siphon pipes*.

anti-skinning agent [pai.] A substance such as *pine oil* added to a *paint* or *varnish* to prevent skin forming at the surface during storage. *Skinning* can also be prevented by filling the empty part of the tin with nitrogen or another inert gas.

anti-slip paint A paint containing sand, cork dust, asbestos fibre, or similar material, used for finishing wood floors or decks.

anti-sun glass, solar control g., heat-absorbing g., anti-actinic g. Several types of window glass which reduce the sun's heat, and usually also the light by at least 25%. Some types reject 75% of the heat but these stop much more light. Heat-absorbing (body-tinted) glasses become hot and give off inwards a third of the absorbed heat; used for the outer pane of *double glazing* this falls to a sixth. Reflecting (surface-modified or coated) glasses perform better because they warm up less and reflect the heat outwards. Fixed overhangs (balconies) or adjustable awnings, blinds or louvres probably admit more light. Such glass gets hotter than its frame, so may need protection by fixing it in *non-setting glazing compound*. *See* **solar control film**.

apartment (mainly USA) *See* **flat, maisonette**.

apartment house (USA) A block of *flats*.

appraisal A judgement of quality; for the building industry this generally means an estimate of the suitability of a building technique for a particular use. Appraisal certificates for *industrialized building methods* are issued by the *Agrément Board*. *TRADA* appraises timber frames.

apprentice A youth who agrees to work under a skilled master for small pay for a number of years on condition that the master teaches him a *craft*. Technical schools are displacing the system.

apprenticeship An *apprentice's* bond with his employer, that the latter shall teach him a *craft*. The agreement is an indenture.

approximate quantities [q.s.] A preliminary estimate of the *building components* in a project before the processes of architectural and structural design have fixed the details of floors, walls, *columns*, *roof*, and so on. It often involves *cubing*.

apron (1) A vertical panel indoors below a *window board*. *See below and C.*
  (2) Vertical asphalt on a fascia or overhang of a roof.

apron eaves piece, T-plate A T-shaped section formed by bending and folding an edge of zinc roofing sheet to fix the eave of the zinc sheet and act as a *flashing*.

apron flashing A one-piece *flashing*, as at the lower side of a chimney penetrating a sloping roof. *Compare* **soaker, stepped flashing**.

apron lining (Scots **breastplate**) [joi.] Horizontal boards forming a vertical face to a stair *well*, and covering the apron piece.

apron piece [carp.] A *pitching piece*.

apron wall (USA) A *spandrel* in a multi-storey building.

arbitration [q.s.] When a dispute over a building *contract* has reached deadlock, both parties may agree to its settlement by an individual mentioned in the contract. Most contracts prescribe this, and name a *building surveyor*.

arcade An arched passage, often with shops on one or both sides.

arch bar A steel bar of rectangular section under a brick *flat arch* to hold it in place, particularly a fireplace arch; obsolescent, reinforced concrete lintels usually being preferred.

arch-brick, voussoir A wedge-shaped brick for building an arch (or lining a well).

arched construction Building by arches; carrying floor or wall loads on arches instead of on *lintels* or *beams* (*C*).

architect One who designs and supervises the construction of buildings. He prepares drawings and *specifications*, inspects sites, obtains *tenders*, and handles legal negotiations needed before work can start. His functions now extend into town planning and the study of the social and work activities that need buildings. The Architects (Registration) Acts 1931 to 1969 protect the title 'architect' in the United Kingdom so that only those who are registered with the Architects Registration Council may practise as architects. To qualify for registration a person must pass an architectural examination of university degree level as well as one in professional practice.

architectural assistant [d.o.], **a. draughtsman** A man or woman working for an architect, normally in the drawing office but sometimes on a site; often a registered architect.

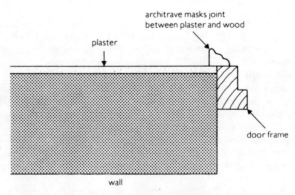

Architrave round a door frame.

Weepholes to an area. In a house with no damp course, the excavation of the earth and the building of the wall to the right of the drawing help to dry out the house wall. Where the height of earth to be held up is only 0.6 m (2 ft) or less, a much weaker wall (e.g. half-brick) will suffice, with an area only 250 mm (10 in) wide, costing about a quarter of the work shown above.

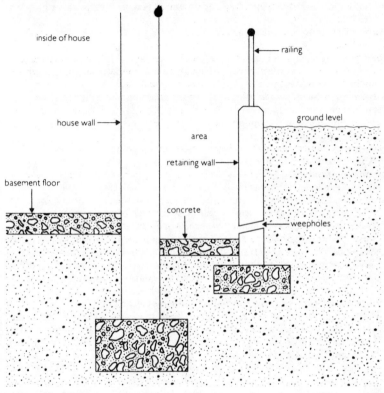

architectural sections, drawn s. Drawn or *extruded sections* in copper, aluminium, or their alloys used as *trim* round the outside of windows, the porches of monumental buildings, and so on.

architrave [joi.], **lining** *Trim* which is *planted* to cover the joint between the frame within an opening and the wall finish, particularly plaster, at a door or window. (Illus.)

architrave block [joi.], **plinth b., skirting b.** A block at the foot of an *architrave* into which the skirting board fits.

arch-stone, voussoir A wedge-shaped stone in a stone arch.

area, dry a. (USA **areaway**) A space separating the *basement* of a building from the surrounding earth, to keep it dry. (Illus. above)

armoured cable [elec.] *Cable* wound round with steel strip or wire (USA BX cable); *see also C.*

23

arris (1) A sharp edge of a *brick*, of *plaster*, or of other *building elements*.
(2) The upper edge, sharp or rounded, of *asphalt (C) skirtings*.

arris gutter [carp.] The V-shaped wooden *Yankee gutter*.

arris rail [tim.] A triangular fence rail made by ripping a square cross-section of wood along a diagonal to make two pieces of triangular cross-section. The rail may be mortised into the fence posts. It is always set with its long side (the diagonal) vertical.

arris-wise, arris-ways Diagonal laying of bricks, slates or tiles, or sawing of timber.

artificial aggregates These include nearly all *lightweight aggregates* except pumice, but also *blast-furnace slag*, and *clinker*, sometimes regarded as a lightweight aggregate.

artificial marble *Scagliola* or *marezzo marble*, both made with *gypsum plaster*.

artificial stone *Cast stone*.

artisan An old term for *tradesman*.

asbestine [pai.] Talc; an *extender*.

asbestos A mineral crystal, consisting of thin, tough fibres like textile, which can withstand high temperatures without change when pure. *See* **sprayed mineral insulation**.

asbestos and health Health risks from machining of asbestos may be severe, but if the asbestos is wetted, especially when drilled or sawn by hand tools, the risk is less. It is not yet proven that glass, ceramic, and other substitutes for asbestos, which also yield fine fibres that enter the lung, are completely harmless. B S 3958 specifies materials for thermal insulation, including preformed sections for covering pipes. If in doubt refer to the Health and Safety Executive's publications or the Asbestos Regulations, 1969. Sawing or drilling should be done at floor level; sweepings should be disposed of in sealed bags.

asbestos-bitumen, semi-rigid asbestos-bitumen sheet, S R A B S A substitute for *flexible-metal roofing* which is softened by heating with a blow lamp and then easily bends to shape. *Sealing compound* is used to join it to neighbouring sheets. B S C P 143 part 16 describes the construction, with many clear diagrams (marketed as Nuralite).

asbestos blanket [plu.] A small blanket wrapped round pipes being welded or annealed or brazed, to keep the heat in.

asbestos cement Cement mixed usually with 10% *asbestos* fibre to make non combustible and cheap sheets for roof and wall *cladding*, also flue pipes and water pipes strong enough for pressures of 250 m (800 ft) head of water. Though non-combustible, not all asbestos cement is tough enough to withstand fire, particularly the common type with 10% asbestos. It can be cut with a tenon saw or hacksaw, preferably wetted and near ground level to reduce the dust.

asbestos-cement slates Large asbestos-cement slates either 500 mm (20 in.) or 600 mm (24 in.) by at least 250 mm (10 in.), laid like ordinary slates, centre-nailed with two nails. Copper nails, 32 mm ($1\frac{1}{4}$ in.) long are used, but the tail of each slate is also drilled for a copper rivet. This 'disc rivet' is slipped into the slot between the two slates in the course immediately below, before the nails are driven. The disc is 22 mm ($\frac{7}{8}$ in.) diameter and the shank passing up from it is bent over after passing through the upper slate. Asbestos must be drilled not punched. A straight cut is most easily made, and without dust, if the slate is cut like glass by scoring each surface deeply along the same line and then pressing it over a straight edge (BS 690).

asbestos rope [plu.] *See* **joint runner**.

asbestos sheeting Corrugated, *profiled*, or plain sheets for roofing and wall *cladding*, made of *asbestos cement*.

asbestos string A *caulking* in the bottom of a socket in a clay *flue lining* to prevent leakage of the cement mortar above it into the lining. The cement used may be high-alumina or Portland.

asbestos wallboard Sheets with a higher proportion of asbestos, consequently a higher fire resistance and better insulating value, than *asbestos-cement* sheet.

ash [tim.] (Fraxinus excelsior) English or European ash is a pale *hardwood* from white to light brown in colour, used for handles of striking tools (navvy's or miner's picks or sledge hammers). It can be easily bent when steamed. Figured varieties are used as *veneers*.

ash dump (USA) A labour-saving device in houses, consisting of a container beneath the fireplace, into which the ashes fall, to be removed later through a *cleanout* door in the cellar or outside the house.

ashlar, ashler (1) Walls or facings of stones, finely dressed to given dimensions, laid in *courses* with thin joints, about 3 mm ($\frac{1}{8}$ in.) thick. The facing may be plain, vermiculated, with *drafted margin*, etc. It was used by the Egyptians in 3000 BC. *Compare* **rubble walls**.

(2) In USA ashlar also includes walling of burnt clay blocks larger than brick size and would therefore include what is called *terra cotta* in Britain and sometimes also brickwork.

(3) A *stud* in *ashlering*, a vertical timber which joins *ceiling joists* to *rafters*.

ashlaring Setting *ashlars*.

ashlering, ashlaring, ashler pieces [carp.] Vertical timbers (studs) about 1 m long, fixed in an attic from *joists* to *rafters* to carry the plaster or other facing of the *partition* which cuts off the acute angle where the roof meets the floor. *Blockwork* partitions are now commoner.

ASHVE The American Society of Heating and Ventilation Engineers.

asphalt roofing Roofing with *bitumen felt* or with *mastic asphalt* (*C*) laid in two or three coats.

assembly gluing, constructional g., secondary g. [tim.] Gluing together *plywood* or timber components to make wooden aircraft or similar structures. *See* **primary gluing**.

Association of Building Technicians A specialist section of *UCATT*, that includes building design and supervisory staffs – *architects, civil engineers* (*C*), *clerks of works, foremen*.

ASTM The *American Society for Testing and Materials*.

astragal [joi.] Scots for *glazing bar*.

atmospheric siphon The *Knapen system* and similar ways of drying out walls through holes drilled from outside the house. (Illus. p. 26)

atomization [pai.] The breaking up of e.g. fluid *paint, lacquer,* or *varnish* into fine drops on ejection from a *spray gun*.

attic A room next to the roof with a ceiling (if any) following the roof slopes.

audiograph An *acoustic* instrument which measures the rate at which sound dies away. It thus gives a measure of the sound *absorption* in a room.

auger [carp.], **Scotch eyed a.** A drilling tool shaped like a cork-screw, for boring

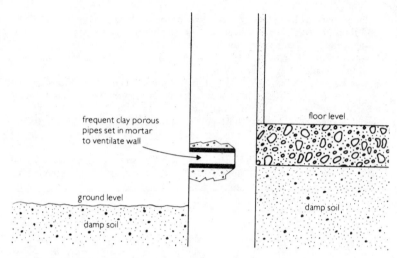

frequent clay porous
pipes set in mortar
to ventilate wall

floor level

ground level

damp soil

damp soil

Atmospheric siphon for drying out old walls with no damp course.

holes in wood. A loop (eye) is forged in the top end, through which a wooden handle is passed. The auger can thus be twisted without a *brace*. Each auger can drill a hole of only one diameter but of considerable depth.

auger bit [carp.] A *bit* of *auger* shape which lacks the eye of an auger and can thus be inserted in a *brace*. *See* **carpenter's tools** (illus. p. 59).

autoclave A pressure vessel in which (for example) *calcium silicate bricks* are cured at high temperature and pressure in live steam.

automatic fire alarm *See* **smoke detector**.

automatic flushing cistern [plu.] A *cistern* which periodically flushes a urinal or a drain of inadequate slope.

automatic immersion heater [elec.] An electric tube- or blade-shaped heater which is submerged in a hot water *cylinder* or tank and controlled by a *thermostat* built into it or in contact with the water.

autumn wood [tim.] Another name for *summerwood*.

awl, scribe a., scratch a. [carp.] A wooden-handled tool with a steel point, parallel to the handle, for marking or scribing wood or piercing hardboard or thin plywood. *Compare* **gimlet**.

axe (1) [carp.] A tool for rough-dressing timber.
   (2) A *bricklayer's hammer*.

axed A stone surface struck with a *bush hammer* (*C*) or axe. Once-axed is rough, fine-axed is smooth.

axed bricks, rough-axed b. Bricks cut to shape with *axe* or *bolster*, not rubbed, therefore laid with joints which are thicker than in *gauged brickwork*. The work is nevertheless skilled, the final trimming being done with a *scutch*.

axle pulley A *sash pulley*.

B

back (1) The *extrados* of an arch.

(2) [joi., tim.] The contrary of *face*, thus the following edge of a *sawtooth* or the hidden surface of a sheet of plywood or plasterboard.

(3) The upper surface of a slate, *compare* **bed**.

back boiler A small *boiler* fitted at the back of the hearth of an open fire or *roomheater* to provide hot water. Large back boilers may also heat *radiators*.

back boxing [joi.] *Back lining*.

back drop, d. connection, d. manhole [plu.] A connection at a manhole, at which the branch drain enters by a vertical pipe.

back filling, b. fill (1) Earth, stone, or hard rubbish used for filling excavations after *foundations* (C) have been laid in them.

(2) (USA) *Backing* brickwork or *bricknogging*.

back-flap hinge [joi.] A door hinge screwed on to the face of a thin door resembling a *butt hinge* but wider, used when the door is too thin to be carried by a butt. (Illus.)

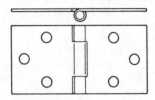

Back-flap hinge.

background, backing, base [pla.] The surface on which the first coat of plaster is laid.

background heating The cheapest possible room heating, the opposite of full central heating, supplemented by electric, paraffin, coal or gas fires in cold weather.

back gutter, chimney g. A *flexible-metal* gutter between the 'uphill' side of a chimney and a sloping roof. *See* **cricket**.

backing (1) The bricks in a wall which are hidden by the *facing bricks*.

(2) Stone which can be used as random rubble.

(3) Coursed masonry built over an *extrados*.

(4) Fitting small wooden *furring* pieces on to *joists* to make a level surface for floorboards.

(5) The shaping of the top of a hip *rafter* to suit the roof slopes.

(6) A *backup strip*.

backing coat [pla.] Any coat other than the finishing coat.

backings [carp.] *Furring* strips on joists.

back iron, cap i., cover i., break i. [carp.] The steel plate which stiffens the *cutting iron* of a *plane* and breaks up the shavings. In a metal plane it is held down by the *lever cap*. *Compare* **block plane**. *See* **carpenter's tools** (illus.).

back lining, b. boxing [joi.] A thin strip closing a *jamb* of a *cased frame* of a *sash window*. It prevents the sash weights from rubbing against the brickwork.

27

back lintel The lintel supporting the *backing* of a wall, and not seen on the face.

back mortaring (USA) *Back plastering.*

back nut [plu.] A nut, on the long thread of a *connector*, which helps to make a tight joint. *See* **fittings** (illus. p. 138).

back painting Painting the unseen face of hardboard, asbestos cement sheets, etc., so as to prevent the buckling or cracking that may happen when an impervious paint system is applied to the face alone. The back may be painted with a cheaper paint such as a bitumen.

back plastering, pargetting (USA) Rendering or plastering the part of a wall which is not seen. It may mean putting an additional plaster skin between the outside *boarding* and inner plaster in *frame construction* to make two air spaces instead of one, or rendering the inner face of the outer leaf of a cavity wall.

back putty *Bed putty.*

back saw [joi.] A saw stiffened by a heavy fold of steel or brass along its back, such as a *tenon saw* or *dovetail saw*. *See* **carpenter's tools.** (illus. p. 59).

back shore, jack s. [carp.] An outer support in *raking shores*, under the *rider shore* (illus. p. 268).

back siphonage [plu.] Sucking back of dirty water from within a building into a water main under low pressure. All water authorities have regulations to prevent this pollution of the main, including insistence on *check valves* (C), *cisterns* to supply all household water except that for drinking, prohibition of *silencing pipes*, etc.

backup strip, lathing board, backing (USA) A narrow strip of wood nailed at the angle of a *partition* as a base on which to nail lathing.

back vent (USA) A *fresh-air inlet.*

badger [joi.] A large wooden *rebate plane.*

baffle A slat of polychloroprene or other durable material, slotted into grooves in the front edges of adjoining concrete *cladding panels* to prevent direct entry of rain and wind into an *open-drained joint; see also* C.

bag moulding [tim.] *See* **flexible-bag moulding.**

bag plug [plu.], **expanding p.** An inflatable drain plug.

bakelite One of the earliest *plastics*, produced by Dr Baekeland in 1916 for making electrical fittings, door handles, drawer pulls, and so on.

baking [pai.] *See* stoving.-

balanced construction [tim.] A description of *plywood* which has an equal thickness of wood in both directions of the grain, is symmetrical about its centre line, and has an odd number of plies. In balanced *three-ply* the face and back *veneers* are of equal thickness and the core is twice as thick as either of them.

balanced-flue appliance A gas heater with its combustion air inlet next to its flue gas outlet in a windproof terminal outside the dwelling. (Illus. p. 29)

balanced sash [joi.] A *sash window. Compare* **sliding sash.**

balanced step, dancing s. A *winder* with its narrow end little narrower than the *fliers*. It is therefore more comfortable to walk on than a winder in which the nosings radiate from a common centre.

balancing valve *See* **lockshield valve.**

balcony A platform projecting from an outside wall at a window of an upper floor and usually with access from it. If it is carried on beams fixed in the wall and not on posts below it, the beams should continue into the floor

Balanced-flue gas fire, diagrammatic cross-section. This one is hung on a wall.

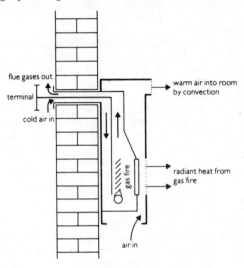

behind and the designer must make sure the floor is heavy enough to hold it up.

bale tack A *tingle*.

balk [tim.] *See* **baulk**.

ballast Unscreened gravel containing sand, grit, and stones of less than boulder size. *See also* C.

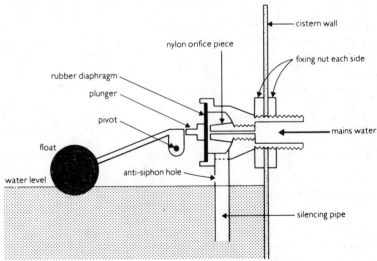

Silencing pipe at a ball valve.

ball catch, bullet c. [joi.] An automatic door fastening in which a spring-loaded ball, projecting slightly from a *mortise* in the door, engages with a hole in a *striking plate* on the *door frame*.

ball cock *See* **ball valve.**

balloon framing [carp.] Modern American timber house construction in which the *studs* run to the roof *plate* past the floor *joists* which are nailed to them. *See* **braced frame, ribbon board.**

balloon structure *See* **air house.**

ball-peen hammer [mech.] An engineer's *hammer* with a round *peen.*

ball valve, float v., b. cock [plu.] Automatic water supply operated by a floating copper or plastic ball in a flushing or other *cistern*, connected by lever to a valve that closes the water supply when the cistern is full and opens it when it is empty. Many types exist. *See* **emergency water stop, silencing pipe, cistern** (illus. p. 29).

balsa wood [tim.] A *hardwood* which is as soft as *cork* and lighter. It is used for making structural models and lightweight, highly insulating *coreboards.*

baluster, banister [joi.] A post in a balustrade of a bridge or *flight* of *stairs*. Wooden turned balusters were first used in England in Elizabethan times and were then about 8 cm (3 in.) in diameter.

balustrade Collective name to the whole infilling from handrail down to floor level at the edge of a *stair*, bridge, etc.

bamboo houses Most houses are built of bamboo in countries where this fast-growing plant thrives, and usually they are built by their occupants.

band Scots for *bond.*

band-and-hook hinge, strap h., band-and-gudgeon h., hook-and-ride h. A gate hinge made of a heavy wrought iron strip (the band), which drops on to a pin fixed in to a wall, often a *gate hook.* (Illus.)

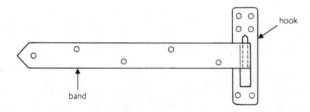

Band and hook hinge.

banding, railing, lipping, edging [tim.] Inlays or strips to cover edges of *veneer* or core ends. On *flush* doors the *shutting stile* is always banded (slamming strip or clashing strip) and, in the best work, also the other edges. *See* **fire-check door**, diagram p. 135.

band saw [tim.] A power saw for cutting intricate shapes or converting timber, having a steel belt with teeth at one edge, running on two pulleys. The saw loop is closed either by *brazing* the ends together or by hooking them with built-in hooks and eyes. Band saws move at about 30 m/s (100 ft/s).

banister A *baluster.*

banker (1) A board on which *concrete, mortar,* or *plaster* is mixed by shovel.

It measures about 1·8 x 1·3 m (6 x 4 ft) with boards 23 cm. (9 in.) high on three sides.

(2) A mason's workbench, of stone or heavy timber.

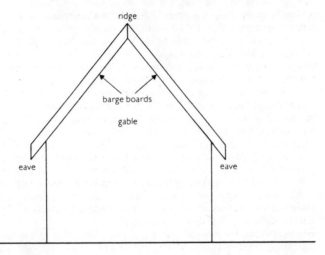

Gable with barge boards.

banker mason, stone dresser, hewer (Scotland) **blocker and dresser** A *mason* working at a *banker* who marks out, shapes, and finishes by hand or by machine, stones cut to size by the *stone-machine hand*. *See* **machine mason**.

bar A *glazing bar*.

barbed dowel pin [joi.] (USA) A barbed piece of steel wire pointed at one end, for fastening *mortise-and-tenon joints*.

bar door [joi.] (Scotland) A *batten door*.

bareface tenon [carp.] A *tenon* with a shoulder cut on one side only, needed when the piece on which the tenon is cut (e.g. a door *rail*) is thinner than the *stile* containing the *mortise*.

barge board, verge b., gable b. A sloping board (built in pairs) along a *gable*, covering the ends of roof timbers, and protecting them from rain. Old barge boards were often beautifully carved. (Illus. above)

barge course, verge c. A brick *coping* to a gable wall, or the tiles next the gable, slightly overhanging.

barium plaster A plaster used in X-ray rooms to reduce the amount of radiation penetrating the walls. It contains barytes aggregate with *gypsum plaster* or *Portland cement* as a *binder*.

barn door hanger (USA) A steel rail and pulleys over a heavy door. The pulleys, attached to the door, carry it sideways along the rail.

barrel [plu.] That part of a pipe throughout which the bore and wall thickness remain uniform. Gas pipes were, at first, made from musket barrels, surplus after the battle of Waterloo. *See also C*.

barrel bolt An ornamental-metal or steel cylindrical rod, running in a case and pushed home by the finger. It does not form part of a lock. *See* **foot bolt**.

31

barrel light A roof *light* made with curved glass and *glazing bars*.

barrel nipple [plu.] A short length of pipe, with a *taper thread* outside at each end, bare in the middle; a *tubular*.

barrow run A smooth path for wheeling loaded barrows on a building site, usually made by laying *scaffold boards* on the ground.

base (1) The base course of a wall. *See also C.*

(2) A widening or *moulding* at the foot of a wall or column.

(3) or **sub-base** (USA) A *skirting board*.

(4) The part of a floor or *stair* tread or *riser* below the finish, sometimes a *grano* or similar surface laid with a trowel.

(5) [pai.] The *ground*; or the main ingredient of a paint, either its main *pigment* (lead base, zinc base) or the main part of the *medium* (oil base).

baseboard, base (USA) *Skirting* board.

base course The lowest or lowest visible *course* of a masonry wall, often provided with a *water table*.

base exchange A *water-softener* process in which water passes through a tank of *zeolite*, a mineral reagent, to absorb the salts that harden the water. Periodically the zeolite tank must be flushed with a salt solution to remove the hardness from the zeolite and rejuvenate it. Common in small houses, the process can completely soften water, but adds sodium, which may affect heart sufferers. *See also C.*

basement A *storey* of which, in USA, less than half is below ground level. In Britain it can be wholly below ground but is generally living space. *Compare* **cellar, sub-basement.**

base shoe, s. mold [joi.] (USA) A quarter-round *bead, planted* at the junction or *skirting* board and floor boards to cover the joint.

base trim (USA) Any *mouldings* which decorate the foot of a wall, column, pedestal, etc.

basic lead sulphate [pai.] A *white pigment*, formed by burning galena (PbS) or zinc minerals containing it, resembling *white lead*. It contains some lead monoxide (PbO), but generally not more than 5% zinc oxide. *See* **leaded zinc oxides.**

bastard ashlar (1) **b. masonry** Facing stones of a *rubble wall*, dressed and built like *ashlar*.

(2) Stones for ashlar work which are not completely dressed at the quarry.

bastard-sawn [tim.] *Flat-sawn.*

bastard tuck pointing, bastard p. *Pointing* shaped with a projection from the face of the brickwork, to emphasize the joint. *Compare* **tuck pointing.**

bat (1) A brick cut across, larger than a quarter brick; *see* **closer.**

(2) A *lead wedge.*

(3) **bat insulation** (USA) A rectangular, paper-wrapped, flat-surfaced insulating *blanket* inserted between the *studs* of external walls, some 5 to 8 cm (2 to 3 in.) thick, 38 to 58 cm (15 to 23 in.) wide, and 20 to 120 cm (8 to 48 in.) long.

batch One mixing of concrete, mortar, plaster, etc.

batch box, measuring frame, gauge b. A box of size calculated for the *mix* (C) in which the stones or sand are measured, before mixing with cement and water, to make concrete. The box has four sides and no bottom, and before being filled is placed on a mixing platform or *banker*, so never needs to be lifted full. (Illus. p. 33)

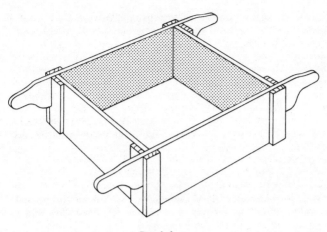

Batch box.

baton, b. rod [joi.] Scots for a *sash stop*.
batted surface, tooled s. A vertically incised *ashlar* surface made with a *batting tool*, after the surface has been rubbed smooth.
batten, baton [tim.] A piece of *square-sawn* softwood timber 50 to 100 mm (2 to 4 in.) thick and 100 to 200 mm (4 to 8 in.) wide (BS 565).
(2) Horizontal strips 5 × 2 cm (2 × 1 in.) or less used for fixing lathing or slates or tiles (*slating-and-tiling batten*). *See* **cleat, battening**.
batten door, ledged d. [joi.] A door faced with vertical boards fixed on to two or more horizontal *ledges* at the back, which are often *clench-nailed* to the facing and sometimes diagonally braced. It has no frame round the edges.
battening [carp.] *Common grounds* put on to a wall as a base for *lathing*.
batter, rake An artificial, uniform, steep slope or its inclination, expressed as one horizontal to so many vertical units.
batter board (USA) A *profile*.
batter brace [carp.] (USA) A *diagonal brace* (C), usually in a *truss*.
batter peg, b. post Pegs which are driven into the ground to set out the limits of an earth slope.
batting, broad tooling, droving, angle dunting Surfacing a stone with a batting tool in parallel strokes, each traversing the full depth of the stone face. The strokes may be vertical, when it is often referred to as tooling, or oblique at 45° to 60°. The result is a regular pattern of fluted cuts in the stone face. *Compare* **boasting**.
batting tool, broad t. A mason's chisel 7 to 11 cm (3 to 4½ in.) wide for surfacing sandstones.
baulk [tim.], **timber, squared log** A square-sawn or *hewn* softwood timber of equal or approximately equal cross dimensions but greater than 100 × 125 mm (4 × 5 in.) (BS 565).
bay (1) One of several uniform divisions of a building, such as the space enclosed between four columns or two beams.
(2) A development of (1) – the volume of concrete poured, or the area of plaster, asphalt, or other roofing, etc., laid at any one time.

bay window A *window* formed in a projection of the wall beyond its general line. Unlike an *oriel* window, it is carried on foundations outside the general building line and an oriel is carried on *corbels*. *See* **bow window**.

bead (1) [joi.] **beading** Usually a semi-circular *moulding* that masks a joint, sometimes alongside a *quirk*. But a *sash stop* (or *guard bead*) is nearly rectangular while a *glazing fillet* (or *glazing bead*) is often a *quarter round*.

(2) [pla.] *See* **angle bead**.

(3) In zinc or copper roofing, at eaves or flashings, an edge bent round to a tube shape or to 180° for stiffening and fixing the edge of the sheet.

(4) [pai.] An accumulation of *paint* or *varnish* at a lower edge due to excessive *flow*.

beading [joi.] A *bead*.

beading tool [joi.] A *bead plane* or its *cutting iron*.

bead plane, b. router, beader, beading tool [joi.] A *plane* for moulding beads on wood or for cutting grooves in which to insert beads. *See* **hollow**.

beam box A *wall box*, or the formwork for a beam.

beam filling, wind f. *Brick nogging* or masonry between floor or ceiling *joists* at their supports to stiffen the joists and provide a *fire stop* in the floor or ceiling.

beam hanger A *stirrup strap*.

bearer [carp.] A horizontal timber, often a *joist*, which spreads load.

bearing bar A steel bar laid on brickwork, instead of a *wall plate*, to provide a level support for floor joists.

bearing plate A plate in a wall which supports a *beam* (*C*) or *column*, spreading the load from the beam over an area of wall large enough to prevent the wall failing.

bearing wall A *loadbearing wall* (*C*).

bed The under-surface of a *brick*, building stone, *slate*, or *tile*, as laid in a building, or mortar touching this surface. *See also* **back**.

bedding A layer, or the act of placing a layer on which something rests continuously. For example, *glazier's putty* under glass, *concrete* under a drain, the *mortar* under bricks or stones, the jute serving under the steel wire armour of a cable.

bedding stone A plane marble slab used by bricklayers and masons to check that rubbed surfaces are flat.

bed dowel A *dowel* in the centre of the *bed* of a stone.

bed joint The horizontal *joints* in *masonry* or brickwork and the radiating joints of an arch.

bed putty, back p. The *glazier's putty* under glass, on which it is bedded. *Compare* **face putty**.

beech [tim.] (Fagus sylvatica) A *hardwood* of Europe, Asia Minor, and Japan with typical spindle-shaped markings on *flat-sawn* boards. It is light reddish-brown in colour and slightly more easily worked than English oak.

beeswax [pai.] The wax from honeybees, used in *stains, stoppings, matt varnishes*, and polish.

beetle (1) **maul, mall** A heavy *mallet* used for striking pegs, paving slabs, and material which would be damaged by a sledge hammer.

(2) *Death-watch* beetle, *pinhole* borer, and *powder-post* beetles are examples of insects which damage *timbers*.

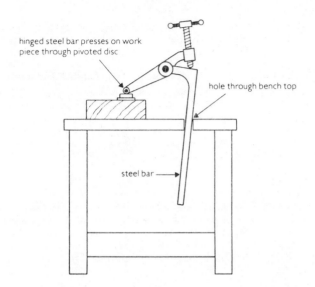

hinged steel bar presses on work
piece through pivoted disc

hole through bench top

steel bar →

Bench holdfast.

Belfast truss [carp.] A wooden *bowstring girder* (*C*) for spans up to about 15 m, built of relatively small boards. The *truss* is curved at the top and has a horizontal tie, called the string, joined by sloping members to the curved top *chord* (*C*).

bell-and-spigot joint [plu.] (USA) A *spigot-and-socket.*

bellcast eaves (Scotland) Eaves with *cocking pieces.*

belt sander [joi.] A portable or bench machine with a replaceable belt made of emery cloth, for the coarse or fine grinding of joinery or occasionally metal or masonry.

bench holdfast [joi.] A *cramp* for holding wood to the bench while it is being worked. (Illus. above)

bench hook, b. stop, side h. [joi.] A flat Z-shaped board set on a bench or a kitchen table to protect it from chisels and saws, made by fixing a *cleat* to opposite faces, at each end (illus. p. 36)

benching *Concrete* cast in a *manhole* (*C*) round a half-round drainage channel to ensure that after a flood the flow falls gradually and no solids are left behind. It is stood on when *rodding.*

bench knife [joi.] A knife blade projecting about 4 cm (1½ in.) above a bench surface and used, like a *bench stop*, for steadying the end of a timber being worked.

bench planes [joi.] Planes used more at the bench than elsewhere, for reducing and smoothing flat timber, the *jack*, *smoothing*, and *try planes*. It may also include the *block plane* and *compass plane*. *See* **carpenter's tools** (Illus. p. 59).

bench sander [joi.] A fixed *sanding machine* used in the workshop. The wood is brought up to it. Three types exist: *belt sanders*, *disc sanders* or *grinders* and *orbital sanders*. All of them grind with strong glasspaper or glass cloth, unlike the *grinder.*

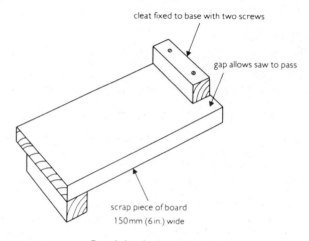

cleat fixed to base with two screws

gap allows saw to pass

scrap piece of board
150mm (6 in.) wide

Bench hook showing cleats.

bench screw [joi.] The thread of a wooden vice.

bench stop [joi.] A peg projecting through a hole in the top of a workbench by an adjustable amount. A board placed against it can be planed without clamping.

bench trimmer [joi.] A *trimming machine*.

bench work Hand work done at the bench rather than by machines.

bend A curved length of pipe, tubing, or conduit. A 90° bend is called a quarter bend, 45° is a one-eighth bend. *See* **fittings** (illus. p. 138).

bending iron, b. bolt, b. pin [plu.] A curved steel bar up to 60 cm (2 ft) long for straightening or widening lead pipe. *See* **plumber's tools** (illus. p. 250).

bending spring [plu.] Helical steel springs of circular cross-section inserted into copper or lead tube to maintain the circular shape during bending (diameters 12 to 50 mm (0·5 to 2 in.)). Smaller diameters of tube are inserted into the spring. This is the most convenient way of *loading of pipe* but for diameters above 22 mm it is probably impossible for one man to bend a pipe however soft. The spring must be well oiled or it may be impossible to extract it.

bent [tim.] A timber piece curved by lamination or steaming. *See* **C**.

benzene [pai.] A volatile flammable paint-remover and *solvent*, derived from coal, usually considered to be C_6H_6.

best reed (Arundo phragmites) The true thatching *reed*. *Compare* **mixed stuff**.

bevel [joi.] (1) One surface meeting another at an angle not a right angle. A *chamfer* is a special bevel.

(2) **tee-bevel, bevel square, sliding bevel** A movable blade for setting out angles. It passes through a stock (handle) to which it can be clamped by a screw and *wing nut* at any desired angle. *See* **mason's and bricklayer's tools** (illus. p. 211), *also* **mitre square**.

bevel halving, bevelled h. [carp.] A *halving* joint in which the contact surfaces are at an angle to the plane of the timbers, to prevent them pulling apart.

bevelled closer A brick cut longitudinally along a vertical plane, starting at the middle of one end, to a far corner. One-quarter of the brick is cut off. *See* **closer**.

bevel siding [tim.] *Clapboard*.

bib, bibcock [plu.] A water tap which is fed by a horizontal supply pipe, not, as in the usual washbasin, by a pipe from below (*pillar tap*).

bid (USA) A *tender*.

billet [carp.] A piece of wood with three sides sawn and the fourth left round. *See also* C.

billing [q.s.] Writing out a *bill of quantities* with the description and *quantities* of each *item*.

bill of quantities [q.s.] A list of numbered *items*, each of which describes the *quantity* of some work to be done in a civil engineering or building *contract*. When the procedure of tendering is adopted (as is usual in Britain), the bill is sent out to *contractors*. Those contractors who wish to do the work write an *extended price* opposite each item. This *priced bill* is the contractor's offer (or *tender* or bid) to do the work. *See* **abstracting, specification**.

binder (1) *Cement*, tar, bitumen, *gypsum plaster*, *lime*, *synthetic resin*, etc. for joining stones, sand, glassfibre, etc.

(2) **binding joist** [carp.] A wooden or steel beam covering the full span of an opening from wall to wall, and supporting *common joists*, now unusual.

(3) [pai.] That part of a paint *medium* which holds the *pigment* in a coherent *film* and is therefore not *volatile*. It may be *linseed oil*, another drying oil, or a *size*, or *resin*.

binding rafter [carp.] A *purlin*.

birch [tim.] (Betula pendula) The silver birch. This and other birches are the hardest European *hardwoods*. The silver birch grows farther north and at higher altitudes even than pine or fir trees. It is white to pale brown, usually without *figure*, more workable, but stiffer than *oak*. It is used for making furniture and *plywood*. Norway *burr* birch resembles *birdseye* maple, and is used as a *face veneer*.

birdseye, peacock's eye [tim.] The *figure* formed by small pointed depressions in the *annual rings* of many consecutive years, one of the few figures which show up well when cut in a lathe (*rotary cutting*), particularly with maple.

birdsmouth joint [carp.] (USA **foot cut**) (1) A cut into the end of a timber to fit it over a cross timber, particularly the cut in a *rafter* to fit it over a *wall plate*.

(2) A *bridle joint*.

bit [carp., etc.] (1) An interchangeable cutting point used by a carpenter in a *brace*, by a miner in a rock drill, or by an oil-well driller in a *rotary drill* (C), etc. *See* **carpenter's tools** (illus. p. 59).

(2) [plu.] The working head of a *soldering iron*, usually made of copper.

bitch A steel spike like a *dog* with the spikes pointing in directions at right angles to each other. Instead of being two-dimensional like a dog, it is three-dimensional. *See* **fasteners** (illus. p. 130).

bit extension, brace e. [carp.] A steel rod of which one end is held by a brace, the other grips a *bit*, for drilling holes deeper than the length of the bit in use.

bit gauge, bit stop [joi.] A small metal piece that can be fixed to a *bit* to ensure drilling stops at the right depth.

bit stock [carp.] A *brace*.

bitty [pai.] A paint or varnish is bitty if small *nibs* of paint skin, etc. stick up above the paint surface.

bitumastic A bituminous, anti-corrosive coating.

bitumen felt, bituminous f., roofing f., (USA **roll roofing, rag f., composition roofing**) Asbestos, flax or other fibres matted into sheets of felt for roofing or *underlays*, generally treated with bitumen or pitch. It can be used in a single layer on a sloping roof or in multiple layers as *built-up roofing* joined with *compound* on a *flat roof*. *See* **impregnated flax felt, mineral-surfaced bitumen felt, sarking felt,** and BSCP 144.

bituminized fibre pipe *Pitch fibre pipe* (USA).

bituminous paint A paint with a high proportion of bitumen, usually dark in colour; e.g. *black Japan*. It consists usually of *drying oil* with *resin* and black *pigment*.

black Japan [pai.] The best black *varnish*, also called *bituminous paint*.

blade [pla.] The part of a plasterer's *trowel* which touches the plaster.

blanc fixe [pai.] Barium sulphate ($BaSO_4$), an amorphous *extender* made fine by chemical precipitation, not, like barytes, by crushing.

blank door or **window** A walled-up door or window.

blanket, quilt *Insulating material* consisting of *eel grass, glass silk, mineral wool,* etc., with paper lining on each face. Some quilts are backed with *aluminium foil* to reduce heat losses by radiation. Blankets can be bought in strips 30 to 90 cm wide in lengths which vary with the material. *See* **asbestos blanket, bat**.

blank wall A wall without openings.

blast cleaning [pai.] *Shot blasting* (C) or similar methods of removing *mill scale* (C) from a steel surface before it can be painted.

blast-furnace slag Slag from iron smelting, sometimes ground with *Portland cement* to form a water-resisting concrete for dams, etc. *Compare* **foamed slag**.

bleaching [pai.] Removal of *colour* by chemical action, often an oxidation caused by sunlight and air.

bled timber Timber from trees which have been tapped for *resin*, usually inferior to other timber.

bleeder tile (USA) Pipes through the basement *retaining wall* (C) to drain water from behind it into drains provided in the building.

bleeding, bleed-through (1) [tim., pai.] penetration of glue through a *veneer*, or of a *paint* through one above it, often preventable by a *sealer*. *See* C.

(2) [plu.] See **air lock** (3).

blemish [tim.] Anything which mars the appearance of timber without affecting its strength and is therefore not a *defect*.

blender [pai.] A round softish *brush* of badger hair with a blunt tip, used for blending colours and removing brush marks left by coarser brushes.

blind area An *area*.

blind floor (USA) A *sub-floor* or *rough floor*.

blind header A half-brick or a *header* not seen on one face.

blind hinge [joi.] A concealed *hinge*.

blind hole A drilled or cored hole which does not pass right through the material. The opposite of a *bottomless hole*.

blind mortise [joi.] A *mortise* which does not pass through the timber.

blind nailing [joi.] *Secret nailing*.

blister figure [tim.] A *quilted figure*.

blistering [pai.] (1) Bubbles in a paint surface, caused by vaporization of moisture or resin under the surface.

(2) (USA **blub**) Local swellings on finished plaster often caused by badly matured lime, a fault which may cause the finishing coat to fall away from the backing. *Compare* **blowing**.

bloated clay *Expanded clay*.

block (1) [carp.] *See* **angle block**.

(2) A masonry unit larger than a brick, laid usually in mortar; also any preformed building unit such as glass blocks, or solid or hollow clay, or hardwood floor blocks. *See* **building blocks**.

(3) A *glazing block*.

blockboard [tim.] Board built up from wooden *core* strips up to 30 mm (1¼ in.) wide, glued between outer *veneers* whose grain runs in the opposite direction – cheaper than *laminboard*.

block bonding Connecting several *courses* of brickwork of one wall into the courses of another, often for *bonding* shallow facing bricks into thicker common bricks in the backing, and for bonding new work into old. *Compare* **toothing**.

block bridging [carp.] (USA) *Solid bridging*.

block flooring *See* **wood-block floor**.

blocking [joi.] An *angle block*.

blocking course One or several courses of bricks or *masonry* in the wall over a stone *cornice* to hold it in position by weight.

block plan A small-scale plan showing the broad outlines of existing buildings or a project.

block plane [joi.] A small metal *plane* about 15 cm long for cutting end-grain, originally the end-grain of butcher's blocks. Compared to other *bench planes*, the cutting *bevel* is reversed; also there is no *back iron*.

block tin [plu.] Commercially pure tin.

blockwork Masonry of *precast concrete* (*C*) blocks that now usually have 45 × 22·5 cm (18 × 9 in.) face size to course with the metric *brick format*. Another block of face size 40 × 10 cm (16 × 4 in.) exists to meet the demand for a 10 cm (4 in.) *module*. These dimensions include 10 mm (½ in.) for jointing. Blockwork is usually more thermally insulating and sometimes cheaper than brickwork. *See* **building blocks**, *also C and* BSCP 121, 122.

bloom [pai.] (1) A thin film, like the bloom on fruit, which forms on old glossy paint or varnish, veiling colour or reducing gloss for no known reason. It can sometimes be removed by wiping with a cloth.

(2) *See* **efflorescence**.

blowing, popping, pitting [pla.] Small pits formed by the expulsion of plaster from the surface by material expanding behind it. The cause may be lime which slakes slowly, or the slow oxidation of coal in the lime.

blow lamp (USA **b. torch**) [plu] A burner with a powerful flame for soldering, leadburning, burning paint, etc., now usually fuelled by *bottled gas*, formerly by paraffin. *See* **oxy-acetylene flame**.

blown oil [pai.] *See* **boiled oil**.

blub [pla.] (1) (USA) *Blistering*.

(2) A hole in a plaster cast, formed by an air bubble.

blue bricks *See* **Staffordshire blues**.

blueing [pai.] Increasing the apparent whiteness of a white *pigment* or paint by adding a trace of blue.

blue stain, sap s. [tim.] A blue fungal discoloration of *sapwood* which does not reduce its strength.

blushing [pai.] Milky opalescence in a *lacquer*, a fault usually caused by application in cold or wet weather, or a lack of *compatibility* in the paint.

board [tim.] (1) Softwood: *square-sawn* timber less than 50 mm (2 in.) thick and wider than 100 mm (4 in.), e.g. *scaffold board, floor board*.

(2) Hardwood: timber thinner than 50 mm (2 in.) and of width varying with the country of origin, as for *planks* (B S 565).

(3) (U S A) *Lumber* 20 cm (8 in.) or more wide, and less than 5 cm (2 in.) thick.

board finish plaster, board p. Usually a retarded *hemihydrate plaster* suitable for single-coat work on *gypsum plasterboard*, it is one of the few plasters to which lime should never be added.

board foot [tim.] The North American unit of *board measure*, formerly used in UK. The amount of *lumber* in a piece which before sawing, planing, and *shrinkage* measured $30 \times 30 \times 2\cdot5$ cm ($12 \times 12 \times 1$ in.). It may be short in all three directions. *See* **dressed size**.

boarding, close b., sheathing [carp.] Boards, often *tongued-and-grooved*, laid over *rafters* or *studs* to act as a surface for fixing insulation, *cladding*, tiles, slates, *flexible metal* sheet, and so on. *Compare* **weather-boarding**.

boarding joists [carp.] *Common joists*.

board measure [tim.] Timber measurement (1) In the U K by the *board metre* (2) In the U S A by the *board foot*.

board metre [tim.] The timber in a piece measuring 1 m² in area and 25 mm thick (B S 565 and 4471).

boasted ashlar, b. surface A rough finish to ashlar made by *boasting*.

boaster, bolster (Scots **drove**) A mason's *boasting* chisel, 4 to 8 cm (1½ to 3 in.) wide, which is struck by a *mallet* in dressing the surface of stone, and used after the *claw chisel*. *See* **mason's and bricklayer's tools** (illus. p. 211)

boasting Surfacing a stone with roughly parallel, oblique, or vertical strokes from a *boaster*, which are not usually uniform nor carried across the face of the stone. There are about nine strokes per inch. *Compare* **batting**.

boat scaffold A *cradle*.

boat spike [carp.] A *ship spike*.

bobbin [plu.] *See* **boxwood bobbin**.

body [pai.] The stiffness of a paint or the solidity of the dried *film*.

bodying in, b. up [pai.] The early stages of French polishing, including staining, filling, and the first polishing before *spiriting off*.

boiled oil [pai.] *Linseed oil* which has been heated (not boiled) for a short time at about 260° C. (500° F.) with soluble lead or manganese *driers*. Air may also be blown through it (blown oil). The drier and the air oxidize the oil, so that paint made with it dries more quickly than with *raw linseed oil*. Boiled oil can be pale or dark. Dark boiled oil contains litharge as *drier*. *See* **pale boiled oil**.

boiler A domestic water heater in which, generally, the water should not boil. It is heated by coal, oil, gas, or electricity. *See* **back b., boot b., electrode b., immersion heater, magazine b., pot-type b.** *See also* C.

bolster, corbel piece, crown plate, head tree, saddle [carp.] (1) A short timber cap over a post to increase the bearing area under a beam.

(2) A bricklayer's *chisel* about 11 cm wide. *See* **boaster**.

bolt (1) [joi.] A *draw bolt* or the tongue of a *lock*, which prevents a door opening.

(2) [mech.] *See C.*

bolting iron [joi.] A narrow *chisel* for mortising drawer locks.

bolt shooting *See* **stud shooting**.

bond (1) Laying bricks or stones in a wall in a regular pattern, devised when mortars were weaker and had less *adhesion* than now. It was important then for every vertical joint to be at least a quarter of the length of a brick or stone from the next vertical joint above or below. It is not now so essential. Common bonds include: *American, diagonal, English, English cross, Flemish, garden-wall, heading, stretching.*

(2) The placing of *slates* or *plain tiles* to exclude rain in such a way that the joint between adjoining units is at or near the centre of the unit in the course below them.

(3) [pla.] *Adhesion* (also called interface strength) resulting from *mechanical bond* (*C*) and *specific adhesion* (*C*).

(4) [tim.] The layer of *glue* in a *plywood* joint.

(5) *See* **lashing**, *also C.*

bond course A course of *headers* (USA).

bonder A *bond stone*.

bond failure [pla.] The commonest fault in plasters – detachment of a coat from the background or from an earlier coat. Defects that can cause it, either alone or in combination, include: lack of key in the background or the earlier coat, sometimes caused by dirt or grease or the formation of salt at the interface; unset plaster caused by premature drying; too wet or too dry background (suction faults); movement caused by *moisture expansion* or contraction or settlement of the building (BS 5492).

bonding agent, keying compound Many *bonding treatments* exist, often of secret composition. They are put on to a base, so that the subsequent asphalt, paint, plaster, timber lamination or veneer will stick to it. (A *bonding compound* usually is a glue.) See **concrete-bonding plaster, spatterdash**, BS 5270.

bonding brick A specially moulded Z-shaped brick used instead of a *wall tie* for holding together the two leaves of a *cavity wall*. It fits as a *header* into the facing and into one *course* higher in the *backing*.

bonding compound Hot molten bitumen put on to a roof to stick *bitumen felt* to the roof and to other felt. *Sealing compound* is applied cold.

bonding conductor [elec.] A length of wire or cable which earths cable sheaths or the metal frames of electrical apparatus. It should have very low resistance to earth, so as to ensure that nothing to which it is connected can rise appreciably above earth potential, even if there is a power leakage.

bonding tape Tape glued on both faces for joining embedded sheets in *damp courses, vapour barriers*, etc., whether of *bitumen felt, pitch polymer*, or polythene.

bonding treatment [pla.] Any pre-treatment for very smooth backgrounds (dense concrete, glazed bricks or tiles or smooth sound paint) that makes plaster stick to them. Bituminous solutions; polyvinyl acetate emulsion or other polymers are used on *soffits* as well as on walls and for reducing suction. *See* **bonding agent, concrete-bonding plaster**.

bond stone, bonder, through s. A long stone laid in a wall as a header, and seen on one face, or in a thin wall on both faces. In thick walls it is best for bond stones not to be of the full thickness of the wall but about two-thirds of it, and to be laid alternately from opposite faces to cross in the middle. When the facing is a *veneer* held by metal cramps, no bonders are needed, nor are they practicable.

bone black [pai.] A black *pigment* consisting of pure carbon. It is extremely fine grained, and, like *lamp black*, after screening only 0·5% is left on a mesh with openings 0·07 mm (1/400 in.) square. It is made from charred bones, ivory chips, etc., and sold as ivory black or drop black. *See also* **carbon black**.

boning pegs Small hardwood cubes placed at the corners of large stones to help in dressing their faces truly plane. *See also* **winding strips**.

bonnet (1) A roof over a *bay window*.

(2) A wire netting sphere inserted into the top of a vent stack or chimney to prevent birds coming in and sparks going out.

bonnet tile, b. hip, cone t. A *hip tile* with a rounded top. It is bedded in mortar on the next bonnet tile.

bonus system of wages An *incentive system* of payment where direct piece rates are not used. Men receive a day-wage which is increased by an additional payment, the bonus, if a set quantity of work is achieved.

book matching, herring-bone m. [tim.] A way of placing successive sheets of *veneer* sliced from the same *flitch*, so that alternate sheets are placed face up and face down as they come from the knife. If the veneers are laid side by side, each sheet will be a mirror image of its neighbour.

boot A projection from a concrete beam or floor slab to carry the *facing brickwork*.

boot boiler A small *back boiler*, L-shaped to increase its heating surface.

borrowed light A window in an internal wall or partition (BS 565).

boss (1) A rounded projection down from a ceiling, often at a newel post or at an intersection of ribs, sometimes a keystone to a dome. It may be carved, whether of wood or stone.

(2) [plu.] A boxwood cone for opening an end of lead pipe.

(3) [plu.] A screwed hole at the top of a hot-water *cylinder*, through which an *immersion heater* can be inserted and fixed.

bossing [plu.] The shaping of sheet lead, zinc, etc., to fit a roof or other shape, with boxwood shapes and a mallet. *Compare* **hammering**.

bossing stick [plu.] A *boxwood* shaper about 30 cm long for shaping a sheet lead lining to a tank, etc.

Boston hip, B. ridge, shingle ridge finish (USA) *Weaving.*

bottled gas [plu.] *Propane* or *butane* (C) or a mixture of them, compressed and sold liquid in steel cylinders for use by plumbers or in caravans or houses where there is no piped gas. Since their *calorific value* (C) is higher than natural gas per unit volume, the distribution pipes are smaller. Unlike *methane* (C) which is lighter than air, they are heavier than air, so a leak in an unventilated boat or cellar can be exceedingly dangerous.

bottle-nose drip, b.-n. curb [plu.] A rounded edge to a *drip* on a sheet lead roof.

bottle nosing [joi.] (Scotland) A half-round *nosing*.

bottom glazing flashing In corrugated asbestos roofing, an accessory below *patent glazing*, which receives a *flexible-metal flashing*.

bottomless hole A hole which passes through a material and is therefore difficult to plug except with a *screw anchor* or similar fixing. *Compare* **blind hole**.

bottom rail [joi.] The horizontal bottom member of a door, casement, or lower sash.

boule [tim.] A *hardwood* log, *flat-sawn* and reassembled into the shape of the log.

bow, camber [tim.] A warping of timber at right angles to its face. *Compare* **cup, spring, twist**.

bow drill, fiddle d. [carp.] A primitive boring device in which the *bit* is rotated by the grip of a cord attached to a bow pulled to and fro like a saw.

bowled floor (USA) A floor sloping down towards one end, at about 1 in 25, as in a theatre or church.

bow saw, turning s. [carp.] An ancient type of saw with a removable blade held in a wooden frame which is tightened by twisting a string. It saws easily round curves.

bow window A *bay window* which is curved in plan.

box casing [joi.] (USA) *Inside lining*.

box cornice, closed c. (USA) [carp.] A hollow *cornice*, built up from wood, and enclosed by gutter or shingles above, *fascia* in front, the *soffit board* below, and the wall of the building behind. Unlike the *open cornice*, the *soffits* of the *rafters* are hidden.

boxed frame, boxing, box f. [joi.] A *cased frame*.

boxed heart [tim.] Timber sawn so that the *pith* is cut out, usually within a 10 cm. square. This is done with some Australian and other *hardwoods* which have poor heart.

box gutter, trough g., parallel g. [plu.] A wooden *gutter*, lined with *flexible metal*, *asphalt* or *roofing felt*, often with one or both sides built along the roof slope, used in *valleys* or behind *parapets*.

boxing (1) [joi.] A *cased frame*.

(2) [joi.] The part of a window recess hollowed out to take a *boxing shutter*.

(3) [carp.] (USA) *Boarding*.

boxing shutters, folding s. [joi.] *Shutters* inside a window which fold away into a recess at the side, the *boxing*.

boxing up [carp.] (USA) Nailing *boarding* to studs, or otherwise encasing something with timber.

box stair (USA) *Closed stair*.

box staple (USA **b. strike**) [joi.] The metal box on a door post into which the latch of a *rim lock* passes when the door is shut. *See* **striking plate**.

boxwood [tim.] A hard hardwood used for making chisel handles, chessmen, *boxwood dressers*, etc.

boxwood bobbin [plu.] An egg shape drilled through the centre and used for truing bends in lead pipes. It is threaded on a strong cord with a brass follower behind it, and pulled through the pipe until the distortions are removed. The follower is used as a sort of hammer, being pulled back and forth until the bobbin passes the obstacle.

boxwood dresser [plu.] A tool like a *bossing stick* for shaping lead sheet. It may be of some *hardwood* cheaper than boxwood, such as hornbeam.

boxwood tampin, turning pin [plu.] A conical *hardwood* tool used by plumbers for opening out the end of a lead pipe.

brace, bit-stock, carpenter's brace [carp.] A cranked tool used for turning a drilling *bit* to make holes in wood. *See* **carpenter's tools** (illus. p. 59).

braced frame [carp.] A wooden building frame with widely spaced, heavy corner posts into which *binders* or girders are framed. The studs between the posts carry no floor load, unlike *balloon framing*. The corner posts rise to the roof, being framed into each floor or ceiling as they pass it. Some bracing is needed in the frame, though it is appreciably stiffer than balloon framing. The term is also used for any *frame construction* intermediate between this and balloon framing.

brace extension [carp.] A *bit extension*.

brace jaws, b. chuck [carp.] The clamp for a *bit* in a *brace*.

bracket (1) A projecting support, of any material, in *masonry* or brickwork called a *corbel*, in metal or concrete, a *cantilever* (*C*).

(2) [carp.] A short vertical board fixed to the *carriage* of a *stair* to support the *tread* directly.

bracketed stairs [joi.] Stairs carried on a *cut string*, usually with overhanging *nosings*.

bracketing [pla.] *Cradling* consisting of shaped wooden *brackets* which carry the lathing for the plaster of cornices.

brad, floor b. [carp.] (1) A *cut nail* of constant thickness but tapering width, with a square head projecting on one edge only. Used for fixing floorboards, they are 5 to 6·2 cm (2 to 2½ in.) long.

(2) An *oval-wire brad*.

bradawl [joi.] A short *awl* with a narrow *chisel* point, pushed in to make holes for nails and screws.

brad setter, b. punch [joi.] (USA) A *nail punch*.

branch An outlet from a *run* of pipe or cable.

branch circuit, final sub-circuit [elec.] The conductors installed between the wall *socket outlet* or other *point* and the fuse which protects them.

branched knot [tim.] Two or more knots branching from a common axis (BS 565).

brander, counter-lath [pla.] A *fillet* sometimes nailed at 30 to 38 cm (12 to 15 in.) centres on to the soffit of joists as a base for ceiling *lathing*.

brandering, counter-lathing [pla.] When ceiling joists are over 8 cm (3 in.) wide, it may be difficult to get a good *key* on *lathing* nailed directly to them. Branders are therefore nailed to the joists, to take the lathing.

brash, brashy A description of timber which breaks with small resistance to shock and little or no splintering. This 'short grain' may be due to fungus.

brass Old-established non-corroding alloy of copper and zinc, used for builders' *hardware*, and in paints for gilding, etc.

brazing [mech.] An ancient method of *capillary jointing* of metals with a film of copper-zinc alloy (hard *solder*) between the red-hot contact surfaces, e.g. for brass, copper, steel, and cast iron in any combination, using a flux such as borax. Unlike *bronze welding* (*C*), any method of heating may be used, though gas is usual. For copper tube, *silver brazing* was introduced to British plumbers in 1959 for diameters up to 100 mm (4 in.).

breaking down [tim.] *Conversion*.

break iron [joi.] (1) A *back iron*.

(2) A *dressing iron*.

break joint, breaking j. *See* **staggering**.

44

breast (1) A projection of a wall into a room, containing the flue and hearth of a fireplace.
(2) [joi.] (Scotland) A *riser* of a *stair*.
(3) The wall under the *sill* of a *window*, down to floor level.
breast drill [mech.] A drill which, like the *brace*, is held with both hands. Unlike the brace, it is provided with an upward extension, topped by a flat bar on which the user can bear the weight of his chest to increase his drilling speed in metal. Breast drills can usually take *twist drills* up to 12 mm dia. The bit is turned by a handle through bevel gears, often with a choice of two speeds. The *hand drill* is a small breast drill without the bearing for the chest.
breast lining [joi.] Wooden panelling inside a window below the *window board*.
breast wall A breast-high *retaining wall* (*C*) for earth.
breather membrane A *vapour check* where *condensation* will evaporate, e.g. behind the tiles on a tile-hung wall.
breeze Small coke which, before 1939, may have been used in Britain to make *building blocks*.
breeze blocks *Building blocks* of coke *breeze*, no longer made; usually means *clinker blocks*. *See* **pan breeze**.
bressummer, breastsummer A long heavy *lintel*, usually timber, carrying a considerable load of brickwork or *masonry*, often placed over a shop window. Steel or concrete girders are now more usual.
brick In temperate climates, bricks are made of clay with some coarser material such as silt or sand. They are burnt, not baked, in a kiln and slightly fused. This fusion can be seen from the surface glaze of *hard-burnt* bricks. In hot climates bricks are often sun-dried (baked) from *adobe* with straw to bind it (as in the Bible). In Roman Britain, bricks varied from 15 × 15 to 45 × 30 cm (6 × 6 to 18 × 12 in.). From 1936 until metrication, the standard British brick had an actual size of $8\frac{3}{4} \times 4\frac{3}{16} \times 2\frac{5}{8}$ in. (222 × 106 × 67 mm) making a *brick format* of 9 × $4\frac{1}{2}$ × 3 in. (228 × 114 × 76 mm). Four courses made 12 in. height, 30·5 cm instead of the present 30·0 cm. American sizes are less uniform than the British. The 'standard modular brick' measures 190 × 89 × 55 mm ($7\frac{1}{2} \times 3\frac{1}{2} \times 2\frac{1}{8}$ in.), lays up three courses to 8 in. (203 mm) and has a brick format in plan of 203 × 101·5 mm (8 × 4 in.) including the half-joint each side. The 'standard common brick' is about 190 × 95 × 57 mm ($7\frac{1}{2} \times 3\frac{3}{4} \times 2\frac{1}{4}$ in. high) but many other sizes exist. *See* **calcium silicate, concrete, economy, engineered, engineering, moulded, Norman, pressed, Roman, solid masonry unit, tolerance, wirecut brick.**
brick-and-a-half wall In Britain a brick wall 34 cm ($13\frac{1}{4}$ in.) thick.
brick and stud *See* **brick nogging**.
brick axe A *bricklayer's hammer*.
brick construction Building with *loadbearing* (*C*) brick walls.
brick core Brick filling under the *soffit* of a *relieving arch*, or hidden behind the lintel of a *flat arch*.
brick damp course An adequate *damp course* against *rising damp* can be made with two courses of *engineering bricks* laid breaking joint, but such bricks cost about four times as much as common bricks. So far as water running down a wall is concerned, a brick or slate damp course, because of the cracks that occur between mortar and brick or slate, does not prevent rain penetration. Such cracks do not allow water to creep up, however.
brick definitions The B S I defines four types of clay or concrete brick: 'cellular'

bricks with indentations (*frogs*) exceeding 20% of the volume; 'solid' bricks with a frog less than 20% of the volume, alternatively with small holes passing through that do not exceed 25% of the volume; thirdly 'perforated' bricks with small through holes exceeding 25% of the volume; fourthly 'hollow' bricks with large through holes exceeding 25% of the volume. 'Small holes' are less than 2 cm across or 5 cm² in area. But the bulk of UK bricks in current use are 'solid' according to these definitions. Bricks with small through holes are nevertheless known as 'perforated' although the BS call them 'solid' (BS 3921, 6073).

brick-and-a-half wall In Britain a brick wall 34 cm (13½ in.) thick.

brick elevator A small endless-chain elevator for raising building materials on to a *scaffold*. Like the *portable belt conveyor* it is easily moved.

brick format The dimensions of a brick plus one half-mortar-joint each side (two half-joints = 10 mm). Thus with UK metric bricks of 215 × 102·5 × 65 mm, the brick format is 225 × 112·5 × 75 mm (9 × 4½ × 3 in.). Four bricks long thus make 90 cm (3 ft) and four courses high make 30 cm.

bricklayer A *tradesman* who builds and repairs brickwork, lays and joints *vitrified clayware* drains, sets chimney pots, manhole frames, and fireplaces, and renders brickwork, including the insides of manholes. In some districts, bricklayers also fix wall and *flooring tiles*, and slating, and lay plaster and granolithic floors, but elsewhere these are plasterer's specialities. *See* **mason**.

bricklayer in firebrick A *bricklayer* specialized in setting firebrick or refractory blocks in fireclay or other *refractory mortar*, with thin joints not more than 3 mm. thick.

bricklayer's hammer, brick axe (USA **ax, axhammer**) A small *hammer* with a sharp *cross peen* as well as a striking face, used for dressing bricks. *Compare* **scrutch**. *See* **mason's and bricklayer's tools** (illus. p. 211).

bricklayer's labourer A skilled *labourer* who mixes *mortar* and carries it either on a hod (hod carrier), on a *head board* (tupper), or in a wheelbarrow to the bricklayer. Before bricklaying on the site has begun, he helps digging, concreting, drainlaying, and shoring.

bricklayer's scaffold A *scaffold* supported by *putlogs*, of which one end is supported in holes in the brickwork, the other end being carried on *ledgers* held by the *standards*. *Compare* **mason's scaffold**.

brick mason (USA) A *bricklayer*.

brick masonry (USA) *Brickwork*.

brick nogging Brickwork infilling between the studs of a wooden frame. *See* **nogging**.

brick-on-edge coping A *coping* of *headers* laid on edge.

brick-on-edge sill A door or window *sill* of *headers* laid on edge.

brick set (USA) A *bolster* for cutting bricks.

brick trowel A bricklayer's large triangular trowel for spreading mortar, with a blade about 28 cm (11 in.) long.

brick truck A modern barrow with one or two wheels, pushed by one man and used for moving bricks from place to place without restacking them each time (a necessity with the ordinary *wheelbarrow*).

brick veneer An outer covering, usually to a timber house, consisting of a half-brick wall, used in North America and Australia over *frame construction*. *See* **veneered wall**.

brickwork (1) *Bricks* built into a wall or other structure. *See* BSCP 121.

(2) The art of building with bricks; in USA known as brick *masonry*. *See* **bond**.

brickwork chaser, keyway miller [mech.] A power tool that cuts a neat groove in masonry to receive a pipe or cable.

bridge A broken brick or lump of mortar dropped into the cavity of a *cavity wall* can join the two leaves of the wall, forming a bridge for water penetration which is also a *cold bridge* (illus. p. 75) and is doubly harmful. *See also C.*

bridge board [carp.] A *cut string*.

bridging [carp.] (1) The spanning of a gap with *common joists*.

(2) The stiffening of adjacent common joists against each other by a row of *solid* or *herring-bone strutting* against the joists, under the floorboards, at the midspan of the joists. This ensures that the joists deflect together when one is heavily loaded, and increases the effectiveness of the floor, since the load on each joist is shared by its neighbours. Because of the possibility of confusion between these two meanings, it might be better to use only the word strutting for this sense. *See* **double-bridging**.

(3) [pai.] The covering over of a gap in a *ground* by the film.

(4) By-passing of a *damp course* (dpc) that allows water to pass up into the wall above it. This can occur because of earth piled against the wall above the dpc, because of rendering or pointing that covers it, or inside the house, because of a *screed* at dpc level. Mortar droppings piled above dpc in the cavity of a wall often form a *bridge* for water to pass across the cavity.

bridging floor [carp.] A floor carried on *common joists* only.

bridging joist [carp.] A *common joist*.

bridging piece [carp.] A short bearer either between or across *common joists* to carry a *partition*.

bridle [carp.] (Scotland) A *trimmer joist*.

bridle joint [carp.] *See* **birdsmouth joint**. A development of the *mortise-and-tenon* joint for heavy framing. The tenoned member is usually a post, cut at the sides to leave a central tongue which enters a notch or mortise in the upper member, usually a beam carried by the post. (Illus. below)

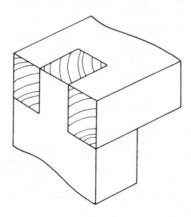

Bridle joint.

bright [tim.] A description of freshly sawn timber without discoloration.

brilliance [pai.] (1) The clearness of a *varnish* or *lacquer*, the absence of opalescence and similar defects.

(2) The cleanness and brightness of a *colour*.

brilliant cutting Cutting a design on *glass* by pushing it down on a revolving sandstone wheel.

brindled bricks Striped bricks unsuitable for *facing* but otherwise perfect.

brise-soleil A shield from the sun, used in tropical or Mediterranean countries, e.g. vertical or horizontal precast concrete strips which prevent hot, direct sun from entering a room.

bristle brush [pai.] A *brush* made from hog's hair, because of their scarcity being replaced by synthetic fibres.

British Board of Agrément *See* **Agrément Board.**

British Standard, BS, BS specification A numbered publication of the *British Standards Institution* describing the quality or the dimensions of a manufacture, such as pipes or *bricks*. Frequently the dimensions and the quality are described in two separate standards. The use by architects or engineers of British Standards in their *specifications* can reduce the volume of the description to a reference (for steel frames, for example) to B S 449.

British Standards Institution, BSI The British organization for standardizing, by agreement between maker and user, the methods of test and dimensions of materials as well as *codes of practice* and nomenclature. Corresponding organizations in other countries are A F N O R (Association Française de Normalisation); A S T M (American Society for Testing and Materials); A S A (American Standards Association). A German standard number is prefixed by D I N (Deutsche Industrie Norm).

British thermal unit The amount of heat needed to warm one pound of water from 39° to 40° F. *See* pp. 8, 9.

brittleheart [tim.] Weak brittle wood at the heart which may need to be *boxed*, common in tropical timbers.

brittleness [pai.] A finish is brittle if it cracks when stretched or when a knife or needle is pulled across it. The opposite of flexibility.

broach (1) A pin inside a *lock* to locate the barrel of its key.

(2) The *mason's* pointed *chisel*.

broached work *Punched work*.

broad axe [carp.] A wide-edged axe with a cutting *bevel* on one side only. It was used for log-cabin building in U S A, and is still used for rough-dressing timber. The handle may be offset sideways from the blade.

broad tooling *Batting*.

broken-range ashlar (U S A) *Uncoursed rubble*.

broken white [pai.] A white which has been toned down, usually to a creamy colour.

bronze An alloy usually of copper and tin without other elements. Aluminium bronze is mainly copper and aluminium.

bronze powder [pai.] *Gold bronze* powder.

bronzing fluid [pai.] A *varnish* or *lacquer* with aluminium or *gold bronze* powders mixed in with it.

brooming [pla.] Scratching a floating coat with a broom to make a *key* for plaster. *See also* C.

browning, brown coat [pla.] A *floating coat* of *gypsum plaster* and *sand*, used with mixes from 1:1½ to 1:3 of sand.

brown rot [tim.] A *decay* of timber to a brown, soft mass.

Brunswick black [pai.] A *bituminous paint.*

Brunswick green [pai.] *Lead chrome green.*

brush [pai.] A tuft of animal, or artificial (nylon), or vegetable fibres held on to a handle, usually wooden (the stock), and used for putting on *paint* or for wetting or dusting down surfaces. Holding the fibre to the stock is a metal ring (the ferrule) or a binding of twine or copper wire. The fibres of all large brushes and some small ones are set in *synthetic resin*, vulcanized rubber, pitch, etc. Brushes may be of *bristle, sable,* badger, squirrel hair, etc. *See* **blender, camel-hair mop, dabber, distemper brush, dusting brush, fitch, flat paint brush, flat wall brush, ground brush, lining tool, mottler, overgrainer, rigger, sable pencil, sable writer, sash tool, stippler.** *See also* **house painter** (illus.) and B S 2992.

brushability [pai.] The ease with which a liquid can be brushed on. Brushable paints are not *gummy* or *ropy* and can be joined easily with paint put on some minutes earlier.

B S *British Standard.*

B S C P British Standard *Code of Practice.*

B S I *British Standards Institution.*

bubbling [pai.] A defect of films containing very volatile *solvents* – bubbles of air or solvent vapours which may disappear before the film dries.

buckle A *spar* in thatching.

budget A leathern pocket to contain nails, carried by *slaters and tilers.*

buff To polish or grind down a floor finish of *terrazzo* or screeded material. It is derived from the high-speed buffing wheels of mechanical engineering which were originally made of buffalo leather and are used for polishing with slight abrasion.

builder's equipment Plant used by builders, from *scaffold boards* to 200-ton *Goliath cranes* (*C*). Also called builder's plant and machinery, a term which has the advantage that it cannot be confused with *building equipment.*

builder's handyman A *jobber.*

builder's labourer A *semi-skilled man* who can mix *mortar* or *concrete*, dig, clean old bricks, load or unload material, place *concrete*, demolish houses, and so on. Like the *jobber*, who does everything inside a house, the builder's labourer does everything outside a house except those trades which are best paid. *See* **bricklayer's labourer.**

builder's ladder, pole l. A wooden *ladder* with half-round *stiles*. Its rungs are made of *oak, ash,* or *hickory*. The stiles may be a *spruce* or *silver fir* pole sawn in two. *Compare* **standing ladder**.

builder's level (1) A *level tube* (*C*) set in a long wooden or *light-alloy straight edge.*

(2) A *dumpy level* (*C*) used on a building site, and therefore sturdy, but not usually very sensitive.

builder's staging or **scaffold** A *mason's scaffold.*

builder's tape A linen *tape* (*C*) or steel tape, often 30 m (100 ft) long, which rolls into a round leather or plastic pocket case.

building approvals (1) Building components, elements or systems are approved in Britain by the *Agrément Board* and by the *National Building Agency*. BRE Digests 166 and 167 describe approval procedures in Denmark, Federal Germany, France, the Netherlands and Sweden.

(2) Approval of a project for a particular building is obtained from the local planning authority, often within the district council offices in the UK.

building blocks Hollow or solid walling olocks of *burnt clay, concrete*, or other material, larger than *bricks*, often 46 × 23 × 23 cm (18 × 9 × 9 in.) and therefore quicker to lay. Used for building *partitions*, they can be as thin as (6·4 cm (2½ in.), hollow or 5 cm (2 in.) solid, and may also be of *diatomite* brick or other insulating material. *See* **blockwork, clinker blocks, hollow blocks, lightweight aggregate, soil stack** (illus. p. 313), **Lignacite**.

building board *Fibreboard, gypsum plasterboard, insulating board, wallboard,* etc. *Woodwool slab* and *corkboard* are intermediate between *building blocks* and building board.

building brick (USA) A *common brick*.

Building Centre An organization established in 1930 to provide information for specifiers and users of building materials. Helped by the makers of building materials, it has seven provincial information centres and one in London.

building certificate *See* **certificate**.

building code (USA) Local building laws corresponding to *Building Regulations* in Britain. *Compare* **code of practice**.

building component A part of a building too complex to be called a *building element*; for instance, a wall, door, roof, or window, all of which may be built of several elements. The electrical, plumbing, gas or other services also contain building components.

building element An elementary part of a building, only one stage removed from a *building material*. *Bricks*, and *joists* of metal, wood or precast concrete are building elements.

building equipment *Services*, furniture, and other plant used in a completed building. *Compare* **builder's equipment**.

building in Fixing a wall tie, air brick, bracket, or other building part into a wall or other part of a building by bedding it in mortar and laying bricks or stones over it and round it. Building in may be done while the wall is being built, or later, by leaving a hole, or breaking a hole afterwards. The part can then be grouted into the hole or fixed into it with *dry pack* (C).

building inspector An employee in Britain of a *local authority*, building society, or insurance company, who tells his employers whether a building is built in accordance with the law or advises them on its rateable value, fire risk, and mortgage value. He needs wide knowledge of building construction, which may be attested by the Building.Inspector's Certificate of the Institution of Municipal Engineers. *See* **inspector** (C), **building official**.

building line (1) The line fixed, usually by the *local authority*, as a limit to building near a road.

(2) The outside face of the wall of a building, shown, in plan, as a line on a drawing.

building materials The materials of which *building elements* are made, for example, sand, ballast, clay, cement, round timber.

building module A *module* which may be small, such as 75 or 100 mm (3 or 4 in.), or large, such as 900 mm or 1 m (36 or 40 in.).

building official (USA) An employee of a *local authority* whose duty it is to enforce a *building code*. He may correspond to the British *building inspector*.

building paper Fibre-reinforced bitumen between layers of kraft paper, laid under concrete to prevent loss of cement into the earth and damage by acid in the soil. It is also used for many other purposes – over the *boarding* of a wall or roof, for example. In Britain it is made in rolls up to 1·8 m (6 ft) wide and 231 m (250 yd) long. It may also be called roofing paper, sheathing paper, Willesden paper, waterproof paper, concreting paper, etc., some of which may be less strong or less waterproof than that described above. Many types are now based on polythene or polyvinyl chloride instead of bitumen (BS 1521).

Building Regulations British national regulations, that superseded local by-laws, were first put into operation in 1966 and metricated in 1972. In principle it was an excellent idea to make building laws uniform throughout the country but by 1980 architects had found them so difficult to understand and apply that there were hopes that they would be completely recast.

Building Research Digest, B R E Digest Inexpensive leaflets stating the conclusions of the *Building Research Establishment* about a building topic. They are issued monthly, covering hundreds of subjects from 'Co-ordination of building colours' to 'Materials for making concrete'. The full title is Building Research Establishment Digest.

Building Research Establishment (BRE) The BRE of the British Department of the Environment was created in 1971 by the fusion of four government bodies, the Building Research Station (Watford, Herts), the BRE Scottish Laboratory (East Kilbride, Glasgow), the Fire Research Station (Boreham Wood, Herts), and the former Forest Products Research Laboratory (Princes Risborough, Bucks). One example of the international reputation of the BRE is its work on *single-stack* drainage.

building society Organization for financing building, in Britain usually backed by an insurance company. Most private building is financed by these societies. The society is repaid by the buyer in the form of rent, usually for not less than ten years, a large part of the rent being interest on the *mortgage*. The buyer must make a down payment of at least 10% of the value of the house, often 25%. *Co-operative housing societies* are very much cheaper in rent and first payment, but demand some physical work or other co-operative effort from the co-operative buyers.

building surveyor [q.s.] A person trained in the techniques, costs and law of building construction. He advises on alterations, building defects, *easements*, extensions, renovations, energy conservation, planning applications, improvement grants, maintenance, fire insurance, and structural surveys in buildings in use. 'Chartered' building surveyors are Fellows or Associates of the Royal Institution of Chartered Surveyors. Others belong to the Incorporated Association of Architects and Surveyors or the Faculty of Architects and Surveyors.

building system An arrangement of the *building elements* to form a connected whole. *Box-frame construction* (C) is one system, *industrialized building methods* are others.

building trade One of or all the occupations of *tradesmen* in building.

built in *See* **building in**.

built-up [carp.] A timber piece built of several smaller ones, usually glued, but sometimes screwed, nailed, bolted, or *fished* (*C*). *See* **compound beam**.

built-up roofing Two or more layers of *bitumen felt*, laid to break joint and jointed with *bonding* or *sealing compound*. This roof covering is cheap, lightweight, and popular, but its life is not exactly known. Guarantees for 3-ply roofing are often given for twenty years and for 2-ply roofing for ten years. They can be white-topped if the final layer is of polyvinyl fluoride or neoprene asbestos (National Building Specification). *See* **roof-decking panels**.

bulkhead A roofed box-shape built above a roof to cover a water tank, lift shaft, stair well, etc.

bulldog clip A *floor clip*.

bulldog plate, tooth p., [carp.] A timber *connector*. (Illus. p. 83)

bullet catch A *ball catch*.

bullet-resistant glazing A type of *security glazing*.

bull header A *header* with the upper exposed arris rounded, used in brick window *sills*.

bullnose The rounding of an *arris*; in general, any rounded end or edge of a brick, a step, a joiner's plane, etc.

bull's eye A small, circular or oval, window or opening.

bull stretcher A *stretcher* with an exposed *arris* rounded.

bund An uninterrupted wall of earth, brick, etc., built around a tank containing oil or other hazardous liquid, to such a height that the volume of liquid it could contain is slightly larger than the maximum volume of liquid in the tank. If the tank leaks, therefore, the bund prevents dangerous spreading of the liquid. Surface-water drains are not provided within the bund. It is drained by pumping.

bur [mech.] A *bit* used in a drill by dentists and by wood carvers for widening holes rather than for drilling them.

burglar alarms. *See* **security**.

burl [tim] *Burr*.

burlap (USA) Hessian canvas – a cheap reinforcement for plaster, much weaker than *metal lathing*.

burning in [plu.] *See* **leadburning**.

burning off [pai.] Removing old paint by heating it with a *blow lamp* and scraping it off while hot. A safer method is the *hot-air stripper*.

burnisher [mech.] A hard steel tool for smoothing and polishing the cutting edge of a chisel, axe, knife, etc.

burnt clay *Ceramics*, not *adobe*.

burnt lime *Quicklime*, calcium oxide (CaO).

burnt sienna, umber [pai.] *See* **sienna, umber**.

burr (1) **burl** [tim.] The curly, much-valued *figure*, got by cutting through the enlarged trunk of certain trees, particularly walnut, formed of the dark *pith* centres of many undeveloped buds.

(2) Jagged metal left on a freshly cut surface. *See below*.

burring reamer [plu.] A tool turned in a brace so as to remove the *burr* left by a *pipe cutter* inside a pipe. *See* **plumber's tools** (illus. p. 250).

bus bar [elec.] A bare copper or aluminium *conductor*, usually fixed on a slate slab, or wall, parallel to the other bars of its *circuit*, to carry a heavy current.

bush (1) [plu.] A short screwed pipe fitting connecting two others of different

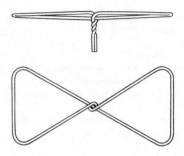

UK butterfly wall tie, made of 5 mm ($\frac{3}{16}$ in.) wire. Length of tie 150 to 200 mm (6 to 8 in.).

diameters. It is threaded inside and outside, and is convenient to use where there is little space.

(2) [elec.] An insulated tube, sometimes of porcelain, which protects cables. *See* **conduit bushing**.

butane *See* **propane blowlamp, bottled gas**.

butt (1) To meet without overlapping.

(2) [tim.] The thick end of a *shingle* or a log, generally the thicker end of anything.

(3) [joi.] A *butt hinge*.

butterfly wall tie A *wall tie* made from galvanized steel wire about 3 mm ($\frac{1}{8}$ in.) dia., bent to the form of a figure 8. These ties transmit less sound than the stronger, stiffer ties of steel strip. (Illus. above)

buttering The spreading of *mortar* on a vertical face of a brick before laying, usually to form a *cross joint*.

buttering trowel A trowel smaller than the *brick trowel*.

butt gauge [joi.] A *marking gauge*.

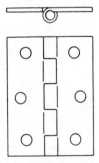

Butt hinge.

butt hinge [joi.] The commonest *hinge* for doors. When the door is shut, the two halves are folded together, one half being on the *door frame*, the other on the *hanging stile*. The ordinary steel butt hinge is very cheap and durable, but ball-bearing butts can be obtained which are smoother running, noiseless, longer lasting, and much dearer.

butt joint [joi.] A joint between two pieces of wood (or metal) which meet at their ends without overlapping.

button [joi.] A small piece of wood or metal held loosely by a screw so that it can turn and thus hold a cupboard door shut.

button-headed screw, half-round s. [joi.] A *screw* with a hemispherical head.

butt stile [joi.] The *hanging stile* of a door.

butt veneer [tim.] *Veneer* having a strong curly figure like *crotch*, caused by roots growing out of the trunk at all angles.

buzz-saw [tim.] A *circular saw*.

B X cable [elec.] (USA) An *armoured cable*.

by-laws (USA **building codes**) Regulations that formerly controlled British building and were made by each *local authority*, but are superseded by the *Building Regulations. See* **code of practice**.

by-pass [plu.] An arrangement of pipes (or conduits) for directing flow around instead of through a certain pipe or conduit.

C

cabinet file [joi.] A smooth, half-round, single-cut file with which a joiner forms a smooth finish on a joint. *See* **cut** (*C*).

cabinet finish [joi.] A varnished or polished finish on *hardwood*, like that on good furniture. *Compare* **carpenter's finish**.

cabinet maker A *joiner* who makes fine furniture and is therefore capable of the finest workmanship.

cabinet scraper (USA **s. plane**) [joi.] A flat piece of steel drawn over a wood surface to prepare it for sandpapering by removing plane marks.

cabin hook [joi.] A hooked bar on a cupboard door or window frame which engages in a *screw eye* on the door to hold it shut or open.

cable [elec.] Insulated, sometimes *armoured cable*, containing copper conductors supplying power to a consumer. Each conductor is separately insulated but laid with the others in a common insulating sheath often made of *polyvinyl chloride*. The cable layout is shown on the wiring diagram.

cadmium plating A *protective finish* for steel articles such as wood *screws*. If *chromated* it takes paint or lacquer better.

calcicosis A disease of the lungs caused by breathing marble dust.

calcium carbonate ($CaCO_3$) The chemical name for chalk, limestone, marble, and so on.

calcium chloride, $CaCl_2$ An *accelerator* now rarely used because it is not suitable for any concrete containing metal. It increases the corrosion of metal and the shrinkage of concrete, and mixed with brickwork mortars may be a source of permanent dampness in the bricks because it is hygroscopic.

calcium hydroxide ($Ca(OH)_2$) *Slaked lime*.

calcium oxide (CaO) *Quicklime*. When water is added, it becomes calcium hydroxide; thus, $CaO + H_2O = Ca(OH)_2$.

calcium silicate bricks, sand-lime b., flint-lime b. Low-cost, pale bricks made from sand, crushed flints or other crushed rock. They do not effloresce, and collect dirt less readily than other bricks, so are a good choice of facing brick for use in *air shafts* or other places where light reflection is essential. Made by compressing the damp sand with slaked lime and maturing in a steam oven for some hours, they are as dense as clay bricks and have an average crushing strength that may reach 48·5 N/mm^2 (7000 psi). Their main difference from clay bricks is that they do not expand but shrink up to 0·35% (1 in 300) on drying, so that walls not designed with this in mind may crack. They should not be soaked before laying and shrinkage joints should be provided every 7·5 m (25 ft). *Aerated concrete* also is calcium silicate (BS 187).

calcium sulphate ($CaSO_4$) The mineral anhydrite which has the same composition as calcined *gypsum*.

calcium sulphate hemihydrate, plaster of Paris, casting plaster *See* **hemihydrate plaster**.

Calculon A brick size introduced about 1972 to create a wall thickness (178 mm, 7 in.) halfway between the 225 mm (9 in.) and the 112 mm (4½ in.) walls. It measures 229 × 178 × 76 mm (9 × 7 × 3 in.). Metric sizes also exists, e.g. 300 × 100 × 100 mm (12 × 4 × 4 in.).

calk, caulk *See* **caulking, tang**.

callus, rindgall [tim.] A mass of wood formed by a growing tree over a surface wound.

calorifier [plu.] A *heat exchanger*, not necessarily for storage, in which water is heated, usually by a submerged coil of pipe with steam or hotter water passing through it. An *indirect cylinder* is one type of calorifier.

cam [mech.] A non-circular wheel, bearing on a part which is made to move by the variations in the radius of the cam. For example, the *lever cap* fixed to the *back iron* of a steel *plane* holds the back iron in place by the wedging action of a cam.

camber, hog (1) Curvature which is domed to allow water off a road, to hide the deflection of a girder, and so on. 'Camber' is used mainly for roads, 'hog' for structures.

(2) [tim.] *See* **bow**.

camber arch, straight a. An arch with a level *extrados* and just enough rise in the *intrados*, about 1%, to counteract the appearance of sagging.

camber beam [carp.] (1) A beam cambered on its upper surface.

(2) An old term for the tie-beam of a truss.

camber board A *template* for forming a *camber*.

camber slip, turning, trimming piece A shaped piece of wood, cambered on its upper surface, used in the *centers* for a flat brick arch to ensure that the arch *soffit* at the midspan is slightly cambered above the springing line.

cambium [tim.] The growing wood just below the bark.

came An H-section strip of lead or of soft copper, shaped to fix each piece of glass to the next one, in *leaded lights* or stained-glass windows, developed in the 1940s into the *structural gasket*.

camel-hair mop [pai.] A *brush* like a *dabber*, made of squirrel's hair.

Canadian latch A *thumb latch*.

Canadian spruce [tim.] (Picea glauca) Several species of *spruce*, softwoods exported from Canada, second in quantity after *Douglas fir* alone, almost white, with a slight lustre, both stiff and resilient. It is used for *joinery* and structural *timbers* including *ladder* stiles.

cant (1) To tilt.

(2) A cant *moulding* is one with flat surfaces and no curves.

(3) Stone built 'on cant' has the natural bedding vertical.

(4) [tim.] To cut *wane* from a log.

cant bay A bay *window* with three straight sides.

cant brick A *splay brick*.

canted Splayed, bevelled, or off-square.

canting strip A *water table*.

canting table [tim.] A *saw bench* with a working surface which can tilt and thus *rip* at any angle required (bevel cutting).

cant strip (USA) A *tilting fillet*.

cap (1) The uppermost, decorative part of a *newel* post.

(2) [plu.] A cover, with internal threads, screwed over the end of a pipe. It thus closes, or caps, the pipe.

cap and lining [plu.] A *plumber's union*.

capillary entry, soakage *Dampness* caused by *capillarity (C)*.

capillary groove, c. break, storm g. A groove or space between two surfaces, large enough to prevent *capillary entry* of water, as in a *water-checked casement*. Tiny holes can suck soil water up to great heights unless the movement is blocked by a *damp course* or an air gap.

capillary joint (USA **sweat j.**) [plu.] A strong joint in *light gauge copper tubing* made by inserting one pipe into a fitting very slightly larger in diameter so that the space between the two pipes can accurately be described as a capillary (hair's breadth) space. Molten *solder*, flowing into this space, immediately spreads round the perimeter. Several types of capillary joint exist, of which most can be made by unskilled, even amateur, labour. They also are neater and smaller than the *compression joint*, but the latter does not need heating. *See* **copper fittings**.

cap iron [carp.] A *back iron*.

cap lever [carp.] *See* **lever cap**.

capping (1) In *flexible metal roofing*, a metal strip covering the wood *roll* either separate from, or welted to the edge of the roofing sheets which are dressed up the sides of the roll. *See* **ridge capping**.

(2) A metal section held outside some *patent glazing* bars to fix the glass and protect the stem of the bar from the weather.

(3) The crowning part of a screen or panelling which does not reach to the ceiling, such as *dado capping*.

(4) A *coping*.

(5) [plu.] The closing of an end of screwed pipe by a *cap*.

capping plane [joi.] A *plane* which rounds off the top of a handrail.

cap sheet The top layer of *mineral-surfaced bitumen felt* in *built-up roofing*.

capstone A *coping*.

carbonating, carbonation The natural, slow, hardening of lime mortars; their conversion into stable *calcium carbonate* by their absorption of carbon dioxide from the air. On the surface of *cast stone*, *crazing* has been caused by the shrinkage which occurs with carbonation, and this can now be eliminated by carbonation during manufacture. In dense concrete, carbonation usually does not penetrate deeply, and this protects the reinforcement. So long as the lime in the concrete is not carbonated, the steel in contact with it remains protected.

carbon black, hydrocarbon b. [pai.] A black *pigment*. Chemically, *bone black*, and lamp black, being pure carbon, are identical with it, but British Standard carbon black is extremely fine powder of which only $0·05\%$ remains on a mesh with $0·07$ mm square openings. It is usually made by burning a hydrocarbon gas in insufficient air, or by cracking acetylene gas. Carbon black is very opaque and of high *staining power*, but it absorbs *drier* and therefore slightly retards the drying of *oil paints*.

carbon dioxide fire extinguisher Reduction of the normal oxygen content of the air from 21% to 15% extinguishes most fires but to achieve this involves about 30% CO_2 in the air, which is a toxic level. Even 5% can lead to shortness of breath and slight headache. This danger is less than the dangers of fire, however, and 100 000 CO_2 systems have been installed by industry since 1929. Several methods exist. For enclosed spaces the preferred method is total flooding. Forced ventilation should stop before, or simultaneously with, the discharge of CO_2. Provided that losses of CO_2 are not high, this method can extinguish deep-seated fires, and is also suitable for electrical fires, fires in fuel tanks and others where water cannot be used. Where total flooding is impracticable other methods are applied (B S 5306 part 4).

carcase, carcass, fabric The loadbearing part of a structure without windows, doors, plaster, or finishes.

carnauba wax [pai.] A hard wax, obtained from the leaves of the Brazilian carnauba palm, or tree of life. It is used as a polish for wood and in *matt* and stoving varnishes.

carpenter A man who erects wooden frames, fits joints, fixes wooden floors, *stairs* and window frames, asbestos sheeting and other *wallboard*, and builds or dismantles wooden or metal *formwork* (*C*). The two trades of carpenter and joiner were originally the same, and most men can do both, but specialize in one or the other. In U S A the term carpenter includes *joiner* (French 'charpente', a wooden or metal framework).

carpenter's finish (U S A) What in Britain would be called joiner's finish, since it includes all *joinery* but no roughly finished work such as *rafters*.

carpenter's hammer [carp.] A *claw hammer*. Compare **joiner's hammer**.

carpentry The craft of cutting timber to make structural frameworks, the *carcassing* of wooden buildings. In U S A (but not in Britain) carpentry includes *joinery*.

carpets B S 3655 'Informative labelling of textile floor covering' contains recommendations to makers of carpets which, so far as its 2½ pages go, may also help buyers in their inquiries into quality. A complementary code for laying is B S 5325, which also advises on choice of carpets and carpet tiles.

carpet strip [carp.] Fixed below a door, originally a hardwood strip, of about the thickness of a carpet, now usually a metal strip clipped to the edge of the carpet.

carport A shelter for a car near a house, usually roofed, but not wholly walled-in, therefore not a garage.

carriage [carp.] (1) **c. piece, rough string, bearer, stair horse** An inclined timber placed between the two *strings* against the underside of wide *stairs* to support them in the middle.

(2) (U S A) A carriage can also be a *string*.

carriage bolt (U S A) A *coach bolt*.

carrying capacity [elec.] The current which a *fuse* or cable can carry without being overheated or having too big a voltage drop.

cartridge fuse (U S A **enclosed f.**) [elec.] A *fuse* sold in a tube of insulating incombustible material which eliminates flashing or danger of fire when the fuse melts. Sometimes they are designed so that cartridges of different *carrying capacities* cannot be interchanged.

carved brickwork Brickwork laid with very fine *joints*, about 1·5 mm ($\frac{1}{16}$ in.) like *gauged brickwork*, sometimes much wider than standard *bricks* to allow for material to be carved off. About 1680, much brickwork in the best houses was carved, but this became unfashionable soon afterwards. *Compare* **moulded bricks**.

case (1) The *facing brick* or stone of a building.

(2) [joi.] (Scotland) A *cased frame*.

cased frame, boxed f. [joi.] The hollow, fixed parts of a *sash window*, containing the sash weights and pulleys and bounded by visible boards called the *outside lining* and *inside lining*.

case hardening [tim.] During seasoning, the outer skin of timber often dries out, shrinks, and hardens more quickly than the inner part. Therefore, *checks* or warping may occur as the inner part dries out, and the timber is said to be case-hardened. *See also C*.

casein glues [joi.] *Glues* made from milk are water-resistant. They abrade edge tools, and are not always proof against moulds, but they have *gap-filling*

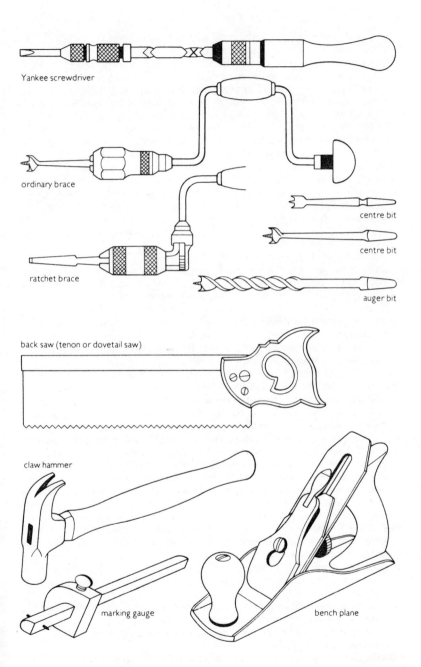

Yankee screwdriver

ordinary brace

ratchet brace

centre bit

centre bit

auger bit

back saw (tenon or dovetail saw)

claw hammer

marking gauge

bench plane

Carpenter's tools.

59

properties and can be used where the *glue line* may be up to 0·8 mm (0·03 in.) thick. Casein is water-soluble before it hardens, and is sometimes mixed with lime to improve its resistance to bacterial attack. It is often used as a *binder* for painting over cement or lime.

casement The hinged or fixed sash of a *casement window* (BS 565).

casement door, French d., French window A pair of glazed (usually outside) doors, hung on opposite sideꞓ of an opening and meeting in the middle. In Britain they open outwards, in France inwards, but in cold countries like Austria they are installed in parts: the outer pair opens outwards and the inner inwards. *See* **espagnolette bolt**.

casement stay A bar used for fixing open a casement. *See* **peg stay**.

casement window A window in which one or more lights are hinged to open (BS 565). Generally, as in door hinges, the hinge pins are vertical. Casements are the simplest, cheapest *opening light*, but for small children, less safe than *sash windows*.

casing [joi.] (1) A *cased frame* or wooden trim or a finishing board, such as the timber lining round a wooden stair.

(2) A *lining* (1) or window frame of light timber.

(3) A timber or similar enclosure on the face of a wall, floor, or ceiling, made to accommodate pipes or cables in a *chase* or other duct. *See also C*.

cassava glue [tim.] A starch *glue* made from the tapioca plant, little used in Britain.

casting resin, cast r. A *synthetic resin* in which shapes can be cast, often a *phenol* or *epoxide* resin.

cast stone, reconstructed s., patent s. Imitation stone for facing buildings, now made from a **strong** concrete core poured on to a crushed-stone *face-mix* about 2·5 cm thick, laid first in the mould. Examples of cast stone can be seen in the fortifications of Carcassonne, repaired in 1138. The technique was only recently revived. *See* **carbonating**.

catalyst A substance which increases the speed of a chemical reaction, generally without taking part in it itself.

catch bolt [joi.] A spring-loaded door *lock* which is normally extended and locked, but is drawn in when the door is shut or opened.

cat ladder, duck board A ladder or board with cleats nailed on it, laid over a roof slope to give access for workmen to repair the roof.

cat walk A gangway round the upper outside walls of high buildings, such as rolling mills, giving access to the roof and eaves for painting or other purposes.

caul [tim.] A sheet of 1·5 mm ($\frac{1}{16}$ in.) thick aluminium in *hot pressing*, or 6 to 9 mm ($\frac{1}{4}$ to $\frac{3}{8}$ in.) thick *plywood* in cold pressing, to protect *veneers* from contact with the presses.

caulking (1) [carp.] *See* **cocking**.

(2) Splitting and twisting the ends of a metal bar to increase its adhesion to mortar when built in.

(3) [plu.] Making a tight spigot-and-socket joint with lead wool or other material driven in by a *caulking iron*. *See also C*.

caulking gun, pressure g. An injecting tool for sealing joints with *mastic*, for instance in *patent glazing*.

caulking iron, c. chisel [plu.] *See* **plumber's tools** (illus. p. 250).

cavil, kevel, jedding axe An axe for stone-cutting, with a pointed *peen*. It may weigh up to 8 kg (18 lb), but is usually much smaller.

cavity barrier A *fire stop*.

cavity block Precast concrete blocks, shaped so that if laid over each other they form a *cavity wall*. *See* **V-brick**.

cavity flashing A *flexible-metal* or other damp-proof *flashing* across a cavity, elaborated into a *cavity tray* in exposed places.

cavity inspection Because of the harm that can be caused by a *bridge* across the cavity in a *cavity wall*, it is important to inspect cavities during construction and to ensure that they are kept clean. If, after construction, the cavity has to be inspected because of a suspected *bridge*, the two vertical joints each side of the chosen brick should be sawn out, then the bed joint over it. It may then be possible to prise out the brick with an electrician's thin bolster. This way ensures that no large lump, only powder, drops into the cavity. If the whole cavity is to be inspected the bricks removed should be at an outside corner. Bridges, where seen, should be broken up by a bar, removed if possible, but if not, pushed so that they drop below the damp course where they can do no harm. A small mirror often helps to detect bridges. Water drops can be seen more easily after or during rain. Another help is to insert a piece of paper, that shows up any drops of water falling on it.

There are several ways of cleaning out cavities when the wall is complete or nearly so. A thin layer of sand spread over the bottom of the cavity at the start of bricklaying prevents mortar sticking to it and the droppings can easily be raked out with a broomstick towards purpose-made holes. Lengths of rope also may be left in the bottom of the cavity, passing through these holes. When pulled out, they should bring most of the mortar droppings with them. The ropes also can be seen while the wall is being built – a great advantage. Occasional blocks also may be left out of the inner leaf so as to reduce the number of bricks to be replaced in the facing. The outer replacement bricks are difficult to lay and are highly noticeable afterwards. *See* **cleanout of wall cavities**.

cavity insulation A *cavity wall* can be insulated during construction by boards of 25 mm (1 in.) thick expanded polystyrene fixed to the inner leaf. There should preferably be a 50 mm (2 in.) gap between the insulating board and the outer wall, making a 75 mm (3 in.) total gap. Though slightly lower in insulation value than the cavity filling mentioned below, it is preferable because it is more waterproof, the construction can be supervised and the gap needed for waterproofing is maintained so long as the boards are fixed to the inner face. By 1980 more than 500 000 houses had had their cavities filled with urea-formaldehyde (UF) foam blown into them as a 'shaving cream' which later hardens and shrinks and in so doing may crack, creating leakage paths for water from the outer face to the inner. Formaldehyde is a poisonous gas. The filling reduces ventilation of the cavity, and obstructs drainage down the inside of the outer leaf so may delay its drying. In contact with flame, UF chars, emitting little smoke, but is not a *fire stop*. Indicator sticks, inserted into holes not being used for injection, show by movement that the foam has reached them. *Loose-fill insulation* blown into the cavity may include fibres of glass or rock, polyurethane foam granules, expanded polystyrene beads or polyurethane foam (BS 5618 and BRE Digest 236).

cavity tray, c. flashing *Cavity walls* exposed to driving rain, e.g. in tall buildings or at abutments with roof slopes, may need special drainage to the outer leaf, that can be obtained only by a *damp course* across the cavity, a cavity flashing or cavity tray. Short proprietary types are sometimes only two or three bricks long, overlapping each other in neighbouring courses to suit the slope. A long cavity tray of *flexible metal* shaped to suit the roof slope may be L-shaped with the vertical part of the L next the inner leaf. If designed to drain to a single point, the tray next to the drainage point will be deepened to a U-shape, at least in a long tray. Many designs exist (BSCP 121).

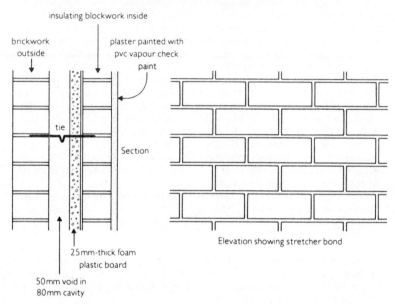

Cavity wall with insulation in the cavity. The wall ties pass through or between the insulation boards.

cavity wall, hollow w. A warm, dry wall, popular in the UK since 1920, often built of two 110 mm (4½ in.) thick leaves separated by a minimum 50 mm (2 in.) continuous gap. The two leaves are connected by at least two wall ties per m². The modern tendency is to build the inner leaf of insulating blocks that are either one, two or three brick courses high. Its *U-value* is 1·93 W/m² deg. C. (0·34 Btu/ft² h deg. F.). It is occasionally 39 cm (15½ in.) thick, in which case the inner leaf is the thicker, 23 cm (9 in.), since it carries the floor joists.

ceil To cover the *soffit* of a room or other space with plaster, board, or other finishing material.

ceiling (1) A plastered or panelled or boarded upper surface to a room.

(2) [tim.] (USA) Matched boards with beads grooved in them, used as a ceiling covering.

ceiling floor [carp.] (USA) *Ceiling joists* or other supports for a ceiling.

ceiling joist [carp.] A joist which carries the *ceiling* beneath it but not the floor over it. Normally the ceiling is carried on the underside of the floor joists, but to improve the *noise insulation* between floors, the ceiling joists may be separate.

ceiling strap [carp.] A strip of wood nailed to *rafters* or floor joists for suspending ceiling joists.

cellar A room or rooms, of which more than half is below ground level, usually reserved for storage or for the central-heating boiler, whereas a *basement* is living space.

cellular brick A brick with deep *frogs*. *See* **brick definitions**.

cellular concrete *Aerated concrete*.

cellular plastics *See* **expanded plastics**.

cellulose acetate butyrate A non-flammable material, a *glass substitute*, which can be an excellent insulator over ceiling linings when appropriately laminated. It is not porous and will not rot.

cellulose enamel, c. nitrate *See* **lacquer**.

cellulose paint [pai.] Very flexible, tough paints, based on *nitrocellulose*, with solvents and *alkyds*. They are best applied by spray and are therefore common on factory-finished units.

cellulose sheet A sheet floor finish made from a mixture of cork dust, sawdust, wood flour, and pigments with gelatinized *nitrocellulose* on a backing of woven jute. It is suitable for restaurants, showrooms, and domestic floors.

cement (1) The bond or matrix between the particles in a rock, particularly that binding the sand grains in a sandstone.

(2) A *binder*, such as *Portland cement*, which binds aggregates into a hard *concrete* or *mortar* within a few days.

(3) [tim.] A term occasionally used for glue.

(4) *See* **Perspex**.

cement fillet, weather f., mortar f. A triangular section of mortar which fills the re-entrant corner at an *abutment* between slates or tiles and a wall. The practice, though common, is forbidden by B S 5534. Slate or *tile fillets* also are not recommended but where used, the roof should be protected by *soakers* of *flexible metal*. *See* **fillet**.

cement mortar Mortar composed of four (or fewer) parts of sand to one of cement, with water, and either *lime* or *plasticizer*. *See* **lime mortar**.

cement paint (1) A mixture of cement and water which applied to concrete, masonry, or brickwork makes it waterproof. Ordinary cement is not very pleasantly coloured, but it is cheap. Coloured cement paints are very much dearer. Cement paint must not come into contact with *gypsum plasters*.

(2) A paint based on *tung oil* or *casein* or other *alkali-resistant* material which can be used over cement.

cement rendering [pla.] The covering of surfaces with a mix of *Portland cement* and sand. As weather-resistant surfaces, these have failed badly in the past by shrinkage and cracking so weaker mixes are now recommended. Neat cement:sand *renderings* are used inside manholes and in other wet positions. *See* **strong mortar**.

cement-rubber latex A *jointless floor* which is also flexible, thanks to its rubber content. The *aggregate* may be marble or other stone chippings or cork or wood chips. A floor made of this can be ground and buffed like a *terrazzo*. It can be as thin as 6 mm ($\frac{1}{4}$ in.). The highly adhesive mixture of cement and rubber has also been used as a protective coating over steel reinforcement in *aerated concrete* and, with marble chippings, as a vandal-proof protective coating over bridge steelwork. *See* **latex**.

cement screed A *screed* of *cement mortar* laid on a floor, particularly on a concrete slab.

cement slurry A liquid cement-water mix for injection, or used as a wash over a wall.

cement-wood floor A *jointless floor* made of *Portland cement*, sawdust, sand, and pigment, which can make a non-dusting quiet floor suitable for offices or living-rooms, though it is unsuitable for bathrooms, kitchens, or workshops.

centers, centering (centres, centring) Curved temporary supports, usually wooden, for an arch or dome during casting or laying.

Central American mahogany [tim.] *See* **Honduras mahogany**.

central heating [plu.] Heating of building space by hot water or steam which circulates through the building in pipes, or by warm air which circulates

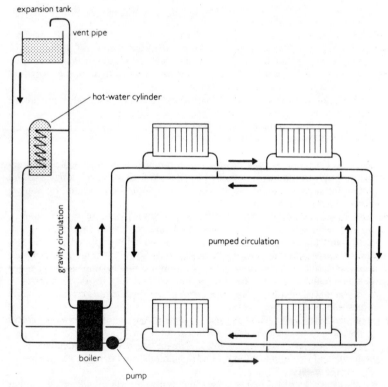

Central heating, two-pipe system. The hot-water supply to the taps is not shown. It comes from the cylinder. (With acknowledgements to Central Heating, the Consumers' Association, 1975.)

through it in *ducts*. *Warm-air heating* is perhaps more logical than piped systems and is certainly faster in its starting effect because much of the heat from pipes goes to parts of the building, not to the human beings who need it. In small houses, usually the circuit for the domestic hot water has a *gravity circulation*, while the radiators are on a pumped, *one-* or *two-pipe* circuit. (Illus.) *See* **small bore, three-pipe, four-pipe systems, warm-air heating**.

centre bit [carp.] A simple bit for drilling with the *brace*. It has a central plain or gimlet point and two side cutters, one of which, the nicker, cuts a circle, while the other, the *router*, ploughs under the wood which has been cut round by the nicker and lifts it out. This simple, cheap bit is, for deep holes, replaced by the *auger bit*.

centre nailing A slate fixing preferred to *head nailing* in windy places. The nail hole is just above the middle of the slate, slightly above the head of the slate in the *course* below (BS 5534).

centre plank [tim.] The plank or planks free of heart, produced from either side of the heart of a log, usually fully *quartered*. Usually applied to hardwoods. *See* **flat-sawn, heart plank**.

centring *See* **centers**.

ceramic flooring tile *See* **clay tile**.

ceramic mosaic (USA) *Flooring tiles* sold in sheets.

ceramics Burnt clay ware. (Cerami was the potters' district of ancient Athens.) Ceramics always excludes sunbaked clays but some specialists have now extended its sense to include pure, dense oxides of metals, many of which like *alumina* (C) are abrasive; carbides and nitrides ('new ceramics'); cement and concrete; glasses; and cermets (ceramics in a metal matrix, to make points for cutting tools). For building, the most important ceramics are *bricks, blocks, clay tiles, vitrified clayware, terra cotta*.

ceramic veneer (USA) *Terra cotta* from 3 to 6·3 cm (1⅛ to 2½ in.) thick, of large sizes, hand-moulded or machine-extruded, and of very wide colour range. The thinner slabs are held by *mortar* only to the wall; the 5 cm (2 in.) or thicker slabs are held on by wires round 6 mm (¼ in.) dia. vertical bars grouted into a grout space between wall and slab.

certificate, building c. A statement signed by the *architect* (or engineer) that the builder is entitled to an instalment on work done. Certificates are usually completed and paid monthly during the progress of building.

cesspit, cesspool, cess box, cess (1) A *rainwater head*.
(2) A pit in which sewage collects. *See also* C, and BSCP 302.200.

chain dogs *See* **nippers**.

chain mortiser [tim.] A *mortising machine*.

chain saw [tim.] (1) A power-operated (petrol-engine) *cross-cut saw* with a projecting jib round which the chain travels. The chain carries cutting picks for cross-cutting logs.
(2) A power saw for cutting building stone. *Hard-faced* (C) metal picks must be used.

chain tongs [plu.] A plumber's heavy pipe grip, which holds the pipe by a chain linked to a bar toothed at the end touching the pipe.

chair rail [joi.] A *dado capping*.

chalking [pai.] The break-up of pigmented *films* on exposure. The binder is so much decomposed by the weather that the *pigment* can be removed by lightly rubbing it. The term is used for all colours, not only for near-white colours, although it originates from these. Washing may restore the original appearance.

chalk line A length of bricklayer's *line* well rubbed with chalk, held tight and plucked against a wall, floor, or other surface to mark a straight line on it. It is also used by plasterers, surveyors, and mural painters.

chamfer An *arris* between two perpendicular surfaces, cut off symmetrically, that is, at 45°. When cut off unsymmetrically, the surface may be called a *bevel. See* **splay**.

chamfer stop (1) [joi.] A *stopped chamfer*.

(2) A brick shaped to form a stop to a chamfer.

channel pipe An open pipe, semi-circular or three-quarter round, used in drainage, particularly at *inspection chambers* (*C*).

channel tile The under-tile of *Spanish* or *Italian tiling*.

charge hand A man in charge of work, the next grade below *foreman* or *ganger* (*C*).

chartered building surveyor, c. quantity surveyor A *building surveyor* or *quantity surveyor* who is a member of the *RICS*.

Chartered Institution of Building Services, CIBS Members of the CIBS are concerned with water supply, sanitation, drainage, fire equipment, heating, lighting, ventilation, electrical and gas supply, telecommunications and any other building service, especially those concerned with human comfort. It was formed in 1976 by a union between the Institution of Heating and Ventilation Engineers and the Illuminating Engineering Society.

chase A groove cut or built into a wall or floor to receive pipes, conduits, cables or a flashing (*see* **raglet**). A pipe chase in a floor is either filled with sand and surfaced with a mortar screed, or covered with some other facing. A *duct* can be a large chase.

chaser *See* **progress chaser**.

chase wedge [plu.] A wooden wedge with a handle, used in *bossing* lead.

cheapener [pai.] A term sometimes used rather unfairly for *extender*.

check (1) [joi.] (Scotland) *See* **rebate**.

(2) [tim.] A crack in converted timber along the grain and across the rings, not passing right through the wood, caused by *shrinkage* during seasoning. In figured *veneers*, fine checks may add character to the pattern and thus be of considerable value. *Compare* **shake**.

(3) [pai.] A crack which penetrates one or more *coats* and usually causes complete failure. *See* **crazing**.

checked back Recessed, *rebated*.

checked ground [carp.] (Scotland) A timber *rebated* (checked) on the edge, to receive lathing or an architrave round an opening. It is flush with the plaster, which may be covered with an *architrave* at its joint with the timber.

checker A storeman or his helper who counts stores or supplies as they arrive on site and checks that they agree with the invoices.

check-fillet An asphalt kerb formed on a roof surface to control rainwater.

check lock [joi.] An arrangement for holding in the locked position the bolt of a door *lock*.

check rail [joi.] A *meeting rail*.

check throat [joi.] A *capillary groove* under a window or door sill.

cheek The side of a *dormer, mortise, tenon*, etc.

cheek cut [carp.] (USA) The bevelled cut at the foot of a *hip-*, *valley-*, or *jack-rafter*.

cheek nailing (Scotland) Double-nailing of slates through a hole at one side of the slate and a notch at the other side.

cheesiness [pai.] A paint film which is soft and incompletely dry is called cheesy and is the opposite of a flexible, tough film. However, a film which is tough on the surface may be cheesy underneath.

chemically resistant cements BRE Digest 120 describes corrosion-resisting cements other than pure Portland cements (which have poor corrosion resistance). They are made with: bitumen; cashew nut resin; epoxy resin; furane resin; rubber-latex-Portland (or aluminous) cement; silicates; and molten sulphur. Some of these expensive cements can be used for bedding and jointing chemically resistant floor tiles.

chemical plumber A craftsman who installs and repairs lead tanks and tank linings. He builds large-diameter pipes (30 cm (12 in.) or more) from sheet lead by joining the ends of sheets bent into a circle. *Compare* **plumber**.

chemical test [plu.] A type of *scent test* in which a chemical is put into the drain, giving off a strong recognizable smell when it comes into contact with water.

chestnut, sweet c., Spanish c. [tim.] The castanea species. The timber resembles oak but lacks *silver grain*, is more easily workable, splits easily, and is nailable. It is much used for fencing and for gates and ladder rungs, since it is as durable as oak when cut young.

chilling [pai.] A deterioration of *paints* or *varnishes* which have been stored at a low temperature. *See* **blushing**.

chimney Any structure containing a vertical *flue*.

chimney back The 23 cm (9 in.) (or thicker) wall behind a fireplace.

chimney bar, camber b., turning b. A wrought iron or steel bar built into the jambs of a fireplace and carrying the brickwork over it.

chimney block (USA) Precast, circular concrete pipe used as *flue lining*.

chimney bond *Stretching bond*, as used for half-brick partitions in chimneys.

chimney breast The chimney wall which projects into the room and contains the fireplace and flues.

chimney can (Scotland) A *chimney pot*.

chimney cap, c. hood An ornamental finish to the *chimney stack*, excluding the chimney pot, often designed to improve the draught.

chimney cowl A revolving metal ventilator over a chimney.

chimney gutter A *back gutter*.

chimney lining (1) A *flue lining*.

(2) *Wall tiles* fixed to chimney *jambs* to protect them from smoke.

chimney pot, flue terminal (Scots c. **can**) A burnt-clay tapered pipe at the top of a chimney stack which leads the smoke clear of the brickwork and may improve the draught.

chimney shaft The part of a chimney which stands free of other structures, usually restricted to a large chimney containing one or two flues only.

chimney stack The brickwork containing one or more *flues* and projecting above a roof.

chipboard *See* **wood chipboard**.

chipped grain, torn g. [tim.] The surface left when small pieces of wood are torn out in planing or machining.

chisel (1) [carp.] A generally wood-handled steel cutting tool, of which the commonest examples are the *firmer*, *paring*, *socket* and *swan-neck* chisels. The British gas industry uses all-steel chisels, saving gasfitters the labour of carrying a mallet as well as a hammer.

(2) Bricklayer's and *mason's* chisels may be *hammer-headed* or *mallet-headed*.

(3) [mech.] *See* **cold chisel** (*C*).

chisel knife [pai.] A narrow *stripping knife* with a square edge not wider than 4 cm (1·5 in.). *Compare* **stopping knife**. *See* **house painter** (illus. p. 180).

chlorinated rubber pai..ts Fire-resisting paints that extinguish when the flame is removed. Since, like all paints, they are a blend of several materials, they also contain flame retardants, such as calcium carbonate. They often contain chlorinated paraffin waxes and are blended with *alkyd resins*. Some chlorinated rubber paints are highly resistant to chemicals and are thus suitable for protecting outside concrete, asbestos-cement sheets or cement renderings. Because they dry by evaporation, two coats can be applied in a day by spray, but care is needed in applying the second coat to avoid lifting the first.

chop [joi.] The movable outer plate of the jaw of a bench *vice*.

chromating [pai.] (1) Priming with lead or zinc chromate to prevent rust forming under the paint.

(2) A protective coating for magnesium alloys (like *anodizing* (*C*) but without electrolysis) formed by dipping the article in hot solutions of alkaline dichromate or of chromic and nitric acids.

chrome green [pai.] A *pigment* which may be *lead chrome green*, a mixture, or pure chromium oxide (Cr_2O_3), which is naturally green.

chrome yellow, Leipzig y. [pai.] A yellow *pigment*, lead chromate ($PbCrO_4$), often mixed with *lead chromes*.

chromium plating, c. plate A *protective finish* consisting of an electroplated surface of chromium. When put on to iron or steel, the chromium is best deposited on nickel previously electro-deposited on copper, which is the first coating on the steel. Electro-deposited chromium is almost as hard as diamond. Hard plating is chromium plate without the interposed copper and nickel.

chute *See* **drain chute, laundry chute**.

CIBS The *Chartered Institution of Building Services*.

cill The spelling usual in the British building industry for *sill*.

cinder block (USA) *Clinker block*.

circuit (1) [elec.] A ring made by conductors carrying power to a consumer, or the conductors themselves.

(2) [plu.] A set of pipes through which water circulates.

circuit vent, loop v. [plu.] (USA) That part of a *ventilation pipe* above the last *soil* connection.

circular plane [joi.] A *compass plane*.

circular saw [tim.] A circular steel disc with teeth cut round the rim. It turns at a rim speed of about 50 m/s (170 ft/s). *See* **swage-setting**.

circulating water The water contained in the closed circuit of a *central-heating* system.

circulation (1) In *planning*, the proper arrangement and proportioning of rooms and spaces to facilitate movement of people from room to room.

(2) [plu.] A system for *circulating water*, or the flow through the system.

CI/SfB classification An arrangement of the information subjects in the building industry, promoted, administered and developed by an agency of the *RIBA* for the building industry as a whole. It is based on the *international SfB* system and is set out in two manuals. The CI/SfB Construction Indexing Manual, which also describes the use of the classification for general information (office libraries, contents of documents, etc.) and for project information (drawings and other *contract documents*). *See* **sequence of trades**.

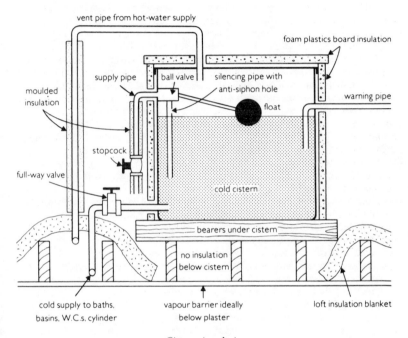

Cistern insulation.

cissing [pai.] *See* **crawling**.

cistern [plu.] (1) **storage tank** A rectangular, commonly open-topped, cold-water tank usually fixed in the *roof* of a house (*compare* **combination tank**). Nowadays usually made of asbestos cement, galvanized steel sheet, or various plastics. In the past they were made of slate slabs bolted together, or of wood lined with lead or zinc or copper sheet. (Illus. above)

(2) **flushing cistern, water-waste preventer** A small tank above a WC fitment which contains enough water to flush the WC once. Usually both types are supplied with water by a *ball valve*.

(3) Any tank for storing water, often underground and of concrete.

city planning *See* **town planning**.

cladding (USA **siding**) The non-loadbearing clothing of the walls and roof of a building, the skin used to keep the weather out. *See* BSCP 143, 297, 298.

cladding panels Buildings can be clad with cheap, heavy (concrete or brick) panels or expensive, lightweight ones, but both types are now generally made of several layers, including an outer layer to resist knocks and weather, an insulating core, a *vapour barrier* on the warm side of the insulation, and an inner finished surface. *See* **curtain walling, glassfibre-reinforced polyester, glass-reinforced cement, large-panel construction**, and BRE Digests 217, 223.

clamp A *cramp* in *joinery*.

clamping plate [carp.] A timber *connector*.

clamping time [tim.] The time for which a glued joint must be clamped. It is greater for curved *plywood* than for flat, and varies also with the type of *glue*.

clamp nail [joi.] (USA) A fastener for picture frames and similar mitred (*see* **mitre**) corners. It is a simplified *corrugated fastener*.

clapboard (USA **bevel siding, lap siding**) [tim.] *Weather-boarding*, from 8 to 28 cm (3 to 11 in.) wide, 16 mm ($\frac{5}{8}$ in.) thick on the lower edge, 6 mm ($\frac{1}{4}$ in.) thick along the upper edge (which is covered by the lower edge of the board above). It is *feather-edged* (neither *tongued and grooved* nor *rebated*).

clapboard gauge, siding g. [carp.] A measure to show the amount of board which should be exposed, used by *carpenters* fixing clapboard.

clasp nail A *cut nail* of square section. Its head has two points which sink into the wood.

claw [carp.] A bar with a split end for drawing nails.

claw bar [carp.] A *pinch bar*.

claw chisel A mason's *mallet-headed chisel* with several broad nicks in the cutting edge, used in roughly shaping stone.

claw hammer, carpenter's h. [carp.] A hammer with one split, claw-shaped peen for drawing nails, used for erecting and dismantling formwork. *See* **adze-eye hammer, carpenter's tools** (illus. p. 59).

claw hatchet A *shingling hatchet*.

claw plate [carp.] A *connector* for timber.

clay lath A base for plastering, made from copper-plated steel-wire mesh on which clay pellets have been kiln-burnt to the wire intersections.

clay mortar mix (USA) Clay powder for *masonry cement*.

clay tile (1) *Roofing tiles*.

(2) Two types of clay flooring tile exist, 'floor tiles' and '*quarry tiles*', both of them *ceramic* in the sense that they are burnt clay ware, but one of them is called ceramic, the other is not. Ceramic 'floor tiles' are made from powder to closer limits and with much lower water *absorption* than quarry tiles. The fully vitrified 'ceramic' floor tile has only 0·3% maximum water absorption, the vitrified grade 4% maximum. Quarry tiles on the other hand are made from clays, usually by extrusion, and have either 6% or 10% maximum water absorption. *See* **underlay**.

clean aggregate Sand or gravel which is free from clay or silt.

clean back The seen face of a header stone. *See* **rough back, skewback**.

cleaning eye An *access eye*.

cleaning hinges, easy-clean h. Long-leaved metal hinges for outward-opening metal *casements*. The outside of the glass can be cleaned by passing the hand through the gap between the hinges. (Illus.) *See* **tilt-and-turn window**.

cleanout (USA) An *access eye*, soot door, etc.

cleanout of wall cavities Some *specifications* forbid the cleaning out of wall cavities and insist that cavities be kept clean during construction by laths, straw rope, etc., laid in the cavity on the foundation, to catch mortar droppings or

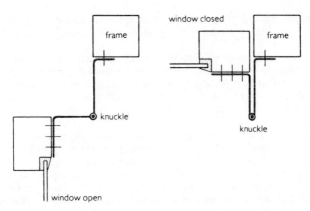

Cleaning hinge.

brick bats. Others allow bricks to be left out at the bottom of the cavity so that it can be cleaned on completion. *See* **cavity inspection.**

clean timber Timber which is free from knots (B S 565). *See* **clear timber.**

clearcole, clairecolle [pai.] Diluted glue *size* containing *whiting*, formerly applied to ceilings and walls before *distemper*.

clear timber, c. stuff Timber which is free from visible *defects* (B S 565). Since knot-free timber is generally only found in the lower part of the trunks of closely grown trees in virgin forests, clear and clean timber is now scarce and *stress grading* has been adopted. *See* **second-growth timber.**

cleat (1) **batten** [carp.] A small piece of wood or metal to reinforce or locate positively another timber, or plugged to a wall to carry a shelf.

(2) A *tingle* in *flexible-metal roofing*. *See also* C.

cleavage [tim.] Wood has cleavage along the grain, particularly *western red cedar* and other woods used for split *shingles*. *See below*.

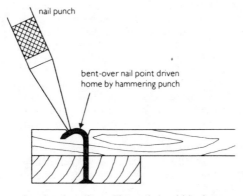

Nail punch in use for clench nailing. The nail should be bent over parallel to the grain of the wood.

cleft-chestnut fencing Fencing made from split-chestnut sticks about 10 cm (4 in.) apart, held with twisted wire to large posts at about 2·1 m (7 ft) apart.

cleft timber Split timber.

clenching, clinching, clench nailing [carp.] Driving a nail right through timber, then bending the point over and on to the back of the timber, a technique used in building *ledged-and-braced doors*, and boats. *See* **nail punch** (p. 71).

clench nail [carp.] A nail used for clenching, such as a *duckbill nail*.

clerk of works The representative on a building site of the *client*. He usually works under the instructions of the *architect* or engineer, and ensures that the work done is exactly as specified in the *contract*, keeping records of such work as foundations which are later covered up. He has a wide knowledge of building construction, which may be confirmed by membership of the Institute of Clerks of Works of Great Britain Incorporated, or he may hold the *Building Inspector's* certificate of the Institution of Municipal Engineers. He is usually an experienced *tradesman* who has done considerable evening study.

client The person or organization by whom a builder or consultant is employed, to whom he is responsible, and from whom he draws his fees. In a building *contract* he is usually the building owner's senior consultant, the *architect*, but to the architect, the client is the building owner.

clinker Sintered or fused ash from furnaces. If properly burnt and containing very little unburnt coal, it is an excellent *hardcore* (*C*) or concrete aggregate for precast *building blocks*, sometimes mistakenly called *breeze*. When clay and chalk are burned together, the clinker formed is crushed to a powder from which *Portland cement* is made.

clinker block (USA **cinder b.**) A cheap, strong *building block* (sometimes insulating if hollow) of *clinker* concrete. If kept dry they have very little *moisture movement* (*C*), but laid wet in a wall they can cause the plaster over them to crack badly while they dry out and shrink.

clip A *tingle* or *tile clip*.

clipped eave An *eave* with the minimum overhang.

clipped gable (USA) A *jerkin head roof*.

cloak [plu.] A waterproof covering formed from *flexible metal*, or other damp-proof material, placed over a projection above the general roof surface to protect it against rain, snow, etc. *See* **overcloak**.

close-boarded, close-sheeted [carp.] *See* **boarding**.

close-boarded fencing Vertical *feather-edged boarding* nailed to two or three horizontal rails which span between posts about 2·7 m (9 ft) apart. A *gravel board* is often provided along the bottom.

close-contact glue [tim.] A *glue* which will not stick if the surfaces to be joined are further apart than about 0·13 mm (0·05 in.). *See* **gap-filling glue**.

close-couple, couple-close [carp.] Term describing a roof of *common rafters* joined at the wall plate level with a *tie-beam*, suitable for spans of about 4 m (13 ft).

close-cut hip or **valley, cut-and-mitred h.** or **v.** A *hip* or *valley* in which the slates, shingles, or tiles are cut to meet on the hip or valley line. A *flexible-metal* or *asbestos-bitumen* gutter or *soakers* beneath them keep out the rain.

closed cornice [carp.] A *box cornice*.

closed stair, box s. (mainly USA) A *stair* walled in on each side and closed by a door at one end. *See* **open stair, fire break**.

closed valley (USA) A *secret gutter*.

close grain, fine g. [tim.] A description of *fine-textured wood. Compare* **close-grained wood.** .

close-grained wood [tim.] *Narrow-ringed wood.*

closer (1) **bat** A brick or stone cut or moulded to complete the *bond* at the corner of a wall.

(2) The part of a brick which is cut to 57 mm (2¼ in.) on face. *See* **bevelled closer, king closer, queen closer**.

close string, housed s., (USA **closed stringer**) A *string* with parallel top and bottom edges. The treads and risers are housed in its face. *See* **step.** *Compare* **cut string**.

closet lining [joi.] (USA) Thin tongued-and-grooved boards of North American red cedar, used for lining clothes cupboards, because their smell repels moths. .

closing stile [joi.] A *shutting stile*.

clothes chute A *laundry chute*.

clouring *Picking*.

clout nail, felt n. A short galvanized *nail* from 9·5 to 63 mm (⅜ to 2½ in.) long with a large round flat head, used for fixing *sash cords*, roofing felt, plasterboard, etc.

club hammer, lump h., (Scots **mash h.**) A double-face *hammer* with a head weighing from 0·7 to 1·8 kg (1·5 to 4 lb) used by bricklayers and *masons*.

clunch Hard chalk, of which English cottages and barns were built in medieval times. It weathers badly but was protected by a skin of *limewash* which was often renewed. *See* **cob**.

coach bolt (USA **carriage b.**) A round-headed bolt enlarged under the head to a square section, enabling it to grip the wood without turning as the nut is tightened up. *See* **fastenings** (illus. p. 130).

coach screw (USA **lag bolt, s. spike**) [carp.] A large, *gimlet-pointed* screw for making fixings to wood, usually 6 mm (¼ in.) dia. or larger. It is driven into wood by turning the square head with a spanner. Part of the hole must be drilled for it. *See* **fasteners** (illus. p. 130).

coarse-grained [tim.] *Wide-ringed. Compare* **coarse-textured**.

coarse stuff [pla.] Originally neat lime *mortar* used in the first and second coats of plaster, out of use because it hardens too slowly and is weak. *Lime putty* is now usually *gauged* with *cement* or *gypsum plaster* (never both). *See* **hydrated lime**.

coarse-textured [tim.] The *texture* of timber with relatively large wood elements (coarse grain or open grain), or unusually wide *annual rings* for the type of wood. Such timber needs a *filler* before it is varnished. *Ash, chestnut* and *oak* are coarse-textured. *Compare* **fine-textured wood**.

coat (1) A single layer of asphalt, plaster, etc. applied to a stated thickness.

(2) [pai.] The *paint, varnish, lacquer*, etc. laid on a surface in one film. *See* **full coat, glaze coat, ground coat, guide coat, mist coat, priming coat, sharp paint**.

cob (1) An unburnt brick, with straw binder.

(2) (south-west USA), **pisé de terre, rammed-earth construction**. Walling of damp earth sometimes mixed with cement, rammed without reinforcement into *formwork* (C). Some mixtures can be laid without formwork. This cheap walling has in the past been practised in France, East Anglia, and the west

of England, and is now used in Australia and other semi-arid countries. *See* **adobe**.

cobwebbing [pai.] The ejection from a *spray gun* of a series of spiderweb like threads (of chlorinated, natural, or synthetic rubbers). The same difficulty may occur in brushing.

cobwork (USA) Log house construction.

cock [plu.] A control for cutting off a supply of water, gas, or other fluid in a pipe. *Plug cocks* are usual for gas, *full-way valves* for water with low circulating pressure, and *screw-down valves* for a water supply with good flow. The taps at a sink, bath or basin are usually *pillar taps* or *bibcocks* but since these regulate the flow as well as cutting it off they are not regarded as cocks (BS 1010, BS 4118).

cocked hinge [joi.] *See* **cocking**.

cocking (1) **cogging, corking** [carp.] Where a beam rests on a *wall plate*, a *mortise* is cut out beneath the beam and two mortises are cut out of the wall plate so that the beam drops into them. *See* **cog**.

(2) [joi.] *Hinges* fixed askew to make a door rise when it opens are said to be cocked. *Rising butts* do the same work more expensively but more elegantly.

cocking piece, sprocket p., sprocket [carp.] A short board nailed to each *common rafter* at the *eaves* to give an eaves overhang with a slightly flatter slope than the rest of the roof. It is used where the overhang obtained with a *tilting fillet* is not enough. For *single-lap tiles* or *asbestos-cement slates* this practice is not recommended by BS 5534.

cockscomb A mason's *drag*.

cockspur fastener A metal fastener for *casement windows*, provided in addition to the usual *casement stay* and pin.

code of practice, BSCP A publication issued by the *BSI* describing what is considered to be good practice in the trade described. Codes of practice do not generally have the force of law, but supplement the *Building Regulations*. American *building codes* generally have the force of law. Many engineering institutions publish codes of practice on their own subjects.

coffer A panel in a *ceiling*, strongly recessed to make a decorative pattern.

cog (1) A *nib*, in roofing tiles.

(2) [carp.] In a *cocking* joint, the tenon left projecting upwards from the *wall plate* into the beam.

coil heating (1) Heating of a concrete floor slab by water pipes cast into it.

(2) Heating of a concrete floor slab by *Pyrotenax* or similar electric cables cast into it.

(3) *See* **panel heating**.

coin A *quoin*.

cold bridge, heat b., thermal b. A piece of metal such as a pipe or wall tie (or any other conducting substance) that passes through a wall can carry heat through it. This means that the inner surface of the wall around the pipe or wall tie will be warmer in summer and so much colder in winter than the remainder of the wall that *condensation* may even occur there. Dense concrete is one substance that has low insulation and can create a heat *bridge*. (Illus. p. 75)

cold-cathode lamp, fluorescent tube [elec.] An electric lamp consisting of a fluorescent glass tube about 0·3 to 2·7 m (1 to 9 ft) long and 3·8 cm (1½ in.)

inside air 20°C.

| 16°C. | | 13°C. | | | 16°C. |

inner leaf

| cavity | bridge | | cavity |

outer leaf

| 2°C. | | 3°C. | | | 2°C. |

outside air 0°C. Equivalent temperatures

| 0°C. | 2°C. | 3°C. | 13°C. | 16°C. | 20°C. |
| 32°F. | 36°F. | 37°F. | 55°F. | 61°F. | 68°F. |

Effect of cold bridge on temperatures on cavity wall in winter. After Environment and Services, *Peter Burberry, Mitchell's Building Series, B. T. Batsford, 1979.*

dia. containing no filament. Alternating current passing through the vacuum in the tube gives no visible light but emits other radiation, which on passing through the glass is changed into visible light by the fluorescence of the glass. These costly tubes give out more light with better diffusion (less dazzle) for a smaller power consumption than a filament lamp. They are used in drawing offices and to save electricity.

cold roof, c. deck In a flat timber roof, a roof void in which the air is at the same temperature as outside. A *warm roof* is one in which the air in winter is warmer than outside. For a cold roof the insulation is placed near the ceiling. For a warm one it is away from the ceiling on top of the roof, covered only by the waterproofing. The conventional tiled or slated, pitched roof is also cold but not usually so-called. The danger with a cold roof is that warm damp air from inside the house can enter it and create *condensation* inside, rotting the timber. To prevent this a *vapour barrier* should be installed under the ceiling, which may create difficulties in the ceiling decoration. In a warm roof there is no danger of condensation. In a pitched roof there is little danger of hazardous condensation because any water drains away harmlessly on the underside of the roof *underlay* felt and such roofs are usually well ventilated (BRE Digest 221). (Illus. below)

Flexible metal or roofing-felt covering

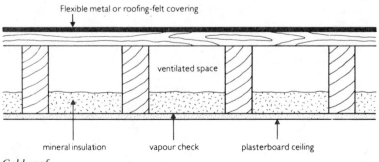

ventilated space

mineral insulation   vapour check   plasterboard ceiling

Cold roof.

cold-setting resins [pai., tim.] Formaldehyde or *epoxy resins* which, when cold, form *polymers* when mixed with an acid accelerator. The action is usually faster if the mixture is heated. *See* **thermo-setting resin**.

cold-water service [plu.] The piped cold-water supply into a building, usually brought into the building by a *rising main*.

collapse [tim.] Irregular, sometimes corrugated, *shrinkage* in eucalyptus timbers. *See* **reconditioning**.

collapsible pans *See* **telescopic centering**.

collar (1) A ring of asphalt built up round a vertical pipe passing through an asphalt roof to ensure a watertight joint at the pipe.

(2) [plu.] An enlargement outside a pipe or a reduction within its bore. It is often made to bear on another collar and ensure a tight joint between pipes as in a *union*.

collar beam, top b., span piece [carp.] A horizontal tie-beam as in a *collar-beam roof*.

collar-beam roof [carp.] *Common rafters*, joined half-way up their length by a horizontal tie-beam. This roof gives more headroom in the centre of the building than a *close-couple* roof.

collar boss [plu.] A *polyvinyl chloride* pipe fitting inserted in a *soil stack* for making branch connections from bath or wash basin or sink. It carries bosses that may be drilled through to make connections.

collection line [plu.] (USA) A house drain.

collections [q.s.] Preliminary calculations made by the *taker off* in the *waste* of *dimensions paper* to record minor dimensions and how he arrived at them. After adding them he writes the sum in the dimension column.

colloids [pai.] Gums or substances like them, such as gelatin, starch or flour paste, which stick fast when their solvent evaporates. *See also C*.

colonial siding [tim.] Plain, square-edged *weather boards*, 23 to 30 cm (9 to 12 in.) wide, of which a considerable width is exposed, used in early American buildings.

colour [pai.] Colour in normal speech includes hue, lightness, and saturation. Hues are red, yellow, green, blue, purple, etc. Lightness is the amount of light reflected (regardless of hue) and is also called value or tone. Saturation is the colourfulness or intensity of a hue compared with a neutral grey of similar lightness. The colours of the spectrum are the most intense. Black is considered to be a colour in painting, but white is not. *See* **pigment**, *also* BS 4800, 5252.

coloured cement White, rapid-hardening, or ordinary *Portland cement* mixed with mineral *pigments*.

column An upright shaft, generally rectangular or round, of concrete, stone, brick, cast iron, steel, or aluminium, normally designed for carrying axial load (weight) in compression. *Compare* **stanchion** (*C*).

comb (1) **c. board** A *ridge* of a roof.

(2) A mason's *drag*.

(3) **scratcher** [pla.] A tool for scratching plaster to give a key for the following coat. It is like a paint brush stock with nails or wire protruding. *Compare* **devil float**.

(4) [pai.] A thin steel, celluloid, rubber, etc. tool used in *graining*.

combed joint, cornerlocked j., laminated j. [joi.] An *angle joint* in which the ends of the pieces are slotted to mate with each other. *See* **dovetail**.

combination cylinder and tank [plu.] A sheet copper container for hot water (usually a cylinder, either *direct* or *indirect*) which has a *cistern* built over it. One advantage of this arrangement is that there is no cold cistern in the roof space and freeze-ups are less likely. The cistern is at atmospheric pressure and the feed to it from the main is controlled by a ball valve. The cylinder can be heated by *gas circulator*, or *immersion heater*, or if indirect by a water coil connected by flow and return pipes to the boiler.

combination door, c. window [joi.] (USA) A *coupled window* or door, removable for the summer.

combination plane A *universal plane*.

combination pliers (USA) A tool resembling the British *footprints*.

combination square [mech.] A most useful, but costly, adjustable tool which can be used as an inside or outside *try square* or *marking gauge, mitre square, plumb rule*, protractor, etc.

combination tank [plu.] A *combination cylinder and tank*.

combined extract and input system A ventilating system which combines the *extract* and the *input systems*. It is more complicated than either, having two fans, and includes automatically controlled heating of the cleaned air.

combing (1) Smoothing the face of soft stone with a *drag* after sawing or chiselling it.

(2) In shingle roofing, a top course of *shingles* which projects above the *ridge* to protect it from the rain blown by the prevailing wind.

(3) [pai.] Partly removing a coat of wet paint with a comb in *graining*.

comfort zone A conception in the design of *air-conditioning* systems. For winter in Britain and for people doing very light work, the most comfortable *equivalent temperature* is 16·8° C. (62·3° F.), corresponding to an *effective temperature* of 16° C. (60·8° F.) and a dry bulb temperature of 18·1° C. (64·7° F.). In summer the temperature should be about 2·2° C. (4° F.) higher. For heavy work it should be lower. For 70% of people to feel comfortable the temperature should not vary more than 2·2° C. (4° F.) from these figures, giving the comfort zone for 70% of people. *See* **degree-day value**.

commode step A *riser* curved in plan, generally at the foot of a stair.

common ashlar Pick-dressed or hammer-dressed *ashlar*.

common bond (USA) *American bond*.

common brick (USA **building b.**) The locally cheapest *brick*, not necessarily used for *facing*, nor for loadbearing work except in great thicknesses. It may or may not be the *stock brick*.

common dovetail [joi.] A *dovetail joint* in which both members show end grain.

common ground, rough g. A strip of wood nailed, *plugged*, or otherwise solidly fixed to a wall or sub-frame as a base for plaster, *joinery, building board*, and so on. *See* **framed ground**.

common joist, floor j., boarding j. [carp.] Wooden boards laid on edge to span a gap between walls. Floorboards are nailed directly to them. The greatest span of wooden joists is usually 5 m (16 ft), but they can be longer at greater cost.

common partition [carp.] A wooden *framed partition* consisting of a *head* and *sill* joined by vertical *studs* at about 45 cm (18 in.) centres, strutted apart by short horizontal wooden struts (*nogging* pieces). It carries no load, unlike the *trussed partition*. A common partition 2·4 m (8 ft) high, built of 76 × 50 mm (3 × 2 in.) softwood, weighs about 5 kg/m² (1 lb/ft²) without coverings. They

Service pipe for gas or water supply from a main, including communication pipe.

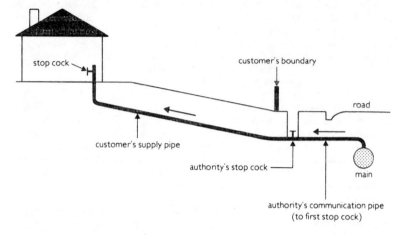

have been superseded in the U K by *building blocks* which are much cheaper.

common rafter, r. spar, intermediate r. A sloping timber, about 10 × 5 cm (4 × 2 in.) fixed to a *wall plate* at the foot and to a *ridge* at the top, in a *single roof*. On a roof system with *principal rafters* bridged by purlins, the common rafter is a sloping timber carried by the purlins above the principals.

common wall (USA) *Party wall.*

communication pipe The pipe, between the supply main and the consumer's stop valve or his boundary, whichever is nearer to the main. It is the part of his *service pipe* which belongs to the water authority or gas board (above).

comparator [pai.] An instrument for comparing, e.g. *colour* intensities.

compartment, fire cell Large buildings are divided into compartments by *fire-resisting doors*, floors, walls, etc. so as to prevent fire spreading beyond the compartment of origin.

compass brick, radial b., radiating b. A brick for building circular brickwork. It tapers in at least one direction.

compass plane [joi.] A metal *plane* with an adjustable curved *sole*, to smooth convex or concave surfaces of various radii.

compass saw, keyhole s., locksaw, fretsaw [joi.] A handsaw with a blade which tapers to a point. It is used for cutting round sharp curves.

compatible, compatibility More used in *painting* but also applicable to plasters. Compatible coats of paint (or materials in the same coat) are those which blend perfectly and look well. An incompatible mix will be cloudy, coagulating, gelling, or precipitating *pigment*. An incompatible film may show *pinholing, lining, sheariness*, low adhesion, poor *gloss*, slow drying, greasiness or *crawling*. For timber, it is important that *glues* are compatible with the preservatives already used.

compo (1) Cement-lime mortar of any composition such as 1 cement: 2 lime: 9 sand.

(2) Lead alloy for gas pipes, that makes a flexible connection to an appliance such as a meter.

composite board [tim.] Many types of *blockboard, hardboard, laminboard, plywood* or *gypsum plasterboard* glued to an insulating sheet such as asbestos or cork or expanded polystyrene, sometimes with a metal surfacing bent over four edges as a *vapour barrier* or simply with aluminium foil backing as a *vapour check*.

composite construction Different materials in conjunction, for example facing and backing bricks in walls, reinforced concrete in-situ *screed* over a precast *prestressed concrete* (C) floor beam, or brickwork carried on a concrete or steel beam and considered to form its *compression flange* (C). See B S C P 117.

composition block floor Flooring blocks measuring about $150 \times 50 \times 9$ mm ($6 \times 2 \times \frac{3}{8}$ in.) which are laid on concrete in a 13 mm ($\frac{1}{2}$ in.) thick bed of wet mortar. The blocks are made of a mix of cement, wood particles, gypsum, calcium carbonate, pigment and linseed oil in a dozen colours and resemble wood block flooring especially when sealed with oleo-resin or polyurethane varnish. They are often used for flooring in laboratories, workshops, hospitals, or churches, and can be washed with soap and water or polished intermittently.

composition floor layer, granolithic worker [pla.] A *floor-and-wall tiler* who lays *jointless floors*.

composition nails Brass nails used for slating and tiling.

compound (1) *See* **bonding compound, dressing compound, sealing compound**.
    (2) [elec.] An easily melted material like pitch which is poured into a joint box to make a solid, insulating, water-excluding filling round the *conductors*.

compound beam, built-up b., keyed b. [carp.] A wooden rectangular beam *built-up* from several timbers by nailing, bolting with *connectors*, jointing with scarfs, *glue*, or any other method. *See* **compound girder** (C).

compound walling Walls laid in two or more skins of different materials.

compreg [tim.] *Improved wood* that has been both compressed and impregnated with *synthetic resin*.

compressed cork *See* **cork board**.

compressed straw slab, strawboard Fire-resistant slabs 1·2 m (4 ft) wide, 2·4 to 3·6 m (8 to 12 ft) long, and 5 cm (2 in.) thick, made from compressed straw faced with strong paper each side. It weighs 19·5 kg/m^2 (4 lb/ft^2) and can be used for making 5 cm (2 in.) thick *partitions* or for insulating walls or roofs.

compressed wood [tim.] Wood whose density and strength have been increased by pressure, like *high-density plywood*.

compression glazing A modern glazing system in which the glass is held in glazing *gaskets* in a metal surround. The gaskets are compressed by a metal bead bolted to the surround.

compression joint [plu.] A joint in *light-gauge copper tubing*, made by screwing together the ends of the two pipes to be joined, by brass nuts outside them. In the commonest type, the *non-manipulative joint*, the nuts force *glands* into close contact with the copper tube to make a watertight or gastight joint. This joint is less neat than the *capillary joint* and needs more space to make it but no flame. *See* **copper fittings, manipulative joint**.

concave joint A durable *mortar* joint, hollowed out by pushing a 13 mm ($\frac{1}{2}$ in.) dia. bar along it while it is *green*. *See* **jointing**.

concealed gutter (U S A) In timber construction, a *box gutter*. There is no *parapet*, but looked at from the ground the gutter is concealed, since it is hidden by, and in, the *cornice*.

79

concealed heating *See* **panel heating**.

concrete An intimate mixture of water, sand, stone, and a *binder* (nowadays usually *Portland cement*) which hardens to a stone-like mass. Lime and other concretes were used in ancient Rome and in Britain for foundations in the nineteenth century, but the production of strong, cheap, uniform Portland cement has enormously increased its use. Cement concrete is now the most widely used engineering material, with an annual consumption above 1 tonne per head – 5 to 10 times the consumption of steel. *See C*, **aerated, lightweight**, B S C P 110.

concrete blocks *See* **blockwork**.

concrete-bonding plaster [pla.] A low-expansion retarded *hemihydrate plaster* to BS 1191 with not more than 5 per cent by weight of shredded wood fibre, *retarder*, etc., used on concrete where other plasters have failed to stick. *See* **bonding treatment**.

concrete bricks Bricks moulded from sand and cement. They can be obtained in many different colours but they represent only one twentieth of the market for clay bricks.

concrete insert A fibre or metal *plug* built into *concrete* or brickwork or fixed into it by drilling. It is used as a fixing for a wood *screw* or *coach screw*.

concrete interlocking tile A standardized British *single-lap tile*, ordinarily measuring 38 × 23 × 1 to 1·3 cm (15 × 9 × $\frac{3}{8}$ to $\frac{1}{2}$ in.), provided with a central nail hole at the top end. *Nibs* are provided at both ends, those at the bottom end fitting the water channel of the tiles in the course below. The side lap is 2·5 cm (1 in.) minimum.

concrete nail (USA) A thick, hard steel nail from 1 to 8 cm ($\frac{1}{2}$ to 3 in.) long, for fixing to brick or concrete. *Compare* **masonry nails**.

concrete pumping A concrete pumping sub-contractor owns expensive mobile *concrete pumps* (C) and *placing booms* (C) which can raise concrete many storeys above ground or lower it to the third sub-basement or send it 500 metres away horizontally with equal efficiency. He can place up to 100 m³ of concrete per hour with only two men, one at the placing lorry carrying the pump, the other at the delivery end of the hose. Other methods, apparently cheaper in rate per m³ of concrete, demand many more men. But if properly planned, with concrete designed to be pumpable, pumping is a fast, economical way of placing high-quality concrete. The time saved on the job makes for overall economy. To maintain good compaction of the concrete, it is possible to keep the delivery hose submerged.

concrete tiles Concrete tiles are made to the same shapes and sizes as many of the traditional clay tiles but about eight times more of them are now sold than clay tiles.

concreting paper *Building paper*.

condensation (1) *Polymerization*.

(2) Surface condensation is seen as dewdrops or damp patches on indoor surfaces, caused by the release of water from air as it is cooled below its *dewpoint* (C). Warm, damp indoor air striking cold surfaces, releases the water it holds as vapour. The other type, *interstitial condensation*, is ordinarily never seen. The average family gives out 12 kg (21 pints) of water daily into the air of their home because of breathing, cooking and washing. Coal fires can draw all this up the chimney. Ideally the structure should be warmed to 10° C. or more throughout the winter. Flueless heaters, burning

paraffin or gas, should never be used to heat a house suffering from condensation. They release one volume of water in burning one volume of oil. Gas produces even more water per unit of heat than oil.

Insulation of the cold wall can help, or if it is already insulated, a *vapour check* should help to keep it dry and thus to maintain its insulation value. Vinyl-faced paper is one of the easiest vapour checks to install. Adding insulation such as 5 mm (0·2 in.) thick expanded polystyrene also helps. None of these improvements should be made before the wall is completely dry.

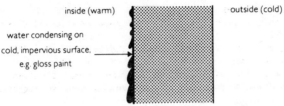

inside (warm)   outside (cold)

water condensing on
cold, impervious surface,
e.g. gloss paint

Surface condensation.

An electric extract fan of 150 or 200 mm (6 or 8 in.) diameter over the cooker, vented to the outside air, removes much of the steam from the kitchen. Condensation on cold pipes can usually be prevented by moulded insulation or other efficient *lagging*. Occasionally the heat of a small refrigerator will keep a wall surface warm enough to prevent condensation on it. In laundries, cold stores or other places where condensation must at all costs be prevented, the most expensive solution may be needed – *de-humidification* – a problem for the heating and ventilation engineer.

Water is not the only vapour that condenses. Grease from a chip shop can condense in the plaster and bricks of the house next door to such an extent that clothes hung in the cupboards become greasy. See below, also B S 5250. (Illus.)

condensation groove A part of the *lead sheath* of a lead-clothed glazing bar which projects under the glass to catch water and channel it to the *condensation gutter* at the foot of the glazing.

condensation gutter, sinking, channel A small gutter at the foot of skylights, *patent glazing*, etc., to carry condensed water through a small hole, pierced to the outside.

condensation in flues *Condensation* is rarely severe in a flue from an open fire in continual use, though it may occur for a short period just after the fire is lit. It may also occur in the flue from a modern, efficient boiler because the flue gases are cooled too much – a result of the efficiency of transfer of the heat in the flue gas to the water in the boiler. If the moisture in the flue results in staining of decorated surfaces in rooms above the boiler, one solution is to install a flexible *flue lining* but this is not practicable with coal firing. Most of the liquid in the flue is water but it contains some sulphur dioxide that makes it acid, and converts mortar into calcium sulphate. This substance occupies a larger volume than the mortar it replaces, causing free-standing chimneys to lean, usually to the south in the northern hemisphere. Such stacks must be pulled down, if necessary below roof level, and the sulphate-saturated bricks should not be re-used. Building Regulations require new flues to be lined with acid-resistant, usually ceramic, flue lining, in which the joints are so arranged (spigot up) as to prevent condensate leaking out. If neither a flexible nor a clay flue lining can be installed, the re-decoration can sometimes be saved (after re-plastering) by stripping the stained plaster and covering the bricks with an impervious coating such as bitumen lathing, over which re-plastering can safely start.

condensation washer A shaped fitting which raises the lower end of a *glazing bar* in *patent glazing* above a *purlin*, to drain off condensed water.

conditioning [tim.] Bringing timber, hardboard, etc. to the condition in which it will be used, reducing or increasing the *moisture content* to the right value. This can be done by wet sponging hardboard or by exposing timber to the air in the room.

conductance The thermal conductance of a building material of a given thickness is the heat in watts which passes through 1 m² of it under a temperature difference of 1° C. between the two faces. It is thus the *conductivity* divided by the thickness in m. For the conductance the temperatures are measured on the face of the material, for the *U-value* they are measured in the air beyond it. For this reason, the *U-value* is always lower than the conductance of the same wall by an amount corresponding to the *surface coefficient*.

conductivity, K-value The thermal conductivity of a substance is the number of watts (Btu/h) passed through an area of 1 m² (ft²), 1 m (in.) thick under a temperature difference of 1° C. (° F.) between the two sides. For constructional materials as a whole there is a roughly proportional relationship between conductivity and density. Thus at densities of 720 kg/m³ (45 lb/ft³), $K = 0.144$ W/m deg. C. (1 Btu in./ft²h deg. F.) while at densities of 2240 kg/m³ (140 lb/ft³), normal for dense concrete, the conductivity is very much higher, $K = 1.15$ W/m deg. C. (8 Btu in./ft²h deg. F.). *See also* **U-value, conductance, sound-reduction factor** B S 3533 and B S 874.

conductor (1) **leader** pronounced 'leeder' (U S A) A *downpipe*.

(2) A substance with a high *conductivity* for heat, electricity, or other energy. Generally metals are good conductors.

(3) A *lightning conductor*.

(4) [elec.] **lead** pronounced 'leed'. A wire or cable of copper, tinned copper, or aluminium, used for leading power from the supply to the consumer.

conductor head (U S A) A *rainwater head*.

conduit [elec.] A metal, or plastic, or fibre tube fitted to a wall or ceiling or other part of a building and used as an encasement to cables. For cables laid in the street, earthenware pipe is used, not conduit. *See below.*

conduit box [elec.] A *distribution box*.

conduit bushing [elec.] A short, internally-rounded, threaded, insulating sleeve at an outlet from a *conduit* to protect the cable insulation.

cone tile, cone-hip t. A *bonnet tile*.

congé (U S A **sanitary shoe**) A small concave *moulding* joining the base of a wall to the floor. *See* **cove**.

conical light A *roof light* or *lantern* built up from straight *glazing bars* and flat panes of glass. It is shaped like a many-sided pyramid.

conical roll, batten r. (U S A) A joint between sheets of *flexible-metal roofing*, formed over a triangular *wood roll*.

conifers [tim.] Trees of the botanical group gymnosperms, which provide all building *softwoods*, mostly fir or pine trees.

Bulldog plate timber connector, held by 12 mm ($\frac{1}{2}$ in.) dia. bolt and nut and washers.

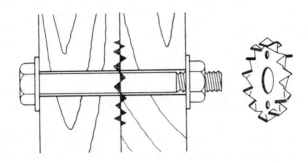

connector, timber c. [tim.] (1) Joint fasteners for roof *trusses* and similar timber frames which increase the shear strength of the joint. Steel split rings, shear plates, toothed plates, and corrugated toothed rings, sometimes inserted in precut sinkings made by a *hole saw*, are held to the timbers by a bolt passing through them and the timber. The bolt is screwed up tightly on to large washers at each end to make a rigid joint (B S 1579). (Illus.)

(2) **longscrew** [plu.] A piece of pipe with an ordinary *taper thread* at one end and at the other end a long *parallel thread* with a back nut. The length of the parallel thread allows the *coupling* to be screwed back on to it completely so that the connector can be removed and the pipe run unmade at will. The backnut forms a watertight joint with the coupling if a hemp *grommet* soaked in jointing liquid is inserted between them before they are screwed up. *See* **double connector, fittings** (illus. p. 138), **plug-in connector**.

consultant A registered architect or professional engineer or surveyor who acts on behalf of a *client*. His functions often go very much further than consultation when he, with his staff, provides the complete design of a building.

consumer's supply control [elec.] The electricity undertaking's meter, together with the consumer's main switch and *cutout box*.

consumer's terminals [elec.] The point where the electricity board's cable ends, and the consumer's wiring begins. It is usually at or near this point that the main switch and the distribution switches and fuses are placed.

contingency sum [q.s.] A *provisional sum* for unforeseeable work, such as pumping after storms.

continuity [elec.] The continuous effective contact of all parts of an electrical circuit to give it high conductance (low resistance). *See also* C.

continuous handrail [carp.] A handrail to a *geometrical stair*. *See* **continuous string**.

continuous string [joi.] An *outer string* continued without interruption round a stairwell, usually under a *continuous handrail*.

contour The cross-section of a decorative *moulding*. *See also* C.

contract An agreement between a *client* and a building or civil engineering *contractor* to do certain types of work at certain rates. Contracts in Britain are usually based on a *bill of quantities* which is mainly a list of numbered *items*, each describing a certain type of work and its extent. The price for supplying the material and labour and doing the work is set against each item by the contractor. If the bill is accepted in this form by the *client* and signed by him, it becomes the main document of the contract. *See also* **cost-plus, etc., tendering, variation order**.

contract documents These form the legal *contract*, and consist of the drawings, the *specification*, the *bill of quantities* or *schedule of prices*, the general conditions of contract, and finally a legal *deed* making these all binding on both parties, *contractor* and *client*.

contractor A person who signs a *contract* to do certain specified work at certain rates of payment, generally within a stated time. *See* **main contractor**.

contractor's agent *See* **agent**.

contracts manager A senior architect, surveyor, civil engineer, or tradesman, employed by a building or civil engineering contractor, who has worked for many years in building construction, and takes full responsibility for the completion of his contracts. He deals with the architect or engineer (or other client) of each site.

convection When a fluid is warmed, it expands, becomes lighter and rises taking heat with it, while it is replaced by denser, cooler fluid. This is the reason for *gravity circulation* and the *stack effect* and explains why air moves about in rooms where there is no draught. *See* **radiator**.

convector heater [plu.] Usually a *fan convector*. (Illus. below)

conversion (1) **breaking down** [tim.] Sawing logs parallel to their length so as to reduce them to convenient rectangular cross-sections. *Compare* **cross-cut**.

(2) *Aluminous cement* concrete that has been mixed with too much water can lose its strength by a chemical conversion especially in warm, damp places. Therefore since the collapse of a swimming-pool roof in 1974 this cement is no longer used in such structures and some engineers no longer use it at all.

converted timber [tim.] *Square-sawn timber*.

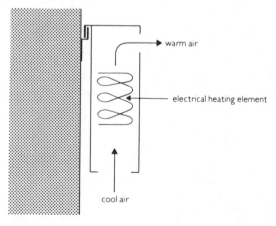

Electrical convector.

cooking vat [tim.] A concrete water tank containing steam-heated water pipes. Every *flitch* is stewed in it for some hours before *slicing* or *rotary cutting*.

cooling tower [mech.] A wooden or concrete tower, used for cooling condenser water by evaporation. These towers lose expensive heat to the air but this waste of heat can be reduced, in closely populated areas, by *district heating*.

cooperative apartment house (USA) A number of *flats* contained in a building owned by a *cooperative housing society*, of which only the tenants are members.

cooperative housing society In Britain, a group, approved by a local authority, consisting of individuals each of whom requires a house or flat. The group buys the site, commissions the *architect*, orders him to send for *tenders*, and obtains from its members one tenth of the cost of the site and building. The remaining nine tenths are lent by the *local authority* borrowing at a low rate of interest from the Treasury. The loan is paid back by rent from the tenants. *See* **cooperative apartment house, mortgage, self-build housing society**.

coordination *See* **dimensional coordination**.

copal [pai.] Natural hard *resins* such as Congo, *kauri* and *dammar*. They provide the hard dark shiny coating of *varnishes* or *oil paints*.

cope (1) To cover a wall with stones, bricks, or precast slabs which usually overhang as a protection to the wall from rain.

(2) A *coping*.

(3) To fit one *moulding* over another without *mitring* by cutting the first to the profile of the second. A wooden moulding is cut with a *coping saw*.

coped joint, scribed j. A joint between *mouldings* at an angle, in which an end of one moulding is cut out but not *mitred* to receive the other. *See* **cope** (3).

coping (1) **c. stone, cope** A brick, stone, or concrete protection, usually overhanging, for weathering the top of a wall.

(2) Making a coped joint in a *moulding*.

(3) Splitting stones by drilling them and driving in steel wedges along a line of holes.

coping saw [joi.] A *modern bow* saw for cutting sharp curves. One type has a steel frame carrying a blade that is a file of circular cross-section about 15 cm long and 1·5 mm diameter.

copper A *flexible metal*, red when freshly cut, used for roofing monumental buildings, where its green *patina* is prized. Copper pipe, used by the Egyptians 5000 years ago, is now common. Copper is durable, malleable, and easy to work but costly. Rainwater should not be allowed to flow even from a small *flashing* of copper on to aluminium, zinc or their alloys, unless they are protected by bitumen or some other suitable coating from the danger of corrosion. *See below, also* **mole plough** (C).

copper bit [plu.] A *soldering iron*. *See* **plumber's tools** (illus. p. 250).

copper fittings [plu.] *Fittings* for *light-gauge copper tube*, many of them not made of copper, but of brass or gunmetal, either capillary or compression joints. *Capillary joints* must be completed by heat. *Compression joints* do not need heat, the joint being completed by tightening *screw threads*. *Silver brazing* can eliminate the use of fittings because all joints can be formed in the tube itself after softening it, by the use of special tools. *See* BS 864, p. 86.

copper glazing *Glazing* with copper *cames* welded to each other. *See* **electrocopper glazing**.

copper nails Used for *roofing nails* or for fixing lead sheet on a *dormer cheek*.

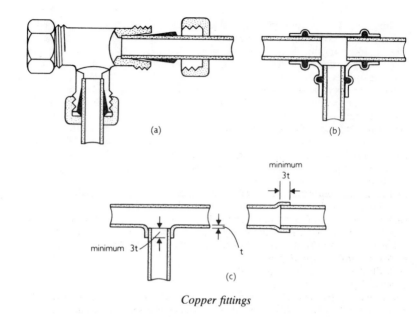

Copper fittings

'Open' nailing is at 7 to 15 cm spacing (3 to 6 in.), 'close' nailing is at 2 to 5 cm (1 to 2 in.). In contact with *Keene's* also, copper nails must be used to prevent corrosion. *See* **silicon bronze**.

copper pipe Pipe from 3 to 100 mm bore ($\frac{1}{8}$ to 4 in.) and from 0·6 mm to 3·3 mm (0·024 to 0·128 in.) in wall thickness, used for every plumbing service in building. *See* **light-gauge copper tube**.

copper plating Electro-plating with copper, a *protective finish* to steel nails, wood *screws*, wire, and so on. Used also under *chromium plate*.

copper roofing *Flexible metal roofing*, of copper sheet generally from 0·4 to 0·5 mm thick, but in the best work 0·6 mm and in good conditions as little as 0·3 mm. It can be laid in large areas but usually no single sheet should be larger than 1·3 m² (14 ft²). The sheet alone weighs 5 kg/m² (1 lb/ft²).

copper slate *See* **lead slate**.

coppersmith's hammer A hammer with a long, bent *ball peen*, used for copper beating.

corbel Brick, masonry, or concrete projecting from a wall face, usually as a support for a beam or roof truss.

corbelling Brickwork projecting successively more in each course to support a chimney stack, *oriel window*, etc.

corbelling iron, corbel pin A metal support built into brickwork to carry (with other corbelling irons) a *wall plate* instead of corbelling the brickwork out to carry the plate.

corbel piece [carp.] A *bolster*.

corded way A path on a steep slope, protected from erosion by steps formed with wooden or stone *risers*.

core (1) The chips cut from a *mortise*, the steel rod beneath a *handrail*, the innermost layer of *composite board*, the part of a *flush door* that is not seen, *brick core* below a relieving arch, etc.

(2) [pla.] A base to a cornice or other complicated plaster work. It may be *bracketing* (hollow core) or a mass of *coarse stuff* reinforced with hair (solid core).

coreboard (USA **lumber core**) [tim.] (1) *Particle board* intended to form the *core* of sandwich construction (BS 565).

(2) Formerly a generic term for *battenboard*, *blockboard*, and *laminboard*.

core driver [carp.] A *hardwood* cylinder the exact size of a hole, pushed through it to clear out chips.

cork The bark of the cork oak, grown in Mediterranean countries and North America. Granulated cork is used as a *loose-fill insulation* weighing 80 to 100 kg/m³. *See below* and BS 3519.

cork board, compressed c., baked c. Granulated cork which has been compressed and baked to form slabs for flooring or insulation.

cork carpet A floor finish from 3·2 to 6·7 mm thick made like *linoleum* in rolls 1·8 m (6 ft) wide. It is insulating, quiet, and suitable for heavy domestic use but not for hard traffic. It is obtainable in about four colours.

corkscrew stair A *spiral stair.*

cork tile *Flooring tile* of *corkboard.*

corkwood [tim.] *Balsa wood.*

corner chisel, drawer-lock c. [carp.] A *chisel* used for cutting out *mortises*. It is L-shaped, with no handle so that both ends are sharpened and used for cutting.

cornerlocked joint [joi.] A *combed joint.*

corner trowel [pla.] (USA) *Angle trowels* of two sorts, used either for internal or for external corners.

cornice A moulding at the top of an outside wall, overhanging it to throw the drips away from the wall, or where an inside wall joins the ceiling.

corrosion inhibitor Chemicals like sodium nitrite or chromate, and some *inhibiting pigments* protect metals, when used in paints or otherwise.

corrugated aluminium A wall and roof *cladding* which is lighter and far more durable, though dearer, than *corrugated iron.*

corrugated asbestos *Asbestos-cement* sheeting for roof or wall *cladding* (BS 690, 5247).

corrugated fastener, joint f., wiggle nail, dog, mitre brad [carp.] A corrugated piece of metal, generally steel, driven into the end grain of two boards to join them at a place where fine appearance is not needed, in boxes, etc.

corrugated iron Steel sheet, corrugated and galvanized on both sides, rusts in damp climates, and therefore needs painting. The paint flakes off new galvanizing, but some months later, it sticks. *See* BSCP 143, **profiled steel sheet**.

corrugated sheet *Cladding* of *PVC*, steel, aluminium, asbestos, or opaque or translucent *glassfibre reinforced resin.*

corrugated toothed ring [carp.] A timber *connector.*

costing Calculation of the cost of a unit of work, from the total work completed with a certain amount of labour and materials. The contractor's *agent* or general foreman calculates his costs per *item* at frequent intervals so as to be sure that they are below the rate which has been written in the *priced bill* by his firm.

cost-plus-fixed-fee contract Like a *cost-plus-percentage contract*, this form is used only for the most urgent work which cannot await preparation of final drawings. The *client* pays to the *contractor* the full cost of all labour, materials, plant, and services used on the site. Contractor's *overheads* and profits are paid for by a fixed fee.

cost-plus-percentage contract A *contract* used only for very urgent work which cannot await completion of the drawings. The *contractor* is paid the full cost of all labour, materials, plant, and services used on the site plus a percentage of these for his *overheads* and profit. Since the contract is in this form, the contractor has a direct incentive to enlarge the scope of the work and to delay completion. For this reason it is undesirable, except under close, strict site supervision.

cost-reimbursement contract Any *contract* based on *cost plus percentage*, *cost plus fixed fee*, or *value cost*. Whenever time is available to complete the drawings before handing over the site to the contractor, a *fixed-price contract* is used, and this type of contract avoided.

cottage roof A roof without *principals*, having only *common rafters* resting on *wall plates*, surmounted by a *ridge*, usually having *ceiling joists*.

cotter A steel wedge driven into a *cottered* or similar joint to tighten it.

cottered joint [carp.] A joint used between the *king post* of a *truss* and the *tie-beam* below it. The king post is held to the tie-beam by a metal U-strap passing below the tie-beam. The strap holds the tie-beam tight to the king post by wedges and *gibs* through king post and strap. *See* illus. p. 328.

coumarone resins, c.-indene r. [pai.] *Synthetic resins* used as a *medium* for painting on metal, as electrical insulating varnish, or as an *alkali-resistant* finish.

counter battens [carp.] (1) *Battens* fixed across the back of several boards to stiffen them, often held by screws in slots to allow *moisture movement*. They were used on drawing boards.

(2) Battens parallel to the *rafters* and nailed over them on a boarded and felted roof. The *slating* or tiling battens are nailed over them. Counter battens are used to ensure that any water passing on to the roofing felt flows straight down. Otherwise it might be held by the slating battens.

counter cramp [joi.] A *batten* with small pieces of wood fixed to it, against which several boards can be cramped with *folding wedges* when they are being glued at the edges (*counter wedging*).

counter flashing A sheet metal *flashing* built into a joint of a chimney or parapet wall and left projecting, to be turned down later when the roof is covered.

counter floor, sub-floor (USA **blind f., rough f.**) [carp.] The lower of two sets of floor boards, often laid diagonally to carry *parquet* or other finished flooring.

counter gauge [joi.] A *mortise gauge*.

countersink (1) **c. bit** A bit for metal or wood, with conical cutting edge to make a conical sinking at the upper edge of a hole drilled to receive a screw.

(2) The conical sinking made by a countersink bit.

counter wedging [joi.] The use of *counter cramps* for fixing boards together as if for a shop counter.

coupled window, double w., storm w. An outside window with a wide air space between it and the inner window to reduce heat loss and *noise*. The outer window is often removable in summer. Noise reduction can reach 35 decibels. *Compare* **double glazing**.

couple roof [carp.] A pitched roof with *common rafters* and no *tie-beam*, used for short spans of up to 3 m (10 ft).

coupling, coupler (1) [plu.] **socket** A *fitting* that joins two pipes whether of copper, plastics or steel. It may be *capillary, compression* or screwed.

(2) In *tubular scaffolding*, a piece which clamps two or more tubes together, usually by a screwed clamp.

coursed ashlar (USA) *Regular-coursed rubble.*

coursed snecked rubble *Snecked rubble* built to occasional courses.

coursed squared rubble (USA **random ashlar**) *Squared rubble* built to occasional courses.

courses Parallel layers of bricks, stones, blocks, slates, tiles, shingles, etc. usually horizontal and of uniform height, including any mortar laid with them. The term is also used for setts or wood blocks laid in rows or for any horizontal layer of material.

coursing joint (1) A *bed joint.*

(2) A *joint* in an arch, concentric with, and separating, two *string courses*.

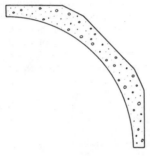

Precast plaster cove for ceiling-wall junction obtainable in lengths of 10 m (33 ft).

cove, coving A concave moulding joining a wall to ceiling or floor (above).

coved ceiling A ceiling curved at its junction with the walls.

cove lighting *Indirect lighting* from above a *cove* or *cornice*. The light is thrown up to the ceiling which reflects the light in a pleasant, diffuse way downwards with no glare.

cover The covered width of a slate, tile, or shingle. *See also C.*

cover fillet, c. strip, c. moulding [joi.] A narrow strip covering the joints in wall or ceiling board.

cover flashing [plu.] A usually vertical *flashing* overlapping the vertical parts of *soakers, lead slates* or the turn-up from the *flexible metal* at the edge of a flat roof. On a sloping roof it may also be a *stepped flashing*.

covering power [pai.] *See* **hiding power, spreading rate.**

coverings for partitions These are used where the stiffness and sound insulation of rigid *infillings* (*bricknogging*) are not needed or where for other reasons (e.g. weight) they would be unsatisfactory. Apart from timber panelling, *plywood, fibreboard, gypsum plasterboard, plaster, insulating board* and *wallboards*, there are *woodwool* and *compressed straw slab*, which, being

89

5 cm (2 in.) thick or more, can be built up to form a partition without framing. *See* **framed partition**.

cowl A metal cover, often louvred or rotating, fixed on a *chimney* to improve the draught.

crab A portable windlass or hand winch for lifting heavy loads. *See also C.*

cracking in paint The breakdown of a paint film on exposure, with cracks through at least one *coat*. Some of the various sorts of cracking are *crawling, crazing, crocodiling, hair cracking*.

cracking in plaster Plaster cracks when it shrinks, when laths twist or are too thinly plastered, or when the structure settles differentially. *Gypsum plasters* do not shrink on hardening; they expand slightly (Portland cement plasters shrink). All cracks except those due to building settlement and shrinking can be avoided. *See* **fire cracks**.

cracking of walls Cracks in outside walls result from *differential settlement (C)* on a clay or silt foundation, at least in the UK, where most people live in areas of clay or silt. They may be caused by a heavier load on one wall than another in a house with the same width of *strip footing (C)*, or by the roots of a *poplar* or other fast-growing tree sucking the water from the clay under the house and making it shrink in summer. The felling of a tree also may cause later cracking because of the slow expansion of the clay afterwards. *See also* **calcium silicate bricks, sulphate expansion, frost heave** (C) and BRE Digest 63.

cradle, boat scaffold A movable *scaffold* hanging on ropes, used by painters for painting tall buildings. *See also C.*

cradling [pla.] Rough timber fixed round steel beams as a ground for *lathing*. *See* **bracketing**.

cradling piece [carp.] A short *joist* from the wall each side of the *chimney breast* to the *trimmer joist*, carrying floor boards.

craft, trade An occupation which needs intelligence and manual skill, and for which an *apprenticeship* has been served, usually accompanied by attendance at evening classes. A man with a craft is a craftsman or *tradesman*.

craftsman *See above.*

cramp (1) **clamp** [joi.] A tool for squeezing together wooden parts during gluing, for example a *counter cramp, floor cramp, hand screw*.

(2) A metal U-shaped bar, from 15 to 30 cm (6 to 12 in.) long and 9 to 25 mm (⅜ to 1 in.) wide, which holds ashlars to each other or to a steel or concrete beam behind. It is often called a cramp iron although for monumental work it is often made of 3 mm (⅛ in.) dia. copper wire or other non-rusting metal. *See* **lead plug, slate cramp**.

(3) A metal strap built into a wall and holding a door frame or lining.

crampon, crampoon *Nippers.*

crank [mech.] A bar with a right-angle bend in it which gives a leverage in turning, for example the starting handle of a car, a carpenter's *brace*, or a crankshaft of an internal combustion engine.

crank brace [carp.] A carpenter's *brace*.

cranked sheet An asbestos-cement corrugated sheet bent to fit the junction of two roof slopes.

crawling [pai.] A *cracking* in gloss-finish topcoats containing *drying oils*, which shrink and reveal a *ground* (3). It may be caused by grease on the ground. Cissing is mild crawling.

crawlway A *duct* high enough and wide enough with all its pipes and cables installed for a man to crawl through (BSCP 413).

crazing (1) Hair cracks on the surface of concrete or *cement rendering*, caused generally by excessive water or by steel trowelling of a too rich mix. Map crazing is random crazing over the whole surface.

(2) **shelling** [pla.] A fault in a *finishing coat* which forms many intersecting cracks on its surface, and leaves its bed, owing to a weak *floating coat*. The cure is to cut out bad patches down to the brick, and relay.

(3) [pai.] *Cracking*, consisting of broad deep *checks*. *See* **crocodiling**.

creasing, tile c. Under a brick-on-edge coping, one or two courses of plain tiles are laid, projecting about 3·8 cm (1½ in.) from the face of the wall. The projection is covered with a *cement fillet*. *See* illus. p. 285.

cremone bolt A vertical bolt on a casement, or casement door, that locks by entering vertically into the door frame at top and bottom, unlike the *espagnolette bolt*, which rotates. The two half-bolts meet at the mid-height on a rack and pinion worked by the door handle.

cricket (USA) In a chimney *back gutter*, a small *saddle* built to throw off the water in both directions.

cripple (1) A bracket anchored at the ridge, carrying a scaffold for slaters.

(2) Any framed member shortened at an opening. A *jack rafter*, for example, is a cripple rafter.

critical path scheduling A valuable development of the *progress chart* on urgent, complicated contracts. As on the progress chart, the expected time required for each operation is written down. From these times can be obtained the time required to reach the end of the contract (the critical path). Application of extra resources to the critical path shortens it, it ceases to be critical and another path then becomes critical. If a computer or punched card machine is used, with each card carrying the duration of an operation and its location in the sequence, a new critical path can be determined in only a minute, even with 1000 cards.

crocodiling, alligatoring [pai.] Bad *crazing* showing a pattern like alligator skin.

crook [tim.] (1) A *knee*.

(2) (USA) The *warping* called *spring* in Britain.

cross [plu.] A *fitting* consisting of two branches meeting at right angles on a *run*. *See* **fittings** (illus. p. 138).

cross band, c. banding, crossing [tim.] In *plywood* or *composite board*, the layers with *grain* perpendicular to the core grain. They reduce shrinking and cracking or expansion. In five-ply the cross bands are the layers between face and core and between back and core (face crossing, back crossing). In *three-ply* they are the two outer veneers.

cross bridging [carp.] (USA) *Herring-bone strutting*.

cross-cut [carp.] To cut with a saw at right angles to the grain of wood, or a saw-cut so made.

cross-cut saw [carp.] A saw with its teeth set and sharpened to cut across the grain of wood. The larger the saw the coarser are its teeth; thus a 35 cm (14 in.) cross-cut has 8 to 10 points per 25 mm (1 in.), while a 66 cm (26 in.) cross-cut has 6 to 8 points per 25 mm (1 in.). *See* **panel saw, pendulum, rip saw, setting**.

cross furring [pla.] (USA) *Brandering*.

cross garnet [joi.] A hinge like those on the entrance doors of ancient ca-

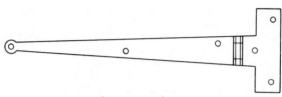

Cross garnet hinge.

thedrals, made of a long steel or wrought iron strap fixed to the face of the door. It is often used for hanging gates or *ledged and braced doors* but not in the best joinery since it is so massive. (Illus.)

cross grain [tim.] Fibres which do not run parallel with the length of the piece. They may be partly *end grain*, *diagonal grain*, *spiral grain*, *interlocked grain*, or alternating. All of these, the contrary of *straight grain*, make the wood hard to work.

cross-grained float [pla.] A wooden float about 30 × 10 × 2·5 cm (12 × 4 × 1 in.), like the *hand float* but thicker, with the grain parallel to the short side, and used for *scouring*. See **plasterer** (illus. p. 246).

crossing (1) [tim] A *cross band*.

(2) [pai.] Laying on a *coat* of *paint* with a *brush* by a series of strokes each at right angles to the previous series. With *oil paints* each series becomes progressively lighter, helping to give a uniform coat.

cross joint (U S A **head joint**) Vertical mortar *joints* perpendicular to the face of a wall. They are less easy to fill than *bed joints* and are usually weaker, being made by *buttering*.

cross-lap joint [carp.] (U S A) A *halved joint* between two pieces of wood which cross each other.

cross peen In the description of hand *hammers*, a wedge shape opposite the face of the hammerhead. This wedge is horizontal when the handle is vertical. The opposite of *straight peen*.

cross tongue, loose t. [joi.] A piece of *plywood* or a slip of wood with *diagonal grain*, glued into a saw cut between two members to stiffen an angle joint. *See* **feather, key, straight tongue**.

cross welt A *seam* between adjacent sheets of *flexible-metal roofing*, usually parallel to the *ridge* or *gutter*. See **staggering, double-lock cross welt**.

crotch, crutch [tim.] The join between a large branch and the tree trunk. The *grain* is curly, since the fibres of the branch must be locked into the fibres of the trunk. The *veneer* is often highly figured and therefore valuable. *See* **curl, plume**.

crown course A *cranked* or curved corrugated asbestos sheet used as an alternative to *ridge capping*.

crown plate [carp.] A *bolster*.

crown post [carp.] A *king post* or the short vertical posts near the middle of a *hammer-beam* roof.

crowsfooting [pai.] Minor wrinkling like the imprint of bird's feet, with the wrinkles not joined up. It can be regarded as an incompletely *crystallized finish*.

cruck house The earliest medieval house of timber that has survived. Only a few remain. The roof is carried on pairs of timbers from ground level to ridge.

Timbers (crucks) with the right curve had to be chosen. Several varieties exist.

cruiser, timber c. [tim.] (USA) A timber estimator who measures and counts some of the trees in a stand and so arrives at a figure for the amount of *standing timber*.

crystallized finish [pai.] The wrinkles formed in paints which contain *tung* or similar oils, or the true crystallizing of certain *lacquers*. *See* **gas-checking**.

Cuban, San Domingo, Spanish, West Indian mahogany [tim.] (Swietenia mahogoni). The first exported mahogany, now very scarce. A close-grained red timber with a fine silky texture, hard, with little *moisture movement* obtainable in large sizes, stronger than *oak* but slightly easier to work, used for the very best *joinery*.

cubing [q.s.] (1) Determining volumes in m^3 (ft^3), etc.

(2) From the volume of a proposed building, in the earliest stage of its design, determining its probable cost by multiplying the cost per m^3 (ft^3) of recently completed similar work by the volume of the building in m^3 (ft^3). Other methods of approximate estimating exist.

culls American term for material which has been rejected as of too low a quality to be used, particularly bricks or timber.

cup (1) [tim.] The natural *warp* in the cross-section of a *flat-sawn* plank, caused by drying *shrinkage*, concave towards the bark.

(2) A *screw cup*.

cupboard latch [joi.] A ball catch or other simple catch for securing a cupboard door.

cup shake [tim.] *Ring shake*.

cup-square bolt A *coach bolt*.

curb [carp.], **kerb** A timber upstand, sometimes used as a *roll*. *See below*.

curb rafters [carp.] The rafters of the flatter, upper slope of a *mansard roof*.

curb roll (USA **c. joint, knuckle joint**) The horizontal joint between the two surfaces of a *mansard roof*.

curb stringer, c. string [joi.] (USA) A three-member *outer string*, consisting of one *close string* carrying the stair, surmounted by a *moulding*, called the shoe rail, from which the *balusters* rise, and faced with a facing string.

cure, curing [tim.] The chemical change (polymerization or condensation) which occurs when *thermo-setting* resins are heated, or when an *accelerator* is added to a *cold-setting resin*. They become insoluble in water, strong and hard, a result of additional linkages between the molecules. *See* **polymers** *and* **C**.

curl [tim.] The fine *figure* obtained by skilful *conversion* of *crotch*.

current-carrying capacity [elec.] *Carrying capacity*.

curtaining, sagging [pai.] Excessive *flow* in paint films, particularly on vertical surfaces, producing bow-shaped ridges, which look like hanging curtains and may collapse and tear down. *See* **run**.

curtain walling Quickly erected, metal-framed, thin, lightweight cladding used on multi-storey buildings, usually clear of the building structure but suspended from it at widely spaced points. It may be partly or wholly glazed. Its opaque panels of vitreous enamel or of synthetic sheet, sometimes under glass, of any desired colour, give the designer a freedom unheard of with conventional materials. Many problems in curtain walling have been previously met in *patent glazing*.

curtilage The land occupied by a dwelling house and its garden.
cushion (1) A *padstone*.

(2) A seating for glass along the full length of a *patent glazing* bar, usually of oiled asbestos, plastics or lead.
cut-and-mitred string [carp.] A *cut string* in which the end grain of the *risers* is hidden by mitring with the vertical part of the notch in the string.
cut-and-mitred hip or **valley** A *close-cut hip* or *valley*.
cut brick A brick cut to shape with an *axe* or *bolster*. It is much rougher in shape than a *gauged brick*.
cut nail [carp.] A heavy *nail* of rectangular cross section made by cutting (shearing) it from steel plate, as opposed to the *wire nail* forged from round or oval wire. It cannot be bent over and clenched like a wire nail since it breaks easily.
cutout (1) [elec.] A circuit-breaking device such as an electric *fuse* or circuit breaker. *See* **short circuit**.

(2) The upper end of a *patent glazing* bar which is cut away to enable the glazing to be flashed.
cutout box, fuse b., lighting panel [elec.] The cast-iron box on an electricity consumer's premises, containing the *fuses* or circuit breakers. *See also* **house service cutout**.
cut stone, natural s. A stone cut to shape with *chisel* and *mallet*. *Compare* **cast stone**.
cut string, open s., bridge board [carp.] An *outer string* with its upper edge cut in steps so that the treads overhang it, used for the dignified stairs of the eighteenth century. *See* **bracketed stairs, string**.
cutter, cutter and rubber A *rubbed brick* for *gauged brickwork*.
cutter block [tim.] A steel block fixed to the spindle of a *spindle moulder*, *surface planer*, or similar wood-working machine. It carries two or more knives which shape or smooth the timber. Cutting is done by an adzing action. All cutter blocks turn at high speeds, at least 4,000 rpm. *See* **solid-moulding cutter**.
cutting gauge [joi.] A tool like a *marking gauge* with a thin blade in place of the marking pin. It is used for cutting laths or rebating timber.
cutting in [pai.] Painting a clean edge, usually a straight line, at an edge of a painted area.
cutting iron [joi.] The sharpened steel blade of a *plane*, wedged to the *back iron*. *See* **carpenter's tools** (illus. p. 59).
cutting list [carp.] A list showing the sizes and sorts of timber needed for a job. *See also* **C**.
cutting pliers [elec.] A pair of pliers with wire cutters on one side as well as the usual flat jaws.
cyclone cellar (USA) A *storm cellar*.
cylinder, storage calorifier [plu.] A closed circular tank for storing under pressure the hot water to be drawn off at the taps, usually of copper. If it is horizontal it is domed at both ends, if it is vertical its top is domed and its bottom is concave. *See* **calorifier, cistern, direct, indirect cylinder**.
cylinder lock, Yale l. [joi.] A *lock* for an entrance door (of rim or *mortise* type) which is opened by key from outside and by knob from inside. It can usually be set with the *latch* permanently in the shut or open position by a catch inside the door. The latch has the same metal tongue as the lock.

D

dab [pla.] See **plaster dab**.

dabber [pai.] A dome-shaped *brush* of soft hair for applying *spirit varnish* or for polishing and finishing gilding.

dado [joi.] A border or panelling over the lower half of the walls of a room above the *skirting*.

dado capping, surbase, d. rail, d. moulding, chair rail [joi.] The highest part of a framed *dado*.

dado joint [joi.] (USA) A *housed joint*.

damages, liquidated d. Sums payable for contractor's delays amounting to a breach of contract, can generally be recovered from the *contractor* only if it can be proved that they are related to a loss caused by the delay.

dammar [pai.] A natural *resin*, soluble in many organic *solvents*, of a pale yellow colour or colourless, used in *varnishes*.

damp course, damp-proof c., dpc A layer of impervious material laid in a wall to exclude water, usually at least 150 mm (6 in.) above ground level, as well as above the junctions of *parapet* walls with a roof and above or before door or window openings. Vertical damp courses (*tanking*) of asphaltic material keep basements dry. Damp courses may be *flexible* or *rigid*. They were not required by law until the Public Health Act 1875. (Illus.) *See* **dampness**, also BSCP 102.

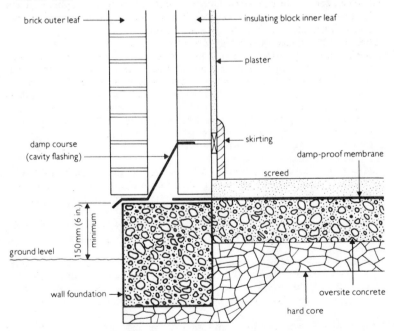

Damp-proofing at a house foundation (*After* GLC Good Practice Details, *Architectural Press, 1979*).

dampness Dampness in buildings is usually first seen on walls, and has many causes including *bridging, condensation, draught stripping, dry rot, overflowing rainwater gutters, rising damp. See also* **moisture expansion of bricks, pore treatments, sawing in a damp course**.

damp proofing Putting a horizontal or vertical *damp course* in a building.

damp-proof membrane A wide *damp course*, usually up a wall as *tanking*, or under a slab.

dap, dapping [carp.] (mainly USA) A sinking such as those made for timber *connectors*, or a *housing* for a *ribbon board* in a *stud*.

dancing step A *balanced step*.

Darby float, Derby f. [pla.] A two-handled wooden or light alloy float 1 to 1·5 m (3½ to 5 ft) long, about 13 cm (5 in.) wide and 1·6 cm (⅝ in.) thick used for levelling surfaces, particularly ceilings.

day The *daylight width*.

daylight factor, sky f. At a given point in a room the daylight factor is the percentage illumination of a horizontal surface at that point compared with the illumination which it would have from the whole hemisphere of sky (BRE Digest 41).

daylight-factor protractor An instrument which simplifies the calculation of *daylight factors* and the solid angles and slopes involved.

daylight prediction, d. forecasting An architect designing buildings, their heights and spacings needs to know, for each living room, whether enough light will reach all parts of it at all seasons. He can forecast the amount of daylight in any part of the room at any season by using the methods of the *Building Research Establishment*.

daylight width, sight w. The width of the opening which admits light through a window. *See* **sight size**.

daywork A method of payment for building work, involving agreement between the *clerk of works* and the *contractor* on the hours of work done by each man, and the materials used. The clerk of works signs the contractor's daysheets. Payment to the contractor consists of his expenses in labour and materials, plus an agreed percentage for overheads and profit. Daywork is *cost-plus-percentage* payment on a small scale.

dead [elec.] The contrary of *live wire*, said of any conductor which is disconnected from its source of power.

dead bolt [joi.] A square-section *bolt* which is driven home by turning a key in a *lock*, as opposed to the ordinary bevelled *latch* worked by a door knob, or the *barrel bolt*.

deadening, deafening, dead sounding The *pugging* of floors or walls.

dead knot, encased k. [tim.] A knot whose fibres are not intergrown with surrounding wood. It is easily knocked out and is thus a worse defect than a *live knot*.

dead leg [plu.] A hot-water connection in which the water is stationary (not circulating) except when it is being drawn off. The water cools down between draw-offs and the dead leg therefore wastes both water and heat. Some water authorities specify the maximum allowable length of dead leg. *See* **hot-water cylinder**, illus. p. 179.

deadlight, fixed sash, fast sheet, stand sheet A *window* in which the glass is fixed directly to the surround, i.e. that does not open.

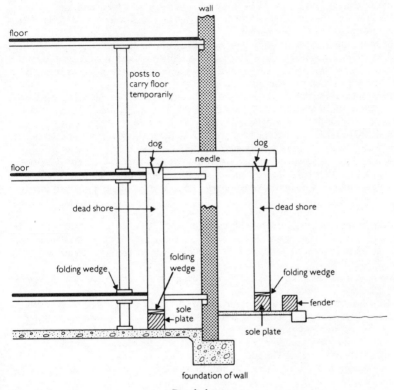

Dead shores.

dead lock [joi.] A *lock* which is worked by key only from both sides and therefore has no door knobs.

dead shore [carp.] A heavy upright timber (one of two) carrying the weight of a wall below a *needle*. (Illus.)

dead-soft temper The softness of *copper* sheet required for roofing. The copper may suffer *hardening* (C) during placing but can easily be *annealed* (C) again by heating it to a dull red heat with a *blow lamp* and allowing it to cool in air or water.

deal [tim.] (1) A piece of square-sawn softwood 50 to 100 mm (2 to 4 in.) thick and 225 to 300 mm (9 to 12 in.) wide (BS 565). It is usually about 230 by 75 mm (9 by 3 in.). *See* **plank**.

(2) *See* **redwood**.

deal frame [tim.] A *frame-saw* used for cutting *deals*, having vertical feed rollers to keep the deal close to the fence.

death-watch beetle [tim.] A *beetle* which burrows deeply into structural timber, in particular the *sapwood* of English *oak*, and is therefore difficult to kill. The adult makes a ticking noise.

decay, fungal d., rot [tim.] Decomposition of *timbers* by fungi and other micro-organisms, for example, brown, *dry, pocket,* and *wet rot. See also* **dote, moisture content, weathering**.

decibel A unit of sound reduction, defined as one tenth of the logarithm to the base 10 of the ratio of the two sound intensities, used in calculating *sound-reduction factors* of *partitions* and floors. (For loudness of sound the unit is the *phon*). See **reverberation period**.

deciduous trees [tim.] Trees which lose their leaves every year, that is all *hard-woods* and a few *softwoods. See* **larch**.

deck *See* **roof-decking panels**, *also* C.

deducts [q.s.] Quantities such as areas of door or window openings deducted from areas of wall or pointing or painting or plaster; *but see* **adds**.

deed (1) A document forming part of a *contract* which, when signed by both parties, is legally binding, and holds the contractor to perform the work according to the *contract documents*. The *client* is equally bound to pay for the work.

(2) A legal document which gives a right to property.

deep bead, draught b., sill b., ventilating b. [joi.] An upright board fixed to and rising about 8 cm above the *window board* of a *sash window*. It allows some ventilation without draught at the *meeting rail* while the bottom *sash* is nearly closed.

deep cutting, deeping [tim.] The *re-sawing* of timber parallel to the faces (B S 565). *Compare* **flat cutting**.

deep-seal trap [plu.] An *anti-siphon trap* with a *seal* 7·6 cm (3 in.) deep or more.

defect [tim.] An irregularity or weakness in wood which lowers its usefulness or structural suitability, such as *decay*, insect damage, poor conversion or machining, *knots, shake, wane* or *warp. Compare* **blemish, open defect**.

defects liability period The *maintenance period*.

de-greasing A preparation for painting on metal. Even concrete, which has been cast against formwork treated with mould oil or other *release agent* (C) may need de-greasing, or paint may not stick. Non-ferrous metals readily hold grease and must be carefully de-greased either by successive wipes with white spirit and clean swabs or by immersion in a solvent. *See* **pre-treatment primer**.

degree-day value Annual figure describing the relative coldness of a site. In Britain, where it is assumed that buildings need no heating when the outside temperature is 15·5° C. (60° F.) or warmer, it is based on the number of days yearly on which the average temperature is lower. Such days are 'weighted' as follows. Each day with an average temperature of 14·5° C. (58·1° F.) counts as 1; 13·5° C. (56·3° F.) counts as 2; 12·5° C. (54·5° F.) counts as 3 and so on. These degree-days for the whole heating season are then added together. Thus London has a degree-day value around 1950. Aberdeen, also at sea level but 644 km. (400 miles) further north, 3050. The effect of altitude generally is to add half a degree-day for each metre of height above sea level. The degree-day value is used by heating and ventilation engineers to calculate the annual fuel consumption for warming a building, as well as the sizes of its boilers and radiators. French measurements are in degrees C. below 18° C. US measurements are in degrees F. below 65° F. (18·3° C.)

de-humidification Reduction of the amount of water vapour in a space or an air stream, sometimes by the use of *desiccants*.

de-humidifier An air-conditioning unit which cools the air below the dewpoint

(*C*), and thus reduces its humidity. It may dry the air by a cooling spray or a chemical *desiccant* or refrigeration. It can save energy because of the latent heat released by the water as it condenses.

Delabole slates Grey, green, or red, *sized* or *random slates* from Delabole, Cornwall, an English quarry worked since the sixteenth century.

deliquescence The liquefying of certain salts by their absorption of water, generally from the air. When patches of chlorides occur in plaster or brickwork, they may deliquesce and be seen as damp dark areas on the plaster. The opposite of *efflorescence*.

demolisher, mattock man, topman, housebreaker A *skilled man* who pulls down a wall by standing on top of it and breaking pieces off below him, or by pulling a loose wall with a winch and rope, or by means of a *concrete breaker* (*C*).

demolition contract A *contract* for building on a city site is usually preceded by demolition of the old building. Although the demolition may be included in the building contract, work is sometimes started more quickly by separating the two, since very few drawings need to be prepared for demolition work. *See* BS CP 94 Demolition.

densified impregnated wood [tim.] *Impreg.*

desiccant A substance that absorbs so much water that it can be used to dry air in a *de-humidifier* or elsewhere.

desiccation [tim.] The drying e.g. of *timbers* in a *kiln*.

design-and-build contract [q.s.] A *package deal*.

detector, automatic call point A *smoke detector*.

devil float, devil [pla.] A *hand float* with a nail head projecting from each corner about 3 mm. The nail heads scratch the surface of fresh plaster to make a *key* for the next coat. *Compare* **comb**. *See* **plasterer** (illus. p. 246).

devilling [pla.] Scratching plaster to make a rough surface for the next coat.

dextrin, starch gum [pai.] A water-soluble gum made from starch, used as a binder in *water paints* and distempers, and for hanging heavy wallpaper.

diamond matching [tim.] *See* **four-piece butt matching**.

diamond saw A *circular saw* about 1·8 m (6 ft) dia., and 9 mm ($\frac{3}{8}$ in.) thick which cuts stone with *black diamonds* (*C*) set in its perimeter.

diamond washer A curved washer used with a *hook bolt* or other fixing through roof sheeting. It fits its corrugations like the *limpet washer* and may be of galvanized steel, plastics or bitumen felt.

diaphragm tank A closed tank with one connection to the hot circulating water of a *sealed* heating system, and with its inner space divided in two by a rubber wall which allows more space for the hot water as it gets hotter. The space the other side of the skin contains nitrogen which is compressible and the pressure in the system therefore does not rise excessively. (BS 4814) (p. 100).

diatomite, diatomaceous earth, moler earth, kieselguhr A soil composed of the hollow siliceous skeletons of tiny marine or freshwater organisms (diatoms) found in Denmark and elsewhere. It is an *extender* in paints, and an *aggregate* for lightweight, insulating *building blocks* or flue bricks. It can be used as a *refractory* (*C*) at temperatures up to 1300° C.

die (1) [joi.] At the upper and lower ends of a *baluster*, the enlarged square part which meets the rail or plinth.

(2) An internally threaded metal block for cutting male threads on bars or pipes, held in a *die stock*. *Compare* **tap**. *See also* C.

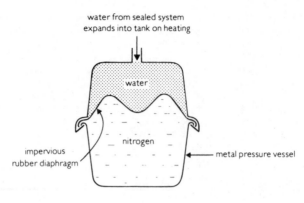

Diaphragm tank.

die stock [plu.] A holder for *dies* with which *screw threads* can be cut by hand.

diffuse porous wood [tim.] *Hardwood* in which the pores are uniform in size throughout the *annual ring*, without any abrupt transition in size between *springwood* and *summerwood*. Compare **ring-porous wood**.

diffuser A *register* (2).

diffuse reflection Reflection of light from a surface as smooth, matt, white paper reflects light equally in all directions.

diffuse-reflection factor The ratio of the light which is diffusely reflected from a surface, to that which falls on it.

diluent [pai.] A *thinner*.

dimensional coordination Agreement between *building-component* makers and *architects* about the dimensions of components so that they can fit into a *modular system*, to simplify their work and help standardization (B S 2900).

dimensional stability A material is dimensionally stable if it has no *moisture movement*, little temperature movement, and does not shrink or expand for any other reason. Cement and wood products are generally unstable, but *plywood* is much more stable than wood, owing to the different directions of the grain in alternate *veneers*.

dimension lumber [tim.] (U S A) *Lumber* stocked in a lumber yard, from 10 to 30 cm (4 to 12 in.) wide, and from 5 to 13 cm (2 to 5 in.) thick, not planed.

dimension shingles *Shingles* cut to uniform instead of to random widths. They are 13 and 15 cm (5 and 6 in.) wide by 40, 46, or 61 cm (16, 18 or 24 in.) long, and usually of *western red cedar*.

dimensions paper [q.s.] Paper used for *taking off*, having the eight columns of vertical ruling shown on p. 101. Columns *a* and *e* are for *timesing*. In columns *b* and *f* the dimensions are written. The squaring columns *c* and *g* are for writing the areas, volumes, etc. calculated from *b* and *f*, while columns *d* and *h* are for the descriptions of the items. The right-hand part of *d* and *h* is called the waste.

dimension stone *Ashlar*.

diminishing courses, graduated c. Courses of slating so laid that the *gauge* between them diminishes from eaves to ridge. The slate sizes also diminish.

Extremely careful work is needed but the appearance is very pleasant. *See*
random slates.

a	b	c	d		e	f	g	h	
timesing	dimensions	squaring	description	waste	timesing	dimensions	squaring	description	waste

Dimensions paper

diminishing piece, d. pipe [plu.] A *taper pipe*.

diminishing stile, gunstock s. [joi.] A door *stile* which is narrowed from the *lock rail* upwards and is glazed above the lock rail. The stile is made narrower to give more space for glass.

DIN Deutsche Industrie Norm (German industry standard).

dinging [pla.] Rough, single-coat *stucco* on walls, consisting of cement and sand, sometimes marked with a *jointer* to imitate masonry joints.

direct cylinder [plu.] All the earliest hot-water systems (and some modern ones) use a direct cylinder; with this, the water passes directly from the boiler to the hot-water cylinder, and then out through the hot tap. Unlike an *indirect cylinder* it contains no heating pipe though it may contain an electrically heated coil, for use mainly in summer.

direct heating The heating of a room by a heat source within it, such as an electric or gas or coal fire. *See* **central heating**.

direct labour The employment of building *tradesmen* and *labourers* by the *client* or his agent (engineer or *architect*) directly, without the mediation of a *contractor*. About one in every three *local authorities* in Britain makes use of direct labour.

dirty money Additional pay to a building worker for working in difficult or unusual conditions. *Compare* **boot man** (*C*).

disappearing stair A *loft ladder*.

discharging arch A *relieving arch*.

disconnecting trap [plu.] An *intercepting trap*.

discontinuous construction Breaks in the continuity of a structure, usually to reduce the amount of impact sound passing through it. This complicates the construction and makes it more expensive but is cheaper than alternative methods of *noise insulation* and very efficient. There are many varieties, including the *double-leaf party wall* and the *floating floor*. (Illus. pp. 102, 144) *See also* **maisonette**.

disc rivet In the fixing of *asbestos-cement slates*, a copper rivet with a large washer that secures the centre of the *tail* of these large slates.

disc sander A small *sanding machine* with a rotating stiff rubber disc which acts as a backing for *glasspaper*, used for *sanding* awkward corners of wood floors which the ordinary floor sander cannot approach. It can be fitted to a hand electric drill.

dispersion [pai.] Finely divided drops of liquid in an *emulsion paint* or other *emulsion* (*C*).

distemper [pai.] Originally (as 'soft' distemper) a heavily pigmented, matt *water* *paint* with *whiting* as *pigment*, bound with glue *size*, that was laboriously removed by washing. When made with *casein* and *lime* or *drying oils* ('hard' or 'washable' distemper) it was more difficult but still possible to remove by washing. Distempers are largely superseded by *emulsion paints* and have so many disadvantages that their British Standard has been withdrawn. 'Calcimine' was the name given in USA to casein distempers. *See* **limewash**.

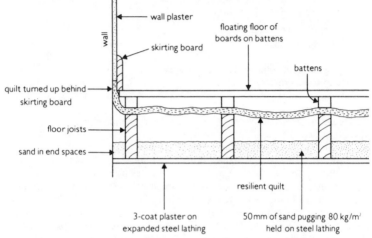

Discontinuous construction (after B R E Digest 103).

distemper brush [pai.] A flat *brush* from 12 to 25 cm (5 to 10 in.) wide, well packed with long bristle. The older two-knot brush is wire bound with two knots fixed on to one stock. *See* **house painter** (illus. p. 180).

distribution box [elec.] A small metal box joined to *conduit* to give access for connecting branch circuits.

distribution panel, d. fuseboard [elec.] An insulated board, at which connections are made to the *branch circuits*. It includes *fuses* or circuit breakers for each branch.

distribution pipe [plu.] A pipe leading water from a storage *cistern*.

district heating Any method of heating flats or houses in one part of a town from a central supply of heat. This generally means using waste heat from electric power stations or other industrial plant. Battersea power station, London, sent hot water through a tunnel under the Thames to the Pimlico (Churchill Gardens) flats. The *cooling tower* requirements of the power station were correspondingly reduced, and its thermal efficiency increased.

district surveyor A *civil* or *structural engineer* (*C*), an official peculiar to London, whose responsibility is the approval of building design and construction from the point of view of safety (fire, stability, etc.) in his district, usually a former London borough. He is an employee of the Greater London Council.

diversity [elec.] It is unlikely that all the appliances in a building will be switched on simultaneously, if only for the reason that one appliance may have to be disconnected from a socket outlet in order to reconnect another. For other reasons also the mains do not need to carry the full load of all the appliances in the building, but only a proportion of it. This proportion, the diversity factor, is the actual maximum demand divided by the sum of the full power demands of all the appliances in the building. Diversity factors apply also to water distribution networks.

division wall (USA **fire w.**) A *fire-resisting* wall from the lowest floor up to the roof. It continues 45 or 90 cm (18 or 36 in.) above the roof, if this is not fire resisting. In London its purpose is to limit each building to 7000 m³ (250 000 ft³) max. capacity between division walls. *Compare* **fire division wall**.

dog (1) A *dressing iron*.

(2) A dog and chain is the same as a pair of *nippers*.

(3) A steel U-shaped spike used for fixing together heavy timbers, for instance a *dead shore* to a *needle*. *See* **fasteners** (illus. p. 130), *also* (*C*).

dog ear (Scots **pig lug**) A box-like external corner formed by folding a *flexible-metal roofing* sheet without cutting. *See* **gusset piece**.

dog-leg chisel [joi.] A chisel bent for cleaning out groves. *See* **swan-neck chisel, corner chisel**.

dog-legged stair A *stair* with two *flights* between storeys, a rectangular *half-landing*, and no stair *well*, so that the *outer string* of each flight is housed in the same *newel post*.

dolomitic lime *Lime* which is roughly half CaO, half MgO. *Compare* **magnesian lime**.

dome A hemispherical *vault*, circular in plan. The horizontal thrust from the dome must generally be carried by *reinforcement* (*C*) in the ring at the foot of the dome. Domes are often crowned with a *lantern*.

dome light A *roof light* with glass curved in one or two directions. Glass domes are cast in Britain up to 1·8 m (6 ft) dia. with 25 cm (10 in.) depth, spherically curved. *See* **saucer dome**.

door casing [joi.] (USA) The *architrave* or other *trim* round a door opening.

door check and spring A *door closer*.

door cheeks, d. posts [joi.] The vertical members (stiles) of a door frame.

door closer, d. check and spring A spring-operated or pneumatic device fixed to a door and its frame to prevent it slamming or opening violently. It can be the most costly piece of *door furniture*.

door frame [joi.] The surround to a door opening, usually *rebated*, carrying the door. It is much stronger than a *lining*, being made of timber about 10 × 8 cm (4 × 3 in.). It consists of two *door posts* (the *jambs*) and a horizontal (the *head*).

door furniture Any *hardware* for a door, including its *bolt*, *door closer*, *escutcheons, finger plates, hinges, lock*, etc.

door head [joi.] The horizontal wooden member forming the top of a *door frame*.

door jack [joi.] A wooden frame made by a *joiner* to hold a door vertical with one edge on the ground while the other is being planed.

door jamb [joi.] A *door post*.

door lining [joi.] *See* **liner** (3).

door post [joi.] A vertical in a *door frame*.

door set [joi.] A door with its frame, architrave or cover moulding, stops and hardware, usually to a standard size.

door sill [joi.] A horizontal timber at the foot of the frame of an outside door. It is connected to the *door posts* and is specially designed to keep out rain.

door stop (1) A strip of wood nailed to the door frame (on expensive frames cut out of the solid) on the head and both jambs, to prevent the door passing through the frame, and to make, so far as possible, an airtight seal.

(2) A catch set in the floor to hold a door open or to prevent it opening too far (floor stop).

door switch [elec.] A switch operated by the opening or closing of a door.

door tidy [joi.] Because no *letter plate* achieves a finished appearance inside the door, a draught-excluding, spring-loaded metal plate, the door tidy, may be installed inside to cover the letter slot.

dormer, d. window A vertical window through a sloping roof, usually provided with its own pitched roof, often with a *gablet* or *hips*. An *internal dormer* has no roof other than the general roof.

dormer cheek The upright side to a *dormer*.

dosy timber [tim.] Wood which is beginning to decay. *See* **dote**.

dot and dab fixing A refinement of *plaster dab* fixing using small pieces (75 × 50 mm or 3 × 2 in.) of insulating board (usually bitumen-impregnated-fibre) of suitable thickness. They are bedded on the wall in *board finish* plaster smears and levelled with a straight edge. They are placed about 450 mm (18 in.) apart horizontally and not more than 1 m (3 ft 4 in.) apart vertically. These pieces of board are the dots. When the plaster has set, plaster dabs are placed on them. Plasterboards are pressed on the dabs and held in place with *lifting wedges*. The dabs should not be less than 25 mm (1 in.) from the edges of the boards to keep the correct alignment of the boards. (One dab may interfere with a neighbouring board.) Once the plasterboard has been trued it can be temporarily fixed with a few rust-resisting *double-headed nails* (*C*) that are withdrawn when the dabs have set, leaving only a few small holes to fill.

dote, doat [tim.] Early *decay*, indicated by dots or speckles, described as dosy, foxy, etc., sometimes a *defect*.

dots (1) A wiped *soldered dot* is a fixing for sheet lead to timber on a *dormer cheek* or other steep surface. The lead is fixed by a wooden screw through it, which is then covered with solder. On a horizontal surface a dot can be formed by *leadburning* – a poured-lead dot, p. 198. *See* **soldered dot**, p. 314.

(2) [pla.] *See* **dot and dab fixing**.

dotting on [q.s.] In the *timesing column* of the sheet on which the *quantities* are taken off, a dot added to the timesing figure indicates that the quantity occurs once more. Some surveyors regard it as a source of error and condemn the practice. *See* **taking off**.

double-acting hinge [joi.] *See* **floor spring, helical hinge**.

double-bridging [carp.] Two rows of *herring-bone strutting* to each span, dividing the floor area into three equal parts, usual for spans above 4·5 m (15 ft).

double connector [plu.] A short piece of pipe with, at each end, a long *parallel thread* fitted with a back nut and a socket. It enables a gas supply to be interrupted in an emergency since it is a convenient method of connecting and disconnecting pipes in any position, however awkward. *See* **connector**.

double-dovetail key, dovetail feather, hammerhead key [joi.] A hardwood key shaped like two *dovetail* pins joined at their narrow ends, driven into mortises cut in a butt joint between two timbers to hold them together. It is of the same shape as a *slate cramp*.

double dwelling *See* **double house**.

double eaves course, doubling c. A double row of *shingles, plain tiles,* or *slates* laid at the foot of a roof slope or vertical section of slating, tiling, or shingling. *See* **eaves course, tilting fillet, undercloak**.

double Flemish bond Brickwork which shows *Flemish bond* on both faces of the wall.

double glazing *Glazing* in which two layers of glass are separated by an air space for thermal or acoustic insulation. *Sealed units* are commonly installed for thermal insulation. Heat losses are therefore nearly halved and *condensation* usually prevented, but this type only slightly reduces the volume of sound passing through the window.

Double glazing can reduce the sound passing through a window by 40 to 45 decibels compared with only 20 to 25 dB for a single-glazed window. Heavy glass improves the performance, so does an absorbent lining round the edges of the air space, and effective sealing. The best spacing between

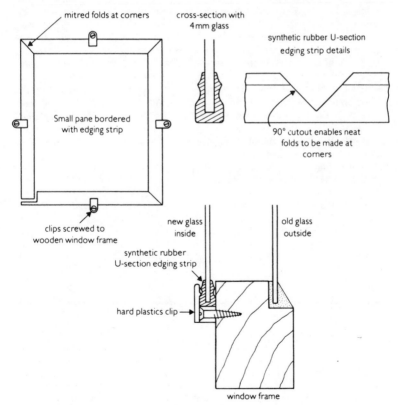

Double glazing (DIY). Applying a second pane of glass to an existing window.

the panes is 200 mm (8 in.); less than 100 mm (4 in.) is not recommended. Two frames are needed with this large spacing. Other means of ventilation may be needed since sealing is so important.

Householders can make their own double glazing on wooden frames or windows by adding a pane of glass framed all round in a synthetic rubber, U-shaped *edging strip*, held down by hard plastics clips. The fixings cost 40% as much as the glass, for a pane 0·5 m (20 in.) square. These panes can be removed in summer to clean or paint the window frame without cutting the hands, since the U-strip stays on (see diagram). A minimum 31 mm (1¼ in.) all round the glass is needed for fixing to the wood. (Illus. p. 105) *See* **coupled window**.

double-handed saw [carp.] A long *cross-cut* saw pulled by one man at each end.

double header [carp.] (USA) A *trimmer joist*, made by nailing together two ordinary joists.

double house (USA) A pair of *semi-detached houses*.

double-hung sash window [joi.] A *sash window* (BS 565).

double-leaf party wall A lightweight, sound-insulating method of housebuilding, a type of *discontinuous construction* in which the houses have separate timber frames, lined sometimes with *laminated plasterboard* 40 mm (1⅜ in.) thick. The cavity between the two leaves is 225 mm (9 in.) or more, measured between the backs of the lining panels. The timber frames thus project into the cavity. One (or two) glass wool or mineral wool quilts 13 to 25 mm (½ to 1 in.) thick inserted in the cavity are stapled on one (or both) sides. Other types exist.

double-lock cross welt [plu.] In *flexible-metal roofing*, a *cross welt* in which neighbouring copper sheets are turned through 360° in the joint and hammered flat, the usual joint for a *flat roof* (illus. below). *Compare* **single-lock cross welt**. (Illus. p. 306.)

double-margined door, double-margin [joi.] A door hinged at one side only, that looks like a pair of doors.

double partition [carp.] *See* **double-leaf party wall**.

double-pitch roof (1) A *mansard roof*.

(2) A *pitched roof*.

double rebated [joi.] A description of a wide *door post* or jamb lining which is

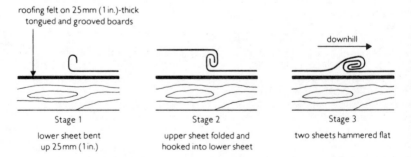

Double-lock cross welt in flexible-metal roofing.

rebated on both edges. The door may thus be hung to open inwards or outwards.

double-return stairs, side flights A ceremonial *stair* with one wide *flight* up from the lower floor to the *landing* and two flights from the landing to the next floor.

double Roman tile A *single-lap* standardized British clay *roofing tile* measuring ordinarily 42 × 36 × 1·3 to 1·6 cm (16½ × 14 × ½ to ⅝ in.). It has 7·6 cm (3 in.) side lap. There are two nail holes but no *nibs*. It differs from the single *Roman tile* in having a roll up the centre. *Compare* **Poole's tile**.

double-skin roof An *asbestos-cement* profiled roof covering which consists of an upper layer, the weathering, and a lower underlay, which is flat and forms the ceiling.

double skirting [joi.] A *skirting* made higher than normally by rebating a second, upper board into the ordinary skirting board.

double step [carp.] In heavy timber framing, such as the support of a *rafter* on a tie-beam at *eaves* level, a W-shaped notch designed to reduce the likelihood of horizontal shear in the tie-beam. (Illus.) *See* **step joint**.

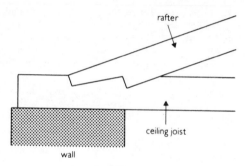

Double step.

double time The double payment customary in the UK for men working any hours between 4 pm on Saturday and Monday morning, or later than 3 hours after normal finishing time from Monday to Friday. *See* **time and a half**.

double window A *coupled window*.

doubling course A *double eaves course*.

doubling piece [carp.] A *tilting fillet*.

Douglas fir (Pseudotsuga taxifolia), **Oregon pine** or **fir** or **British Columbian pine** The most important building *softwood* in the British Commonwealth, also very important in USA. It deflects only half as much as other softwoods and resembles European *redwood*, though it is less dense. *See* **fir**.

dovetail [joi.] A joint often used in the corners of boxes or fine joinery. Unlike the *combed joint*, the interlocking tenons (called pins) are fan-shaped, like a pigeon's tail. They are thicker at the end than at the root, and can therefore not easily be pulled out.

dovetail cramp A *cramp* for stone which is of double-dovetail shape and may be of slate or metal.

dovetailed lathing, d. sheeting [pla.] Steel or plastics or *asbestos-bitumen* sheet bent into dovetailed corrugations of about 19 mm (¾ in.) depth and width. It may be plastered both faces or only one and can be used for *damp-proofing* a wall or as *permanent formwork* (*C*) for a concrete floor, or as *metal lathing*.

dovetail feather [joi.] A *double-dovetail key*.

dovetail halving, d. halved joint [carp.] A joint made by *halving*, in which the halved pieces are dovetailed.

dovetail saw [joi.] A *back saw* about 20 cm (8 in.) long, with about 18 points per 25 mm (1 in.).

dovetail sheeting *Dovetailed lathing*.

dowel (1) A short, round wooden rod used instead of or together with a *tenon* for holding two wooden parts together, by inserting it into a hole drilled in each. It should be grooved (keyed) to enable air and excess *glue* to escape. (Illus.) *See* **treenail**

(2) A short steel rod cast into a concrete floor, over which a door post can be fixed by dropping the bored post over the dowel.

(3) A piece of slate or a *cramp* used for locking adjacent stones to each other in a wall.

dowel pin [joi.] (1) A short round *wire nail* pointed at both ends.

(2) (USA) A headless nail with one point and a barbed shank. It is driven into a *mortise-and-tenon joint* to fasten it permanently.

(3) A *dowel*.

dowel plate [carp.] A steel plate in which holes are drilled to the diameters of

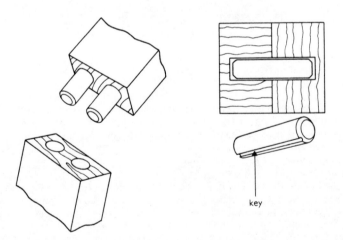

key

Dowelling. (Above). Two dowels have been inserted into one piece, which is now ready to be joined to the other. (Right). Dowels to be glued are keyed with a veegroove to release surplus glue. The hole is drilled a little deeper than the dowel length. Acknowledgements to Carpentry *by Percy Blandford, Macdonald Guidelines, 1979.*

dowels. It can be used for verifying the diameter of a dowel, or by driving through, for trimming it to size.

dowel screw, handrail s. [joi.] A wood *screw* threaded at each end.

downcomer [plu.] A pipe leading water from the cistern to the W C, water heater, wash basin, and bath. Some of these are now directly connected to the main supply. *See also* **downpipe**.

downpipe, downcomer, rainwater pipe (U S A **downspout, conductor, leader**) A vertical or steep pipe which brings rainwater to the ground from roof *gutters*, the successor to the gargoyle. The earliest pipes were of lead, which began to be replaced in Britain by cast iron in the nineteenth century. This in turn is being superseded, mainly by plastics.

dozy [tim.] *See* **dote**.

draft A *drafted margin*.

draft chisel, drafting c. A *chisel* struck with the *mallet* and used for making a *draft* on the face of a stone.

drafted margin A smooth, uniform border 1·9 to 5 cm (¾ to 2 in.) wide, worked round the edges of the face of a stone.

draft stop (U S A) A *fire stop*.

drag (1) A steel plate about 15 cm long, 10 cm wide (6 × 4 in.), with toothed edges, used for levelling plaster surfaces, for producing a key for the next coat of plaster, or for smoothing *ashlars*. *See* **plasterer** (p. 246), **mason's and bricklayer's tools** (illus. p. 211), *also* C.

   (2) [pai.], **brush drag, pulling** A resistance to the *brush* from a *paint* or *varnish* while it is being put on, sometimes a serious defect. *See* **gummy**.

dragged work Stone which has been smoothed with a *drag*.

dragon beam, d. piece [carp.] A horizontal timber into which the end of the *hip rafter* is framed. The outer end of it is carried on the corner of the building where the *wall plates* meet, the inner end at the *angle tie*.

dragon tie [carp.] An *angle tie*.

drain Removal of surplus water by downhill flow, usually through *drain pipes* below ground. *See also* C.

drain chute A special *drain pipe* shaped to make *rodding* easy, tapered in its upper half.

drain cock A cock placed at the lowest point of a water system, through which the system can be drained.

drained joint An *open-drained joint*.

drain ferret A thin glass bottle containing strongly smelling vapour which is broken inside a drain to reveal leaks.

drain pipes Pipes, as well as their joints, may be either rigid or flexible. Flexibility is desirable in areas where the ground may move, e.g. near mines. Flexible pipes, of *pitch fibre*, *plastics*, ductile cast iron, or steel, deform appreciably before collapse. Rigid pipes, of asbestos cement, *vitrified clay*, concrete, or grey cast iron, break before their deformation becomes noticeable. Pipe joints made flexible by a plastics or rubber ring, as in the *sleeved joint*, allow rigid pipes to settle without breaking. But rigid pipes are not softened by standing in the sun as PVC or pitch-fibre pipes may be (p. 110). *See* **flexible pipe** (*C*), **sewer** (*C*), *also many* B S and B S C P.

drain plug, d. stopper A *bag plug* or *screw plug*.

drain tests [plu.] Drains must be tested for leakage, after installation and before

Drain pipe, rigid type with flexible rubber-ring joint, showing concrete bedding and its interruption at joint.

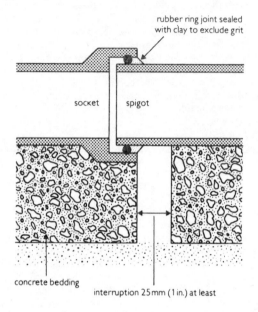

rubber ring joint sealed
with clay to exclude grit

socket   spigot

concrete bedding

interruption 25 mm (1 in.) at least

they are covered up with earth, so that the water authority can have alterations made if it does not approve the work. Prospective house buyers or building societies also may insist on a drain test. *See* **air test, chemical test, hydraulic test** (*C*), **rocket tester, scent test, screw plug**.

draught (1) The pressure difference at the foot of a *chimney* between the air outside and that inside it. This pressure difference (because the air inside is hotter and lighter than that outside) draws air up through the fuel bed into the chimney. The draught can be measured in millimetres of water. It is the *stack effect* in the chimney.

(2) [carp.] In *drawboring*, the amount by which the holes are out of line so as to ensure a tight joint.

draught bead [joi.] A *deep bead*.

draught stabilizer (U S A **barometric damper**) A vertical metal plate in the wall of a *flue*, pivoted horizontally and counterbalanced so that the *draught* cannot be excessive for long. When the draught increases too much, the plate is sucked inwards, admitting cool air and thus reducing the draught through the fire. It automatically closes when the draught diminishes, thus usually ensuring correct draught. It is unusual in small boilers. (Illus. p. 111)

draught stop (1) A *fire stop*.

(2) [joi.] The sill member, sometimes on a *deep bead*, that joins *sash stops* each side in mitred joints, guiding the inner *sash* of a *sash window* so that it does not swing into the room.

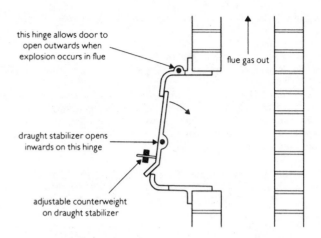

Draught stabilizer for oil-fired boiler.

draught strip A strip of sprung metal, sponge rubber, etc., fixed in the gap between the frame and a door or window to prevent draughts, often very efficiently.

draught stripping Installation of *draught strips*. Sometimes they are so effective that they increase *condensation* and thus the *dampness* in the house (BRE Digest 176).

draw bolt [joi.] A *barrel bolt* or other simple bolt pushed by hand, not driven by a key.

drawbore [carp.] To drill holes through a *tenon* and the mortised piece about 3 mm (⅛ in.) out of line so that a tapered steel pin driven through both pieces will draw them closely together. The steel pin is replaced by an oaken *treenail*. This method of cramping during gluing is much stronger than *cramps* since the pressure is never relaxed – so much so that gluing is sometimes dispensed with. See **draught, drawbore pin**.

drawbore pin, drawpin [carp.] A tapered steel pin used in drawboring to bring the holes into line, and then withdrawn before the *treenail* is inserted.

draw-in system [elec.] A carefully planned wiring system, in conduits or ducts; the cables can be pulled in through the *pull box* and replaced when required.

drawknife [carp.] A knife blade bent into a U-shape with *tangs* at each end in the plane of the blade, each tang carrying a handle so that the knife can be pulled by both hands towards the user.

drencher system A *sprinkler system*.

dress (1) [carp.] To plane and sandpaper timber.

(2) To cut stones to their final shape.

dressed size [joi.] [tim.] The size after planing. It may be 9 mm (⅜ in.) less than the *nominal size* in both directions of the cross section because of the removal of wood in planing and sawing as well as *shrinkage* from a higher *moisture content* (BS 4471).

111

dressed stone Stone which has been squared all round and smoothed on the face.

dressed timber *Surfaced timber.*

dresser [plu.] A *hardwood* tool shaped for beating lead; *see* **bossing**.

dressing (1) Shaping and finishing building stones. *See also* **dressings**.
(2) [plu.] *Bossing.*

dressing compound Bituminous liquid used hot or cold for dressing the exposed surface of *roofing felt*. *Compare* **bonding compound, sealing compound**.

dressing iron, break i., dog, traverse A 46 cm (18 in.) long steel straight edge with spikes at each end for fixing into a work bench. A *slate* is laid on the dressing iron and the *zax* brought down to cut it neatly. *See* **plasterer's tools** (illus. p. 246).

dressings *Masonry* or *mouldings* round openings, or at the corners of buildings, of better quality than the remainder of the facing brick or stone. Rubble walls or brick walls were often built with dressings of stone or *gauged brick*.

drier [pai.] Any compound of lead, cobalt, manganese, etc. which encourages the *oxidation* of *drying oil* in a paint or varnish. *See* **lead drier, paste drier, soluble drier**.

drift bolt [carp.] A steel pin usually not less than $2 \cdot 2$ cm ($\frac{7}{8}$ in.) dia. driven into holes bored $1 \cdot 5$ mm ($\frac{1}{16}$ in.) smaller as a fixing between heavy timbers. *See also* **drift** (*C*).

drift plug [plu.] A wooden plug driven through a lead pipe to straighten a kink.

drill bow [joi.] The bow of a *bow drill*.

drip (1) **throat** A groove or projection under an overhanging edge of an overhang, designed to stop water flowing back to the building and to throw it off at the outer edge.
(2) In *flexible-metal roofing*, a step formed in a flat roof at right angles to the direction of fall. The lower sheet is turned up and over the riser, under the *overcloak*, which is bent down the riser and sometimes on to the flat. *See also* **drop apron**.

drip channel A *drip*.

drip edge A *drop apron*.

drip-free paint *See* **non-drip paint**, also **thixotropy** (*C*).

dripping eave An *eave* with no gutter.

drip sink A *tray*.

dripstone, hood mould A projecting moulding of stone or brick over the outside of a door, window or arch, to throw off rain. A rectangular dripstone is a 'label'.

drive screw, s. nail [carp.] A galvanized nail 2 mm ($0 \cdot 08$ in.) or more thick, with a twisted shank that looks as if it might be a steep *thread*. It can be driven in by a hammer but is very difficult to withdraw. It is used for fixing roof sheeting. The spring-head roofing nail is similar, with an even steeper thread (BS 1494).

drop annunciator An *annunciator* in which a signal drops to show the number of the room from which the signal originated.

drop apron, drip In *flexible-metal roofing*, a strip of metal fixed vertically down at *eaves*, *verges*, and *gutters*, held by a *lining plate*.

drop ceiling A *false ceiling*.

drop connection, d. manhole A *back drop*.

drop elbow, tee [plu.] A small *elbow* or tee with *ears* for screwing it to a wall.

drop escutcheon, d. key plate [joi.] A small metal plate pivoted above a keyhole to cover it when the key is not in the *lock*. It matches the *escutcheon*.

drop system [plu.] A heating circuit in which the *flow* pipe rises directly to its highest level, from which it feeds downward branches which drop as nearly vertically as possible to a return main.

drop window [joi.] A *sash window* which descends completely into a pocket beneath the *sill*, leaving the whole space for ventilation.

drop wire [elec.] A cable from the nearest pole of an overhead supply line, connecting a house with the supply.

drove (Scotland) A *boaster*.

drowning pipe [plu.] A *silencing pipe*.

drunken saw, wobble s. [tim.] A *circular saw* which is deliberately set slightly off the perpendicular to its own shaft so that it makes a wide cut. It is used in *joinery* for cutting *open mortises*.

dry area, blind a. *See* area.

dry construction, d. walling Building without mortar or systematic plastering as in methods using *dry partitions*, plywood, *precasting (C)* or other *industrialized building methods*. The building is ready for occupation quickly but may be expensive. In spite of the name, these methods must not be used in a damp structure. *See* **dry lining**.

dry hydrate [pla.] *Lime*, $Ca(OH)_2$, that has been slaked by the manufacturer with exactly the calculated amount of water and sold in bags as powder. It should be soaked overnight to give *plasticity*.

dry joint A joint with mortar, *see C*.

drying [pai.] The hardening of a coat of paint or varnish by *evaporation* of the *vehicle* or chemical change (usually *oxidation*) or the two together. Air drying is drying at air temperature; forced drying or *stoving* is drying at higher temperatures. *See* **dry to handle, drying oil, hard dry, dust dry, surface dry, touch dry**.

drying of screeds *Screeds* that are to take a glued-down floor finish, such as thermoplastic, asbestos or pvc tiles or sheet flooring, must be dry before the glue is applied or it will fail. Usually one month is allowed per 25 mm of screed thickness for forward planning purposes but a moisture meter should be used for the final decision (BRS Digest 18 and BSCP 203).

drying oil [pai.] An oil such as *linseed oil* which forms a tough film when exposed to air in a thin layer. Drying is often made more rapid by a *drier*.

drying out Several thousand kilograms of water have to be evaporated from new brick houses before they can be decorated with certainty that the paint will not spoil, and each kg of water needs 0·7 kilowatt-hour of heat to evaporate it. Several thousand kWh are therefore needed to dry out the building. Evaporation removes heat, i.e. cools the building. Evaporation can be helped and its cooling effect reduced in fine weather by opening all windows, and by heating the house, but heaters not connected to a flue should not be used unless they are electric. A kg of oil or gas in burning produces another kg of water to be removed from the house. The usual rule for the time needed for drying out a wall or slab is : 'one month per 25 mm of thickness in good conditions' but this is often not enough. If earlier painting is essential, a porous paint (some *emulsions*) will not prevent the drying out process, and is relatively cheap. *See also* **dampness**.

dry lining A lining to the inside of a room, e.g. with *tapered-edge plasterboard*, plywood or any *wallboard* that needs no plastering. Dry linings reduce *condensation* during construction and enable the building to be painted, warmed and occupied sooner. Secure fixings for heavy pictures, etc. can be made to dry linings by drilling a hole through the wallboard and pushing stiff plaster of Paris through the hole. It sets in a few minutes, enabling a hole to be drilled and a firm plug inserted. Several other methods are equally good. *See* **dry construction, dry partition**.

dry masonry Walling laid without *mortar*.

dry partition A modern partition wall, prefabricated often in areas as large as 4 m × 1 m (13 × 3 ft) that can be erected without plastering, and very quickly. Some are made of plasterboard with honeycomb paper core, others are of expanded polystyrene faced both sides with hardboard. Another type uses *gypsum wallboard* screwed to thin, 0·7 mm (0·03 in.), thick steel U-sections with hard steel self-tapping screws. A precast plaster *cove* may complete the joint between ceiling and wall.

dry-press brick (USA) A *brick* of good quality pressed from nearly dry clay.

dry riser A vertical pipe in a tall building, with inlet connections at the fire brigade's access point, through which water can be pumped in by the fire brigade for them to fight the fire from any point upstairs where *fire hydrants* are located on it.

dry rot [tim.] Decay of timber because of dampness feeding the fungus, Merulius lacrymans, at least 20% *moisture* in the timber being essential. At much below this level the fungus dies. Dry rot has threads like plant stems that transmit moisture even through brickwork, and is difficult to eradicate without burning the infected wood and heating the bricks nearby with a blow-lamp or disinfecting them. Dry rot cannot pass a barrier of *magnesium oxychloride* plaster.

dry sprinkler *See* **sprinkler system**.

dry stone wall *Dry walling*.

dry to handle [pai.] The last stage in the *drying* of a paint film when it can be freely handled without damage.

dry walling (1) Walls built without mortar.

(2) *See* **dry construction**.

dry wood, d. stock [tim.] *Timber* after seasoning, having, in Britain, from 15% to 23% *moisture content*.

dual fuel system A heating system in which the fuel in use, gas, oil or coal, may be replaced by another.

dubbing out [pla.] Filling hollows in a wall surface with *coarse stuff* or roughly forming a *cornice* before running the *finishing coat*.

duckbill nail [joi.] A chisel-pointed nail, very easy to *clench*.

duckboard A *cat ladder*.

duck-foot bend, rest b. A right-angle bend often used at the foot of a column of vertical cast-iron pipes. It is provided with a flat seating to carry the weight of the pipes and water and the thrust due to the change in direction of the water.

duct (1) A *casing, chase, crawlway* or *subway* that accommodates pipes or cables. Ducts transmit both sound and fire so they must be designed to reduce *noise* as well as having *fire stops*. *See* **honeycomb fire damper**, also BSCP 413, and **cable duct** (*C*).

(2) Metal, wood, or *asbestos-cement* or plastics tubes, round or rectangular ventilation ducts, for distributing conditioned air to rooms or for withdrawing stale air or fumes from them (BS 5720).

dug anchorage An anchorage to an *airhouse*. *See* illus. below.

dumb waiter (1) (USA) An *elevator* which raises or lowers food or crockery from one level to another.

(2) (Britain) A piece of table furniture standing at the centre of a table – a rotatable circular tray carrying condiments.

dummy (1)[plu.] A lump of lead or iron fixed on the end of a long cane or iron rod, used as an internal mallet for straightening large lead pipes. *See* **plumber** (illus. p. 250).

(2) A round lump of zinc or lead weighing 1 to 2 kg (2 to 4 lb), with a short wooden handle, used as a hammer by *masons* who are working soft stone, such as Bath stone, with wooden-handled chisels or gouges.

dunnage [tim.] Waste timber used for packing (p. 211).

dunter A *monumental mason* who prepares large faces of granite for polishing with a pneumatic surfacing machine, or the machine itself.

duodecimal system The feet and inches system or other systems in which 12 small units make up a large unit. Calculations can be made in this system, but British *quantity surveyors* were the only people to use duodecimal calculation.

duplex apartment (USA) A *maisonette*.

duramen [tim.] The *heartwood* of a tree.

dust dry (USA **d. free**) [pai.] A stage in the *drying* of a finish, after which dust will not stick to it.

dusting [pla.] Wear of a concrete floor surface, usually caused by excess water in the mix, careless laying or poor *curing* (C).

Dutch arch, French a. A brick arch, flat at top and bottom, of which only the central bricks are wedge shaped.

Dutch bond A confusing term, either *English cross bond* or *Flemish bond*.

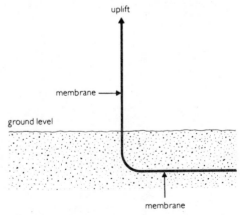

Dug anchorage for an air house, showing the membrane. Suitable in soil with particles that will not cut the membrane.

115

Dutch door (USA) A *stable door*.
dwang (1) [carp.] (Scotland) *Strutting* between floor joists.
    (2) A crowbar.
dwarf partition A *partition* which does not rise to the ceiling.
dwarf wall A low wall, e.g. that supporting the ground floor *joists* of a dwelling house.
dye [pai.] A colouring material which, unlike a *pigment*, is soluble and colours materials by penetration. When a dye colours an insoluble base, such as aluminium hydroxide, the resulting pigment is called a *lake*.
dyke (Scots **dike**) *Dry walling* in stone.
dyker, stone ditcher, stone hedger A *walling mason* who builds boundary walls of stone.

E

ear [plu.] *See* **lug** (1).

earth (1) Excavated material; strictly speaking only *topsoil* (*C*) is earth.

(2) [elec.] (USA) **ground** An electrical connection to earth through an *earth electrode* and suitable conductors to it. *See* BSCP 1013.

earthed concentric wiring [elec.] A cable in which one conductor, a metal tube, is earthed and contains the other conductor insulated within it. *See* **Pyrotenax**.

earth electrode [elec.] A metal plate, water pipe, or other conductor electrically connected to earth, preferably in a position where the earth is always damp, to ensure low electrical resistance.

earthenware *Ceramics* of lower strength than *vitrified clayware*.

earthing lead [elec.] The conductor which makes the final connection to an *earth electrode*.

earth plate [elec.] An *earth electrode*.

earth termination network [elec.] Those parts of a lightning protective system which distribute the discharge to earth.

easement In law, a right which a person may have over another man's land, such as the right to walk over it or to run a pipe through it.

easing the wedges Slackening the *folding wedges* of *shoring* after the hardening of mortar or concrete that they support.

easy-clean hinge [joi.] A *cleaning hinge*.

eave The lowest, overhanging part of a sloping roof, or the area under it. *See* illus. pp. 31, 279, 305.

eaves board, e. catch A *tilting fillet*.

eaves course A first course of *plain tiles*, *slates*, or *shingles* on a roof, including the course of plain tiles at *eaves* on which the first course of *single-lap tiles* is bedded. *See* **double eaves course, eaves tile**.

eaves fascia [carp.] *See* **fascia board**.

eaves flashing A *drop apron* from an asphalt roof dressed into an eaves gutter.

eaves gutter A rainwater *gutter* along the *eaves*. (Illus. p. 129)

eaves plate [carp.] A wall plate spanning between posts or piers at *eaves*, carrying the feet of the rafters over the gaps.

eaves pole [carp.] A *tilting fillet*.

eaves tile A short tile about 21·5 cm (8½ in.) long used in the *eaves course* (or *under-eaves course*) in *plain tiling*. *Compare* **under-ridge tiles**.

echo Repetition of sound by reflection from walls such as the rear wall of an auditorium; echo is reduced by *absorption*.

economy brick (USA) *Brick* to fit the 10 cm (4 in.) height *module*, therefore measuring about 19 × 9 × 9 cm (7½ × 3½ × 3½ in.) to make, with its mortar joints, 20 × 10 × 10 cm (8 × 4 × 4 in.). *Compare* **engineered brick**.

economy wall (USA) A 10 cm (4 in.) thick brick wall plastered or rendered, stiffened at intervals with 20 cm (8 in.) *piers* carrying the roof *trusses*, and projecting outwards at each side of doors and windows.

edge bedding *See* **face-bedded**.

edge bend (USA **crook**) [tim.] *Spring*.

edge grain, vertical g., comb g. [tim.] A grain seen in *quarter-sawn* wood. The best quarter-sawn oak shows *silver grain*.

edge isolation *See* **expansion strip**.

edge joint [tim.] A joint in the direction of the *grain*, between two *veneers*. *Compare* **butt joint**.

edge nailing [carp.] *Secret nailing* of floor boards, etc.

edge runner A grinding mill consisting of circular rolls driven round in a circular steel bowl containing the material to be ground (mortar, putties, etc.).

edge-shot board [carp.] A board with a planed edge.

edge tools [carp.] Tools with a cutting edge, particularly the *hatchet*, *chisel*, *plane*, *gouge*, knife, *saw*.

edging strip (1) A U-shaped synthetic rubber strip 4 mm wide completely enclosing the edges of a pane of glass and enabling it to be used for the *double glazing* of any single-glazed wooden window or frame that has 31 mm (1¼ in.) margin available all round. This margin is needed for screwing the hard plastics clips down to hold the glass. No putty is needed.

(2) A *banding* glued to the edge of a door.

edging trowel A rectangular trowel with one edge turned down so as to trim the fresh concrete edges of kerbs, etc.

eel grass An *insulating material*, a sea plant (Zostera marina) whose dried leaves when loosely packed are very sound absorbent.

effective temperature A measure of comfort that takes account of radiant heat, air movement, and the temperatures of both dry and wet bulbs (B S 5643). *See* **comfort zone**.

efflorescence Powdery white salts left on a wall surface as it dries out. They are unsightly though usually harmless unless they lift paint or plaster. They come mainly from gypsum or pyrite in the clay and coal the bricks were fired with, occasionally from the mortar. B S 3921 describes tests on bricks for efflorescence. Air-entraining plasticizers generally contribute no salts, but lime and cement do. If efflorescence cannot be removed by light brushing, and breaks up plaster, the plaster must be removed, asbestos-bitumen lathing or other impervious backing nailed to the bricks and the wall re-plastered. It can be greatly reduced if not prevented by keeping bricks dry during laying, which includes covering them at night. *See* **deliquescence**.

eggshell (1) [pai.] *See* **gloss**.

(2) A smooth, matt face to building stone.

elastomer Any synthetic or natural rubber, sometimes in the rubber industry defined as material resilient enough to be stretched to twice its length and, on release, to snap back to the original length. *See* **polymer, fleximer, Neoprene**.

elastomeric sealant A liquid or paste that hardens after application, to become a rubbery *sealing compound*.

elbow, ell [plu.] A sharp right-angled pipe *fitting*, as opposed to a bend, which is gentler. *See* **fittings** (illus. p. 138).

elbow lining [joi.] The panelling over a window *jamb*.

electric-blanket heating [tim.] A method of accelerating *assembly gluing* by covering the glued joint with an electrically heated blanket.

electric hand-held tools *See* **hand electric tools**.

electrician A *tradesman* who instals or repairs electric circuits (wiring), machines, or plant (B S C P 1017).

electric-panel heater A panel heated by electrical resistances. It may be surfaced with marble, plastics, etc., and can work at a high temperature of about

290° C. (550° F.), at a medium temperature below 120° C. (250° F.), or at a low temperature below 81° C. (180° F.). *See* **panel heating**.

electric screwdriver A tool like a hand-held *electric drill* (*C*), used on mass-production work because of its speed of operation and the exactness to which all screws are driven with the same force, using a clutch which slips at the final *torque* (*C*).

electro-copper glazing (USA **copper g.**, **copperlite g.**) Pieces of glass are accurately cut and assembled between copper *cames* and pressed tightly together. (The copper strips are brought into electrical contact by soldering.) The assembly is then placed in an electrolyte containing copper salts and the copper strips are made the cathode so that more copper is deposited on them. The glass is thus held tightly. *See* **fire-resisting glazing**.

electrode boiler A *boiler* with submerged electrodes that heat the water by electric current passing through it. It is generally larger than domestic size and has the advantage that no surfaces can be harmed by flame. No overheating or short-circuiting can occur if the boiler is empty when the power is switched on.

electrolier (USA) A hanging electric light fitting.

electro-osmosis Protecting a wall against *rising damp* by controlling the flow of electric current between it and the underlying wet earth (Rentokil Ltd). For water under pressure this method is unsuitable, so are *water-repellent liquids*, and generally *tanking* alone can succeed. *See also* C.

elemi [pai.] An *oleo-resin* from the tropics, particularly the Philippines, used for making spirit lacquers and *nitrocellulose* products.

elevation A view of something as if projected on to a vertical plane. The front view of a house is its front elevation. *See* **plan** (illus.).

elevator (USA) A *lift* for passengers or goods.

ell [plu.] An *elbow*.

elm, common e. (Ulmus) [tim.] A dull brown *hardwood* which *warps* badly if not carefully seasoned. It should be kept either wet or dry but not allowed to alternate between the two. It has twisted grain and is even harder to split than *oak*, but in other respects is slightly weaker. It is cut as *burr* for veneers, or used in the solid for *piles* (*C*), *weather-boarding*, and panelling.

emergency water stop Where the *stopcock* is inaccessible, a flow of water into a *cistern* can be stopped by tying up the *ball valve*. (Illus. p. 120)

emery cloth *See* **glasspaper**.

eminently hydraulic lime *Hydraulic* lime burnt from a limestone containing more than about 25% of aluminium silicates. Such limes cannot be obtained as *dry hydrate* without loss of hydraulic strength.

emissivity of a surface *See* **absorptive power**.

emulsifier system A *sprinkler system* which works at high pressure, at least 345 kN/m^2 (50 psi) and is installed in places where oil may catch fire, for example, near *transformers* (*C*). A powerful spray is directed on to the escaping oil, which is emulsified by the jet, and prevented from burning, since each drop is thus surrounded by water. After some hours the oil may separate from the water and be re-used, but this does not occur with all oils.

emulsion paints [pai.] Paints that are often called 'vinyl', '*latex*' or 'plastic' and may be based on *polyvinyl acetate* emulsion. They dry by evaporation, therefore quickly, have no fire hazard, and brushes are easily washed in water.

119

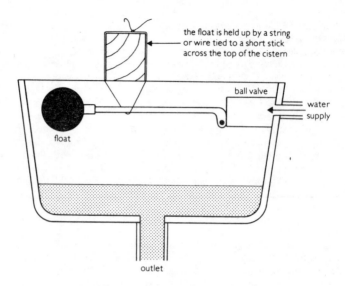

the float is held up by a string or wire tied to a short stick across the top of the cistern

ball valve

water supply

float

outlet

Emergency water stop for a ball valve.

Many different colours are available but oil-bound *stainers* must not be used. They are usually matt but some have a sheen. Though porous enough to allow some drying of new plaster, they should not be applied to a wall that is really wet. If old emulsion is well cleaned, it can be re-coated without failure, using emulsion or oil paint. Emulsion should not be used in a kitchen or bathroom unless recommended by the maker. *Polyvinyl chloride* emulsion paints have been used as *vapour checks. See* **emulsion** (*C*).

enamel (1) [pai.] A *hard gloss paint* whose high *gloss* is obtained by a high proportion of *varnish* with reduced *pigment* content. Enamels *flow* well but need good *undercoats* since they are not opaque.

(2) Vitreous enamel is a glass surface, often white, attached by firing to cast-iron or pressed-steel articles like baths. It is very much more resistant to wear than enamel paint but it chips when struck a hard blow. During sawing, the chipping can be prevented by first covering the surface with adhesive tape.

encase [joi.] To cover with a case or lining.

enclosed fuse [elec.] (USA) A *cartridge fuse.*

enclosed stair A *closed stair.*

enclosure wall (USA) *Curtain walling.*

end grain [tim.] The surface of timber exposed when a tree is felled or when timber is *cross-cut* in any other way.

end joint [tim.] A *butt joint.*

end-lap joint [carp.] An *angle joint* formed between two timbers by *halving* each for a length equal to the width of the other.

endless saw [tim.] A *band saw.*

engineered brick (USA) A *brick* which measures, with its mortar joint when laid up, 20 × 10 × 8 cm (8 × 4 × 3·2 in.), that is 5 courses for 40 cm (16 in.) height. *Compare* **economy brick**.

engineering brick Bricks defined in UK by BS 3921, 'Clay bricks and blocks', of uniform size, high crushing strength and low *absorption*. Class A bricks crush at stresses above 69 N/mm^2 (10 000 psi) and have an absorption below 4·5%. Class B have 48 N/mm^2 (7000 psi) crushing strength and maximum 7% water absorption. Class A are used for *damp courses*.

engineer's hammer, fitter's h. [mech.] A *hammer* with a head weighing from 0·1 to 1·4 kg (4 oz to 3 lb) on which are a striking face, and a *ball peen*, or a *cross peen*, or a *straight peen*.

English bond A brick *bond* in which alternate *courses* are composed entirely of *stretchers* and entirely of *headers*.

English cross bond, Saint Andrew's c. b. A *bond* like *English bond*, except that in alternate stretcher courses a *header* is placed next to the *quoin* stretchers. Therefore the vertical joints of alternate stretcher courses are displaced a half-brick from each other and are not in the same vertical line as in English bond. Therefore, this bond can be much more decorative than English bond, since the *cross joints* in the stretcher courses line up, with a quarter-brick displacement, with alternate cross joints in the header courses. In this way a pattern of diagonal lines crossing each other shows on the face of the brickwork. With the judicious use of *flared headers*, diagonal patterns can be picked out in it. *See* **Flemish diagonal bond**.

English garden-wall bond *American bond*.

English roofing tile (USA) A *single-lap* clay roofing tile, whose sides overlap within its thickness so that both the visible and the hidden surfaces of the tile are smooth.

epoxide resin, epoxy r., ethoxylene r. [pai.] *Two-pack* glue or paint, useful in carpentry or for repairing masonry but dangerous to breathe if put on with a *spray gun*. It can be used for patching shallow (3 mm, ⅛ in.) deep holes in concrete surfaces, and can act as a *damp course* if the concrete base is not too damp. *See* **levelling compound**.

epoxy-resin-sand mortar This expensive mortar can be used as a *damp course* if it contains about 15% resin. It is strong and sticks well so is suitable for bedding *copings*.

equilibrium moisture content [tim.] The *moisture content* at which timber neither gains nor loses moisture, when subjected to constant humidity and temperature. *See also* C.

equivalent temperature A measure of comfort that takes into account radiant heat, air movement and dry bulb (not wet bulb) temperature (BS 5643). Unlike the American *effective temperature*, equivalent temperature does not take humidity into account and is not therefore used in heavy industry where men sweat.

erection The positioning and fixing of a metal, or timber, or precast concrete frame.

ergonomics The interactions between work and people, particularly the design of machines, chairs, tables, etc. to suit the body, and to permit work with the least fatigue.

escalator, moving stair [mech.] A moving endless belt with steps on it, which allows crowds to move more quickly into or out of shops, underground stations, etc. than by stairs or lifts. It does however need more space than lifts or stairs. One upward and one downward moving stair are needed, preferably also a third. *Compare* **inclinator**.

escape stair, fire e.s. A stair of metal or concrete, required by law as an escape in the event of fire in a tall building, sometimes the only stair built, either inside or outside it. *See* **pressurized escape route**.

escutcheon, scutcheon, key plate [joi.] A metal plate round a key hole, covered by a *key drop*. (Illus.)

Escutcheon.

escutcheon pin [joi.] A brass nail 1 cm (0·5 in.) long for fixing an *escutcheon*.

espagnolette bolt A vertical bolt on a *casement door*, consisting of a round rod with a hook at each end. A handle at the mid-height turns the rod, engaging the hooks in slots at the top and bottom of the other door, locking and tightening it. The handle is then held firmly by slipping it over a bar on the casement (Spanish refinement of the *cremone bolt*).

establishment charges *Overheads*.

estate agent One who manages, buys, or sells land and buildings. He may belong to the Royal Institution of Chartered Surveyors, to the Auctioneers and Estate Agents Institute, to the Incorporated Society of Auctioneers and Landed Property Agents or he may hold a university degree in estate management. Any of these is a qualification for the work.

estimating [q.s.] Determining the probable cost of future work, by *cubing* or other methods.

etching Cutting (usually a decorative pattern) on the surface of glass, metal or concrete with an acid. Metal engravings are cut away (etched) by acid where they are not covered by a 'resist' such as a wax, which protects them from the acid. Concrete may be etched to expose its aggregate.

etch primer [pai.] *See* **pre-treatment primer**.

evaporation (1) The loss of moisture in vapour form from a liquid.

 (2) [pai.] The drying of *varnishes*, *emulsions* and *lacquers* may be solely by the loss of vapour, as opposed to the hardening of *drying oils* which always occurs by *oxidation*, never by evaporation alone.

even-textured, even-grained [tim.] A description of timber with little variation in the size of the wood elements, for example, timber in which there is little contrast between *springwood* and *summerwood*.

exfoliated vermiculite *Vermiculite* which has been heated and thus expanded to many times its original volume.

exfoliation The scaling of stone, caused by the weather.

exhaust shaft A ventilating passage to remove air from a room.

exhaust system of ventilation An *extract system*.

expanded clay, bloated c., (U S A **haydite**) Vitreous cellular, insulating clay pellets which have been burnt in a cement kiln in such a way as to form hard, air-filled cells. *See* **lightweight aggregate, LECA**.

expanded plastics, foamed p., cellular p. Substances like expanded *polystyrene*. *See also* BRE Digest 224, BS 3379, BS 4840, BS 4841, BS 5241, BS 5608.

expanded polystyrene An *insulating material* obtainable as *loose fill*, or in blocks or sheets, weighing less than any known insulator, 16 kg/m³ (1 lb/ft³). Its maximum recommended temperature of use, 70° C., is low, but it is strong for so light a material, having a compressive strength of 173 kN/m² (25 psi) and a tensile strength of 207 kN/m² (30 psi). Wall and ceiling linings made of it melt at about 80° C. but are not a severe fire hazard if fully bonded to a substance that will not burn. This means that they must not be 'spot-glued' but glued all over, to prevent 'blobs' of burning material falling. They should also never be painted with an oil paint, and preferably should be left unpainted. *See* **sandwich construction**.

expanding bit, expansion b. [carp.] A drilling bit with a cutter which can be adjusted to varying radii. One bit can thus cut holes from 1 to 4 cm (½ to 1½ in.) or from 2·2 to 7·6 cm (⅞ to 3 in.) dia. Expanding bits have no twist.

expanding plug A *bag plug* or *screw plug*.

expansion *See* **coefficient of expansion** (*C*); **dimensional stability, moisture content, moisture expansion, temperature movement,** *and below*.

expansion bay A recess in the side of a pipe *duct* to make space for *expansion bends* (*C*).

expansion of brickwork *See* **moisture expansion, sulphate expansion of brickwork, temperature movement**.

expansion pipe, vent p. In *open vented* domestic hot-water systems, a pipe leading from the *cylinder* to a point over the expansion tank so that, if the water boils, steam (or water) will discharge harmlessly into it. The boiling water expelled from the boiler into the tank will eventually fill it and overflow through the *warning pipe*, showing the owner that either the fire should be damped down or hot water drawn off or both. *See* illus. p. 69.

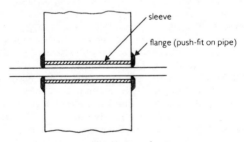

Expansion sleeve.

expansion sleeve, pipe s. A metal, cardboard, asbestos, or plastics pipe built into a wall or floor, through which another pipe passes. This allows the inner pipe to expand or contract without cracking the wall. (Illus.)

expansion strip, e. tape, edge isolation, insulating strip, isolating strip Resilient *insulating material* used to fill the joint between a *partition* and a structural wall or column, or to separate a *glass block* wall from any structural material and thus to prevent damage to the glass.

expansion tank *See* **diaphragm tank, expansion pipe, central heating**. (Illus.)

123

expediter (USA) A *progress chaser*.

extended prices, e. rates [q.s.] The rates or prices for the items in a *bill of quantities* which have been multiplied by their appropriate *quantities* to give a sum of money, written in the bill on the same line as the rate. When all the items have been so multiplied, the bill becomes a *priced bill*.

extender (1) [pai.] **inert pigment** A white powder, often a crystalline mineral with low *hiding power*. It is added to paint to adjust its film-forming and working properties such as *thixotropy* (C). Most extenders are crushed as finely as *pigments*. The commonest are *asbestine*, barytes, *blanc fixe*, *diatomite*, kaolin, *mica*, silica, *whiting*.

(2) [tim.] A substance such as wood flour added to expensive *glue* to dilute it and thus increase its spreading capacity.

extending ladder A telescopic *ladder* which, if wooden, consists of two or three *standing ladders*. They can normally be obtained up to an extended length of 15 m (50 ft).

extension rule A wooden *rule* in two parts which slide relatively to each other. Interior measurements, for example the width of a door or window opening, can be taken with it.

extensions [q.s.] *Extended prices*.

exterior trim [carp.] (mainly USA) Wooden *mouldings* for *barge boards*, *cornices, eaves gutters, water tables*, etc.

exterior-type plywood [tim.] *Plywood* in which the *glue* (not the wood) is moisture resistant. *See* **interior-type plywood**.

external glazing *Glazing* on the outside wall of a building. It may be *outside* or *inside glazing*.

external hazard *See* **fire hazard**.

external wall A wall of which at least one face is exposed to the weather or to the earth.

extra, e. work Work which was not included in the original *contract* and has to be ordered by the *architect* or engineer in writing, generally by a *variation order*.

extract system A ventilation system consisting of an electrically-driven fan connected to air *ducts*. The fan sucks the air from the room and blows it into a duct which leads it to the open air through louvres or a cowl. *Compare* **input system**.

extrados The upper surface of an arch, or of *arch stones*. *See* **intrados**.

extra over [q.s.] In *bills of quantities*, items may be stated and paid for either separately in full, or as 'extra over' another item. Thus in excavating to foundation level, breaking up old foundations with explosives could be priced either extra over the general cost of excavation or separately at its full cost, according to the decision of the writer of the bill of quantities. Similarly, excavation below water level also may be paid as extra over ordinary excavation.

extruded section The commonest *light alloy* structural sections, formed by *extrusion* (C).

eye (1) *See* **access eye**.

(2) [mech.] An opening formed in a metal member, for example, the eye of a hammer head into which the handle fits, or the ring formed at the end of an *eye bolt* (C).

eyebrow, e. dormer A window or ventilator opening in a roof surface. The roof to the window forms no sharp angles with the general roof, unlike a *dormer*. Instead, the general horizontal line of the roof is continuous, with an upward curve at the eyebrow. It resembles an *internal dormer* apart from the curved roof.

F

fabric (1) The *carcase* of a building.

(2) *See* **wire-mesh reinforcement** (*C*).

face (1) [tim.] A broad surface of *square-sawn timber* (BS 565).

(2) **f. side** The wide surface of *plywood*, blockboard, timber, etc., with the best appearance, identified by the *face mark*.

(3) [carp.] The front (cutting) surface of a *saw-tooth*.

(4) The surface of *gypsum wallboard* which can be painted without plastering. It is ivory coloured. A surface to be plastered is grey.

(5) The exposed surface of *ashlars* or of other wall *cladding*.

(6) [mech.] A working surface such as the part of a *hammer* which drives the nail in, the opposite end of a hammer head from the *peen*.

face-bedded, edge-bedded Stone laid so that the *natural bed* is vertical. The stone is liable to flake away, as at the Houses of Parliament, London. Only arch-stones are correctly laid like this.

face brick (USA) *Facing brick*.

faced wall A wall in which the *facing* and *backing* bricks are bonded to act together under load. *Compare* **veneered wall**.

face edge, working e. (USA **work e.**) [joi.] The first edge of *joinery* to be prepared, from which the other edges are measured.

face hammer A *mason*'s hammer with a striking *face* and a cutting *peen*.

face joint The part of a *cross joint* which is seen on the face of a wall.

face mark, X-mark [carp.] A mark pencilled on the *face* to show that other surfaces are to be trued from it. One of the two corners of the face is also trued to form a straight line from which setting out begins.

face measure, surface, superficial m. [tim.] The area of one face of a board. It is not the same as *board measure* except when the board is 25 mm (1 in.) thick.

face mix A mixture of cement and crushed stone, placed on the surface of a mould for *cast stone* and backed with a cheaper, stronger concrete mix which is poured immediately afterwards and therefore bonded to it. *See* **slip-form** (*C*), **granitic finish**.

face mould A *templet* or full size cut-out drawing which is applied to the face of stone (or to moulded *joinery* such as a handrail) to verify its shape in plan. *See* **falling mould**.

face plate [joi.] That part of a *marking gauge* which is pressed against the *face* of timber while the timber is being marked.

face putty, front p. The triangular fillet of *glazier's putty* on the exposed surface of glass. *See* **bed putty, glazing bar**.

face side, working f. (USA **work f.**) [joi.] *See* **face** (2).

face string [joi.] (USA) An *outer string*.

facia *See* **fascia board, fascia bracket**.

facing, lining [joi.] Fixed non-structural joinery, such as an *architrave*. *See below*.

facing bond Any *bond* showing mainly *stretchers*.

facing bricks (USA **face b.**) Bricks of pleasing but not necessarily uniform colour and texture, covering *blockwork* or common brickwork.

facing hammer (USA) A *hammer* with a notched rectangular head for dressing stone or precast concrete.

factory-chimney builder A *steeplejack*.

fadding [pai.] Applying *shellac* lacquer with a pad called a fad.

fading [pai.] Bleaching of a colour by ageing or weathering. *Chalking* looks like fading, but the colour can be restored by a coat of varnish.

faggot A facing brick made about 2 in. wide to cover a *boot*.

faience Glazed *terra cotta*. It is fired twice, once without and once with the glaze, often very large glazed tiles.

fair cutting [q.s.] Cutting of facing brickwork, always assumed 11·5 cm thick, therefore measured by length, and not as an area. Like *rough cutting*, the work is done with *bolster* or *trowel* or *scutch*, less often with the saw.

fair-faced brickwork A brickwork surface which is built neatly and smoothly. It is generally impossible to build both faces fair, one brick thick, in *English bond* but this can be done in *Flemish bond*.

fall bar [joi.] (1) A wooden bar pivoted on a primitive door and controlled by the finger through a hole in the door.

(2) A steel bar like (1) but smaller and neater, used in the *thumb latch*. Both types fasten the door by dropping into a catch fixed on the *door post*.

falling mould [joi.] The developed elevation of a handrail centre line. It does in elevation what the *face mould* does in plan.

falling stile The *shutting stile* of a door.

fall pipe A *downpipe*.

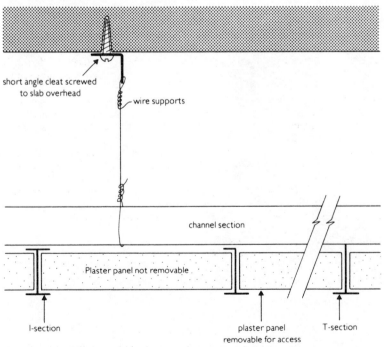

short angle cleat screwed to slab overhead

wire supports

channel section

Plaster panel not removable

I-section

plaster panel removable for access

T-section

False ceiling. General support scheme showing access panel.

false body [pai.] The high *viscosity* (*C*) of a *thixotropic* (*C*) paint which is always reduced when the paint is stirred.

false ceiling, drop c., counter c., suspended c. A ceiling built with a gap between it and the slab above from which it hangs, allowing space for *services*, thermal insulation etc. The ceiling panels may be removable to give access, but in any case at intervals *fire stops* must be formed of sheet steel or asbestos or plasterboard, mineral wool, etc. at least 25 mm (1 in.) thick. Ceiling surfaces exist in extraordinary variety. Perforated metal strips with an absorbent quilt backing can absorb as much sound as an acoustic tile ceiling and need few supports, even as far as 7 m (23 ft) apart. Open grids of timber or metal look good and give excellent access to services but only slightly reduce fire hazard and noise (BSCP 290). (Illus. p. 127)

false tenon, inserted t. [carp.] A *hardwood* tenon inserted where the *tenon* of the jointed timber would be too weak.

fan During demolition or building of a wall beside a street, a floor of scaffold boards projecting out and sloping slightly upwards over the street, so that any falling objects which hit the boards are deflected back to the wall, and not out into the street.

fan convector A *heat exchanger* that usually receives pumped hot water from a boiler and is provided with an electric fan that sucks air over its heating tubes to blow out warm air. Any fan convector, because of its fan, has a much higher output of heat than a conventional radiator of the same size,

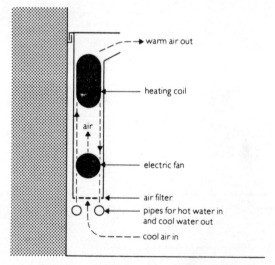

Fan convector.

although the electrical power demand of the fan is usually well below 100 watts. The *unit heater* is at ceiling height but the fan convector is a domestic appliance and is usually on a wall at low level under a window. (Illus.)

fanlight [joi.] A *light* over a door, originally semicircular, now of any shape within the main door frame.

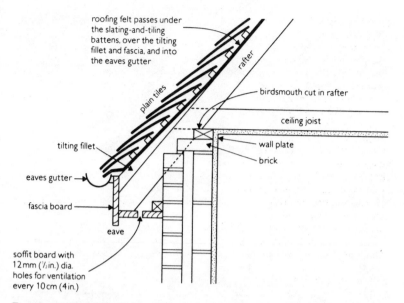

roofing felt passes under
the slating-and-tiling
battens, over the tilting
fillet and fascia, and into
the eaves gutter

rafter

plain tiles

birdsmouth cut in rafter

ceiling joist

tilting fillet

wall plate

brick

eaves gutter →

fascia board

eave

soffit board with
12mm (½ in.) dia.
holes for ventilation
every 10cm (4 in.)

Eaves gutter on plain-tiled roof. Plain tiles slope less steeply than the rafters they are laid on, so they must be placed only on a steep roof, and never at less than 40° to the horizontal, even at eaves.

fascia board (1) **eaves f**. A board set on edge, fixed to the rafter ends or wall plate or wall to carry the gutter under the *eave*. The fascia board's top edge is level with the top of the *tilting fillet* and may act as one, ensuring the correct slope for the eaves tiles. The *underlay* is draped over it into the *eaves gutter* (Illus. above) (BS 5534).

(2) The wide board over a shop front, carrying the shop name.

fascia bracket A light *bracket* screwed on a *fascia board* to carry an *eaves gutter*.

fasteners, fastenings Metal pieces for fixing wooden members together, such as *bolts*, *bitches*, *connectors*, *dowels*, *nails*, *screws*, *ship spikes*, *staples*. In carpentry, flat steel plates with holes drilled in them are used for fishing joints. They may be rectangular, T-shaped, L-shaped, or *angle sections* (C) which replace the *mortise-and-tenon joint*. (Illus. p. 130) *See* **three-way strap**.

fast to light [pai.] A description of a *colour* which is unaffected by light of a certain sort.

fat board A bricklayer's board for carrying *mortar* when pointing.

fat edge [pai.] A ridge of wet *paint* which collects at the lower edge of a painted area because too much has been put on, or because the paint *flows* too well.

fat lime Lime with high volume yield and good workability, usually *high-calcium lime*.

fat mix A rich mix with more cement, lime, or other *binder* than usual.

fat mortar [pla.] A *mortar* which sticks to the trowel. *Compare* **lean mortar**.

fattening, thickening [pai.] Increase in the *viscosity* (C) of paint during storage but not sufficient to make it unusable. *Feeding* is severe fattening.

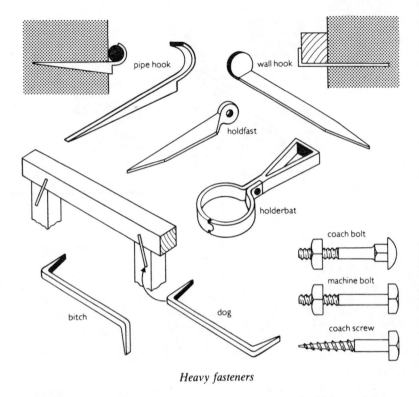

Heavy fasteners

fattening up, maturing [pla.] Increasing the *plasticity* of *slaked lime* by soaking it in water at least overnight.

faucet [plu.] (1) (USA) A small tap, for example at a household sink.

(2) (Scots) A *socket*.

faucet ear [plu.] A projection from a pipe socket, for nailing the pipe to the wall.

feather (1) **slip tongue, spline** [carp.] A *cross tongue* joining *matchboards*, not always glued.

(2) **pendulum slip** [joi.] The wooden slip separating the *sash* weights in a sash window.

feather edge [pla.] A *feather-edge rule*.

feather-edged board [carp.] Tapered boards used as *weather-boarding* or *close-boarded fencing*, tapering from about 16 to 6 mm from edge to edge, p. 131.

feather-edged coping, splayed c., wedge c. A coping stone with one edge thicker than the other, thus with its upper surface sloping one way only (BS 5642).

feather-edge rule [pla.] A *rule* from 0·45 to 2 m (18 in. to 6 ft) long with one edge tapered to 3 mm or 1·5 mm ($\frac{1}{8}$ or $\frac{1}{16}$ in.) thick. It is used after a *floating rule* or for working angles.

feather joint, ploughed-and-tongued j. [joi.] A joint made with a *cross tongue* between *ploughed edges*.

Feather-edged board used as weather-boarding outside a house. (It can also be used in fencing, but then the boards are upright.)

feathering compound A *levelling compound*.
feather tongue [joi.] A *cross tongue*.
feed [pai.] *See* **feeding**, *also C*.
feed cistern, f. tank [plu.] A *cistern* that supplies cold water to replace hot water drawn off in the taps, usually not an *expansion tank* (B S 4118).
feeding, livering [pai.] A thickening-up of liquid *paint* or *varnish* in the container to a rubbery jelly which cannot be used. *See* **fattening, setting-up**.
feint In *flexible-metal roofing* a slightly bent edge of *cappings* or *flashings* to form a *capillary break*.
felt *See* **bitumen felt**.
felt-and-gravel roof (USA) A roof covered with *bitumen felt*, protected by gravel to reduce its *U-value*.
felting down [pai.] *Flatting* a dry *varnish* or *paint* film by a felt pad charged with *abrasive* powder and lubricated with water or other suitable liquid.
felt nail A *clout nail*.
fence [mech.] (1) A guide for timber on a saw bench or other timber cutting machine, or a sheet steel or strong wire mesh guard fixed around a moving machine to prevent injury to people who put a hand inside.
(2) In the joiner's *plough*, a piece of wood or metal parallel to the cut, holding the blade at a constant distance from the edge of the wood so that the groove is ploughed paralled to the edge of the wood.
(3) An enclosure, such as a *palisade*.
fender A *baulk* laid on the ground in a street to protect scaffold *standards* from the wheels of traffic. *See* **dead shore** (illus. p. 97).
fender wall A *dwarf wall* carrying the hearth slab to a ground floor fireplace and sometimes also *joists*.
fenestration The architectural arrangement of the windows and other openings in the walls of a building, mainly in the façade.
ferrule (1) [carp.] A metal band round the handle of a tool to prevent it splitting.
(2) [plu.] Generally a short length of tube such as a *sleeve piece*.
fettle (1) [mech.] To remove the roughness from a casting and to verify that it

is free from flaws by hanging it from chains and striking it with a hammer. *See* **flash** (2)

(2) An extension of the first sense, the finishing-off work in any trade.

fibre board, f. building b. Boards or sheets, commonly sold in sizes 1·2 by 2·4 m and larger, built up by felting from wood or other vegetable fibre. They fall into two main classes, *insulating boards* that are not compressed during manufacture, and *hardboards* that are. Their main bond is by the felting of woody fibres and not by added cement or glue. They burn and have in the past been the cause of rapid *flame spread*, but suitable surface treatment can improve this property up to class 1 (very low flame spread) of BS 476. The density of hardboard is always above 480 kg/m^3, sometimes as high as 960 kg/m^3, and its commonest thickness is 3 mm, though it can be made 13 mm thick. Insulating board is always less dense than 400 kg/m^3 and it is not made thinner than 11 mm.

fibre conduit [elec.] Moulded-fibre, insulating *conduit*.

fibreglass *See* **glass-reinforced cement**.

fibre-reinforced concrete *See* **glass-reinforced cement**.

fibre saturation point [tim.] The *moisture content* (about 30%) above which the strength and dimensions of timber remain roughly constant, and below which the strength increases and the wood shrinks progressively as the moisture content falls.

fibrous concrete *Concrete* containing fibrous *aggregate* such as asbestos or sawdust, used for its lightness or nailability.

fibrous plaster, stick and rag work [pla.] *Plaster of Paris* shapes made in the workshop by casting in gelatin or plaster moulds. They are reinforced with coarse, open canvas and wood laths, and sometimes with wire netting and tow.

fibrous plasterer [pla.] A *plasterer* who makes or fixes *fibrous plaster* work. He is specialized either as a 'shop hand', or as a 'fixer' who sets the cast plaster work in place and joins the pieces to each other with wet plaster.

fiddleback [tim.] A *mottle* figure, a *ripple* in sycamore or maple, used for veneering violin backs.

figure [tim.] The natural markings of timber, including both *grain* and colour. Figure usually adds to the beauty and value of a timber but is not always a sign of strength.

figuring (USA) Calculating or taking off *quantities* or estimating costs from a drawing.

filled joint A way of making the joints between panels in *large-panel construction* by filling them with *sealing compound*, consuming much expensive

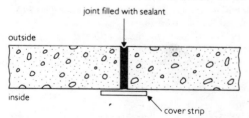

Filled joint in large-panel construction. This type of joint wastes sealant.

sealant and using it in the wrong place. The *open-drained joint* corrects this by using the sealant in a sheltered position where it is more useful, p. 229.

filler (1) [pai.] **surface filler** A creamy paste, put with a *filling knife* over rough areas of wood to smooth them before high-class painting. *See* **hard stopper**.

(2) Substances added to *plastics* including paints, to vary their properties and sometimes also to lower their cost, resembling *extenders* in glue.

fillet [joi.] (1) A narrow strip of wood fixed to the angle between two surfaces, for example, a shelf *cleat*.

(2) A small square wooden *moulding*.

(3) A *weathering* to replace *flashings* at *abutments* or under *verges*, often a *cement fillet*, or an asphalt seal separately formed from the rest of the roof asphalt, etc.

fillet chisel, f. rasp, f. saw Tools used by masons for working stone to fine limits.

filling [pai.] *See* **filler**.

filling knife [pai.] A knife like a *stopping knife* but having a thinner, springier blade, used for laying on paste *filler*.

filling-in piece [carp.] A timber such as a *jack-rafter*, shorter than its neighbours.

fillister (1) **sash f.** [joi.] A *rebate* cut in a *glazing bar* to receive glass and putty.

(2) **filletster** A *plane* for rebating *glazing bars*.

film [pai.] The dried *paint* or *varnish* of one or several coats.

film building, f. forming [pai.] The property of forming an adhesive, strong, continuous, flexible paint *film*, possessed in a high degree by *linseed oil*, a medium which is fluid enough to be laid on with no thinner; therefore all the *medium* contributes to the film.

film glue [tim.] A thin, solid sheet of *phenol formaldehyde resin* laid between thin, costly, decorative, *face veneer* and the cheap, stronger, thicker, backing veneer. Film glue is easily applied. Since it neither wets the veneer nor causes it to expand, it is the only *glue* possible with very thin veneers less than 1 mm thick. It is *thermosetting*.

final sub-circuit [elec.] A *branch circuit*.

fine solder [plu.] An alloy of ⅔ tin, ⅓ lead, more costly than *plumber's solder*, used in making the *blown joint*, for tinning, and for copper-bit soldering. It has the lowest melting point of all *solders*, about 183° C.

fine stuff [pla.] The material of the *finishing coat*.

fine-textured wood [tim.] Wood like birch or maple, with small pores which need no *filler* before varnishing, the opposite of *coarse-textured* wood.

finger joint [joi.] A longitudinal, glued joint between two timbers, usually machine made. (Illus. below)

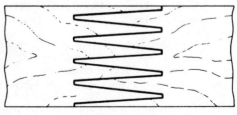

Finger joint.

finger plate [joi.] A plate fixed near the *latch* of a door to protect the door from finger marks.

finger slip [joi.] A small curved-edge *hone* for smoothing the inner surface of *gouges*.

finial A usually pointed ornament at the top of a *gable* or pinnacle or *newel*. *See* **hip knob**.

fining off [pla.] Applying the *finishing coat* of external rendering.

finish (1) [joi.] (USA) Fixed *joinery*.

    (2) **finishing coat** The final coat of *paint* or plaster.

    (3) [pai.] The appearance of the final coat of paint, varnish or polish which may be *crystallized, gloss, matt, polychromatic, textured,* or *wrinkle finish*.

finished floor, finish floor The visible, completed floor surface.

finisher, trowel man A *skilled man* who gives a smooth finish to precast concrete units with a wooden *float* or steel trowel, sometimes patching gaps with concrete of matching colour. A specialist architectural stone finisher smooths the surface with a stone and polishes it with an emery wheel or buffing wheel.

finish hardware [joi.] (USA) *Hardware* which is seen and therefore given a good finish, such as *door furniture*, clothes hooks, and so on, as opposed to *rough hardware*.

finishing carpentry [joi.] American term describing what is called *joinery* in Britain, that is doors, *skirtings, architraves,* etc.

finishing coat, setting c., skimming c., fining c., white c. [pla.] A final layer of plaster about 3 mm thick, usually of *gypsum plaster*.

finishing off [joi.] Preparing the finished surface of *joinery*.

finishings (USA **finish**) The fixed *joinery* in a building; also the *plaster, paint,* or other final details to the walls, doors, etc.

finishing tools Plasterer's or *composition floor layer*'s trowels or floats for shaping curved or other difficult surfaces.

fir [tim.] A loose term which should properly be confined to the Abies family, that is *whitewood, silver fir,* and others. It is also often used for *redwood* and *Douglas fir*.

fire alarm Automatic fire alarms are often linked to a *smoke detector*.

fireback The wall behind a fireplace.

firebars Cast iron bars on which solid fuel is burnt.

fire block [carp.] (USA) *Solid bridging* in floors or wooden walls, a *fire stop*.

fire breaks The *fire-resisting doors, closed stairs, concrete* floors, *division walls,* etc., which reduce the risk of fire in a building to an amount acceptable to insurance companies or the law. *See* **fire stop**.

firebrick *Brick* made from any clay difficult to fuse, generally one with a high content of quartz. It can usually be used up to temperatures between 1500° and 1600° C. *See* **refractory linings** (*C*).

fire cell *See* **compartment**.

fire cement Refractory cement such as a *fireclay,* or *high-alumina cement* (*C*).

fire-check door [joi.] An old (BS 459:1951) type of door still provided by makers, that gives 30 or 60 minutes' fire resistance because it is protected by 3 mm ($\frac{1}{8}$ in.) plywood glued over plasterboard panel infilling on each face, or over asbestos sheet for the 60-minute type. It is not *fire-resisting* because it does not fully comply with BS 476 part 8, p. 135. *See* **intumescent sealant, pressed steel**.

Fire-check door and frame (60-minute type). The 30-minute type has no asbestos sheet under the plywood. No nails, screws or other metal fastenings are allowed on the lipping, plywood or asbestos (after BS 459 and BRE Digest 155).

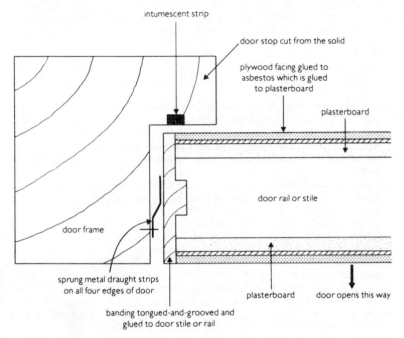

intumescent strip

door stop cut from the solid

plywood facing glued to asbestos which is glued to plasterboard

plasterboard

door rail or stile

door frame

sprung metal draught strips on all four edges of door

plasterboard

door opens this way

banding tongued-and-grooved and glued to door stile or rail

fireclay Clay which is rich in minerals containing quartz, SiO_2, and alumina Al_2O_3, used for making *firebrick*.

fire cracks [pla.] Cracks in a plastered surface caused by exposure to the sun or other heat during drying. *See* **cracking, crazing**.

fire division wall (USA) A wall which divides up a building to resist the spread of fire. Unlike a *division wall* it does not necessarily rise through more than one *storey*.

fire door (1) A door to a furnace.

(2) A generally metal-plated door designed to slide shut when a *fusible link* melts so that it holds back a fire for an hour or more.

fire escape stair An *escape stair*.

fire-extinguishing equipment Drenchers, fire hydrants, sprinklers, emulsifiers, hand-operated foam sprays and so on.

fire grading, fire-resistance g. In Britain structural members such as roofs, beams, columns, walls or doors can be tested by fire under BS 476 and graded for their fire resistance (endurance). Fire resistance is usually measured by the time for which the member continues to satisfy three criteria: absence of collapse, flame penetration, or excessive temperature rise on the 'cool' face. If it satisfies all three criteria for four hours it has four hours' fire resistance. Thirty minutes is often adequate for small houses, while

6 hours could be needed for a warehouse with a *fire load density* of 380 000 Btu/ft² (4000 MJ/m²). The fire resistances needed by buildings are laid down in *Building Regulations* (BS 4422).

fire hazard Danger of fire. Internal hazard arises from fuel in the structure or contents of the building. External hazard arises outside. Hazards include combustibility, flammability, *ignitability*, heat or smoke release, smoke penetration and toxicity (BSCP 3, chap. 4).

fire hydrant An outlet from a water main to which a fireman can connect his hose. It may be of 63, 38 or 19 mm (2½, 1½ or ¾ in.) nominal bore and can be provided inside or outside a building, in colliery yards, timber yards. *See* **dry riser**.

fire load density The fuel in the structure or its contents, per unit area (BS 4422). This refers to floor area but others have recommended that fire load density should be calculated on wall area. A 'low' fire load density is less than 1135 MJ/m² (100 000 Btu/ft²) of floor area and this is usual for dwellings and offices. A 'moderate' one is from 1135 to 2270 MJ/m² (100 000 to 200 000 Btu/ft²). Warehouses often have a 'high' fire load density, 2270 to 4540 MJ/m² (200 000 to 400 000 Btu/ft²). *See* **fire grading**.

fire point (1) The lowest temperature at which a substance ignites and continues to burn when a flame is put to it. *See* **flash point**.

(2) A place where fire-extinguishing equipment is kept.

fireproof A term which should not be used since no practical construction can withstand fire indefinitely. In USA the term means a construction which will safely withstand the complete burning of the contents of the building. *See* **fire resisting**.

fire protection Every measure for the prevention, detection and extinction of fire, as well as the reduction or prevention of fire damage or loss of life and the design of buildings to resist fire (structural fire protection). *See* **smoke detector**, *also* BS 4422.

fire protection of structural steelwork Bare steel frames are liable to fail rapidly in fires, much more quickly even than thick wood joists. Fire protection is given by covering the frame with material which delays the arrival of heat to the steel. This covering may be brick, concrete, hollow clay, foamed slag or gypsum blocks, plaster on *metal lathing*, etc. The thicker the cover, the more protection it provides. *See also* **fire grading, vermiculite-gypsum plaster**.

fire-resisting door, floor, or **wall** Any *door set*, floor or wall that can satisfy for a stated period of time the three criteria of *fire grading*. *Protected openings* in it must endure as long, and the period chosen has to be suitable to the occupancy and fire load of the building.

fire-resisting finishes, fire-retardant finishes [pai.] Paints based on silicones, *polyvinyl chloride, chlorinated rubber, urea formaldehyde* resins, *casein*, borax, and other flame retardants which form a coating about 0·02 to 0·05 mm thick and thus considerably reduce the rate of *flame spread* of a *combustible* material. *See* **intumescent sealant**.

fire-resisting glazing In London, wired glass or *electro-copper glazing* built into lights not exceeding 61 cm (2 ft) square is usually considered to have half an hour's fire resistance if it is at least 6 mm (¼ in.) thick and the panes do not exceed 10 cm (4 in.) square. The frame of the light must have at least half an hour's fire resistance also.

fire stop, draught s., cavity barrier A barrier to fire, such as a brick wall built across an attic space at intervals or a horizontal barrier through the hollow part of a wall. These fire stops must be non-combustible, or of timber 5 cm (2 in.) thick at least. *See* **beam filling, compartment, false ceiling, fire block.**

fire terms Apart from those beginning with 'fire', *see also* **compartment, flame spread, ignitability**, and **roof screen**, but many more are printed in BS 4422.

fire testing of materials Small specimens of building materials can be tested by the methods of BS 476, in particular for fire propagation, *ignitability*, non-combustibility, and *flame spread*.

fire tower (USA) In tall buildings, a stair designed as a fire escape with entries at each floor, protected by fire doors so that smoke cannot enter the stair.

fire venting Inducing hot gas and smoke to leave a building by *smoke outlets*, so that firemen can see to fight the fire.

fire wall (USA) A *division wall*.

firing Exposure of *bricks* and other clayware to heat in a kiln.

firmer chisel [carp.] A carpenter's or joiner's ordinary *chisel*, stronger than a *paring chisel*, less strong than a *socket chisel*. It should not be struck with a hammer or mallet.

firmer gouge [carp.] A *chisel* with a blade curved like a *gouge*.

firring [carp.] *See* **furring**.

first fixer [carp.] A *carpenter* cutting or fixing *joists*, *rafters*, floorboards, *stairs*, or window frames.

first fixings (1) [joi.] *Grounds*, *plugs*, and so on which carry the *joinery*.

   (2) [carp.] Structural timber, *joists*, *rafters*, floors, etc.

first floor (1) (Britain) The floor which is next above the floor at ground level and is therefore about 2·75 m (9 ft) above ground. This definition is also accepted in USA for houses with neither *basement* nor *cellar*.

   (2) (USA) In buildings with a basement or cellar the first floor is the first above ground level (which in Britain is the *ground floor*).

first storey The space between the *first floor* and the floor above.

fished joint [carp.] *See* **splice**.

fish glue, isinglass [tim.] A *glue* like *animal glue* but prepared from fish bladders and skins.

fish-tailed fixing A split and twisted end of a metal bar, mortared into a mortar joint or hole in masonry.

fitch [pai.] A long-handled small *brush* bound with tin, with which nearly inaccessible details are painted. *See* **lining tool**.

fitter's hammer [mech.] An *engineer's hammer*.

fittings, pipe f. [plu.] *Bends*, *couplings*, *elbows*, *unions*, etc. For screwed pipe they are usually of *malleable cast iron* (C). For *copper* or *plastics*, they may also be *capillary* or *compression* fittings. *See* illus. p. 138.

five X, 5 X Western red cedar *shingles* cut to 41 cm (16 in.) lengths. When placed together, five butts measure 5 cm (2 in.) thick.

fixed light, f. sash A *dead light*.

fixed-price contracts [q.s.] These may be of three types, *lump sum*, *schedule of prices*, or *measure-and-value contracts*. Fixed-price contracts are generally recommended by consultants and preferred by clients, since the contractor has an incentive to work fast and economically. Compare the slow, expensive *cost-reimbursement contract*.

fixer (1) **f. mason** (Scotland & Cornwall **builder mason**) A *mason* who sets prepared stones in walls.

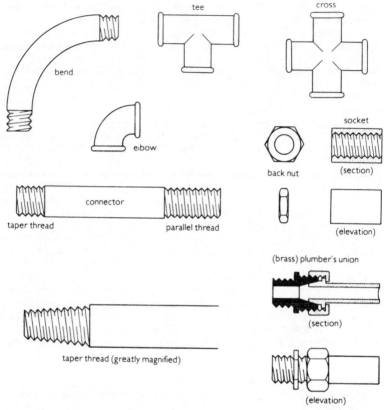

Fittings for screwed gas or water pipe, mainly of dead mild steel or malleable cast iron.

(2) [pla.] A plasterer who fixes *fibrous plaster* as opposed to a 'shop hand'.

fixer's bedding *Lime putty* used by *fixer masons*.

fixing Glass panes are fixed when they are secured to ceilings or walls for such purposes as flush lighting fittings. Otherwise the word *glazing* is used.

fixing brick, f. block, nailing block, nog, wood brick A brick made from wood, or sawdust and clay, or from *diatomite*, or *lightweight concrete*, or other nailable material, used for fixing joinery. *Fixing fillets*, being thinner, shrink less and are a better fixing.

fixing compound A *glazing compound*.

fixing fillet, f. slip, pad, pallet, pallet slip [joi.] A piece of wood, the thickness of a mortar joint 23 × 11·5 cm (9 × 4½ in.), inserted into a *joint* as a fixing for *joinery*. *See* **fixing brick**.

fixings [joi.] *Common grounds, plugs, fixing fillets*, etc., for holding joinery, sometimes called *first fixings*. *See* **fasteners**.

fixing slip [joi.] A *fixing fillet*.

fixing strip A steel, non-ferrous metal or plastics device for fixing board or sheet *coverings for partitions* or for fixing *cladding* to the wall frame or *sub-frame*.

fixture, fitment Anything fixed to a building. It becomes the landlord's property if its removal would damage the building, e.g. plumbing, wash basins, ceiling lamps.

flagstone, flag, flagging A slab of concrete, or cast or natural stone used for paving footways or gardens, originally sandstone which splits into flat sheets.

flaking (1) A ground on which *thatch* is laid, consisting of reeds woven over the rafters. No *battens* are used.

(2) The detachment of stone, brick, paint or plaster.

flame cleaning [pai.] Removing mill scale and water from weathered structural steelwork by a flame. The surface is primed with *pre-treatment primer* immediately afterwards.

flame-retardant treatment A *fire-resisting finish*.

flame spread Building materials in Britain used for wall or ceiling lining are tested under BS 476 by intense radiant heat, together with a gas flame, to determine how quickly their surface ignites. They are classified as follows: 1. very low, 2. low, 3. medium, 4. rapid.

flammable The term used in Britain and USA by fire authorities instead of inflammable, meaning that which burns with a flame. *See* **non-combustible**.

flanking transmission of noise A type of noise transmission experienced between neighbouring terrace houses. Noise passes from one to the other mainly by two paths – direct transmission through the *party wall* – and flanking transmission through the outside walls. The outside walls are continuous with each other. The sounds in the source house pass into its outside wall and along it to the neighbour's house.

flanking window A window beside an outside door, with its sill at the doorsill level.

flanks The *intrados* of an arch, near its *springings*.

flank wall A wall at one side of a building.

flared header, flare h. A brick which is dark at one end through being close to the fire during burning. It can be used for patterning the face of brickwork. *See* **English cross bond**.

flash (1) To make a weathertight joint, called a *flashing*.

(2) **mould mark** In any casting, a narrow strip of surface metal, indicating leakage from the mould, projecting along a line that was the boundary between the two halves of the mould. It is usually removed by *fettling*.

flash drying [pai.] Rapid drying by exposing paint or varnish to radiant heat for a short time. *See* **stoving**.

flashing (1) A strip of impervious material usually *flexible metal* (such as zinc 0·8 mm thick or copper 0·56 mm thick or lead 1·8 mm thick, or *asbestos-bitumen* which is even thicker) that excludes water from the junction between a roof covering and another surface (usually vertical). Flashings, at their upper end, are usually wedged tightly into mortar joints raked out to receive them. *See also* **apron flashing, counter flashing, cover flashing, raking flashing, stepped flashing**.

(2) Burning bricks alternately with too much and too little air to give them varied colours.

(3) [pai.] The defect of glossier patches in a *finish*, particularly at joins or laps.

flashing board A *layer board*.

flash point The lowest temperature at which a substance momentarily ignites when a flame is put to it. *See* **fire point**.

flat (1) A level platform, generally a roof, particularly a lead-covered roof (lead flat).

(2) (USA **apartment**) One floor of a multi-storey building or a dwelling, originally only on one floor. *Compare* **maisonette**.

(3) [pai.] Matt, *see* **gloss**.

(4) [pai.] *See* **flatting down**.

(5) [tim.] *See* **flat cutting**.

flat arch, straight a., French a. (USA **jack arch**) An arch with a level *soffit* and *extrados* made usually of wedge-shaped, *gauged*, or moulded bricks which radiate from one centre. It is used over doors, windows, and fireplaces. *See* **soldier arch**.

flat coat [pai.] A coat of *filler*.

flat cost The cost of labour and material only.

flat cutting, flatting, ripping, ripsawing [tim.] The *re-sawing* of timber parallel to the edges (BS 565). *Compare* **deep cutting**, *see* **sliced veneer**.

flat-drawn sheet glass Ordinary *sheet glass* for windows.

flat grain [tim.] The grain of *flat-sawn* timber, most of which has annual rings at less than 45° with the face of the piece.

flat interlocking tile A *single-lap* standard British clay roofing tile normally measuring 39 × 20 × 1·9 cm (15½ × 8 × ¾ in.) provided with two nail holes and no *nib*. It has a 7·6 cm (3 in.) side lap.

flat joint, flush j. A mortar joint whose surface is flush with the brickwork.

flat-joint jointed A *flat joint* in which a narrow groove has been cut with a *jointer*.

flat paint brush, f. enamel b. [pai.] A metal-bound *brush* used by the *house-painter*. It is of black bristle stiff enough to carry heavy *varnish*, *paint*, or *enamel* and is from 1 to 15 cm (½ to 6 in.) wide. *See* **house painter**, p. 180.

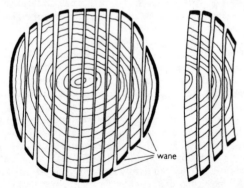

Flat-sawn log. The log has been seasoned after sawing, and the illustration shows the effects of shrinkage on it. The surfaces are curved because the redial shrinkage is only two thirds of the tangential shrinkage. On the right is part of the same log showing the (concave outwards) warp which the shrinkage causes. The two central planks are fully quarter-sawn.

flat-pin plug [elec.] A common type of fused plug suitable for insertion into a *shuttered socket* outlet on a *ring main*. Its three contact pins are rectangular in cross-section.

flat pointing Pointing of brickwork to make *flat joints*.

flat roof (Scots **platform r.**) A roof which slopes at less than 10° to the horizontal. Its surface should slope at least at 1 in 60 for drainage.

flat sawing [tim.] Sawing logs with parallel cuts, a method of *conversion* which wastes less timber than any other.

flat-sawn timber, plain-s., slash-s., (U S A **bastard-s.**) Two thirds of the boards made by *flat sawing* have *annual rings* meeting the surface at less than 45°. The remaining one third, the centre planks, are *quarter sawn*. (Illus. p. 140.)

flatting See **flat cutting** [tim.], **flatting down** [pai.].

flatting down, rubbing [pai.] *Sanding* with powdered pumice and felt, cuttle fish, glass paper, or other *abrasives*.

flat varnish [pai.] A *varnish, lacquer,* or *enamel* with its *gloss* reduced by adding wax, soap, *pigment,* or *filler*.

flat wall brush [pai.] A *brush* like a *distemper brush* but narrower, being only about 12·5 or 15 cm (5 or 6 in.) wide.

flaunching A cement mortar *fillet* round the top of a *chimney stack* to throw off the rain, surrounding the *chimney pot*.

fleaking *Flaking* with reed, to make a ground for *thatch*.

Flemish bond A *bond* which shows, in every course, alternating *stretchers* and *headers*. See **double Flemish bond, single Flemish bond, monk bond,** and *below*.

Flemish diagonal bond By laying a *course* of *stretchers* alternating with a course of headers and stretchers alternately, a face *bond* is obtained in which, as in *English cross bond*, a diagonal pattern can be seen.

Flemish garden-wall bond, Sussex g.-w. b A *bond* showing, in each course and on both faces of a 23 cm (9 in.) wall, a sequence of three *stretchers* and one *header*. In thicker walls, one face is formed in English bond. Like *English cross bond* and *Flemish diagonal bond*, the face shows a diagonal pattern.

Fletton A village near Peterborough, hence the low-cost bricks made from the Oxford clay of the neighbourhood.

flex, flexible cable (U S A **lamp cord**) [elec.] Flexible copper *conductors* enclosed in rubber and a textile or *polyvinyl chloride* binding. It is used for the final connection to an electrical fitting in a house, for example a lamp or heater. See **flexible cord**.

flexible-bag moulding [tim.] A process for making *moulded plywood*. Pressure, during gluing up, is applied to the hot *veneers* through a rubber bag, which forces the veneers on to a mould. In the vacuum process, the veneers are placed inside the bag, which is evacuated. In other methods, the bag is under strong internal pressure and is outside the plywood. See **skin**.

flexible cord [elec.] A *flex* in which each *conductor* has an area not larger than 4·5 mm^2 (0·007 in.^{2}).

flexible damp course A *damp course* of *flexible metal* or bitumen or plastics sheet.

flexible metal Sheet metal, originally zinc, lead, copper, or painted tinplate, but now also aluminium for *flashings* or roofing. See *below*.

flexible-metal conduit [elec.] *Conduit* made from spirally wound steel strip.

flexible-metal roofing Roof coverings or *flashings* of *flexible-metal* sheet. Like

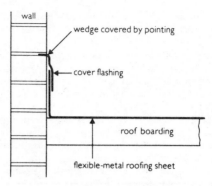

Flexible-metal roofing.

roofing felt, these roof coverings need to be laid on *boarding*, covered with an *underlay*. Painted tinplate is used only in dry climates. *See* **double-lock cross welt**, *also* BSCP 143. (Illus. above)

flexible mortar *See* **strong mortar**.

fleximers Expensive *jointless flooring* materials that may be only 6 mm ($\frac{1}{4}$ in.) thick, containing some *elastomer* to reduce cracking and increase flexibility and adhesion. *Epoxides*, though not strictly fleximers, have many of their properties. *See* **cement-rubber latex, levelling compound**.

flex plug and socket [plu.] *See* **plug-in connector**.

flier, flyer (1) A rectangular *tread* in a *stair* (not a *winder*).

(2) [carp.] A *flying shore*.

flight A series of *steps* which joins a floor or landing to the next one (below).

flint wall A wall built of flints showing their dark-grey broken faces, with brick or stone *quoins*.

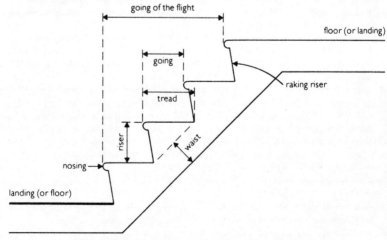

Flight of reinforced concrete stairs with raking risers.

142

flitch [tim.] (1) A large timber, intended for conversion.

(2) Timber from which *veneers* are to be cut, usually with *wane* on one or more edges.

(3) The stack of veneers after cutting, piled in the order in which they were before cutting. *See* **swatch**.

flitched beam, sandwich b. [carp.] A beam built from two wooden beams sandwiching a vertical steel plate. The three are bolted together through the plate.

flitch plate [carp.] The steel plate which reinforces a *flitched beam*.

float (1) [pla.] (USA **floater**) A wooden plastering tool such as the *cross-grained float* or *Darby float*. *See* **blade, plasterer** (illus. p. 246), **trowel**.

(2) [plu.] A metal drain pipe, usually cast iron, hung just below floor level, draining the floor above.

(3) A hollow ball of plastics or incorrodible metal fixed to the end of the operating lever of a *ball valve*.

floated coat [pla.] A plaster coat smoothed by a *float*.

float glass Glass of equal quality to *plate glass*, that has superseded it for all thicknesses from 3 to 25 mm. Its surface is smooth because, during manufacture, it floats on molten metal. *See* **sheet glass**.

floating (1) [pla.] Levelling with a *floating rule* the second coat, the *floating coat* of *three-coat plaster*.

(2) [pai.], **flooding** The re-arrangement or separation of *pigment* grains at the surface of a paint film. When two pigments are mixed, this sometimes happens because of insufficient wetting, different densities or particle sizes, etc. Although it may in other paints be a defect because the final colour is not known before the coat is dry, floating is desired in aluminium and other metal paints. *See* **leafing**.

floating coat, browning c., [pla.] The second of three coats in *three-coat plaster*. It is levelled with a *floating rule* between *screeds*, resembles the first coat and is not more than 1 cm (⅜ in.) thick. It is usually the same mix as the *rendering coat*.

floating floor *Discontinuous construction* for sound insulation, by separating the wearing surface of the floor from the loadbearing part, whether concrete or wooden. A *glass-wool* quilt is laid on the rough floor, 5 × 5 cm (2 × 2 in.) battens laid on it without nailing, and finished floor boards nailed to the battens. If the final floor is a concrete *screed*, this should be not less than 65 mm (2⅝ in.) thick, reinforced at least with chicken wire, and separated from the glass wool by a layer of *building paper* or polythene sheet. The floor finish over it can improve the insulation against impact noise, sometimes considerably, for example 8 mm cork tiles overlain by thick carpet with rubber underlay. The ceiling below is fixed in the usual way (BRE Digest 104). (Illus. pp. 102, 144)

floating rule (USA **rod**) [pla.] A long wooden *rule* with which a *floating coat* is levelled to a plane surface between *screeds*. *See* **feather-edge rule**.

floating screed A *floating floor* of mortar, not timber. (Illus. p. 144)

float valve [plu.] A *ball valve*.

flock spraying (USA **flocking**) [pai.] Blowing soft, fluffy fibres from cotton, silk, or other textiles on to a sticky surface to form textile effects, such as suedes or felts of various colours.

floor-and-wall tiler [pla.] A *tradesman* who chooses, matches, cuts, and trims *wall tiles* and beds them in *mortar, glue,* or *plaster*. He also builds up hearths

floor finish (parquet, carpet, etc.)

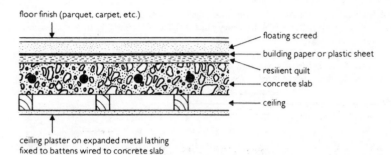

- floating screed
- building paper or plastic sheet
- resilient quilt
- concrete slab
- ceiling

ceiling plaster on expanded metal lathing
fixed to battens wired to concrete slab

Floating screed for noise reduction between floors.

and fireplaces and sets large *faience* tiles, and maybe a *composition floor layer*. *See* **tile slabber, floor-layer's labourer**.

floorboards The most usual boards for floors are planed square-edged wooden boards, nominally 15 × 2·5 cm (6 × 1 in.), that measure in fact about 14·5 × 2·2 cm (5¾ × ⅞ in.). Tongued and grooved boards provide a better floor because they are more fire-resistant, draughtproof and strong for the same thickness. Recently large flooring panels made of 19 mm (¾ in.) *wood chipboard* have become available which are quicker to lay, need fewer nails and are cheaper than wood. If tongued and grooved all round they are better than wood in fire resistance and strength (BSCP 201, 209).

floor chisel A *bolster* about 5 cm (2 in.) wide for pulling up floorboards.

floor clip, bulldog c., (USA **sleeper c.**) Strips of 0·9 mm thick *sherardized* steel sheet pushed into and anchored in the surface of a *concrete* floor slab or *screed* just after it has been levelled. When the concrete has hardened, the two ends of the strip can be pulled up into a U-shape and nailed to flooring *battens*, to which the finished wooden floor is fixed. A pad of asbestos or rubber sometimes forms part of the clip to reduce sound transmission from the floor to the room below (acoustic clip).

floor cramp, flooring c. [carp.] A *cramp* for forcing floorboards together before they are nailed down. It is clamped astride a *floor joist*.

floor framing [carp.] The *common joists*, their *strutting* and support.

flooring brad *See* **brad**.

flooring saw, floor s. [elec., plu.] A short saw with a curved point, toothed also on the back of the point, that enables the tradesman to cut his way fairly easily through a floorboard.

flooring tiles [pla.] Usually *concrete* or *clay tiles* set in cement mortar or in bituminous or other *adhesive*. For a more sound-absorbent, heat-insulating, decorative, or comfortable surface, tiles of *linoleum*, glass, *cork*, rubber, asphalt, or plastics are used. More durable floors are made of brick, or of steel *anchor plates* filled with concrete, or of cast-iron anchor plates, p. 145. *See* **slab floor, thermoplastic tiles**. *See* BSCP 202, 203.

floor joist [carp.] A *common joist*.

floor-layer's labourer A helper to the *floor-and-wall tiler* who loads and unloads tiles or other materials for him, soaks tiles, mixes mortar or *jointless flooring* composition, sometimes helps in rubbing a *terrazzo* floor, and cleans up when the floor is laid.

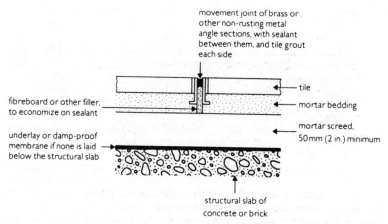

movement joint of brass or
other non-rusting metal
angle sections, with sealant
between them, and tile grout
each side

tile

fibreboard or other filler,
to economize on sealant

mortar bedding

mortar screed,
50 mm (2 in.) minimum

underlay or damp-proof
membrane if none is laid
below the structural slab

structural slab of
concrete or brick

Laying clay floor tiles.

floor lining [carp.] *Building paper* laid over a *rough floor* before the finished floor is placed on it.

floor plan A drawing of a building showing the *layout* of all rooms, wall thicknesses, and other building information needed on a particular floor.

floor sander A *sanding machine* used for smoothing wooden floors.

floor spring, s. hinge [joi.] A sprung *pivot* housed in the floor to control the opening and closing of a *swing door*. *Compare* **helical hinge**.

floor stop [joi.] A *door stop* set in the floor.

floor strutting [carp.] *Herring-bone* or *solid strutting* between floor *joists* at midspan.

floor tile *See* **clay tile, flooring tile.**

floor varnish [pai.] A *varnish* put on floorboards must be quick drying, tough, abrasion-resistant, washable, and must take wax polish.

floor warming *See* **underfloor heating.**

flow, level [pai.] To spread into a smooth film, a property of liquid paints or varnishes which ensures that they will show neither brush marks nor *orange peeling*, though they may *run* badly.

flow pipe A pipe by which hot water leaves a boiler and enters a radiator or hot-water *cylinder* in a water heating system. *See* **primary flow and return pipes.**

flue A passage for smoke either in a chimney or leading to it. The 230 × 230 mm (9 × 9 in.) square pargetted brick flue has been superseded by clay *flue linings* which, for an open fire may have an equally large flueway, or for a gas fire may be much smaller. Except for gas fires, each flue serves one fire only.

flue block *See* **flue lining** *and* illus.

flue gathering A *throat* (2).

flueless heaters *See* **condensation.**

flue lining (1) **f. liner, f. block, chimney block** *Terra cotta* or fireclay pipes of 23 × 23 cm (9 × 9 in.) or smaller, circular or rectangular and 30 or 60 cm (12 or 24 in.) long, which have superseded *pargetting* (BS 1181).

(2) When a modern gas- or oil-fired furnace is installed at an old flue, a

145

pliable flue lining tube should be inserted along its full length. Because these boilers are so efficient, they have cool flue gases liable to leave *condensation* water in the flue. The condensate is likely to pass through the brickwork and to stain the plaster in the rooms severely. These flue linings, made of aluminium, asbestos, etc. contain the condensate because they are sealed to the chimney at the top and to the boiler at the bottom. The space between lining and brick may be filled with lightweight concrete, or other insulation material. They are made in sizes from 80 mm (3 in.) diameter upwards. Where an old flue is accessible for its full height on one side, it is possible to re-line it by breaking out a suitable width of brickwork and inserting clay liners. Built with the socket up they prevent any outward leakage of condensation. The jointing mortar may be of *aluminous cement*.

flue pipe A metal or *asbestos-cement* pipe which leads smoke from a *roomheater* to the flue. To prevent flame striking asbestos cement (which would break), the first 1·8 m (6 ft) next the stove should be of metal.

fluorescent lighting [elec.] *Cold-cathode lamps.*

fluorescent pigments [pai.] Metallic tungstates, borates, and silicates, and some organic dyes. They form brilliant paints when effectively used, particularly in dull surroundings, because they convert invisible radiation to visible, and therefore are brighter than neighbouring surfaces. Some of them deteriorate quickly on exposure. *See* **phosphorescent paint**.

fluorocarbon resin *See* **ptfe**.

flush (1) Description of a surface wholly in one plane, for example, a flush door.

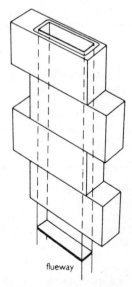

flueway

Flue blocks for a gas fire, forming part of a partition. These blocks for a straight flueway can be bonded into brickwork without difficulty. Curved flueway blocks also can be bonded in.

146

(2) To flake off, said of the face of walling stone. *See* **hollow bed**.

(3) [plu.] To send a quantity of water down a pipe or channel to clean it.

flush door [joi.] A smooth-surfaced door, built of *plywood, hardboard,* or *coreboard,* either a *hollow core* or *solid door.*

flushed joint A joint above or below which the surface stone has flaked off.

flushing trough [plu.] A long water tank extending above and across a range of WCs, and supplying them with flushing water. It has the advantage that any WC can be flushed at short intervals without the waiting period needed for the filling of a *cistern.*

flushing valve (USA **flushometer**) [plu.] A valve which supplies a precise quantity of water to flush a WC and therefore replaces the usual *cistern.* It has the advantage that there need be no wait while the cistern refills, but, because of its direct connection with the water main, not all water authorities allow it.

flush panel, solid p. [joi.] A panel which is flush with its framing.

flush soffit A smooth under-surface, particularly of *spandrel steps.*

fluxes In *soldering, brazing,* and *welding* (*C*), fusible substances like borax which cover the joint, prevent oxidation and so help the molten metal to stick. *See also C.*

flyer A *flier.*

flying bond (1) *Monk bond.*

(2) *American bond.*

flying scaffold A scaffold hung usually by ropes from an *outrigger*. *See* **cradle**.

flying shore, flier A horizontal strut fixed between two walls above ground level, often placed between two houses in a street when the house between has been demolished. For spans much longer than 10 m (33 ft), timber flying shores long enough are difficult or impossible to find. Consequently tubular steel scaffolding is then used, with intermediate scaffolding towers to the ground where convenient. *See* **straining piece, needle, raking shore**, p. 268.

fly wire Fine wire mesh used as *scrim* between the joints in *wallboards.*

foam *Lightweight concrete* made from foamed cement. *See below.*

foamed plastics *See* **expanded plastics**.

foamed slag Blast-furnace slag which has been foamed during cooling to make a useful *lightweight aggregate* (BS 877).

foil A description of copper, zinc, aluminium, or lead which is thinner than *sheet* or *strip,* that is, less than 0·16 mm.

folding casement, f. door [joi.] Either a *casement door* or two or more casements or doors hinged together in a confined space to open or close by folding or unfolding (BS 565).

folding rule A *fourfold rule* or a *zigzag rule.*

folding shutters [joi.] *Boxing shutters.*

folding stair A *loft ladder.*

folding wedges, easing w., striking w., lowering w. [carp.] Wedges, often of hardwood, used in pairs to tighten up or slack off *dead shores, flying shores, raking shores,* and *falsework* (*C*), and *centers* of all sorts. *See* **easing the wedges, sand box** and illus. pp. 97, 268.

follower [plu.] *See* **boxwood bobbin**.

Fondu *Aluminous cement.*

foot block An *architrave block.*

foot bolt [joi.] A strong *tower bolt* set vertically at the foot of a door.

foot cut, plate c., seat c. [carp.] (USA) The horizontal saw-cut in the *birdsmouth* at the foot of a *common rafter*. *See* **plumb cut**.

footing A foundation to a wall. *See also* C.

foot plate [carp.] (1) A horizontal timber laid over and crossing the *wall plate*. It joins the foot of the *rafter* to the foot of an *ashler* piece.

(2) A *sole plate*.

footprints, pipe tongs (USA) **combination pliers** [plu.] A pipe fitter's adjustable wrench with serrated jaws, made in different sizes to grip pipes from 7·6 cm (3 in.) dia. down to a few mm. It also turns nuts but burrs the flats so that they cannot afterwards be turned with a spanner. *See* **gas pliers, plumber**, p. 250.

footstone A *gable springer*.

force cup [plu.] An essential household tool for unblocking sinks, basins, baths, etc., generally the first tool tried by plumbers. This rubber cup on a short stick is pushed up and down over the waste plug so as to drive the retained water down, and suck it back alternately. (Illus. below)

rubber

Force cup.

forced circulation, mechanical c. [plu.] A pumped circulation, as opposed to a *gravity circulation*.

forced drying [pai.] *Drying* at a temperature not above 65°C. (150° F.). *Compare* **stoving**.

foreman An experienced *tradesman* in charge of other men working at his trade. He may work with the tools or merely supervise others. *See* **general foreman**.

foreman bricklayer An experienced *bricklayer* who gives out instructions concerning dimensions, levels, and *bonds* for brickwork.

foreman carpenter and joiner An experienced *carpenter* and joiner who is generally specialized either as an outside foreman, or as an inside foreman (shop foreman) supervising bench workers and wood machinists. The outside foreman works on a building site, supervising carpenters and joiners, working under the *agent* or *general foreman* and sets out work from *architects'* or engineers' drawings. The shop foreman also sets out work but on a smaller scale, and his work is usually less heavy.

foreman glazier An experienced *glazier* who measures work, estimates cost, and may choose glass and plan the cutting of it. He may prepare *templates* for curved glass and be able to work with stained glass.

foreman plasterer A capable *plasterer*, usually with experience in both *fibrous* and solid plaster, able to work to the instructions of an architect. In Britain he may have the technical certificate of the City and Guilds of London Institute. The best foremen can give a price for work before doing it.

fore plane [joi.] A plane between the *jointer* and the *jack plane* in length.

forked tenon [joi.] A joint in which a *tenon* cut in the middle of a long *rail* is inserted into an *open mortise*.

formaldehyde *See* **synthetic resin.**

format dimensions The plan dimensions of a brick or block plus half a joint all round, usually 10 mm (⅜ in.) for two half joints.

form of tender [q.s.] In *tendering*, documents including a *bill of quantities*, sent out by an architect to contractors, on which they state their price for doing the work.

fossil resin, fossil, f. gum [pai.] *Resins* such as *copal* which have become hard through ageing in the ground.

foul-air flue A ventilating duct which draws air out of a room.

foul drain [plu.] A *soil drain*.

foul water Sewage, also called *soil*.

foundation stone A large stone set in a wall near ground level, generally well above the foundation. Carved outside it are the date of setting, usually also the *building owner*'s, the builder's, and the *architect*'s names. A hollow within the stone may be filled with contemporary objects such as coins.

four-coat system [pai.] The accepted way to paint new wood. There is agreement that it should include *primer*, *undercoat* and *gloss* coat, but some authorities insist on two undercoats, others on two gloss coats. (Some gloss coats cannot be put on to a gloss coat.) For internal work a good finish may be had by using two undercoats and rubbing down. For outside work, better protection should be had from two gloss coats.

fourfold rule, folding r. A two-feet (or in Scotland three-feet) long, wooden pocket rule divided into inches and eighths, hinged at three joints, to fold into one quarter of its length. *See* **push-pull rule, zig-zag rule.**

four-piece butt matching, diamond m. [tim.] Joining four adjacent sheets of figured, *sliced veneer* so that the richest *figure* is at the centre of the panel. Each sheet is cut square, near the edge of the best figure. These four right-angles join to make a richly figured veneer nearly four times as big as each separate sheet. The method gives a vivid effect with strongly striped veneers.

four-pipe system A system with separate *flow* and *return pipes* for *central heating* and for hot water (B S 5643).

foxtail wedging, fox w. [carp.] *See* **secret wedging.**

frame [carp.] The timber members of *joinery* or a building frame may be connected by *halving*, by *mortise-and-tenon*, or by similar joints. But in American *frame construction* now there are few carpentry joints and nearly all the joints are nailed. *See also* C.

frame construction [carp.] (U S A) Wooden house building, including *balloon framing*, *braced frames*, *platform frames*.

framed and braced door, f. ledged and b.d., f.b. and boarded d. [joi.] A door which shows, on the face side, vertical boards as well as the two *stiles* and the top *rail* which is rebated to take the ends of the boards. On the back can be seen, in addition, the horizontal *ledges* at the bottom and middle of the door, as well as the two diagonal *braces* (*C*). (Illus. above)

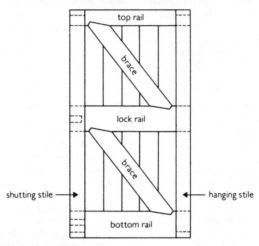

Framed and braced door (*braces do not function if hanging stile and shutting stile are reversed*).

framed and ledged door [joi.] A door like a *framed and braced door* without the diagonal *braces* (*C*.).

framed door [joi.] A door with a rigid frame (generally with tenon and mortise joints) consisting at least of top, bottom, and *lock rails*, *hanging stile*, *shutting stile* and panels.

framed ground [joi.] *Grounds* framed like a door frame round openings with the head tenoned to the posts, used as a fixing for *joinery*.

framed partition A *partition* built up on its own frame of timber. *See* **common partition, coverings, head, nogging, sill, stud, trussed partition**.

frame house [carp.] The American sawn timber house of *frame construction*, sheathed usually with *weather-boards* or *shingles* outside.

frame saw [tim.] (1) A power saw for wood or stone with one or several vertical or horizontal blades held tight in a frame.

(2) [carp.] A heavy *bow saw*.

framing square [carp.] A *steel square*.

freemason A term which in the Middle Ages meant a skilled *mason*, capable of cutting *freestone*, that is of carving.

free-standing, self-supporting A description of a part of a building which does not touch other parts, for example, a *chimney stack* or a *column*.

freestone Building stone which is fine-grained and uniform enough to be worked in any direction and can thus be carved – generally limestones or fine-grained sandstones.

free stuff [tim.] *Clear timber*.

freight elevator, trunk lift (USA) A goods lift, used for hoisting furniture and other heavy loads in a building, but not for carrying passengers. *See* **dumb waiter**.

French arch *See* **Dutch arch**.

French casement, F. door or **F. window** [joi.] A *casement door*.

French fliers The *fliers* round an *open-well stair* which has *quarter-space landings*.

Frenchman A kitchen knife with the end bent over, used with the *jointing rule* for trimming mortar *joints*.

French polish, F. varnish [pai.] *Shellac* dissolved in *methylated spirits*. *See* **spiriting off**.

French tiles Clay *single-lap tiles*, occasionally imported to Britain.

fresco [pai.] Painting on wet lime plaster with pigments mixed in water. The *pigments* are limited to those few which are sufficiently *alkali resistant*. Considerable skill is needed, and plasterer and painter must work together. For these reasons fresco painting is now rare.

fresh-air inlet A pipe connected to the open air, admitting fresh air to the lower end of a house drain, near its connection to the *sewer* (*C*). It is fitted with a hinged mica flap at its upper end to prevent it working as a foul-air outlet, because in country or suburban districts it is fixed near ground level. Since these flaps are not reliable, many authorities do not now insist on a fresh-air inlet, allowing the drains to be ventilated by the *ventilation pipe* at the upper end of the house drain. *See* **intercepting trap**.

fret saw [joi.] A saw for cutting round sharp curves. It consists of a thin, narrow, replaceable blade held in a frame. The blade can be released from the frame to insert it into a drilled hole in the wood from which sawing begins. Many sizes are obtainable, from very small handsaws to power-operated *jig saws*.

fretwork (1) [joi.] Work done with a *fret saw*.

(2) *See* **leaded light**.

friction latch, f. catch [joi.] A small spring catch mortised into the edge of a door like a *ball catch*.

frieze The part of the wall of a room above the picture rail.

frieze panel [joi.] The highest *panel* in a door of more than four panels.

frieze rail [joi.] In a door with four *rails*, the one below the top rail.

frit Treated and finely ground sand, glass, and flint used for glazing bricks and other *ceramics*.

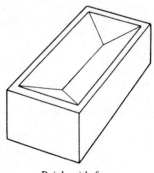

Brick with frog.

151

frog An indentation on a bed face or faces of a brick to reduce its weight. At least for V-shaped frogs, walls built frog down (frog empty) are stronger than walls built frog up. (Illus. p. 151)

frontage The length of a site in contact with a road.

frontage line A *building line*.

front hearth The concrete floor of a fireplace projecting into the room.

front lintel The *lintel* supporting the visible wall over an opening.

front putty *Face putty*.

frost *See* **winter working** *and below*.

frosting [pai.] A translucent, finely wrinkled finish formed during *drying* of *tung* and other oils that have not been properly heat-treated. *See* **gas-checking**.

frost in houses There may be a risk of boiler explosion when the cold feed to a hot water system is blocked by ice. Water from an open reservoir or filter beds may be not much above 0° C. when delivered into the supply mains in winter. To ensure the main does not freeze, it should be covered by at least 750 mm (2 ft 6 in.) of earth. In Sweden, 2 m (6 ft 6 in.) is usual. Water mains should therefore rise into the house well inside the outer walls. Overflow pipes from roof cold water *cisterns* should have obstructions to the inward flow of cold air. One of the best ways of doing this inside the building is to put a right-angle downward bend on the entrance to the overflow pipe, submerging it in the *cistern*. This obstructs the overflow, so it may sometimes be preferable to put the bend (or a tee) at the outside end of the overflow pipe (BSCP 99). (Illus. p. 69)

froststat [plu.] An automatic control, a type of *thermostat* that turns on the heat when the *circulating water* temperature falls nearly to 0° C.

fugitive pigment [pai.] A *pigment* which fades quickly.

full coat [pai.] As thick a *coat* of *paint* or *varnish* as can be properly applied.

full gloss [pai.] The highest grade of *gloss*.

full size (1) The *tight size* of an opening for glass.

(2) Full size slates in Scotland are 36 × 20 cm (14 × 8 in.) or larger.

full-way valve, gate v. [plu.] A cock which does not impede the flow of water, essential where the water pressure is barely enough for the flow required.

fungicidal paint [pai.] A *paint* which discourages fungus even in tropical conditions. Many disinfectants can be blended with paint for this purpose.

fungus [tim.] The cause of the *decay* of wood, *dry rot* being the commonest in buildings in Britain.

furniture [joi.] *See* **door furniture**.

furred [plu.] Said of pipes, boilers, tanks, etc., which become encrusted from *hard water* heated in them. *See below*.

furring, firring (1) Lathing fixed to *common grounds* and plastered, leaving an air space between brick and plaster.

(2) (USA) A cavity within an outer wall to keep out damp and for insulation. It may be formed with lath and plaster or with *hollow blocks* or bricks.

(3) [carp.] Timber strips laid, for example, on uneven joists to pack them out, and make a plane surface for floor boards, or for the close boarding of a roof or wall.

furring strip [carp.] A *common ground*. *See* **furring**.

furrowed surface Horizontal or vertical flutings at about 1 cm (⅜ in.) centres on *ashlar*, often on a face projecting between *drafted margins*.

fuse, f. element [elec.] A small piece of wire in an electric circuit which melts when the current exceeds a certain value. It is a fire protection for the house and the wiring. If the fuse is properly designed no *short circuit* can last more than a fraction of a second. *See* **cartridge fuse**.

fuse box, f. board [elec.] A *cutout box*.

fused plug [elec.] A plug that fits into a wall *socket outlet* and contains a fuse to protect the wiring and appliance connected to it. Without 13-amp fused plugs, *ring mains* would not be possible.

fuse link [elec.] A container, generally of porcelain, which holds the *fuse* element. It can be pulled out of the *cutout box* to insert a new element.

fuse switch, s. f. [elec.] A switch containing a *fuse*. *Compare* **switch and fuse**.

fusible link A metal part which, until it melts, holds open a *fire door*. It then releases the fire door, which closes.

fusible plug [mech.] A metal plug of low melting point, screwed into the part of a boiler just above the furnace, under the water. If the water level drops below the fusible plug, this will melt and steam will blow down into the fire and put the fire out. A similar plug is used in *sprinklers* and *drenchers*.

G

gabbart scaffold (Scotland) A sturdy *scaffold* of squared timber. The *standards* are three *deals* bolted together, the middle deal being cut off at platform levels to let the *ledger* pass between the two outer deals. The ledger thus rests on the middle deal.

gable, g. end The triangular part of the end wall of a building with a sloping *roof*, between the *barge boards* or *rafters*. A gable may be of any material – weatherboards, brick, stone, hung tiles, etc. (Illus. p. 31)

gable board A *barge board*.

gable coping A coping to a gable wall which projects above the roof and is coped mainly with *kneelers*.

gable post [carp.] A short post at the apex of a *gable* into which *barge boards* are *housed*.

gable roof A roof with a *gable* at one or both ends. *See* **pitched roofs**, p. 279.

gable shoulder The projection formed by the *gable springer* at the foot of a gable coping.

gable springer, foot stone, skew block The overhanging stone at the foot of a gable coping, below the lowest *kneeler*. *See* **rubble wall** (illus. p. 282).

gable wall A wall crowned by a *gable*.

gaboon, g. mahogany, okoume [tim.] An *African mahogany* (Aucoumea klaineana).

gain [carp.] A *mortise* or notch to receive another timber or a timber *connector*.

gallery apartment house (USA) A block of flats with access at all levels from open corridors.

gallet, garnet A *spall*, a chip of rock.

gallows bracket [carp.] A triangularly-framed bracket which projects from a wall.

galvanized pipe [plu.] Galvanized steel *screwed pipe* for water.

gambrel roof (1) **half-hipped r.** A roof having a gablet near the ridge and the lower part hipped. *See* **pitched roofs** (illus. p. 279).
    (2) US term for a *mansard roof*.

gamma protein [pai.] Protein from soya bean meal, an *extender* for *casein* in water paint.

gang saw [tim.] A reciprocating mechanical saw such as a *frame saw*.

gangway A path of *scaffold boards* laid for men to walk on or to wheel barrows along.

gap-filling glue [tim.] Unlike *close-contact glue*, a gap-filling glue is strong even with a joint 1·5 mm thick (BS 1204). Sawdust mixed with close-contact glue fills gaps also.

Garchey sink A *waste-disposal unit* installed in some modern flats. All kitchen garbage can be emptied through it and dustbins are needed only for tins, bottles, and bulky waste.

garden-wall bonds Brickwork usually one *brick* thick, built to show a *fair face* each side. Since garden walls are not heavily loaded, the number of stretchers can be high. *See* **American bond, Flemish bond**.

garnet hinge [joi.] A *cross-garnet hinge*.

garnet paper *Abrasive* paper covered with finely powdered garnet.

gas-checking, gas-crazing [pai.] *Crystallizing*, webbing, crows-footing or *frost-*

ing of *paints* or *varnishes* containing vegetable *drying oils*, so called because it occurs when these oils dry in heating gas.

gas circulator [plu.] An appliance for heating water by gas, which is connected to a container for hot water, normally a *cylinder*. In warm weather, coal- or oil-fired boilers are not needed for *central heating*. An *immersion heater* or gas circulator can take the place of the boiler for supplying domestic hot water. Both are expensive to run but labour-saving.

gas concrete The lightest, weakest, most insulating *aerated concrete*. It contains no sand and is made by foaming the mixing water with cement alone.

gasket [plu.] (1) Hemp fibres wound round the threads of a screwed joint in a water pipe before it is screwed up. When wetted, the hemp expands and makes a watertight joint.

(2) **gaskin** In the jointing of socketed *vitrified clayware* pipes with cement mortar, a ring of old rope, etc., pushed into the base of the *socket* around the *spigot* before any mortar is inserted; superseded by the **sleeved joint**, etc.

(3) A permanently flexible, puttyless protection to the edge of glass, consisting of a strip of compressed foam rubber enclosing its edge. It may be held by a *glazing bead* or merely fit into a groove in the surround. Some types compress with a *zipper*. *See* **Neoprene, structural gasket**.

gas pliers Strong pliers with concave jaws for gripping gas pipe, serrated like the jaws of *footprints*.

gas proof [pai.] Description of a film which does not *gas check* in heating gas.

gate hook, gudgeon A metal bar driven by its point into a wooden post or built into a *masonry* or *brick* gate pier. It has an exposed, upstanding pin on which the *hinge* of the gate is dropped to hang the gate. *See* **band-and-hook hinge**.

gate pier A gate post of *concrete*, *brick*, or stone.

gauge (1) The proportions of different materials in a *mortar* or *plaster* mix.

(2) [pla.] To strengthen a lime mortar by adding a little *Portland cement* or *gypsum plaster*.

(3) **margin** The exposed depth of a *slate* or *tile*, that which is seen. It is the distance between the bottom edge of one row of slates or plain tiles, and the bottom edge of the next row above or below. This is the same as the distance between the centres of the *battens* or the fixing nails. *See* **lap**. The following rules apply to *sized*, not to *random* slates, nor to *single-lap tiles*.

For *centre-nailed slates*, gauge $= \dfrac{\text{length} - \text{lap}}{2}$. For plain tiles or *head-nailed* slates, gauge (cm) $= \dfrac{\text{length} - \text{lap} - 2 \text{ cm}}{2}$, nailing 2 cm from the head.

(4) A wooden or metal boundary strip used in asphalting to show the correct thickness of asphalt, like a *screed* in plastering.

(5) [joi.] *See* **mortise gauge**.

(6) *See below*.

gauge board (1) **spot b., mortar b.** [pla.] A board about 90 cm (3 ft) square for carrying *plaster* and tools. It is usually placed on a stand about 68 cm (27 in.) high. *See also* **gauging board**.

(2) [carp.] A *pitch board*.

gauge box A *batch box*.

gauged arch An arch built from *gauged bricks*, that is, soft bricks sawn to shape or rubbed smooth on a stone or another brick. They are laid with very fine joints, often of *lime mortar* without cement or sand (pure *lime putty*), which may be 3 mm ($\frac{1}{8}$ in.) thick or even less.

gauged bricks, rubbed brickwork Brickwork like that used for a *gauged arch*. It was in fashion in England from 1650 to 1750 and in Colonial Virginia, then sporadically in fine Victorian buildings but even more rarely in the present century.

gauged mortar Cement-lime *mortar*. *See below*.

gauged stuff, g. plaster, putty and plaster [pla.] *Lime putty*, usually for the finishing coat of interior *cornices, ceilings* and *mouldings*, to which either *gypsum plaster* or cement has been added to hasten the set. Gypsum plaster counteracts shrinkage but cement shrinks.

gauge pot Container for pouring liquid *grout* (C).

gauge rod A *storey rod*.

gauging (1) [pla.] Adding *Portland cement* or *gypsum plaster* to a mix to hasten its set.

(2) [carp.] Marking timber with a *mortise gauge* or *marking gauge*.

(3) Sawing and rubbing bricks to size and shape for *gauged brickwork*.

gauging board A *banker* for mixing mortar, plaster, etc.

gauging box A *batch box*.

gauging plaster *Plaster of Paris* or other *gypsum plaster*.

gauging trowel *See* **plasterer's tools** (illus. p. 246).

gaul [pla.] A hollow in a *finishing coat* caused by bad trowelling.

G-cramp [joi.] A steel, G-shaped screw *cramp* used by *joiners* when gluing wood.

gelling [pai.] Conversion of liquid to jelly. *See* **feeding**.

general contractor A *main contractor*.

general foreman The *main contractor*'s representative on a site, in charge of all labour under the *agent*. He coordinates the work of trades *foremen*, whether employed by the main contractor or by a *sub-contractor*. He has usually graduated from a trade and been a trade foreman. *Compare* **ganger** (*C*).

geometric stair A stair which in plan may be circular, semi-circular or elliptical. It has no newel posts and often no landings between floors.

Georgian glass A *wired glass*.

German siding, novelty s. [carp.] *Weather-boards* concavely rounded on the top edge and rebated on the inner face of the bottom edge.

gesso [pai.] A brilliant white composition of *whiting* and *glue*, or *plaster of Paris* and *size*, or of other materials, used as a background for painted designs on wood or plaster, sometimes in relief.

gib [carp.] An iron or steel packing piece which clasps together the parts of a *cottered joint*, passing through a hole in the *king post*. It is wedged tight with steel wedges, the *cotters*.

gig stick [pla.] A *radius rod*.

gimlet [carp.] A small tool with a wooden handle at right angles to the point, used for boring holes smaller than 6 mm ($\frac{1}{4}$ in.) dia. in wood. It was used by the ancient Greeks. *Compare* **awl**.

gimlet point [joi.] A description of the point of wood *screws* or *coach screws* which are intended to form at least part of their own hole and to grip the wood at their point.

gin A tripod and *gin block* or other simple *lifting tackle* (*C*).

gin block, g. wheel, jinnie wheel, rubbish pulley A single pulley for fibre rope, carried in a steel frame with a hook at the top from which it can be hung.

girder casing Material which covers and so protects from fire that part of a steel *girder* (*C*) that is below ceiling level. It may be of concrete, brick, terra cotta, etc. *See also* **formwork** (*C*).

girt [carp.] A *rail* or intermediate beam in wooden-framed buildings, often carrying floor *joists*, a small girder. *See below.*

girth, girt [tim.] The circumference of a round timber, measured by tape. Timber is paid for at a price per m^3 (ft^3) calculated from the *quarter-girth*.

girt strip [carp.] A *ribbon board*.

gland (1) [plu.] **olive** A compressible copper or brass ring which in *non-manipulative joints* is slipped over the copper tube and under the screwed fitting. When the fitting is tightened, the soft metal of the gland is compressed and deformed, thus sealing the gap between the tube and the fitting.

(2) [elec.] A seal used at the end of a cable to prevent water entering. A similar gland is used at water taps and stop valves to prevent leakage outwards.

gland joint A joint on a copper hot-water or soil pipe which allows temperature movement.

glass *See* **anti-sun g., float g., obscured g., safety g.**

glass blocks, g. bricks Hollow translucent blocks of glass obscured by patterns moulded on one or both faces. When used as *partitions* they give a pleasant diffused light, but they have low heat insulation value and low *fire resistance*, though they are non-combustible. In pavement lights solid glass is used.

glass-concrete construction (1) Reinforced concrete *pavement lights* or floor or roof slabs with glass lenses cast in.

(2) Walls with loadbearing concrete *mullions* between which hollow *glass blocks* are built in.

glass cutter A tool for cutting glass, either by a diamond or by a hard, sharp, metal wheel.

glassed surface *See* **polished work.**

glassfibre-reinforced concrete *See* **glass-reinforced cement.**

glassfibre-reinforced polyester (GRP) *Cladding panels*, church spires, gargoyles, roof trim, window sills and frames have been made of GRP and are likely to have at least 30 years' life when properly made (BRE Digest 69). Caravan roofs, boat hulls, large pipes, sports car bodies and corrugated roofing sheet also can be made of it. As a translucent shell roof it has spanned 15 m (49 ft). Cladding panels vary in thickness from 3 to 6 mm ($\frac{1}{8}$ to $\frac{1}{4}$ in.) and weigh from 5 to 10 kg/m^2 (1 to 2 lb/ft^2). Extra thickness needed at edges and fixing points may double these figures. If insulation against heat and sound and for fire resistance is added, the weight may rise to 40–60 kg/m^2 (8 to 12 lb/ft^2) (BRE Digest 161).

glassfibre-reinforced resins Many substances other than polyesters are reinforced with glassfibre, in particular the two-part resin tubes sold for car repairs, that harden in 15 minutes. These are very useful even without the glassfibre, for repairing holes in pipes that are impossible to mend with hot metal, such as rainwater gutters at eaves 6 metres (20 ft) above ground.

glasspaper, sandpaper, garnet paper, emery cloth *Abrasive* paper made from glass, flint, garnet, corundum, or similar powders glued to cloth or paper. About fifteen different finenesses exist. Some types can be used wet and thus produce no harmful dust.

glass-reinforced cement, glassfibre-reinforced concrete, GRC Factory-made, precast or spray-moulded units reinforced with alkali-resistant glassfibre (Cem-FIL). The products are only 10 to 15 mm ($\frac{3}{8}$ to $\frac{5}{8}$ in.) thick and include *cladding panels*, sewer pipes and linings, cable ducts, and street furniture but are not approved for structural use in the damp climates of Europe (Fibreglass Ltd, St Helens).

glass silk, g. wool Fire-resisting, flexible fibre made from molten glass and used as an *insulator* for heat and sound, obtainable as *blanket* between waterproof papers, or resin-bonded or bitumen-bonded or loose. *Compare* **mineral wool**.

glass size The *glazing size*.

glass slate, g. tile A piece of glass made to the same size as a *slate* or *tile* and laid among the slates or tiles to give light to an attic. Several glass slates must be used together if any light is to be let in. Apart from glass some translucent plastics are allowed: unplasticized PVC, *polyester resin* with glassfibre reinforcement (both stabilized against ultra-violet light), or acrylic material. For roof coverings in towns, fire hazard must be carefully considered, and some plastics have poor fire resistance.

glass stop (1) A device at the lower end of a *patent glazing* bar to prevent panes sliding down.

(2) A *glazing fillet*.

glass substitutes *Perspex, cellulose acetate butyrate, polycarbonate, polystyrene,* and vinyl polymers are common glass substitutes, all of which break less easily than glass and weigh less than half as much but expand with heat ten times as much. They therefore need more clearance and more flexible fixing. Polycarbonate is the strongest and most expensive. The others are roughly comparable in price with glass but softer and so more easily scratched and less easily cleaned.

glaze (1) To instal glass in any outside *light. Compare* **fixing**.

(2) A glass-like waterproof protection fired on to the surface of pottery, bricks, walls, and occasionally, roofing tiles. It may be transparent, coloured, or white.

glaze coat [pai.] A nearly-transparent, thin, coloured *coat* put on to enhance the colour below. The process of putting on the coat is called glazing.

glazed tile Earthenware *wall tiles* mainly for interior use, obtainable with a cream or white earthenware glaze or an *enamel* glaze of many possible colours. All glazed wall tiles craze, particularly where the temperature is variable. The only tiles which do not craze are unglazed tiles such as *quarry tiles*.

glazed ware, g. stoneware Common but outdated terms for *vitrified clayware*, a survival from the time when the best clayware was glazed by the vapour of common salt thrown into the kiln during firing.

glazier A *tradesman* who cuts glass and fixes it in a window or door frame with putty and *glazing sprigs* or spring-clips or *glazing beads* of wood, metal, or plastics. He also removes old putty.

glazier's chisel A glazier's *putty knife* shaped like a chisel.

glazier's putty, painter's p. A plastic material used for bedding glass in wooden *lights* and for making a weatherproof fillet of *face putty* outside the glass, holding it to the frame. It is made of *whiting* mixed with *linseed oil*. Linseed-oil putty usually needs to be 48 hours old before it is hard enough to take oil paint but, within 21 days, it should be painted to protect it. Most *hard stoppings* shrink very much less than putty. *See* **glazing compound**.

glazing (1) To fit glass or other transparent sheet into *lights*. *See above and below*; *also* **fixing, patent glazing**. *See* B S C P 153, B S 6262.
   (2) [pai.] *See* **glaze coat**.

glazing bar, sash b., astragal A T-shaped bar of wood or metal to hold glass and subdivide a window. Some windows are not subdivided, have no glazing bars and let in more light but their glass is more expensive, because it must be thicker. (Illus. above)

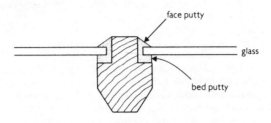

face putty

glass

bed putty

Glazing bar.

glazing bead The usual term, though deprecated by B S 565, for a *glazing fillet*.

glazing block, location b., setting b., distance piece A piece of lead, wood, unplasticized P V C or similar material some 75 mm (3 in.) long, of the thickness of the glass, under, above, or beside a large piece of glass or double-glazed unit (larger than 0·2 m^2 or 2 ft^2) to centralize it in the frame.

glazing compound Substances that hold glass, like *glazier's putty, metal-casement putty, non-setting glazing compound*, or pre-formed solid strips. *See* **gasket**.

glazing fillet, g. bead, glass stop A wooden metal, or plastics strip, often *quarter round*, with holes drilled through it for screwing to the rebate in a glazing bar, that replaces *face putty* over glass. In a door the glass may be bedded in wash leather. In the best work, hardwood is used, with mitred corners. (Fillet is also a term used for face putty.) A neat job is quickly done in re-glazing because old putty does not have to be hacked out. See **patent glazing**.

glazing size, glass size The size of a piece of glass cut for *glazing*. The clearance between glass and window should be 1·5 mm ($\frac{1}{16}$ in.) all round. The glass size both ways should thus be 3 mm ($\frac{1}{8}$ in.) less than the distance between the extreme edges of rebates in window bars, or *tight size*. Glass measurements should be stated as length times height. For double-glazed units the space all round should be increased to 3 mm, thus the glass size should be 6 mm less both ways than the rebate size.

glazing sprig, glazier's point, brad A small headless *nail* buried in the *face putty* round a pane of glass to hold it while the face putty is hardening.

gloss [pai.] The reflection of light by a painted surface. The stages of gloss in *finish* recognized by the British Standards Institution are:
   (1) flat (or matt), practically without *sheen*, even from oblique angles.
   (2) eggshell flat.
   (3) eggshell gloss.
   (4) semi-gloss.
   (5) full gloss, that is, a smooth, almost mirror-like (specular) gloss from any angle.

glossing up [pai.] The defect of a *gloss* which develops on a matt surface when it is handled.

glue, adhesive [tim.] *Animal glue* for sticking wood has been known for centuries and is still used indoors but for outside gluing it has been superseded by the *synthetic resins*. B S 5442 lists 20 types of glue for sticking wood to wood, 12 types for the 26 floor finishes it lists, and 18 glues for the 29 wall or ceiling surfacings. A glue should be compatible with any preservative or fire-retardant used on the timber. *See also* **colloids, gap-filling glue, vegetable glue**.

glue block [carp.] An *angle block*.

glue line [tim.] The thin surface of *glue* between two parts.

glue spread [tim.] *See* **spreading rate**.

glu-lam [tim.] *Laminated wood* used structurally, e.g. to build a roof *truss*.

glycerin, glycerine, glycerol [pai.] An alcohol which, like other alcohols, mixes in all proportions with water and is used in preparing *synthetic* and natural *resins* for *paints* and *varnishes*.

going The horizontal distance between two successive *nosings* is the going of a *tread*. The sum of the goings of the treads is the going of the *flight* (p. 142).

going rod A rod for setting out the *going* of a *flight* of *stairs*. Compare **storey rod**.

gold bronze [pai.] A copper or copper alloy powder for *bronzing*.

gold size [pai.] Two types of gold size exist, both *oleo-resinous varnishes*. One dries quickly to the tacky state and remains tacky for some time, which helps for sticking down gold leaf. The other has more *driers*, hardens quickly and is used in *fillers*.

gold stoving varnish [pai.] A transparent *varnish* which forms a yellow film on tinplate or other silvery surfaces, either by means of a dye or by discoloration of the film during *stoving*.

gore A *lune* for covering a dome.

gouge (1) [joi.] A chisel with a curved cutting edge for hollowing out wood, more used by carvers than *joiners*. Carving gouges are very numerous. Joiner's or turner's gouges are less varied and are generally curved like part of a cylinder, except for the *parting tool*.

(2) A *mason*'s tool for carving stone. It may be wooden-handled and struck with the *dummy*, or all-steel and struck with the mallet.

gouge bit [carp.] A drilling bit with a rounded end.

gouge slip, slipstone [carp.] An *oilstone slip*.

graduated courses *Diminishing courses*.

graffito, sgraffito, scratch work [pla.] A *plaster* surface decorated by scoring a

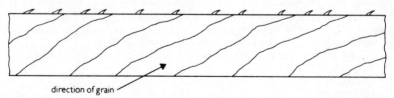

direction of grain

Grain of wood. This rough surface, planed to the left, would have been smooth if planed to the right.

pattern on it while it is soft, and exposing a lower coat of a different colour. The upper layer is often white, the lower layer black or dark red. More than two colours can be used if required.

grain [tim.] The general direction, size, and arrangement of the fibres and other elements in wood. (Illus. p. 160) *See* **figure**.

grainer [pai.] A painter who can paint wood or stone to imitate wood *grain* and knot marks, marble veins, and so on.

graining [pai.] Painting a surface to look like the *grain* of wood or marble, etc., by manipulating a wet coat of semi-transparent 'graining colour' with graining combs, brush, rags, and other implements.

granitic finish A *face mix*, resembling granite, on precast concrete.

grano, granolithic screed A *jointless floor* of cement, sand and granite chippings, floated over a concrete floor, preferably as a *monolithic screed*, to create a smooth, hard-wearing surface. Emery or Carborundum powder (1 kg/m^2 or 3 oz/ft^2) scattered over the wet surface should make it non-slipping.

granulated cork *See* **cork, corkboard**.

gravel board, g. plank A horizontal board fixed to the underside of a *close-boarded fence* to prevent the vertical boards from reaching the ground. It is more easily replaced than a vertical board and less easily rotted than the end grain of the vertical boards.

gravity circulation of hot water [plu.] A system which circulates water by *convection* from the boiler to the hot water system upstairs and back again. It works only because of the temperature and density differences between the water in the *flow* and the *return pipes*. Most systems which supply hot water only without *central heating* are of this type. No pump is needed but the boiler should be as low in the house as possible to achieve a good circulation. It is unusual in heating circuits, which are usually pumped (pp. 64, 179).

greasiness [pai.] A greasy surface on a paint film, caused by lack of *compatibility*.

green (1) *See* **green concrete**.

(2) [tim.] A description of unseasoned timber, which, unless otherwise specified, can be taken to be of 50% *moisture content*.

green concrete, g. mortar Concrete or cement mortar after its initial set and before it has begun to harden properly, when it has a dark green colour. It remains green up to about seven days or more in cold weather, less in hot weather.

greenheart [tim.] (Ocotea rodiaei) A hardwood from Guyana which is remarkable for its very high stiffness. It is used for docks, piles, and similar structures where high strength is more important than low cost of timber and labour. *Compare* **Douglas fir**.

grid plan A plan in which setting-out lines called grid lines coincide with the most important walls and other *building components*. Prefabricated buildings may be set out on a grid plan. *Compare* **planning grid**.

grillage A metal frame carrying *slates, shingles,* or *tiles,* and replacing slating battens. The horizontal bars can be set at the gauge of the tiles, slates or shingles. *See also* (*C*).

grille (1) An open, often decorative screen of metal or wood.

(2) A grating or screen through which air passes usually into (rather than from) a ventilating duct. A grille has no damper and connects to a return air duct, unlike a *register*.

161

grinder [mech.] An *abrasive* wheel turned by hand or by electric motor, used for sharpening tools and removing metal from other surfaces. *See* **grindstone**.

grinding slip [joi.] An *oilstone slip*.

grindstone [carp.] An *abrasive* wheel of natural sandstone which is turned at a low speed, often by hand or treadle, so as to enable a *carpenter* or *joiner* to sharpen his edge tools. Electrically driven, fast-turning grinders have the disadvantage that they heat the tools and may thus spoil the *temper (C)* of the steel.

grinning through The showing through plaster of lathing beneath, or the showing of a lower coat of paint through a top coat. *See* **pattern staining**.

groin The curved line at which the *soffits* of two *vaults* are seen to intersect. For **groyne** *see C*.

grommet, grummet [plu.] A hemp washer soaked in jointing compound and fitted between the back nut and the socket of a *connector* to make a tight joint. Many other grommets exist.

gross features [tim.] In considering the stress to which a timber part may be subjected, gross features are *knots, wane, slope of grain, shakes, checks, splits,* each of which is defined in B S C P 112. *Rate of growth* is also limited. *See* **stress-graded timber**.

ground (1) [carp.] A *common ground* or framed ground.

(2) [elec.] (U S A) *Earth* or earth connection.

(3) Any surface which is or will be painted, tiled or plastered, or the first of several coats of paint or plaster. *See* **ground coat**.

ground brush [pai.] A wire- or string-bound paint *brush*, round or oval in section, used for painting large areas (grounds). *See* **house painter**, p. 180.

ground coat [pai.] An opaque coat put on under a *glaze coat* or *scumble*.

grounded work [joi.] *Joinery* fixed to grounds.

ground floor The floor which is nearest the ground, generally about 30 cm (1 ft) above ground level. *See* **first floor**.

ground plan A *plan* of the ground floor of a building. It may also show the foundations.

ground plate, sole p. [carp.] The lowest horizontal timber of a wooden building frame.

grounds [carp.] *Common grounds* or *framed grounds*.

ground sill [carp.] A *sole plate*.

ground storey The part of a building between *ground floor* and *first floor*.

growth ring [tim.] Usually the same as an *annual ring*, though it is possible in a year of exceptional weather for two growth rings to occur.

G R P *Glassfibre-reinforced polyester* (or plastics).

grub screw, set s. [joi.] A short *screw* fitted into threads on the metal part of a door handle to grip the spindle tightly. It has a slotted head small enough to pass into the hole on the handle and thus should not scratch the finger if properly fitted.

guard bead, guide b. [joi.] A *sash stop*.

guard board A *toe board*.

gudgeon (1) A metal dowel for locking neighbouring stones together.

(2) A *gate hook*.

guide coat [pai.] A very thin *coat* of loosely bound paint applied over a *surfacer* before it is rubbed down. It is removed during rubbing, but guides the person doing the rubbing, showing him the high places.

guillotine [joi.] A *trimming machine*.

gullet [joi.] The gap between the teeth of a file or saw; also the length of a *saw-tooth* from point to root.

gum arabic [pai.] A fine, white powder obtained from certain acacia trees, used in making transparent paints.

gummy [pai.] Sticky, of a paint that causes *drag* because the *solvent* evaporates fast or because of cold weather, etc. *Compare* **slip**.

gum vein [tim.] Local accumulation of *resin* as a streak in some hardwoods.

gunstock stile [joi.] A *diminishing stile*.

gusset piece In *flexible-metal roofing*, a piece of metal soldered over an external corner between a roof sheet and two intersecting upright surfaces. *See* **dog ear**.

gusset plate [tim.] A piece of strong *plywood* nailed or screwed, sometimes also glued to the ends of two or more timbers in a *trussed rafter* or other timber *truss* instead of a timber *connector*. (Illus. below) *See also* C.

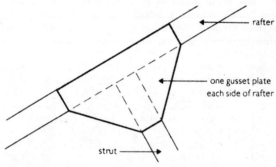

Plywood gusset plates at a joint in a timber roof truss.

gutter A channel along the edge of a road or an *eave*, to remove rainwater. *Eaves gutters* may be of cast iron, pressed steel, concrete, plastics, etc. *Valley gutters* can occur where two roof slopes meet. *See* **box gutter**.

gutter bearers [carp.] (1) Short 5 × 5 cm (2 × 2 in.) timbers under a *box gutter* which carry the *layer boards*.

(2) Timber bearers each side of a *box gutter*, carrying *snow boards*.

gutter bed A *flexible-metal sheet* laid over the *tilting fillet* behind an *eaves gutter* to prevent overflow from entering the wall.

gutter board A *gutter bearer*.

gutter plate [carp.] (1) A wall plate below a *flexible-metal* gutter.

(2) A side of a valley gutter. It is lined with flexible metal and carries the feet of the rafters. *Compare* **pole plate**.

gymnosperm [tim.] Trees with naked seeds, that is conifers (fir, pine, yew), called *softwoods*, though some may be very hard.

gypsum CaSO$_4$.2H$_2$O The raw material for *gypsum plasters*, also the final stage of these plasters when they have set. It is an *extender* in *water paints* or *distempers*, rarely in *oil paints* because it is slightly soluble in oil and not very opaque.

gypsum baseboard [pla.] Square-edged *gypsum plasterboard* which is made for plastering with gypsum or anhydrite plaster after *scrimming*.

gypsum lath [pla.] *Gypsum plasterboard* in relatively small sheets, nailed to a wall or ceiling for plastering. It is usually plastered two coats, like *fibre board*, gypsum wallboard, or base board. The first coat is a mix of 1 volume of *gypsum plaster* with 1½ of sand, the finishing coat being any neat gypsum or retarded *hemihydrate plaster* gauged with lime.

gypsum plank (USA **board lath**) [pla.] *Gypsum plasterboard* thicker than 13 mm (0·5 in.), and not wider than 600 mm (2 ft), with a surface to take plaster.

gypsum plaster [pla.] Many plasters made from *gypsum* by heating it to drive off water, for example, anhydrous gypsum plaster ($CaSO_4$), *Keene's* ($CaSO_4$ with borax or alum as an *accelerator*), *plaster of Paris* ($CaSO_4.\frac{1}{2}H_2O$), and retarded *hemihydrate plaster*. Unlike cement, they expand on setting and therefore do not crack unless there are faults in the backing. They must never be mixed with *Portland* cement.

gypsum plasterboard [pla.] *Building board* made of a core of *gypsum* or *anhydrite* plaster, usually enclosed between two sheets of heavy paper. It includes *gypsum baseboard*, lath and plank, *gypsum wallboard, insulating plaster-*

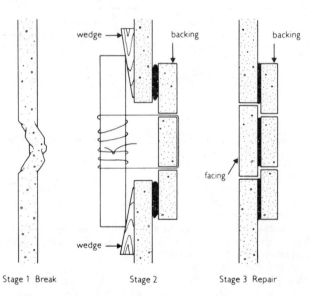

Stage 1 Break   Stage 2   Stage 3 Repair

Gypsum plasterboard, repairing a break.
1. Saw a neat rectangle around the break.
2. Insert a backing piece of plaster or wood, anchored with a piece of wire or string through it. Glue it in place with plaster or glue.
3. Cut a facing piece to the shape of the hole and glue it to the backing with plaster. Sandpaper the edges and fill gaps with plaster joint filler.
Acknowledgements to British Gypsum Ltd.

board, tapered edge plasterboard, etc. All types are now of aerated plaster, which has slightly better thermal insulation and is less heavy than dense plaster. Straight-line cuts in plasterboard are made either by sawing with a fine-tooth saw, or in the same way as glass is cut, by scoring both surfaces along exactly the same line. The scored line is then placed over a sharp straight edge and the board is snapped. Apart from being mainly non-combustible, any gypsum plasterboard has good fire resistance because of the cooling effect of the steam driven out of it when it is heated (BS 1230, 5492). (Illus. below)

gypsum wallboard Gypsum plasterboard with its *face* self-finished or designed to be decorated directly. (Illus. below) *See* **wallboard**.

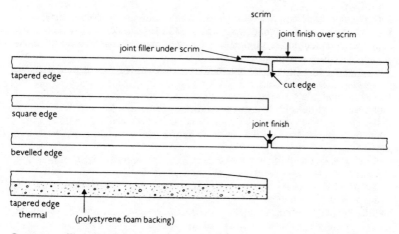

Gypsum wallboards, common types, and some jointing possibilities as dry lining. Acknowledgements to British Gypsum Ltd.

H

hacking (1) A course of *rubble walling* composed of stones alternately one and two to the height of the course.

(2) (USA) Laying bricks in such a way that the bottom edge of each course is set in from the line of the course below.

(3) Roughening a surface to make plaster or *rendering* stick.

hacking knife A knife with which old *putty* is removed from a *light* before reglazing it. *See* **house painter** (illus. p. 180).

hacksaw A handsaw or mechanical saw for cutting metal, consisting of a steel blade stretched tight in a frame. The blade is replaceable and wears out quickly by breakage of the teeth, which must be hard and are therefore brittle.

haft The handle of a light tool such as a knife or an awl. *Compare* **helve**.

hair [pla.] Bullocks' or goats' hair was used in lime undercoats (*coarse stuff*) as reinforcement in the proportion of 1 kg of hair to 120–180 litres of coarse stuff to reduce cracking.

hair cracking [pai.] Fine, erratic, random cracks which do not penetrate the top coat.

haired mortar [pla.] *Mortar* containing fibres.

half bat, snap header A half-brick, cut in two across the length.

half-bed [q.s.] The *labour* of laying a stone on its bed is called a half-bed since the *bed-joint* is thus laid for the stone above. *See* **half-plain work, half-sawn stone**.

half-brick wall A wall the width of a brick, entirely built of *stretchers*, therefore in Britain, 10·2 cm (4 in.) thick in standard bricks.

half-hatchet (USA) A *carpenter*'s hatchet with a notch for drawing nails, like a plasterer's *lath hammer*.

half-landing (1) **landing** A platform intermediate between two floors of a building, and joined to them by *flights* of stairs.

(2) A *half-space landing*.

half-lap joint [carp.] A joint formed by *halving*.

half-plain work [q.s.] The *labour* of laying *ashlar*.

half rip-saw [carp.] A *rip-saw* with closer teeth than the usual rip-saw.

half-round Semicircular, such as a semicircular drainage channel, or *ridge tile*, or a file flat on one face, curved on the other.

half-round veneer [tim.] *Veneer* cut on a lathe from a *flitch* which is roughly semicircular. The figure is intermediate in character between *sliced* and *rotary veneer*, since the cut radius can be made very large and the curvature very flat. The curve of the face of the flitch from which the veneers are cut may therefore be much less than a half-circle. *See* **stay log**.

half-sawn stone [q.s.] Stone which has been sawn only, the term half being used because half of the sawing cost is charged to the stones each side of the cut. *See* **half-bed**.

half-space landing [joi.] A landing of width equal to two *flights*, at which there is an angle of 180° between flights (BS 565). *Compare* **quarter-space landing**.

half-timber A piece of timber measuring not less than 13 × 25 cm (5 × 10 in.) in cross section, made by halving a baulk along its length.

halving [carp.] A general way of forming an *angle joint*, or occasionally a *lengthening joint*, between two timbers of the same thickness. One half of

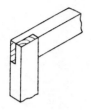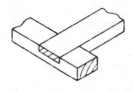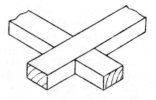

Halved joints, various types.

each is cut away, the cut surfaces placed together, and the result is a joint in which the outer faces are flush. *See* **dovetail halving, end-lap joint, lap joint, splice**, *and* illus. above.

hammer A steel tool (the head) with a central eye to which a handle is fixed at right angles. One end of the head has a flat, hardened face for driving nails. Its other end, the *peen*, may be hemispherical or wedge shaped. *See also* **claw, club, engineer's, joiner's, lath hammer**.

hammer-dressed stone, hammer-faced s. Stone which has been only roughly faced, that is with the hammer at the quarry.

hammer finish (1) [pai.] A *finish* like hammered metal, produced by coloured *enamels* containing metal powder applied with a spray gun.

(2) *See* **hammering**.

hammer-headed chisel Any *mason's* chisel with a flat conical steel head, which is struck by a hammer and not by a mallet. *Compare* **mallet-headed chisel**.

hammer-headed key (1) A *double-dovetail key*.

(2) A stone *cramp* like a *slate cramp* for locking stones together.

hammering Bending sheet metal such as copper into decorative shapes with a hammer. *Compare* **bossing**.

hammer pitching, h. pinching Working the surface of *pitch-faced stone*.

hand (of doors) [joi.] The hand (right or left) of doors and windows is important when hinges and some door springs, latches or rim locks are ordered, but mortise locks, butt hinges, H-hinges, and some others are not handed. In Britain a door is right-hand hung if the hinges are on the right of a person opening the door towards himself, but its rising butts or lift-off hinges would be left hand. American terminology is different, but both in Britain and USA a right-hand lock fits a right-hand hung door, a right-hand screw tightens clockwise, and a right-hand stair has the handrail on the right going up.

hand brace [carp.] A carpenter's *brace*. *Compare* **hand drill**.

hand drill [mech.] A small boring tool usually of 8 mm (5/16 in.) or smaller capacity, like the *breast drill* but lighter and lacking its upward extension. It is more suitable for drilling in confined spaces or for drilling metal than is the carpenter's *brace*.

handed A description of building parts, including *joinery*, which match each other as an object matches its image in a mirror. Handed objects form a matching *pair*, one left-handed, the other right-handed. *See* **hand (of doors)**.

hand electric tools *Circular saws*, drills, *grinders*, *sanders*, rotary planers, etc. on a building site should for safety be supplied by a transformer at 110 volts.

hand float, straight-grained f., skimming f. [pla.] A wooden tool for laying on the *finishing coat* of plaster. It measures about 30 × 10 × 1 cm (12 × 4 × ⅜ in.), the *grain* being parallel to the length.

handrail, guard r. [joi.] A rail forming the top of a *balustrade* on a balcony, a bridge, stair, etc.

handrail bolt, joint b. [joi.] A bolt threaded at both ends to bring two ends of a handrail together. A square nut at one end is gripped in a *mortise* in an end of one handrail. In the other handrail, a similar mortise is provided, but the nut is circular and notched. This nut can be tightened by striking the notches with a *handrail punch* inserted into the mortise from beneath the handrail.

handrail punch [joi.] A small tool inserted into a *mortise* under a wooden handrail to tighten a nut on a *handrail bolt*.

handrail screw [joi.] Either a *dowel screw* or a *handrail bolt*.

handrail scroll [joi.] A spiral ending to a handrail.

hand rotary electric planer [joi.] An electrically driven planing machine, held and handled like a bench *plane*, except that no force is required, and the cutting is done by the adzing action of a *cutter block*. Planing is therefore quick and relatively effortless. A 1-hp motor is needed for a 63 mm (2½ in.) wide cutter.

handsaw [carp.] Any joiner's or carpenter's saw held in the hand, such as a *rip saw*, *cross-cut*, or *tenon saw*, not a power-operated saw. *See* **setting**, p. 298.

handscrew, screw clamp [joi.] A *cramp*, generally with wooden jaws and screws.

hang [joi.] To fit a door or a window to a building by its hinges.

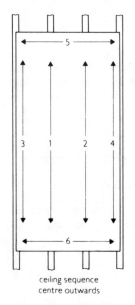

Spacing 100mm (4 in.)
along the perimeter and
200mm (8 in.) elsewhere.

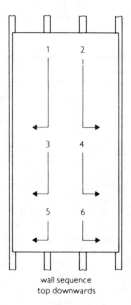

ceiling sequence
centre outwards

wall sequence
top downwards

Hardboard nailing sequences.

hangar A building which shelters aircraft.

hanger Generally a steel member from which other parts are hung, such as a vertical steel bar carrying the weight of the *walings* (C) in a deep excavation; also a *stirrup strap*.

hanging gutter (USA) An *eaves gutter* fastened to *rafter* ends or to a *fascia*.

hanging post, hingeing p. The post from which a door or gate hangs.

hanging sash [joi.] A *sash window*.

hanging shingling, weather s., vertical s. *Shingles* fixed to steep slopes.

hanging stile [joi.] The *stile* carrying the hinges of a door or casement.

hardboard *Fibreboard* formed under pressure to a density of 480 to 800 kg/m^3 (30 to 50 lb/ft^3) is medium hardboard. Standard hardboard is denser, and tempered hardboard is both denser, more than 960 kg/m^3 (60 lb/ft^3) and more resistant to water. Most hardboards have one smooth and one textured face. Sometimes the smooth face is covered with plastics, metal or wood veneer or embossed with a pattern to represent wood, leather, etc. It is usually 3 mm ($\frac{1}{8}$ in.) thick but boards are made in thicknesses up to 12·7 mm ($\frac{1}{2}$ in.). (Illus. p. 168)

hard-burnt (1) A description of a burnt clay *brick*, *tile*, etc., which has been burnt at high temperature, giving high compressive strength and durability and low *absorption*.

(2) [pla.] Usually also a hard plaster, this type of *gypsum plaster* has been heated to a higher temperature than *plaster of Paris* or *retarded hemihydrate plaster*. It reacts more slowly with water, enabling a dead-flat surface to be perfected by the plasterer. *Keene's* is one type.

hard dry [pai.] A stage in the drying of a paint film when it is nearly free from tackiness and is dried throughout its depth. It can therefore be flatted or another coat can be safely applied.

hardener (1) An *accelerator* for a *synthetic resin*.

(2) [pla.] A material used to harden plaster casts or gelatine moulds, such as alum, dextrine or polyvinyl acetate.

(3) **surface h.** A solution in water of sodium silicate, zinc silico-fluoride, etc., applied to a concrete floor to strengthen it and so reduce *dusting*. A hardener cannot hold together a poor concrete but may improve a good one. *See* **levelling compound**.

hard finish [pla.] A smooth *finishing coat* containing *gypsum plaster*. *See* **hard plaster**.

hard gloss paint [pai.] A popular *oil paint* like *enamel*. It obtains its hard glossy finish from *resin* in the oil *medium* (like varnish). It is hard by comparison with *oil gloss paint*.

hard plaster [pla.] Plasters resist knocks in the following order, the hardest first: (1) cement and sand mixes, (2) plasters like *Keene's*, (3) retarded *hemihydrate plasters*, (4) *gauged* lime plasters. Generally the greater the lime content the softer is the plaster. Soft plaster has better sound *absorption*, does not show *condensation* so badly, and has a texture which many architects prefer to that of hard plaster. Hard plaster generally means a *hard finish*.

hard plating Low-cost *chromium plating*.

hard solder [plu.] *Solder* containing copper, which therefore melts at a higher temperature than *soft solder*. *See* **brazing**.

hard stopper, stopping [pai.] Stiff paste for filling deep holes, wide cracks, etc., that may be of the same composition as *filler*. Both are sold also as powder for mixing with water or oil. Modern *two-pack* materials for repairing car bodies are excellent stoppers for deep holes.

hardware Originally builders' iron and steel supplies, now also non-ferrous metal and plastics parts. This vast subject is covered by B S 3827, glossary of builders' hardware, in 50 pages of definitions. *See* **finish hardware**.

hard water Water containing calcium or magnesium salts in solution which react with soap and thus prevent a lather forming easily in the water. When hard water is heated, its salts are deposited in pipes, boilers, or channels, which become *furred* up. *See* **water softener**.

hardwoods [tim.] Wood from broad-leaved, usually *deciduous trees*, botanically *angiosperms*. Not all hardwoods are hard though most British ones are. *See* **softwood, timbers**.

hardwood strip floor *See* **parquet-floor layer**.

harl (Scotland) *Rough cast*.

hasp [joi.] A hinged, slotted arm or plate. *See* **hasp and staple**.

hasp and staple [joi.] A fixing for doors, gates, or box lids, in which the *hasp* is locked over a *staple* by a padlock or peg which passes through the staple.

hatchet [carp.] A small axe for dressing timber, held in one hand. Some, like the plasterer's *lath hammer*, are called hammers.

haunch, hauncheon [joi.] In a *tenon* made the full width of the wood from which it projects, but narrowed near the point, the wide part near the root is called the haunch. *See* **haunched tenon**, *also C*.

haunched tenon [joi.] A *tenon* which is narrower at the tip than at the root. *See* **haunch**.

haunching (1) Concrete round the sides of a buried *stoneware* pipe to support it above the bedding concrete.

(2) [joi.] A *mortise* for a *haunched tenon*.

hawk, mortar board [pla.] A small pinewood square about 30 × 30 × 2 cm (12 × 12 × ¾ in.), with a handle below, for carrying *mortar, stopper*, etc. *Light alloy* hawks are also made. *See* **mason's and bricklayer's tools**, p. 211.

hay band A straw rope left inside the cavity of a *cavity wall* to collect mortar droppings. *See* **cavity inspection**.

haydite (U S A) *Expanded clay*, a *lightweight aggregate*. *See* **perlite**.

head The upper horizontal member of a door frame, window frame, *sub-frame, partition* frame, etc. It is also the larger end of a bolt or hammer or the upper end of a slate, rainwater pipe, etc.

head block [carp.] A block bolted to the end of a timber tie to take the thrust of a *rafter*. It may also be keyed into the tie.

head board A board carried on the head of the *bricklayer's labourer* in the north of England, and used by him instead of a *hod* for carrying mortar. *See also C*.

head casing [joi.] (U S A) The part of the *architrave* outside and over a door. It may be topped by a *weathering*.

header (1) A *brick* laid across a wall to *bond* together the different parts of a wall, and, by extension, the exposed end of a brick.

(2) **h. joist** [carp.] (U S A) A *trimmer joist* in floors or walls of *frame construction*. For the confusion between American and British senses *see* **trimmer**.

head flashing A *flashing* like a small *gutter* round the edge of a projection through a roof.

170

head guard A *cavity flashing* over the head of a door or window frame.
heading bond Brickwork *bond* of headers only, used for footings and for all curved walls.
heading course A course of *headers*.
heading joint (1) A *cross joint*.
(2) [carp.] A *lengthening joint*. *See* **splayed heading joint**.
head moulding A *dripstone*.
head nailing The nailing of *slates* at about 2 cm from the head. Each nail is thus covered by two slates and a better covering is formed than with *centre nailing*, but the method is unsuitable for exposed windy sites. Since the *gauge* is slightly smaller than with centre nailing, the cost and weight per unit area of roof are slightly more.
headroom, headway *See* **stair clearance**.
heart [tim.] The centre of a log. *See* **boxed heart, heart centre**.
heart bond A *bond* for walls which are too thick for *through stones*. Two *headers* meet within the wall and their joint is covered by another header.
heart centre, pith [tim.] The core of a tree, also called *parenchyma*. *See* **balsa wood, burr**.
heart plank [tim.] A plank containing the heart of a *hardwood* log and thus most of its defects. *See* **centre plank**.
heartshake [tim.] A radial *shake* originating at the heart (BS 565).
heartwood, duramen [tim.] Sometimes the best timber in a log, to be distinguished from the *sapwood* which, before the tree was felled, was living tissue, and is softer, and paler in colour. *Compare* **heart centre**.
heat-absorbing glass *See* **anti-sun g.**
heat bridge *See* **cold bridge**.
heat capacity, thermal c. A concept used in connection with space heating and *condensation*. A room of low heat capacity (hardboard walls and ceiling) heats up more quickly than one of high heat capacity (thick masonry). Consequently when warm, damp air enters a room with cool walls of high heat capacity, *condensation* on the walls may result until the walls warm up.
heat exchanger A device containing one fluid, usually air or water, that is heated (or cooled) by a hotter (or cooler) fluid passing through special tubes inside it. A *calorifier* is one type.
heating [plu.] *See* **boiler, central, coil, district, space, unit heater**.
heating and ventilation engineer A *mechanical engineer*, often a member of the *Chartered Institution of Building Services*, concerned with all building services including *heating*, *air changes*, *sprinklers* and centralized *vacuum-cleaning plant*. *Compare* **hot-water fitter**.
heating battery A *heat exchanger*.
heating element [elec.] That part of an electric heater which consists of a wire heated by an electric current.
heat insulation The ability of a material to impede heat flow. It is inversely proportional to the *U-value* of the material. *See* **insulating materials**.
heat-recovery wheel A wheel mounted across the incoming and outgoing air ducts of an air-conditioning system that, by slowly rotating, transfers heat in winter from the outgoing to the incoming air. In summer it can function in reverse to cool the incoming air. High efficiencies are claimed but stationary *heat exchangers* working on the same principle also exist.
heat-resistant paint, enamel *Paint* or *enamel* which can be *stoved* at high tem-

peratures or used on *radiators* or similar equipment. They often contain silicone resins.

heat-resisting glass A glass with a low *coefficient of expansion* (*C*), like borosilicate glass, that has superseded *mica* for the windows of *roomheaters*.

heavy-bodied paint [pai.] Either a viscous paint or one that makes a strong *film*.

heel [joi.] (1) The rear end of a *plane*.

(2) The lower end of the *hanging stile* of a door. *See* **nose**.

(3) The part of a beam or *rafter* resting on a support.

heel strap [carp.] A U-shaped steel *strap* (*C*) bolted to the *tie-beam* of a wooden *truss* near the *wall plate*. The strap passes over the back of the *principal rafter*, joining it to the tie-beam, and transmits the rafter thrust to the tie-beam.

helical hinge [joi.] A hinge for a *swing door* which is hung from its frame. *Compare* **floor spring**.

helical stair The correct but not the usual name for a *spiral stair*.

helve The handle of an axe, pick, sledge hammer, or similar heavy tool, usually made of *ash* in Britain, or *hickory* in U S A. *Compare* **haft**.

hemihydrate plaster, browning, class B plaster (to BS 1191) [pla.] *Plaster* obtained by gently heating *gypsum* ($CaSO_4 \cdot 2H_2O$) which loses part of its water and becomes half-hydrated, the hemihydrate ($CaSO_4 \cdot H_2O$), the quick-setting *plaster of Paris*. To make it suitable for plasterer's work a retarder of set, usually *keratin*, is added to form retarded hemihydrate plaster. Hemihydrate plaster in contact with iron or steel should have 5% of its weight of hydrated lime mixed with it to prevent corrosion. The plaster is sometimes sold with the lime mixed into it. *See* **gypsum plaster**.

herring-bone bond *Diagonal bond*.

herring-bone matching [tim.] *Book matching*.

herring-bone strutting (U S A **cross bridging**) [carp.] Stiffening floor *joists* at their midspan by fixing a light strut from the bottom of each to the top of its neighbours and the top of each to the bottom of its neigbours. *See also* **bridging, solid bridging**.

hessian (U S A **burlap**) Strong coarse material woven from jute or hemp for making sacks, wrapping for electric power cables, or reinforcement for *fibrous plaster*.

HEVAC, HVAC Heating, ventilation and air conditioning.

hew [carp.] To shape timbers with hatchet or axe. *See below*.

hewn stone Stone with a good finish (dressed stone).

H-hinge, parliament h., shutter h. [joi.] A *hinge* screwed through holes on two lengthened parts (legs of the H) away from the joint. The knuckle (the cross-

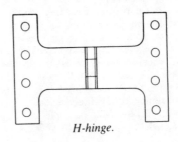

H-hinge.

bar of the H) projects beyond the face of the closed door or shutter allowing the door to clear *architraves* and lie flat against the wall when opened. It is used for outside shutters. (Illus. p. 172.)

hickey A portable steel tool used in USA for bending steel tube, conduit, or reinforcement.

hickory [tim.] A strong north American timber used like English *ash* for tool handles, ladder rungs, etc., where high shock resistance and bending strength are needed.

hiding power, opacity [pai.] The ability of a paint to obscure colour beneath it.

high-alumina cement *Aluminous cement.*

high-calcium lime, fat, rich, white, white chalk, non-hydraulic lime [pla.] A pure lime (mainly CaO) giving a very plastic *lime putty*. It can safely be mixed with *Portland cement.*

high-density plywood [tim.] *Improved wood.*

highlighting [pai.] Emphasizing the relief of a surface by making certain parts of it paler than the general colour.

high-pressure system A method of *central heating* with small pipes and rapid circulation of water at about 205° C. (400° F.) and 16 atmospheres. It was preferred to the low-pressure system when this required awkwardly large pipes before *small bore systems* were used.

hinge [joi.] A metal, pinned connection between a door or gate and the jamb or post on which it swings. The commonest hinges in building are *back-flap, band and hook, butt, cross garnet, helical, H-hinges, lift-off butts, rising butts.* The following hinges are symmetrical and therefore not handed: back-flaps, butts, H-hinges (p. 172). All other types of hinge are *handed* and the *hand* must be stated. For heavy doors or *swing doors, pivots* may be preferred to hinges.

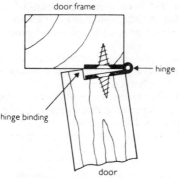

door frame

hinge

hinge binding

door

Hinge-bound door.

hinge-bound door [joi.] A door which is hard to close because the hinges have been screwed in with the door set too close to the frame. With *butt hinges* this can easily be remedied. The door is unhung, slips of cardboard are inserted behind the butts, and the door rehung. The process is repeated until the door closes easily. (Illus. below)

hip (Scots **piend**) The outstanding edge formed by the meeting of two roof surfaces near the ends of roofs which do not finish with a *gable*. Rainwater flows away from a hip and towards a *valley*. *See* **hipped roof** *and* **pitched roofs** (illus.).

hip capping (1) The uppermost strip of *roofing felt* or other protection over a hip.

(2) *Weaving*.

hip hook, h. iron (Scots **piend strap**) A galvanized steel bar nailed to the foot of the *hip rafter* to hold the lowest *hip tile* in place. It projects and is seen (B S 5534).

hip knob A *finial* to a *ridge* where it meets a *hip* or *gable*.

hipped end The sloping triangular end of a *hipped roof*.

hipped gable roof A *jerkin-head roof*. *See* **pitched roofs** (illus. p. 279).

hipped roof A roof which has four slopes instead of the two slopes of the ordinary gabled roof. The shorter sides are roofed with small sloping triangles, the hipped ends, bounded by two hips above (meeting at the ridge) and an *eave* below. Normally the eaves are at the same level all round. *See* **pitched roofs** (illus. p. 279).

hip rafter, angle ridge, angle r. A rafter forming a *hip*. The *jack-rafters* meet on it.

hip roll (1) **ridge r.** [carp.] A round timber with a V-cut beneath to cover a hip.

(2) The *flexible-metal* covering which fits over a wooden hip roll.

hip tile Clay, concrete or asbestos-cement tiles over the roofing tiles that meet at a *hip*. Angular, round and *bonnet* hip tiles are standardized in the UK. Hip tiles should be nailed as well as bedded in mortar at their lower edges. The lowest hip tile is held by a galvanized steel *hip hook* (B S 5534). *See* **ridge tile**.

hod A tray measuring $40 \times 23 \times 23$ cm ($16 \times 9 \times 9$ in.) shaped like a $40 \times 23 \times 23$ cm box cut diagonally in two. It is fixed to a long handle by which it can be held on the shoulder with one hand and thus carried up a ladder. It contains twelve bricks or 9 litres (2 gallons) of mortar and is therefore very heavy when loaded. *See below*.

hod carrier A *bricklayer's labourer* who carries a *hod*.

holderbat A fixing for holding a pipe firmly, and clear of the surface of the wall or *soffit* (B S 4118). *See* **fasteners** (illus. p. 130).

holdfast A steel or cast-iron spike driven into a joint of brickwork. At its outer end is a flattened eyed piece, through which a screw can be driven to fix *joinery*, etc. *See* **fasteners** (illus. p. 130).

holding-down clip A *tingle* shaped like a *capping*, to anchor and join adjacent lengths of capping.

hole saw, tubular s., h. cutter, annular bit [mech.] A drilling tool which cuts a ring-shaped sinking and can if necessary cut out a complete cylinder of wood or metal. In carpentry it is used for fitting the *shear plate* and the split ring timber *connectors* and consists of a pipe with one serrated end. It greatly increases the maximum diameter of hole which can be made with any given drill.

holidays, skips [pai.] Areas which have been left unpainted.

holing of slates For *head nailing*, each slate should be holed as close as practicable to each edge. Both holes should be 20 to 25 mm (0·8–1in.) from the edge and 25 mm (1 in.) from the *head* of the slate. The punching should be from the *bed* (underside) towards the *back* (top) creating a countersink on

Hollow clay block for building plastered partition. Similar blocks are used lying flat in hollow-tile floors.

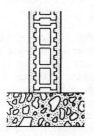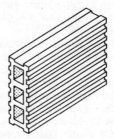

the back in which the nail head can sit. For *centre nailing* the holes are so placed that the nails just clear the head of the slate below. The thicker end of the slate, if there is one, should be exposed (the *tail*).

hollow (1) A concave surface.

(2) **hollow plane** [joi.] A plane for forming convex surfaces. *Compare* **round**.

hollow bed A *bed joint* which is not filled in the middle, a method of laying *sills* so as to prevent them breaking if the *masonry* settles unequally. If other stones are laid like this, they may flake off.

hollow blocks, h. tiles Concrete or burnt clay hollow *building blocks* are used for making partitions or external walls, or for forming reinforced concrete *hollow-tile floors* (C) (Illus. above) Lightweight, thermally-insulating, hollow blocks are also made of *foamed slag* concrete, diatomite, gypsum, etc. (below). *See* **solid masonry unit, flue lining**.

hollow clay tile *Hollow blocks*.

hollow-core door [joi.] A *flush door* in which the plywood or *hardboard* of both faces is glued to a skeleton framework (or core). It is less heavy and cheaper than a *solid door*.

hollow glass blocks *See* **glass blocks**.

hollow partition Usually now one built of *hollow blocks*, but before about 1920 all partitions were hollow, built of 100 mm or 75 mm (4 or 3 in.) *studs* plastered both sides, leaving a 100 or 75 mm gap in the middle, occasionally closed with *nogging*. See **discontinuous construction**.

hollow plane [joi.] *See* **hollow**.

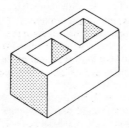

Hollow concrete block. 440 × 215 × 215 mm (17¾ × 8½ × 8½ in.) and many smaller sizes.

175

hollow roll, seam r. A method of jointing two pieces of *flexible-metal* sheet in the direction of the fall of a sloping roof. The edges of adjacent sheets are laid together, lifted up, and bent round to form a cylindrical roll without a *wood roll*, but sometimes with a metal fixing strip, a *tingle*.

hollow wall (1) A *cavity wall*.

(2) (USA) A wall built of two leaves which are bonded together, not with wall ties, but with bricks, such as a wall built in *rat-trap bond*.

hollow-wood construction [carp.] Wood construction with *plywood* (decorative or structural or both) glued on both faces as in hollow-core doors.

homogeneous fibre wallboard A wallboard made of the same material as *insulating fibreboard* but generally thinner. It is used as a cheap wall and ceiling lining where high insulation of sound and heat are not needed. It can be used as a base for plaster and as a permanent shuttering for concrete or as an underlay below linoleum or carpets. It is made in thicknesses of 10 mm ($\frac{1}{2}$ in.) or less, up to 1·2 m (4 ft) wide and 3·6 m (12 ft) long.

Honduras mahogany [tim.] (Swietenia macrophylla) A Central American mahogany of the same family as *Cuban mahogany* but slightly paler, softer, less dense, and easier to work.

hone, oilstone [carp.] A smooth quartz stone that gives a final, uniform, long-lasting polished edge to a cutting tool previously rubbed on a coarser stone such as a *grindstone*. The surface is oiled before the blade is rubbed on it. Hones are also used for rubbing *terrazzo* or interior stonework.

honeycomb fire damper Under the *Building Regulations* an automatic device must be fitted in a ventilation *duct* to close it in the event of fire, where it passes through a wall, floor or ceiling of a fire *compartment*. Mechanically operated fire dampers, worked by a *fusible link*, need regular maintenance but may be inaccessible though they work well when they do work. The honeycomb fire damper needs no maintenance and is based on *intumescent paints* introduced about 1950 to prevent rapid flame spread over wallboard. The paint film, on heating, froths to a dough which sets into a carbon foam several hundred times its original volume, sealing and insulating the protected surface. BRE Digest 158 claims that it provides an effective fire barrier for air speeds up to 10 m/sec (33 ft/sec) but should not be used where it is likely to be wet. Water affects the paint.

honeycomb wall, sleeper w. A *half-brick wall* built of *stretchers* with gaps between, so that they are held by bed joints only at their ends, above and below, e.g. under the wooden ground floor of a house with no basement, supporting the floor *joists*.

honing gauge [joi.] A small clamp with one wheel attached. The clamp holds a *chisel* while it is being rubbed on a stone and thus keeps the same angle for the chisel edge throughout the rubbing process.

hood A *dripstone*.

hook [joi.] The extension of the *cutting iron* past the *sole* of a plane.

hook and eye [joi.] A fastening for a door or a casement window consisting of a *cabin hook* on the frame which engages with a *screw eye* on the door.

hook bolt A galvanized bolt with an unthreaded end bent into a U-shape to hook securely under a steel angle *purlin* or angle *rafter*. The threaded end passes through a wall or roof sheet with a nut and washer holding the sheet. (Illus. opposite)

hook joint [joi.] A joint used between the meeting edges of *casement doors* and showcases which must be airtight. The *rebate* on one *stile* is cut to an F-shape,

Hook bolt holding profiled roofing sheet to a steel angle purlin or rafter. Acknowledgements to Alan Everett, Finishes, Mitchell's Building Series, B. T. Batsford, 1979.

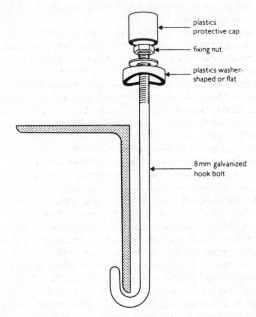

plastics protective cap

fixing nut

plastics washer-shaped or flat

8mm galvanized hook bolt

which fits into a similar groove on the opposite stile. A similar arrangement can be made for the *meeting stiles* of double windows.

hook rebate [joi.] The F-shaped rebate in a hook joint.

hook strip [joi.] (USA) A cleat fixed to a wall as a base to which clothes hooks can be screwed.

hopper The draught-preventing, triangular *deadlights* at the side of a *hopper light*. Compare **rainwater head**.

hopper head [plu.] An enlarged top, usually to a vertical pipe, where it receives water from a rainwater *gutter* or *waste pipe*. Forbidden for waste pipes since 1965, this practice is usual for *rainwater heads*.

hopper light [joi.] A *light* hinged at the bottom with draught-preventing glazed hoppers each side, or between deep *reveals* where there is no space for *hoppers*.

hopper window, hospital w. [joi.] A window formed of one or more *hopper lights* above each other.

horizontal shore A *flying shore*.

horn [joi.] Originally an extension beyond the frame of a mortised member (usually a *stile*) to strengthen the *mortise* during wedging up. Since it protects the frame during transport, it is also used with dowelled joints. It helps to build a frame into brickwork. *See* **racking back** illus. p. 266.

horse (1) [carp.] Framing used as a temporary support, such as a *trestle*.

(2) [carp.] A *string* carrying the *treads* and *risers* of a *stair*.

(3) [pla.] A short board housed to receive the *stock* (or wood backing) to

the shaped metal *templet* which forms a plaster *moulding* to the required profile. *See* **running mould**, *also below*.

(4) [plu.] A wooden *finial* which is to be covered with lead.

horsed mould [pla.] A wooden stock (carrying zinc plates cut to the profile of the desired plaster *moulding*) housed firmly into a *horse* and fixed to it by wooden stays. The horsed mould is pushed along the angle between ceiling and wall by one plasterer. It is held in position by a *running rule* nailed to the wall and a *nib guide* nailed to the ceiling. A second plasterer feeds the plaster on to the moulding. *See* **muffle**.

horsing up [pla.] Building up a *horsed mould* for running a plaster *cornice*, etc.

hose cock, h. bib, sill c. (USA) A tap at sill height outside a building, with a *fitting* which will take a hose.

hospital door [joi.] A *flush door*.

hospital window [joi.] A *hopper window*.

hot-air heater *See* **warm air heating**.

hot-air seasoning [tim.] Drying timber in a *kiln*.

hot-air stripper [pai.] A safer method than *burning off*, for removing old oil paint, is to use hot air at 600° C. (compared with 1900° C for the blow lamp) but the device is much more elaborate, involving an electric fan and an air heater.

hot pressing [tim.] Gluing *plywood* in a *press* between heated *platens*, usual for *thermo-setting resins* and common for other *glues* which set more quickly when heated. *See* **caul**.

hot spraying [pai.] Spraying of *paints* and *lacquers* which have been heated to reduce their viscosity instead of adding volatile *thinners*. In this way a thicker coat can be formed.

hot-water cylinder A *cylinder* for storing hot water. *Compare* **storage water heater**. (Illus. p. 179).

hot-water fitter, heating and domestic engineer A *tradesman* who instals and maintains small boilers, furnaces, etc., sometimes also *air-conditioning* systems, usually working under a *heating and ventilation engineer*. He may hold the technical certificate of the City and Guilds of London Institute but with further qualifications may eventually become a heating and ventilation engineer himself.

housebreaking The demolition of buildings.

housed joint [joi.] (USA **dado j.**) A shallow sinking in the face of one board to enclose (or house) the end of another timber in the way that steps are housed into a *close string*.

housed string [joi.] A *close string*.

house painter A craftsman who paints buildings and prepares them for painting with wire brush, scraper, pumice stone, blow lamp, or chemicals, filling in cracks with *hard stopping*, etc. *See* illus. p. 180.

house painter and decorator A *housepainter* who can also hang paper and do gilding and marbling. *See* **painter's labourer**.

house service cutout [elec.] A cast-iron or plastics *cutout box* in which the *service cable* ends. It is sealed by the electricity undertaking.

housing [joi.] A *housed joint*.

housing society *See* **cooperative housing society**.

hub [plu.] (USA) The enlarged end (or bell or *socket*) of a cast-iron pipe.

hue [pai.] *See* **colour**.

humidifier Plant such as washers or sprays for raising the air moisture content

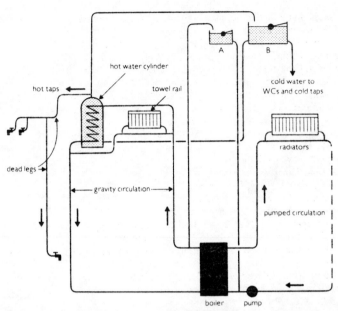

Hot-water cylinder heated by gravity circulation with a few radiators heated on the one-pipe system. The towel rail, not on the heating circuit, but on the primary flow-and-return, is an exception, enabling it to heat the bathroom even when the central heating is turned off. A = expansion tank; B = cold cistern. With acknowledgement to Central Heating, the Consumers Association, 1975.

and modifying its temperature in *air-conditioning*.

humidity The water content, usually, of air.

hungry, starved (1) [pai.] Description of a surface which is too absorptive for the amount or kind of paint put on it. The paint film is therefore thin and patchy.

(2) [pla.] Description of a plastering mix of low *plasticity*.

HVAC, HEVAC Heating, ventilation and air conditioning.

hydralime [pla.] *Hydrated lime*.

hydrant A connection to a water main, usually a *fire hydrant*.

hydrated lime Slaked lime, $Ca(OH)_2$ bought either as *dry hydrate* or as *lime putty* in polythene bags.

hydraulic A description of *limes* or mortars which, like *Portland cement*, set and harden under water because of their content of burnt clay (aluminium silicate). They also harden more quickly than lime mortar but cannot all be mixed with Portland cement in plastering. Non-hydraulic limes (pure CaO) are the most workable or 'fat'. *Eminently hydraulic* limes are 'lean', the least workable, and set under water in three days whereas *feebly hydraulic* limes require twenty-one days. *See* **semi-hydraulic lime**.

hydraulic cement *Cement* which hardens under water, like Portland. *See* **hydraulic**.

hydraulicity The property of a mortar (not possessed by *high-calcium lime* mortar) of setting in the absence of air or in excess water.

179

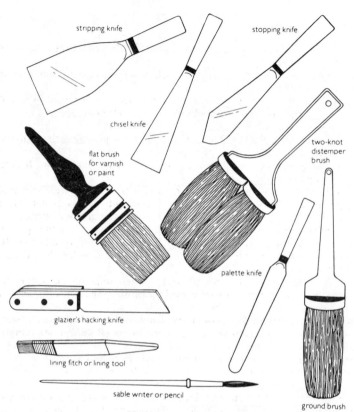

House painter's tools.

hydraulic lift A hydraulic lift may be direct-acting, with a hydraulic ram in contact with the floor of the lift cabin, raising or lowering it. The ram must be located below the lift well, in a borehole as deep as the height of the building. An indirect-acting lift is not in contact with a ram but is raised and lowered by ropes above it. Both types need an electrically driven hydraulic pump as a source of power. The pump is usually on the lowest floor of the building, unlike the usual rope-operated lift, for which the motor room is on the roof (BS 3810, part 8).

hydraulic test [plu.] *See* C.

hygroscopic salts Salts which attract moisture. In damp walls these travel up from the ground dissolved in water. The water dries out on the face of the wall in a warm room but the salt is left behind and may concentrate in the wall, so that the bricks are never dry even in persistent drought. Several possibilities exist, described in BRE Digest 27. All are expensive but some have been successful.

hyperbolic paraboloid roof A shell roof which looks like a butterfly in elevation. It began to appear in the 1950s, built in timber or concrete.

I

ignitability The ability of a material to be ignited by a small flame – one of the *fire hazards* (BS 476).

imbrex In *Italian tiling*, the over-tile which is semicircular and fits over the *tegula* or under-tile.

immersion heater [elec.] An electric resistance heater submerged in a water tank. *See* **automatic immersion heater**. *Compare* **electrode boiler**.

impact noise *See* **airborne noise**.

imperfect manufacture [tim.] Defects in conversion or planing such as variation in sawing, *mismatching*, torn or *chipped grain* or other tool marks, *skips* in planing, machine burn, insufficient *tongue* or groove, and so on. It is less weakening than a *defect*.

impreg [tim.] *Improved wood* that has been impregnated with *synthetic resin*.

impregnated flax felt *Bitumen felt* made of felted jute or flax or hair, waterproofed with fluxed coal-tar pitch, brown wood tars, or wood pitches.

impregnation [tim.] Timber protection with *preservatives* (*C*) under pressure or with alternating vacuum and pressure. It is much more effective than application by brush, but needs special plant and is therefore best done by a timber wholesaler.

improved nails [carp.] Nails formed with upstand rings on the shank, that greatly increase their withdrawal load. Like ordinary nails they do not make fully rigid joints. They may be rust-proofed.

improved wood, high-density plywood *Plywood* that has been specially treated to strengthen it or improve its other properties (BS 565). *See* **compreg, impreg**.

improvement line A *building line*, the line of an improved road.

incentive system of wages A wage system in which men receive more pay if they do more work, for example, *bonus* or piece rates. However if, as may occur in Britain, the extra pay increases disproportionately to the amount of tax paid, the incentive may not be an incentive to work steadily. It may encourage a man to work hard for a short time and then to stay away from work so that some tax is paid back to him.

incise To cut or carve stone, glass, wood, etc.

inclinator [joi.] An armchair which carries the occupant upstairs, installed in his home by the celebrated comedian Groucho Marx, who also invented the word.

inclined shore A *raking shore*.

incombustible building material *See* **non-combustible**.

incompatibility [pai.] The opposite of *compatibility*.

increaser [plu.] A *taper pipe* increasing in diameter in the direction of flow.

incrustation (1) **fur** [plu.] Hard lime or other materials deposited in water pipes or conduits. *See* **scale**.

(2) A layer of corrosive material which collects on stone or brick in an industrial district and should be removed periodically to prevent the wall wearing away.

indent A gap left in a course of brickwork or stone between *toothers* to *bond* with future work.

indented joint [carp.] A joint in which the wooden fishplates and the main timbers are cut with mating notches (which may be wedged). The fishplates are bolted to the main timbers.

indenting *Toothing*.

indenture A legal agreement used, for example, between an *apprentice* and his master.

indicating bolt [joi.] A door bolt installed on a WC door to show whether it is vacant or engaged.

indirect cylinder [plu.] *Direct cylinders* fur up quickly in *hard water* districts. To prevent or reduce furring, indirect cylinders have two circuits for hot water. The *primary flow-and-return* pipes are at least 19 mm ($\frac{3}{4}$ in.) in diameter and are connected to the boiler and cylinder only, usually using *gravity circulation*. The water in this circuit is never changed, therefore it does not fur up. Circulating through a coil in the cylinder it heats the water that passes out of the cylinder through the draw-off pipes and hot taps. Long draw-off pipes (*dead legs*) cool quickly and hot taps connected to them must be run for a long time before the water comes out hot. Their water may be kept hot by connecting them to the cylinder through a secondary circulation. This pipe, connected to the bottom of the cylinder, allows the water in the draw-offs to pass back into the cylinder and be re-heated but it wastes heat though it may save water.

indirect heating *Central heating*.

indirect lighting Lighting a room by any means which hides the lamp. It generally involves hiding the lamps behind a *cornice* so that the light is thrown down into the room by the white ceiling. It is more restful to the eyes than direct lighting. *See* **cove lighting**.

industrialized building methods Not industrial building, but a high degree of prefabrication applied to domestic or other construction so as to reduce site work to the minimum; this involves careful planning, and the maximum of standardization. The quantity of factory work on the *building components* is deliberately increased so as to reduce the cost, and improve the quality and speed of construction. *See* **large-panel construction, mechanical core**.

inert pigment [pai.] A *pigment* or an *extender* which, unlike a *drier*, does not react chemically in a paint.

infilling Material placed within a building frame or *partition* for fire resistance, insulation, weather protection, or stiffness. Brickwork is the usual infilling in Britain, but *insulating materials* are also used. *See* **coverings**.

inflated structure *See* **air house**.

infra-red drying [pai.] *See* **stoving**.

ingo, ingoing (Scots) A reveal to a window, fireplace, etc.

ingo plate [joi.] (Scots) A *reveal lining*.

inhibiting pigment [pai.] Zinc or other chromates, red lead, zinc, aluminium, or graphite powders added to paints, particularly *priming coats* to prevent corrosion. *See* **pigment**.

inhibitor [pai.] Materials such as arsenic or antimony compounds which delay a chemical action in *pickling* (C) acids, or small proportions of anti-oxidants which reduce *skinning*. *Compare* **corrosion inhibitor, inhibiting pigment**.

injection of a damp course In walls of old buildings where the *sawing in of a damp course* is impracticable, the injection of a *water-repellent* silicone may provide a good *damp course* even in a rubble wall, as is claimed by the National Coal Board. Holes are drilled into the bricks or stones (not mortar) at about 15 cm (6 in.) centres and are connected by polythene tubes to the waterproofing liquid, which can be injected at any desired pressure. Water under pressure cannot be held back but *rising damp* may be.

inlaid parquet [joi.] *Parquet* flooring glued in blocks about 60 cm (2 ft) square on to a wood backing and then fixed to floor boards.

inlay A decorative design which has been cut into a surface of *linoleum*, wood, or metal and filled with material of a different colour, often by gluing.

inner bead [joi.] A *sash stop*.

inodorous felt A brown, bitumen-impregnated flax *roofing felt* used as an *underlay* to roofs covered with *flexible metal sheet*.

input system A method of ventilating by sucking air into an electric fan from the roof to the rooms through *ducts*. A simple air cleaner is usually included, together with an automatically controlled air heater. *See* **combined extract and input system**.

insert, patch, shim [tim.] An inlay of *veneer* which fills a knot hole or other hole in *plywood*. *See* **joint tape**.

inside-angle tool [pla.] (USA) A float for shaping internal angles.

inside facing [joi.] (Scots) *Inside lining*.

inside glazing *External glazing* placed from within the frame. *See* **internal glazing, outside glazing**.

inside lining [joi.] (USA **i. casing, box casing**) Any part of a *cased frame* with its *face* toward the building.

inside trim, casing t. [joi.] (USA) The *architrave* within a door or window.

in situ A description of work done on the site rather than in the prefabrication works or factory, e.g. to contrast site concrete with *precast concrete* (*C*).

in-situ floor finishes *Jointless floors*.

inspection certificate A note from a local authority certifying that the drains of a building are satisfactory, and that it is ready for occupation.

inspection fitting, i. eye An *access eye*.

inspection junction [plu.] A *lamphole* (*C*).

installation, internal i. The gas pipes and appliances on the consumer's side of the control cock at the board's gas meter. *See* BSCP 331.

instantaneous (sink) water heater A small, non-storage gas or electric water heater usually with its own taps and swivel spout for fitting over a sink. *See also* **multi-point water heater**.

insulate To protect a room or building from sound or heat (or heat loss) usually by the use of *discontinuous construction* to break up the sound paths, combined with *insulating materials*. *See* **conductivity, insulators**.

insulated metal roofing *Roof decking*.

insulating fibre board *Fibre board* at least 11 mm ($\frac{1}{2}$ in.) thick, and of low density for high insulation.

insulating glass *Double glazing*.

insulating materials Materials for insulating rooms or buildings from heat or cold or sound. They can be divided into several classes, that is (a) *insulating fibre boards, plasterboard, asbestos, corkboards*, (b) *loose fills*, (c) *blankets*, (d) *woodwool* or *compressed straw slab*, (e) *building blocks*, (f) *double glazing*, not properly a material but a special use of a material. *See* **insulators, expanded polystyrene**, BSCP 3, chaps 2, 8.

insulating plasterboard *Plasterboard* backed with brightly polished aluminium *foil* (total weight 7 kg/m² (1·5 lb/ft²)).

insulating strip An *expansion strip*.

insulators (1) *Insulating materials*, that is materials having a low heat *conductivity*. Heat insulators are not good sound insulators, but most of them have good sound *absorption*. The effectiveness of a sound insulation increases with its weight, but heat insulators generally improve with a reduction in weight and a corresponding increase in the number of air cells enclosed. Insulating materials that become damp lose efficiency as insulators. *Condensation* is one of the most common causes of dampness. See **discontinuous construction, loose-fill insulation**.

(2) [elec.] Materials which have low electrical conductivity, such as dry paper, timber, or cotton, certain resins or varnishes, rubber, many plastics, mica, porcelain, glass, and so on.

integral waterproofing The *waterproofing* of concrete by including an *admixture* with the mixing water or cement. Probably no admixture can make a bad concrete waterproof. See **watertight basements**.

integrity In *fire testing*, the absence of cracks through the unit and of flames on the cooler side.

intercepting trap, interceptor, disconnecting t. A *trap*, fitted between a house drain and a sewer, to disconnect the air in the two. In many towns, these traps are no longer being installed, as they are unnecessary for well-laid modern house drains and they hinder the ventilation of the *sewer* (*C*). Where a fresh air inlet is used, it is connected to the upstream side. *Compare* **petrol intercepting chamber**

intergrown knot [tim.] A *live knot*.

interim certificate A payment for building work, but not the final *certificate*.

interior-type plywood [tim.] *Plywood* made with *glue* which does not resist moisture well. Many of the *synthetic resins* and some *casein glues* are moisture-proof and can thus be used without difficulty out of doors (unlike *animal glue*). Moisture-resistant glue does not prevent wood from rotting.

interlaced fencing, woven board, interwoven f. Fencing made by weaving together straight, very thin boards so that no space remains to be seen through.

interlocked grain, interlocking g., twisted fibres [tim.] A *grain* in which the fibres slope one way in one series of rings, then slowly reverse their slope in the next growth rings, and so on. *Spiral grain* is one example. *Ribbon grain* is shown when the wood is quarter sawn. Wood with this grain is difficult to cut or split.

interlocking joint A joint in *ashlar* in which a projection on one stone beds in a groove on the next one. See **joggle**.

interlocking tile See **single-lap tile**.

intermediate rafter A *common rafter*.

internal dormer A vertical window in a sloping roof, within the general line of the roof so that the flat surface outside the window sill must be waterproofed (in the past often with lead). See **dormer**.

internal glazing Glazing on internal walls. See **external glazing**.

internal hazard See **fire hazard**.

International SfB (Samarbetskommittén för Byggnadsfrågor) An international classification of building information subjects. The system originated in Sweden but is now sponsored and administered by C I B (International Council for Building Research Studies and Documentation). The *CI/SfB* English language version is the responsibility of the *RIBA*.

interstitial condensation *Condensation* not on a visible surface but within a wall, floor or ceiling, therefore usually invisible. Since wetting of any building material reduces its insulation value, this aggravates the effect of cold weather. If a *vapour barrier* or *vapour check* is placed on the warm face of the building material, it should never occur. (Illus. below)

intertie [carp.] An intermediate horizontal member in a *framed partition*, to stiffen it at a door head or elsewhere between floor levels.

intrados, soffit The visible under-surface of an arch or *vault*.

intruder alarms. *See* **security**.

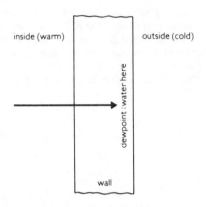

inside (warm)   outside (cold)

dewpoint : water here

wall

Interstitial condensation. This takes place when the warm surface is not impervious. The air then passes through it and drops its water as dew wherever it is cooled to its dewpoint.

intumescent sealant, strip, mastic or paint Liquids or solids inserted around a *fire-check door*, often into a special groove, that swell when heated, blocking the air gap and preventing penetration of smoke. They can be painted over. *See* **fire-check door** (illus. p. 135), also **honeycomb fire damper**.

inverted roof, upside-down r., inside-out r. On flat roofs the insulation material is normally below the roof waterproofing to keep dry. In the inverted roof it is placed on top of the waterproofing. It must be some insulator such as foamed glass or expanded polystyrene which does not lose insulation value when wet and also must be weighed down by gravel or concrete slabs. It is not a *cold roof*.

iron [joi.] A *cutting iron*. *See also* C.

iron core [joi.] A steel bar covered by a wooden handrail, connecting the tops of *balusters*.

ironmongery Cast or wrought iron, or *hardware*.

iron oxide [pai.] Iron oxides are used in *pigments* both manufactured and natural, for instance Venetian red (haematite). Magnetite (Fe_3O_4) or a mixture of oxides make black or purple pigments. The *umbers, siennas,* and *ochres* are oxides or hydrated oxides of a yellow to chestnut or dark brown colour and were among the earliest pigments used by man.

irregular coursed rubble *Rubble walling* built to *courses* of various depths.

isocyanate [pai.] Poisonous material in some *two-pack* polyurethane paints that can be dangerous if breathed as a 'spray mist'. Through ventilation reduces the danger.

isocyanurate foam Foam like *polyurethane* foam.

isolating membrane An *underlay*.

isolation strip An *expansion strip*.

Italianized roofing Roofing of Italianized zinc sheet, that is zinc sheet with three or more equally spaced, parallel, half-round corrugations running down the slope.

Italian tiling (USA **pan and roll tiles**) *Single-lap tiles* which form a roof covering with two different sorts of tiles, the curved over-tile or imbrex and the flat, tray shaped under-tile or tegula. *Compare* **Spanish tile**.

item [q.s.] A description of a volume of material and work supplied, or of one *labour* in a *bill of quantities* followed by its unit (metres, ft, m^2, ft^2, kg, lb). When *tendering*, the *contractor* writes his price opposite each item.

J

jack arch (USA) A *Welsh arch* or a *flat arch*. *See also C*.

jack plane [carp.] A *bench plane* used for cleaning wood from the saw, or from any preliminary rough work. A wooden jack plane is about 43 cm (17 in.) long; steel jack planes are shorter.

jack rafter A short *rafter* between *hip rafter* and *eave* or between *valley* and *ridge*.

jack rib, cripple, j. timber [carp.] A curved *jack rafter* used in a small dome roof.

jamb The vertical flank of a wall opening, to the full thickness of the wall, often also the joinery covering the flank. *Compare* **reveal**.

jamb lining [joi.] A timber facing covering a jamb.

jamb post, j. stone A post or stone, forming a door jamb.

Japan [pai.] *Black Japan*.

Japanese lacquer [pai.] A glossy coating obtained by tapping the sap from the Japanese varnish tree (Rhus vernicifera) or sumach.

jedding axe A *cavil*.

jemmy A *pinch bar* about 38 cm (15 in.) long.

jenny A *gin block*.

jerkin-head roof, hipped gable, shread head (USA **clipped gable**) A roof which is *hipped* from the *ridge* halfway to the *eaves* and gabled from there down, the contrary of a *gambrel roof*. *See* **pitched roofs** (illus. p. 279).

Jetfreezing Several methods of temporarily freezing a central heating or water supply pipe, enabling the pipe to be opened without draining it. One of these functions by the use of liquid nitrogen at − 196° C., another, Jetfreezing, uses liquid carbon dioxide that changes into the solid 'dry ice' as soon as it leaves the cylinder. A closely fitting jacket around the pipe, injected with the cold gas, enables pipes up to 10 cm (4 in.) diameter to be frozen, the smaller diameters usually within 15 minutes. The method is also used for maintenance work on oil-filled electrical power cables.

jib door, gib d. A door whose face is flush with the wall and decorated to be inconspicuous.

jig A clamp or other device for holding work or guiding a tool so that repetitive jobs can be accurately worked without repeating the marking out.

jig saw, scroll s. [tim.] A reciprocating, power-operated saw like the *fret saw*, used for cutting sharper curves than those which can be cut by the *band saw*. One weighing about 3 kg (7 lb.) will also cut 6 mm ($\frac{1}{4}$ in.) thick mild steel, 15 mm ($\frac{3}{8}$ in.) thick *light alloys*, 30 mm ($1\frac{1}{4}$ in.) thick *improved wood* or 60 mm ($2\frac{1}{2}$ in.) thick softwood.

jinnie wheel A *gin block*.

jobber, builder's handyman A semi-skilled man who can do any house repair such as bricklaying, plastering, painting, plumbing, *joinery*, roofing. *Compare* **builder's labourer**.

jog (USA) An offset or change in the direction of a line or a surface. *See* **joggle**.

joggle [carp.] A small projection at the end of a mortised piece to strengthen it, e.g. a *horn* or a *stub tenon*. For *blockwork* or *masonry, see C*.

joggle piece [carp.] A post shouldered like the foot of a *king post* to form an abutment for a strut.

joiner (1) A man who makes *joinery* and works mainly at the bench on wood which has been shaped by the machinists. His work is finer than the *carpenter*'s, much of it being finished in the good conditions of the joinery shop where it is not exposed to the weather.

(2) (Scots) A *carpenter*-and-*joiner*.

joiner's gauge A *marking gauge*.

joiner's hammer, Warrington h. A *hammer* with a *cross peen* head weighing from 110 to 570 g (4 to 20 oz.).

joiner's labourer, carpenter's mate A helper to a *carpenter* or *joiner*, who may be known as a gluer-up if he prepares *glue* and joints. He can generally stack timber.

joinery (1) (USA **finishing carpentry**) Making and fixing the wooden finishes to a building such as doors, *skirting boards, architraves*, linings, *windows*, picture rails.

(2) (USA) The joints in *carpentry* as well as joinery, or even cabinet making.

joint (1) The *mortar* between adjacent bricks or stones, *bed joints, cross joints*, and *wall joints*. *See* **concave, flat, keyed, weather-struck**.

(2) [carp.] A connection between two members to form a corner (*angle joint*) or for lengthening or widening a timber surface.

(3) Expansion joint. *See C, also* **movement joint.**

joint bolt [joi.] A *handrail bolt*.

joint cement, j. filler, j. finish, j. tape Proprietary materials used in *dry lining*.

jointer (1) Bricklayer's tools, used after bricklaying, for putting various surface finishes on to mortar *joints* in *pointing* or *jointing*. *See* **mason's and bricklayer's tools** (illus. p. 211).

(2) [carp.] **jointing plane** A *plane* longer than the *try plane*, and used for smoothing long edges to be joined. Steel jointers are about 60 cm (2 ft) long, wooden ones may be 76 cm (2·5 ft) long. *See* **rubbed joint.**

jointer saw A machine for sawing stone.

joint fastener [carp.] A *corrugated fastener*.

joint filler *See* **joint cement**.

jointing Working the surface of mortar *joints* to give a finished face while the mortar is *green* rather than raking them out and refilling them as in *pointing*. Because jointing involves the use of the same mortar in the face as in the bed it is stronger than pointing and preferable for a durable joint. *See* **tooling, weather-struck joint.**

jointing compound, j. paste [plu.] Any substance inserted in a pipe joint to make it leak-proof. In threaded steel pipes even old paint has served the purpose. In practice many plumbers used a creamy substance like fluid putty laid over the threads before joining them, in conjunction with tow, but this combination has been superseded by the more convenient *ptfe* tape.

jointing material [mech.] *See* **gasket** (*C*).

jointing plane [carp.] A *jointer*.

jointing rule A long *straight edge* used by bricklayers with the *jointer* in pointing. *See* **plasterer** (illus. p. 246).

jointless flooring, composition f., in-situ f. Floor surfaces laid usually by plasterers or by specialist *composition floor layers*, consequently without the close joints of tiled floors. They include asphalt, anhydrite, cement-bitumen, *cement-rubber latex, cement-wood, grano, magnesite flooring, pitch mastic,* *terrazzo*. In spite of the name, many jointless floors are best laid with joints about 2·5 m (8 ft) apart, particularly those containing cement, to allow for *shrinkage* (*C*). Those mentioned so far are not expensive in materials but they all are of mortar screed thickness 25 to 50 mm (1 to 2 in.) minimum (BSCP 204). *See* **fleximers**.

joint mould, section m. [pla.] A zinc, plywood, or cardboard *template*, shaped for a plaster member.

joint rule [pla.] A steel *rule* from 5 to 46 cm (2 to 18 in.) long, used by *plasterers* in forming the *mitres* at the junctions of cornice *mouldings*. One end is cut at an angle of 45°. *See* **plasterer** (illus. p. 246).

joint runner, pouring rope [plu.] Asbestos rope or similar material, used for packing the outside of a pipe joint which is to be cast in molten lead. *See* **pipe-jointing clip**.

joint tape (1) Paper or paper-faced cotton tape (sometimes embossed) which is fixed over the joints between wallboards. *Compare* **scrim**. *See* **joint cement**.

(2) [tim.] Gummed brown paper with which the *face* of *veneer* is reinforced before it is glued to its backing, mainly to hold *inserts* in place. Fusible tape is converted to glue in *hot pressing*. *See* **film glue, tapeless splicer**.

joist (1) A wooden or steel beam directly supporting a floor, usually a *common joist*. Steel joists are often distinguished by calling them RSJs or *rolled-steel joists* (*C*).

(2) In USA, rectangular *lumber* from 5 cm (2 in.) up to 12·7 m (5 in.) thick and 10 cm (4 in.) or more wide, graded for its bending strength loaded on edge. Graded for its bending strength loaded on face it is a *plank*.

joist anchor A *wall anchor*.

joist hanger A steel plate or *strap* (*C*) or cast-iron shoe which carries the end of a wooden *joist*. (Illus. below).

joist trimmer [carp.] A galvanized steel plate bent and drilled for nailing to one *joist* so that it can carry another at right angles to it. (Illus. p. 190).

journeyman *See* **tradesman**.

jumbo brick (USA) A *brick* larger than usual, whether intentionally or by mistake.

jumper (1) In *snecked* or *squared rubble* a *stretcher* which covers more than one *cross joint*.

(2) [elec.] (USA) A temporary electrical connection made round part of a circuit.

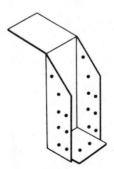

Joist hanger, of galvanized steel, for building into brickwork.

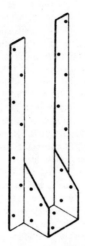

Joist trimmer, of galvanized steel, nailed or screwed to a joist so as to hang another at right angles to it.

(3) [plu.] A brass, mushroom-shaped part in the domestic water tap, whether for sink or basin or bath, which carries the washer on the lower face of the mushroom disc. The stalk of the mushroom points upwards into a hollow guide, the screw-down part of the tap. When the tap opens, the force of the water lifts the jumper into this guide, raising the washer with it. Jumpers, or their washers, need replacing every few years, when the tap begins to drip.

junction [plu.] A *special* drain pipe made with a *socket* to take a *branch*.

junction box [elec.] A box which covers the joints between the ends of conductors in house wiring or underground cables.

K

kauri [pai.] A fossil *copal resin* from the largest conifer of the North Island of New Zealand which is believed to live 3,600 years. It was at one time much used in hard-drying *varnishes*.

Keene's cement, Parian plaster, hard-burnt plaster, Class D plaster (to BS 1191) [pla.] An anhydrous *gypsum plaster* with an *accelerator* of set, a *hard plaster* with a smooth, vermin-proof finish. It is used for *finishing coats*, often over a Portland cement rendering and a coarse variety of Keene's in the *floating coat*. It should not be mixed with lime. Its gradual set enables it to be trowelled smooth without danger.

keeper [joi.] (1) A metal loop over the fall bar of a *thumb latch* to limit its travel.

(2) A *striking plate* or other guide for a bolt in a door.

keeping the gauge Maintaining the spacing of the brick *courses*, usually four per 30 cm (12 in.) height for a metric English *brick* of 6·5 cm (2⅝ in.) depth.

keeping the perpends Laying *bricks* or stones or *slates* or *tiles* accurately so that the *cross joints* (perpends) or the visible edges of slates and tiles in alternate *courses* shall be in the same vertical line.

keratin A *retarder* for *plaster of Paris*, obtained from the horns, hoofs, nails, or scales of animals.

kerf A saw-cut in wood or stone etc. *See* **setting** (illus. p. 298).

kerfed beam [carp.] A beam cut with several saw-cuts to allow it to be bent.

kerfing [carp.] Making saw-cuts on one side of a piece of wood so as to bend it towards that side, a convenient way of curving the risers of bullnose steps.

kevel *See* **cavil**.

key (1) The roughness of a surface, the texture which enables *plaster, mortar, glue*, etc., to grip it with a *mechanical bond* (*C*). *See* **concrete bonding plaster**.

(2) [carp.] A special *hardwood* piece let into a joint to strengthen it, such as a *double-dovetail key* or a *feather*, or a small hardwood slip let into a *mitre* joint or a *counter batten* dovetailed across boards to prevent them warping.

(3) [mech.] A bar driven between a drive shaft and the hub of a wheel to ensure that the shaft drives the wheel.

(4) A *cotter*.

(5) A bricklayer's pointing tool for making a *keyed joint*.

key drop [joi.] An *escutcheon* cover.

keyed [joi.] (1) Held or locked by a *key*.

(2) Said of a dowel which is grooved, to allow air and excess *glue* to be driven out.

keyed beam [carp.] A beam with a *lap joint* into which slots have been cut in each member. *Hardwood* or metal rectangular wedges (keys), driven into these holes, increase the bending strength of the joint. *See also* **compound beam**.

keyed joint Concave *pointing* of a mortar *joint*.

keyhole saw [joi.] A *compass saw*.

keying-in *Bonding* a *brick* wall to another already built.

keying mix [pla.] A *bonding treatment*.

key plan A *location plan*.

keystone The central wedge-shaped *arch-stone* at the crown of an arch, put in last. It is no more important than the other arch-stones, but its insertion means the completion of the arch.

keyway [mech.] A slot cut along a shaft, and another along its matching hub, to receive a *key*.

Khaya [tim.] *See* **African mahogany**.

kick The difference in slope between *patent glazing* and the surrounding roof.

kicking plate, kickplate [joi.] A protective metal plate fixed to the bottom *rail* of a door.

kiln A furnace in which cement, brick, or lime is burnt, or a chamber through which warm air passes to dry timber.

kiln dried, k. seasoned [tim.] A description of timber dried in a kiln. *Compare* **natural seasoning**.

kilojoule *See* pp. 8, 9.

king bolt, k. rod A vertical steel rod hanging from the ridge to the *tie-beam* of a wooden roof truss, taking the place of a *king post*.

king closer A three-quarter brick used as a *closer*. A diagonal piece is cut off one corner by a vertical plane passing from the centre of one end to the centre of one side. (It is actually $\frac{7}{8}$ of a brick but is usually called a $\frac{3}{4}$ brick.)

king post (USA **joggle post**) [carp.] A vertical timber which hangs from the ridge of a king-post roof truss and carries the tie-beam of the *truss* at its foot. Its foot is joggled to carry two struts (*see* **joggle piece**) and the tie-beam is often held to the king post by a *cottered joint*.

king-post truss [carp.] A wooden roof *truss* consisting of a pair of principal rafters held by a horizontal *tie-beam*, a vertical *king post* between tie-beam and *ridge* and usually also two struts to the rafters from a thickening (joggle) at the foot of the king post. It is suitable for spans up to about 11 m (36 ft) but like the *queen-post truss* is now not being built in Britain.

kiss marks Marks on bricks which have touched in the kiln.

kite winder Of three *winders* turning a right angle, this is the central one, so called because in plan it looks like a kite.

Knapen system, atmospheric siphon A proprietary method of drying out damp walls by drilling holes into them from outside at about the level of the floor inside. The holes do not pass right through the wall and are left open for ventilation. Several methods exist, some drilled down, others drilled up, but in all types, ventilation is provided. Water vapour is much lighter than dry air at the same temperature, so theoretically downward drilling from outside would be best, if there is no chance of water draining in from the face of the wall. Near ground level also, upward drilling becomes impossible. (Illus. p. 26).

knapped flints Flints broken across the middle, therefore dark coloured, often grouped to form a square on the wall face.

knapping hammer A *hammer* for shaping stones.

knee (1) **elbow** [plu.] A sharp right-angle bend in a pipe.

(2) [joi.] A curve in a handrail which is convex above like a human knee. *Compare* **ramp**.

(3) **crook** [tim.] A naturally-curved short timber.

kneeler, skew table, skew The sloping-topped, level-bedded stones in a *gable coping*, above the *gable springer*. *See* **rubble wall** (illus. p. 282).

knifing filler [pai.] A *filler* that is fine-grained and soft enough to be put on with a *filling knife*.

knob-and-tube wiring [elec.] An early American method of concealed wiring of buildings, still used in districts liable to be flooded. The conductors are carried in rubber-insulated cable on porcelain knobs fixed to floor *joists*. The cable passes through timber in a porcelain tube.

knobbing, knobbling, skiffling Dressing stones roughly in the quarry by removing protruding humps.

knocked down (mainly USA) Description of building components, delivered to a job completely cut and shaped, but not assembled.

knocking up Mixing and making workable a batch of *plaster*, *concrete*, *mortar*, or *paint*. (The adding of fresh water to stiffened mortar or concrete is usually forbidden, since such material should be thrown away.)

knockings Stone chips smaller than *spalls*.

knot [tim.] A place in a tree trunk from which a branch has grown out. Knots which reduce the strength of wood are *dead*, *loose*, or *unsound* knots. Harmless knots are *live, pin, sound*, and *tight knots*.

knot brush [pai.] A thick *brush* with its bristles or fibres bunched in round or oval shapes, for painting walls (one-, two-, or three-knot brushes).

knotting [pai.] *Shellac* dissolved in *methylated spirit*, used as a local *sealer* over *knots* in new wood so that it can be painted without danger of the knots exuding sap through the paint. Other quick-drying compositions are also used. *See* **aluminium primer**.

knotting, priming and stopping [pai.] After *surface preparation*, the first three treatments of new wood should take place in this order.

knuckle [joi.] The holes in a *hinge* through which the pin passes.

knuckle joint [carp.] A *curb joint* in a *mansard roof*.

knuckle soldered joint [plu.] A right-angled joint made between two lead pipes.

kraft paper Strong brown paper used in building as the containing sheet of insulation *blankets*, in *building paper*, and in other ways.

K-value The thermal *conductivity* of a material. *Compare* **U-value**.

L

labour [q.s.] Work which is done with material already itemized and paid for elsewhere. A labour is often a separate *item* in a bill, although one item may contain several labours.

labour constant [q.s.] The amount of labour required to do a unit of work, e.g. for 1 m² (ft²) of brickwork 22·5 cm (9 in.) thick.

labourer A man who has not been apprenticed to any trade and is therefore paid less than a *tradesman*. In practice he may have some skill in many trades, like a *jobber* or a *builder's labourer*, and thus be very useful.

laced valley A *valley* formed by *tiles* or *slates* without a *valley gutter*. Slates or tiles of 1½ times the normal width are laid on a *valley board*. The two slopes intersect sharply and do not blend into each other as in a *swept valley*. See **valley tile**.

lacquer [pai.] A glossy finish which dries rapidly by *evaporation* of the *vehicle*. Lacquers are used for decoration (*Japanese lacquer*) and for coating tin cans and bright metal surfaces such as brass (transparent lacquer). Unlike *varnish* and *enamel*, modern lacquers are based on cellulose compounds including *nitrocellulose*, also *acetone*, and *resins*.

ladder Ladders consist of two long wooden *stiles* spaced apart by *rungs* wedged tightly into holes mortised in the stiles at 20 to 30 cm (8 to 12 in.) centres. *Light-alloy* is much lighter than wood. Different types are the *builder's ladder*, *standing ladder*, *extending ladder*, *step ladder*, and *steps*.

ladder scaffold A *scaffold* quickly erected on ladders braced together, used for painting or other light work.

ladkin, latterkin A *hardwood* tool for opening the *cames* of *leaded lights*.

lag To wrap pipes or tanks with insulating material, thus protecting cold surfaces against frost or *condensation* and reducing heat losses from warm ones.

lagging (1) Horizontal boards nailed across the *centers* and supporting an arch during construction.

(2) *See* **lag, moulded insulation**.

lag screw, l. bolt (USA) A *coach screw*.

lake [pai.] A *pigment* consisting of a *dye* precipitated on to an inorganic base (or carrier or filler) such as aluminium hydroxide.

laminate To compress, at high temperature, layers of paper, textile, or veneer with *synthetic resin*, so as to make a sheet of durable material. *See below*.

laminated arch [tim.] An arch built of *laminated wood*.

laminated fibre wallboard *Hardboard* used for panelling walls, ceilings, etc. with a surface which is smooth or pebbled, painted or prepared for painting. Preformed boards made to curves from 15 to 60 cm (6 to 24 in.) dia. can be used for clothing *columns* or as column *formwork* (*C*), and have been made in England since 1906.

laminated glass *Safety glass* of annealed or toughened glass sheets interlaminated with *glass substitute*. With the glass (as usual) outside it is possible to achieve a high (for glass) *fire grading* of 90 minutes.

laminated joint [joi.] A *combed joint*.

laminated lead sheet A *cladding* of thin layers of lead glued to other material.

laminated plasterboard A plasterboard used in the *double-leaf party wall*, 40 mm (1⅝ in.) thick, which may be made up from two layers of 20 mm

($\frac{7}{8}$ in.) plasterboard or three layers of 13 mm ($\frac{1}{2}$ in.) plasterboard or four layers of 10 mm ($\frac{3}{8}$ in.), at least partly glued together in the factory and there enclosed in timber frames. The last layer is often fixed on the site with its joints in the opposite direction from those made in the factory. Joints that open up can then not form air paths through the wall. The 40 mm ($1\frac{3}{8}$ in.) thickness of plasterboard weighs only about 25 kg/m² (5 lb/ft²).

laminated plastics, synthetic-resin-bonded paper sheet Sheets of paper or textile, soaked with a *synthetic resin*, and pressed together to make a stiff board or glossy-surfaced covering for a wall or board. In spite of the name they are obtainable not only as sheet but also as bars, cylinders and other sections. *See* **laminate**.

laminated wood Layers of *veneer* or wood glued or mechanically fastened together without *cross bands*. In practice many constructions intermediate between this (pure) laminated wood and *plywood* exist and it is rare to find one devoid of crossings. Laminated wood is built of *plies* which are thicker than the usual plywood veneers. (Illus. below).

laminboard [tim.] A fine quality wooden board built up from core strips not more than 7 mm wide, glued between two or more outer plies. The finished board can be from 12 to 50 mm thick. *Compare* **blockboard**.

lamp black, vegetable b. [pai.] A *pigment* like *bone black* but made by burning coal tar products with very little air. *See* **carbon black**.

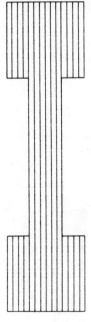

Long-span beam made of laminated wood. The plies, 25 mm (1 in.) thick, can be joined by gluing, nailing or bolting, or all three (vertical cross-section).

lamp cord [elec.] (USA) A *flex*.

lampholder, lamp socket [elec.] A wall fixture or fitting at the end of a *flex*, which carries an electric light bulb.

lampholder plug [elec.] *See adaptor*.

landing A platform between two *flights* or at an end of a flight, a *half-landing*, *half-space* or *quarter-space landing*.

lantern, lantern l. A frame raised above the general level of a roof, glazed all round to admit light and sometimes air. It may have a *roof light*. *See* **saucer dome**.

lap (1) In *centre-nailing*, the effective length of a *slate* or *plain tile* which is covered by two others, or as BS 5534 puts it, the amount by which the *tails* of slates in one course overlap the *heads* of slates in the *course* that is next but one below them. On tiles or *head-nailed slates*, it is measured from the centre of the nail hole. Because an increase in lap decreases the slope of each tile, it should not exceed one third of the tile length, and should be less on a flat slope than on a steeper one with similar exposure. The combined effects of lap and the *camber* of a plain tile make the slope of its upper half much less than that of the rafters below it. *See* **weather, gauge**.

　(2) [pai.] To place one coat of paint or varnish beside another and over its edge to make an invisible join; also the join so formed.

　(3) [plu.] *See* **passings**.

lap cement *See* **sealing compound** (2).

lapis lazuli The sapphire of the Bible and the ancients, used like marble for decorating walls, now a semi-precious stone, no longer ground to make the pigment *ultramarine*.

lap joint, lapped j. [carp.] A joint between timbers made by laying one over the other and bolting through them or clamping them with U-bolts. *Halving* is a development of the lap joint. (Illus. below) *See also* C.

lapped tenons [carp.] Two *tenons* which enter a *mortise* from opposite ends and lap each other within it.

lap siding [tim.] *Clapboard*.

larch (USA **tamarack**) [tim.] (Larix) A hard, strong, resinous *softwood*, not easy to convert owing to knots and *resin* and therefore used in the round in mines, in piling, and in *carpentry*, although it is also used in *joinery* and flooring. Larch is one of the few *deciduous* conifers.

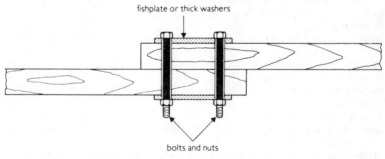

fishplate or thick washers

bolts and nuts

Bolted lap joint.

large-panel construction An *industrialized building method* first used in the USSR with reinforced concrete panels one or two storeys high, sometimes made of lightweight insulating concrete. Between panels, the *open-drained joint* is usual. For large-panel timber walls, which have been prefabricated for many years both in Europe and America, the term is not used.

larmier A *drip*.

larry (1) [pla.] A tool 2·1 m (7 ft) long, shaped like a hoe, used for mixing *plaster*.

(2) Fluid *mortar*.

larrying, l. up (USA) Using fluid *mortar* in which the *bricks* are slid into position and not laid, after which mortar is poured in to fill the vertical joints.

lashing, whip, bond A short fibre rope or steel rope for use as a crane *sling* (*C*), tying *scaffold* timbers, etc.

latch [joi.] A door fastening which may be of several types, the two most important of which are: (1) The *thumb latch*, a bar, pivoted on the door, which catches in a hook on the frame.

(2) The bevelled metal tongue operated by a door handle and controlled by a spring in the common *mortise lock*, *rim lock*, or *cylinder lock*. Unlike a lock, it engages by spring when the door is closed, without any key being turned.

latchet [plu.] A *tingle*.

latex Originally the sap of the rubber tree, but now in the plastics industry, an *emulsion* (*C*) in water of a *synthetic resin*. See **emulsion paint**.

latex emulsions [pai.] *See* **emulsion paint**.

lath, lathing Any base for plaster including types of *plasterboard* made for the purpose, *metal lathing, fibre board, clay lath*, etc., but originally split wooden slats which demanded thick plaster, were weak, and often moved after the plaster was put on, causing it to crack.

lathe [tim.] A machine on which wood or metal is turned to a circular shape, such as the powerful machine on which *rotary* and *half-round veneers* are cut.

lath hammer, claw hatchet, shingling hatchet [pla.] A plasterer's *hammer* for nailing laths. It has an axe edge as well as a hammer face, the axe side being nicked near the handle to form a claw for drawing nails. *See* **plasterer**, p. 246.

lathing Any base for *plaster*. *See* **lath**.

lath, plaster, and set [pla.] *Two-coat work*, a *floating coat*, and a *finishing coat* often used on modern backings such as plasterboard or *insulating board*.

lath, plaster, float, and set [pla.] *Three-coat work*.

latterkin A *ladkin*.

lattice window A *light* in which small *panes* of glass are bedded in metal *cames*. The usual type is a *leaded light*.

laundry chute, clothes c. A duct from a bathroom to a lower floor, into which dirty clothes are dropped.

laundry tray, l. tub (USA) A deep, wide sink fixed to a wall for washing clothes.

lay bar A horizontal *glazing bar*.

layer board, lear b. [carp.] A board on which the lowest *flexible-metal* sheet of a *box gutter* is laid.

laying off [pai.] Final, gentle brushing of a wet paint surface with a 'dry' brush to eliminate brush marks or roller stipple marks.

laying trowel (1) A *brick trowel*.

    (2) [pla.] **laying-on trowel** A rectangular steel trowel about 260 × 110 mm (10½ × 4½ in.) with which *plaster* is laid on to a surface. *See* **plasterer**, p. 246.

lay light A *light* fixed horizontally in a ceiling.

layout A *plan*, usually showing the general arrangement of buildings, rooms, equipment, streets, etc.

lay panel [joi.] A door or other *panel* with its length horizontal.

leaching cesspool (USA) A *cesspool* which leaks. Cesspools also leak in Britain although this is forbidden by water authorities. *See* **tight cesspool**.

In all the terms below down to 'lead wool' (except where otherwise indicated) the syllable 'lead' is pronounced 'led' and refers to the heavy metal.

lead [plu.] (1) A metal used for *plumbing* by the Romans and for roofing since early Saxon times. Lead rainwater pipes often of very beautiful design were used until the nineteenth century, when cast iron became common, and lead is now too expensive for any but the most extravagant *architect*. The sheet lead used for building is from 1 to 3 mm thick; *see* **lead flat**.

    (2) A lead *came* of a *lattice window*.

lead (pronounced 'leed') (1) [elec.] A *conductor*.

    (2) **corner lead** (USA) A section of brickwork, plumbed exactly and built up ahead of the remainder by steps in the courses, called *racking back*.

lead burner [plu.] A specialized *plumber*.

leadburning [plu.] The welding of lead without solder. A higher temperature is needed (about 327° C. for pure lead, against about 180° C. for solders) but expensive solder is not used. Joints can be made which are impossible by other means. Thus lead sheets for making *lead slates* can, if necessary, be joined at an acute angle by melting the lead at the junction between them, producing a joint that is strong, malleable, and sometimes inexpensive. Lead pipe can be joined to brass by leadburning. An oxy-acetylene or oxy-hydrogen flame is best because of the intense local heat needed. Some toxic gases are emitted during leadburning.

lead-capped nail A nail with a lead washer forming the underside of the head. When driven on to a roof sheet, it makes a watertight joint.

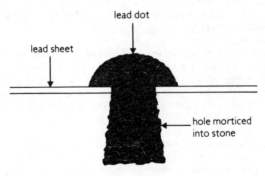

Poured lead dot in stone, formed either in fine solder or by leadburning.

lead cesspool A lead *rainwater head* at the lower end of a parapet gutter to collect rainwater before it enters a downpipe.

lead chromes [pai.] Yellow to orange *pigments*, very opaque and of high *staining power*, consisting of basic lead chromate often with *chrome yellow*. Some primrose shades may contain a small percentage of precipitated aluminium compounds with up to 4% of Al_2O_3. *Compare* **zinc chromes**.

lead chrome green, Brunswick g. [pai.] Composite *pigments*, prepared from *lead chrome* and *Prussian blue*. *See* **chrome green**.

lead-clothed glazing bar, lead-covered g. b. *See* **lead sheath**.

lead dot [plu.] For **poured-lead dot** *see* illus. p. 198. *See* **dots**.

lead driers [pai.] Lead compounds which quicken the hardening of *drying oils*, e.g. *litharge*, lead linoleate, lead resinate, and other organic salts of lead. *See* **drier**.

leaded light, lead glazing A *light* in which small diamond-shaped panes of glass are held in lead *cames*.

leaded zinc oxides [pai.] *White pigments* which are mixtures of ZnO (zinc oxide) and $PbO \cdot 2PbSO_4$ (*basic lead sulphate*). They are described in Britain as 15%, 25%, or 35% leaded. This means that the pigment contains 15% or 25% or 35% of $PbO \cdot 2PbSO_4$ ($\pm$ about 2%), the remainder being ZnO. These pigments are made from sulphide ores of lead and zinc, burnt without separating them.

leader head (pronounced 'leeder') (USA) A *rainwater head*.

lead flat A *flat roof* covered by lead sheet with *rolls* and *drips* at suitable intervals. Lead flats are best laid in areas smaller than 2·2 m² (24 ft²) and shorter than 3 m (10 ft), falling at 1·2 per cent (12 mm per m). The lead should be placed on waterproof *building paper* that does not stick to the wood or the lead, covering either planed boards or 2·5 mm plywood. Oak should never touch lead because its tannic acid attacks the metal. Lead can be corroded by mortar and should therefore be protected on both faces with a coat of bitumen or bitumen paint. It is not now used for large areas because it is costly and heavier than other *flexible metal*. Lead is unsuitable for steep slopes because it creeps unless it is fixed to the boarding with lead *dots* 76 cm (30 in.) apart both ways. Lead was formerly described by its weight in lb/ft², the heaviest for flats being 7 lb/ft², which is now known as code 7 lead. Code 3, the lightest for flat roofs, weighs 3 lb/ft², is 1·25 mm thick, and is used on roofs with no traffic where the lead needs no *bossing*.

lead-free paint Paint without lead compounds, used in food packing, etc. *See* **lead restricted, lead paint**.

lead glazing *See* **leaded light**.

lead joint [plu.] A *spigot-and-socket joint* in large cast iron water pipes, made by pouring molten lead into the gap or caulking it with *lead wool*.

lead-light glazier, l.-l. maker A *tradesman* who sets out and solders lead or copper *cames*, cuts glass, *glazes* the light, and fixes it. If he is specialized in stained glass he may be known as a fret glazier or decorative glass worker. If he is also *fixing*, he is called a stained-glass fitter and fixer. *See* **leaded-light**.

lead nail A small copper alloy *nail* for fixing lead sheet to a roof.

lead paint Paint containing lead *pigment*, particularly *white lead*. All lead pigments are poisonous because they are soluble in the juices of the stomach and can thus be absorbed by the body. The greatest danger from white lead is the inhaling of its dust. Involuntary swallowing and absorption through the skin are less likely. *See* **lead-restricted**.

lead plug (1) A small cylinder of lead driven into a *joint* or hole in a wall. It is a tight fixing for a *screw*.

(2) A lead *cramp* cast between neighbouring stones in a course into a groove cut in each to hold them together.

lead-restricted paint Paint which contains less than 5% of PbO calculated according to the British *lead paint* regulations of 1927. Such paints are regarded as *lead-free*.

lead roof A *lead flat*.

lead safe A *tray*.

lead sheath An enclosure to the steel core of a *glazing bar* which embodies *lead wings* and *condensation grooves* (lead-clothed *glazing bar*). *See also C*.

lead slate, copper s., l. sleeve [plu.] A specially made lead, copper, or other *flexible-metal* flashing to fit round a pipe where it passes through a roof. It is shaped like a top hat with the top cut off. *Compare* **soaker**.

lead tack A *tingle*.

lead wedge, bat A tapered piece of lead made by beating folded scrap lead or by casting, used for fixing a *flashing* to a *raglet*. *See* **tag**.

lead wing *See* **wing** (3).

lead wool [plu.] Lead cut up into thin strands and used for caulking iron pipes (*spigot-and-socket joints*) when for some reason it is impossible to pour molten lead into the socket.

leaf (1) One of a pair of doors or windows or one of the slates at a slate ridge.

(2) One half of a *cavity wall*, generally a *half-brick wall* tied by *wall ties* to the other half. *See* **withe**.

leafing [pai.] The *floating* of metallic paints containing aluminium powder, mica, etc. The flat grains protect the paint film by lying flat, and show up the aluminium. Often used as primers or *sealers*, e.g. over bitumen, tar, etc. *See* **aluminium primer**.

lean mix A *mortar* or *concrete* mix with little cement, or a plaster which is unworkable.

lean mortar [pla.] *Mortar* which is harsh, difficult to spread; the contrary of *fat*.

lean-to roof, half-span r. A roof sloping one way only, whose summit is carried on a wall higher than the top of the roof. *Compare* **penthouse roof**.

lear board A *layer board*.

LECA Light Expanded Clay Aggregate, a *lightweight aggregate*.

ledge [joi.] One of the two or three horizontal timbers on the back of a *batten door* or on a *framed and braced door*.

ledged and braced door [joi.] A *batten door* diagonally braced across the *ledges*, an unframed, medieval door, still used. *See* **clenching**.

ledger A horizontal pole, parallel to the wall in wooden *scaffolding*, lashed to the *standards* and carrying the *putlogs*. In *tubular scaffolding* similar terms are used, but different fixings.

ledger board [carp.] A *ribbon board*.

leggatt A *thatcher*'s wooden tool for striking the butts of *reeds* to bring them into line.

let in [joi.] *Housed*.

letter plate [joi.] A front-door fitting to receive letters, consisting of a slotted plate fixed to the outside of the door. The best types have a *door tidy* inside. *See* **postal knocker**.

level, mechanic's l., spirit l. A *level tube* (*C*) set in a *straight edge* from 23 to 90 cm (9 in. to 3 ft) long or even longer. *See* **mason's and bricklayer's tools** (illus. p. 211).

levelling [pai.] *See* **flow, pulling over**.

levelling compound, feathering c., self-levelling floor finish, underlayment A fine-grained *mortar* or similar substance that can be safely placed on a floor in a thin layer of 5 mm (0·2 in.) or even less (which is impossible for cement *screeds* since they break up even at 12 mm ($\frac{1}{2}$ in.) thickness) and so is used to finish off smoothly the top of a rough concrete, e.g. where it has been impossible to place a *monolithic screed*. It can also be used to make repairs or fill holes. It must be spread with a trowel but the trowel marks disappear after a minute or two. It may be either a relatively cheap (3 times as expensive as cement mortar) but non-wearing mortar or an expensive *resin* with its curing agent, often an *epoxy* or a *polyester* or a *polyurethane*. Both types can be used for smoothing a floor to receive *thermoplastic* tiles or sheet rubber or *polyvinyl chloride* sheet but the resins are also hard-wearing and fairly chemical-resistant and can be laid on concrete, timber or metal.

levelling rule [pla.] A *straight edge* about 3 m (10 ft) long used with a spirit *level* for bringing *dots* and *screeds* to a uniform surface. *See* **rule**.

lever boards Adjustable wooden *louvres*.

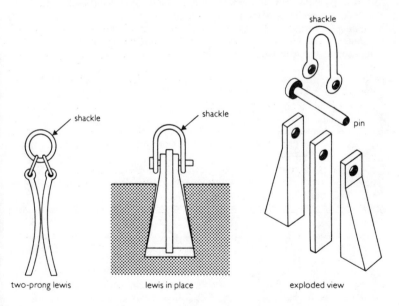

two-prong lewis   lewis in place   exploded view

Lifting lewises.

lever cap [joi.] The metal piece above the *back iron* of a metal *plane* which holds the back and *cutting irons* in place by a cam action.

lever lock [joi.] A good-quality *lock* in which the key must move several levers to shoot the bolt.

lewis, lifting pins An arrangement of several wedges or of curved steel bars which grip into a dovetailed *mortise* in the top of a heavy block of stone or concrete. Lewises are of several different types. Some can be released at a distance by the banksman who pulls a string attached to a releasing wedge. (Illus. p. 201).

lewis hole A hole cut in stone or cast in concrete to enable it to be lifted with a *lewis*.

lewising tool A *mason*'s chisel for cutting *lewis holes*.

lift (USA **elevator**) [mech.] An enclosed platform for carrying goods or passengers from one level to another in a tall building. *See* **hydraulic lift**, *also* BSCP 407.

lifting, raising, pulling up [pai.] Failure caused by the swelling of a dry film of *paint* or *varnish* when another coat is applied over it, usually manifested by wrinkling.

lifting beam A *strongback*.

lifting pins A *lewis*.

lifting wedge, foot lifter A block of inverted pyramid shape, used when working single-handed to hang a door or fix plasterboard on *plaster dabs*. With the foot weighing on the outer end of the wedge and the door or plasterboard on the inner end, the weight is held up without labouring. (Illus. below).

lift-off butts, loose butt hinges (USA **loose-joint butt**) [joi.] *Hinges* which can be taken apart by lifting one leaf from the other. A door can thus be easily unhung by lifting it. (Illus.)

lift shaft, l. well The vertical opening in a building, through which the lift and its counterweight travel.

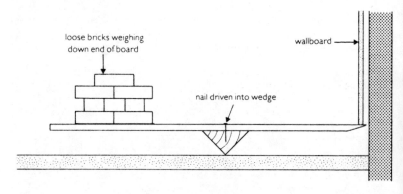

Lifting wedge for holding large wallboards in position while they are being fixed single-handed. If dabs of plaster of Paris are being used, the bricks may be unnecessary and weighting with the foot may be enough, because plaster of Paris hardens quickly.

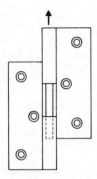

Lift-off butt hinge.

ligger (1) A hazel or willow stick, 1·5 m (5 ft) long, held down by *spars* at the ridge of *thatch*.

(2) [pla.] Scots for a *spot board*.

light One glazed or unglazed window (usually of several panes), whether fixed or opening, for instance the part between two *mullions*. *See* **deadlight**.

light alloys Alloys of aluminium and alloys of magnesium. Their specific gravities are: Al alloys 2·8, Mg alloys 1·8 (compared to steel 7·8). *See* **duralumin** (*C*), BSCP 118, 143.

light-gauge copper tube [plu.] BS 2871 describes many different types of copper tube, with outside diameters from 6 to 159 mm ($\frac{1}{4}$–6$\frac{3}{8}$ in.), and corresponding wall thicknesses from 0·6 to 7·6 mm (0·02–0·3 in.), in a dozen tables of tube dimensions. Tubes may be supplied in one of several different conditions, the main three being annealed (soft), half-hard, and hard-drawn. Tube bought in a coil is invariably annealed which makes it easy to straighten or to bend. Hard-drawn tube has the least wall thickness but is difficult to bend. The commonest tube for domestic use is half-hard, 15 mm (0·6 in.) diameter outside, light-gauge, thin-walled (0·7 mm (0·03 in.) thick). When specifying copper tube it is important to state which dimensions table in BS 2871 is to be followed – usually Table X or Y or Z for *compression* or *capillary joints*.

lighting panel [elec.] A *cutout* box for protecting lighting circuits.

lightning conductor, l. rod [elec.] A thick copper *lead* (pronounced 'leed') connected to *earth*, projecting above a building, and provided with sharp points which very much reduce the chance of the building being struck by lightning. *See* **air termination network**, BSCP 326.

lightning shake [tim.] Compression failure of wood, seen as a cross break.

lightweight aggregate *Vermiculite* and *perlite* are lightweight aggregates used instead of sand in plaster, but also in concrete for roofs of large span. *Pumice* or *foamed slag* or *clinker* aggregates can also be used to make *lightweight concrete*. As early as 1919 *expanded clay* aggregates were in use in USA for shipbuilding, and they are now used very widely for the structures of multi-storey buildings.

lightweight concretes are of two main types: (a) *aerated concretes*, weighing around 800 kg/m³ (50 lb/ft³) or less, which are highly insulating and not very strong; (b) concretes made from *lightweight aggregate*. These can be used for structural purposes (columns, beams, and slabs), are less good insulators though better than dense *concrete* (*C*), and usually weigh less than 1760 kg/m³ (110 lb/ft³). *See also C*, B R E Digest 123, B S 6073, 3797.

light well An *air shaft*.

Lignacite *Building blocks* made of sawdust, sand and cement since 1947 in the U K. The material is nearly three times as insulating as dense concrete, easy to nail and saw, inexpensive and sometimes cored with slots to provide insulating air spaces.

lignified wood [tim.] *Improved wood* impregnated with lignin at high pressure.

lignin [tim.] The main part of wood after cellulose, resins which cement the wood fibres together.

lime Chalk and other forms of calcium carbonate burnt in a kiln are called *quicklime* (CaO). When soaked in water this becomes *hydrated lime*. Both forms are lime. *See* **high-calcium lime, hydraulic**.

lime concrete A mixture of gravel, sand, and *lime* used since Roman times until *Portland cement* was made.

lime mortar Mortar containing lime, sand and water only. It is now rarely used in building, though often supplied to the site *ready-mixed*.

lime plaster [pla.] Neat *lime* or a mixture of *lime* and sand.

lime putty [pla.] Wet *hydrated lime* that has been soaked overnight or longer to give it *plasticity*.

lime tallow wash [pai.] *Limewash* mixed with tallow, used for roof and wall surfaces; one of the few coatings which do not damage bituminous roofing.

limewash, whitewash, whiting, whitening [pai.] A slightly germicidal 'milk' made with *quicklime* by soaking in excess water. Alum, *casein*, *size*, and other binders have been used. Though obsolescent for interiors and being superseded by *emulsion paints*, it is still used for farms or other buildings with no *damp course*.

limpet washer A conical *washer* (*C*) fixed under the nut of a *hook bolt* to hold down a corrugated sheet. It is shaped to fit the top of the corrugation. A *diamond washer* has the same function.

line A cord used for setting out building work, particularly by *bricklayers*. It is also used in tunnelling by mine surveyors, who chalk the line, then, when it is properly set, flick it against the roof. The resulting line marked on the rock shows the direction of the tunnel.

line level A small spirit *level* which, suspended at the middle of a taut bricklayer's line, can be used to level it to within about 1 mm per m (⅛ in. in 10 ft)..

linen tape A tape used for rough measuring and setting out. It is light and easily handled but less accurate than a steel *tape* (*C*), particularly if no steel wire is interwoven in it.

line pins Steel pins about 8 cm (3 in.) long inserted in the mortar *joints* at the ends of a wall and used for holding a bricklayer's *line*. *See* p. 211.

liner, lining (1) [pai.] *See* **lining tool**. 'Lining' is also a painting defect in which parallel troughs or ridges run in the direction of brushing or draining of a *paint* or *varnish*. It shows that the *media* were not *compatible*. Silking is very fine-grained lining.

  (2) [plu.] A *sleeve piece*.

  (3) [joi.] *Wallboards* and other *coverings for partitions*. It may also be an

architrave. A door lining or door case is a surround to a door, made of thinner wood than a *door frame*.

lining paper Paper pasted on to a wall as a base for wallpaper or paint.

lining plate In *flexible-metal roofing* a *tingle* at *eaves* or *verge*.

lining tool, liner [pai.] A small flat *fitch* with a slanting edge used for painting lines with the help of a *rule. See* **house painter** (illus. p. 180).

link dormer A large *dormer*, sometimes with lights at the sides. It may join one part of the roof to another part or include a projection from the roof such as a chimney.

linked switch [elec.] Two or more switches joined by bars so as to open or close simultaneously or in sequence.

link fuse [elec.] A *fuse* which is not protected by a cover plate.

linoleum, lino A detachable floor covering built up from *linseed oil* and *hessian* canvas. Its thickness is measured in mm and varies from 2 to 6·7 mm, made in widths up to 2 m. If glued to the floor all over, it has longer life than if nailed. It must only be laid on a dry floor. Rubber floor finishes are an improvement on lino, but more costly and not removable (BS 810, 1863).

linseed oil [pai.] The most valuable oil in the *paint* and *varnish* trades, obtained by crushing the seed of flax. When exposed to the air it darkens and thickens to a tough *film* by *oxidation*, called *drying*. It is also called Baltic, or Black Sea, or Plate oil, after the sea or river of despatch. *See* **boiled oil, raw l. oil**.

linseed-oil putty *Glazier's putty* to BS 544 should keep for three months in the unopened tin without caking or hardening.

lintel, lintol A small beam over a door or window *head*, usually carrying wall load alone.

lintel-damp-course A galvanized sheet steel lintel bent up to act also as a *damp course* across the cavity of a *cavity wall*, and into the inner leaf of brickwork. It may carry both leaves or only the outer leaf.

lip, lipping [joi.] A *banding* on a *flush door*.

liquidated damages *See* **damages**.

litharge, lead monoxide (PbO) [pai.] A *drier* and *pigment* of pale yellow to brown colour.

lithopone [pai.] A very opaque white *pigment*, a co-precipitated mixture of barium sulphate ($BaSO_4$) and zinc sulphide (ZnS), used in interior paints, *water paints*, *distempers*, and in *enamels* with *synthetic resins*.

little joiners [joi.] Small pieces of wood which are used to hide and fill holes in wood; for example, *pellets* and *inlays*.

live edge [pai.] An edge of paint is said to be live if it can still be blended with newly applied paint without the *lap* showing.

live knot, intergrown k. [tim.] A *knot* whose fibres are intergrown with the wood. It is allowable in structural timber within certain size limits. *Compare* **dead knot**.

livering [pai.] *Feeding*.

live wire [elec.] A conductor with the electrical power switched on to it, therefore dangerous to touch. It may be called alive (opposite, dead).

loadbearing *See* (*C*), *also* BS 5628.

loading coat, l. slab A concrete slab laid over asphalt *tanking*, to ensure that it is not pushed upwards by water pressure below it.

loading of pipe [plu.] Before bending a pipe, it is filled with a *bending spring*, or with molten lead, low melting-point alloy, pitch, *resin*, or compressed sand. This loading prevents the pipe distorting during bending.

lobby Entrance area to a hall or house, sometimes with two or more spring-controlled doors to create an *air lock*, as in an *air house* or *pressurized escape route*, to reduce draughts and loss of air pressure. *See* **tambour**.

local authority In the UK a city, town, borough, burgh, district, island or county council or similar body which controls the quality of building by enforcing the *Building Regulations*. It is not always the planning authority but is usually in the same building.

location plan, block p., key p. A *plan* which shows the dimensions and position of a building site, usually also the building proposed.

lock [joi.] A fastening for a door, operated by a key which shoots a bolt, the commonest types being *mortise*, *rim*, and *cylinder locks*. *Compare* **latch**.

lock block [joi.] A wooden block in a *flush door* into which a *lock* can be fixed.

locking bar A development of the *hasp and staple* for fastening gates or barn doors. The long hasp or bar pivots on a pin on the frame, hooks over the staple, and is secured with a padlock.

locking stile [joi.] A *lock stile*.

lock joint, l. seam A *seam* in *flexible-metal roofing*.

lock rail [joi.] The *rail* in a door, which carries the *lock*.

lockshield valve, balancing v. [plu.] One of the two valves attached to a radiator, that enable the radiator to be removed for repair or replacement without stopping the heating system and necessitating the laborious work of draining the *circulation*. The other is the control valve, in daily use for turning the radiator on or off. The lockshield valve is only used once in the lifetime of a circulating system, on the occasion when the system is balanced to ensure that each radiator receives its adequate share of hot water.

lockspit A narrow V-shaped cut in the ground surface made by a *ganger* (C) to mark the line of a dig.

lock stile [joi.] A *shutting stile*.

loft (1) A storage space under a roof. Where access to it is by a trapdoor, this must be made large enough for the cold-water *cistern* to pass through. Otherwise part of the roof may have to be removed when the cistern is replaced.

(2) (USA) An entire upper floor of a commercial building, let to a tenant who subdivides it as he thinks best.

loft ladder, disappearing stair A folding ladder which is fixed on the top of a trap door into a loft or attic space and is invisible from below when the trap door is closed. The trap door is hinged to open downwards and is counter-balanced to carry the ladder by weights or springs. These ladders are indispensable for transforming an inaccessible loft into usable living space. They were made of wood but are now often of *light alloy*.

London stocks *See* **stock brick**.

long dummy [plu.] A *plumber*'s tool for straightening kinks in lead pipe. *See* **plumber's tools** (illus.).

long float [pla.] A *float* which needs two men to handle it.

long oil [pai.] A high ratio of oil to resin in a varnish (mainly for outside use). Compare **short oil**. *See* **oil length**, *also* BS 2015.

longscrew [plu.] The steel tube of a *connector*.

looping in [elec.] A method of reducing the number of T-joints in house wiring conduits by keeping one conductor permanently connected to the lampholder, the other passing through the switch. More wire is needed, as the conductor must double back on itself, but the cable is cut at fewer points and there are therefore fewer joints.

loop vent, circuit v. (USA) A *ventilation pipe* which is a continuation of a soil pipe above the last soil branch.

loose butt hinges [joi.] *See* **lift-off butts**.

loose-fill insulation Insulating materials such as granulated *cork*, loose *expanded clay*, or other *lightweight aggregate*, or *mineral wool*. Loose fill is placed between or over ceiling rafters or in the gap of a cavity wall to increase the insulating value of a dry air space. *See* **cavity insulation**.

loose knot [tim.] A *knot* which is not held tight and may drop out, and is therefore a *defect*.

loose-pin butt, pin hinge [joi.] A *butt hinge* with a withdrawable hinge pin which enables the door to be unhung merely by removing the pins from the hinges, without the labour of unscrewing the butts.

loose side, slack s. [tim.] Of *sliced veneer*, that side which was in contact with the blade. It is bent outwards and slightly broken, being the inner side of the veneer when it was cut from the log. *Compare* **tight side**.

loose tongue [joi.] A *cross tongue*.

lost-head nail A round wire *nail* with a very small head.

lot (USA) A site in a town.

loudness Loudness is measured by phons. For instance, a sound judged by a normal observer to be '*x*' *decibels* above the threshold of audibility has an intensity of *x* phons.

louvre (USA **louver**) A ventilator originally with horizontal wooden slats to keep out rain, now often of glass strips horizontally pivoted in a window. It was a combined chimney and window in a medieval hall.

low-pressure system The normal way of heating domestic water, usually with *gravity circulation*.

LPG, liquefied petroleum gas *Bottled gas*.

lug (1) **ear** A small projection from a frame or pipe for fixing purposes, for example, a steel door frame is fixed to a wall by a steel lug built into the wall.
(2) [elec.] A terminal on the end of a wire to make good electrical connection.

lug sill A *sill* with its ends built into the *jambs*. *See* **slip sill**.

lumber [tim.] (1) In USA the term for converted logs which have been sawn and sometimes *re-sawn*. Boards of lumber may be up to 7·3 m (24 ft) long while *timber* may be 18 m (60 ft) long. In flat-sawn lumber the maximum width is the diameter, in quarter-sawn lumber it is half the log diameter. *See* **dimension lumber**.
(2) Imported square-edged sawn hardwood of random width (BS 565).

luminaire [elec.] A light fitting or lighting standard.

luminous ceiling A *false ceiling* containing horizontal translucent panels which illuminate the space below from lamps above them.

lump hammer A *club hammer*.

lump-sum contract A *contract* in which the contractor submits a price for construction (and maintenance for a short period) of the work shown on the contract drawings. A *bill of quantities* is sometimes drawn up by the engineer or *architect* to help the contractor, but not normally. This is a simple type of *fixed-price contract* which is suitable for small buildings but not for large work of any sort. It has the further disadvantage that *tender* prices submitted by different firms cannot be compared since they are not usually based on the same quantities.

lune, gore A figure enclosed by two arcs of circles. A number of the figures, fitted together, form a balloon shape. Similarly, if cut in two and fitted together they form a hemisphere or dome. Half lunes are therefore used in cutting out metal, felt, or timber to cover a dome.

M

machine mason A *banker mason* at a stone-working lathe or planing machine.

machinist A skilled *tradesman* or at least a semi-skilled man who sets and operates a wood- or metal-working machine.

made ground, made-up g. Ground which has been raised by *fill* (*C*).

magazine boiler A coal- or coke-fired boiler for a hot-water or central-heating system, which has a bunker fitted to it, large enough to contain 24 hours' fuel. It thus needs attention only once a day.

magnesian lime, m. quicklime *Lime* with 5% to about 40% MgO. *Compare* **dolomitic lime**.

magnesite flooring A *jointless floor* of oxychloride cement (Sorel's cement) made by mixing magnesia (MgO) and magnesium chloride ($MgCl_2 \cdot 6H_2O$) with sawdust, sand, or similar fillers. When wet it corrodes metal and should not be used in kitchens or bathrooms for this reason. Even in dry conditions, the metal of gas, water and electrical services should be protected by at least 25 mm (1 in.) of dense concrete to eliminate any chance of their corrosion by the magnesium chloride.

magnesium alloy *See* **light alloy**.

magnesium-oxychloride cement *See* **magnesite flooring**.

mahogany [tim.] Many hardwoods – *Cuban mahogany*, Honduras mahogany, *African mahogany*.

main The supply authority's pipe or cable. *See* **communication pipe** (illus. p. 78).

main contractor, general c., prime c. A *contractor* who is responsible for the bulk of the work on a site, including the work of *sub-contractors*.

maintenance period, retention p. The period, after completion of a *contract*, during which a *contractor* is required to make good at his own expense any work which needs repair. *See* **retention money**.

maisonette (USA **duplex apartment**) A self-contained *flat* on two levels having its own internal stairs. Large blocks of flats are sometimes built in this way, to obtain quiet for the occupants, avoiding the costly methods of *discontinuous construction*.

make good To repair as new.

makore [tim.] (Mimusops heckelii) An *African mahogany*.

mall, maul A heavy *mallet* or beetle.

mallet A tool like a *hammer* with a wooden, rawhide, or rubber head. Wooden mallet heads should be of beech, hickory, or well-chosen applewood. (Illus. p. 211)

mallet-headed chisel A *mason's* term for those of his *chisels* which have a rounded steel head, so must be struck with a *mallet*. *See* **hammer-headed chisel**.

management contract A contract in which the *main contractor's* chief function is not as a builder but as a manager of sub-contractors and an adviser to the architect, structural engineer and other consultants. He is appointed early, to give advice. Later his main functions are programming and running the job. Abroad, especially in the USA, the system is well known, but by 1973 fewer than 50 such contracts had been let in Britain. The system is most suitable for buildings with complicated electrical and mechanical equipment that is difficult to price. It allows procedures to be telescoped because of the intelligent co-operation that is possible from the start between consultant and contractor. Various parts of the job can thus be simultaneously at completely different stages, whether at design or detailing or tendering or construction. This is not possible with most ordinary contracts when the job must be completely billed, and partly designed and detailed before the contractor can price it.

manganese drier [pai.] Manganese dioxide (MnO_2), and other organic and inorganic salts of manganese. *See* **drier**.

manipulative joint [plu.] A *compression joint* in which the ends of the copper tubes are slightly opened out. This laborious joint is usual only for large pipe diameters, in which the belled-out pipe makes a strong seal.

man-made fibres The first man-made fibre, artificial silk, was made in 1885 from nitrocellulose, viscose was first made in 1910, cellulose acetate in 1911, nylon in 1936 and others more recently.

mansard roof, curb roof (U S A **gambrel r.**) A roof which has on each side a relatively flat top slope and a steeper lower slope, usually containing *dormers* to use the attic space of the building. *See* **pitched roofs**, p. 279. The lower roof space contains dormers.

manufactured gas Gas piped to customers after processing originally of coal (town gas), mainly now of oil. In the U K all but 2% (in remote districts) has been phased out and replaced by natural gas. Its calorific value is about half that of natural gas.

marble facing Marble about 19 mm ($\frac{3}{4}$ in.) thick with 13 mm ($\frac{1}{2}$ in.) air space between it and the wall. It is fixed to the wall by 3 mm ($\frac{1}{8}$ in.) dia. copper wires or other non-corroding *cramps* dowelled into the marble and sealed into *plaster dabs*.

marbling [pai.] Copying the appearance of marble or other stone with paint.

marezzo marble An artificial marble like *scagliola*, which differs from it mainly in having no chips of added coloured material. It is precast on to a smooth sheet of plate glass or slate to give a polished surface.

margin (1) **gauge** The exposed depth of a slate or tile. *See* **gauge**.

(2) [joi.] The projection of the *close string* of a stair above the line of *nosings*. (Illus. p. 326).

(3) [joi.] The exposed flat face of a *stile* or *rail*.

(4) [joi.] A border mitred round a hearth.

(5) *See* **drafted margin**.

margin templet [joi.] A *pitch board* with an edge strip equal to the width of the *margin*.

margin trowel [pla.] A narrow rectangular trowel used for working in a narrow width (B S 4049).

marked face [joi.] The *face* (2).

marking gauge, butt g. [joi.] A beechwood bar with a steel point projecting at right angles from it near one end and a *hardwood* block sliding along it which can be locked at any point along the bar. It is used for marking lines parallel to that face of the wood which the block travels along. *See* **carpenter** (illus. p. 59), **cutting gauge, face plate, mortise gauge**.

marking knife [joi.] A steel bar with a cutting edge at one end, like a skewed chisel, and a point at the other end, used for marking wood before cutting or drilling.

marouflage [pai.] To *glue* a canvas to a wall which is to be covered by a mural

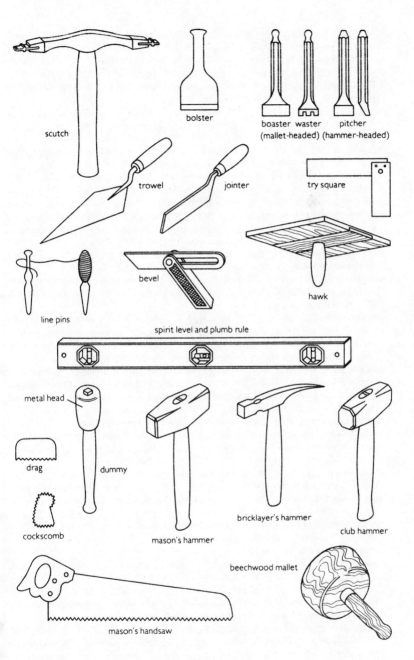

Mason's and bricklayer's tools.

211

painting. It is put on by rollers, glued with a paste (often of *gold size*), and forms a strong, matt *ground* for the painter.

mash, m. hammer Scots for a *club hammer* or *sledge hammer* (*C*).

masking [pai.] During painting, the edges of a painted surface are protected from paint by masking them with tape or paper stuck on, or by holding a paper, metal, or cardboard mask over them.

mason A stone worker or stone setter. In Scotland or USA a *bricklayer* is usually also a mason. He is generally in England either a *fixer* or a *walling mason*. *See* illustration.

masonry Stone and the craft of stone wall building, including the preparation and the fixing of the stones. In Scotland masonry includes brickwork and laying tiles. In USA it also includes *concrete* block, *hollow block*, and sometimes also poured *concrete* or *gypsum* walls. *See* BS 5390.

masonry cement A *cement* consisting mainly of ordinary *Portland cement* together with *plasticizers*, clay, *whiting*, or secret materials to form a plastic, *water-retentive* mortar for building walls. At the site only clean sand and water need to be added to make a good *mortar* (BS 5224).

masonry fixings *Cramps, anchor bolts* (*C*), *lewis bolts* (*C*) and plates for fixing stonework in place.

masonry nails Cadmium-plated nails or *drive screws* which can be driven into ordinary bricks with a hammer or into predrilled holes in harder material. *Compare* **concrete nail**.

masonry paint, stone paint Thick (up to 2 mm (0·08 in.)) weather-resistant, durable outside paints well known on the Continent, usually emulsion-based. Some types are called 'organic renderings'. Others include sand, mica or fibre mixed in to thicken them. *Compare* **cement paint**. *See* **textured finish**.

mason's joint A mortar *joint* consisting of a projecting triangle of mortar.

mason's labourer A skilled *labourer* who helps in the *mason's* yard, lifting stones and cutting *lewis holes* with a compressed-air tool. On the site he helps the mason *fixer* generally, supplies him with *mortar* and grout and other materials, and cleans down stonework. *See* **rubbing-bed hand**.

mason's mitre, m. stop A corner formed out of solid stone. The actual joint is not a *mitre* but usually a butt joint away from the corner. It is also sometimes used in joinery.

mason's putty *Lime putty* mixed with stone dust and *Portland cement* for jointing *ashlar*, with a mix usually from 1:1:6 to 1:4:15 cement:lime:stone dust.

mason's scaffold A *scaffold* which stands free of the wall, is supported on two rows of *standards*, and built of baulks or steel sections, with *braces* (*C*). Mason's scaffolds cannot (like bricklayer's scaffolds) be partly supported on the wall because the *putlog* holes would disfigure the stonework.

mason's stop A *mason's mitre*.

mastic (1) Resin from the Levantine mastic tree, that may be chewed or used as varnish when dissolved in alcohol.

(2) Any permanently plastic and sticky waterproofing material, that can be used for sealing all outdoor joints in buildings or as a *glazing compound*. *See* **sealing compound**. *Compare* **mastic asphalt** (*C*), **pitch mastic**.

matchboard, matched boards, match lining [tim.] Boards laid side by side, and shaped with *mouldings* or *rebates* on each edge so that the *straight tongue* on one fits (matches) the groove on the other. They are used for flooring, wall lining, and so on. *See* **vee-joint**.

matched floor [carp.] A floor made of *matchboard*.

matching [joi.] (1) *Matchboard*.

(2) [tim.] The arrangement of sheets of specially figured *veneer* in ways which bring out, by contrasts, the best in the colour and *figure* of the wood. Matching is practically confined to *sliced veneers*, since *rotary veneers* rarely have a figure which is interesting enough. *See* **book matching, four-piece butt matching**.

match planes [joi.] Pairs of *planes* which cut the tongue and the groove of *matchboard*. Sometimes the same plane will take both cutting irons (at different times). Most matchboard is now cut by machine. *See* **universal plane**.

matt [pai.] A very low *gloss*.

mattock A tool like a *navvy pick*, except that one end is broadened out like a hoe, the other being sharpened like a pick or a chisel or an axe blade. It is used for cutting tree roots and digging in stiff ground.

matt varnish [pai.] *Dammar* dissolved in turpentine with wax added will give a matt finish.

maturing The improvements obtained by the *ageing* of *varnishes*, or by the soaking of *hydrated lime* in water, etc.

maturing bin, m. pit [pla.] A bin or wood-lined pit on the building site, where formerly *lime putty* was left to mature for a month. Superseded by *ready-mixed lime-sand mortar*.

maul, mall, beetle A heavy wooden *mallet*.

maximum demand [elec.] The greatest instantaneous power demand from a consumer. It is important because some methods of charging for electricity are based on the maximum demand, but *see* **diversity**.

measure-and-value contract [q.s.] A *fixed-price contract* in which the *contractor* receives, with the tender drawings, a *bill of quantities*. When there is time to prepare the bill as well as the drawings, this sort of *contract* is preferred by consulting engineers or *architects* because it simplifies the comparison of *tenders* from different contractors. Contractors have precise information for tendering and less work to do to make up their prices than with unbilled contracts.

measurement [q.s.] The *quantity surveyor*'s duties of estimating from drawings the amount of work to be done and billed, and, later, his measuring on the site of the work done and to be paid for. On civil engineering *contracts* this work is often done by engineers using simple, civil engineering methods. *See* **Standard Method of Measurement**.

measuring frame A *batch box*.

mechanic (1) [mech.] A *fitter (C)*, a man skilled in mechanical engineering.

(2) A *tradesman* in any of the building trades.

mechanical core, sanitary c., plumbing services [plu.] Prefabricated pipes for hot and cold water supplies, wastes, drains, and gas, as well as prepared cable for electric services, all ready for installation with the minimum of site work in an *industrialized building method*.

mechanical engineer A person qualified in *mechanical engineering*, in Britain usually a member of the Institution of Mechanical Engineers, often a university graduate. *See* **heating and ventilation engineer**.

mechanical engineering The design and construction of engines and machines of every sort. It merges with electrical engineering but does not include the design of electrical circuits.

213

mechanical plastering [pla.] Modern plasterers use mechanical mixers, grinding and polishing machines, sprays, vibrators, *plastering machines* and pumps for raising mixed plaster to a multi-storey building.

mechanical saw [tim.] The *circular saw*, *band saw*, and *jig saw* are the best known mechanical saws for wood.

mechanic's level A *level*.

medium, vehicle Vague terms for the liquid in *paint*, excluding *pigment*. Some writers think that vehicle includes *thinner*, medium does not. *Varnish* and *lacquer*, since they contain no *pigment*, have a higher proportion of medium than paint does.

medullary ray, pith r. [tim.] *Ray*.

meeting rails, check r. [joi.] The *rails* of *sash windows* which touch when the window is closed.

meeting stile [joi.] A middle *stile* (or shutting stile or closing stile) of a *folding door* or casement.

melamine formaldehyde [tim.] A *synthetic resin* used for gluing or surfacing *veneers* or *laminated plastics*. It is not damaged by cigarette burn, is used for making stoved finishes, and keeps colour well.

melamine-surfaced chipboard [tim.] Resin-bonded *chipboard* with a decorative, smooth, *melamine formaldehyde* surface, is cheap, stable, fairly strong, and became available in Britain about 1963.

membrane A skin – a term often used in the expression damp-proof membrane, a *damp course*. A curing membrane may be a tarry liquid poured on to a concrete road slab immediately after casting, so as to prevent evaporation from it while the concrete is gaining strength for the critical first week at least. Membranes are also the main part of an *air house*.

mending plate A flat steel plate drilled with holes for countersunk screws, used for repairing *carpentry* work by screwing it on to sound wood on each side of the break. (Illus. below)

mensuration [q.s.] The measurement of lengths, and the calculation of lengths, areas, and volumes.

Merulius lacrymans [tim.] The fungus which usually causes *dry rot* in Britain.

metal-casement putty A *glazing compound* used on hardwood, concrete, or

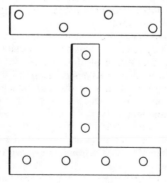

Common mending plates.

stone surrounds that have been sealed to prevent absorption of oil, as well as on metal. It may crack or detach if the finishing coat of paint is not put on within 28 days of glazing. Mixed with an accelerator these compounds can have a much shorter hardening time, enabling them to be painted soon after glazing.

metal coating, metallizing, metal spraying A thin film or films of nickel, copper, cadmium, *chromium*, aluminium, or zinc laid over corrodible metal surfaces. The coating protects either by completely enveloping the surface or by *sacrificial protection* (*C*) when it is locally worn through. *Galvanizing* (*C*), *sherardizing*, and *chromium-*, *cadmium-*, or nickel-*plating* are usually applied before a part is built in. Zinc or cadmium coatings can, however, now be sprayed on after erection by a special oxy-acetylene blowpipe (metal spraying). The cost of such a metal coating on a structure is higher than the best painting, but metal coating is likely to last five times as long as paint, and because of this may allow the structural designer to use thinner metal in his structure. The metal can be applied thickly enough to be polished after grinding off the surface roughness. *See* **protective finishes to metal**.

metal lathing *Expanded metal* (*C*) not less than 0·56 mm thick weighing 1·6 kg/m^2 (3 lb/yd^2) at least, used as a base for plaster. It should be galvanized or painted. It is stronger and more fire-resistant and vermin-resistant than *laths* and generally easier to fix. Expanded metal lathing may be with or without stiffening ribs. Other types are perforated steel sheet, and *dovetailed lathing*. Cut edges of galvanized metal lathing should be bitumen painted to prevent rusting.

metallic paint [pai.] Paints containing tiny flakes of metal, usually aluminium or zinc, for *priming* or rust-inhibiting or sealing a loose coat or as a *sealer* before re-decoration. *See* **aluminium primer**.

metal painting [pai.] Painting with *bronzing fluid* as a vehicle.

metal-sheathed mineral-insulated cable [elec.] Cable like *Pyrotenax*.

metal sheeting *See* **flexible-metal roofing, profiled steel sheet**.

metal trim *Architraves, skirtings*, picture rails, and *angle beads* of *pressed steel*, which are fixed before plastering and incorporated in the plaster surface. They are flush with the plaster and therefore do not collect dust.

metal valley [plu.] A *valley gutter* lined with lead, zinc, copper, or aluminium.

methylated spirit [pai.] Industrial alcohol containing some wood alcohol (methyl alcohol) to make it doubly poisonous, used for making *knotting, French polish*, etc.

mica Minerals with such excellent cleavage that they can be made thin enough to be transparent. They are also very good electrical insulators and are used as *extenders* to help the *leafing* of aluminium paint and thus to resist the penetration of moisture. *See* **heat-resisting glass**.

mica-flap valve A sheet of mica at a *fresh air inlet*, hinged to allow air to flow inwards only.

microbore [plu.] *See* **minibore**.

mid-feather (1) [joi.] A *parting slip*.

(2) A central *withe* in a chimney.

milkiness [pai.] The defect of a whitish or translucent appearance in a *varnish* film.

milk of lime [pla.] *Slaked lime* in water. *See* **maturing bin**.

milled lead Lead rolled into sheets from cast slabs.

mill-run mortar *Mortar* made in a *pug mill* or other mixer.

millwork [tim.] (USA) *Prefabricated* joinery (doors, windows, panels, stairs) made at the mill and partly assembled there. *See* **planing-mill products**.

mineral black [pai.] Black *pigments* which may be the carbonaceous clays of Devon or the crushed *slate* of the Continent of Europe. Graphite also is a black mineral pigment but is not called mineral black.

mineral-insulated cable [elec.] *See* **Pyrotenax**.

mineral-surfaced bitumen felt A heavy *bitumen felt* whose upper surface is dressed with particles of *slate* or other stone, its lower surface with talc or sand, used as a single layer on sloping roofs or as a top layer in multiple roofing. It is made 1 m wide in rolls 10 m (33 ft) long.

mineral wool, rock w., slag w. A flexible, resilient, flocculent *insulator* made from slag or mineral fibres. It can be used loose or made up in 1 to 5 cm ($\frac{1}{2}$ to 2 in.) thick *blankets* in waterproof paper, *scrim* cloth or aluminium foil, etc. *Compare* **glass silk, perlite, vermiculite**.

minibore, microbore [plu.] A description of a central heating circuit using circulation pipes smaller than those used for *small bore*, usually of 6, 8, 10 or 12 mm outside diameter. Since the advent of small-bore systems, low-cost circulating pumps have been developed that can adequately deal with the higher pressures needed in these smaller tubes. The tubes are easy to bend and install, less conspicuous than larger pipes and they lose less heat. Water distribution manifolds of suitable diameter, to which the main flow and return pipes are led, provide convenient connections for up to nine radiators – 18 joints (BS 5449).

mist coat [pai.] (1) A very thin sprayed coat, usually of cellulose *lacquer*.

(2) A very thin coat of *emulsion paint*, laid on a surface as a *sealer* before *emulsion paint* if the surface is liable to detach.

mitre (USA **miter**) [joi.] A joint made between two members of similar cross section that are to be at 90° to each other. Each is cut at 45° to its axis, so that the line of the joint is seen to cut the corner. A stronger joint than the simple glued and butted mitre is the *dovetail*.

mitre block, m. box [joi.] A U-shaped or L-shaped block of wood with saw cuts in it at 45° to the axis of the block. The piece of wood to be cut is held firmly, or clamped to the block and can thus be sawn to an exact mitre.

mitre board [joi.] A *mitre shoot*.

mitre brad [carp.] A *corrugated fastener*.

mitred-and-cut string [carp.] A *cut-and-mitred string*.

mitred knee [joi.] A mitred intersection between a horizontal part of a *handrail* and a steeply falling part, curved like a bent human *knee*.

mitre dovetail, blind or **secret d.** A *dovetail* joint in which the pins cannot be seen and only the line of the *mitre* joint shows.

mitred valley, hip A *close-cut valley* or hip.

mitre saw [joi.] A *tenon saw*.

mitre shoot, m. board [joi.] A frame for holding a *moulding* while the *mitre* is being planed.

mitre square [joi.] A *bevel* with the blade fixed at 45° to the stock.

mitre templet [joi.] A small rebated frame made to guide the *chisel* when *mitring* small *mouldings*.

mitring machine [tim.] A *trimming machine*.

mixed glue, ready-mixed g. [tim.] *Synthetic resin* glue mixed with an *accelerator*. *Compare* **separate application**.

mixed stuff *Best reed* containing some gladden (Iris pseudacorus or foetidissima) and lesser reed mace (Typha angustifolia).

mixing varnish [pai.] A varnish *medium* which can be mixed into an *oil paint* to give additional *gloss*.

model by-laws Predecessors to the *Building Regulations*, issued by the UK Ministry of Housing.

modular masonry unit (USA) A *brick* or *building block* which measures, laid up with its mortar joint, a multiple of 4 in. in plan both ways. Vertically a whole number of courses (1, 2, 3 or 4) lays up to 4, 8, 12, or 16 in. (10, 20, 30 or 40 cm). *See* **brick format**.

modular system The planning of buildings and their components to fit a *planning grid* related to a *module*. *See* **dimensional coordination**.

modulated control [mech.] Automatic control of *central heating* is usually by simple on-or-off switch from the room *thermostat* or water thermostat. For a hot water system the switch may open or close the boiler air supply. For a *warm-air system*, the switch will stop or start the fan. This method is widely used because it is cheap and sturdy, but it is abrupt and often noisy. A modulated control does not switch on or off abruptly, it reduces or increases the heat flow gently. It is therefore smoother, more responsive, and (most important) quieter.

module (1) A unit of length by which the planning of buildings can be to some extent standardized. Before metrication some British *architects* used plan modules of 1·015 m (40 in.) based on the width of one person at shoulder height plus construction thickness and tolerances. When a module is used, few dimensions are put on the architect's drawing, all main dimensions being indicated by the grid lines. The module thus saves drawing-office work and *quantity surveyor*'s work. Japanese architecture was standardized, long before any European influence came to Japan, by the module of the 3 × 6 ft (0·90 × 1·80 m) floor mat. *See* **brick, blockwork**.

(2) Any prefabricated assembly.

moisture barrier A *vapour barrier, vapour check, damp course*, etc.

moisture content [tim.] The amount of water in wood expressed as a percentage of its *oven-dry* weight, often exceeding 100% for freshly felled timber. At the time of erection the moisture content should not exceed 22% in carpentry or 17% in joinery. In dried-out buildings these figures are reduced to about 16% and 14% with a further 2% reduction if the building is continuously heated. The smallest moisture content at which *fungus* can grow in wood is 20%. The lowest moisture content demanded is 8% to 12% for wood-block floors in hospitals. Below 25% moisture, the moisture content can be measured to an accuracy of 2% or slightly closer by electrical moisture meters, which measure the electrical resistance of the wood between two sharp electrodes driven into it with a special hammer. Reduction of moisture content from the green state to about 25% has little or no effect on the strength, but a reduction from 25% to 12% may double the compressive strength. With any moisture content above 18% wood should be neither painted nor primed. In the conditions of building sites it is unrealistic to insist on moisture contents being closer than ± 2% (BRE Digest 156). BS 4471 states that the cross-sectional dimensions of softwood are to be based on 20% moisture content. By comparison, the dimensions at 25% moisture shall be 1% more and at 30% moisture 2% more, while for lower moisture contents, 1% of the dimensions should be subtracted for each 5% smaller than 20%. Moisture contents above 30% are regarded as 30% for this BS. Bricks and concretes, lightweight or dense, also expand slightly when wetted, as well as losing some of their thermal insulation value. The *U-value* of a material increases as its moisture content rises – its insulating value falls (BRE Digest 108). *See* **fibre saturation point, shrinkage** (illus. p. 302, also *C*).

moisture expansion of bricks Bricks begin to take up moisture and expand irreversibly as soon as they cool. According to BRE Digest 165, typical bricks expand by nearly 1 mm per metre (⅛ in.: 10 ft) in the first eight years, half of it in the first week. The brickwork containing them expands less, about half (0·6 mm/m). In addition there is a reversible wetting-and-drying *moisture movement* that is unlikely to exceed 0·02%. The long-term moisture expansion is not accelerated by soaking the bricks in water. Brickwork should therefore be built with bricks at least a week old, having well detailed, generous *copings, damp courses, flashings,* etc. *See* **sulphate expansion of brickwork, temperature movement**.

moisture gradient [tim.] The variation of *moisture content* between the outer and the inner part of a piece of wood.

moisture movement Bricks, concrete and timber expand when their moisture content increases, often merely in response to a change in the weather, without 'getting wet' at all. Metals, glass, etc. have no moisture movement. Granites, plastics and some hard plasters have very little. *See* **movement joints, temperature movement**.

molding (USA) *Moulding*.

moler brick Brick made of *diatomite*.

monitor, m. roof A continuous *lantern* light like the *north-light roof*, but with vertical sides. *See* **roof light** (illus. p. 280).

monk bond, Yorkshire b., flying b. *Flemish bond* modified to show on the face two *stretchers* and a *header* repeating in each course.

monkey tail [joi.] A downward scroll at the end of a *handrail*.

monkey-tail bolt [joi.] An *extension bolt*.

monolithic screed A *screed* of *grano, terrazzo,* or other mix laid on a fresh concrete slab within three hours of casting, consequently undergoing the same *shrinkage* (*C*). Such a screed need be only 10 mm (⅜ in.) thick and will never separate from the slab, a common fault with other screeds. Up to 20 mm (⅝ in.) thickness of monolithic screed may be accepted as part of the slab structure. *See* **levelling compound**.

monumental mason A *mason* who carves stone, cuts lettering, creates *polished work,* etc.

mortar Many types of mixture of *sand* with *Portland cement* and *lime putty* or *mortar plasticizer* or of sand and *masonry cement,* for *rendering* or for laying bricks, blocks or stones. For example a (strong) 1:1:6 cement:lime:sand mix corresponds in strength and *plasticity* to a 1:5 masonry cement:sand mix or to a 1:6 cement:sand mix with *plasticizer*. Until the use of Portland cement became general, lime:sand mixes were usual. Cement:sand mortar without either plasticizer or lime is too strong for use above ground. It can cause cracking where there is only slight settlement, but below ground level where

218

it stays damp, shrinks less and cracks less easily, its strength is useful. It is also less easy to lay than other mortars. Mortars should have *water retentivity* and plasticity (should cling to the trowel). Ready-mixed lime-sand mixes are sold to which only the dry cement and some more water need to be added. Because of the slowness of hardening of mortar, the greatest height of wall that may be placed in one day is 1·5 m (5 ft), usually less. *See* **fat mortar**, and BRE Digest 160.

mortar board A *hawk*.

mortar-cube test A test for a cement performed by crushing a cube of it made in a standard way with standard sand and measuring the crushing strength.

mortar mill A mixer for *mortar*, often a *pug mill*.

mortar plasticizers BS 4887 specifies *admixtures* used in mortar, which entrain air during mixing and thus improve its *plasticity* and frost resistance, for laying bricks, blocks or stones or for *rendering*. The tiny air bubbles also reduce mortar strength but not excessively if the total percentage of air is kept low by a short mixing time. *See* **air-entraining agent** (*C*), BRE Digest 160.

mortgage An agreement by which a house owner (the mortgagor) gives his property conditionally to the mortgagee, usually a *building society* or insurance company, as a security for the payment of a debt. Very often the mortgagee lends the money to buy the house, but the house does not become his unless the mortgagor defaults in payment.

mortise, mortice A slot cut in wood or stone, in which a *tenon* from another member is glued or pinned, or a *lock* or *lewis* is placed. It should not be wider than one third the thickness in wood, much less in stone.

mortise-and-tenon joint [joi.] A joint between members at right angles to each other, such as a door *rail* tenoned into its *stile*. *See* **mortise**.

mortise chisel [carp.] A *chisel* strong enough to be struck by the *mallet*, for cutting mortises; stiffer than the *firmer chisel*.

mortise gauge, counter g. [joi.] A *marking gauge* with two marking points, of which one is movable. It is used for marking out *mortises* and *tenons*.

mortise joint [joi.] A *mortise-and-tenon joint*.

mortise lock [joi.] A lock set in a *mortise* (within the door thickness). The lock is hidden and the joinery is of better quality than with the *rim lock*.

mortising machine [tim.] A power-operated machine which cuts *mortises* in timber. It may be one of two general types, the square chisel, or the chain mortiser, which has a projecting jib and chain with cutting teeth. The latter is used for cutting large mortises. The square chisel is an *auger bit* rotating in a square steel shell with holes cut into the sides through which the chippings are thrown out.

mosaic Floor, ceiling, or wall surfaces built up from small cubes of marble, glass, or pottery laid in cement to a pattern, a technique known to the ancient Romans. Such a surface abraded smooth after laying is called *terrazzo*.

mosaic cutter A *floor-and-wall tiler* who fixes *Roman mosaic*, cuts the cubes, and glues them to paper. If he makes his own designs he is known as a pattern maker.

mosaic parquet panels, wood mosaic BS 4050 describes these 400 to 500 mm (16 to 20 in.) square chequered assemblies, of rectangular wooden strips glued to paper, mainly quarter sawn. The strips are 18 to 25 mm (¾ to 1 in.) wide and 100 to 125 mm (4 to 5 in.) long. If they are of hardwood, the slips may be as little as 6 mm (¾ in.) thick. Softwood and soft hardwood strips should be thicker, preferably 10 mm (⅜ in.).

motorized valve [plu.] A valve that closes or opens the heating *circulation*; it can easily be fitted into an automatically controlled central heating system, being operated by an electric motor.

mottle [tim.] A *figure* which greatly increases the value of *veneer* for cabinet work, for example *fiddleback*.

mottler [pai.] A flat thick *brush* for *graining* and *marbling*. *Compare* **overgrainer**.

mould [pla.] A zinc sheet cut to the profile of a *moulding* and fixed to a wooden stock cut to the same profile. *See* **horsed mould**.

moulded A description of any material, on which a *moulding* has been cut or cast.

moulded bricks (1) *Bricks* of ordinary quality, generally for *facing*, which are neither *pressed* nor *wirecut*.
   (2) Bricks moulded to shape in Tudor times so that when laid they formed an ornamental brick *corbel*, *chimney-stack*, arch, window, or door *jamb*, *transom*, or *mullion*. All of these moulded bricks, except in chimney stacks or *finials*, were at times plastered to imitate stone. In about 1650 moulded bricks lost their vogue in favour of *carved brickwork*.

moulded insulation, sectional i. *Insulating material*, shaped to fit round steam, hot water, or refrigerator pipes and *fittings*, a ready-made *lagging*.

moulded plywood, ply plastics [tim.] *Plywood* curved during gluing by pressure, usually from *flexible bags*, using heat and *thermo-setting* glues.

moulding (1) A continuous projection or groove used as decoration to throw shadow, sometimes also to throw water away from a wall. It may be in stone, brick, plaster, joinery, cast iron, aluminium, plastics, and so on. In joinery, mouldings are either formed on the solid (*stuck*) or applied by gluing or nailing (*planted*).
   (2) [joi.] The operation of cutting mouldings with woodworking machinery or hand *planes*. The *spindle moulder* is the most versatile machine for cutting mouldings, but other machines are used.

moulding cutter [joi.] A *solid-moulding cutter*.

moulding machines Machines for cutting *mouldings* on wood or stone. *See* **spindle moulder**.

moulding plane [joi.] A hand *plane* used for cutting *mouldings*. *See* **universal plane**.

mouse, duck [joi.] A short, curved piece of lead tied to a string and slipped over a *sash pulley*. The other end of the string is tied to the *sash cord*, which can be pulled over the pulley by the string as the mouse is drawn through the *pocket*.

mouth [joi.] The slot in the *sole* of a *plane* through which the *cutting iron* projects and into which the shavings pass.

movement joints in brickwork B R E Digest 165 suggests that *movement joints* (*C*) in brickwork should allow for 10 mm (⅜ in.) of movement every 12 metres (40 ft) of wall, to accommodate *moisture expansion* and drying shrinkage as well as some *sulphate expansion*. In structural frames of steel or concrete, compressible joints should be provided at tops and sometimes at ends of walls. Walls below *damp course* generally need no movement joints. In factory floors or other large areas of *clay tile* flooring, movement joints are also needed. *See* **flooring tile** (illus. p. 145).

mudsill [carp.] A *sole plate*.

muffle [pla.] A layer of *gauged stuff* covering a *horsed mould* to the thickness of the *finishing coat*, used for roughing out the core of a *moulding* which is too large to be made without a core. Before the finishing coat is run, the muffle is chipped off the mould.

mullion A vertical dividing member of a frame between the *lights* of a door or window, each of which may be further subdivided into *panes* by *glazing bars*. (Illus. above) *Compare* **transom**.

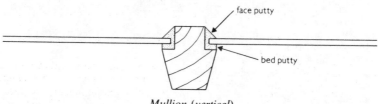

Mullion (vertical).

multi-ply [tim.] *Plywood* with more than three plies. *See* **balanced construction**.

multi-point water heater An instantaneous (non-storage) gas water heater that supplies hot water to several taps. So as to reduce its running cost it should be installed next the tap most frequently used. A typical multi-point unit heats 7 litres (1½ gal.) of water per minute through 45° C. (81° F.) whereas a single-point heater (instantaneous sink heater) heats only 3 litres (5 pints) per minute through 45° C. (81° F.) The Building Regulations allow only *balanced flue* gas heaters in bathrooms.

multi-unit wall (USA) A wall built of two or more half-brick thicknesses, called *withes*, a British *cavity wall*.

muntin [joi.] (1) A subsidiary vertical framing member in a *panelled door*, framed into the *rails*, separating the *panels*, usually of the same width as the *stiles*.

(2) (USA) A *glazing bar* or a *mullion*.

N

nail The commonest nails are cold-forged from bright round steel wire of diameter between 1·2 mm (0·05 in.) and 6 mm (¼ in.). The largest nails (over 13 cm (5 in.)) are known as spikes; the smallest are pins, tacks, oval brads (not to be confused with flooring brads), and *glazing sprigs*. Clout nails are large-headed, galvanized *wire nails* for fixing *slates*, *roofing felt*, or *sash cords*. Those nails which are not made from wire are usually black and of rectangular cross section. They are either sheared from steel plate (cut nails) or have forged heads like the rose-head nail (wrought nails). *Sherardized* nails are made for nailing *gypsum plasterboard*. Nails are usually sold by weight. *See* **roofing nails**.

nailable A material which holds *nails* and into which nails can be driven.

nail float [pla.] A *devil float*.

nailing ground A *common ground*.

nailing machine *See* **stapling machines**.

nailing strip *See* **no-fines concrete**.

nail puller, pry bar [carp.] A tool used for drawing *nails*, more delicate than a *claw hammer*, shaped something like a screwdriver with a curved, forked blade.

nail punch, n. set (USA **brad setter, brad p.**) [joi.] A short blunt steel *punch*, tapering at one end to the diameter of a small *nail*. It is struck by the *hammer* when a nail head is to be driven below the surface. Its point is concave to hold the nail head. (Illus. p. 71)

naphtha [pai.] A *thinner* distilled at temperatures from 160° to 270° C., resembling *white spirit* and used in painting but with caution owing to its strong smell.

narrow-ringed timber, close-grown, close-grained, fine-grained, fine-grown wood Wood which has grown slowly, has narrower, less conspicuous *annual rings* and is therefore stronger than wood which has grown quickly. *Compare* **wide-ringed timber**.

National Building Agency (NBA) A government-sponsored, non-profit organization, which aimed to improve design, construction and management in building. Founded in 1964 it was then concerned with the *appraisal* of *industrialized building methods* for housing, with demonstration building projects and with metrication.

National Building Specification (NBS) A six-volume (small jobs, 2 volumes) loose-leaf publication updated quarterly, obtainable on subscription from NBS Services Ltd, Newcastle upon Tyne. Owned by NBS Services Ltd, a subsidiary of the *RIBA*, it is a 'library' of clauses of specifications from which architects or other consultants can selectively copy when writing *specifications* or *preambles* to bills of quantities. The clauses are simple, short and, unlike most specifications, easy to understand. Ample references are given to BSS and to other authorities. The information can be supplied in at least four different possible forms: (1) conventionally printed on loose-leaf sheets, (2) on magnetic disk suitable for at least 35 word-processing or computer systems, (3) by computer-to-computer transfer over the telephone on some 30 other systems, (4) by IBM magnetic card for some six word-processor or computer systems. NBS is also a word-processing bureau for building specifications based on its publications.

natural bed A stone is laid on its natural bed when its bedding planes are horizontal, advisable for loadbearing stones, especially out of doors. Sometimes the natural bed must be marked on the stone at the quarry, since, particularly with igneous rocks, it is not always obvious. *See* **face-bedded**.

natural cement A limestone containing clay or a clay containing *lime*, which, when burnt, makes without additions a *hydraulic* cement.

natural gas Any fuel gas that flows from the ground. Usually it is mostly methane (CH_4) with other paraffins and olefines.

natural seasoning [tim.] The drying of timber by stacking it so that it is exposed to the air all round but sheltered from sun and rain, a process which usually takes years and is therefore costly. This old method may be preferred to *kiln seasoning*.

natural stone Stone which has been quarried and cut, not *cast stone*.

navvy pick A heavy double-pointed *pick*, or one with a point and a chisel edge, generally with a *helve* 90 cm (36 in.) long.

neat size [carp.] The dimensions of a piece after cutting and planing.

needle (1) **n. beam** A short, horizontal, wooden or steel beam which passes through a shored wall, carries the wall, and transfers its weight to *dead shores* (illus. p. 97).

(2) In *flying* or *raking shores* (p. 268) a short (about 45 cm (18 in.) long) horizontal, *hardwood* or steel piece which passes through the vertical *wall plate* (2) and the wall. It thus holds the wall plate in place and forms an abutment for the shores.

needle scaffold A *scaffold* hung on *needles* driven into the wall.

Neoprene Trade name for an oil-resistant American synthetic rubber (like PVC), which has other excellent properties of non-flammability and light-resistance. Puttyless glazing, with weathertight Neoprene *gaskets* enclosing the glass on both inside and outside edges, is now often used on large buildings, partly because of the speed of glazing. This type of mounting for glass, which is both resilient and sealed, improves *noise insulation*, in which flexible sealing is important.

nest of saws [joi.] Several saw blades which can be used at different times in the same handle.

neutralizing [pai.] Preparation of *concrete* or cement *mortar* or *plaster* surfaces for painting, so that the free *lime* of the ground does not attack the paint. *See* **alkali-resistant paint**.

newel, n. post [joi.] A post in a *flight* of stairs carrying the ends of *outer string* and *handrail* and supporting them at an end or corner. *See* **solid-newel stairs, open-newel stair**.

newel cap [joi.] A wooden top to a *newel* post.

newel drop [joi.] A downward decorative projection of a newel post through a *soffit*.

nib (1) **cog** A downward-projecting lug at the head of a *roofing tile*, for hooking over the tiling *batten*. Continuous nibs can be obtained that enable the tile to be used, e.g. with the nib downhill to act as a *drip* for a windowsill or *coping*.

(2) The part of the top edge of a vertical sheet of asphalt which fits into a chase in the wall which it protects.

(3) [pai.] A small solid particle which projects above the surface of a film, usually of *varnish*. A film with nibs is called *bitty*.

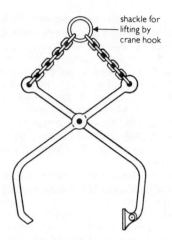

shackle for
lifting by
crane hook

Nippers (or crampon or stone tongs).

nib guide [pla.], **n. rule** A 5 × 2 cm (2 × ¾ in.) *straight edge* nailed on the floating coat of a ceiling on which a *cornice* mould is to be run. It holds the upper end of the *horsed mould* in position as the *running rule* holds the lower edge.

nicker (1) [carp.] *See* **centre bit**.

(2) A mason's broad *chisel* for grooving stone before splitting it.

nidged, nigged ashlar Stone, particularly granite, dressed roughly with a pointed hammer. The hardest granite can be dressed only in this way.

night lock [joi.] A *cylinder lock*.

night vent, v. light, v. sash, ventilator [joi.] A small *opening light* with horizontal *hinges* above a *casement window*.

nippers, crampon, stone tongs, dog and chain Two curved levers hinged together near their middle and lifted by a crane at their upper ends. The pull of the crane at the upper end draws the lower ends of the nippers together and they are thus forced to nip the block of stone being lifted. (Illus. above)

nipple (1) [plu.] A short pipe threaded outside at each end with a *taper thread*, used for joining two *couplings* or internally threaded pipes.

(2) A small valve at the high points of a hot-water system by which air can be released to prevent air locks.

(3) [mech.] A small brass tube screwed into a machine part for injecting grease into it through a grease gun.

nitrocellulose, cellulose nitrate, guncotton An important part of most modern *lacquers* used on metal, wood, or textiles. It is also used for making *plastic wood* and some *glues*. *See* **cellulose paint**.

no-fines concrete Concrete made without sand. It therefore contains large pores, and for this reason provides no *capillary* passage for water. It has been used in Britain for building house walls (Crawley new town) in roughly the same thickness as the *cavity wall* which it replaces. A typical no-fines aggregate consists of 95% between 19 and 9·5 mm (¾ and ⅜ in.) and 5% smaller than 9·5 mm (⅜ in.). Since it is not *nailable*, *chases* are formed during casting and a *foamed slag* nailing strip is plastered into the chase after the shuttering has been stripped. No-fines concrete must not be vibrated or rammed, but lightly punned. It is usually not reinforced except for a few diagonal bars across the corners of openings. It must be rendered outside to strengthen and protect it. It is often regarded as a *lightweight concrete* especially when made of *lightweight aggregate*.

nog A *fixing brick*.

nogging (1) **n. piece, nog** [carp.] Horizontal short timbers which stiffen the *studs* (verticals) of a *framed partition*.

(2) *See* **brick nogging**.

noise The best way of reducing noise in dwellings is by planning, to keep noisy things together and separated from quieter things like housing. This applies not only to *zoning* but also within the dwelling – *maisonettes* are an example. Noise reduction by means other than planning is usually less effective and many times more expensive than noise reduction put in by the design of a building, though planned noise reduction also may be expensive (tunnel for a motorway under a housing estate). A fan used for forced ventilation will emit 17 decibels more noise if its speed is doubled. If the fan speed is halved, however, a larger, more expensive fan and housing will be needed to achieve the same air speed. Duct air speeds of 5 m/sec (16 ft/sec) or less are satisfactory for most buildings but 2·5 m/sec (8 ft/sec) will help to create especially quiet conditions. The possibilities open to a local authority in creating noise abatement zones are set out in BRE Digests 203 and 204. *See* **discontinuous construction, pugging**, *also* BSCP 3.

noise absorption The *noise* level within a room can be reduced before it is built, by design, or after it is built by noise *absorption*, that is by surrounding it or filling it with absorbent (non-echoing) material.

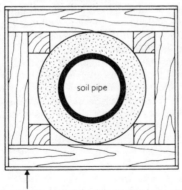

soil pipe

hardboard or other covering over frame to casing, consisting of 25 × 25mm (1 × 1 in.) timber, fixed to a wall along any side

Noise insulation for a soil pipe passing through a living room or bedroom. (After National Housebuilding Council, 1974). The soil pipe is surrounded with a 25 mm (1 in.) ring of sound-absorbent fibre, preferably with more sound-absorbent material filling the casing.

noise insulation Reduction of the sound passing through a wall depends on its mass, the weight per m², with the exception that a *cavity wall* built on the principle of *discontinuous construction* reduces the noise passing through it nearly twice as much as a normal one. A wide cavity is needed, preferably 150 mm (6 in.) with absorbent infill and there should be either no wall ties or very flexible ones. (Illus.) *See* **acoustic screen, airborne noise, double glazing, double-leaf party wall, flanking transmission, Neoprene, staggered-stud partition**, and above.

nominal size [tim.] The dimension of timber after sawing but before planing or otherwise working it. It is usually about 3 to 4 mm (⅛ in.) larger than the final size after planing (*dressed size*).

nominated sub-contractor When the client or his *consultant* wishes one company to do some work, he states this, usually in a *bill of quantities*, thus nominating a *sub-contractor*. The work is described in the bill and is allowed for by the *main contractor* as a *prime cost sum*.

non-bearing wall A wall which carries its own weight and wind load only, as opposed to a *loadbearing wall* (*C*).

non-combustible The term preferred by the Fire Protection Association and other fire authorities to the old word incombustible, meaning that which does not burn.

non-drip paint [pai.] Modern paints that do not drip from the brush, because they are not liquids but jellies. They are none the less easy to apply and flow well.

non-flammable Description of material which will not burn with a flame. *See* **flame spread**.

non-hydraulic lime [pla.] *High-calcium lime*.

non-manipulative joint [plu.] A *compression joint* which requires no work on the pipe other than cutting the ends square, and is therefore more used, at least for the smaller diameters of pipe, than the manipulative joint. *See* **gland**.

non-return valve [plu.] A fitting occasionally inserted into a water supply pipe to prevent backward flow into the main. The *jumper* in domestic taps or in a *screw-down valve* has the same function.

non-setting glazing compound A permanently flexible *glazing compound* (of many different types) used on *anti-sun glass* or other glass that needs a flexible fixing. If the thickness is at least 3 mm (⅛ in.) the core should stay flexible even if the surface hardens. *See* **sealing compound**.

non-slip floors or **treads** Non-slip floor surfaces may be formed by creating a chessboard pattern from prefabricated abrasive cubes of carborundum or alumina or by sprinkling a *grano* floor with abrasive powder or by filling grooves or squares in the floor with abrasive powder mixed with cement (B S 5395).

Norfolk latch [joi.] A *thumb latch*.

normal roll pantiles *Pantiles* which have rolls of the same width from head to tail.

Norman brick (USA) A *brick* measuring 30 × 10 × 6·7 cm (12 × 4 × 2⅔ in.) including the mortar *joints*. Three courses lay up 20 cm (8 in.) in height.

north-light roof, saw-tooth r. A factory roof having one steep and one gentle slope. In the northern hemisphere the steeper slope is glazed and faces north. In the southern hemisphere it is built facing south. *See* **roof light**, p. 280.

nose (1) Any blunt overhang, a *nosing*.

(2) The lower end of the *shutting stile* of a door or *casement*. *See* **heel**.

nosing A half-round, overhanging edge to a stair tread, flat roof, window sill, etc., in concrete, stone, or timber. *See* **flight** (illus. p. 142).

nosing line A line touching the edges of the nosings of a stair. The *margin* of a *close string* is measured from it (Illus. p. 326).

notch, gain [carp.] A groove in a timber to receive another timber.

notch board [carp.] (1) A *cut string*.

(2) (USA) A *close string*.

notching [carp.] Joining two timbers by cutting a part out of one or both. *See also C*.

novelty siding [tim.] *German siding*.

Nuralite [plu.] *See* **asbestos-bitumen**.

nylon One of the stronger plastics, though it has only one tenth the strength of steel and 100 times its thermal expansion, nylon is so wear-resistant, corrosion-resistant and cheap that it is now used for making such hardware as barrel bolts for cupboard doors, wood screws up to 6·5 cm (2½ in.) long and even gear wheels.

O

oak [tim.] (Quercus robur, Quercus petraea, etc.) *Hardwoods* which grow in temperate climates throughout the world. English oak is difficult to work because of its hardness and twisted grain, but it has for long in England been a valued structural timber which is very decorative when *quarter sawn*. It is not generally so stiff nor so strong as either beech or ash. All imported oak is more straight-grained than English oak, and therefore easier to work. *See* **death-watch beetle, workability**.

oak shingles *Shingles* made from oak heartwood, generally 300 × 90 × 16 mm (12 × 3½ × ⅜ in.) at the butt to 13 mm (½ in.) thick at the tip.

oakum Untwisted rope or hemp, tarred or oiled and used sometimes as a caulking in prefabricated buildings, between precast concrete pieces and so on.

oak varnish [pai.] An oil *varnish* with a high proportion of oil to resin, 1½ to 1 or less, normally used indoors. Elastic oak varnish can be used out of doors.

oblique butt joint [carp.] A *butt joint* at an angle other than 90° to the length of the piece.

obscured glass, vision-proof g., translucent g. *Glass* through which light can pass, although things cannot be distinguished through it. It is sand-blasted or moulded to roughen the surfaces.

ochre [pai.] Hydrated iron oxide used as a *pigment*. It is yellow or yellowish brown, paler than *umber* or *sienna*, and may contain a little clay.

offset A ledge in a wall where the wall thickness changes, or a curve like an S joining two parallel lengths of a pipe, such as a *swan neck*.

offset screwdriver [carp.] A screwdriver which turns screws at right-angles to its length.

offshoot A *water table*.

oil-burning stove *See* **condensation**.

oil-fired central heating [plu.] The most expensive and probably the most luxurious *central heating*. *See* **flue lining**.

oil gloss paint Paint made with *boiled oil* and some *raw linseed oil*. It is suitable for interior use. *Compare* **hard gloss paint**.

oil length [pai.] The ratio of oil to *resin* in a varnish *medium*. *See* **long oil, short oil**.

oil-modified alkyd [pai.] Very durable paint, now in more general use than lead or *oleo-resinous paints*.

oil paint Paint with a binder of *drying oil* or oil *varnish* mixed with *thinner*.

oil paste, colours in oil [pai.] A concentrated paste of *pigment* and oil used for *tinting* or for making paint by adding oil or *thinners* and *driers*.

oil stain [pai.] A thin *oil paint*, with very little *pigment*, used for staining wood floors. *Compare* **spirit stain, water stain**.

oilstone [joi.] A *hone*.

oilstone slip, s. stone, gouge s. [joi.] A small *hone* with a curved edge or edges for sharpening *gouges* and concave *cutting irons* of *planes*.

old woman's tooth [joi.] The original form of the plane now called a *plough*. It has a *cutting iron* like a chisel, wedged in a beechwood block.

oleo-resin [pai.] Mixed oil and resin from the sap of plants or trees, used in *varnish* and *paint*. *See* **turpentine**

oleo-resinous paint or **varnish** [pai.] A paint or varnish containing *drying oils* with natural or *synthetic resins*. They have good *gloss* and last longer than lead paints. *See* **gold size**.

oncosts *See* **overheads**.

one-pipe system (1) [plu.] House drainage in which *soil* and *sullage* flow together through one pipe to the drain. It may need *anti-siphon pipes*. *See* **single-stack, two-pipe systems**, B S 4118.

(2) A *central heating* circuit in which all the flow and return connections to the radiators come from the same pipe. The furthest radiator is therefore much cooler than the radiator next to the boiler. *See* **hot-water cylinder** (illus. p. 179), **two-pipe system**.

opacity, opaqueness [pai] The *hiding power* of a paint, the opposite of transparency.

open assembly time [tim.] The time which elapses between the application of the *glue* to a *veneer* or joint and the assembly of the veneers or parts of a joint.

open cornice (UK **open eaves**) [carp.] In American timber house construction, an eaves overhang in which the rafter *soffits* and usually also the slates or roof *sheathing* can be seen. *Compare* **box cornice**.

open defect [tim.] Any hole or gap in timber or ply, such as *checks*, splits, knothole, wormhole, or open joints.

open-drained joint, drained j. A way of making joints between concrete panels in *large-panel construction*, which involves an airtight joint usually with *sealing compound* at the back (inside) of the panel, protected by a *baffle* in front that stops any driving rain. (Illus. below) *Compare* **filled joint**, p. 132.

open floor [carp.] A floor, in which the *joists* are exposed beneath, since it is not ceiled.

open grain [tim.] *Coarse-textured*.

open-grained [tim.] *Wide-ringed*.

opening, clear opening (of a door or window) The clear horizontal width between *jambs*, available for installing a frame, usually about 6 mm ($\frac{1}{4}$ in.) more than the width of the frame.

opening leaf [joi.] A leaf of a *folding door* which opens, as opposed to a *standing leaf*.

opening light [joi.] A *window* which opens, not a *deadlight*.

open mortise, slot m., slip m. [joi.] A *mortise* open on three edges. It is not a

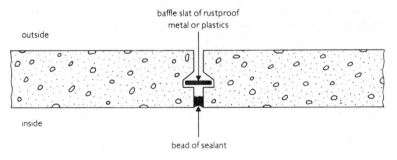

Open-drained joint between large concrete panels.

true mortise but is used for table legs and can be cut with a circular saw. *See* **forked tenon**.

open-newel stair A *geometric stair* (one without newels).

open planning Planning of tall buildings without *air shafts*, often also the designing of a house with few fixed *partitions*.

open roof A roof in which the *principals* can be seen from below, since it has no ceiling.

open slating, spaced s. *Slates* or *tiles* laid with a gap between those in the same *course*, sometimes used to ventilate cowsheds, etc. The gap should not be more than the slate width minus 20 cm (8 in.).

open stair (USA) A *stair* which is open on one or both sides. *Compare* **closed stair**.

open string [joi.] A *cut string*.

open tendering [q.s.] *See* **tendering**.

open valley A *valley* in which the *slates, tiles*, or *shingles* are so cut and laid that the *flexible-metal* sheet or other waterproof material under them in the *valley* is exposed. *Compare* **secret gutter**.

open vented system [plu.] The usual water heating circuit, with an *expansion pipe* open at the top, not a *sealed system*.

open-well stair A *stair* with a generous *well*.

orange peeling [pai.] *Pinholing* in a sprayed finish – a *flow* failure caused by incorrect air pressure, solvents or lacquer.

orbital sander [joi., pai.] An electric şander capable of producing a dead-smooth (satin) finish on timber, also used for *flatting* paint, plaster or masonry. A popular machine weighs 2·4 kg (5 lb), has a base (sanding area) 115 × 228 mm (5 × 9 in.) and is rated at 250 watts.

ordinary Portland cement A *hydraulic cement* made by heating to *clinker* in a kiln a slurry of clay and limestone. This is the cheapest and most widely used *cement*. *See also* **C**.

organosol [pai.] A polyvinyl chloride coating applied in the steelworks to the inner face of galvanized *profiled steel sheet* to a thickness of about 0·05 mm (0·002 in.).

oriel window An upper-storey, overhanging window. Unlike the *bow window*, it is carried on corbels.

O-ring joint A joint between *drain pipes*, made watertight by a rubber ring between *spigot* and *socket*. Since it is flexible it allows the pipes to settle. The concrete bedding around the pipe should therefore be left out for some 2 cm at the joint to ensure that it can flex, otherwise settlement might break the pipes. (Illus. below, pp. 110, 310)

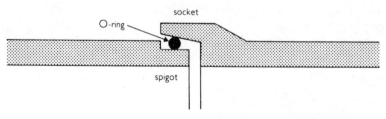

O-ring joint in concrete drain pipe, about 5° movement is possible.

orpiment [pai.] Arsenic sulphide (As_2S_3), a lemon-yellow mineral *pigment*.

outer lining [joi.] An *outside lining*.

outer string (USA **face s.**) [joi.] The *string* of a wooden *stair* furthest from a wall, as opposed to the *wall string*.

outlet (1) A vent, in particular an opening in a *parapet wall* through which rainwater discharges into a rainwater hopper.

(2) [elec.] A *socket outlet*.

outrigger A beam projecting from a building and wedged against a ceiling within it. It carries a *fan* or *flying scaffold*. *See also C*.

outside casing, o. facing [joi.] An *outside lining*.

outside glazing *External glazing* placed from outside the frame.

outside lining [joi.] (USA **o. casing**) The boards forming the outside of a *cased frame*.

oval-wire brad A *wire nail* formed from oval wire in lengths from 19 mm ($\frac{3}{4}$ in.) to 10 cm (4 in.). It is supplanting *wrought* or *cut nails*. Not to be confused with *brads* for flooring.

oven-dry timber Timber which loses no moisture in a ventilated oven at 103° $\pm$ 2° C. (BS 565).

overcloak In *flexible-metal roofing*, that part of the upper sheet which laps over the lower at a *drip* or *roll* or *seam*. *See* **undercloak, cloak**.

overflowing rainwater gutters Blocked rainwater gutters probably originate more *dampness* than any other cause, at least in modern houses. To prevent it, gutters should be cleaned out every autumn after the leaf fall.

overgrainer [pai.] A brush like a *mottler*, but thinner and longer, used also for *graining* and *marbling*.

overhand work Facing bricks laid from inside a building by men standing on the floor or a scaffold inside. Overhand laying reduces the scaffolding costs but the bricklayer cannot see properly, so bricklayers with experience of this work are needed.

overhang A projection of a roof, floor, or other horizontal part beyond the wall which carries it.

overhanging eaves *Rafters*, tiles, slates, etc. projecting, as usual, clear of the wall.

overhead door, up-and-over d. [joi.] A door which opens by being lifted up and slipped into a horizontal position at the door *head*. It may be in one or two leaves.

overheads, overhead expenses, establishment charges, oncosts [q.s.] The costs of electric light, roads, supervision, accounting, director's fees, etc., which cannot fairly be charged to one job and must therefore be distributed over all the *items* on a *contract*.

oversailing course A brick or stone *string course* or corbelling.

oversite concrete A layer of about 15 cm (6 in.) of concrete to seal the earth under the ground floor of a house, whether this is of wood or of other flooring material. *See* **solum.**

over-tile The imbrex of *Italian* or *Spanish tiling*.

overtime Additional payment tor time worked above the normal number of hours. *See* **double time, time and a half**.

oxidation [pai.] The hardening of *drying oils* in air by their absorption of oxygen to form a durable *film*, not by evaporation alone.

oxter piece [carp.] An ashler piece, the vertical in *ashlering*.

oxy-acetylene flame [plu.] A flame obtained at a gas jet supplied from large steel cylinders of oxygen and of acetylene, through high-pressure hoses. The most powerful flame in common use, it is hot enough to weld steel or to cut it by burning, or to make brazed joints or for *lead burning*. For most plumbing purposes the modern *propane blowlamp* is adequate, needs short hoses or none, and is safer and more portable.

oxychloride cement *See* **magnesite flooring**.

P

package deal, turnkey contract, etc. An arrangement whereby a *contractor* agrees with his *client* to take full responsibility for design and construction. This eliminates some of the delays involved in co-operation with consultants but it increases the risk to the client of unsuitable construction. Only conceivable with a sophisticated, conscientious contractor, it is less secure for the client than a *management contract*.

pad (1) **padstone, template** A stone or precast concrete block placed under a heavy load such as the end of a girder to spread its load in a *loadbearing wall* (*C*).

(2) A *tool pad*.

paddle mixer (USA **twin pug**) A *mortar* mixer with two horizontal shafts rotating in opposite directions. *See* **pug mill**.

padsaw A *saw* blade in a *tool pad*.

paint A liquid applied to building materials in *coats* which dry hard within a few hours. It protects them from corrosion, and is usually decorative. Paint consists of *pigment* and *medium*. *See below;* also **dispersion** (*C*), **emulsion paint, fire-resisting finishes, oil paint, plastic paint,** also BS 6150.

painter *See* **house painter** (illus.).

paint brush. *See* **brush.**

painter's caulk, sealing compound Names used by different makers for a fluid *sealing compound* of gun grade supplied in tubes about 20 cm (8 in.) long and 4 cm (1⅜ in.) diameter, from which it is conveniently expelled by a screw gun. An easy filler to use but some types have considerable shrinkage.

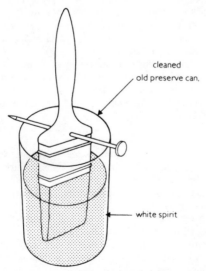

cleaned
old preserve can.

white spirit

Paint brush maintenance. A nail passed through a hole, drilled in the stock of the brush, preserves the bristle while the brush hangs in white spirit between jobs.

painter's labourer A skilled labourer who helps a *house painter* by preparing surfaces, stripping old wallpaper, washing ceilings, etc. He may apply the first coat of *emulsion paint*, or creosote fences or rough timber, in which case he is called a brush hand.

painter's putty *Glazier's putty*, used as a *filler*.

paint harling Throwing paint-coated stone chips on to a sticky paint film to make a rough surface.

painting Putting on *paints, varnishes* and *stains* for protection and decoration. It begins with *surface preparation* followed by *priming* and *stopping*, after which comes the *undercoat* and *gloss coat*. (Not all these stages are needed for all surfaces.) Painting must generally not start before the *drying out* is complete. A *four-coat system* is usual (BS 6150).

painting damp walls Because about a year is needed for a house to dry out properly, walls of new houses are often painted while still damp. Painting of really wet walls usually fails completely. The paint chosen should therefore allow water vapour to pass through it. Many *emulsion paints* are suitable, but *see* **alkali-resistant paint**.

painting on galvanized steel The effect of rain and wind on galvanized steel is to make paint stick to it better, but the period of weathering needed may vary from a week or two to more than a year.

paint remover A liquid which softens a *paint* or *varnish* film, so that it can be easily scraped or brushed off. They may be of two types: (1) Those containing soda which may damage the surface and always injure the hands. (2) Those containing organic *solvents* which cannot damage either the surface or the hands. These can easily be distinguished from soda-based liquids, as they do not mix with water.

paint system A succession of *coats* designed to protect a surface and give a decorative finish. On wood the first treatments are *knotting, priming and stopping*; on plaster a *sealer*; or on metal, *surface preparation, pre-treatment primer* or *primer*, then an *undercoat* with good *hiding power*, and a high *gloss* coat and sometimes a *varnish*.

pair Two oppositely *handed* but otherwise similar objects.

pale, paling Pointed, upright, metal or wooden stakes in a *palisade*.

pale boiled oil [pai.] A *linseed oil* through which a little air has been blown at about 150° C. It contains a small amount of *driers* and is used for making oil and *hard gloss paints*.

palette board [pai.] A small thin board with a handle or a hole through it for the thumb, used for mixing colours, mainly by artists.

palette knife [pai.] A knife with a long, narrow, symmetrical, springy blade rounded at the point, for handling colours on a palette board. *See* **house painter** (illus. p. 180).

palisade An enclosure of pointed wooden or metal *pales* driven into the ground.

pallet, p. slip A *fixing fillet. See also* C.

pallet brick A brick rebated at one edge to receive a *fixing fillet*.

pan-and-roll roofing tiles (USA) *Italian tiling*.

pan breeze The mixture of small coke (coke breeze) and furnace clinker from the pan beneath a furnace burning coke breeze. It was used as an aggregate for making concrete blocks (*breeze blocks*).

pane, square A sheet of glass cut to size to fill part of a *light* between *glazing bars*.

panel (1) [joi.] An infilling of glass, wood, or other material let into grooves or rebates in *panelled framing*, leaving the panel free to move relatively to the *frame*.

(2) The brick infilling to the steel or concrete frame of a structure.

(3) A single span or *bay* of a continuous concrete slab.

panel box, p. board [elec.] A *cutout box*.

panel heating [elec.] Electrical resistance heating by flat panels with a surface temperature of about 38° C. (100° F.) flush with the wall, or by panels about 5 cm (2 in.) clear of the wall at a higher temperature. Coils of hot-water pipes hidden in walls or floors are now usually called concealed heating or *coil heating. See also* **electric-panel heater**.

panelled door [joi.] A door built of a framed surround with the spaces between the framing members (*stiles, rails, muntins*) filled with *panels* of thinner material. These were the best doors in existence before *plywood* was made, and they are so built as to have no excessive *moisture movement*. However, plywood flush doors, even of the cheapest sort, have less moisture movement than *panelled framing*. (Illus. below)

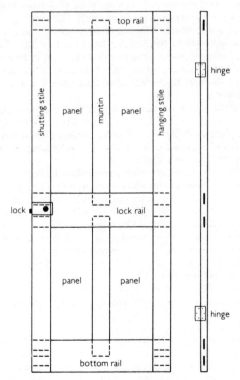

Panelled door: (right), edge view showing seen tenons. Mouldings round panel edges are not shown.

panelled framing [joi.] Framing consisting of *stiles* (vertical) with *rails* (horizontal) tenoned into them and, in wide frames, *muntins* (vertical) tenoned into the rails. The frames contain panels.

panel pin [joi.] A round wire *nail* between 1 and 1·6 mm thick and from 1 to 5 cm (½ to 2 in.) long. It is very slender, has a small head, and is used for *joinery*. It can be nearly invisible when driven below the surface.

panel saw [joi.] A *cross-cut saw* about 56 cm (22 in.) long with closely set teeth. It has about 10 points per 25 mm (1 in.).

panel wall Brickwork or other walling in *skeleton construction*. It is restrained by the building frame, generally on at least three of its four edges, carries only its own weight, and is carried at each floor by the building frame.

panic bolt [joi.] A door bolt often used at the double exit doors of theatres. It is opened by pressure from inside on to a waist-high horizontal bar within the door.

pantile A *single-lap tile* shaped like an S laid horizontally – thus ~. The British standard size is about 34 × 24 × 1 cm (13½ × 9½ × 0·4 in.). Each tile overlaps its neighbour on the right (looking at the roof from the ground in front of the house) and is overlapped by its neighbour on the left by about 5 cm (2 in.). About 205 tiles are needed per 10 m² (107·6 ft²) and the weight of the pantiles alone is about 49 kg/m² (10 lb/ft²). Pantiles generally have a nail hole and a *nib* at the head. Larger, heavier pantiles exist, up to 42 × 33 cm but they weigh less per 10 m² than the small ones.

parallel coping A coping, not *weathered* but of uniform thickness, for covering a sloping surface such as a *gable*.

parallel gutter, p. parapet gutter A *box gutter*.

parallel thread [mech.] A *screw thread* of uniform diameter used on mechanical connections such as *bolts* (*C*) but not in pipe fittings except on *connectors*. Compare **taper thread**.

parapet A low wall guarding the edge of a roof, bridge, balcony, etc.; that part of a house wall which passes above the roof. Since it is exposed on its face, back and top to the weather, it needs detailing with more care than other walls. BRE Digest 165 therefore recommends that parapets should either be avoided completely or given generous detailing with a wide *coping* and good *damp courses*. At roof level the damp course should be in the form of *engineering bricks* of low *absorption* to provide a good bond with the roof. Bricks in the damp course should be laid preferably with sulphate-resistant cement. Low-sulphate bricks should be used where possible and *movement joints* provided every 12 m (40 ft). Similar recommendations apply to free-standing walls.

parapet gutter *See* **box gutter**.

parenchyma [tim.] The wood tissue of the *medullary rays*, seen in the *silver grain* of oak, also the main part of the *heart centre*, soft and weak.

parge [pla.] The mixture used in *pargetting* (1) either cement mortar or *coarse stuff* with *hair* and cowdung.

pargetting, parging [pla.] (1) *Rendering* the inside of a brick *flue*, superseded by modern *flue blocks* and *linings*.

(2) Decorative plastering to the outside walls of Elizabethan houses with lime plaster. Repetitive patterns, sometimes very beautiful, modelled in the plaster before it hardened can be seen in East Anglia.

(3) (USA) *Back plastering*.

paring chisel [joi.] A long, thin, bevel-edged *chisel* which is never struck with the *mallet*.

paring gouge [joi.] A thin, long *gouge* sharpened on the inside.

Paris white *See* **whiting**.

parliament hinge [joi.] An *H-hinge*.

parquet floor A wooden floor covering of *hardwood* blocks in geometrical patterns glued to the floor and polished. It can now be obtained fixed to *plywood* so that large areas can be quickly laid (plywood parquet).

parquet-floor layer, wood-block floor l., hardwood-strip flooring l. A *tradesman* who lays prepared *parquet floor* on a wooden *sub-floor* by gluing or pinning. As a wood-block floor layer he lays *hardwood* blocks in adhesive on concrete. As a hardwood strip-flooring layer he lays prepared *parquet strip* on a wooden sub-floor covered by three-ply. He works to a drawing if need be, finishes the floor with a hand scraper or *sanding machine*, and sometimes stains and polishes it. *See* **wood-block floor**.

parquet strip, strip, overlay flooring [tim.] A floor consisting of tongued and grooved *hardwood* boards 1 cm (⅜ in.) actual thickness which are *secret nailed* and glued to a wooden *sub-floor*.

particle board [tim.] *See* **wood chipboard**.

parting bead, p. strip [joi.] A narrow vertical strip of wood fixed to the *pulley stiles* of *cased frames* of *sash windows* to separate the upper sash from the lower sash when they are being opened or closed and therefore sliding past each other.

parting slip, mid-feather, wagtail, pendulum [joi.] A long narrow vertical slip of wood, which hangs from the pulley level to the bottom of the *cased frame* of a *sash window*, and keeps the sash weights from colliding when the window is being opened or closed.

parting tool, vee t. [joi.] A V-shaped *gouge* used by wood carvers and wood turners.

parting wall or **fence, party w.** or **f.** (USA **common w.**) A fence or wall separating two properties and shared by them.

partition A wall between rooms, non-loadbearing and generally one storey high. Partitions can be built in an enormous variety of ways, the commonest permanent ones now being of plastered brick or *blockwork*, but *dry construction* is possible, e.g. in expanded plastics slabs faced both sides with *hardboard*, which are only 50 mm (2 in.) thick. *See also* **compressed straw, corkboard, framed partition, woodwool**, BS 5234.

partition coverings, infillings *See* **coverings, infillings**.

partition plate, p. cap, p. head [carp.] The uppermost timber of a *trussed partition*, on which the joists rest.

passings, laps [plu.] The distance by which one *flexible-metal* sheet overlaps the next in *flashings*, ridge coverings, *gutters*, etc.

paste drier, patent d. [pai.] A stiff paste consisting of *drier* mixed with *drying oil* and an *extender*. *Soluble driers* are now more popular.

patch, shim [tim.] An *insert* of veneer in *plywood*.

patent glazing Any dry (puttyless) *glazing* in a roof or wall, not usually in housing, and often with metal *glazing bars* that usually span 2·1 m (7 ft) but spans of 3·3 m (11 ft) are known. Concrete, galvanized steel or aluminium bars are protected by cappings of zinc, copper, lead, aluminium, plastics, etc. The glass is bedded on a *cushion*. It can be *double-glazed*. *See also* illus.,

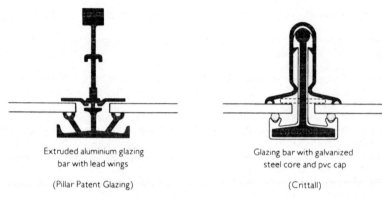

Extruded aluminium glazing
bar with lead wings

(Pillar Patent Glazing)

Glazing bar with galvanized
steel core and pvc cap

(Crittall)

Patent glazing.

condensation groove, monitor, north light, shoe, storm clip, and B S 5516.

patent plaster [pla.] *Hard plaster* like *Keene's*.

patent-roofing glazier A *glazier* who fits glass in roof lights with metal frames, fixes assembled *roof lights*, and makes them weather-proof. He is often specialized either in assembling the frame or in the fixing of it in the roof or in the *glazing*. *See* **patent glazing**.

patina A thin, stable, protective film of oxide which forms on metals exposed to air, particularly the green coating on copper or its alloys (verdigris) which usually takes many years to form, but has recently been made artificially by chemical means in much less time.

pattern staining [pla.] The discoloration of plasterwork caused by the different conductances of backings. Where *gypsum plasterboard* is fixed over steel *joists*, the part in contact with the joists becomes darker than the part with no backing. This part has a bigger temperature difference, from the air in the room, than the surrounding plaster. The air therefore circulates over it more freely and drops more dust on to it.

pavement light, vault l. A *light* formed of solid glass blocks cast into concrete or set in a cast-iron frame over a basement.

pavement prism A *glass block* fitted in a *pavement light*.

pean [mech.] The *peen* of a *hammer*.

pearlite *See* **perlite**.

pebbledash, spardash, dry dash An outside finish to a wall, in which clean, washed natural (or artificial) pebbles are thrown on to the fresh, final *rendering* coat, pushed in and left exposed (BS 4049). Compare **roughcast**.

pebble walling A wall built of rounded pebbles. It can be as beautiful as *flint walling*.

peeler log [tim.] A log chosen for *rotary cutting*, particularly a *Douglas fir* log.

peeling (1) [tim.] *Rotary cutting* of veneers.

(2) The dislodgement of plaster or paint from its backing.

peen [mech.], **pein, pean, pene, pane**, etc. The blunt, wedge- or ball-shaped end of a *hammer* head, opposite the striking *face*. *See* **ball p., cross p., straight p.**

peen hammer A *mason's* hammer with no flat striking face but two cutting *peens*.

peg (1) An *oak* or galvanized steel rod 6 mm (¼ in.) dia. passed through a *roofing tile* to hold it in place.

(2) [joi.] A *dowel*.

(3) [joi.] A metal pin which secures glass to a metal window frame.

peg stay A casement stay which holds a window in place by a peg through one of its holes.

pein [mech.] *See* **peen**.

pellet [joi.] A small circular piece of wood, cut to match the grain of wood into which it is inlaid to cover the head of a countersunk screw.

pelmet [joi.] A built-in board or very short curtain over a window, that hides the curtain rail, blind fittings, etc.

pencilling Painting mortar joints of brickwork with white paint to contrast the joints with the brickwork.

pendulum saw, swing s., swinging crosscut [tim.] A *circular saw* which hangs on a frame pivoted at ceiling level and is brought down to a log to *cross-cut* it.

penthouse (1) An *apartment* built on the flat roof of a building, with walking space round it. *See* **bulkhead, penthouse roof**.

(2) **pentice** A projecting hood over a window or door or wall to protect it from rain.

penthouse roof, pen r. A roof sloping in one direction only. It differs from a *lean-to roof* because it covers the wall.

perfections *Western red cedar* shingles 46 cm long and 1·4 cm (18 in. and $\frac{9}{16}$ in.) thick at the *butt*.

perforated brick A *brick* with vertical perforations through the *frog*. They reduce the weight, allow the brick to dry quickly, and thus lower the cost of burning. They are much used on the Continent of Europe particularly in Germany. (Illus. below) *See* **brick definitions, V-brick**.

perimeter diffuser In *warm-air heating*, a diffuser placed at the edge of a room, for example under a window, to neutralize its cold effect.

perlite, pearlite A volcanic glass found in USA. When heated, it expands to lightweight, glassy, spherical particles about the size of small peas. It is an

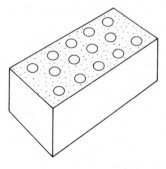

Perforated brick.

239

insulating *aggregate* for plaster or precast concrete and absorbs less water than exfoliated *vermiculite*.

perlite plaster [pla.] Gypsum plaster which contains only *perlite* aggregate, and no sand. It is a good insulator, and is easy for the plasterer and his labourer to work with because it is light in weight.

permeability [pai.] The rate of movement of a fluid through a material. The permeability of wood affects its rate of drying, also the amount of pre-servative it can absorb, and any paint put on it. Heartwood is usually denser and less permeable than sapwood except in *Douglas fir*, hemlock, *larch* and *spruce*. For a *damp course*, only the most impermeable bricks are suitable, but elsewhere with permeable bricks the permeability may be an advantage, helping them to dry out. *See also* C.

perpends (1) **face joints** The visible part of *cross joints* in brickwork or masonry. *See* **keeping the perpends**.

(2) The corners of a brick wall erected first and carefully plumbed to serve as a guide for the wall between.

(3) The sloping (so-called vertical) joints between adjacent slates or tiles.

(4) (USA) *Perpend stones*.

perpend stone, parpend A *bond stone* which passes through a wall and is seen on both faces.

Perspex, Plexiglas *Glass substitute* made of methyl methacrylate, obtainable tinted or colourless, in thicknesses from 1 to 25 mm ($\frac{1}{24}$ to 1 in.), flat or cor-rugated, domed or moulded. It is stronger and lighter than glass, admits more ultra-violet light and ordinary light, and does not splinter into sharp pieces. It can be made to the shape of slates, tiles, or asbestos-cement sheets and used with them to light an attic. Perspex sheets can be joined together by gluing or by cementing, that is by coating the edges with an organic solvent and pressing them together. Tinted Perspex is used for interior panelling or *partitions* to give a tinted *borrowed light*. Perspex is inferior to glass in fire resistance since it is *thermoplastic*, so is not allowed for *glazing* in London for *fire resisting* purposes.

pet cock [mech.] A small valve on a pressure vessel, pump casing, etc. that is opened to release air.

petrifying liquid [pai.] *See* **clearcole**.

petrol intercepting chamber, petrol trap A *trap* into which the waste from petrol (gasoline) filling stations or washdown yards for cars flows before entering the *sewer* (C). It consists of three separate chambers with scumboards across the top to keep the floating petrol from flowing out. The chambers are ven-tilated so that the *volatile* and explosive part of the petrol evaporates and is removed. *Compare* **intercepting trap**.

phenol-formaldehyde resin, phenolic r. Originally made as *bakelite*, these *syn-thetic* resins are highly moisture resistant and immune to attack by bacteria, and have formed useful glues since 1930. *See* **film glue**.

phenolic foam Foamed phenol-formaldehyde resin insulating boards, weighing only about 48 kg/m^3 (3 lb/ft^3), have the advantage over many other foam boards that they burn only with considerable difficulty, with very little smoke or toxic gases and are usable at temperatures up to 150° C. They are not strong enough to carry the feet of a ladder but, covered with quarry tiles, their performance is greatly improved (BS 3927).

Phillips recessed-head screw [joi.] *See* **recessed head screw**.

phon The unit of loudness of sound. Painfully loud sound is at 130 phons, a pneumatic drill at 3 m (10 ft) 90 phons, soft speech 40 phons, a very quiet room 30 phons. *See* **decibel**.

phosphating Protection of a metal surface by hot phosphoric acid. Like *pickling* (*C*) it is a pretreatment and *inhibiting* coat rather than a finished surface. Phosphating should therefore be followed by surfacing with oil, wax, paint, or *lacquer*, and many proprietary processes make use of it.

phosphorescent paint A *paint* which emits visible light for some minutes or hours after visible or ultra-violet light has fallen on it. There are several types of phosphorescence, shown respectively by zinc sulphide, strontium sulphide, and calcium sulphide. *Fluorescent* material emits visible light immediately, not after the radiation has fallen on it.

pick A digging tool like an axe, but with two sharp points, used for breaking loose rock or digging stiff clay or gravel. *See* **navvy pick**.

pick and dip, New England method *Shoved joints*.

pick axe A *navvy pick*.

picket A *pale* in a fence or driven into the ground.

pick hammer A *slater*'s tool for holing *slates* and drawing or driving *nails*. *See* **plasterer** (illus. p. 246).

picking, wasting, stugging (Scots **clouring**) Surfacing a stone in *rubble walling* with a steel point struck at right angles to the surface to make many small, closely spaced pits.

picking up [pai.] (1) *Pulling up*.
    (2) Joining *live edges*.

pieced timber A timber from which a damaged part has been cut out in a *dovetailed* shape. A good piece of timber which matches the grain is cut and fitted to the dovetail.

piece moulding [pla.] A moulding process used for fibrous plaster when a single reverse mould is not possible. The mould is made in several pieces held together by a case made of fibrous plaster.

piecing (1) **dry p.** [pla.] A line where plastering finished one day and was started again next day or later. Piecings are often a disfigurement but they can be made less conspicuous by locating them carefully, for example at a corner or behind a rainwater pipe. If the whole of a wall can be plastered in a day, there will be no piecing.
    (2) [joi.] *See* **pieced timber**.

piend Scots for a *hip*.

pier (1) The loadbearing brickwork in a wall between openings.
    (2) A short *buttress* (*C*) on one or both sides of a wall, bonded to it to increase its stability. *See* **pilaster**.

pig lug (Scotland) In *flexible-metal roofing* a *dog ear*.

pigment [pai.] An insoluble, finely ground, usually opaque powder. Its solubility in water is generally below ½%, and it is so fine that only ½% is allowed to be larger than 0·06 mm for most British standard pigments. This fineness makes a smooth *paint* with high *spreading rate*. Pigments are generally ground in a *vehicle*, often oil. Most pigments are either minerals or *lakes*. White pigments are not considered to have *colour*, black pigments are. Pigments are therefore classified as white or coloured. *See* **extender, stainers**.

pilaster A rectangular *pier*, sometimes fluted, projecting from the face of a wall, having a cap, shaft, and base. It buttresses the wall.

pile *See C.*

piling [pai.] The behaviour of a very quick drying *paint* which during application by *brush* becomes so sticky that the resulting *film* is thick and uneven (BS 2015). *See also* **pile** (*C*).

pillar A *column* or *pier* of stone or cast iron.

pillar tap [plu.] A water tap used on washbasins and baths, having a long vertical screw thread below, that passes through the edge of the basin or bath to the supply pipe (not a **bibcock**).

pilot hole [carp.] A guiding hole, usually of smaller diameter than the main hole.

pilotis A reinforced concrete column projecting through an open ground-floor space to carry the structure above.

pilot nail [carp.] A temporary *nail*, driven to hold timber while the main nails are being driven.

pin (1) [joi.] A slender *wire nail* such as a *panel pin*.

(2) [carp.] A *treenail* or *dowel*.

(3) [joi.] The *dovetail* tenon inserted into a dovetail joint.

(4) To wedge a *pile* (*C*), wall or other foundation to a structure over it with *dry pack* (*C*) (formerly with slates bedded in mortar). *See* **underpin** (*C*).

(5) A *pintle*.

pinch bar, jemmy, claw b., wrecking b., case opener A bent piece of hexagonal or round steel 13 to 19 mm ($\frac{1}{2}$ to $\frac{3}{4}$ in.) dia., about 45 cm (18 in.) long, with a claw bent to a U at one end and a rough *chisel* point at the other. When longer than 90 cm (36 in.) it is called a *crowbar* (*C*) and the U-shaped claw becomes straight.

pinch rod A rod used like a *storey rod* for checking the width of a gap such as the dimension between floor slabs, or a door or window opening.

pine [tim.] (Pinus) Many *softwoods* are called pines but the only one mentioned in this book is *redwood*.

pine oil [pai.] A strong *solvent* made from the *oleo-resin* of pine trees or synthetically. It is an *anti-skinning agent* that gives good *flow* properties to paints.

pin hinge [joi.] A *loose-pin butt*.

pinhole [tim.] *Worm hole* not larger than 1·5 mm ($\frac{1}{16}$ in.), without bore dust and usually dark stained. Pinhole borers do severe damage but only to green timber.

pinholing [pai.] Tiny holes in a dry paint or varnish, whether sprayed or brushed. *See* **orange peeling**.

pink primer [pai.] A *priming coat* for wood, originally containing mainly white and red lead *pigments* but now of very vague composition.

pinnings (Scotland) Stones of different colour or texture set in a *rubble wall* to give a chequered effect.

pintle [joi.] The pin of a hinge for a door, lock gate, etc. If fixed to the gate it projects downwards. If fixed to the post it projects upwards.

pipe Pipes for most purposes may be of *plastics*, copper, cast iron, steel, or asbestos cement. Water supply pipes are often of galvanized *dead-mild steel* (*C*), originally *wrought iron* (*C*); *see also* **drain pipes**.

pipe cutter [plu.] A tool for cutting metal pipes. It carries hard-metal cutting discs which bite into the pipe as the tool is twisted round it. Some of the metal is forced inwards as the pipe is cut, reducing the pipe dia. The pipe bore is recovered with a *burring reamer.*

pipe drill A tubular *plugging chisel* which cuts round holes in brickwork for wooden *plugs.*

pipe duct A *duct.*

pipe fitter [plu.] A *tradesman* who instals pipes for water, steam, gas, oil, or chemical plant. The pipe may be screwed, flanged, loose-flanged, Victaulic, or gas- or arc-welded and he may specialize with any sort.

pipe fittings [plu.] *See* **fittings, copper fittings**.

pipe hook A spiked *fastener* driven into a wall *joint* or a timber. It has a curved end for holding a pipe. *See* **fasteners** (illus. p. 130).

pipe-jointing clip [plu.] An asbestos and metal ring that envelops a pipe joint which is to be filled with molten lead.

pipe layer, drain l. A *skilled man* who joints, in the trench, pipes of glazed stoneware, concrete, iron, steel, or asbestos cement, laying them to correct levels. A service layer can also cut threads in the ends of metal pipes.

pipe sleeve *See* **expansion sleeve**.

pipe wrench, cylinder w., Stillson [plu.] A heavy wrench with serrated jaws for gripping, screwing, or unscrewing steel pipe. *See* **plumber's tools** (illus. p. 250).

pisé de terre Walling made of *cob.*

pitch (1) The ratio of the height to the span of *patent glazing* or a *stair* or roof, or its angle of inclination to the horizontal. For example, the pitch of a plain-tiled roof should not be less than 35°.

(2) The distance between parallel objects at uniform spacing, such as nails in wood, reinforcing bars in concrete, rivets in steel, the threads of a *screw*, or the distance from one *nosing* to the next of a stair. *See* **pitch board**.

(3) **rake** [carp.] The slope of the *face* of a *saw-tooth* measured from the perpendicular to the line of the points.

pitch board, step mould, gauge b. [carp.] A triangular *templet* for a stair, cut with one side equal to the rise, the second to the *going*, and the third, the hypotenuse, equal to the distance from one *nosing* to the next (pitch). It is used for setting out the lines to which the *strings* should be cut or *housed*. A *margin templet* gives the correct distance from the top of the string to the *nosing line*. Additional templets for treads and risers are used for marking out their thicknesses on the string.

pitched roof The commonest type of roof, usually one with two slopes at more than 20° to the horizontal, meeting in a central *ridge*, pp. 279, 354. *See* **flat roof**.

pitch-epoxy glue A glue suitable for fixing *expanded polystyrene*.

pitcher tee [plu.] A *sweep tee*. *See also* **mason's tools**, p. 211.

pitch-faced stone, pitched-face s., rock-face s. Stone which has been worked at the quarry with the *pitching tool*. It may be *rubble* or *ashlar* but is always rough.

pitch fibre pipes Black pipes made 25% of wood or asbestos fibre, and 75% of refined coal tar pitch. They are usually buried, and are suitable for soil and rainwater drainage, but not for continuously flowing hot liquid, nor for pitch solvents such as any petroleum spirit. In first cost they are competitive with concrete or *vitrified clayware*, they are also more flexible and lighter in weight. They are very quickly laid (120 m (400 ft) per hour) for two reasons: the average pipe length is 2·5 or 3 m (8 or 10 ft) and the jointing method is quick. Being smooth the pipes can be laid at flat gradients, e.g. 10 cm (4 in.) pipes at 1 in 85.

pitch-impregnated fibre pipe *Pitch fibre pipe*.

pitching piece, apron p. [carp.] A horizontal timber fixed into the wall near the *landing* of a *stair* to bear the *carriages*, strings, and landing-floor *joists*.

pitching tool, pitcher A *hammer-headed chisel* about 23 cm (9 in.) long with a thick broad edge (about 6 mm ($\frac{1}{4}$ in.) thick). *See* **pitch-faced stone**; *also* **mason** (illus. p. 211).

pitch mastic A *jointless floor* made from *aggregate* and coal-tar pitch, fluid when hot, spread to a thickness of 16 to 19 mm ($\frac{5}{8}$ to $\frac{3}{4}$ in.) like *asphalt* (*C*). Not the same as *mastic*.

pitch pocket [tim.] A *resin pocket*.

pitch-polymer damp course A *damp course* supplied in rolls of various widths, 15 m (50 ft) long and 0·9 or 1·25 mm (0·03 and 0·05 in.) thick. Pitch polymer dpcs are made of coaltar pitch with PVC, fillers and plasticizers, are reinforced with synthetic fibres, and do not squeeze out under pressure or in hot weather.

pitting [pla.] The *blowing* of plaster.

pivot The point about which something rotates. A seesaw pivots about its mid-point. The *hanging stile* of a *swing door* may be pivoted at top and bottom without *hinges*. Pivots are stronger but much more costly than hinges, though not every floor is strong enough to tolerate the deep *mortise* in it needed for the bottom pivot.

plain ashlars Surfaced stones, smoothed with a *drag* or other smoothing tool.

plain-sawn timber *Flat-sawn timber* (illus. p. 140).

plain tile The common, flat *roofing tile* of concrete or burnt clay, which in reality has a slight spherical camber, convex above. Its size is standardized in Britain at 26·5 × 16·5 cm by 1·0 to 1·5 cm thick (10$\frac{1}{2}$ × 6$\frac{1}{2}$ in. by $\frac{3}{8}$ to $\frac{5}{8}$ in.) with at least two *nibs* at the head and two nail holes nearly 6 mm ($\frac{1}{4}$ in.) dia. Each tile overlaps two *courses* below it, and for this reason plain tiling is heavy, about 590 being needed to cover 10 m² (107·6 ft²) of roof at 10 cm (4 in.) gauge, and weighing 78 kg/m² (16 lb/ft²). *Single-lap tiles* are lighter per unit area of roof, though individually heavier. Plain tiles should not be laid on a roof sloping at less than 35° to the horizontal, preferably 40°. (Illus. below) *See* **pantiles, tile-and-a-half tile, under-ridge tile**.

with two nibs

with continuous nib

Plain tile.

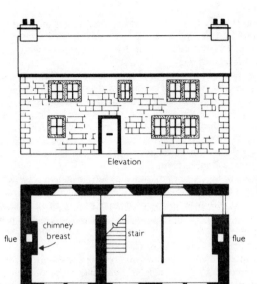

Elevation

Plan of first floor of a stone house, and elevation.

plan A drawing showing a layout in a horizontal plane. Much of the architect's work is *planning* and the drawing of plans. (Illus. above)

plane [carp.] A tool for smoothing and shaping wood, of which very many different sorts exist. Many of the *moulding planes* have been superseded by machinery which can cut mouldings much more quickly than they can be cut by hand. The *bench planes* are still much used. *See also* **back iron, badger, bead plane, cutting iron, hollow, match plane, plough, round, sole, spokeshave, universal plane**.

plane iron [carp.] The *cutting iron* of a *plane*, not its *back iron*.

planer [mech.] A *planing machine* for surfacing metal or stone or timber.

plane stock [carp.] The body of a *plane*, holding the *cutting iron* and *back iron*.

planing machine [tim.] A machine which smoothes wood surfaces by the adzing action of a *cutter block*. It will also, with care, remove twist from a surface, do bevelling, chamfering, moulding, and tongueing and reduce different pieces of wood to the same thickness. Many types exist. *See* **surface planer**.

planing machinist [tim.] A *woodworking machinist* who sets and operates a *planing machine* to give true face and edge to timber. Working as a thicknessing machinist, he sets the *thicknessing machine* to give precise thickness.

planing mill [tim.] (USA) A sawmill where timber is also planed and made into match or floorboarding.

planing mill products [tim.] (USA) Floorboards, ceiling boards, and *weatherboarding*, as opposed to *millwork*.

plank [tim.] (1) In softwoods, *square-sawn* timber 50 to 100 mm (2 to 4 in.) thick and 250 mm (10 in.) or more wide (BS 565). In hardwoods it is always over 50 mm thick but of various widths, and sometimes *waney*, according to the country of origin. *See* **deal**.

(2) (USA) Lumber thicker than 1 in. (25 mm) laid with its face horizontal like a floorboard. *See* **joist**.

plank-on-edge floor (UK **solid-wood floor**) [carp.] A floor used in USA for its fire resistance and solidity. The floor *joists* are laid touching each other; no rough floor is laid, the finish floor being fixed to the joists.

planning In house or building design, the planning is the organization of the details of the layout, and is best done by an *architect*, though many owners prefer to do it themselves. Municipal or civil engineers with an architectural bias, or architects with an engineering bias, have the best qualifications for leading a *town-planning* team.

planning grid A network of perpendicular lines usually one *module* apart, used by *architects* to help them arrive at a building layout. It is not a *grid plan*.

planted [joi., pla.] A description of *fibrous plaster* or of a *moulding* or strip fixed by nailing, screwing, or gluing on to the piece which it decorates, and not cut or moulded in the solid. *See* **sticking, stuck moulding**.

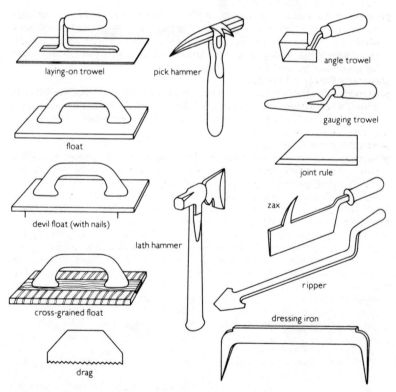

Tools of the plasterer (left) and the slater (bottom right).

plaster [pla.] A substance which later hardens, but is applied to walls and ceilings while it is *plastic*. Plasters may be of *Portland cement* or *gypsum plaster* or *lime putty* with sand. *See* **rendering, finishing coat, plasterer, stucco**, *also* BS 5492.

plaster base [pla.] A ground for plaster. It may be wood, *metal lathing*, brickwork, *masonry, insulating board, gypsum lath*, etc.

plaster bead [pla.] An *angle bead*.

plasterboard The usual name for *gypsum plasterboard*.

plasterboard nail A galvanized or *sherardized* nail for fixing *plasterboard*.

plaster dab [pla., joi.] Small lumps of *board finish* gypsum plaster stuck at regular intervals to walling or lathing for fixing plasterboard, wall tiles, marble facing, joinery, etc. For plasterboard they are about 300 mm (1 ft) apart horizontally and 450 mm vertically (18 in.), and about 50 mm (2 in.) thick, levelled with a straight edge and plumb rule. The sheet of plasterboard should be cut at least 25 mm (1 in.) shorter than the ceiling height. It is pushed on to the dabs with its lower edge resting on one or two short boards used in the same way as *lifting wedges*. The boards can be weighted with (say) ten bricks at the end farthest from the wall so that they hold the plasterboard up until the plaster has hardened.

plasterer A *tradesman* who may be a *fibrous plasterer* or a plasterer in solid work. The latter lays successive coats of plaster or rendering and fixes *fibrous plaster* such as mould *cornices* and wall patterns. He can use a *horsed mould*, erect *lathing* for plaster, and apply stucco. Plasterers in some districts also lay *grano* and fix *wall tiles*. *See* above.

plasterer's float [pla.] *See* **float**.

plasterer's labourer A helper who mixes plaster or brings it from the mixer in a *hod*, wheelbarrow, etc. He may also sieve materials, fix *lathing*, work a *gin block*, raise *scaffolding*, and prepare a wall surface for plaster.

plasterer's lath hammer A *lath hammer* (illus. opposite).

plasterer's putty *Lime putty*.

plastering machine A hopper-fed machine that blows or pumps *pre-mixed plaster* or *thin-wall plaster* 5 to 25 mm (0·2 to 1 in.) thick on to a wall or ceiling, using a metal applicator rotor placing the full thickness of plaster in one coat through a flexible hose. The plaster is then smoothed by hand, the men using a metal *feather-edge rule*. The final process is electrically powered trowelling followed by hand finishing.

plaster of Paris, hemihydrate p., casting p., Class A p. (to BS 1191) [pla.] *Gypsum* which has been heated to drive off some of its water and has become $CaSO_4 \cdot \frac{1}{2}H_2O$. When mixed with water it warms up and sets in about ten minutes, expanding slightly; because of this expansion it is an excellent casting plaster, but is mainly used in building in *fibrous plaster* work or for quick, small repairs or as retarded *hemihydrate plaster*.

plaster stop An *angle bead*.

plastic [pla.] *See* **plasticity, plastics**.

plastic emulsion [pai.] *See* **emulsion paint**.

plastic, plastics glues *Synthetic resin* glues for timber, *epoxide resins* for gluing *light alloys*, etc. *See* below.

plasticity, workability, fatness [pla.] The property in a plaster or mortar, of sticking to the trowel, and of being smooth to work with, obtained with cement mortars by adding an *air-entraining agent* (C) or matured slaked lime,

247

or by using a *masonry cement*. *Lime putty* and *gypsum plasters* are naturally plastic, unlike sanded *mortars*.

plasticizer (1) An *admixture* in *mortar* or *concrete*, which can increase the *plasticity* (*C*) of a mix so much that the water content can be extremely low, and the mortar or concrete strength can be high. *See* **mortar plasticizer**.

(2) [pai.] A non-volatile substance mixed with the *medium* of a paint, varnish, or lacquer to improve the flexibility of the hardened *film*.

(3) In plastics, plasticizers are added during manufacture to make them soft, flexible and easy to process, but unplasticized plastics may be stronger, e.g. unplasticized polyvinyl chloride (UPVC) is used for making corrugated transparent roofing sheet.

plastic paint, texture p. A paint which can be manipulated after application to give a patterned or *textured finish*. On conscientiously scrimmed plasterboard, there is no need for even a skim coat of plaster under this paint. It is a powder usually based on *gypsum* and mixed with water for use indoors sometimes to hide a rough surface, by its stippled or combed texture. (BS 6150).

plastics Some of the most important plastics are *polyvinyl chloride* (PVC) which has been in production since the early 1930s; *polythene* (since the early 1940s), polypropylene, polymethyl methacrylate (Perspex), and *glassfibre-reinforced resins*. Not all plastics are *synthetic resins*. Plastics are either *thermo-setting* (those which harden once for all when heated), or *thermoplastic* (those which soften whenever they are heated). (The word plastics is used in the singular as a noun to distinguish it from the adjective plastic.) Most plastics burn, none are non-combustible, but *UPVC* is self-extinguishing and some others can be made so. *See also* **acetal resins, glues, polycarbonate,** etc., **resins, temperature movement, ultraviolet radiation,** and BS 1755.

plastics coatings [pai.] Enamels, lacquers, varnishes, paints and even *jointless floorings* made of plastics are becoming usual, particularly *alkyds*, amides, polyamides related to *nylon*, phenolic resins, silicones, polyvinyl resins and *chlorinated rubber*.

plastics pipes Plastics pipes all have a smooth bore which discourages any deposit of scale, makes for low friction losses and good flow. They weigh only about one sixth as much as iron or steel pipes but are not so strong, have very low electrical conductivity and cannot be used for earthing an electrical circuit. The four main types in use are unplasticized PVC (UPVC), polyethylene (*polythene*), polypropylene, and ABS. They are not yet commonly accepted for hot water services because their expansion with increase in temperature is five to twelve times as much as with metal pipes. As they are less stiff than metal this creates problems of support. UPVC pipes are commonest for soil and rainwater above ground, and can be joined by solvent welding (which cannot be done with polythene) or by a rubber ring joint, in which one pipe is pushed into the spigot of the other. Compression joints like those used for copper tubing are also available for most plastics tubes, using a rubber sealing ring (BSCP 312).

plastic wood [tim.] A paste of *nitrocellulose*, wood flour, *plasticizers*, *resins*, and other materials dispersed in *volatile* solvents. It is used for repairing wood, filling holes, etc., and its surface can be painted over in about one hour.

plastisol [pai.] A plasticized *polyvinyl chloride* protective coating, usually textured, laid 0·2 mm (0·008 in.) thick over galvanized *profiled steel sheet*. Long life is expected in this outer coating, used since 1965.

plate [carp.] (1) A horizontal timber about 5 × 10 cm (2 × 4 in.) supported throughout its length, particularly one along the top of a wall on which the ends of roof timbers are laid (*wall plate*). In *frame construction* it is the corresponding member capping the studs.

   (2) (Scotland) A broad thin board, planed on one or both sides.

   (3) [mech.] *See C.*

plate cut [carp.] A *foot cut.*

plate glass, polished p. g. High quality, expensive glass, made in thicknesses from 25 to 38 mm (1–1½ in.). *See* **float glass.**

platen [tim.] The hot steel plates used in *hot pressing* for making *plywood* with *thermo-setting* glues. *See* **phenol formaldehyde resin**, *also C.*

platform frame, Western f. [carp.] A timber *frame house* in which wall, floor, and roof frames are independently built. The floor platforms are carried over the full thickness of the wall frames which are built in separate *storeys*. Diagonal boarding braces the floor, all external walls and the roof; additional stiffer braces are usually provided in the wall frames.

platform roof Scots for a *flat roof.*

plenum chamber An air chamber kept at a pressure slightly above atmospheric.

plenum system *Air conditioning* a factory or large building by keeping the pressure in it above atmospheric pressure. Clean air is blown into rooms near the ceiling level and foul air is withdrawn near floor level at the same side of the room, or allowed to escape through cracks in doors and windows. *Unit heaters* which draw fresh air directly from outside through a hole in the wall are often now preferred. *See* **pressurized escape route.**

Plexiglas *See* **Perspex.**

pliers A pair of pliers is a gripping tool, pivoted like a pair of scissors, usually with blades for cutting thin wire, built into its jaws. *See* **seamer.**

plies [tim.] Plural of *ply*, a sheet of *veneer, bitumen felt*, etc.

plough (1) **router** (USA **plow**) [joi.] A *plane* which makes grooves, usually along the *grain* of wood. By varying the position of the *fence*, the distance of the groove from the edge of the wood can be adjusted. The plough was invented in about the sixteenth century together with the *panelled* construction for which it is an essential tool.

   (2) *See C.*

ploughed and tongued joint [joi.] A *feather joint.*

plough strip [joi.] A strip of wood which has been ploughed.

plow (USA) A *plough.*

plug (1) A small pointed wooden peg pushed into a hole in a wall where a *screw, nail*, or other *fastening* is to be driven. Factory-made plugs exist, but wood is cheap and very effective for small loads. *See* **plugging.**

   (2) [plu.] A *bag plug* or *screw plug.*

   (3) An electrical connection to fit into a *socket outlet.*

   (4) [plu.] A pipe *fitting*, threaded outside, which closes an end of pipe by screwing into it.

plug-centre bit [carp.] A *bit* used for widening holes. The central part is a plug inserted in the hole already drilled.

plug cock, p. tap [mech.] A simple valve, in which the fluid passes through a hole in a tapered plug. The valve is closed by turning the plug through 90°.

plug-driving gun *See* **stud gun**.

plugging Drilling a hole in *masonry*, which is to be filled with a *plug* of wood or fibre or metal as a fixing for a nail, *drive screw*, wood *screw*, etc.

plugging chisel or **drill** (USA **star drill**) A short steel bar held in the hand, and struck with the *hammer* to make holes from about 3 mm (⅛ in.) to about 13 mm (½ in.) dia. in brick, concrete or masonry. It is used like the *jumper* (*C*). *See* **pipe drill**.

plug-in connector, flex cock, plug-and-socket gas connector [plu.] A method of connecting a short, flexible gas pipe to a wall plug as conveniently as electrical flex. The plug is pushed into a bayonet socket and, when turned, allows gas to pass to the appliance. Removal of the plug automatically closes the gas-way.

plugmold [elec.] (USA) A hollow, pressed steel or plastics *moulding* fitted to the wall as a *chair rail* or *skirting board* containing electric cables, with power plugs as required. *See* **raceway**.

plug tenon, spur t. [carp.] A *stub tenon* shouldered on all four faces (BS 565).

plumb Vertical.

plumb bob, plummet A weight hanging on a string (the *plumb line*) to show the direction of the vertical.

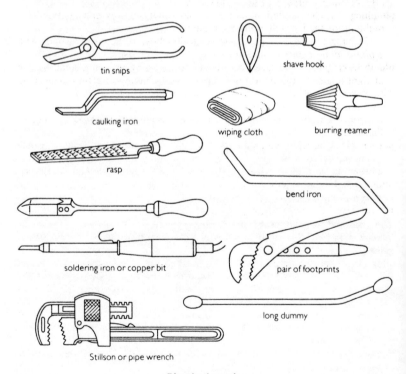

tin snips

shave hook

caulking iron

wiping cloth

burring reamer

rasp

bend iron

soldering iron or copper bit

pair of footprints

long dummy

Stillson or pipe wrench

Plumber's tools.

plumb cut [carp.] (USA) The vertical cut in the *birdsmouth* at the foot of a *rafter* where it fits over the wall plate; also the vertical cut at the *ridge* (top cut). *Compare* **foot cut**.

plumber A *tradesman* who shapes and fixes *flexible-metal roofing*, cuts, bends, and joins water pipes, instals *soil pipes*, waste pipes, and water systems, sometimes gas pipes also. The usual metals he works in are copper, lead, iron, zinc, and mild steel, though the term plumber originally meant lead worker. In the north of England, plumbers are usually *glaziers*. In Britain a plumber may hold the technical certificate of the City and Guilds of London or the highest qualification, that of Registered Plumber (R.P.). *See* **lead burning, chemical plumber**.

plumber's labourer or **mate** A skilled *labourer* who helps the plumber by carrying his tools and bringing his materials to him and may help to make *wiped joints*, etc.

plumber's solder, p. metal, coarse s. [plu.] An alloy of lead and tin varying from 1:1 to 3:1, used in the *wiped joint*. Unlike fine solder it is plastic at temperatures above 183° C. up to 260° C. when it melts.

plumber's union, cap and lining [plu.] A *union* joined to a brass or copper tube (the lining or sleeve) which can be soldered to a lead pipe, enabling this to be joined by the screw fitting of the union to a pipe of other material (BS 4118). *See* **fittings** (illus. p. 138).

plumbing (1) The sanitation, hot and cold water services and heating of a building, or their installation. *See* **plumber**.

   (2) Transferring a point to one vertically above or below it, usually with a *plumb bob* or *plumb rule*, but *see* C.

plumb level, plumb and level, p. rule A spirit *level* fitted with a small bubble at right angles to the main bubble to show the plumb direction. The small bubble is central when the main bubble is held vertical.

plumb line [sur.] A string on which a weight is hung to stretch it in a vertical direction. The string should be braided like fishing line to avoid spinning of the weight.

plumb rule A straight edge, from the top of which a *plumb line* is hung. A hole cut out at the bottom and a slot all the way up give freedom for the string and bob to show the vertical. It was used before *plumb levels* were available.

plume [tim.] The figure formed by *crotch* in mahogany.

plummet A *plumb bob*.

ply (1) [tim.] A thin sheet of wood usually called a *veneer*, used for making *plywood* or *laminated wood*.

   (2) One sheet of *roofing felt* or of other material built up in several layers.

plymetal *Plywood* faced on one or both sides with a sheet of metal which may be galvanized steel, aluminium, Monel metal, or others.

plywood [tim.] Structural board, stronger and more dimensionally stable than wood, because it is glued from an odd number of sheets of *veneer* with the *grain* of adjacent sheets at right angles to each other. *Three-ply* is the commonest and cheapest but *multi-ply* is also much used. Plywood was used by the joiners of Europe, particularly France, in furniture-making some centuries ago, and probably also by the ancient Romans and Egyptians. Plywood, as we know it now, was used by the American piano industry in 1830 for the planks which held the pins to which piano cords are attached. It was then made of *sawn veneer*. At this time, obviously, piano makers understood its superiority over wood in strength and stability in varying conditions of dampness. *Blockboard* desk tops were made in 1883 and plywood *panels* for doors in 1890, flush doors following much later. Plywood was known in USA as 'veneered stock' until 1919 when, to avoid the ignorant but widespread prejudice against veneer, the old Veneer Association changed its name to the Plywood Manufacturers' Association of USA. It differs from *laminated wood*, in which the plies have parallel grain. *See also* **balanced construction, composite board, cross band, moulded plywood, rotary cutting, sliced veneer, synthetic resin.**

plywood parquet, p. squares A form of *parquet* consisting of *plywood* tiles with a top *veneer* 3 mm ($\frac{1}{8}$ in.) thick of *oak*, *birch*, or *ash*. The tiles are 23 to 90 cm (9 to 36 in.) square, pinned to the wooden *sub-floor* (and glued in the best work). The nail holes are filled and the floor *glasspapered* after laying. If no wooden sub-floor exists a 1 to 2 cm ($\frac{3}{8}$ to $\frac{3}{4}$ in.) thick plywood layer must be put down as a base for the parquet. If the sub-floor is rough, it should be made smooth by a plywood underlay about 5 mm thick all over it.

plywood sawyer [tim.] A *tradesman* who sets and works power saws for cutting *plywood* (*bandsaws, circular saws, straight-line edger*, and so on).

pneumatic architecture *See* **air house**.

pneumatic tools Tools driven by compressed air. There is often little to choose between them and electric tools except in wet places. There they add no danger of electric shock. For percussive tools they may be better, also for small, ultra-fast drills (15 000 rpm or more), but with larger tools, exhaust noise may make them more offensive than electric ones.

pneumatic water supply A water-supply system used in isolated houses in North America. The *cistern*, in the basement, is a closed tank from which the water is forced into the house by compressed air.

pocket (1) An opening in a wall in which a beam is to be inserted.

(2) **weight p.** [joi.] The hole in which the *pocket piece* fits. The sash weight is passed through it when it is fixed to the *sash cord*.

pocket chisel, sash c. [joi.] A *chisel* for cutting the pocket in the *pulley stile* of a window frame. It has a wide, thin blade, honed on both sides.

pocket piece [joi.] The piece of the *pulley stile* at the foot of a window frame which can be removed to insert the sash weights or to string new *sash cords* on them.

pocket rot [tim.] Decay of timber in small lens-shaped areas, which eventually become round holes.

pock marking [pai.] *Orange peeling* or other unsightly depressions formed in the *drying* of a *paint* or *varnish*.

pod A bathroom pod is a prefabricated bathroom that can be added to a house that does not have a bath. It can be placed in position on its prepared slab within 20 minutes of its arrival on the site, but connecting to the water supplies, wastes and gas or electricity will need a few hours more. It is then ready for use. Because of the cost of hiring the crane needed to lift the pod over the roof of the house, it is usually not economic to install fewer than six on any particular site. The roof is often flat, and made of *glassfibre reinforced plastics*.

point (1) [carp.] The sharp end of a *saw-tooth*. The number of teeth per 25 mm (1 in.) of a saw is one fewer than the number of points per 25 mm.

(2) A lampholder, *socket outlet*, or other terminal at which electricity or gas can be taken from an installation.

pointing (1) Raking out mortar *joints* 2 cm ($\frac{3}{4}$ in.) deep and pressing into them a surface mortar. The bedding mortar is disturbed and may not bond with the surface mortar. *Jointing* is therefore more durable, but pointing provides the opportunity of using a mortar of different colour. *See* **tooling**.

(2) The completion of joints between ridge or *hip tiles* or tiles on walls with mortar. *See* **torching**.

pole plate [carp.] A horizontal beam resting on, and perpendicular to, the tie-beams or *principal rafters* of a wooden roof *truss*, supporting the feet of the common *rafters* and the inner edge of the *box gutter* if there is one.

polished work, glassed surface, p. face Building stone of crystalline texture (limestone, marble, or granite) which has been smoothed with *abrasives* and buffing to form a glass-like surface.

polishing of thermoplastic floor tiles To keep the 'new' look of thermoplastic or asbestos or pvc tiles or sheets, occasional polishing is essential. The polishes available are emulsions, solutions or pastes of waxes or resins. Emulsions can be used without risk but solutions or pastes should never be used on thermoplastic tiles since the solvents in them dissolve or at least soften the binders in the tiles. Too much polish should not be used, it causes slipperiness and catches dirt. Dirty polish can be removed by detergent washing followed by a rinse with clean water. The black marks made by rubber-heeled shoes can be removed by rubbing with scouring powder and fine steel wool.

polishing varnish, rubbing v. [pai.] A *short-oil* varnish used for fine joinery, generally one which is so hard and dry that it can be polished by *abrasive* and mineral oil without dissolving the resin.

poll (1) [mech.] A striking *face* of a *hammer*.

(2) To split (knap) flints.

pollarding [tim.] Annual lopping of the shoots on the poll (the top) of a tree. It forms a valuable figure, such as the *burr* in *veneers*.

polycarbonates *Glass substitute* with high impact strength, less easily ignitable and less flammable than most plastics, used in vandal-resistant fittings and in *security glazing*. (Illus. below)

polyesters *Synthetic resins* with many uses, that are cheaper than *epoxies* and can be used in *levelling compounds*, or for bonding concrete units together, and are used in painting as *alkyds*. *See* **glassfibre-reinforced resin**.

polymers Organic compounds, including many *synthetic resins* and rubbers. They have large molecules containing many hundreds of smaller molecules

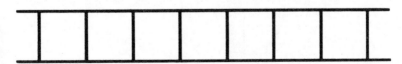

Transparent polycarbonate sheet used instead of glass around a garden centre in London. The twin-walled sheets are 10 mm ($\frac{3}{8}$ in.) thick, 2·1 m (6' 11") wide and 10·5 m (34' 5") long, some of them strongly curved (actual size).

of the monomer linked together. Polymers are usually solid, and are formed when synthetic resins harden (*cure*), whether as *glue* or casting resin. *Polyvinyl chloride* is an example. *See* **cure, elastomer**, also BS 1755.

polymerization, condensation [tim.] The *cure* of a *synthetic resin*. *See* **polymer**.

polystyrene A *glass substitute* comparable in price with glass, also used for making wall tiles though it softens at 60° C. and is marked by boiling water, turpentine or other organic solvents. *See* **expanded polystyrene**.

polytetrafluorethylene *See* **ptfe.**

polythene, polyethylene, alkathene A chemically inert, electrically insulating synthetic rubber, of which bottles are made and pipes for chemicals or cold water. As a cold-water supply pipe, polythene should be laid with some excess length during normal weather. During deep frost, no 'snaking' is needed, this will take place in warmer weather as the tube expands. It needs support frequently – every 200 mm (8 in.) for 12 mm (½ in.) nominal bore tube on a horizontal run (BRE Digest 15). *See* **thermofusion welding**, and below.

polythene film Versatile sheet that can be used temporarily to keep timber dry on a building site or as a *damp course*. The transparent type lasts only three years in shade or one year in sunlight because it is destroyed by *ultraviolet radiation*. More than ten years' life can be expected, however, even in bright sunlight, from the carbon-black-filled variety which is quite opaque and a recommended damp course. The 2·5% carbon black 'hides' the ultraviolet radiation from it (BRE Digest 69). The foil 0·25 mm (0·01 in.) thick may also be used for covering the floors of chemical plants. It is laid on a very smooth floor and covered with a second screed which is usually covered with floor tiles.

polyurethanes *Synthetic resins* that have many uses as varnishes, paint *vehicles*, or *levelling compounds*. They are more flexible than *epoxies* or *polyesters*, and can be foamed.

polyvinyl acetate, PVA, PVAC Rubbery synthetic resins used in building, often in *emulsion* (C) form. PVA is a *glue* for carpenters (BS 3544, 4071), an *emulsion paint*, also a *bonding agent* for plaster, used on smooth concrete before *projection plastering*.

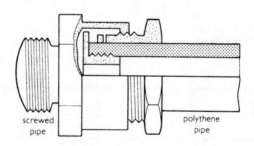

screwed
pipe

polythene
pipe

Polythene pipe. Brass or gun metal fitting for joining polythene coldwater pipe to screwed water pipe. Note the threaded metal sleeve inserted within the polythene tube, and screwed into it to ensure a tight joint.

polyvinyl chloride, PVC A vinyl resin, a *polymer*, a rubbery, almost non-combustible material used in building for making corrugated transparent roofing sheet (unplasticized, *UPVC*), pipes, cable insulation, sheet surfacing to *gypsum plasterboard*, *emulsion paint* that forms a *vapour check*, vandal-resistant glazing or flooring sheet or tile. Like *linoleum* it must be laid on a dry floor. It is impervious to water, oils and many chemicals. As a vapour check on the inner surface of plasterboard it is in the ideal location for preventing *interstitial condensation*.

polyvinyl fluoride, PVF Weather-resistant sheet or surfacing for steel or aluminium *cladding panels*, known in the UK since 1960 and in USA since 1950.

pommel (1) A knob such as a ball *finial* to a roof.

2) *A punner* (*C*), with an iron foot for ramming earth.

Poole's tiles Flat, clay *single-lap tiles* standardized in Britain at 41 × 34 × 1 cm (16 × 13½ × ½ in.). They have 7·6 cm (3 in.) side lap and differ from the *double Roman tile* in that the central ridge extends only half way up. Like the double Roman tile they have two waterways, two nail holes, and no *nibs*.

poplar Poplar trees should not be allowed nearer than 18 m (60 ft) from buildings founded on clay unless the foundations are deeper than the poplar roots. Poplars grow very quickly and cause clay to shrink rapidly in summer because of the water which they draw out of it. They thus damage foundations.

popping [pla.] *Blowing* of plaster.

pores [tim.] The small round holes, seen on the end grain of *hardwood*, which lead the sap upwards.

pore treatments Damp-proofing methods for masonry. Brick surfaces exposed to the weather, that have been sprayed or brushed with a silicone resin solution, absorb much less water than untreated surfaces. They repel the water. In fact a small piece of brick treated with this resin will float on water. 'Synthasil' made by the National Coal Board is one such liquid. Other *water-repellent treatments* exist. It is not yet possible to guarantee the life of these treatments. *See also* **injection of a damp course**.

porous pipes Pipes laid in the ground to drain it may be of different materials. Those made of concrete are ingeniously formed from completely porous *no-fines concrete* in the top half and from non-porous dense concrete in the bottom half (BS 1194). *See* **field drain** (*C*).

porous woods [tim.] *Hardwoods*.

portable belt conveyor A rubber *belt conveyor* (*C*) 7 to 11 m (23 to 36 ft) long with a belt from 35 to 50 cm (14 to 20 in.) wide driven by a motor from 2 to 4 hp, frequently used for loading lorries. The belt is usually troughed and provided with short steel angle cleats riveted on, to prevent material slipping back down steep slopes. It may be used therefore for delivering bricks to second floor level. The conveyor is carried on a two-wheeled frame and can be tilted to any angle. An economical belt speed which gives little belt wear is 30 to 45 m/min. (100 to 150 fpm). Some types have a power drive to one road wheel. *See* **brick elevator**.

Portland cement So called since about 1820 when it was first patented in England, because when hard it resembled the stone from Portland in Dorset. *Roman cement* was its forerunner. *See* **concrete, ordinary Portland cement**, *and C, also* BS 4627.

Portland stone A limestone from Portland on the south coast of England, used for facing important buildings. It weathers well and forms strong contrasts between the parts which get wet and stay white and those which are sheltered and blacken.

post [carp.] A main vertical support of a building frame or *partition* or sub-frame, thicker than a *stud*.

postal knocker [joi.] A *letter plate* which includes a door knocker.

posts and timbers [tim.] (USA) Square timbers 13 × 13 cm (5 × 5 in.) or larger, *stress-graded* for use as struts.

pot floor A *hollow-tile floor* (*C*).

pot life, spreadable l., working l., usable l. The time for which a *glue* remains usable *after mixing*, as opposed to its *shelf life*.

pot type boiler A coal- or coke-fired *boiler* with a plain cylindrical water jacket. It is efficient, but is not aimed to heat the room in which it is placed, since most of its heat passes into the water.

pounce [pai.] A pattern transferred on to a surface below a piece of paper by pricking holes in it and rubbing pumice powder (pounce) through it on to the surface below.

pouring rope [plu.] A *joint runner*.

powder-post borings [tim] *Worm holes*, 1·5 to 3 mm ($\frac{1}{16}$ to $\frac{1}{8}$ in.) dia., with a fine, dust-like flour from the borings. The holes are slightly larger than *shot hole* and are often found in *hardwoods*.

power panel [elec.] A *cutout box*, for power circuits rather than for lighting.

preamble [q.s.] The introduction to each trade in a *bill of quantities*.

pre-boring for nails Boring a hole for each nail enables more nails to be driven into each joint because they can safely be closer than when no hole is drilled. Therefore joints can be stronger. The drill bit should be slightly thinner than the nail – about $\frac{2}{3}$ to $\frac{4}{5}$ of the nail diameter. The least distance of wire nails from the end of the wood should be 20 times the nail diameter (D) if the holes are not bored and 10D· if they are. Similar dimensions apply for the spacing of nails along the grain. The side spacing between lines of nails is 10D for unbored holes and 3D for bored holes. The edge distance is 5D in both instances.

prefabricated building All buildings are to some extent prefabricated, since many building components are brought on to the site completed (doors, roof trusses, etc.). The word prefabricated is therefore usually reserved for those buildings of which walls, roofs, or floors are completed either off the site or in a site factory. *See* **industrialized building methods**.

prefabricated tie (USA) A *wall tie* consisting of one wire of about 3 mm ($\frac{1}{8}$ in.) dia. in each leaf of a *cavity wall* joined by similar wires at right angles, welded to them at intervals, like fabric reinforcement.

preliminaries [q.s.] The introduction to a *bill of quantities*. *Compare* **preamble**.

preliminary works [q.s.] Demolition, road or river diversions, etc.

pre-mixed plaster [pla.] Plaster supplied ready mixed, either wet in drums or dry in bags, sometimes containing *lightweight aggregate*. A dry mix may be based on Portland cement or on gypsum plasters. For *plastering machines* it contains no sand nor lightweight aggregate. The high thermal insulation of these plasters makes them useful in cold climates and for the *fire protection of structural steelwork*. *Thin-wall plaster* is one type.

preparation [pai.] *See* **surface preparation**.

preservatives (1) Preservatives for steel or cast iron are described under **protective finishes to metal**.

(2) For stone, preservative treatment should include washing with liberal amounts of clean, warm water every three years to remove the corrosive salts which collect on the surface. It is generally best to use neither chemicals nor soap. Many proprietary treatments exist. Steam cleaning without chemicals may also be harmless and effective even if the stone has been allowed to accumulate dirt for many years. *See* **pore treatments**.

(3) For wood preservatives *see* B R E Digest 201, *also* B S 1282, 5589, and *C*.

press [tim.] An arrangement of *platens* (steel plates) between which sheets of *veneer* are glued to form *plywood* under pressure. *Hot pressing* is generally worked by hydraulic pressure. Screw presses are used only for cold gluing.

pressed brick Bricks with sharp *arrises* and smooth surfaces formed by moulding under high pressure. The stronger qualities are *engineering* or *semi-engineering bricks*.

pressed glass Bricks, *pavement lights* and so on, of glass pressed to shape.

pressed steel Sheet steel, usually galvanized, hot pressed into various shapes as *trim* in joinery or as window *sills*, *sub-sills* and *sub-frames*. For these uses it is generally 1·6 to 2·5 mm ($\frac{1}{16}$ to 0·1 in.) thick. (Illus. below)

pressure [tim.] Timber may be glued either in presses which have no follow-up pressure (screw presses), or there may be a follow-up pressure, as in a hydraulic press which allows for the yielding of the wood. Fluid pressure, exerted by steam, compressed air, hot water, etc., can be applied by *flexible-bag moulding*.

pressure gun, caulking g. A tool like a grease gun, used for applying joint sealing material to a joint, *mastic* as a *bed putty* to window bars and so on.

pressurized escape route A fire escape route from a building, into which air is blown to counteract the *stack effect* and prevent smoke entering. If pressurized escape routes are used, stairs and *lobbies* do not have to be placed on outside walls, smoke shafts may become unnecessary as a means of alternative ventilation, and some smoke-stop doors may be unnecessary. Another advantage is that the extra stairs needed for a highly populated building may

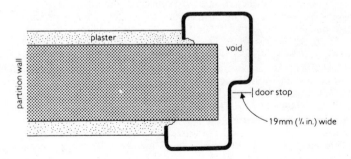

Cross-section of pressed-steel door frame suitable for a fire-check door to B S 459 (welded hinges and fixing lugs not shown).

not be needed. Pressures may reach 50 pascals (nearly 0·2 in. or 5 mm water gauge) but in two-stage designs the first stage may be only 15 pascals. Some buildings have automatic release of pressurizing air, switched on by the device that automatically opens the *smoke outlets*, which in turn may be started by a *smoke detector* (BS 5588, 4422). *See* **escape stair**.

pressurized structure An *air house*.

pre-treatment primer, holding p., etch p. [pai.] *Two-pack or one-pack primers* used on non-ferrous metals or on iron or steel directly after blast cleaning, to protect against rust. Blast-cleaned surfaces need priming within four hours (preferably one hour) of shot-blasting. An ordinary primer must be used afterwards.

priced bill [q.s.] A *bill of quantities* which has been sent out to a *contractor* for him to *tender*. The contractor has entered his price opposite each item, *extended* the prices, and summed the totals. The priced bill with certain formal documents constitutes the contractor's offer or tender to do the work for the price he has stated.

pricking up [pla.] Applying the first coat of *plaster* on *lathing*.

pricking-up coat [pla.] The first coat of plaster on *lathing*. *See* **rendering coat**.

prick post [carp.] A *queen post* or an intermediate post in a frame.

prick punch A tool like a *nail punch* with a point on it, used for pricking holes through sheet metal, for making a small hole to start a *nail* and so on.

primary flow and return pipes [plu.] The pipes in which water circulates between *boiler* and *cylinder* in a water-heating system, the flow pipe being that by which water leaves the boiler, returning to it by the return pipe usually because of *gravity circulation* alone. (Illus. pp. 64, 179)

primary gluing [tim.] The gluing in *plywood* manufacture and other veneering work, as opposed to *assembly gluing*.

prime cost contract [q.s.] A *contract* under which the *contractor* receives his proven costs plus an agreed percentage (or a fixed fee) for *overheads* and profit. The *RIBA* publishes a suitable form of contract with definitions. These contracts are placed only when time is so pressing that there is no alternative.

prime cost sum [q.s.] A sum entered in a *bill of quantities* by the *consultant*. The sum is provided to pay for the cost to the *contractor* of a specific article after deducting all discounts except the $2\frac{1}{2}\%$ discount for monthly settlement of accounts. It specifies the quality required in the article.

primer (1) A bituminous adhesive coating for sticking a *roofing felt* on to a roof boarding.

(2) [pai.] *See below, also C.*

priming coat, primer [pai.] The usual first coat of paint, put on new wood before the *stopping*. It ensures that the *undercoat* and *gloss* coat stick. It must be put on first to ensure that the stopping sticks. Otherwise, e.g. on wood or particle board, the water will be sucked from a water-based stopping or the oil from an oil-based one. Large areas of stopping may have to be re-primed. *See* **pre-treatment primer, sanding sealer, surfacer**.

princess posts, side p. [carp.] Subsidiary vertical timbers between the *queen posts* and the wall, to stiffen a *queen-post truss*.

principal (1) A *principal rafter*.

(2) A roof *truss*.

principal post [carp.] A *door post* in a *framed partition*.

principal rafters [carp.] **principals** The main *rafters*, those in the roof *truss* which carry the *purlins* on which the *common rafters* are laid.

processed shakes Common, sawn, *western red cedar* shingles which have been surface-textured on one face to look like split *shingles*. *See* **shakes**.

profile (1) (USA **batter board**) Horizontal boards set on edge at a datum level outside the foundation dig for a building. The level at which they are set is usually basement or ground floor or a few feet above or below. Nails or saw cuts in the top edges of the boards show the dig lines, footing lines, *building lines*, and any other important lines for setting out the lower part of the building. One profile is fixed at the end of each line, that is, two for each corner, so that strings can be stretched between the boards to show any line at any time.

(2) [pla.] A *templet* for shaping a moulding.

profiled steel sheet, p. cladding Steel sheets of trapezoidal (troughed, not corrugated) cross-section, that have been galvanized both sides as well as coated outside with 0·2 mm (0·008 in.) thick *plastisol* and on the reverse side with an *alkyd* or other durable paint. For permanent buildings they have superseded galvanized *corrugated steel sheet*, in part because of their much longer life and finer appearance, but also because the flat shapes are easier to fix to the structure and to insulation boards. Many colours are available and several textures – smooth, leather grain, etc. Profiled sheets may also be made of asbestos-cement, plastics, etc. (BS 5427)

progress certificate *See* **certificate**.

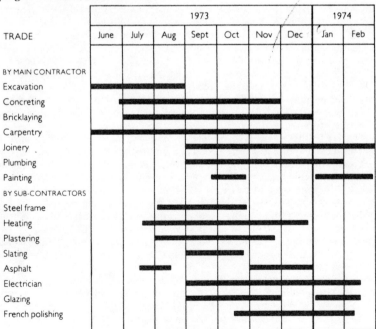

Progress chart

progress chart A wall chart showing the various operations in the construction of a building, such as clearing the site, excavation, concreting foundations, erecting steelwork, casting ground floor, casting first floor, casting roof, building outer walls, partitions, plastering, painting, and so on. Each operation is shown with proposed starting and finishing dates. Immediately, it can be seen at what state each *trade* should be on a certain date, and whether it is delayed. *See* **critical path scheduling** *and* illus. p. 259.

progress chaser, chaser (U S A **expediter**) A clerk employed by a *contractor* on a building site to verify the arrival on time of building materials and plant. He is also expected to know the reasons why any section of work is delayed. The person (and terms) are borrowed from factory production.

progress report A weekly report by a *clerk of works* or *resident architect* on the work done during the week and, more especially, on the work which should have been, but was not, done.

projecting scaffold A working platform built out from an upper storey, not reaching to the ground.

projection plaster [pla.] Special *gypsum plaster* suitable for application by machine. It contains additives that improve the *water retentivity* and *workability* and hold the setting time to 3 or 4 hours.

projection plastering [pla.] The use of *plastering machines* to apply *pre-mixed plasters* in a single coat between 5 and 25 mm (0·2–1 in.) thick, but usually about 13 mm ($\frac{1}{2}$ in.) for walls and 8 mm ($\frac{3}{8}$ in.) for ceilings. For dense concrete or other difficult surfaces, a *bonding agent* may have to be put on first.

propane blowlamp [plu.] A heating torch supplied from a *bottled gas*. The gas is obtainable in small steel bottles containing as little as 0·34 kg (12 oz) of the gas. Because of this and the high calorific value of the gas, a bottle with an appropriate burner screwed on to it can be used instead of the *oxy-acetylene* flame or the paraffin *blow lamp*. Large heavy cylinders with hoses to the blow lamps are also used. It is displacing the paraffin blow lamp although it is twice as expensive in fuel refills.

protected opening An opening in an internal, *fire-resisting floor* or wall which can be closed by a shutter or door of appropriate *fire grading*. *See* **pressurized escape route**.

protective finishes to metal Many surface coatings can protect metal from rust. The most important purely protective finishes are *hot-dip* (*C*) or electro-tinning or *galvanizing* (*C*), *sherardizing, cadmium* or *copper plating*, and *phosphating*. Finishes which are also decorative are *chromium* or *nickel* plating. For large steel structures, *metal coating* is possible. BS 5493 describes sprayed metal, electroplated metal, paint systems, bitumen, asphalt and coal-tar coatings, powder coatings, grease paints, wrapping tapes, cement mortar coatings, etc. BSCP 1021 describes *cathodic protection* (*C*).

provisional sum [q.s.] A sum set aside in the *bill of quantities* by the *consultant* to provide for work whose scope is not clearly foreseen. It may be *subcontractor*'s work.

Prussian blue, ferrocyanide b., Chinese b., etc. [pai.] A synthetic *pigment*, first made commercially in about 1770, consisting mainly of $Fe(CN)_6$ with some water, potassium and additional iron. Some varieties are valued for their metallic lustre, a sheen like bronze when looked at obliquely.

pry bar [joi.] A *nail puller*.

ptfe, polytetrafluorethylene [plu.] A *plastics* which came into use around 1962, with a number of functions in plumbing. As a tape it is wrapped around a screw thread and supersedes the use of tow and *jointing compound* (trade name Teflon).

P-trap [plu.] A trap (illus. p. 261) with an ordinary U-shaped seal and a final horizontal outlet. *See* **S-trap**. (Illus. p. 331.)

puff pipe An *anti-siphon pipe*.

pugging, pug, deafening, deadening *Soundproofing* floors with material inserted between the ceiling and floorboards of a wooden floor. Sand, slag wool, and *coarse stuff* have all been used. In Austria, where timber is plentiful, an effective way used in ordinary housing is to carry the ceiling on ceiling joists that are completely separate from the floor joists alongside them. This adds *discontinuous construction* to the principle of pugging, and the timber is extravagantly heavy by UK standards, which also helps considerably. *See* **sound boarding**.

pug mill A machine for mixing (and breaking up lumps of) clay or *mortar* – an open pan in which two rollers (or knives) on opposite ends of the same horizontal shaft are pushed round, and crush the materials. The pug mill is also used for blending paints (*pugging*).

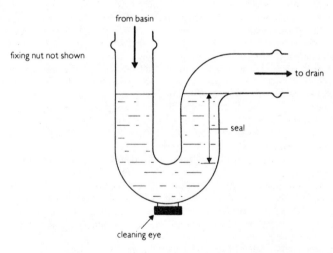

P-trap for a basin, 32 mm (1¼ in.) diameter.

pull [joi.] A handle for opening a door, drawer, etc., called a door or drawer pull or *sash lift* as the case may be.

pull box [elec.] A box placed in a length of *conduit*, at which the cables can be pulled. If pull boxes are placed at short intervals, the work of drawing the cables through the conduit is easier. *See* **draw-in system**.

pulley head (USA **yoke**) [joi.] The horizontal board in the *cased frame* of a *sash window* against which the sashes abut when pushed to the top.

pulley stile, sash run (USA **window s.**) [joi.] The vertical board at each side of the *cased frame* to a *sash window*. The pulleys over which the *sash cords* pass are fixed in them.

pulling [pai.] *Drag*.

pulling over [pai.] Levelling a film of cellulose *lacquer*, usually on wood, by rubbing it in one direction only with a soft cloth or leather pad soaked in a mixture of organic *solvents* which partly dissolve the lacquer.

pulling up, picking up [pai.] *See* **lifting**.

pull-out strength of nails [carp.] *See* **withdrawal load**.

pumice Foamy rock quarried in Germany and elsewhere for use as a *lightweight concrete* aggregate or as an *abrasive* in painting. It floats in water. *See* **pounce**.

pumice concrete *Lightweight concrete* made from pumice. It is *fire resisting* and has, like *foamed slag*, a low thermal *conductivity*. The highest strength is comparable with *clinker blocks*.

pumice stone [pai.] *Pumice* cut with plane faces to use as an *abrasive* for smoothing paint before repainting.

punch (1) [joi.] A *nail punch* or *centre punch* (C) or *handrail punch, solid punch*, or *prick punch*.

(2) A *mason*'s chisel with a cutting edge 10 cm (4 in.) wide. *See also* C.

punched work, broached w. *Ashlar* faced with a *punch*, with rough, diagonal strokes across the face.

puncheon (1) [carp.] A short post in the middle of a *truss*, such as a *trussed partition* or a *queen-post truss*.

(2) (USA) A roughly dressed, sometimes adzed *slab* of wood used for flooring. *See also* C.

purlin A horizontal beam in a roof, at right angles to the *principal rafters* or *trusses*, and carried on them. It carries the *common rafters* if there are any, or the *profiled steel sheet, roof decking*, etc.

purlin roof A roof for small houses, in which the purlins are carried on cross walls instead of on *trusses*.

purpose-made brick Bricks *moulded* to a special shape, such as *compass bricks*. *Compare* **gauged bricks**.

push plate [joi.] A metal plate, on the *lock stile* of a door at the level of the hand, to protect the paint from damage by people's hands.

push-pull rule A steel tape 12 mm ($\frac{1}{2}$ in.) wide, often 3 m (10 ft) long, which can be rolled into a pocket box of about 5 cm (2 in.) dia.

putlogs Short horizontal bearers, which carry *scaffold boards* in a *bricklayer's scaffold*. The putlog rests in a small hole left in the brickwork at one end, and on the *ledger* at the other end.

putlog holes Holes left in brickwork for *putlogs*.

putty *See* **glazier's putty, lime putty, mason's putty**.

putty and plaster [pla.] *Gauged stuff*.

putty knife A *stopping knife*.

PVA, PVAC [pai.] *Polyvinyl acetate*.

PVC *See* **polyvinyl chloride**.

pyramid For many hundreds or thousands of years the Great Pyramid was man's most massive structure with its 20 million m³ of stone.

pyramidal light A *roof light* in which the *glazing* slopes up to a point from a base shaped like a regular polygon.

Pyrotenax, copper-sheathed or **mineral-insulated cable, earthed concentric wiring** [elec.] An electric cable consisting of copper wire contained in a copper tube filled with magnesia, MgO. It is unaffected by fire, can be heavily overloaded without endangering the building, and is so reliable that it is often used in power stations. However, each run of cable must be sealed against moisture by welding or other special treatment of the ends. Pyrotenax cables may be cast into concrete slabs as *coil heating*.

Q

quadrant [joi.] A metal, curved *casement stay*. *See also* **quarter-round**.

quadrant dividers [carp.] A pair of dividers in which one limb slides on an arc fitted to the other limb and may be temporarily clamped to it by a screw.

quaggy timber [tim.] Wood with many *shakes* at the centre.

quantities [q.s] The amounts of building materials and of work put into a building, translated into the terms and units of the *bill of quantities* (in mm, m, m^2, m^3, kg, tonnes, etc.). Whether quantities are provided in the *contract* depends on the amount of information available at the time it was drawn up. Different contracts are used according to whether quantities, approximate quantities, or no quantities are included in the *contract documents*.

quantity surveying [q.s.] The drawing up of *bills of quantities*, their settlement between *building owner* and *contractor*, and the *arbitration* of disputed points after the completion of the work. *See* **quantity surveyor**.

quantity surveyor [q.s.] A person trained in construction costs and contract procedures. He makes feasibility studies, advising the client on selection of *contractor*, prepares *contract documents* such as the *bill of quantities*, controls costs, provides financial statements during building and helps to settle the final account. This profession, unique to the UK, originated in the 19th century, when groups of competing contractors shared the cost of employing one man to draw up a bill of quantities as a basis for tender. Chartered quantity surveyors belong to the *RICS*.

quarrel A *pane* of glass in *leaded lights*.

quarry face, q. pitched, q. dressed A description of stone as it comes from the quarry, that is, squared with a rough face.

quarry sap The moisture in stone freshly cut from the quarry. When this has dried out, the stone is harder to work.

quarry stone bond Any *bond* which exists in rubble walls.

quarry tiles, quarries Burnt clay, black, buff or red *flooring tiles*. They are from 23×23 to 10×10 cm (9×9 to 4×4 in.) in size, unglazed, but not porous.

quarter bend [plu.] A 90° bend in a pipe. Other bends are proportional to this, a one-eighth bend being 45°.

quartered [tim.] *Quarter-sawn*.

quartered log [tim.] A log cut into four quarters for *conversion* by *quarter-sawing*.

quarter-girth rule [tim.] The volume of the *square-sawn* timber in a round log is assumed to be equal to a square of side equal to the quarter girth of the log at the middle of its length, that is $0 \cdot 616D^2$ which is equal to $(\frac{\pi}{4}D)^2$, multiplied by the length.

quartering [tim.] *Quarter-sawing*.

quarter-round, quadrant [joi.] A convex *moulding* like a quarter circle.

quarter-sawing, quartering, rift sawing [tim.] Sawing wood as nearly radially as possible, with no growth ring at an angle of less than 80° to the surface in fully-quartered timber, 45° being usually acceptable for floorboards. It is used for the best floorboards and for oak to give the fine figure of *edge grain*. The log is usually first cut into quarters, after which each quarter is cut radially, wasting timber in wedge shapes. *Compare* **flat-sawn timber**, p. 140.

quarter-space landing [joi.] A small square landing between flights at an angle of 90° to each other, and as wide as one flight (BS 565). *Compare* **half-space landing**.

queen bolt A steel bolt used in place of a *queen post* in the *queen-post truss*.

queen closer A *brick* cut in half along its length to keep the *bond* with a 5 cm (2 in.) face width. Normally in England it measures about 21 × 5 × 6·5 cm deep (8¼ × 2 × 2½ in.). *See* **closer**.

queen posts [carp.] The two posts nearest the midspan in a *queen-post truss*.

queen-post truss [carp.] A *truss* which was used for spans from 10 to 20 m (35 to 70 ft) but is now little used. It differs from the *king-post truss* in having no central post but two queen posts each side of the centre. *See* **Pratt truss** (*C*).

Quetta bond A *bond* with gaps formed in the middle of the wall, like *rat-trap bond* except that the bricks are laid on bed, not on edge, and the usual wall is 34 cm (13½ in.) thick. The cavities in the middle are filled with grout as the wall rises and contain vertical steel. Each course of both faces is laid in *Flemish bond*. *See* **reinforced brickwork** (*C*).

quicklime [pla.] *Lime* (CaO) which has not been slaked, unlike **lime putty**.

quilt *See* **blanket**.

quilted figure, blister f. [tim.] An elaborate *figure* consisting of apparent knolls in *birch* or maple due to uneven *annual rings*.

quirk [joi.] A furrow parallel to a *bead* and terminating it.

quirk bead [joi.] A semicircular *bead* with a *quirk* at one side to mark an edge of a board. A double quirk bead has quirks each side.

quirk router [joi.] A *plane* for cutting *quirks*.

quoin, coin (1) An outer corner of a wall.

(2) A brick or large stone set in a salient corner of a wall.

quoin header A corner *header* in the face wall which is a *stretcher* in the side wall.

R

rabbet A *rebate*.

rabbet plane A *rebate plane*.

raceway [elec.] (USA) A rectangular *duct* for cables or bus bars. It may be a *plugmold*.

racking back, raking b. The normal way of building a *brick* wall consists of first building the corners or ends very carefully in steps rising from the middle part of the wall. The gradual increases of height to the corner are called racking back. (Illus. below)

radial brick, radius b. A *compass brick*.

radial shrinkage [tim.] The drying *shrinkage* of timber at right angles to the *growth ring* is two thirds of the *tangential* shrinkage.

radiant heating (1) (USA) *Coil heating*.

(2) [pai.] *Stoving* a finish by radiation from a hot surface.

radiator [plu.] A gilled container, usually for water, often part of a *central-heating* system. Being at a low temperature it loses less heat by radiation than by *convection*, and in theory it should therefore be called a convector.

radiator key A small spanner. (Illus. p. 267) *See* **air lock** (3).

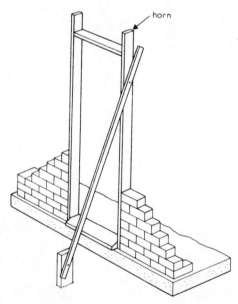

horn

Racking back. The central part of the wall is carefully raised first and accurately plumbed with the corners lowest as shown. It is convenient then to plumb and fix a door or window frame carefully to act as a guide for the rest of the brick-work. Where, as usual, there is no frame to act as a guide, the corners are raised first.

Radiator key – the small hole is about 5 mm (0·2 in.) across.

radio-frequency heating, high-frequency, dielectric capacity, electrostatic h. [tim.] A method of rapidly heating thick *plywood* assemblies for gluing by electrodes placed in the assembly. *Compare* **strip heating**.

radius rod, gig stick [pla.] A strip of wood about 5 × 5 cm (2 × 2 in.) and slightly longer than the radius of an arch to be moulded. The *mould* is fixed firmly to one end of the rod at the correct radius. The gig stick is then pivoted at the centre of the arch by nailing it to a board. The moulding is formed with a *horsed mould*.

radius shoe [pla.] A piece of zinc plate screwed to one side of a plasterer's *radius rod* over its centre point. It is drilled so that the centre pin or nail can pass through the radius rod.

rafter [carp.] A sloping timber extending from the *eave* to the *ridge* of a roof. It may be a *common rafter* or a *principal rafter*.

rafter filling, beam f., wind f. Brick infilling between rafters at wall plate level.

rag felt (USA) *Bitumen felt*.

raglet, raggle, raglin A thin groove, in stone often *dovetailed*, cut in stone or in a mortar joint of brickwork to receive the end of a lead *flashing*, which is fixed by *leadburning* or wedging.

rail (1) [joi.] A horizontal secondary member with a *tenon* cut on it, framed into vertical *stiles*, e.g. in a *panelled door*.

(2) [joi.] The upper, continuous part of a *balustrade*, a handrail.

(3) Any horizontal timber in a fence.

rail bolt [joi.] A *handrail bolt*.

railing (1) An open fence made of posts and *rails*.

(2) [joi.] A *banding*.

raindrop figure [tim.] A *figure* which may be *mottle* alternating with *ribbon grain*.

rain leader (pronounced leeder), **r. conductor** (USA) *Downpipe*.

rainwater head, hopper h., r. hopper (USA **conductor h., leader h., cistern h.**) The enlarged top end of a *downpipe*, that collects the water from the *eaves gutters*.

rainwater pipe A *downpipe*.

raised fibres [pai.] The fibres of wood rise from the surface when it dries naturally or after the application of a coat of paint or varnish. To achieve a glossy paint or varnish surface, the fibres should be sanded off with fine glass paper after every coat but the last.

raising plate [carp.] A *pole plate* or *wall plate*.

rake (1) **batter** An angle of inclination to the vertical.

(2) [carp.] *See* **pitch**.

raked joint A mortar *joint* which has been cleaned of mortar for about 2 cm (¾ in.) back from the face before *pointing* or plastering.

rake moulding (USA) The sloping *moulding* at the top of a *barge board*, just below the *shingles* or *tiles* on a *gable* end.

raking back *Racking back.*

raking cornice or **coping** A *cornice* or *coping* on a slope, e.g. over a *gable*.

raking cutting Cutting not at right angles.

raking flashing A *cover flashing* used e.g. between a stone *chimney* and a sloping roof. It is parallel to the roof slope and is let into a sloping *raglet*. A *stepped flashing* is not practicable with stone, as the joints are too far apart.

raking out Cleaning out mortar *joints* before *pointing*.

raking riser A *riser* which is not vertical and overhangs the *tread* below, to give more foothold. The tread is bigger than its *going*. *See* **flight** (illus. p. 142).

raking shore, shoring, raker A long *baulk* or several baulks erected to hold up

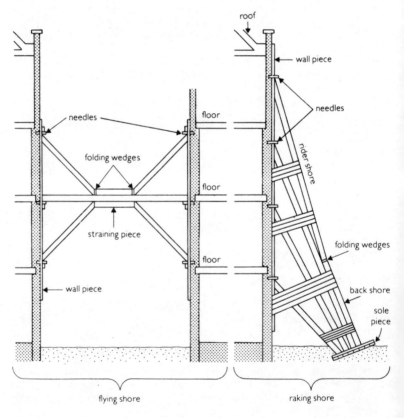

Flying shore and raking shore. Both types of shore bear against vertical wall pieces held in place by needles of timber or steel into the wall f = floors, n = needles.

temporarily a wall of a building. It is carried on a wooden *sole plate* at ground level and designed so that each baulk abuts against the building on a *needle* inserted into the wall near each ceiling level. *See* **rider shore, wall plate**.

rammed-earth construction The *cob* construction of the dry parts of USA.

ramp (1) [joi.] A bend in a *handrail* or coping which is concave on the upper side. *Compare* **knee**.

(2) [plu.] A short, steep length of drain pipe.

ram's horn figure [tim.] A ripple like *fiddleback*.

random ashlar American term for *coursed squared rubble*.

random courses *Courses* of varying depths.

random rubble *Rubble walls* built of stones which are of irregular shape and size and not coursed.

random shingles *Shingles* varying from 6 to 30 cm (2½ to 12 in.) or more wide but of uniform length.

random slates, rustic s. *Slates* of varying width, sold by the ton with a maker's statement of their covering capacity in square metres per ton. They may be laid in *diminishing courses* or at random. Their rustic appearance is often attractive. The best known English randoms are *Delabole* and *Westmorland*. *Compare* **sized slates**.

range masonry, coursed ashlar, r. work (USA) *Regular-coursed rubble*.

ranging line A string stretched between *profiles* to show a face of a wall or other line.

rank set [carp.] A set of the *back iron* of a *plane* which leaves a big space between it and the edge of the *cutting iron*. It is used for rough work, the opposite of a fine set.

rasp *See* **plumber's tools** (illus. p. 250).

ratchet brace, r. drill [carp.] A carpenter's *brace* for use where, in confined spaces, a full turn cannot be given to the brace. It is fitted with a ratchet and pawl mechanism which allows the bit to be turned while in the hole (p. 59).

rate of growth [tim.] The number of *growth rings* per cm of timber measured radially. *Softwoods* with many growth rings per cm are stronger than those with few, an indication of rapid growth and weakness. *See* **stress-graded timber**.

rating [mech.] The rating of an electric drill is the diameter of the largest hole it can drill into mild steel. Nominal ratings vary from 6 to 32 mm (¼ to 1¼ in.). About twice these diameters would be feasible for softwood.

rat-trap bond, all-rowlock wall A brick *bond* in which the bricks are laid on edge in *courses* 11·5 cm (4½ in.) deep to build a 23 cm (9 in.) thick wall. It consists of two leaves 7·6 cm (3 in.) thick in which headers and stretchers alternate. A cavity, 23 × 7·6 cm (9 × 3 in.) in plan, is left opposite each stretcher. The wall is cheap and fairly strong, p. 270. *Compare* **Quetta bond, silver-lock bond**.

raw linseed oil [pai.] Refined *linseed oil* which has not been 'boiled'. Unrefined linseed oil is never used in painting.

Rawlplug A small drilled plug, made usually of wood fibre, occasionally of soft metal (*see* **Rawlbolt** (C)) inserted into a hole in a wall, as a fixing for a nail or screw. Some metal Rawlplugs are made with a wide collar at the outer end to prevent them passing through a bottomless hole (screw anchor).

ray, wood r., medullary r. [tim.] Radial strips or ribbons of attractive *grain*, sometimes seen, especially in the *silver grain* of quartered oak. The growing

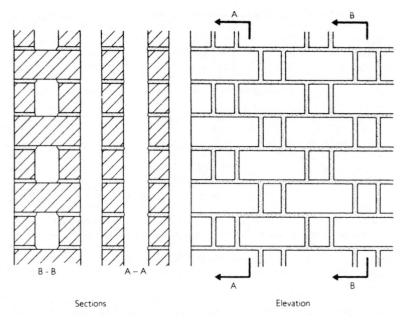

B - B   A – A

Sections   Elevation

Rat-trap bond.

part of the tree is next to the bark, not in the medulla or pith, so 'medullary ray' is obsolescent

ready-mixed concrete *See C.*

ready-mixed lime-sand mortar BS 4721 specifies ready-mixed lime-sand mortars. Lime-sand mixes keep for much longer without deterioration than mixes containing cement. Cement and more water can be added at the site. The strongest usual mix after the cement has been added is 4:1:12 cement:lime:sand, the weakest is 1:2:9. A 1:3 lime:sand mix has only 9 to 14% lime; a 1:3 cement:sand mix on the other hand has 20 to 25% cement. A 1:12 lime:sand mix has only 1·5 to 4% lime. Therefore the effect of even a little cement is considerable. *See* **rendering coat.**

real estate (USA) Land and buildings.

rebate, rabbet (Scots **check**) [joi.] A long, step-shaped rectangular recess cut in the edge of a timber, such as that cut from the side of a *glazing bar* to receive the glass and putty.

rebated weather-boarding [carp.] *Weather-boarding* of wedge-shaped cross section with a *rebate* along the inner face of its lower edge so that the top (thin) edge of the lower boards fits into the rebate in the lower (thick) edge of the upper board. *German siding* and *shiplap siding* are also both rebated but not specially so called. *See* **siding.**

rebate plane, rabbet p., [joi.] A *plane* with a *cutting iron* and mouth reaching to the edge of the *sole*, enabling it to cut *rebates.*

receptacle [elec.] (USA) *Socket outlet.*

receptor [plu.] (USA) The shallow *tray* of a shower bath.

recessed head screw, Phillips s. [joi.] A *screw* with a head not slotted across its full width like the common wood screw but with a cross-shaped recess into which a cross-shaped screwdriver blade fits. The grip between screwdriver and screw is better, the head is stronger and less likely to break off than the slotted head and surrounding finishes are less prone to damage. A possible reason for the unpopularity of these screws is that the recess can become burred and the screw cannot then be turned. It can be removed only by drilling it out.

recessed pointing, r. joint The mortar *joint* in *pointing* is set back about 6 mm ($\frac{1}{4}$ in.) from the face of the wall. It therefore is strongly shadowed. There is less danger of mortar peeling than with joints which are near the face.

reciprocating drill [joi.] A hand drill with a steeply threaded shaft which carries the drill *chuck* (*C*) at its lower end. A sleeve which fits this thread is pushed down the shaft and so rotates it. When the sleeve is drawn back up the drill, the grip within the sleeve does not hold the thread nor turn the shaft. It is used for drilling holes less than about 3 mm ($\frac{1}{8}$ in.) dia.

reciprocating saw [mech.] A power-driven saw capable of similar work to the power *jigsaw* but looking rather like a heavy *handsaw* with an electric motor near the handle.

reconditioning [tim.] High temperature steam treatment of *hardwood* which has suffered *collapse*. It also reduces *warp*. The process was developed by Australians for their hardwoods.

reconstructed stone *Cast stone*.

rectangular tie (USA) A *wall tie* made of a bent rectangle of heavy wire about 5 × 15 cm (2 × 6 in.).

red lead [pai.] A red *pigment* consisting of mixed oxides of lead, mainly Pb_3O_4. It is an *inhibiting pigment*, is used on wood as well as on steel, but like most *lead paints* is poisonous.

red oxide [pai.] Red iron oxide, a *pigment* which does not inhibit corrosion.

reducer (1) [pai.] A *thinner*.

(2) [plu.] A *taper pipe* reducing in diameter in the direction of flow.

reducing power [pai.] The strength of a *white pigment*, that is the paleness of tint produced when a standard amount of it is mixed with a standard amount of a coloured *pigment*. The paler the tint the greater is the reducing power of the white. *Compare* **staining power**.

redwood (Pinus sylvestris), **red deal, yellow deal, northern pine, Scots pine** or **fir**, etc. [tim.] A *softwood* which grows throughout northern Europe and Asia, used for *carpentry* and *joinery*. It is easy to work, durable, machinable, takes *nails* and *screws*, and also *glues*, *paints* and *stains* well. The word redwood is usually confined to timber imported to Britain, often from the Baltic.

reed In *thatching*, the best reed is Arundo phragmites, but in the west of England reed means wheaten straw. *See also* C.

refractory mortar *Mortar* suitable for boiler settings, or other furnaces. One suitable mix is 3 parts of *grog* to 1 of *aluminous cement*.

refrigerant The working fluid in a *refrigerator*, which alternately vaporizes to cool the refrigerator and is compressed to liquid again by a compressor (Freon, sulphur dioxide, etc.).

refrigerator [mech.] The domestic refrigerator consists of a small compressor for the cooling fluid, often Freon or sulphur dioxide (SO_2), which is compressed to about 400 kN/m^2 (60 psi), cooled in a finned tank outside the refrigerator and then expanded to gas inside the tubes of the cold cupboard. This expansion and volatilization of gas takes up heat from the cold cupboard and gives it out in the cooling tank outside it, warming the room.

register (1) A damper to vary a chimney draught.

(2) An outlet into a room from a ventilating duct, provided with a damper to regulate the volume of warm air discharged into it. *Compare* **grille**.

reglet A *raglet*.

regrate To remove the outer surface of *hewn stone* so that it looks new.

regular-coursed rubble (USA **range masonry, coursed ashlar, range work**) Coursed *rubble walling* in courses of different height, generally from 7 to 15 cm (3 to 6 in.)

regularizing [tim.] BS 4471 states that regularizing is the thicknessing, planing or other machining of a timber to make its cross-section uniform throughout its length. The aim is strength not beauty, and regularized timber may have rough, unplaned patches.

regulus metal, antimonial lead [plu.] An alloy of lead which is very much harder than lead, containing about 10% antimony. It is used as a wall *cladding* sheet.

reinforced bitumen felt A light *bitumen felt* made of fibre saturated with bitumen with an embedded layer of loose jute hessian. It is used as *sarking felt* on unboarded roofs.

reinforced concrete *See C*.

reinforced masonry *Masonry* of stone or *building blocks* reinforced with steel in the bed or vertical joints.

reinforced woodwool Building slabs of *woodwool* stiffened lengthwise with *battens*, or pressed steel U-sections.

relieving arch, rough a., discharging a. An arch built over and clear of, a wooden *lintel* or other weak support, to carry load. It is generally of rectangular bricks with wedge-shaped mortar *joints*.

render and set [pla.] Two-coat plaster on walls, *rendering* covered by a *finishing coat*. It is used on *gypsum plasterboard, insulating board*, etc.

render, float, and set [pla.] *Three-coat plaster* on walls.

rendering [pla.] Applying *mortar* to a wall or cement *mortar* to the inner face of a manhole or *stucco* to an outside wall. This is often done by bricklayers, but plasterers usually do any rendering which is to be covered by a *finishing coat* indoors or out of doors (BS 5262).

rendering coat [pla.] A first coat of *plaster* on a wall, usually about 1 cm ($\frac{3}{8}$ in.) max. thickness. A first coat on *lathing* is called a pricking-up coat. A typical strong rendering mix is 1:1:6 cement:lime:sand, and a weak one is $\frac{1}{2}$:1:4$\frac{1}{2}$ (1:2:9). Where *plasticizer* must be used because lime causes *efflorescence*, 1:6 and 1:8 correspond to the mixes above. With *masonry cement*, a 1:5 mix corresponds to a 1:6 mix with plasticizer. *See* **ready-mixed lime-sand mortar**.

re-saw [tim.] To rip sawn timber into smaller sizes.

resident architect An *architect* at a site who watches the interests of the *building owner* during construction, working under the *consultant*.

residual tack [pai.] A fault of finishes which do not harden, caused by vegetable oils such as dehydrated castor oil. It may last indefinitely in damp air.

resin bonded [tim.] Glued with *synthetic resins*, usually moisture-resistant.

resin chipboard [tim.] *See* **wood chipboard**.

resin-impregnated wood [tim.] *Improved wood*.

resin pocket, pitch p., pitch streak [tim.] In some softwoods, an opening between the growth rings, that contains resin.

resins (1) The natural resins are obtained from the sap of plants or pine trees or are found in the ground near where the trees have been. They are of three sorts, the gum resins (asafoetida, frankincense, and myrrh), the hard resins (all varnishes contain some) and the *oleo-resins*. Examples of the hard resins are *copal, mastic* and *rosin*. The oleo-resins include Canada balsam and true *lacquer* from a sumach tree (used in China for about 1300 years). All hard resins are insoluble in water but may be dissolved in organic *solvents* or vegetable oils. Some gums are soluble in water, particularly those used as *glues*.

(2) *Synthetic resins* are organic compounds of which the first members resembled the natural resins. They have outstanding qualities in *glues* and paints.

resistance *See* **surface resistance** The thermal resistance is the reciprocal of the *conductance*, and is analogous to electrical resistance.

resorcinol formaldehyde resin [tim.] A *synthetic resin*.

rest bend A *duck-foot bend*.

retarded hemihydrate plaster [pla.] *See* **hemihydrate plaster**.

retarder [pla.] An *admixture* such as keratin added to *plaster of Paris* to reduce its hardening rate enough for it to be used as *hemihydrate plaster*. *See also C*.

re-tempering [pla.] The practice of remixing *mortar* or plaster which has begun to set. It is forbidden.

retention money [q.s.] A percentage of the money due to a *contractor* who has completed his contract. This money is not paid to him until the end of the *maintenance period* when the building owner and his consultants are satisfied that the contractor has fulfilled his obligations. The amount is usually 5%, of which half or a third is paid on completion.

return (1) A change of direction at the end of a wall, usually at right angles. Returns of brick walls are important for two reasons. First, the return adds strength because of its buttressing effect. Secondly, shrinkage cracks are likely to appear at the return unless it is designed and built with care.

(2) A *return pipe*.

return pipe [plu.] The pipe by which the water leaves a *radiator* or hot-water *cylinder* and returns to the *boiler* in a water-heating system. *See* **primary flow and return pipes**.

return wall, r. end, returned corner A short length of wall perpendicular to an end of a longer wall.

reveal The visible part of a *jamb* in a door or window opening, not covered by the frame.

reveal lining [joi.] The finish over a *reveal*.

reveal pin, r. tie A screw inside a window opening used for clamping *tubular scaffolding* to the opening.

reverberant sound Sound re-echoed from wall or ceiling surfaces. It reaches the hearer after the direct sound and may confuse speech. See below.

reverberation period, r. time of an enclosure The period of time, in seconds, required for sound of a certain frequency to decrease, after the source is silenced, to one millionth of its initial value, that is by 60 *decibels*. It depends mainly on the volume and on the *absorption* of the room. A long reverberation period reduces the clarity of speech. A one-second reverberation period at a distance between speaker and hearer of 30 m (90 ft) might be tolerable with loud, clear speech but a shorter period would be better. For music a longer reverberation period is needed than for speech.

reverse [pla.] A *templet* cut to the reversed shape of a *moulding* and placed on it to check its accuracy.

reversible lock [joi.] A lock in which the *latch* can be taken out and reversed. This enables it to be used on a door of opposite *hand*, or on the opposite *stile* of the same door. The hand of the lock is reversible.

revolving door, swing d. A door with up to four leaves ordinarily perpendicular to each other and pivoted on a central post. They may either rotate or be locked shut or open (parallel). It is a type of *air lock* and need not exceed 1·8 m (6 ft) diameter in plan.

rhone, rone (Scotland) An *eaves gutter*.

RIBA The Royal Institute of British Architects.

riband [carp.] (1) **ribbon board** A timber which runs along the head of the struts under a reinforced concrete beam, to fix the *formwork* (*C*) to the beam sides and to carry the weight during casting.

(2) A *rail* in a palisade.

ribbing [tim.] Corrugation on the surface of timber due to the different drying *shrinkages* of *springwood* and *summerwood*.

ribbing up [joi.] Building up circular *joinery* like *laminated wood* by gluing *veneers* together with parallel grain.

ribbon (1) An occasional course of ornamental slates or tiles.

(2) A *ribbon board*.

ribbon board, r. strip, ribbon, girt strip, ledger b. [carp.] A *joist housed* into the *studs* at ceiling level, supporting the floor joists in *balloon framing*.

ribbon grain, r. stripe, stripe figure, roe figure [tim.] Alternating light and dark strips 3 to 13 mm ($\frac{1}{8}$ to $\frac{1}{2}$ in.) wide in *quartered* timber formed by the different reflections of light in *interlocked grain*.

ribbon saw [tim.] A narrow *band saw* about 5 cm (2 in.) wide only.

ribbon strip [carp.] A *ribbon board*.

ribbon stripe [tim.] *Ribbon grain*.

rich mix A mix of *concrete* or *mortar* which contains more cement than usual, or a plaster mix with less sand and more *gypsum plaster* or *cement* than usual.

RICS Royal Institution of Chartered Surveyors. *See* **surveyor**.

riddle A coarse sieve.

ride [joi.] (1) A door which touches the floor when it opens is said to ride. This can sometimes be prevented by *cocking* the hinges.

(2) A joint which meets in the middle and is open at the ends is said to ride.

(3) A pin in a *strap hinge*.

rider shore A short, topmost *raking shore* which rests not on the ground but on a *back shore* lying along the highest full-length raking shore. Riders are not needed except for tall buildings (illus. p. 268).

ridge, r. board, r. pole, r. piece [carp.] The horizontal board set on edge, at which the *rafters* meet. It is about 2 to 4 cm by 23 cm (1 to $1\frac{1}{2}$ by 9 in.) in cross section (illus. p. 354).

ridge binder [carp.] *See* **trussed rafter**.

ridge capping, r. covering A covering over a *ridge*. It may be of *roofing felt*, purpose-made asbestos-cement sheet, clay roofing tile, sawn slate, sheet metal, or steel angle, depending on the roof construction.

ridge course The topmost course of slates or tiles, next the ridge, cut (or purpose-made) to the required length.

ridge pole [carp.] A *ridge*.

ridge roll [carp.] A *hip roll*.

ridge stop At an intersection between a ridge and a wall rising above it, a piece of *flexible metal* flashing dressed over the ridge and up the wall.

ridge tile A concrete or burnt clay *tile* for covering a *ridge*, often also suitable for covering a *hip*, made in several different shapes. They are either 300 or 460 mm (12 or 18 in.) long and are normally bedded in mortar (BS 402, 5534).

rift sawn [tim.] *Quarter-sawn*.

rigger [pai.] A long-haired *brush* with a flat end for painting lines or bands of different thicknesses. *See also* C.

rigid damp course A *brick damp course* or a slate one.

rim latch [joi.] A metal box screwed on to the inner face of the *shutting stile* of a door. It contains a *latch*, turned by door knobs, for fastening the door. This is cheaper than a *lock*.

rim lock [joi.] A *rim latch* which can be locked.

rindgall [tim.] A *callus*.

ring course The course nearest the *extrados* in an arch several *courses* deep.

ring main [elec.] A convenient method for wiring power circuits in houses, standardized in Britain. A ring of about ten power points is generally allowed. Each *socket outlet* is connected to the main through two lengths of cable which together form the ring. Each *fused plug* contains its own fuse protecting its own appliance, and with the other plug fuses, the ring main. *See* **wiring regulations, spur**.

ring-porous wood [tim.] *Hardwood* containing more and larger pores in the *springwood* than elsewhere. These pores show up as a ring. *Compare* **diffuse porous wood**.

ring shake, cup s., wind s. [tim.] *Shake* along one or more *growth rings See* **shell shake**.

rip [tim.] To saw parallel to the grain, also called *flat cutting*. *See* **cross-cut**.

ripper (1) A slater's long cranked blade which is inserted under the *slates* and pulled back to cut the *roofing nails* when a roof is being repaired. *See* **plasterer's tools** (illus. p. 246), *also* C.

(2) [tim.] A *rip saw*.

ripple [tim.] A beautiful *figure* caused by the buckling of fibres during growth. It is often seen in sycamore. *See* **fiddleback**.

ripple finish [pai.] An intentional uniformly wrinkled finish which is obtained usually by *stoving*.

rip saw, ripping s. [carp.] A *handsaw* made to cut parallel with the grain. It can have as few as 6 points per 25 mm (1 in.). *See* **setting**.

rise (1) The vertical height of an arch measured from *springing line* to the highest point of the *intrados*.

(2) The vertical height from the supports to the ridge of a roof.

rise-and-fall table [tim.] A circular *saw bench*, which can be raised or lowered relatively to the saw.

275

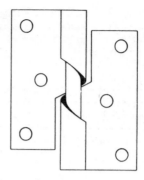

Rising-butt hinge.

rise and run [carp.] The *pitch* (1) of a member expressed as a certain vertical height for so much horizontal run.

riser (1) The upright face of a step. No riser should exceed 220 mm (8⅜ in.). *See* **flight** (illus. p. 142).

(2) In *snecked rubble* a deep stone which is thicker than one *course* and may also be a *bond stone*.

rising and lateral conductors [elec.] Power or lighting cables in a *branch circuit*.

rising-butt hinges, rising butts [joi.] *Hinges* which cause a door to rise about 1 cm (½ in.) when opening. They are made with a helical bearing surface between the two leaves. The door therefore tends to close automatically as well as to clear a carpet when opening. Also the door can be lifted off its hinges without unscrewing them. (Illus. above)

rising damp *Capillary* (*C*) movement of water into a wall from the ground, a complaint that is commonest in houses built before 1875 when *damp courses* became compulsory. In new houses with the necessary damp course it is rare unless *bridges* exist or the damp course has failed. Where it seems impracticable to insert a damp course by *sawing in* or *injection*, it may be possible to hide the damp area and reduce its ill effects. In an old house with no damp course, that has suffered the evaporation of the dampness into the house for years, the wall at the level of the evaporation becomes impregnated with salts brought up with the water. These salts are likely to absorb water and to remain damp. The plaster therefore may have to be stripped. A number of methods of treatment involve stripping, followed either by fixing *dovetailed lathing* to the bricks or the painting of the wall with bitumen emulsion or other waterproofing liquid and then re-plastering. Occasionally the existing plaster is kept and used as a base on to which aluminium or lead foil is glued with bitumen as a base for decoration.

rising main An electrical power supply cable or main gas or water supply pipe which passes up through one or more storeys of a building. (For water, BS 4118 prefers 'rising pipe').

rive [tim.] To split *shingles, laths*, etc., making riven shingles or laths.

riven slate *Slate* that is split, not sawn.

rocket tester, smoke r. [plu.] A rocket which gives off a dense, lasting smoke directed into a drain under test. The drain is plugged at both ends and subjected to a slight excess internal pressure of 3·8 cm (1·5 m) water gauge.

rock face The surface texture of *pitch-faced* stone.

rocking frame An oscillating frame on which moulds are set while they are being filled with *concrete*. The oscillation helps to compact the concrete.

rock wool *See* **mineral wool.**

rod A board on which the dimensions of a piece of *joinery*, etc. are set out full size, for instance, a *storey rod* for setting out stairs. *See below.*

rodding (1) Cleaning out drains with *drain rods* (*C*). (Illus. above)

(2) (USA) Levelling plaster with a *floating rule*.

rodding eye [plu.] An *access eye* at the head of a branch drain, formed by bringing the drain (backwards) up to ground level and sealing it with a cover plate. *See below.*

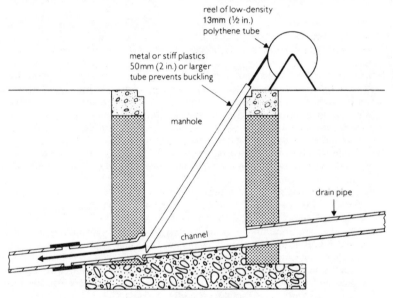

Rodding of drain pipe – cane rods and steel-spring rods are also used.

rodding-point drainage [plu.] An approach to drainage layout that saves investment money because there are fewer *inspection chambers* (*C*). These are replaced by *rodding eyes* at which flexible rods can be inserted – 13 mm ($\frac{1}{2}$ in.) diameter low-density polythene tube carried on 30 m (98 ft) reels. They pass easily round bends. At inspection chambers, to prevent buckling of the tube as it is pushed into the drain, it is passed through a metal tube, to suit the manhole depth.

roll (1) **wood r.** A piece of wood over which *flexible-metal roofing* sheets are lapped and folded.

(2) *See* **double Roman tile, hollow roll, solid roll,** *and below.*

roll-capped ridge tiles *Ridge tiles* with a cylindrical projection above them.

roll capping [plu.] Inverted U-shaped *flexible-metal* strips placed thus ∩ to cover wooden *rolls* and the edges of neighbouring metal sheets.

rolled-strip roofing *Roll roofing*.

roller coating [pai.] Applying paint or emulsion by roller.

roller-coating enamel [pai.] *Enamel* which is applied to steel or other metal sheet by a roller-coating machine.

rolling shutters Wooden or metal shutters used for large doors or windows which are taken up or let down from a roller carried by a *lintel* over the opening. Metal rolling shutters give good fire protection.

roll roofing, rolled-strip roofing US terms for any roofing material sold in rolls like *roofing felt*.

rolok *See* **rowlock**.

Roman bricks (USA) Bricks which measure 30 to 40 × 10 × 5 cm (12 to 16 × 4 × 2 in.) including the mortar *joints*. They therefore lay up six courses per ft (30 cm) height.

Roman cement, Parker's c. Properly speaking *pozzolanas* (*C*), but the term has come to mean, in England, a cement made in the nineteenth century by burning lumps of marl found in the London clay. It was the forerunner of *Portland cement*.

Roman mosaic, tessellated pavement [pla.] A *terrazzo* laid with pieces of marble about 1 cm (½ in.) square (tesserae) placed by hand. Geometrical patterns can be made by gluing the stone on to strong paper, then inverting the paper over the floor covered with wet *mortar*, when the stones and paper are pushed into the mortar. The paper is later removed and the stones are not abraded after laying. *See* **mosaic cutter**.

Roman tile A British, clay *single-lap tile*. The single Roman tile is not standard and has one waterway. The *double Roman tile* is standardized and has two waterways separated by a central roll.

rone, rhone (Scotland) An *eaves gutter*.

roof For domestic roofs and spans up to about 4·5 m (15 ft) *common rafters* are usual. A quickly erected timber roof truss is the factory made *trussed rafter*, spanning from 5 to 11 m (16 to 36 ft). For longer spans, steel or concrete are more economical, but laminated wood arches are more beautiful and costly. *See* **concrete roofs** (*C*), *and* **pitched roofs** (illus. p. 279).

roof boards, boarding, sheathing Boards laid touching each other, usually tongued and grooved, nailed to the *common rafters* as a base for asphalt, *flexible-metal roofing*, or *roofing felt* under slates or tiles.

roof cladding, r. covering Slates, tiles, *asbestos cement* sheet, *flexible metal*, *profiled steel sheet*, etc. *See* **cladding**, BSCP 143, 144.

roof-decking panels Lightweight, insulated waterproof panels, spanning up to 4 m (13 ft) and covering about 2 m² (21 ft²) each, that enable a roof to be quickly, if expensively, completed. They weigh up to 30 kg/m² (6 lb/ft²) and are clad with roofing felt or flexible metal over an insulator (strawboard, woodwool) and a wooden, steel or aluminium structure. *See* **built-up roofing**, BSCP 199.

roof guards *Snow boards* (2).

roofing felt *See* **bitumen felt**.

roofing-felt fixer, r.-f. layer A *skilled man* who cuts to shape, lays, and fixes roofing felt. He joints the felt by lapping it, or mopping it with *sealing* or *bonding compound*, or by heating it with a *blow lamp*.

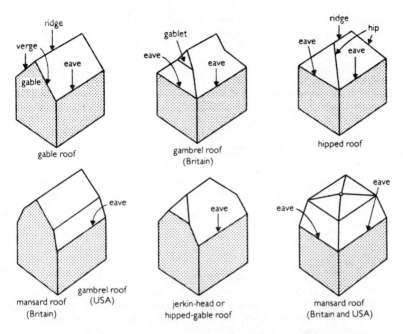

Pitched roofs, usually of span from about 4 to 9 m (13 to 30 ft).

roofing nails There are two types of roofing nail – those that fix the *slates* or *tiles* to the *slating-and-tiling battens* and those that fix the battens to the *rafters*. Nails for fixing slates or tiles should be not less than about 40 mm (1⅝ in.) long. Those for fixing the battens need to be longer, at least 30 mm (1¼ in.) longer than the batten thickness. For fixing slates or *plain tiles*, ordinary steel or galvanized nails are less durable than aluminium, copper or *silicon bronze*; silicon bronze probably being the best. In exceptionally corrosive conditions such as chemical works or animal houses, even these may corrode too fast and special stainless steel nails or oaken pegs may be needed. On roofs at 60° or more to the horizontal, covered with plain tiles, each tile is fixed with two nails, but with slopes of 50° or less, only one course in five needs nailing (twice) (B S 5534).

roofing square [carp.] A *steel square*.

roofing tiles Concrete, burnt clay or even steel tiles for covering roofs. Clay tiles are the oldest and pleasantest to look at, so the other types often copy their shapes and colours. Clay tiles are of three general types: (a) *plain tiles*, (b) *single-lap tiles*, (c) *Italian* or *Spanish tiling* (both expensive and heavy but very decorative) (B S 5534).

roof ladder A *cat ladder*.

roof light, skylight A *dome light, lantern, monitor, north light, patent glazing*, or a *saucer dome* in a roof. It may be an *opening light* or a *dead light*. *See* **thermoplastic**, *also* B S C P 153. (Illus. p. 280)

279

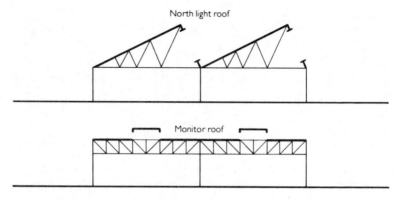

Factory roof lights.

roof-light sheet (1) An *asbestos-cement* roofing sheet with an opening, generally an upstand, in the middle for *glazing*.

(2) A corrugated or flat sheet of *glass substitute*.

roof screen, r. curtain A *fire stop* in the roof space.

roof space Unused space between the roof and the *ceiling* of the highest *storey*.

roof terminal The open end of a *ventilation pipe* at the roof.

roof truss *See* **truss**.

roomheater A solid-fuel-burning appliance, usually now with fire doors of *heat-resisting glass*, formerly known as a slow combustion stove. Many now have *back boilers* that can heat six radiators and domestic hot water (BS 1846).

room-sealed appliance [plu.] A gas heater with its flue outlet and air inlet isolated from the room where it is. *See* **SE-duct**.

root [carp.] The part of a *tenon* which widens out at the shoulders.

ropiness [pai.] A surface in which *brush* marks have not flowed out is called ropy. This is caused by bad *flow* of the *paint* or *varnish* or by brushing after it has begun to harden.

rose (1) A decorative plate through which a door handle passes.

(2) A decorative plate or boss through which an electric light flex hangs from a ceiling (ceiling rose).

rose bit [carp.] A *countersink* bit for wood.

rosin, colophony The solid *resin* remaining after the distillation of *turpentine*, used for making *varnishes, size*, and as a soldering *flux*.

rot [tim.] *Decay* of timber.

rotary cutting, peeling [tim.] A *veneer* cutting method in which the hot soaked log is taken from the *cooking vat*, mounted in a powerful lathe and turned at a speed of 30 to 60 rpm (depending on the log dia.) against a long knife. The knife cuts off a continuous sheet of veneer, which is thus produced at a speed of about 1 m/sec (200 fpm); 90% of veneer is cut in this way, including most of the veneer from which *plywood* is made, but most figured veneers are made by *slicing* or as *half-round veneer*. *See* **birdseye**.

rotary veneer [tim] *Veneer* made by *rotary cutting*.

rotten knot [tim.] An *unsound knot*.

rough arch A *relieving arch*.

rough ashlar A block of stone as brought from the quarry.

rough back An end of a stone hidden in a wall. *See* **clean back**.

rough bracket [carp.] A *bracket* under a stair.

rough carriage [carp.] A *carriage* under a stair.

roughcast (Scots **harling**) [pla.] **slapdash, wet dash** A *rendering* in which the final coat of mortar containing pebbles is thrown on and left rough (BS 4049). Like *pebbledash* it is believed to have good resistance to wet, so is often applied to an inferior brick facing.

rough coat [pla.] The *rendering coat* on a wall.

rough cutting [q.s.] Cutting of common brickwork. It is measured as an area, and if faced is presumed to have a 11·5 cm (4½ in.) thick facing which is measured elsewhere as *fair cutting*. A 34 cm (13½ in.) wall with facing would have 23 cm (9 in.) of rough cutting and a length of 4 m would be measured as $4 \times 0·23 = 0·92$ m². The fair cutting for the same job would be 4 linear m.

rough floor [carp.] (USA) Rough floor boards about 23 cm (9 in.) wide, usually square-edged, on which the finished floor boards are laid. In the best work a layer of building paper separates the two floors. *See* **sub-floor**.

rough grounds *Common grounds*.

rough hardware (USA) Bolts, *nails, fasteners*, and other metal fittings which are not seen and therefore are not *finish hardware*.

roughing in, r. out Doing the first rough work. In plumbing, installing water, gas or other pipes as far as the points where they must join their fixtures. Roughly shaping a piece of wood. Laying the core of plaster of a large *moulding*, for which the *horsed mould* is covered with a *muffle*.

rough string [carp.] A *carriage* under a *stair*.

round (1) A *rung* of a *ladder*.

(2) [joi.] A *plane* which cuts a groove. *Compare* **hollow**.

(3) Viscous, of paint, varnish, etc. A round coat is a thick coat.

round knot [tim.] A *knot* cut roughly at right angles to its length. *Compare* **splay knot**.

round-topped roll In *flexible-metal roofing*, a joint formed over a *wood roll* with vertical sides and rounded top.

rout [joi.] To cut a groove in wood. *See* **router**.

router [joi.] (1) A *plough*.

(2) The side wing in a *centre bit* which ploughs out the wood.

(3) A hand-held *plough* with a *cutter block* driven by an electric motor. Specialized variations of this machine up to 3 hp are used for cutting out for hinge *butts*, for *weather strips*, and even for lock *mortises* 11 cm (4½ in.) deep.

rowlock, rolock A brick-on-edge course. *See* **rat-trap bond**.

rowlock-back wall A wall faced with bricks laid on bed and backed with bricks laid on edge.

rowlock cavity wall, all-rowlock w. A wall built in *rat-trap bond*.

royals *Western red cedar* shingles 60 cm (2 ft) long and 1·3 cm (½ in.) thick at the butt.

r.s.j. A *rolled-steel joist* (C).

rubbed brick, rubber A soft smooth brick without *frog*, suitable for rubbing to shape for *gauged brickwork*.

rubbed finish (1) A finish on concrete obtained by rubbing down with a carborundum stone or similar *abrasive*.

(2) [pai.] *See* **flatting down, polishing varnish**.

rubbed joint [joi.] A glued joint formed between two narrow boards to make of them one wider board. Both boards are planed smooth with a *jointer*, coated with *glue*, and then rubbed together until no more glue and air can be expelled from the joint. No clamp is needed and the joint is very strong.

rubber (1) **polisher, terrazzo polisher, floor r.** A skilled *labourer* who smoothes or polishes *terrazzo* surfaces with carborundum stone or by machine.

(2) A *rubbed brick*.

rubber-bag moulding [tim.] *Flexible-bag moulding*.

rubber latex floor *See* **cement-rubber latex**.

rubber sheet A good but expensive floor covering, 3 to 13 mm ($\frac{1}{8}$ to $\frac{1}{2}$ in.) thick, obtainable in rolls up to 1·8 m (6 ft) wide and 30 m (100 ft) long. Tiles can also be obtained. The sheet or tiles can be glued to a smooth dry floor.

rubbing [pai.] *Flatting down*.

rubbing-bed hand, stone rubber, rubber down, floatsman A *mason's labourer* in the stonemason's yard who helps the masons rubbing the stones to their final surface.

rubbing stone A grit stone on which *bricks* are rubbed to smooth them after they have been *axed* roughly to shape, for a *gauged arch*, etc.

rubbing varnish [pai.] A *flatting varnish*.

rubbish pulley A *gin block*.

rubble (1) Broken bricks, old plaster, and similar material.

(2) Walling stones which are not smoothed to give fine joints like ashlars but are sometimes squared and coursed. *See* **rubble walls**.

rubble ashlar An *ashlar*-faced wall, backed with rubble.

rubble walls Stone walls which differ from *ashlar* walls in the thickness of the

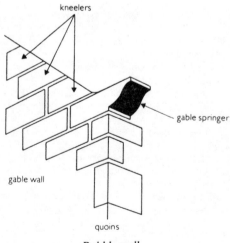

Rubble wall.

mortar *joints*, which may be as much as 2·5 cm (1 in.) thick. *Random rubble* and *snecked rubble* are the main types. They are either uncoursed or occasionally coursed, but *squared rubble* is usually coursed, since uncoursed squared rubble would be the same as snecked rubble (BS 5390), p. 282.

rule (1) A *straight edge* of any length or construction, for measuring, or for drawing straight lines or setting them out on the site (illus. p. 292).

(2) [pla.] A straight edge for working plaster or *dots* to a plane surface or for other purposes. They include: *floating rules, joint rules, levelling rules, running rules, screed rails.*

run (1) A *barrow run.*

(2) The general layout of the pipes or cables in a building.

(3) [plu.] The part of a pipe or *fitting* which is in the main line of flow. *See* **tee.**

(4) [pla.] To pass plaster or *lime putty* through a sieve.

(5) [carp.] The distances between the supports of a *stair* string or of a *rafter*.

(6) [pai.] A narrow ridge of *paint* or *varnish* which has flowed down, advancing from a small bulb or teardrop at the lower end of the painted area, after the paint has begun to set. A tear is a run like a teardrop.

rung, round [carp.] A horizontal bar used as a step in a *ladder.*

run line [pai.] A straight line painted by using a *lining tool* and straight edge, or by stencilling.

runner (1) [joi.] The guide in front of a *plough.*

(2) [carp.] A horizontal timber which carries the *joists* of the formwork under a concrete slab, or the folding wedges of an arch.

(3) A long strip of *withies* laid with others in horizontal bands on *thatch* and held down by *spars*. Straw bands are sometimes used instead.

running [pla.] Forming a *moulding* such as a *cornice*, in place with a *horsed mould*. See **running mould, running rule.**

running bond *Stretcher bond.*

running mould, horse [pla.] A *horsed mould.*

running-off [pla.] Applying the finishing coat of plaster to a *moulding.*

running plank, gang p. A plank in a *barrow run.*

running rule, slipper guide [pla.] A 5 × 2 cm (2 × ¾ in.) *straight edge* nailed to the *floating coat* below a *cornice* moulding which is to be run. The *horsed mould* rests on it and slides along it, its upper end being held by the *nib guide*. *See* **running screed.**

running screed [pla.] A narrow band of plaster used instead of a *running rule* for running a *moulding.*

running shoes [pla.] Metal pieces on a *horsed mould* where it touches the *nib guide* and *running rule* to enable the *mould* to slide easily and prevent it wearing.

rusticated ashlar *Ashlar* on which the face is left rough standing out from the *joints*, the stones being cut back at the edges by bevelling or rebating (*see* **drafted margin**). In other types of rustication (rustic quoins), alternate stones project about 2·5 cm (1 in.) beyond the others.

rustic brick A *brick* with a surface which has been roughened by covering it with sand, by impressing it with a pattern, or by other means. Rustic bricks are often of variegated colours and are then prized as *facing bricks.*

rustic joint The *joints* sunk back from the surface of stone, seen in *rusticated ashlar*.

rustic slates *Random slates*.

rybate, rybat (Scotland) A rebate or *jamb stone* forming a rebate, that is a *reveal* stone.

S

sabin The unit of sound *absorption*, equivalent to the absorption of 1 ft^2 (0·092 m^2) of open window (after Dr Sabine, pioneer of acoustics).

sable pencils [pai.] Pointed *brushes* of sable hair, set in quills varying in size from lark's through crow's to duck's and goose's, or set in a metal ferrule. Sable is very expensive and squirrel hair may be used instead. Used for decorative detail.

sable writer [pai.] A brush like a *sable pencil* but longer, with a flat edge or a point, used for sign writing. *See* **house painter** (illus. p. 180).

saddle (1) **s. piece** A piece of *flexible metal* about 46 × 46 cm (18 × 18 in.) dressed to shape and fixed under *slates* or *tiles* at vulnerable points such as the intersection of a *dormer* ridge and the main roof.

(2) A large *roll* on a flat roof, dividing it into bays.

(3) [carp.] A *bolster*.

(4) A fixing lug passing round a pipe or *conduit* and screwed down each side of it.

(5) To make a connection to an existing pipe run or sewer, a saddle may be bolted over the pipe after breaking into or drilling it. The saddle makes a tight joint to the branch.

saddle-back board [carp.] A narrow board chamfered on both edges, fixed under a door and above the boards on each side of it. If the door is hung to close on this board, it will clear the carpet when open.

saddle-back coping A *coping* with a sharp apex and flat flanks which slope down from it each side. (Illus. below)

saddle bar A horizontal metal bar which stiffens *leaded lights*.

saddle bead A *glazing bead* for fixing the glass to each side of a curved *glazing bar*.

saddle joint, water j. A *joint* between stones in a *cornice* in which the stones meet in a saddle shape to throw the water away from the joint.

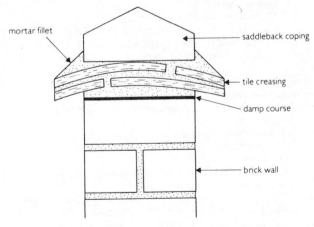

mortar fillet

saddleback coping

tile creasing

damp course

brick wall

Saddle-back coping over tile creasing with mortar fillets.

saddle piece A *saddle* of flexible metal.

saddle scaffold A *scaffold* built over a *ridge*, sometimes supported by *standards* at the side of the building, used for repairing chimneys. *See* **straddle pole**.

saddle stone The *apex stone* of a gable.

safe (1) A *tray*.

(2) A strong box.

safety arch A *relieving arch*.

safety glass Any glass that breaks into small pieces which harm people less than the large splinters of ordinary glass. All glass fixed indoors should be *laminated* or *toughened* or *wired*. *See* **security glazing**.

safety lintel A *lintel*, which carries load, to protect another more decorative lintel.

Saint Andrew's cross bond *English cross bond*.

sally [carp.] A re-entrant angle cut into a timber (birdsmouth).

salt glaze A glaze on clayware used before *vitrified clayware* became available.

sample [tim.] Sheets of *sliced* or *half-round veneer* taken from the top, middle, and bottom of the *flitch* as an indication of the *figure*. These veneers are kept in the manufacturer's sampling trunk with a record of the log number and the area of veneer in the flitch. *See* **swatch,** and *C*.

sand Building sands should be durable, clean and inert, i.e. they should not swell after the mortar or plaster has hardened. Any dirt or grease in a sand reduces the strength of concrete, mortar or plaster. Silica sands, the commonest, are completely inert from the builder's viewpoint. Sand size also is important, and is measured by *screen analysis* (*C*) (sieving). Coarse sands are best for concreting, medium ones for walling mortars (B S 1200) and fine (*soft sand*) for inside plastering (B S 1198). B S 1199 specifies sands for outside *renderings*, floor *screeds* and inside plastering with lime and cement. Since sand can make up two-thirds of the weight of a plaster and unsuitable sand can ruin a finish, it often pays to spend money on improving a local sand which does not reach the specification. This may be done by screening out the oversize particles.

sand box A device which enables *centering* to be quickly and easily struck. The posts supporting the centering are set on small timbers bearing on dry sand in boxes. When the post is to be removed, one side of the box is slipped out, the sand flows away, and the post can then drop out. *Compare* **folding wedges**.

sand-dry surface [pai.] A surface on which sand will not stick. *See* **drying**.

sanded bitumen felt A *bitumen felt* for roofing.

sand-faced brick A *facing brick* coated with sand to give it an attractive rough surface. *See* **rustic brick**.

sanding [joi.] Smoothing wooden surfaces with *glasspaper* by machine or by hand. In painting, the same process of smoothing paint surfaces is called rubbing or *flatting down*.

sanding machine, sander [joi.] An electrically or mechanically powered machine used for cleaning up *joinery* or for smoothing walls or floors with *glasspaper* or other *abrasives*. They may either be portable or *bench sanders*.

sanding machinist [tim.] A *tradesman* who fits an abrasive belt or disc on to a sanding machine and works the machine either in the shop or on the site, smoothing a timber floor.

sanding sealer [pai.] A specially hard first *coat* which seals or fills but does not hide the *grain* of wood. The surface can be sanded after the sanding sealer is put on. *Compare* **filler, sealer, surfacer**.

sand-lime bricks *See* **calcium silicate bricks**.

sandpaper [joi.] *See* **glasspaper**.

sand rubbing Applying a surface layer of sand or chips to a roof covered with *roofing felt*.

sandwich beam A *flitched beam*.

sandwich construction Composite construction of *light alloys*, *plastics*, plaster-board, etc., generally a hard outer sheet glued to an inner core of foam plastics or paper honeycomb. For its weight it is extremely strong, particularly if purposely arched. *Expanded polystyrene* and *polyurethane* are often used in cores.

sandwich damp course A *damp course* laid on a concrete slab and covered by a *screed*.

sanitary shoe [joi.] U S term for a *congé*.

sap, quarry s. The moisture in a freshly quarried stone. If, as is generally believed, stone is harder when the sap has dried out, this is probably because the sap contains the cement of the stone.

saponification [pai.] The action of alkalis (such as the lime in cement) on oils. The oil is converted to soap, which is dissolved by water. Any paint containing oil can be destroyed if it saponifies. *See* **alkali-resistant paint**.

sap stain [tim.] *See* **blue stain**.

sapwood, alburnum [tim.] The outer wood in a tree, lighter in colour than the *heartwood*. It usually decays more easily than heartwood but it also absorbs preservative more thirstily and is not always weaker than the heartwood.

sarking [carp.] In Scotland roof *boarding*, elsewhere *sarking felt*.

sarking felt, underslating f. *Bitumen felt* below slates or tiles, either on roof *boarding* or without it. *See* **reinforced bitumen felt**.

sash [joi.] A window.

sash balance [joi.] A spring which operates a *sash window* and thus eliminates sash weights, pulleys, and cords.

sash bar [joi.] A *glazing bar* (USA *muntin*).

sash chain [joi.] A chain used instead of *sash cord* in the best (or the heaviest) windows. It must be used with a cogged *axle pulley*.

sash chisel [joi.] A *pocket chisel*.

sash cord, s. line [joi.] A cord nailed to the side of a *sash window*, passing over the pulley and held tight by the sash weight. The window is easy to slide up and down, but chains last longer. *See* **sash ribbon**.

sash cramps [joi.] *Cramps* between 0·6 and 1·5 m (2 and 5 ft) long used for clamping *sashes* during gluing.

sash door, half-glass d. [joi.] A door of which the upper half is glazed.

sash fastener, s. lock (U S A **s. fast**) [joi.] A fastening on the *meeting rail* of one sash which swings across to the meeting rail of the other sash and engages with a spur on it.

sash fillister [joi.] A *fillister*.

sash lift [joi.] A *pull* or hook on a *sash window* for opening it.

sash pocket [joi.] *See* **pocket**.

sash pulley [joi.] Pulleys at each side of a *sash window*, set in *pulley stiles* and carrying the *sash cords*.

sash ribbon [joi.] A steel tape which, attached to a spring instead of to a sash weight, holds the window up.

sash run [joi.] (USA) A *pulley stile*.

sash stop [joi.] **window bead, guard bead** (Scots **baton rod**) A moulding mitred round the inner edge of a sash window to prevent the inner window from swinging into the room (BS 565). *See* **draught stop**.

sash tool [pai.] A round *brush*, smaller than a *ground brush*, made in various sizes, bound with metal or string, and used for painting sashes, frames, and other small areas.

sash window, balanced s. (USA **vertical s.**) [joi.] A window in which two *opening lights* slide up and down in a *cased frame*, balanced by *sash cords* tensioned by sash weights and passing over *sash pulleys*. *Compare* **sliding sash**.

saturation coefficient (1) (Britain) The ratio between the volume of water absorbed by a brick in 5 hours boiling and the volume of its pore space.

(2) (USA) The ratio of the water absorbed by a brick soaked in cold water for 24 hours to that absorbed when the brick is boiled for 5 hours.

saucer dome A glass or plastics one-piece *dome light*.

saw A steel blade for cutting wood (or stone or metal). The main power-driven saws for wood are *circular*, *band*, or *jig saws*. For hard stone, frame-saws like large hacksaws or circular saws with diamonds set in the cutting edges are used. *See* **hacksaw, handsaw, sawyer**.

saw bench [tim.] A steel table through which a *circular saw* passes. The *rise-and-fall* table is being superseded by the stationary saw bench, in which the saw is raised or lowered.

saw doctor [mech.] A skilled mechanic who looks after the mechanical saws in a sawmill and sometimes also the *handsaws*.

sawdust cement A concrete made with cement and sawdust. It is sometimes used for making fixing blocks but has very high *moisture movement*, that of timber added to that of cement. In addition, the wood may react with the cement and weaken it, but see **Lignacite**.

saw horse [carp.] A four-legged stool made on the job by a carpenter for hand sawing.

sawing in a damp course To eliminate *rising damp* in old brick buildings with no *damp course*, the first possibility to investigate is whether a bed joint can be sawn through at a suitable level to enable a copper or bitumen-felt damp course to be inserted and pinned up with slates in mortar. *Handsaws* can be used as well as power saws. The method is cheaper and quicker than the old way of cutting out a course of bricks in short lengths, replacing it either with a course of *engineering bricks* or with the same bricks and a damp course bedded in with them. A *chain saw* that will cut a slot only 7 mm ($\frac{1}{4}$ in.) wide will enable a metal sheet to be inserted. The subsidence to be expected when a damp course is sawn in is about 1·5 mm ($\frac{1}{16}$ in.). Walls thicker than about 530 mm (21 in.) cannot be treated in this way (BRE Digest 245).

sawn veneer [tim.] In USA *quarter-sawn* oak is still cut on large diameter *segment saws*, which make a cut 1 mm thick, with a *veneer* of about the same thickness or slightly thicker. Even with this narrow kerf the loss of wood in sawing can amount to half the log volume, but the method is still used because it makes sheets of strong veneer which polish well. *See* **plywood**.

saw set [joi.] An adjustable tool which gives the correct *set* to the teeth of the saw.

saw-tooth [joi.] Each small cutting blade in a *saw* from *point* to root. *See* **angle of saw-tooth, back, face, gullet, pitch, set, space**.

sawyer [tim.] A craftsman who sets and operates mechanical saws. They may be of many types and he can be described according to his saw, as a band-mill sawyer, frame sawyer, circular sawyer, chain-cross-cut sawyer, etc.

sax A slater's *zax*.

Saxon shakes Hand-split western red cedar *shingles* 60 cm (2 ft) long, of random widths varying in butt thickness from 19 to 32 mm ($\frac{3}{4}$ to $1\frac{1}{4}$ in.). They may be halved in thickness by sawing, to provide a flat under surface.

scabbing hammer, scabbling h. A *hammer* with one pick point used for rough dressing, for example, of *nidged ashlar*.

scaffold, scaffolding A temporary steel, *light alloy*, or timber erection to carry men and materials. *See* **bricklayer's scaffold, cradle, mason's scaffold, saddle scaffold, tubular scaffolding**.

scaffold boards *Softwood* boards which form the working platform of a *scaffold*. They measure 23 × 4 cm (9 × $1\frac{1}{2}$ in.) and may be up to 3·7 m (12 ft) long. They also can form *barrow runs* and are bound with hoop iron round the ends to prevent them splitting.

scaffolder A *tubular scaffolder* or *timber scaffolder*.

scagliola [pla.] Precast plaster polished and coloured like marble, used since the 17th C, made of plaster like *Keene's* with added *pigments* and chips of coloured material. It is then polished with a stone and coated with linseed oil. *Compare* **marezzo marble**.

scale (1) The deposit of magnesium and calcium salts formed in a *furred* pipe by *hard water*.

(2) The reduction ratio of a drawing or model compared with the object it depicts. *See also* **blast cleaning** *and* **C**.

scallops Short *withies* placed to hold *thatch* at the *verges* of a roof and held down by *spars*.

Scandinavian plasters [pla.] *Thin-wall plasters*.

scantle, gauge stick, size stick. A strip of wood 4 × 2 cm ($1\frac{1}{2}$ × $\frac{3}{4}$ in.) with two nails projecting from it to mark the position of the hole measured from the *tail* of the slate.

scantling [tim.] (1) In softwood, a piece of square-sawn timber between 50 and 100 mm thick and between 50 and 125 mm wide (B S 565), i.e., between 2 by 2 in. and 4 by 5 in.

(2) In *hardwood*, square-edged timber.

(3) A loose term for the dimensions of the cross section of a timber.

scarcement (Scotland) The narrowing of a brick wall as it rises from the footings.

scarf, scarfed joint [joi.] Ends of boards or veneers glued together after bevelling at 1 in 12 to 1 in 20. (Illus. p. 290)

scent test, smell t. A *drain test*, made by pouring strong scent such as peppermint oil into a drain and plugging it.

schedule of dilapidations [q.s.] A list of repairs to be done by a tenant when a lease expires. It is drawn up by an *architect* or *surveyor* acting for the landlord.

schedule of prices [q.s.] A document that takes the place of a *bill of quantities* in certain *fixed-price contracts* in which no *quantities* appear in the tender documents. Each firm invited to *tender* writes down its rates to a list of *items*

289

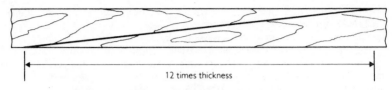

12 times thickness

Glued scarfed joint at 1 in 12.

(the schedule of prices) which are described only. For small-scale work such as general repairs this may be satisfactory, but some idea of the quantity involved must be given to the *contractor* or his prices will be too high.

scissors truss [carp.] A simple *truss* formed of four main members, two of which are *rafters* from wall plate to ridge. The other two extend from the *wall-plate* to the middle of the opposite rafter. These two members intersect at the middle of the span, giving a scissors-like appearance to the truss. A scissors truss may also be of steel. It gives good ceiling height in the centre of the span.

scotch A bricklayer's *scutch*.

Scotch bond *American bond*.

Scotch glue [joi.] *See* **animal glue**.

scouring [pla.] To give plaster a smooth hard surface by working it with a *cross-grained float* in a circular motion. Sometimes water is sprinkled on with a brush at the same time. The finishing process, with a trowel, is called 'ironing in'. Not all plasters are suitable, but *Keene's* and Sirapite can be scoured.

scraped finish [pla.] A finish to lime-cement stuccos, used in Central Europe. The finishing coat *stucco* is scraped with a steel straight edge just as it begins to harden, 1·5 to 3 mm ($\frac{1}{16}$ to $\frac{1}{8}$ in.) of plaster being removed. The aggregate is well exposed and the finish can be patterned if the scraping tool is serrated.

scraper (U S A **s. plane**) A *cabinet scraper*.

scratch awl [joi.] An *awl*.

scratch coat, pricking-up c. [pla.] The first coat of plaster on lathing. *Compare* **rendering**.

scratcher [pla.] A *drag* or *nail float*.

scratching [pla.] Laying the first coat of plaster and roughening its surface for the next coat.

scratch tool [pla.] A *small tool* for completing plaster enrichments.

scratch work [pla.] *Graffito*.

screed (1) A band of plaster or concrete or an *angle bead* carefully laid to the final surface as a guide for the *rule* when plastering or for the *screed rail* when concreting.

(2) A wooden or steel *straight edge* fixed temporarily to a wall, floor, or ceiling as a guide to the rule or screed rail instead of (1) above, p. 292.

(3) A layer of mortar, 12 to 75 mm ($\frac{1}{2}$ to 3 in.) thick, laid on a concrete slab to smooth the surface. *See* **jointless floor, monolithic screed**, B R S Digest 104. (Illus. p. 291)

screed rail A heavy straight edge set at the required surface level for mortar or concrete, usually with another, so that the surface can be easily and accurately formed between them. It is removed when the concrete is hard.

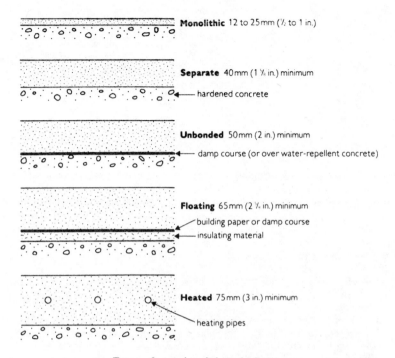

Types of screed and their thicknesses.

screen A rectangular frame about 2 × 1 m (6 × 3 ft) with a mesh built into it for separating pebbles from sand. *See also C. Compare* **sieve**.

screw [carp.] A metal fastening with a *thread* formed on the shank. Wood screws are described by their length and diameter. The diameter is described in numbers called the screw gauge, which vary from 0 (1·5 mm or 0·06 in.) up to 32 (12·7 mm or ½ in.). Generally it is impossible in hardware stores to find screws thicker than No. 14 (6·3 mm or ¼ in.). The British screw gauge is little different from the US screw gauge. See also **bolt** (*C*), **coach screw, dowel screw, grub screw, nylon, recessed head screw**.

screw anchor A metal *Rawlplug* sleeve for a *bottomless* hole.

screw auger An *auger*. *See C.*

screw clamp [joi.] A *handscrew*.

screw cup [joi.] A conical metal ring that protects the mouth of a countersunk hole for a wood screw in fine joinery, a removable plywood panel, etc.

screwdown valve [plu.] A valve with a plate or disc across its waterway that is moved parallel to its own plane to open or close it. It has a higher resistance to flow than a *full-way valve*, so is used only where the pressure is more than adequate.

screwed pipe [plu.] The cheapest and heaviest gas or water pipe, made of *dead-mild steel* (*C*), usually in lengths of 6 m (20 ft) screwed outside with a *taper thread*, and joined by malleable-iron *fittings* threaded inside. Because of the

291

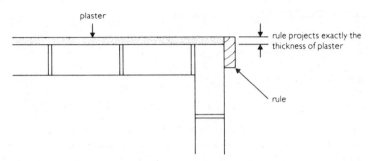

plaster

rule projects exactly the
thickness of plaster

rule

Use of a vertical wooden rule as a screed in plastering a wall.

labour of installation, these pipes have been superseded by *copper pipe* in housing but are still used for building railings, etc.

screw eye [joi.] A metal loop at the head of a screw, used with a *cabin hook* to form a door or window fastening.

screw gauge [carp.] *See* **screw**.

screw nail [carp.] A *drive screw*.

screw plug, disk p. A rubber ring which expands to block the end of a length of drain when the two steel plates each side of it are screwed together in a *drain test*.

screw thread The shape of the *thread* on a *screw* may be *Whitworth* for building fixings, *buttress* (*C*) for force transmission, fine threads for mechanical work, etc., but it is related to the bar diameter; *see* **screw, tap, thread rolling**.

scribe (1) To cut a line on a surface with a pointed tool to the outline of a *templet*.

(2) [joi.] To shape one member to the surface which it touches, thus to fit a board snugly to a surface which is not straight.

scribe awl [joi.] An *awl*.

scribed joint [joi.] A *coped joint* between *mouldings*.

scriber [joi.] A pointed tool or a tool like a pair of dividers for marking out scribing lines.

scrim [pla.] Coarse canvas, or cotton or metal mesh, used for bridging the joints between board, sheet, or slab coverings in *dry construction* with *joint cement*, etc., and as reinforcement for *fibrous plaster*. *Compare* **joint tape**.

scrimming [pla.] Setting *scrim* over joints in *gypsum plasterboard*, masonry, or carpentry, as a base for plastering, painting, or papering.

scrub board [joi.] (USA) A *skirting board*.

scrub plane [carp.] A *plane* with a rounded *cutting iron* for removing a considerable depth of shaving at each stroke.

scumble glaze, s. stain [pai.] Transparent paints used in *scumbling* for enriching or softening or otherwise modifying the *colour* of the coat below the finish coat. *See* **ground coat**.

scumbling [pai.] The achievement of broken *colour* effects by removing or texturing a wet coat to expose part of the coat beneath it.

scutch, scutcher, scotch A *bricklayer's* tool for cutting bricks, also used by the *walling mason*. It resembles a small *hammer* except that there is no striking face but a *cross peen* on both ends of the head.

scutcheon [joi.] An *escutcheon*.

seal [plu.] The water in the *trap* of a drain or *gulley* (C) that prevents foul air passing up out of the drain. Usually 50 mm (2 in.) deep, it is deeper in the *deep-seal trap*. Seals may be lost through siphonage or evaporation. *See* **P-trap, wiping seal**.

sealant *See* **sealing compound**, *also C*.

sealed flue, s. boiler A *balanced flue* of a gas-fired boiler.

sealed system [plu.] Sealed heating circuits, sometimes using a closed *diaphragm tank* instead of an open expansion pipe and tank, have been introduced to Britain from USA and Europe. Since air cannot enter the system, corrosion is less likely than with the *expansion tank*. Sealing also allows the water temperature to be higher and this makes for economy.

sealed unit, double-glazing u. A pair of glass (or *glass substitute*) panes sealed together in the factory, with a cavity between that may be from 5 to 20 mm (0·2 to 0·8 in.) across, and clean, dry air inside to prevent dirtying of the inner surfaces. *See* **tight size**.

sealer, sealing coat [pai.] (1) Liquids, some of which are transparent, used like *size* as priming coats to close the pores of wood, plaster, and other building materials, for instance to prevent the wood of a *glazing bar* absorbing oil from *glazing compound*. Clean pine floorboards may be coated with a sealer (varnish).

(2) **buffer coat** A liquid laid over bitumen, or creosote, etc., to prevent it bleeding through other paints. It must be insoluble both in the paint laid over it and in the substance below it. See **aluminium primer**.

sealing compound (1) **sealant** Modern *mastics* that stick to the sides of a joint to exclude water, wind and grit. When the sides of the joint move, the sealant moves with them. Two-part sealants harden faster than one-part sealants. The stiffest, described as 'strip grade', are semi-solid; the next, 'gun grade', are applied by pressure injection gun; the softest are 'knife grade'. They include polysulphides, silicones, polyurethanes, butyls and acrylics. Most, except the bituminous mastics, are *non-setting glazing compounds*, used in modern glazing systems, *open-drained joints*, etc.

(2) **lap cement** A fluid bitumen applied cold to *bitumen felt* for sealing the laps to each other. *Compare* **bonding compound**.

sealing ring A rubber ring that seals a *sleeved joint* or a *spigot-and-socket joint*. It usually fits into a groove formed by a local enlargement of the socket diameter.

seam, welt [plu.] A joint between two sheets of *flexible-metal roofing* made by turning the edge of each vertically upwards, bringing the two upturned parts together, doubling them over, and dressing them flat. *See* **cross welt, standing seam**.

seamer, seaming pliers [plu.] A pair of *pliers* with jaws specially shaped for forming *seams* between *flexible-metal sheets*.

seam roll A *hollow roll*.

seasoning (1) [tim.] The drying of timber to a specified *moisture content*. It may be *natural* or *kiln* seasoning.

(2) The drying and hardening of stone. *See* **quarry sap**.

seat cut [carp.] A *foot cut* in a *rafter*.

secondary circulation [plu.] *See* **indirect cylinder**.

second fixer [carp.] A *carpenter* or *joiner*, fixing *joinery*.

second fixings [joi.] *Joinery* which is fixed after the plastering, e.g. *skirting boards*, linings, picture rails, cupboards, and in fact most joinery except doors. Plumbing and electrical wiring may also be included in the second fixings.

second-growth timber [tim.] A term used to distinguish wood which has grown later than the first growth of a virgin forest, with less *clear timber*.

seconds Second-quality material, particularly clayware such as *bricks* and drain pipes.

secret dovetail [joi.] A *mitre dovetail*.

secret fixing [joi.] Fixing of *joinery* which cannot be seen at the surface of the joinery. One method is *secret screwing*, another *secret nailing*.

secret gutter (USA **closed valley**) A nearly hidden *valley gutter*, in which the *flexible metal* is covered by the slates or tiles. It is easily blocked by leaves, so is not recommended by BS 5534. *Compare* **open valley**.

secret nailing, blind n. [joi.] Nailing which is not seen on the surface. Tongued and grooved, or *rebated* boards can be slant-nailed through the tongue or rebate. Another method is to shave off a thin chip of wood with a sharp knife, drive the *nail* in where the chip was taken out, and *glue* the chip back over it.

secret screwing [joi.] A joining method used for making a wide board when only two narrow ones are available. *See* **secret screw joint**.

secret screw joint [joi.] A strong glued joint between the planed edges of boards. Stout *screws* (at least No. 14s) are inserted in one edge and left with their heads projecting about 10 mm ($\frac{3}{8}$ in.). Slots are drilled opposite them in the board to which they are to be fitted. The two boards are fitted together first, being pressed towards each other, then one is struck endways to drive the screws to the end of the slots. The same board is then given a blow on the other end, to release the screws from the slots. The joint is unmade, each screw screwed in a quarter turn, and the surfaces are glued and re-assembled.

secret tack A strip of lead soldered on the back of a lead sheet passed through a slot in the roof boarding and screwed to the inside of it, so as to hold a heavy vertical sheet.

secret valley A *secret gutter*.

secret wedging [joi.] Fixing a *stub tenon* by inserting wedges into sawcuts in its end before it is inserted into a *blind mortise*. As the *tenon* is driven in, the wedges are forced in by the pressure of the blind end of the *mortise* on them. If the mortise is *dovetail*-shaped the assembly is called foxtail wedging.

section *See C*.

sectional insulation [plu.] *See* **moulded insulation**.

section mould A *template* of *plywood* or similar material cut to the cross-section required for a member.

security At least three senses of 'security' exist: locks and other physical barriers to entry; intruder alarms; fire protection. Many of these are electronically controlled and some lock makers are concerned with all three. See BS 3621, 4166, 4737, also **sensing equipment**.

security glazing Glazing with *safety glass*, anti-bandit glass, etc. for bank counters or jewellers' windows. Glass should have at least 10 mm ($\frac{3}{8}$ in.) edge cover all round, backed by 3 mm ($\frac{1}{8}$ in.) mild steel. Plastics need even more, 25 mm (1 in.) edge cover between the edge of the transparent sheet and the sight line (BS 5051, 5357, 5544).

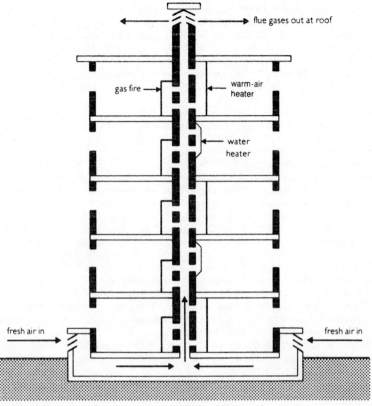

Diagrammatic vertical cross-section of block of flats to show SE-duct connected to gas fires, water heaters and hot cupboards.

sedge (Cladium mariscus) A tall grass from marshy places which forms the ridge of thatch. It is placed wet across the roof and fixed by *liggers*. *See* **straw**.

S E-duct, appliance ventilation duct [plu.] In multi-storey buildings, a vertical duct open at both ends used both as flue and as air intake for all the *room-sealed appliances* in its sector of the building. Only some appliances are suitable for connection to a SE-duct and a check should be made with the gas authority before the appliance is chosen. (Illus. above) *See* **U-duct**.

seediness [pai.] A rough, sandy-looking paint film, sometimes caused by incompatibility.

segment saw [tim.] A special *circular saw* of up to 3·6 m (12 ft) dia. which makes a very thin kerf and is still used in USA for cutting *sawn veneer*.

self-build housing society A *cooperative housing society* whose members subscribe the usual proportion of cost but do not send out for *tender* from builders because they build their houses themselves in their spare time. Lots are drawn for the family to occupy the first house and all the members help to build until the last house is built and the last family housed.

self-centering formwork *See* **telescopic centering**.

self-faced stone Stones like *flagstones* which split cleanly.

self-finished roofing felt *Bitumen felt* which is saturated with bitumen, coated on both sides with it, and sometimes also dressed with fine talc on both sides.

self-levelling floor finish A *levelling compound*.

self-supporting scaffold Any scaffold like the *mason*'s and unlike the *brick-layer's scaffold*.

self-supporting wall (USA) A *free-standing* wall.

self-tapping screw A hardened steel, *gimlet-pointed* screw, which forms for itself a matching *thread* in a pre-drilled hole in steel sheet.

semi-detached house (USA **double house**) One of a pair of houses built simultaneously, with a *party wall* between them. *Compare* **terrace house**.

semi-engineering brick A *brick* with a crushing strength higher than *common bricks* but rather below the second grade of *engineering bricks*, 48 N/mm^2 (7000 psi).

semi-hydraulic lime A *lime* intermediate between *high-calcium lime* and *eminently hydraulic* limes, for example, greystone lime. When run to putty it is nearly as workable as non-hydraulic lime but its *hydraulic* properties are much reduced by *fattening up* . If hydrated to *dry hydrate* at the factory it does not lose its hydraulic properties.

semi-rigid asbestos-bitumen sheet *See* **asbestos-bitumen**.

semi-skilled man A workman such as a *rigger* (C), or *builder's labourer*, who has learnt his work by helping others, and is rather less skilled than a *skilled man* or a *tradesman*. He has risen from *labourer* in his *trade* merely by working at it and may become a skilled man.

sensing equipment Commonly used for door opening and closing, this includes sensitized mats, traffic strips, photo-electric or ultrasonic beams, *smoke detectors*, and other *security* devices.

separate application [tim.] A method of using *urea-formaldehyde glue* in which the *accelerator* is spread on one side of the joint and the *resin* spread over the other side. The two parts are then clamped together. The method is simple and economical since *mixed glue* is not wasted.

separating layer An *underlay*.

septic tank A purifier for sewage where no *sewer* (C) is available. It is a tank through which sewage flows slowly enough for it to decompose and be purified. It is divided into two or more chambers separately by scum boards with an opening below. The receiving compartment capacity is made equal to the house-water supply of at least seven, and at most twenty-four hours. The best method of removal of effluent from a septic tank is by automatic siphons which periodically discharge a quantity of the water into pipes buried in a field, where the water passes to plant roots. *See* BSCP 302.

sequence of trades The order in which (originally) the various trades carried out their work in a new building. The lefthand column shows an early, full sequence. Since the sequence determines the layout of the *contract documents*, it is important to know which one has been chosen. Another possible, and quite different, order is the *CI/SfB classification*. The righthand sequence below, from the Standard Method of Measurement, 1979, is shorter because the trades are grouped.

1. preliminaries
2. demolition and shoring
3. earthwork
4. piling
5. concrete in situ
6. precast concrete and hollow floors
7. brickwork and partitions
8. drainage and sewage
9. asphalt
10. pavings
11. masonry
12. roofing
13. timber and hardware
14. structural steelwork
15. metalwork
16. plastering, wall tiling, terrazzo
17. sheet metal
18. rainwater goods
19. cold-water supply and sanitary
    plumbing
20. hot-water supply
21. gas and water mains
22. heating
23. ventilating
24. electrical
25. glazing
26. painting and decorating
27. provisional sums; items by
    specialists

1. preliminaries
2. demolition
3. excavation and earthwork
4. piling and diaphragm walling
5. concreting
6. brickwork and blockwork
7. underpinning
8. rubble walling
9. masonry
10. asphalt
11. roofing
12. woodwork
13. structural steelwork
14. metalwork
15. plumbing and mechanical
16. electrical
17. floor, wall, and ceiling finishes
18. glazing
19. painting and decorating
20. drainage
21. fencing

service cable The power cable joining the supply authority's main to the *house service cutout*.

service core The *mechanical core* of a building.

service ell, s. tee [plu.] An ell-shaped or tee-shaped screwed *fitting* with an external thread outside it at one end (as usual) and its other end enlarged to form a screwed socket.

service layer *See* **pipe layer**.

service pipe The full length of a gas or water pipe between the main and the premises receiving the supply. *See* **communication pipe, supply pipe** (illus. p. 78), *also* BSCP 331.

service riser A gas pipe which rises to supply an upper floor.

services (USA **utilities**) Supply or distribution pipes for cold or hot water, *sprinklers*, steam, or gas; also power cables, bell and telephone cables, lift machinery, transformers, drains, ventilation *ducts*, etc.

set [joi.] (1) A *nail punch*.

(2) The slight overhang given to the point of each *sawtooth* to make the *kerf* just wider than the saw and enable it to run easily. *See* **setting** (4).

(3) *See* **door set**.

(4) The first hardening (initial set) of concrete, mortar or plaster.

(5) [pla.] To apply a *finishing coat*.

(6) [pai.] A paint or varnish film which has ceased to flow is said to have set.

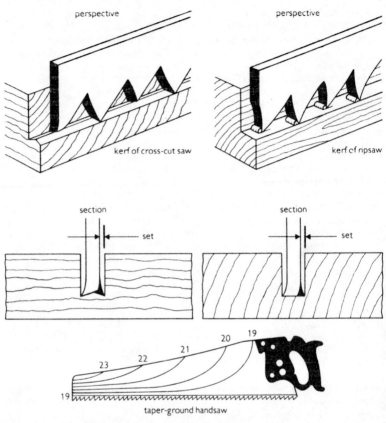

Setting handsaws. The saw is taper-ground, and the contours on it show the tapering thickness of the blade in Standard wire gauge.

setback A withdrawal of the *building line* in the upper floors of a tall building to a distance about one storey height back for each floor above a certain level. This is required by planning laws to ensure that enough light reaches the street.

set screw (1) [joi.] A *grub screw*.

(2) [mech.] A *screw* designed to fit, not into a nut, but into a hole tapped into a block, plate, or machine part, like a *grub screw*.

setter out, marker out [joi.] A skilled *joiner* or *carpenter* of many years' experience who marks out work for other men to shape. *See* **setting out**.

setting (1) The first hardening of *concrete*, *mortar*, *plaster*, *glue*, or *paint* after which they should not be disturbed.

(2) The laying of stones, *bricks*, *lintels*, etc., in a wall.

(3) The brickwork which supports and encloses a furnace or a boiler.

(4) [joi.] The third operation after *topping* and *shaping*, preceding the

298

sharpening of a saw. It is the bending over of the teeth alternately to one side and then to the other of the saw so that the saw-cut is (for *handsaws*) about 1·5 times the thickness of the saw. The commonest mistake in sharpening saws is to give them too much set. *See* illus. p. 298.

setting block A *glazing block*.

setting coat [pla.] The *finishing coat* of plaster.

setting-in stick [plu.] A hardwood tool for bending sheet lead.

setting out Putting pegs in the ground to mark out an excavation, marking floors to locate walls or preparing dimensioned rods for *carpentry* or *joinery*. Large scale setting out is done by a civil engineer, small scale work by a *setter out* or *foreman* of a *trade*.

setting up (1) [pai.] Gelling of a paint during storage, called *feeding* if it cannot be thinned by stirring.

(2) [plu.] *See below*.

set up [plu.] (1) To bend up the edge of lead sheet.

(2) To caulk a joint with lead, driving the lead in with a blunt chisel. *See also* **upsetting** (*C*).

sewer brick (USA) Low *absorption*, abrasion-resistant bricks, used for the same purposes as British *engineering bricks*.

SfB (Samarbetskommitten för Byggnadsfrågor) An international classification of building information subjects, that originated in Sweden but is now sponsored by CIB (International Council for Building Research and Documentation). The English language version, known as *CI/SfB*, is the responsibility of the *RIBA*.

sgraffito [pla.] *Graffito*.

shake [tim.] Separation of wood fibres along the *grain* of the wood in the log due to stresses while standing, felling or seasoning. *See* **check, heartshake, ring shake**.

shakes [tim.] Hand split *shingles*. *See* **processed shakes**.

shaping [tim.] The second operation in putting a cutting edge on a saw. It is the filing of the teeth to a uniform shape and size after they have been topped. The subsequent operations are *setting* and *sharpening*, *topping* being the first.

sharpening saws [tim.] The last operation, preceded by the *topping*, *shaping*, and *setting*, in putting a cutting edge on a *handsaw*. Like shaping and topping, it is done with a taper saw file. The saw is fixed in the vice with not more than 6 mm (¼ in.) of *saw-tooth* projecting from it. The file is held horizontally, and starting at one end each alternate tooth face is given one or two strokes. The other faces are then sharpened after reversing the saw in the vice. The saw should then be sharp and can be dressed on the side with a smooth stone to remove burred metal. A rip saw should be sharpened with the file perpendicular to the saw, a cross-cut saw with the file at about 70° to the saw.

sharp paint A quick-drying paint with a flat finish, usually strongly pigmented, drying by *evaporation* and used for *priming* or *sealing*.

sharp sand Sand grains which are angular, not rounded. Coarse and gritty, it contains no clay, and is therefore clean and suitable for making *concrete*.

shave hook [plu.] A *plumber*'s tool used for shaving lead pipes before *soldering* or by painters for scraping off burnt paint. *See* **plumber's tools** (illus. p. 250).

sheariness [pai.] The oily opalescent surface of a painted *film* which should have a high *gloss* and has failed because of greasy surface, foul air, or lack of *compatibility* in the *paint*.

shear plate [carp.] A timber *connector* of diameter 6·7 cm (2⅝ in.) held by a 19 mm (¾ in.) dia. bolt. *See* **hole saw**.

sheathing (USA **boxing**) [carp.] *Boarding, see also C.*

sheathing paper *Building paper* on roof *boarding.*

sheen [pai.] A *gloss* seen at glancing angles on an otherwise flat *finish.*

sheet A description of copper, aluminium or zinc which is thicker than 0·15 mm (0·006 in.), thinner than 9·5 mm (⅜ in.), and more than 46 cm (18 in.) wide. *Foil* is thinner, *strip* is narrower. Flat lead sheet is rolled, not cast, and is usually described as milled sheet or strip. For steel, sheet is material thinner than *plate* (*C*) (3 mm or 0·12 in.).

sheeter, iron roofer A *skilled man* who fixes *profiled steel,* zinc, or *asbestos-cement* sheeting on roof and walls with *hook bolts, screws,* or clips. He may cut sheeting to shape and is described according to his material as a zinc roofer or asbestos-cement sheeter.

sheet glass Ordinary window glass, less smooth than float or plate. It is made in thicknesses from 2 to 6 mm (0·08 to ¼ in.).

sheeting *Boarding.*

sheet-metal work The working of steel or *flexible metal,* by *plumber* or *sheet-metal worker.*

sheet-metal worker [mech.] A *skilled man* who shapes sheet steel with the hammer or with machines. He joints sheets by riveting, seaming, welding, *soldering,* or *brazing* and may mark them out or cut them by guillotine. He may be specialized as an air-duct maker, chimney-cowl maker, or ventilator maker. Generally, in Britain, workers in metal thicker than 5 mm (3/16 in.) are called sheet-iron workers, those who work very thin metal less than 1·5 mm (1/16 in.) being tinsmiths, regardless of the metal they work.

shelf life The time for which a *glue* or paint can be stored before it becomes unusable. *Compare* **pot life**.

shelf nog A piece of wood built into a wall and projecting out from it to support a shelf.

shellac, lac [pai.] An incrustation formed by an insect on the trees of India and neighbouring regions. It is a natural *resin,* the orange variety being commoner, white shellac being bleached. Soluble in alcohols, it forms part of spirit *varnishes, French polish, knotting, abrasives,* etc.

shellac and white-lead mortar A *mortar* used in brickwork to be carved.

shell gimlet [carp.] An old type of *gimlet* with a parallel hollowed shank.

shelling [pla.] *Crazing.*

shell bedding A way of laying concrete blocks that improves their insulation against cold and wet. The bedding mortar is laid in thin strips only along the two long edges of each block.

shell shake [tim.] A *ring shake* which shows on the surface of sawn timber (shelly timber).

sherardizing [mech.] Coating small iron or steel articles with zinc by heating them with zinc dust in a revolving drum at about 350° C. It gives a penetrated coating which is more durable than *galvanizing* (*C*), does not peel off, and gives less increase in size and distortion.

shim [tim.] An *insert* in *veneer.*

shingle (1) Rounded aggregate of variable size and shape, without sand.

(2) A thin rectangular piece of timber about 40 × 13 × 0·6 cm (16 × 5 × ¼ in.) used like a *tile* for covering walls or roofs. It usually reduces in thick-

ness from *tail* (butt) to *head*. Shingles were used in ancient Rome and split oak shingles were common in mediaeval Britain. In USA, there are shingles of bronze, and other metals. *See* **tip, weather**, and for sizes, *see* **dimension, five X, perfection, royals, Saxon shakes, takspan**.

shingling hatchet, claw h. A hatchet like the plasterer's *lath hammer*, with a notch in the blade for drawing *nails*.

shiplap boards, s. siding [tim.] *Weather-boarding* of a rectangular cross section with a *rebate* cut on each edge, fitting into corresponding rebates on the neighbouring boards. White, opaque, extruded PVC 'planks' are being widely used as a substitute for wooden shiplap board. PVC has more *temperature movement* than wood, especially if it is backed with insulation material, but it should remain sound for 20 years without painting. Timber needs yearly attention.

ship spikes, boat s. [carp.] Steel spikes for fixing large timber, forged from square bar, having a wedge point.

shoddy work (1) Inferior work of any sort.

(2) Squared granite less than 30 cm (12 in.) thick.

shoe (1) A short length at the foot of a *downpipe* bent to direct the flow away from the wall.

(2) An iron or steel socket enclosing the end of a *rafter* or other load-bearing timber.

(3) In *patent glazing*, a fitting which holds the lower end of a glazing bar on to a roof member such as a *purlin* and prevents the glass sliding.

shook [tim.] A small piece of sawn timber or *sliced veneer*, or a set of such pieces for making a box.

shoot (1) *See* **drain chute**.

(2) [joi.] To true the edge of a board with a *jointing plane*.

shooting board [joi.] A board framed to steady another board while its edge is being shot (planed).

shooting plane [joi.] A *jointing plane*.

shop and office fitter [joi.] A *joiner* specialized in building shop fronts, therefore accustomed to the use of *hardwoods*, metals, and metal-faced *plywood*.

shop drawing A manufacturer's drawing which will be worked to in his workshops and may be submitted for approval to a consulting *architect* or engineer.

shopwork Work done in the manufacturer's shop, not on the site.

shore A *raking shore, dead shore* or *flying shore*.

shoring Giving temporary support with *shores* to a building being repaired, altered, or *underpinned* (C).

short (1) **short circuit** [elec.] An electrical fault caused by two power leads being electrically joined and causing a very high current to pass. It should cause the *fuses* to melt or other *cutouts* to come into action.

(2) [plu.] A short piece of pipe.

short grain [tim.] *See* **brash**.

short oil [pai.] A low ratio of oil to *resin* in a *varnish*. *Compare* **long oil**.

short-working plaster Plaster which is difficult to mix, and from which the sand separates when the mix is squeezed on the board. It is caused by deterioration of plaster which has been stored in a damp place.

shot hole [tim.] *Worm hole* between 1·5 and 3 mm ($\frac{1}{16}$ and $\frac{1}{8}$ in.) dia. *See* **powder-post**.

shot sawn A description of the smooth surface given to building stone sawn by chilled shot, fed into the groove during cutting.

shoulder [carp.] The surface at the root of a *tenon* which abuts on the wood outside the *mortise*.

shouldered architrave An *architrave*, round a door, which widens at the top.

shouldering (1) **half-torching** A thin bed of *haired mortar* inserted under the head of each *slate* in exposed places to keep the *tail* down. *See* **torching**.

(2) The small diagonal pieces cut from the bottom left-hand and top right-hand corners of *single-lap tiles*.

(3) The splay cutting of the top corners of slates from Westmorland and some other quarries. B S 5534 allows this.

shoulder nipple [plu.] (U S A) A *nipple* (pipe *fitting*) with a space of about 19 mm (¾ in.) between threads at the middle.

shoved joints, pick and dip (U S A) Bricklaying by *buttering* the end of the *brick* and pushing it against the last brick laid – a bricklaying method common in Britain also. The *cross joints* are usually badly filled. *Compare* **slushed joints**.

shread head A *jerkin-head roof. See* p. 279.

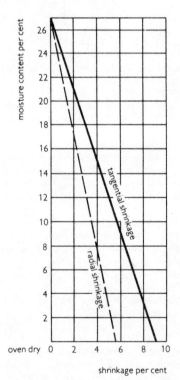

Average shrinkage of wood in drying (shrinkage varies greatly with species). After Fitzmaurice, Principles of Modern Building, *HMSO*.

shrinkage [tim.] The maximum shrinkage of timber during drying is about 0·4% along its length, about 4·5% parallel to the *growth rings*, and about 3% at right angles to them. The tangential shrinkage is about 1·5 times the radial shrinkage, because of the geometry of the circle. *See also*, **moisture content, flat-sawn log** (illus. p. 140) *and C.*

shutter A wooden or steel cover inside or outside a window, that fastens over it at night to protect the occupants.

shutter bar A pivoted bar for holding shutters closed.

shuttered socket [elec.] A *socket outlet* with two holes for the insertion of power prongs and one for an earth prong. The earth prong, being longer than the others, must be inserted first. Small shutters ordinarily block the power holes but are opened only when the earth prong is inserted and the whole plug can then be pushed in. They are therefore not dangerous to children. Standard shuttered sockets are rated at 13 amp (3KW at 240 volts) and often used for *ring mains*.

shutter hinge [joi.] An *H-hinge*.

shutting post The fixed post against which a gate shuts.

shutting stile, lock s., slamming s. [joi.] That *stile* of a door which carries the lock. In a folding door it is called the *meeting stile. See* **hanging stile**.

side [tim.] A broad surface of *square-sawn timber*, usually called a *face*.

side cut, side board, siding [tim.] A piece of wood sawn to exclude the *heart centre*.

side flights *See double-return stairs*.

side gutter A small gutter down a roof slope at the intersection of a *chimney* or *dormer* or other vertical surface with the main roof.

side hook [joi.] A *bench hook*.

side jointing [joi.] (USA) The *topping* of *saw-teeth* at the side of the saw with a *hone*.

side lap For *slates*, tiles or *shingles*, the horizontal distance between the 'vertical' joint in a lower course and the next 'vertical' joint in the course above it. For roofs at a low angle of slope the side lap needs to be more than for steep roofs. For *single-lap tiles* it is the amount by which each tile is covered by the tile beside it in the same course, and is not variable as it is for slates or *plain tiles*.

sidelight, winglight [joi.] A *dead light* such as a *flanking window*.

side posts [carp.] *Princess posts*.

side rabbet plane [joi.] A small metal *plane* for planing the wall of a *rabbet* or groove. Its *cutting iron* is therefore in the side of the plane, not in the *sole*. Normally a right- and a left-hand plane are needed, but some are built with both a right- and a left-hand cutting iron.

siding [tim.] (1) *See* **side cut**.

(2) *See* **weather-boarding**. In USA, any wall *cladding* except *masonry* or *brick*, e.g. *asbestos-cement*, metal, or other sheets.

sienna [pai.] *Pigment* obtained from hydrated mineral iron oxide, and described as raw sienna when it is the yellow-brown clean crushed mineral, or burnt sienna when it is calcined to a rich orange-brown. It is not very opaque, but its transparency can be made use of in oil *stainers. See* **ochre, umber**.

sieve A round tray about 38 cm (15 in.) dia., with one or more meshes per linear cm, used for separating different sizes of sand and gravel. *See* **screen**.

sight size The *daylight width* and the light-admitting height of a window.

silencing pipe, drowning p. [plu.] A vertical, normally submerged tube connected to a *ball valve*, through which the flow enters a *cistern*. It may have a small anti-siphon hole drilled in its top end, but even this may not be enough to avoid contravention of a water authority's regulations against *back siphonage*. *See* illus. p. 29.

silicate paints Water paints containing sodium silicate. They are non-flammable but alkaline and therefore may be covered only with *alkali-resistant paints*.

silicates Very common and chemically complex rock-forming minerals containing the radical SiO_3. Sodium silicate, Na_2SiO_3, is used for waterproofing bricks, stone, or concrete, for hardening concrete floors, and for improving the *fire-resistance* of timber. *See* **Joosten process** (*C*), **clay** (*C*), **calcium silicate**.

silicon bronze Probably the most durable but one of the most costly metals used for making nails, screws, etc., for boats or roofs where steel rusts quickly. It contains 1 per cent manganese, 3 per cent silicon, and 96 per cent copper, but is considerably harder than copper.

silicone [pai.] *See* **water-repellent treatment**.

silk [pai.] Trade term for eggshell *gloss*.

silking [pai.] *See* **lining**.

sill, cill, sole plate (USA **abutment piece**) [carp.] The lowest horizontal member of a *framed partition*, of *frame construction*, or of a frame for a window or door. A wooden door or window sill may be fixed over a stone, concrete, or brick sill. *See* **lug sill**.

sill anchor, plate a. A bolt anchored in the concrete or masonry foundation to a timber house. It passes through a hole drilled in the *sill*, holding the frame down against the wind.

sill bead [joi.] A *deep bead*.

sillboard [joi.] (Scotland) A *window board*.

sill cock (USA) A *hose cock*.

silver brazing, s. soldering [plu.] A method of joining copper tubes, introduced to British plumbers about 1960. The solder is an expensive alloy of copper, silver and phosphorus. Its melting point is appreciably lower than most *brazing* alloys', though well above 600°C. (*compare* **fine solder**). It needs no flux because the phosphorus in it acts as one (BS 1845).

silver fir [tim.] (Abies alba) Many firs go by this name, most of them from central and southern Europe. It is the largest European tree, growing up to 60 m (200 ft) high. Good quality silver fir is used for general building work, including floorboards and *joinery*. It is generally slightly weaker and lighter than *redwood*. *See* **whitewood**.

silver grain [tim.] The fine, pale-grey, shining flecks of *wood ray* seen in *quarter-sawn* oak or beech.

silver-lock bond A 215 mm ($8\frac{1}{2}$ in.) thick brick wall built of alternating courses of *headers* and *stretchers*. The headers are laid in the ordinary way on bed, 70 mm (3 in.) high but the stretchers are laid on edge 110 mm ($4\frac{1}{2}$ in.) high with a continuous cavity behind them. It is cheaper and weaker than *English bond* but stronger than *rat-trap bond*.

silver solder [plu.] Solder used in *silver brazing*, with about 15% silver.

single bridging [carp.] *Herring-bone strutting* at the midspan of floor *joists*.

single-coat plaster [pla.] Modern plaster applied in one coat, e.g. over plasterboard or smooth concrete or as *thin-wall plaster*. It can be less than 2 mm

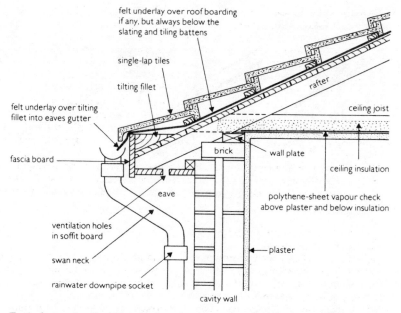

felt underlay over roof boarding
if any, but always below the
slating and tiling battens

single-lap tiles

tilting fillet

felt underlay over tilting
fillet into eaves gutter

rafter

ceiling joist

fascia board

brick

wall plate

ceiling insulation

eave

polythene-sheet vapour check
above plaster and below insulation

ventilation holes
in soffit board

swan neck

plaster

rainwater downpipe socket

cavity wall

*Typical eave detail with single-lap tiles. Usually such a roof would have counter
battens nailed to the underlay.*

($\frac{1}{12}$ in.) thick but scratches or other hollows should first be filled with the same
plaster.

single Flemish bond Brickwork laid in *Flemish bond* which is seen on one face
only, as opposed to *double Flemish bond*. There is generally *English bond*
within the body of a wall faced in single Flemish bond.

single-handed working *See* **air lock, lifting wedge, sprag**.

single-hung window A *sash window* of which only one sash, usually the bottom
one, is movable and balanced by *sash cord* and weights.

single-lap tile, interlocking t. Curved or flat, clay or concrete roofing tiles, so
called because they overlap only the tiles in the course immediately below
them, unlike *slates* and *plain tiles* which lap two *courses*. Modern types interlock with neighbouring tiles, sometimes on three edges. (Older types, *pantiles*
and *Spanish tiles* do not interlock.) All are larger than plain tiles so a roof tiled
with them weighs only about two thirds as much as a plain-tiled roof. They
are holed for nails and some also have nibs. The lefthand edge of each tile,
viewed from the ground, fits under an overlap in the righthand edge of the
next tile in the same course. Makers claim that some types can be laid at a
pitch of only $17\frac{1}{2}°$ but most types need a slope of at least 30°. They include
*concrete interlocking, double Roman, flat interlocking, Poole's tiles, Roman
tiles*. (Illus. above)

single-lock cross welt [plu.] A *cross welt* on a sloping roof, or a sloping part of
a *flat roof*, in which the two *flexible-metal sheets* are single-locked, i.e. each
is held to the other by a 180° fold (p. 306). *Compare* **double-lock cross welt**.

roofing felt on 25 mm (1 in.) thick
tongued and grooved planed boards

Stage 1	Stage 2	Stage 3
lower sheet bent up 20 mm (¾ in.)	upper sheet bent down and hooked into lower sheet	two sheets hammered flat

Single-lock cross welt in flexible-metal roofing.

single-pitch roof A *lean-to roof.*

single-point heater [plu.] An *instantaneous* (*sink*) *water heater.*

single Roman tile *See* **Roman tile.**

single roof [carp.] A roof carried by *common rafters* without roof *truss*, *purlins*, or *principals*. It may be tied by a 15 × 5 cm (6 × 2 in.) timber tie at eaves level (*close-couple roof*) or higher (*collar-beam roof*) or it may be a lean-to or flat roof. The common rafters are generally of 10 × 5 cm (4 × 2 in.) timber at 38 cm (15 in.) centres. In the best work they are *close-boarded.*

single-stack system [plu.] A form of *one-pipe system* from which most of the *anti-siphon pipes* have been omitted, and with *deep-seal* traps to washbasins and sinks (BS 4118, BRE Digest 248, 249).

sink bib, b. nozzle (USA) The tap at a kitchen sink.

sinking [joi.] A recess cut below the surface of wood, for example, where *butt hinges* are fixed on a door.

sinking in, sinking [pai.] Loss of *gloss* of a finish coat due to the absorption of its *medium* by the *undercoat.*

site (USA **lot**) Land which is used, or will be used, for construction.

Sitka spruce [tim.] (Picea sitchensis) A *softwood* from the island of Sitka on the north west coast of Canada. It is the finest *spruce* and is obtainable in large sizes, pinkish white to pale brown with a silky sheen which is absent from the commoner *Canadian spruce*; used for *blockboard* cores, *joinery*, and *ladder* stiles.

size [pai.] A liquid *sealer*, usually transparent, with which wood or plaster is coated so that *varnish* or *paint* or *glue* applied over it will not be too much absorbed. Of the two sorts most commonly used, glue size is glue diluted with water and put on to plaster, varnish size is made from oil, resin, and *thinner* and put on below paint. *See* **gold size.**

sized slates *Slates* of uniform dimensions, not *random slates.*

size stick A slater's *scantle.*

sizing, pre-sizing [tim.] Spreading dilute *glue* (called *size*) on to a surface before gluing it. Since size penetrates more than glue, it reduces the absorption of glue by the wood during gluing. Woods of different densities should be sized before gluing, but the sizing should not be hard before the glue is applied.

skeleton construction A steel or reinforced-concrete frame with floors of concrete. No wall rises higher than one storey without its load being transferred to a *column* through a floor slab or beam, except occasionally, when instead of columns, reinforced-concrete loadbearing walls carry the floor loads.

skeleton core [joi.] The hidden internal frame of a *hollow-core door*.

skeleton steps *Treads*, often of metal, with no risers.

skew (1) Oblique.

(2) A *kneeler*.

skewback The upper surface of a *springer* (or the springer itself). It is so called because the surface slopes to carry the first of the uniform *arch-stones*. *See* **clean back**.

skewback saw [carp.] An expensive *handsaw* with a *back* slightly curved instead of straight, as it is in the cheap but very slightly heavier saws. It is usually taper ground. Some people prefer a straight-back saw because it can be used as a straight edge. *See* **setting** (illus. p. 298).

skew corbel A *gable springer*.

skew flashing A *flashing* between a *gable* coping and the roof below it.

skew nailing, toe n., tusk n. [carp.] Driving *nails* in, not perpendicularly, but obliquely to the surfaces to be joined. Where possible, alternate nails are driven in opposite directions.

skew table A *kneeler* in a *gable* coping.

skid road A road for quarrying, made of partly embedded round logs set 1 to 2 m (3 to 6 ft) apart across the road. Sledges or *stone boats* are the only users of the road. It is greased in summer but in frosty weather needs no grease, being naturally slippery.

skids Short lengths of wood used for packing walling stones to the correct height when laying them.

skiffling, knobbing Dressing stones roughly in the quarry.

skilled man Either a *tradesman* or a leading hand in a modern *trade* which has expanded too quickly for the apprenticeship system to become general (general riggers, bar benders, *steel erectors* (*C*)). Many such men, who are not called tradesmen, may nevertheless have more skill and adaptability than tradesmen. Most of them work to drawings. Since there is no apprenticeship, many skilled men have risen from *labourer*.

skimming coat, skin c. [pla.] A normal *finishing coat* about 3 mm ($\frac{1}{8}$ in.) thick.

skin [tim.] In *flexible bag moulding* a thin piece of *moulded plywood* or a thin *hardwood* covering over the mould to protect it. *See* **caul**.

skinning [pai.] Formation in the tin on the surface of a *paint* or *varnish*, of a skin from the *oxidation* of the *drying oil* when the tin is left to stand, because of a high proportion of *driers*, a viscous *medium* or a very fast drying oil. *See* **anti-skinning agent, inhibitor**.

skips (1) **planing s.** [tim.] An area of timber missed (skipped) by the planing machine.

(2) **holiday** [pai.] Areas left unpainted by mistake.

(3) A large steel container of several m^3 capacity for storage and removal of refuse. For use in a street, a licence from the local authority must be obtained.

Hard-wearing coved skirting of sand and cement (3:1) showing plywood templet for shaping it.

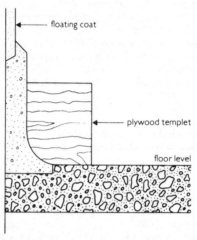

skirting, s. board (Scots **base plate**) (USA **mopboard, washboard, scrub board, base**) Originally a wooden board set vertically round the foot of a wall to protect if from kicks. It may now be built of *wall tiles*, metal trim, *terrazzo*, asphalt or other material more durable than wood, and can also be a low upstand of the roof under the *flashing* at a roof *abutment*. (Illus. above)

skirting block An *architrave block*.

sky factor The *daylight factor*.

skylight A *roof light*.

skyscraper A multi-storey steel-framed building, typical of New York where the bedrock is only 15 m (50 ft) below ground and makes an excellent foundation for a 50-storey building.

slab [tim.] A piece of timber with one sawn face and one *waney*, curved face.

slabbing [tim.] Squaring a log; cutting *slabs* off it.

slab floor (1) A *reinforced concrete* (*C*) floor.

(2) A floor covered with slabs of marble, slate, limestone, granite, *flagstones, cast stone, terrazzo*, etc.

slack side [tim.] The *loose side* of *sliced veneer*.

slag bricks Bricks made from *blast-furnace slag* crushed and mixed with *lime*.

slag strip [carp.] (USA) A strip of wood nailed round the edges of a felt roof to keep the gravel covering in place and to give a finished appearance to the edge of the roof. *See also* **no-fines concrete**.

slag wool, silicate cotton Filaments of metallurgical slag used for their high fire resistance, thermal insulation, and acoustical *absorption*. *See* **mineral wool**.

slaked lime *Hydrated lime*.

slaking The hydration of *quicklime*, thus: $CaO + H_2O = Ca(OH)_2$.

slamming stile [joi.] A *shutting stile*.

slamming strip [joi.] A *banding* over the edge of the *shutting stile* of a *flush door*.

slap dash *Rough cast*.

slash grain [tim.] The *grain* of *flat-sawn timber* (slash-sawn timber).

slat (1) [tim.] A thin strip of wood in a *louvre*, blind, etc.

(2) A *stone slate*.

slate Natural slate, quarried in North Wales and other areas, has been almost entirely replaced elsewhere by *single-lap tiles* or by *asbestos-cement slates*, which are much cheaper in districts far from the quarries. They are quarried in square-sawn blocks about 76 mm (3 in.) thick which are then split to thicknesses from 6 to 13 mm ($\frac{1}{4}$ to $\frac{1}{2}$ in.) They are usually sold by the tally of 1000, but ton slates – either *randoms* or very large ones – are sold by weight. Normal lengths are between 20 and 61 cm, with widths from 14·5 to 40·5 cm (8 to 24 in. by 6 to 16 in.). BS 680 quotes 27 sizes. Only 11 of the largest are needed to cover 1 m² but 74 of the smallest, which consequently make a heavier roof. *See* **roofing nails**, *also* BS 5534.

slate-and-a-half slate A slate half as wide again but of the same depth as those next it, used at *valleys*, *hips*, and *verges*. *See* **laced valley, swept valley**.

slate axe A slater's axe or *zax*.

slate batten A *slating-and-tiling batten*.

slate boarding [carp.] Close *boarding* over a roof under slates or tiles.

slate cramp A piece of slate cut to a shape which in plan is waisted like an hourglass, having dovetailed ends. It is about 5 cm (2 in.) long by 2·5 cm (1 in.) wide at the ends, and 13 mm ($\frac{1}{2}$ in.) wide at the waist. It is from 2·5 to 15 cm (1 to 6 in.) deep, and fits into vertical *mortises* in neighbouring stones to lock them together.

slate hanging, weather slating Slating over a wall.

slate listing Overhanging, horizontal slates, set in the bed joints of an *abutment* between a roof and e.g. a chimney. The slates overhang each other and throw the water away from the abutment, reducing the need for a *cover flashing* of *flexible metal*.

slate nails *See* **roofing nails**.

slate powder [pai.] Very fine powder of slate used as an *extender* in paints. It is fairly opaque and too dark to be used in any pale paint.

slater-and-tiler A *tradesman* who lays *slates*, *tiles*, and lead *soakers*, punches holes in slates by hand or machine, cuts and trims them, and lays *sarking felt*. He may also nail *close-boarding* on to *rafters* which have been fixed by the *carpenter*. He usually nails his own *slating-and-tiling battens* (and *counter battens* if necessary). He also lays *ridge tiles* in *mortar*.

slate ridge, s. roll A ridge made of a circular rod of slate with a V-cut beneath. The roll is bedded on a heavy slate each side called a wing.

slater's iron A light *dressing iron* with a single spike, used by the slater while he is on the roof.

slating-and-tiling batten Square-sawn timbers between 19 × 25 mm ($\frac{3}{4}$ × 1 in.) and 30 × 80 mm ($1\frac{1}{4}$ × 3 in.), nailed horizontally over *common rafters* or *counter battens* to carry *slates* or *tiles*.

slatter A *mason* who shapes stone slates (slats).

sleeper (1) [carp.] A *valley board* carried on the *rafters* of the main roof. It carries the feet of the *jack-rafters* and replaces a *valley rafter*.

(2) [carp.] A *sleeper plate. See also (C)*.

sleeper clip US term for a *floor clip*.

sleeper plate [carp.] A *wall plate* on a *sleeper wall* or a similar wooden plate on a concrete floor carrying floor boards or *joists*.

Polypropylene sleeve with rubber sealing rings for joining vitrified clay pipes.

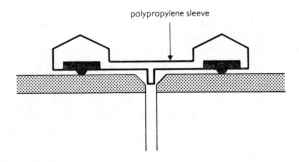

polypropylene sleeve

sleeper wall A *honeycomb wall* (2).

sleepiness [pai.] A reduction of *gloss* as a film dries, a defect sometimes akin to *seediness*.

sleeve *See* **expansion sleeve**.

sleeved joint *Drain pipes* can be joined by a sleeve, a pipe slightly larger in diameter than the drain pipe, that thus fits neatly over it. These joints can be made only on plain-ended (socketless) pipes – an advantage because socketed pipes are expensive. Some sleeves are made of polypropylene tube, grooved inside and fitted with two rubber rings that make a watertight joint which is flexible, enabling clay pipes to settle without breaking. (Illus. above) *Compare* **spigot-and-socket joint**.

sleeve piece, thimble, ferrule, liner [plu.] A short, thin-walled brass or copper tube soldered to a lead pipe so as to join it to one of different metal. *See* **taft joint, plumber's union**.

sliced, flat-cut, knife-cut veneer [tim.] *Veneer* made by a machine with a knife up to 5 m (16 ft) long which cuts straight slices as a hand *plane* does. The *flitch* is first heated in a *cooking vat* so that when cut it is wet and steaming. The slices can be as thin as 0·2 mm but are usually about 1 mm. This method produces no sawdust but may make a slightly weaker veneer than *sawn veneer*. It is the usual method of cutting figured veneer, for which it is preferred to rotary cutting. Sliced veneer has a *loose side* and a *tight side*.

sliding-door lock [joi.] A *lock* designed for sliding doors. It has a hook-shaped bolt which engages with the back of the *striking plate* and holds the door.

sliding sash A window which opens by sliding horizontally. *Compare* **sash window**.

slip (1) A *fixing fillet*, or narrow brick.

    (2) [joi.] A *parting slip*.

    (3) [pla.] Fluid grout made with *gypsum plaster* or *cement*.

    (4) [pai.] A paint which is so little *gummy* that it seems to be lubricated is said to have slip.

slip feather [joi.] A tongue for a joint such as a *feather joint*.

slip joint A joint between pipe ends made merely by passing a pipe into a socket without screwing, soldering or *solvent welding*. With electrical conduit it has the disadvantage that there is no earthing through the conduit.

slip mortise [joi.] An *open mortise* or a *chase mortise*.

slipper [pla.] A metal shoe on a *horsed mould* which slides along the *running rule*.

slipper guide [pla.] A *running rule*.

slip sill A window or door *sill* which fits or slips between the *jambs* of an opening and is not built into the walls, like a *lug sill*.

slip stone [joi.] An *oilstone slip*.

slip tongue, false t. [joi.] A tongue in a *feather joint*.

slope of grain [tim.] The angle between the axis of a timber and the general direction of the *grain*. Timber for structural purposes should not have a slope more than 1 in 8 for beams (or struts less than 10 cm (4 in.) thick). For thicker struts, the slope should be below 1 in 11. *See* **gross features**.

slop sink, housemaid's s. A low sink, large enough to take a bucket under the tap, often installed in hospitals.

slot mortise [joi.] An *open mortise*.

slot screwing [joi.] Screwing of boards through slots which allow some movement. Any *shrinkage* cracking can be closed up by slacking off the screws in the slots, pushing the boards together, and tightening the screws again. *Compare* **secret screwing**, which can never be undone.

slow-burning construction (USA) (1) Heavy-timber construction which is more *fire-resisting* than bare steel frames.

(2) Construction with materials treated with fire-resistant surfacing or impregnation.

slurry A fluid cement-water mix, sometimes containing sand.

slurrying Protection of the finished surface of a stone facing by covering it with a weak mix of lime and stone dust, which is washed off when the builder hands the building over to the client.

slushed joints, slushed-up j. (USA) Brickwork in which the vertical *joints* are filled with *mortar* poured from a watering can (grouting), or by throwing in mortar with the edge of the trowel, a more usual method than grouting, though it fills the joints less well.

small-bore system, small-pipe s. [plu.] *Central heating* with radiators (or other heat exchangers) fed by pairs of pipes, usually of 15 mm (0·6 in.) outside diameter through which the water is driven by a pump. This has superseded older systems, with large-diameter pipes and no pumps. BS 5449 defines small-bore heating as the use of pipes of 15 to 35 mm ($\frac{1}{2}$ to $1\frac{1}{2}$ in.) outside diameter. *See* **minibore**.

small tool, spoon [pla.] A small curved steel tool for moulding, mitring, or scratching an indentation in a *moulding*. It is used for finishing off mouldings by hand and is therefore made in several different shapes.

smell test The *scent test* for drains.

smith's hammer [mech.] A *hammer* weighing from 0·7 to 2 kg ($1\frac{1}{2}$ to 4 lb), shaped like a *sledge hammer* (*C*), with a *cross peen*.

smoke detector, automatic s.d., automatic call point A device that raises a fire alarm and may open *smoke outlets* automatically, can detect changes in visibility, temperature, ionization of the air and so on (BS 5445, 5446).

smoke outlet, s. extract, s. vent An opening, or a fire-resisting shaft or duct provided in a building to act as an outlet for smoke and hot gases produced by an outbreak of fire (BS 4422). The outlet may open automatically. *See* **fire venting, thermoplastic, pressurized escape route**.

smoke rocket A *rocket tester*.

smoothing plane [joi.] A relatively short *bench plane* about 20 cm (8 in.) long used after the *trying plane*. *See* **carpenter's tools** (illus. p. 59).

smudge [plu.], **soil** A mixture of *lamp black* and *size* put over a lead surface to prevent *solder* sticking to it.

snake [plu.] A tool like a long *bending spring*, used for unblocking drains.

snakestone, Water of Ayr s., Scotch s. A smooth stone used for polishing *Keene's cement* to a glass-like finish when making *scagliola* or *marezzo marble*.

snap header, blind h. A half-brick, not a *header*.

sneck In *snecked rubble* a small squared stone, not less than 8 cm (3 in.) deep, whose top surface is level with the top of a *riser*.

snecked rubble (Scotland) A *rubble wall* built of squared stones of irregular size. Its peculiarity lies in the use of *snecks*.

snips *See* **tin snips**.

snow boards, s. slats (Scots **s. cradling**) (1) Horizontal wooden slats nailed with gaps between them on short bearers over a *box gutter* to allow melting snow to drain away.

(2) **s. guard, roof g.** A wire fence or a board on edge about 20 cm (8 in.) high fixed at least 10 cm (4 in.) along the roof slope above the eaves gutter to prevent heavy masses of snow slipping off the roof and breaking the eaves gutter or its supports. BS 5534 states that the clearance between the roof surface and the bottom of the guard should be at least 5 cm (2 in.). Evidently they cannot hold up loose slates slipping off a steep roof.

snow cradling *See* **snow boards** (1).

soakage *Capillary entry*.

soaker A small *flexible metal flashing*, roughly of slate size, cut to shape by the *plumber* and laid by the *slater* to interlock with *slates* or *tiles*. It makes a watertight joint at a *hip* or *valley* or at an *abutment*. It is bent at right angles for an abutment or at an obtuse angle for a valley.

soap A *queen closer*.

socket (1) [plu.] (in USA **bell**) An enlarged end of a pipe into which an end of another pipe can be fixed by ramming in cement mortar, lead, a rubber ring, etc. Sockets made separately for many types of pipe including *vitrified clayware*, are used in the *sleeved joint*. Unsocketed pipes are cheaper than socketed ones, also broken pipes may be used where formerly they could not. *See* **coupling** and **fittings** (illus. p. 138).

(2) A *mortise* to receive the *pivot* of a pivoted sash, door, etc.

socket chisel [carp.] A massive *chisel*, with a socket formed at the base of the *tang*, into which the wood handle fits. It is used for mortising and is strong enough to be struck with a *mallet*.

socket former [plu.] A tool that is inserted into an end of copper tube to widen it to the bore needed for a socket of a *capillary joint*. Pumping fluid into its hydraulic ram causes it to open out the end. The tool is expensive but a hammer-driven socket former can be improvised from a short piece of stainless steel tube of the same diameter as the copper tube to be expanded. Joints made in this way are less conspicuous than any other type and the method enables short ends of tube to be used up, but takes more time than other methods. If the copper hardens or begins to split, the widening must be stopped, the split piece cut off, and the copper softened (annealed) by heating it to a dull red heat.

socket inlet, plug [elec.] An electrical part, fixed generally to the *flex* of an appliance for connecting it to the supply through a *socket outlet*, or sometimes through an *adaptor*.

socket joint [plu.] A *spigot-and-socket joint*.

socket outlet (1) [elec.] (USA **receptacle**) An electrical fixture on a wall, containing two or three holes into which the metal prongs of an *adaptor* or *socket inlet* are inserted. *See* **shuttered socket, ring main,** BS 546.

(2) [plu.] That part of a *plug-in connector* for gas which is fixed to the wall.

soffit, soffite (1) The under-surface of a *cornice, stair,* beam, arch, *vault,* or rib or the uppermost part of the inside of a drain, etc.

(2) [joi.] The *lining* at the *head* of an opening.

soffit board, planceer piece [carp.] A horizontal board nailed to the underside of rafters, forming the *soffit* under an *overhanging eave.* (Illus. p. 305)

soft-burnt A description of clay *bricks, tiles,* etc., which have been fired at a low temperature and therefore have high *absorption* and low compressive strengths.

soft sand *Sand* with small grains, rounded and uniform in size, smooth to the hand when squeezed, quite unlike *sharp sand*. It is used for plastering or for making mortar for rendering, pointing, bricklaying, etc., but not for making concrete.

soft solder [plu.] *Fine solder, plumber's solder,* etc., made mainly of lead and tin, both of which melt below 200° C, unlike *hard solder*.

softwood [tim.] The conventional, common description of timbers of the botanical group gymnosperms, most of which in commerce are conifers. They are sometimes harder than *hardwoods*. The softwood yew is nearly as hard as *oak* and harder than many other hardwoods. *See* **balsa wood.**

soil [plu.] (1) *Smudge.*

(2) Sewage as opposed to *sullage*.

soil branch A branch pipe leading to the *soil stack*.

soil cement (USA) *Cob* construction. *See* **soil stabilization** (*C*).

soil drain, foul d. [plu.] A drain for carrying sewage or trade effluent to the

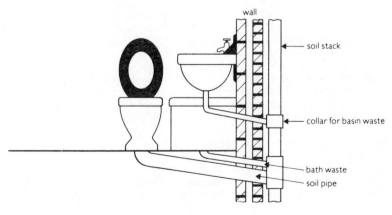

Soil stack for house plumbing.

313

sewer (C). It is of at least 10 cm (4 in.) dia. A soil drain is tested before use by the *smoke rocket* or by the *hydraulic test (C).*

soil stack A vertical pipe which takes sewage down from the parts of a building above ground into the *soil drain.* Its upper end passes above the roof and is left open to ventilate the drain. Cast iron was usual but *plastics* are commoner in new work. (Illus. p. 313)

soil ventilation pipe [plu.] *See* **ventilation pipe**.

solar control film Polyester film coated on one side with aluminium foil and bonded to window glass to reduce the sun's heat and glare by 75%.

solar control glass *Anti-sun glass.*

solar reflecting surface, spar finish A covering of white rock chips (spar) over a flat roof of asphalt or other dark material to reduce its absorption of the sun's heat. *Aluminium paint* should be as effective as spar, and lighter in weight though less durable.

solder [plu.] Any alloys used for joining metals except those which consist mainly of the parent metal. These are called filler rods or electrodes and are used in *welding (C).* *Plumber's solders* and *fine solders* are lead–tin alloys. *Brazing* or *hard solders* are copper–zinc alloys. *See* **silver brazing.**

soldered dot [plu.] (Illus.) *See* **dots**.

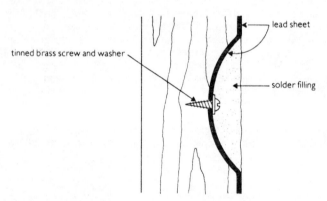

Wiped soldered dot screwed to timber dormer cheek with brass screw.

soldering iron, s. bolt, copper bit [plu.] A small copper block fixed on one end of a thin steel rod to which a wooden (or other thermally insulating) handle is attached. The copper bit may be heated electrically or by other means, but the handle is always kept cool by this construction. *See* **plumber's tools** (illus. p. 250).

soldier (1) [joi.] A short upright *ground* for fixing a *skirting board.*
    (2) An upright brick, a brick on end. *See also C.*

soldier arch A *flat arch* of uncut bricks on end.

soldier course A course of bricks on end, laid usually as a *coping.*

sole [joi.] The smooth under-surface of a *plane,* out of which the *cutting iron* projects.

sole plate (1) **s. piece, mudsill, ground sill** (USA **abutment piece**) [carp.] The timber laid on the ground under the feet of *raking shores* and at right-angles to them, illus. p. 268.

(2) A *sill*.

solid [joi.] Timber without *planted* mouldings.

solid bossing [plu.] The *bossing* of lead to shape.

solid brick *See* **brick definitions**.

solid bridging, s. strutting (USA **block b.**) [carp.] *Strutting* of floor *joists* by rectangular short lengths of *joist* cut to fit tightly between, and at right-angles to, the joists at midspan. Solid bridging needs more precise work than *herringbone strutting* but is stiffer and forms a valuable *fire stop*, for which reason it may also be used in hollow wooden *partitions*. *See* **bridging**.

solid door [joi.] (1) A *flush door* with a solid core resembling *blockboard*, not a *skeleton core*. *Compare* **hollow-core door**.

(2) A *fire-resisting* door built of three thicknesses of tongued and grooved boarding, the inner one horizontal, the outer two vertical. Sometimes this door is plated with sheet metal.

solid floor (1) A *concrete* floor slab, built without *hollow blocks* but with solid concrete throughout its thickness.

(2) [carp.] *See* **plank-on-edge floor**.

solid frame [joi.] An expensive door frame in which each *stile* with its *stop* is a single rebated piece of wood and the stop is therefore not *planted*.

solid masonry unit (USA) Any *brick* whether *perforated* or cellular, provided that its cross-sectional area in every plane parallel to the bed, is 75% or more of the bed area. A hollow masonry unit has less solid than 75% of the bed area. *See* **hollow blocks**.

solid moulding, stuck m. [joi.] A *moulding* cut on the timber, not planted.

solid moulding cutter [tim.] A single piece of steel used on the *spindle moulder*, with perfectly balanced cutters that run at high speeds and do not need frequent sharpening. They are accurate in cutting but costly to buy.

solid-newel stairs *Spiral stairs* of stone in which the inner end of each step is shaped to form a nearly continuous cylinder with the inner ends of the other steps. Partly because they take up very little space they were the commonest means of access to upper floors until about 1550 when the framed wooden stair was introduced. They were also popular because they were easily defended by a single swordsman. If the owner of the house was right handed, he built his stair with the *newel* on the left looking down. *See* **turret step**.

solid partition A *partition* which has no cavity. It may be of *bricks, blocks*, etc.

solid plasterwork [pla.] Plaster with a solid *core* which is formed in place, not in the shop, like *fibrous plaster*.

solid punch A hard steel bar shaped like a *nail punch*, but with an end which is even blunter, for driving a bolt out of a hole, etc.

solid roll A joint between sheets of *flexible-metal roofing* which are folded together over a *wood roll*. *Compare* **hollow roll**.

solid stop [joi.] A *door stop* rebated in a *solid frame*.

solid strutting [carp.] *Solid bridging*.

solid wood floor [carp.] A *plank-on-edge* floor.

soluble driers, liquid d. [pai.] *Driers* which are soluble at ordinary temperatures in *drying oils* or hydrocarbon *solvents*. They are usually resinates, linoleates, or naphthenates of lead, manganese, or cobalt.

solum The ground below the lowest floor in a building. If for any reason this

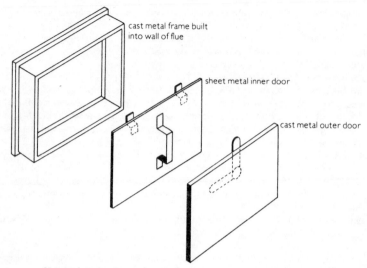

Vertical or horizontal soot door, cast in iron or aluminium.

is not covered with *oversite concrete*, it must be damp-proofed in accordance with the *Building Regulations*, in Scotland with hot pitch or asphalt, or south of the border with thick plastics sheet covered with 50 mm of fine concrete (BS 2832).

solvents [pai.] Liquids like *acetone*, alcohol or water, that dissolve solids. Because they evaporate, *paints* made with them dry quickly except in the coldest weather, and the solvent is absent from the *film*. Most solvents or *thinners* are highly flammable, and the way they may be stored in quantity is controlled by law.

solvent-welded joint [plu.] A permanent joint between plastics tubes, made after smearing both spigot and socket with a solvent, by merely inserting the spigot into the socket.

soot door (USA **ashpit d., cleanout d.**) A door at the foot of a *chimney* through which the chimney is swept and soot is removed. (Illus. above)

soot pocket An extension of a *chimney* below the smoke inlet, usually fitted with a *soot door*.

Sorel's cement *See* **magnesite flooring**.

sound absorption *See* **absorption**.

sound boarding [carp.] Horizontal boards fitted closely between *joists* and resting on them in the thickness of the floor. They carry *pugging*, which increases the sound insulation of the floor.

sound insulation *See* **noise insulation**.

sound knot [tim.] A tight, solid, undecayed *knot* which is at least as hard as the wood round it. *Compare* **unsound knot**.

soundproofing A term which has very little meaning, and is therefore falling out of use in the same way as 'fireproofing'. *See below, also* **absorption, discontinuous construction, noise, pugging,** *also* BSCP 3, chapter 3.

316

sound-reduction factor, acoustical r. f. A value which can be expressed for a given wall or *partition* in *decibels*. This value gives a measure of the reduction in intensity of the sound of any given frequency which passes through the wall. The sound-reduction factor is 5 decibels better if the wall weight is doubled. *Compare* **conductivity**, *see insulators*.

south-light roof A *north-light roof* of the southern hemisphere, with the steeper slope glazed and facing south.

soya glue [tim.] A *vegetable glue* made from soya bean meal after extraction of its oil. It resembles *casein glue*.

space [carp.] Of a saw, the length from one point of a *saw-tooth* to the next.

spaced slating *Open slating*.

space heating The heating of a building by *direct, small-bore, warm-air* or other heating method. See B S 5449.

spall (1) To break off the rough edges of stone with slanting blows of a *chisel*.

(2) **gallet** A flake of stone used for filling the spaces in *rubble walls* or in pitching *revetments* (*C*).

spandrel (1) A roughly triangular space between the *extrados* of an arch, one abutment, and the road carried by the arch.

(2) **apron wall** (U S A) The vertical infilling in a multi-storey building between a window sill and the window head below, or any opaque panel in *curtain walling*.

(3) The triangular infilling under the *outer string* of a stair.

spandrel step A solid stone step of triangular shape, carved to make, with other similar steps, a flush *soffit* to the *stair*.

Spanish mahogany [tim.] *Cuban mahogany*.

Spanish tile (1) (U S A **mission t.**) *Roofing tiles* shaped like a half-cylinder slightly wider at one end than the other. The *over-tile* and *under-tile* are of roughly the same shape, the under-tile being larger. These tiles form a beautiful roof which is flexible both in *side lap* and end lap. However, the amount of timber needed is considerable, as 8 × 5 cm (3 × 2 in.) timbers must be fixed up the slope of the roof (over felt on *boarding*) to secure the under-tiles. *See* **Italian tiling**.

(2) (U S A) A *single-lap tile* which slightly resembles the tile called in Britain a single *Roman tile*.

span piece [carp.] A *collar beam*.

span roof [carp.] An ordinary *pitched roof*.

spar (1) **brotch, buckle** In *thatch*, a split piece of hazel or willow 60 cm (24 in.) long. Eight spars are obtained from a 5 cm (2 in.) dia. branch. They are pointed at both ends, doubled, and driven into the thatch over *runners, liggers*, or *scallops*.

(2) A *common rafter*.

spar finish A *solar reflecting surface*.

sparge pipe [plu.] A perforated pipe for flushing a urinal stall, etc.

spar piece, span p. A *collar beam*.

sparrow peck (1) A texture given to plaster by pitting it with a stiff broom.

(2) A texture given to stone by *picking*.

spar varnish [pai.] A boat *varnish* with outstanding resistance to water and sunlight. It usually consists of *tung* or *linseed oil* with durable *resins*.

spatterdash [pla.] A wet, rich mix of *cement* and sand (1:1½ to 1:3) which is thrown hard on to a smooth *brick* or *concrete* surface and allowed to harden.

and thus provides a *key* for, or reduces the suction of, the first coat of plaster. If these hardened rough splashes of *mortar* do not give enough adhesion, *concrete-bonding plaster* may have to be used, or the same mortar, mixed with some polyvinyl acetate emulsion, should be vigorously brushed into the surface and stippled immediately to form a key (BS 5262).

special A bend or tee or similar *fitting* of a pipe, or a bullnose brick, squint quoin, splay brick, etc., which needs to be specially ordered, usually by number. If it is a piece kept in stock it is called a 'standard special', otherwise it has to be specially made.

specification Descriptive text written by a consulting engineer or *architect* to tell the *contractor* what is neither in the *bill of quantities* nor on the drawings. Written in the order chosen for 'he *sequence of trades*, its function differs with the type of contract. In some *contracts* with an unusually detailed bill of quantities, the specification, though provided, may be no part of the contract. In contracts without quantities it is a part of the contract and in conjunction with the drawings defines the quality and extent of the work. *Preambles* also describe quality. *See* **National Building Specification**.

spigot [plu.] An end of a pipe inserted into a *socket* in the next pipe to form a *spigot-and-socket joint*.

spigot-and-socket joint (USA **bell-and-spigot j.**) [plu.] A joint in clay or other pipes which is made tight by caulking one end of pipe of normal diameter (the *spigot*) into an enlarged end, the *socket*. For cast iron the caulking is with lead wool or molten lead. For *vitrified clayware* it was originally of cement *mortar*, plugged with a ring of old rope at the lower end, a rigid joint which has been improved in the *O-ring* (p. 110), *sleeved joint* (p. 310).

spike knot [tim.] A *splay knot*.

spindle (1) [mech.] A small axle.

(2) [joi.] A turned piece of wood such as a circular *baluster*.

(3) [tim.] A *spindle moulder*.

spindle moulder, spindle [tim.] A *moulding machine* which has a vertical shaft rotating at about 7500 rpm carrying a *cutter block* with two or more specially shaped knives or a *solid-moulding cutter*. Since it is a very versatile machine it usually needs a specialist to operate it. *See* **woodworking machinist**.

spiral grain [tim.] Fibres growing spirally round the trunk of a tree, thus making the wood difficult to work. *See* **interlocked grain**.

spiral stair A circular *stair* in which the *treads* are all *winders*. (The shape is helical, not spiral.) The central parts of the winders are laid on top of each other and form a continuous cylindrical *solid newel*. These stairs can be made of stone, as was customary in the past, or of cast iron. Recently, elegant precast concrete treads have been made. *See* **turret step**.

spiriting off [pai.] The final operation in French polishing, in which the last traces of oil are removed by a rag damped with *methylated spirit*, drawn quickly and often over the surface. *See* **bodying in**.

spirit level *See* **level**; *also* **mason's and bricklayer's tools** (illus. p. 211).

spirit stain [pai.] A dye dissolved in alcohol (methylated spirit), usually with *shellac* or other dissolved *resin* as a *binder*. It is used for darkening a wood surface, but emphasizes the *grain* of the wood less than a *water stain*.

spirit varnish [pai.] *Varnish* made by dissolving a gum or *resin* in alcohol or other spirit. It dries by *evaporation* of the spirit and resembles *knotting* in composition.

spit The depth of one spade blade, about 23 cm (9 in.).

splashboard (1) A board placed on edge beside a *scaffold* against a wall to keep it clean.

(2) A *weather moulding* planted at the foot of an outside door.

splash lap That part of the *overcloak* of a *flexible-metal* drip or roll which extends on to the flat surface of the next sheet.

splat A cover strip over the joints of *wallboards*.

splay A sloping cut across the full width of a surface, often at 45°, a large *chamfer*.

splay brick, cant b. A special brick which is bevelled at about 45° at one end (splay header) or at 45° along one edge (splay stretcher).

splayed grounds [joi.] *Grounds* with bevelled or rebated edge to provide a *key* for the plaster where the ground also acts as a *screed*.

splayed heading joint [carp.] A joint between the ends of floorboards which are not cut vertically but at 45°, so that one overlaps the other.

splayed skirting [joi.] A *skirting* with its top edge bevelled, not moulded.

splay knot, spike k. [tim.] A *knot* cut nearly parallel to its length. *Compare* **round knot.**

splice [carp.], **fished joint** A joint between *halved* timbers which are covered on each side by steel or wooden plates (*fishplates* (C)), bolted together through the timbers.

split [tim.] A crack in wood or *veneer* which passes through it. *Compare* **check.**

split course A *course* of bricks cut lengthwise to reduce their depth to less than that of an ordinary course.

split head [pla.] A steel tripod of adjustable height carrying a standard notched at the top to hold a *scaffold board* on edge. This makes a fairly strong platform for plasterers, but four split heads are needed to carry two boards on edge.

split pipe A pipe cut lengthwise, a channel.

split-ring connector [tim.] A timber *connector* inserted in a pre-cut ring-shaped groove in both timbers, made with a *hole saw*.

split shakes [tim.] *Shingles* which have been split, not sawn.

split system (USA) Space heating, by blowing warm air into a room and using *radiators* simultaneously.

spokeshave [joi.] A two-handed light *plane* for shaping surfaces which are curved like the spokes of a wheel.

sponge-backed rubber floor Solid rubber sheet about 3 mm ($\frac{1}{8}$ in.) thick, backed with sponge rubber 3 to 9 mm ($\frac{1}{8}$ to $\frac{3}{8}$ in.) thick, obtainable in rolls 1·8 m (6 ft) wide, 23 m (75 ft) long. It can be laid on most smooth surfaces which are perfectly dry. A *screed* of about 3 mm of *cement-rubber latex* is a good foundation over wood, metal, or concrete floors. Adhesives based on natural rubber must be used for fixing the sponge to the floor and to the solid rubber surface layer.

spot board, gauge b. [pla.] A plasterer's board about 1 m (3 ft) square on which he works up the plaster before he puts it on. It rests on a stand about 68 cm (27 in.) high.

spotting [pai.] The defect of small areas of a painted surface with a different *colour* or *gloss* from the rest.

spotting in, spot finishing [pai.] *Rubbing* down and refinishing small defective patches in a coating (BS 2015).

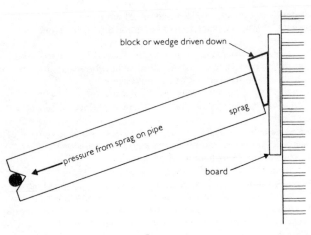

Sprag.

sprag A stout timber or steel pipe wedged against a wall or floor to hold a timber during glueing or a copper pipe during soldering. It can apply as much force as is needed by the single-handed builder. (Illus. above)

sprayed mineral insulation Insulating materials put on with a *spray gun* usually over metal pipes or steel or aluminium structures to reduce their heat transfer or noisiness or to improve their *fire protection*. Expanded *vermiculite* or fibres made from *blastfurnace slag* or rock such as kaolin may be used. Since 1975 these have superseded sprayed *asbestos*.

spray gun, s. pistol, paint s., air brush, etc. Painting with spray equipment is very much faster and easier than brush or roller work provided that the areas to be painted are large and continuous, such as the walls and ceiling of a room. Three methods are used on building sites, the most convenient for small jobs being compressed-air sprays, with a small compressor, driven usually by an electric motor. Airless sprays, however, have no compressor and work with a very high-pressure pump that forces the paint to the spray gun, with the advantage that, as the 'spray mist' produced is less than from 'air guns', the painter does not breathe the spray and there is less wasted paint. Air-assisted airless sprays have a pump working at a lower, safer pressure, as well as a little air at low pressure, allowing as much ease of control as the air spray, but without its spray mist. Some spray guns eject *metal coating* or cement mortar or plaster. *Lacquer* can be put on only by spraying. *Lead paints* are not allowed to be sprayed in the UK, and priming by spraying is not advisable. Brushing gives better penetration. *See* **atomization, gunite** (*C*).

spray painter A craftsman who sprays paint through a *spray gun*, which may be worked by electric motor, or an extension from a vacuum cleaner.

spreading rate [pai.] The surface area covered by unit volume of glue or paint (or unit weight of paste paint). 'Covering power' is ambiguous.

sprig [joi.] A small *nail* with no head, such as a *glazing sprig.*

sprig bit [joi.] A *bradawl.*

320

spring (1) **edge bend** (USA **crook**) [tim.] A variety of *warp* which consists in the curving of a board in a plane parallel to its face.

(2) [plu.] *See* **bending spring**.

springer, springing The first stone laid in an arch. It is bedded on the *springing line* and its upper surface is called the *skewback*.

spring-head roofing nail A galvanized drive screw for fixing *profiled sheet*.

springing line The horizontal line in an arch joining the *springings*.

springings The intersections at each side of an arch between its lower surface (*intrados*) and the faces of the walls or piers which carry it.

spring snib [joi.] A sash fastener which is spring controlled.

springwood, earlywood [tim.] That part of the *annual ring* which is formed in spring and is usually paler, less dense, and weaker than *summerwood*.

sprinkler system A *fire-extinguishing* system consisting of pipes installed near ceiling level. Branches from the pipe project downwards 3·3 m (10 ft) apart. The lower end of the branch is sealed with a *fusible plug* (C) which melts at 68° C. (155° F.), so that water is released from the sprinkler when the air temperature reaches 68° C. The principle of the drencher system is similar. The modern tendency is to replace the metal plug by a plastics plug containing liquid which expands and bursts at a temperature which can be predicted within 5° C. Sprinklers may be 'wet' or 'dry' or 'alternate-wet-and-dry'. The dry sprinkler is fitted with upward-turned sprays, its pipes being laid to a fall of about 1 in 200 and filled with air at a pressure of about 275 kN/m^2 (40 psi). This system is used in Russia, Canada, and other countries with hard winters, since the water is admitted to the pipes only when the air is released from them. The wet sprinkler is permanently filled with water, and operates more quickly when there is a fire, but is not proof against frost. The alternate-wet-and-dry sprinkler can be water-filled in warm weather and air-filled in frosty weather. It is used in temperate countries with occasional frost. The best sprinkler installation requires two independent water supplies, of which at least one is a public main or large reservoir, and the highest spray must deliver water under a pressure of 15 m (50 ft) of water or 173 kN/m^2 (25 psi). Sprinkler installations in the UK conform to the Fire Offices Committee's publication: 'Rules for automatic sprinkler installations'. *See* **emulsifier system**.

sprocket A *cocking piece*.

sprocketed eaves *Eaves* given an outward tilt by *sprockets*.

spruce [tim.] Many species of picea, softwoods which are exported from North America and are very light, weighing only 432 kg/m^3 (27 lb/ft^3) at 12% *moisture content. See* **Canadian spruce, Sitka spruce**.

spud [joi.] A *dowel* in the foot of a door post to fix it to the floor.

spur (1) [elec.] A *socket outlet* from a single cable branching off a *ring main*.

(2) A short concrete post set in the ground to carry a wooden post above ground. The wood thus lasts many years longer than when sunk in the earth.

square [carp.], **try s.** An L-shaped metal or metal-and-wood tool for setting out right-angles. *See* **mason's and bricklayer's tools, steel s., combination s.**

square chisel [joi.] *See* **mortising machine**.

squared log [tim.] (1) A *baulk*.

(2) A *half-timber*, that is, a baulk sawn down the middle, at least 13 × 25 cm (5 × 10 in.) in cross section.

squared rubble *Rubble walls* made with stones of varying size which are squared and not snecked. It is usually *coursed* at every third or fourth stone and may be built almost as carefully and with as thin joints as *ashlar*.

square-edged timber Timber without *wane*, and not *tongued-and-grooved*.

square joint [carp.] A *butt joint*.

square-sawn timber Timber sawn to a rectangular cross section, with or without *wane* (BS 565). *See* **square-edged timber**.

square-turned baluster or **newel** [joi.] A *baluster* or *newel* post with *mouldings* cut on four faces by any method except *turning*.

squaring, s. up, working up [q.s.] Calculating areas, a process which follows *taking off* from drawings or measuring up work.

squeeze [pla.] To take a squeeze of a *moulding* is to press wet plaster over it and thus to take a cast from which a *template* can be cut.

squint quoin A projecting corner of a building which is not a right angle.

squirrel-tail pipe jointer [plu.] A *pipe-jointing clip*.

stability The resistance of a structure to sliding, overturning, or collapsing. *See* C.

stable door (USA **Dutch d.**) [joi.] A door cut through horizontally at about half its height, with each half separately hung.

stack In a building, usually a vertical conduit for fluid, whether a *chimney stack*, a rainwater *downpipe* or a *soil stack*.

stack effect Because the air inside a building is warmer than the outside air, it is buoyant and tends to rise within the building or up a chimney. This can encourage a fire or help to start one. *See* **convection**.

staff *See* **angle staff**.

staff bead (1) [pla.] A moulded external angle normally run in *Keene's* plaster (BS 4049).

   (2) [joi.] *Sash stop*.

Staffordshire blues An extremely hard and dense, deep-blue *brick* which can be obtained *wirecut* or *pressed*. With its remarkably high crushing strength of 110 N/mm^2 (16 000 psi) it is one of the best *engineering bricks* in Britain.

stagger To arrange rivets, bolts, or other fixings alternately so that, for example, rivets do not come opposite other rivets in the next row. *See* **staggering**.

staggered courses *Courses* of *shingles* laid with their butts not in one horizontal line.

staggered-stud partition [carp.] A *partition* formed of two separate rows of vertical timbers (*studs*) each being surfaced by its own *covering* – a type of *discontinuous construction* to reduce noise.

staggering An arrangement of joints or supports spread to give uniform strength. For instance, in *flexible-metal roofing*, *cross welts* are staggered so that they intersect only one *standing seam* at a time.

staging A *mason's scaffold*.

stain (1) [tim.] *See* **blue stain**.

   (2) [pai.] A solution or suspension of dye or other colouring matter in a *vehicle* designed to *colour* a surface by penetrating rather than hiding it. True stains are *water*, oil, or *spirit stains*, according to the vehicle. *Varnish* stains are not true stains, since they do not penetrate the surface but merely leave a coloured coating on it.

stained-glass windows Windows of glass which is coloured by firing.

stainers, tinters [pai.] Coloured *pigments*, ground in a paint *vehicle*, which can be added in small amounts to ready-mixed *paints* to modify their colour. Stainers have intense *staining power* but are not always very opaque.

staining power [pai.] The amount of colour given to a *white pigment* by a certain amount of coloured pigment. It corresponds to the *reducing power* of a white pigment.

stainless steel An *alloy steel* (*C*) with varying amounts of alloying metals, but often with chromium and nickel, commonly 18 per cent Cr and 8 per cent Ni. It resists corrosion well, and so, when polished, is used for shop fronts, door furniture, etc., but it is not invariably stain-free. Water-supply or heating tube made of it is compatible with fittings made for copper tube, but it is stiffer than copper and more difficult to bend. To obtain a good finish, the polished, more expensive grade of tube must be used.

stair, stairs [joi.] A series of steps with or without landings, including necessary *handrails* and *balustrades*, and giving access from floor to floor (BS 565). Minimum recommended dimensions of house stairs are 90 cm (3 ft) overall width, 24 cm (9¼ in.) *treads*, and 21·5 cm (8½ in.) *going*. In a straight flight, twice the rise plus the going should not add up to more than 70 cm (27½ in.) nor to less than 55 cm (21⅝ in.). Stairs may be *bracketed, dog-legged, double-return, geometric* or straight flights, among others. *See also* **flier, nosing, winder.**

staircase Originally the space within which a stair was built, this word has now come to mean *stair.*

stair clearance, headroom, headway BS 5395 (Stairs code) states that the minimum ceiling clearance measured from the *nosing line* at right angles to it should be 1·5 m (5 ft) while the vertical headroom from the treads should not be less than 2 m (6 ft 6 in.). These are absolute minima because a tall man hurrying downstairs will hit a ceiling at only 1·5 m clearance.

stairhead The top of a *stair.*

stair horse [carp.] A *carriage.*

stairway A *staircase.*

stake [carp.] A timber pointed at one end for driving into the ground.

stallboard [joi.] A strong *sill* and its framing beneath a shop window over the *stall riser.*

stallboard light [joi.] A *pavement light* near a stallboard.

stall riser [joi.] The vertical surface of polished granite, armour *plate glass, tile,* wood, marble, etc. from the pavement up to the *stallboard.*

standard (1) **scaffold pole** An upright of a *scaffold.*

(2) *See* **British Standard** *and below.*

standardization Agreement between producer and consumer under the authority (in Britain) of the *British Standards Institution* on certain tests, dimensions, tolerances, and qualities of a certain product for certain purposes. When agreement is reached it is published as a *British Standard.* Building, after coinage, was probably the first subject to be standardized and building standards have been used ever since systematic building began. They are mentioned even in the Code of Hammurabi (2050 BC) (sunbaked bricks). Standard sizes make building cheaper and planning for building easier since makers can plan for and make fewer sizes.

standard knot [tim.] (USA) A knot of 1½ in. (3·8 cm) dia. or less.

Standard Method of Measurement, SMM6 [q.s.] The method of measuring builders' work, approved by the Royal Institution of Chartered Surveyors and the National Federation of Building Trade Employers, and published by them in a book of that title (6th edition, 1979). *See* **measurement**.

standard special A piece made to standard dimensions and quality, such as a *bullnosed* coping *brick* or a *bend* of pipe, which is always stocked but not sent with an order for bricks or drains unless ordered. *See* **special**.

standard specification *See* **British Standard**.

Standard wire gauge (SWG), imperial SWG An old established way of specifying the thickness of steel saws, sheet, wire, tube, cut nails and some non-ferrous metals such as copper. The Birmingham gauge (BG), used for sheet steel, generally differs from the same number of the SWG by less than 20 per cent. There are many other British and American 'gauges' for sheet metal and wire, including the Birmingham wire gauge which is not the same as the Birmingham gauge.

standing ladder A *ladder* with rectangular *stiles*, as opposed to a *builder's ladder*. An *extending ladder* is built of two or more standing ladders.

standing leaf [joi.] A leaf of a *folding door* which is bolted in a closed position, as opposed to the *opening leaf*.

standing seam, stand-up welt [plu.] A *seam* in *flexible-metal roofing*, usually running from ridge to eaves, which stands vertically – no disadvantage since the water flows down parallel to it. The two ends of the sheets to be joined are bent up respectively 4 cm and 3 cm (1·6 and 1·3 in.). A 4 cm high *tingle* is bent up with them, and nailed to the roof boarding with copper nails under one of the sheets. The tingle and the two ends are together folded through 360° forming a final upstand about 18 mm (¾ in.) high. The tingles measure about 8 × 2 cm (3 × 1 in.) and are placed every 30 cm (12 in.) to hold the

SWG diameters in millimetres and inches

SWG	(mm)	(in.)	SWG	(mm)	(in.)	SWG	(mm)	(in.)
7/0	12·700	0·500	13	2·337	0·092	32	0·274	0·01
6/0	11·786	0·464	14	2·032	0·080	33	0·254	0·01
5/0	10·973	0·432	15	1·829	0·072	34	0·234	0·00
4/0	10·160	0·400	16	1·626	0·064	35	0·213	0·00
3/0	9·449	0·372	17	1·422	0·056	36	0·193	0·00
2/0	8·839	0·348	18	1·219	0·048	37	0·173	0·00
1/0	8·230	0·324	19	1·016	0·040	38	0·152	0·00
1	7·620	0·300	20	0·914	0·036	39	0·132	0·00
2	7·010	0·276	21	0·813	0·032	40	0·122	0·00
3	6·401	0·252	22	0·711	0·028	41	0·112	0·00
4	5·893	0·232	23	0·610	0·024	42	0·102	0·00
5	5·385	0·212	24	0·559	0·022	43	0·091	0·00
6	4·877	0·192	25	0·508	0·020	44	0·081	0·00
7	4·470	0·176	26	0·457	0·018	45	0·071	0·00
8	4·064	0·160	27	0·417	0·0164	46	0·061	0·00
9	3·658	0·144	28	0·376	0·0148	47	0·051	0·00
10	3·251	0·128	29	0·345	0·0136	48	0·041	0·00
11	2·946	0·116	30	0·315	0·0124	49	0·031	0·00
12	2·642	0·104	31	0·295	0·0116	50	0·025	0·00

(With grateful acknowledgement to *Specification*)

sheets in place. Standing seams are not used on surfaces where people must walk.

standing timber Growing trees. Their volume in timber is estimated by a *cruiser*.

stand oil [pai.] *Drying oil*, such as *linseed* or *tung oil*, which has been *polymerized* by heat treatment. It is so called because it was originally made by standing it in the sun for a time.

stand sheet A *dead light*.

staple (1) A metal loop for padlocking a door or gate. *See* **hasp and staple**.
(2) A U-shaped nail with two points.

stapling machines *Hardboard* or other *fibre board* can be fixed firmly to wooden studs by stapling machines with less labour and less damage to the board than by hammering, and for difficult fixing (overhead) this can be much easier. Staples with diverging points should be used. Machines fix hardboard four times as fast as hand hammering.

star drill (USA) A star-shaped *plugging chisel*.

star shake [tim.] Several *heartshakes* (BS 565).

starved [pai.] *Hungry*.

stat Abbreviation for *thermostat*.

station roof, umbrella r. A roof carried on a single row of stanchions. It is therefore *cantilevered* (*C*) to one or both sides.

statutory undertaker A UK organization with a duty laid down by law to provide a service to the general public or to a section of it such as shipping interests, e.g. British Rail, electricity boards, gas boards, passenger transport authorities such as London Transport, water authorities and dock, harbour or inland navigation boards. Until 1973 all were immune from noise legislation and could be as noisy as was convenient to them but in that year they lost this immunity.

stave [carp.] A *rung* of a *ladder*.

stay bar (1) A horizontal bar which strengthens a *mullion* or a leaded light.
(2) A bar which holds together the two opposite walls of a building and prevents them falling apart.
(3) A *casement stay*.

stay log [tim.] A large timber fitted to a *veneer* lathe. It is used as a base on to which *flitches* are screwed when *half-round veneer* is cut from them.

steam-brush cleaner A *skilled man* who cleans the outside stone or brick faces of buildings with a steam jet and wire brush.

steam-stripping appliance [pai.] A portable boiler connected to a flat metal distributor which blows steam on to a wall, making it easy to strip *wallpaper* or *distemper*.

steel *See C*.

steel casement Usually the cheapest, most convenient window in the UK, sometimes fixed direct to a wall, but usually to a wooden or steel *sub-frame*. To enable them to receive *metal-casement putty*, galvanized steel *casements* must be de-greased, followed by a coat of a suitable *pre-treatment primer*.

steel core In *patent glazing* a specially shaped rolled steel bearer enclosed within a *lead sheath*.

steel lathing [pla.] Expanded-metal or steel-wire mesh used as *metal lathing*.

steel square, roofing s., framing s. [carp.] A *square*, graduated with data for calculating the length of rafters and the angles of the cuts they need to fit *wall plate* and *ridge*.

steeplejack A *tradesman* who repairs and builds steeples and other tall brickwork or *masonry*, including *lightning conductors, weathercocks*, clock faces, and *chimneys* whether of brick or steel. He usually erects his own staging and ladders and does any incidental carpentry, painting, gilding, roofing, steel erection, cutting, welding, or *grout* (C) injection.

steeplejack's mate A helper to the steeplejack. He works mainly on the erection of *ladders*, staging and tackle.

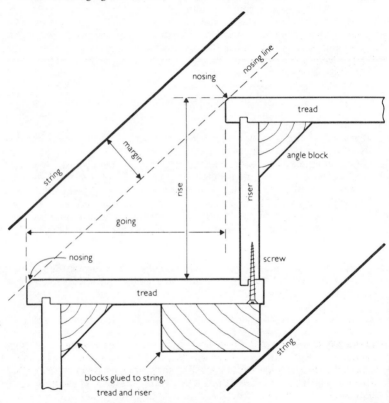

Step in a wooden stair, showing nosings.

step One unit of a *stair*, consisting of a *riser* and a *tread*. It may be a *flier* or *winder*. (Illus. above)

step flashing A *stepped flashing*.

step joint [carp.] A joint between *rafter* and *tie-beam* in which the tie-beam is notched with a *birdsmouth* to receive the end of the rafter p. 327. To reduce the depth of the cut a *double step* may be used.

step ladder A wooden *ladder* built with rectangular *stiles* and *treads* (not *rungs*) which are designed to be horizontal in use. *See* **steps**.

Stepped flashing prepared by plumber and ready for building into the brickwork above roof level. The height between steps is equal to the height of a brick course. The length of the steps varies with the roof slope.

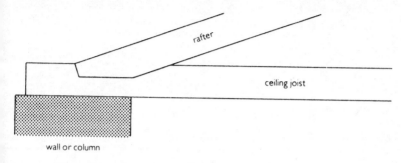

wall or column

Step joint.

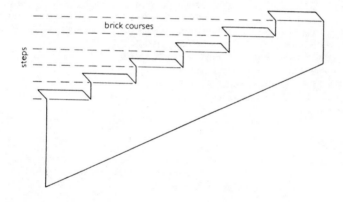

stepped flashing [plu.] A *flexible-metal* or roofing-felt *cover flashing* let into the joints of brickwork to make a weathertight joint between a wall (often a chimney) and the sloping part of a roof. The flashing steps down occasionally, from one mortar joint to the next, so that the vertical part of the flashing is kept to about 8 cm (3 in.) height and the metal is not wasted. (Illus.) *See* **raking flashing, upstand**.

stepped skirting An asphalt *skirting* at an inclined intersection with a roof.

steps, pair of steps A *step ladder* with a framed stay hinged to the top so as to make it self-supporting.

step turner [plu.] A hardwood tool for shaping *stepped flashings*. It has a sawcut 6 mm (¼ in.) wide in one edge. The flashing is inserted into this and it is then turned through 90° so that the flashing is correctly shaped for insertion into the bed joint of the brickwork. (Illus. p. 328)

stick-and-rag work [pla.] *Fibrous plaster*.

sticker [tim.] A small separator laid with others of uniform thickness between

Step turner made of a piece of hardwood about 30 cm (1 ft) long, with a slot 25 mm (1 in.) deep and 6 mm ($\frac{1}{4}$ in.) wide.

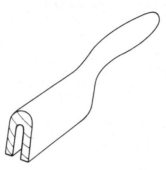

sheets of freshly cut wood to encourage the circulation of air and the drying of the wood.

sticker machine [joi.] A machine for cutting *mouldings* out of the *solid*.

sticking [joi.] The shaping of a moulding with a *plane* or a *sticker machine*.

sticking board [joi.] A framed board in which small pieces are held steady while they are being moulded with a *plane* (or stuck).

stile [carp.] An upright end-framing member *mortised* to enclose a *ladder* rung or a *tenon* of a *rail*. Compare **muntin**.

Stillson [plu.] *A pipe wrench. See* **plumber's tools** (illus. p. 250).

stipple [pai.] (1) To dab paint with a *stippler* immediately after a coat is put on.

(2) To break up the colour of a coat with spots of a different colour, or to break up its texture with a bristle or rubber *stippler*.

stippler, stippling brush [pai.] A brush or other tool for breaking up the texture of a wet coat, or to remove brush marks and to give the surface a uniform, slightly granulated finish. Sometimes it is a large brush whose stock, apart from the handle, resembles a short plank of about 170 × 140 mm (7 × 5 in.)

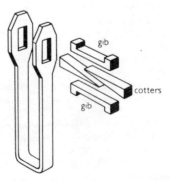

Stirrup strap for a cottered joint.

into which is set an area of soft bristle some 60 mm (2·5 in.) long. Other stipplers are of rubber.

stirrup strap, stirrup, hanger (USA **bridle iron**) [carp.] A steel strap built into brickwork or fixed to a post or beam and holding a horizontal member up to it. One example is the steel strap which holds the tie beam up to the king post in a *cottered joint*. (Illus. p. 328)

stock (1) [tim.] *Converted timber*, also called stuff.

(2) [carp.] The wooden part of a *plane*, the body or handle of a tool.

(3) [pla.] The wooden backing to the zinc profiles made for running a moulding with a *horsed mould*. It is firmly housed into the horse and braced with short wooden stays used as handles.

(4) [plu.] A tool which holds a *die* for cutting an external thread.

stock brick The *brick* which is most commonly available in any district is the stock brick of the district. The former London stock brick (a yellow Kentish brick which blackens with age in towns) has become so well known that it is now generally referred to in the south of England as a stock brick, or stock, but is no longer the commonest London brick. *See* **Fletton**.

stock brush [pla.] A *brush* used for wetting a wall before plastering, to prevent it absorbing too much water from the plaster.

stock lumber [tim.] (USA) Wood sawn·to market sizes.

stone (1) A walling material; either cut natural rock such as sandstone, limestone, and granite, or *cast stone* (BS 2847).

(2) [joi.] A carborundum or other natural or artificial *hone* for putting a cutting edge on to a *chisel, plane iron*, etc.

stone boat (USA) A wooden or sheet steel tray, preferably mounted on sledge runners, used for hauling stone short distances over a *skid road* or similar track.

stone dresser, s. cutter, scabbler, squarer, block chopper A man who roughly dresses stone blocks at the quarry.

stone-machine hand, s. sawyer, sawman, s. polisher, s. turner A *mason* who sets and operates stoneworking machines.

stone paint *See* **masonry paint**.

stone saw A long reciprocating blade, with no teeth, fed with water and an *abrasive* such as sand or carborundum, for cutting stone.

stone slate A *flagstone* for roofing. Stone slates are very heavy and therefore an expensive roofing material but some used in England are beautiful (Horsham, Collyweston, Cotswold).

stone surfacer A heavy *stone tool* for dressing large areas of stone.

stone tongs *Nippers*.

stone tool A percussive tool held in the hand for dressing or carving stone.

stoneware *Vitrified clayware*, etc.

stoning [tim.] With reference to a *circular saw*, running the saw and pressing an abrasive stone in a direction at right angles to the axis of the saw. It corresponds to the *topping* of a handsaw.

stooling, stool (1) The upper surface of the end of a concrete or stone *lug sill*. It is horizontal, to form a bed for the masonry over it.

(2) (USA) A *window board*.

stoothing [carp.] *Common grounds* for joinery, plaster *lathing*, etc.

stop (1) A *bench stop*.

(2) A decorative conclusion to a stuck moulding.

(3) A *door stop*.

stop bead [joi.] (USA) A *sash stop*.

stopcock [plu.] A cock that turns off the water or gas supply. Stopcocks for water allow flow in one direction only and prevent back-flow from the house and possible pollution of the mains thereby. If the stopcock is installed the wrong way round no water will flow through it. Consequently an arrow embossed on the metal shows the direction of flow. Stopcocks for gas do not have the non-return function. *See* **emergency water stop**.

stopped chamfer, stop c. [joi.] A *chamfer* which dies away, gradually merging into a sharp *arris*.

stopped mortise [joi.] A *blind mortise*.

stopper (1) [pai.] **stopping** *Filler* or *hard stopping*.

(2) [plu.] A device such as a *bag plug* or *screw plug* for blocking a drain during a *drain test*.

stopping knife, putty k. A *glazier*'s knife for smoothing putty, also used by painters for putting *hard stopping* into holes or cracks. It is like a *chisel knife* with one rounded edge and one splayed edge, meeting at a point. *See* **house painter's tools** (illus. p. 180).

stop valve [plu.] A valve for regulating flow, not a *stopcock* (BS 4118).

storage tank [plu.] *See* **cistern**.

storage water heater [plu.] An electrical or gas-fired appliance that heats water under thermostatic control and stores it until needed.

storey (USA **story**) The part of a building between one floor and the next above it. Thus the seventh storey is the part of the building from seventh floor level to eighth floor level. *See* **first floor**.

storey rod (USA **story pole**) A *batten* cut to the exact height of a *storey*, often having dimensions marked on it such as the levels of certain brick courses or of window *sill*, window *head*, and *stair* treads. *See* **going rod**.

storm cellar, cyclone c. A cellar in which the people of the house take shelter against the violent cyclones and tornados of central and southern USA.

storm clip A saddle-shaped metal clip, fixed outside a *glazing bar*, to hold the glass down in *patent glazing*.

storm door [joi.] (USA) An additional inner door, used in winter, to insulate a house from hard weather.

stormproof window [joi.] A wooden *casement window* with additional protection against rain, for example, hood mouldings, throatings and lips in the joints.

storm sheet An *asbestos-cement* roofing sheet which is curved down at one edge to protect an eave against rain.

storm window A *coupled window* or an *internal dormer*.

story (USA) *Storey*.

stoving (USA **baking**) [pai.] Drying by heat, generally above 65° C. (150°F.). In convection-oven stoving the heat reaches the painted surface largely by convection. In radiant-heat stoving or infra-red drying the heat reaches the painted surface mainly by radiation. *Compare* **forced drying**.

straddle pole A sloping *scaffold* pole laid along a roof in a *saddle scaffold* from a *standard* to meet the other straddle pole at the ridge.

straddle scaffold A *saddle scaffold*.

straight arch A *flat arch*.

straight courses *Shingles* laid with their *butts* in line like tiles or slates.

straight edge A straight, parallel piece of metal or seasoned wood, used by most of the building *trades* for *setting out*.

straight flight [joi.] A *stair* consisting of *fliers* only, with no *winders*.

straight grain *Grain* which is parallel with the length of the timber.

straight joint (1) [carp.] A *butt joint*.

(2) A vertical joint immediately above another one – a mistake in brick bonding.

straight-joint tiles *Single-lap tiles* made so that their edges in successive courses run in one line from *eaves* to *ridge*.

straight-line edger [tim.] A modern, mechanically-fed *circular saw* which straightens the edges of veneer and smooths them so well that they can be glued without further treatment.

straight-peen hammer [mech.] Any *hammer* which has, opposite the striking face of the hammerhead, a blunt wedge, parallel to the shaft of the hammer. *Compare* **ball peen, cross peen**.

straight tongue [joi.] One edge of a board made thinner by rebates each side of it so that the tongue so made can fit into a groove to match it. *See* **cross tongue, matchboard**.

straining beam [carp.] Any horizontal *strut* (*C*), particularly that between the heads of the *queen posts* in a *queen-post truss*.

straining piece, strutting p. [carp.] A horizontal timber dogged or bolted to the middle of a horizontal *flying shore* as an abutment from which the shorter, sloping *struts* (*C*) at each end of it obtain their thrust, *see* p. 268.

straining sill [carp.] A timber lying on and dogged to the *tie-beam* of a *queen-post truss* between the *queen posts* or between the queen and *princess posts* to keep them in place.

S-trap [plu.] A trap at a sink, basin, WC pan, etc., from which the outlet pipe has a vertically downward direction. (Illus.) *Compare* **P-trap**.

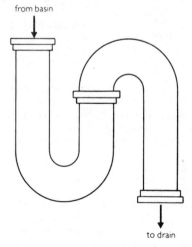

from basin

to drain

Copper S-trap. This two-piece type needs no cleaning eye as it can easily be dismantled and re-assembled.

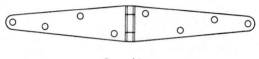

Strap hinge.

strap anchor [carp.] A steel plate joining two floor *joists* which butt at a support. It is fixed on those *joists* which are anchored to the walls with *wall anchors*. In this way the walls are given good lateral support by the floor joists.

strap bolt [carp.] A fastening for heavy timbers, consisting of a metal strap with holes drilled through it at one end and a threaded rod (bolt) at the other end.

strap hinge A *band-and-hook* hinge or *cross-garnet* hinge, or one formed of two metal *straps* (*C*) of equal length. (Illus. above)

strapped elbow [plu.] A *drop elbow*.

strapping *Common grounds* on a wall, used as a base for *lath* and plaster.

straw Straw is sometimes used for *thatch*, wheat or rye straw being the best. *Sedge* may be called sedge straw.

strawboard *Compressed straw slab*.

stress-graded timber [tim.] Converted timber which has been divided into various classes according to the *rate of growth* and the amount of *knots*, *shakes*, *slope of grain*, and *wane*. In practice 80% of good *softwood* can be stressed to 6·9 N/mm^2 (1000 psi) in bending. Stress grading was introduced because strength tests have always been done on *clear timber*, now a very scarce material. Therefore, to enable wooden structures to be economically designed, it became necessary for engineers to have some rational means of assessing the strength reduction due to any particular defect. Machine stress grading, testing timber in bending to measure its stiffness, is slightly more accurate than grading on the basis of visible *defects*. Timber that has been stress graded loses its grade if it is cut. *See* **gross features**.

stretch A surface of single-tier *patent glazing*. Its area is measured by the length overall the end bars times the depth, and expressed in m^2. The depth is the length of the *glazing bar*.

stretcher A brick or stone laid with its length parallel to the length of the wall. *Compare* **header**.

stretcher face The long face of a brick seen after it is laid.

stretching bond, stretcher b. Brickwork half a brick thick (about 10 cm (4 in.)) in which each brick is laid as a *stretcher*. This bond is also seen on the face of *cavity walls* 28 cm (11 in.) or 38 cm (15 in.) thick.

stretching course A course of *stretchers*.

striking off lines [pla.] Lines drawn on wall or ceiling for setting *fibrous plaster*.

striking plate, keeper, strike p., strike [joi.] A plate with a rectangular hole in it, screwed to the *mortise* in a door post. When the door closes, the *latch* of a *mortise lock* slides against it and holds the door shut by passing into the rectangular hole. *See* **box staple**.

striking wedges *Folding wedges*.

string (USA **stringer**) [joi.] A sloping board at each end of the treads housed or cut to carry the treads and risers of a stair. A string is either a *wall string* or an *outer string*, and either a *close string* or a *cut string*.

string course A decorative, usually projecting, thin horizontal course of brick or stone, often continuing the line of the window *sills* or *dripstones*. In modern construction its place is sometimes taken by the floor slab projecting and throwing water away from the walls.

stringer [joi.] (USA) A *string*.

stringing mortar (USA) Spreading enough mortar on the *bed joint* to lay several bricks.

string piece [carp.] The horizontal *tie-beam* of a *Belfast truss*.

strip [tim.] (1) Softwood under 50 × 100 mm, i.e. less than 2 × 4 in.

(2) *Hardwood* 50 × 50 mm to 50 × 140 mm, i.e. 2 × 2 to 2 × 5½ in. (BS 565).

(3) (USA) *Lumber* less than 2 × 8 in. (50 × 200 mm).

(4) [mech.] Copper, zinc or aluminium which is thicker than foil (0·15 mm or 0·006 in.), thinner than 9·5 mm (⅜ in.) and narrower than 45 cm (18 in.) *Compare* **sheet**.

(5) A description of lead sheet.

strip board [tim.] A term sometimes used for *blockboard* in which the core blocks are not glued to each other.

stripe figure [tim.] *Ribbon grain*.

strip flooring *Parquet strip*.

strip heating [tim.] Heating of wood by a bare metal strip carrying a heavy current at low voltage, when gluing with *synthetic resins*. *Compare* **radio-frequency heating**.

stripper A *skilled man* who dismantles moulds or *formwork* (C) for concrete. He may also clean them, oil them, and insert reinforcement.

stripping (1) Clearing a site of turf, brushwood, etc.

(2) [pai.] Removing old *paint*, *distemper*, etc., by a blow lamp, *stripping knife*, or other means. *See also* C.

stripping knife, broad k. [pai.] A knife with a stiff steel blade, widening from the base to a square edge from 2·5 to 10 cm (1 to 4 in.) wide (BS 6150). It is used for removing *wallpaper* and loose *distemper*. *See* **chisel knife, house painter's tools** (illus. p. 180).

strip soaker A *soaker* of *bitumen felt* or other waterproof sheet laid under each course of *shingles* at a *swept valley*.

strongback, lifting beam A beam designed to lift a unit such as a concrete pile, beam, column, etc, so as to reduce the stresses suffered by it during lifting. It is hung directly from the crane hook and itself has several attachments for crane *slings* (C) down to the unit to be lifted. Strongbacks are needed because concrete piles, for example, without one would receive the most severe stressing of their lives while being slung into position by crane. Usually each strongback is designed to lift a particular unit and its expense is justified by the assurance it gives that this will suffer no damage during lifting.

strong mortar *Mortar* made of ordinary or rapid-hardening *Portland cement* without *lime* gains strength quickly, has high shrinkage and may cause cracking in a wall, where a weaker, flexible mortar made with lime or *masonry cement* would not. The weaker mortar allows settlement during construction and acquires its strength later, after settlement is more or less complete, therefore without cracking. Strong mortar is normally used only below *damp course* where it shrinks less than above it. *See* **rendering coat**.

struck joint (1) A *weather struck joint*.

(2) A joint pressed in at the lower edge, sloping in the reverse direction

from a weather struck joint. Mainly for interior work, in which rain does not need to be thrown off.

structural A description of a part of a building which carries load in addition to its own weight, as opposed to *partitions, joinery, plaster*, etc. which carry only their own weight. In USA the term is used in a wide sense; *see below, also C.*

structural clay tile (USA) American term for what might generally be called in Britain non-structural burnt-clay *hollow blocks*. Many different sorts exist: side construction tile with cavities horizontal, end construction tile with cavities vertical, partition tile, facing tile, floor tile (hollow floor blocks), *furring* tile for lining the inner face of outside walls, header tile providing cavities in the backing blocks for *headers* from the *facing brickwork*, and so on.

structural gasket A glazing *gasket*, often of H-section like a lead *came*, first used in 1949 in USA.

structural glass (USA) Rectangular panels or tiles of glass, used for facing walls.

structural lumber [tim.] (USA) Sawn timber 5 × 10 cm (2 × 4 in.) or larger, usually *stress graded* and under calculated stress.

structural steelwork *Rolled-steel joists* (C) or built-up members fabricated as building frames, by riveting, welding, or bolting, or all three.

structure (1) The loadbearing part of a building.

(2) Anything built by man, from a *hydraulic-fill dam* (C) built of earth or a *pyramid* of stone to a hydro-electric power station. A structure is not necessarily roofed, a building is.

strutting (1) Using *struts* (C) as supports, for example, *dead shores*.

(2) [carp.] *Solid bridging* or *herring-bone strutting*.

strutting piece [carp.] (1) A *straining piece*.

(2) A piece of joist cut for *solid bridging*.

stub A *nib* of a *tile*.

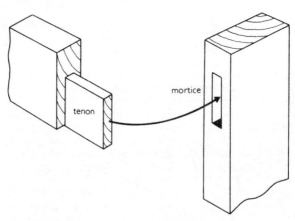

Stub tenon. The mortice is slightly deeper than the tenon.

334

stub tenon [carp.] A *tenon* which is inserted into a *blind mortise*. If it is wedged this must be done by *secret wedging*. (Illus. p. 334).

stuc Plasterwork made to look like stone.

stucco [pla.] *Rendering*, usually painted, on the outside of old buildings, originally of lime and sand, but from the 19th C. with cement. *See* **cement rendering, pebble dash, scraped finish.**

stuck moulding [joi.] A *moulding* cut out of the solid by a plane or *sticker machine*, the opposite of a *planted* moulding.

stud (1) **studding** [carp.] Intermediate vertical members in a framed partition (about 8 × 5 cm (3 × 2 in.)) or in *frame construction* (about 10 × 5 cm (4 × 2 in.)), usually placed about 45 cm (18 in.) from studs on each side. The end members (posts) are heavier. On a *partition* or the inner face of a building frame, *lathing* or *wallboards* are usually nailed to the studs. Timber close-boarding may be nailed to the outside of studs in a building frame to stiffen it.

(2) [mech.] A threaded rod, a *screw* (C) with no head; *see below.*

stud gun An explosive-operated gun which shoots hard steel, pointed studs of 6, 9·5 or 14 mm ($\frac{1}{4}$, $\frac{3}{8}$ or $\frac{9}{16}$ in.) dia. (male- or female-threaded) into concrete, brickwork, or mild steel. A strong hold is obtained in steel by 12 to 19 mm ($\frac{1}{2}$ to $\frac{3}{4}$ in.) penetration. A safety device prevents the gun firing except when it is pressed against a wall, and no licence is needed for it in Britain. Explosive-operated stud guns must not shoot studs into hard materials like cast iron, hard steel, glass or glazed bricks, nor into soft materials like lath and plaster, fibre board, or hollow clay blocks. To attempt this may result in shattering of the blocks and flying splinters of glass or the stud may pass right through. Operators should wear goggles. *See* illus. below. *Compare* **stud welding**.

stud shooting The driving of threaded studs with a *stud gun*.

stud welding Fixing a metal stud on to a steel frame by *resistance welding* (C) after the frame is built. Studs were used as a fixing for *joinery* in the UNO

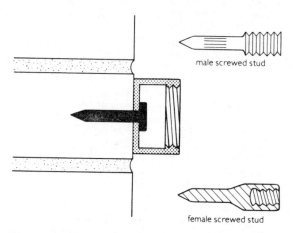

male screwed stud

female screwed stud

Rivet driven by an explosive-operated stud gun to hold an electrical junction box to brickwork.

building in New York. The welding is rapid, the stud being held in place with a sort of gun during welding. *Compare* **stud gun**.

stuff (1) [pla.] Plaster; *see* **rendering coat, finishing coat**.

(2) **stock** [joi.] *See* **square-sawn timber**.

stump foundation, brush block f. The usual foundation for the wooden bungalows built in Australia where wood is cheap. It consists of pits dug at 1 to 2 m (4 to 6 ft) spacing both ways, each pit containing a 10 × 10 cm (4 × 4 in.) 'stump' or round timber upright, resting on a 23 × 15 × 4 cm (9 × 6 × 1½ in.) sole plate on the ground. The wood must be proof against decay, termites, etc., since the pits are back filled.

stump veneer [tim.] *Veneer* from the butt of a tree. That from *walnut* butts is particularly prized for its fine *figure*. *See* **burr**.

sub-base, base (USA) A *skirting board*.

sub-basement The second *storey* below the ground, the storey below the *basement*.

sub-casing (USA) A *blind casing*.

sub-circuit [elec.] A *branch circuit*.

sub-contract A part of a *contract*, often specialist work such as asphalting, which is done by a separate firm from *the main contractor*. The main contractor is responsible for the work, pays the sub-contractor, and is paid by the *consultant* or *client* for it.

sub-contractor A specialist employed by a *main contractor* to perform a *sub-contract*. Sub-contractors must usually be approved by the *architect* before the contractor engages them.

sub-floor A wooden or concrete floor which carries load but is not seen, being covered by a finish of wooden blocks or other material. In USA it is called a blind floor, or if wooden a *rough floor*.

sub-frame A frame attached to the main building frame as a fixing for the *cladding* or for a door or window, often of *pressed steel*.

subletting A *main contractor* can sublet most of his *contract* to *sub-contractors*, but this sub-division of responsibility is usually allowed only with the architect's permission in writing.

subsidence, settlement Downward movement of the ground surface. *See also C.*

sub-sill [joi.] BS 1422 describes pressed steel sub-sills that cover the full width of the wall plus a projection to throw off the water. They fit the pressed steel sub-frame of the window. To resist corrosion they are either galvanized or *sherardized* or sprayed with zinc or aluminium.

sub-station [elec.] A room or building containing electrical equipment such as switches, usually with transformers to reduce high-voltage incoming power to a *voltage* at which the consumer can conveniently use it. It may be provided by the electricity authority or by the consumer.

substrate [pai.] A *ground*.

subway (1) A passage below ground for people to walk through, sometimes (under a building) containing cables and other building services, and mainly provided for their maintenance.

(2) (USA) An underground railway.

suction (1) [pla.] The adhesion of wet mortar or plaster to a surface. Low-*absorption* backgrounds have low adhesion (glazed tiles, engineering bricks, etc.) but there is good adhesion and high suction with most *common bricks*. See **bonding treatment**.

(2) [pai.] Excessive absorption from a paint can be reduced by a *sealer*.

Suffolk latch A *thumb latch*.

suite Of rooms, a set of interconnected rooms. Of locks, a set of locks each of which can be opened by a master key as well as by its own key.

sullage [plu.] Dirty water from basin, bath or kitchen but not from WCs.

sulphate expansion of brickwork Soluble sulphates, present in most bricks, react chemically with the tricalcium aluminate in the *ordinary Portland cement* in mortar to cause an irreversible vertical expansion of up to 0·2% in facing brickwork and as much as 2% in rendered work. Though the horizontal expansion is less because there are fewer mortar joints in this direction, it may be more obvious. Sulphate attack is not usually noticeable before two years after completion and can thus be distinguished from *moisture expansion*, most of which occurs quickly. The effect of sulphate attack on mortar can be reduced by generous detailing of *copings* and *damp courses* to keep the brickwork dry, by building with rich mixes with *mortar plasticizer* instead of *lime*, and by using *sulphate-resisting cement* (C) instead of ordinary Portland. If the sulphate attack is severe the mortar joints disintegrate. The usual first indication is horizontal cracks on internal plaster (B R E Digest 89).

sulphate of lime [pla.] *Gypsum*, anhydrite, calcium *hemihydrate*, etc.

summerwood, latewood [tim.] The denser, darker wood formed in summer. *Compare* **springwood**.

sump pump A pump of small capacity for occasionally emptying a *sump* (C) in a part of a building which is below the level of the drains.

sunk draft A *drafted margin*.

sunken joint [tim.] A defect in veneering, small depressions in the surface of *veneer* above joints in *coreboard* or *cross bands*, caused by gluing faults or variation in thickness of the cross bands.

sunk face An *ashlar* face which is cut below the margins of the stone.

sunk gutter A *secret gutter*, sunk below the roof surface.

super [q.s.] Abbreviation for superficial, and thus for 'area'.

superficial measure [tim.] *Face measure*.

super hardboard The most dense and water-resistant *hardboard*. It is used as a lining to *formwork* (C), as a floor finish, for boat building, and so on.

supply pipe The consumer's part of the *service pipe*, usually the length between the building and its boundary or the stop valve, whichever is nearer to the main. *Compare* **communication pipe**. (Illus p. 78)

surbase [joi.] (1) A *dado capping*.

(2) (USA) A *moulding* which crowns a *skirting board*.

surcharged drain [plu.] A drain that is filled to its crown, consequently under a pressure that is higher than atmospheric. If the surcharging increases until the sewage level reaches the tops of the manholes, their covers may be lifted off and sewage will flow into the streets.

surface coefficient The heat loss per degree of temperature difference between a surface and the air or other fluid surrounding it, per unit area and unit time. Its reciprocal is the surface resistance. The surface coefficient makes the difference between *U-valve* and *conductance*, thus:

conductance × surface coefficient = U-value.

surface damp course, s. damp-proof membrane A *damp course* designed for walking on, such as *asphalt, pitch mastic, epoxy, bitumen*, etc. Some of these must be laid hot on concrete that has had ample time to dry out.

surface dry [pai.] A stage in *drying* when a paint is dry on the surface but wet beneath.

surfaced timber, dressed t., wrot t. [joi.] Timber planed on one or more surfaces.

surface filler [pai.] A *filler*.

surface hardener *See* **hardener**.

surface measure [tim.] *Face measure*.

surface of operation A plane surface on a stone prepared as a datum from which to work the rest of the stone.

surface planer, surfacer [tim.] A steel bed plate with its upper surface in two halves at different, adjustable levels, but parallel and carefully ground plane. Between the two halves the adzing *cutter block* rotates, so that its blades project above one half and are level with the other half. *See* **thicknessing machine**.

surface preparation [pai.] For wood, plaster, etc., preparation may consist only of *stopping* and light sanding after *priming*. For iron and steel it is much more laborious, beginning with the removal of scale by *blast cleaning*, followed immediately by a *pre-treatment primer*. Non-ferrous metals may need both *de-greasing* and a pre-treatment primer after it.

surfacer (1) [tim.] A *surface planer*.

(2) [pai.] A thin, pigmented *filler*, or *sealer*, or both, for smoothing slightly uneven surfaces before painting. It is usually sanded smooth after drying. *See* **sanding sealer, guide coat**.

(3) A *dunter* machine.

surface resistance The reciprocal of the *surface coefficient*.

surface retardant [pla.] A liquid put on to *formwork* (C) to make it easier to strip, and to give the concrete good bonding properties for later plastering. The surface concrete drops away or can be brushed off, leaving a rough surface on which plaster will stick.

surface spread of flame *See* **flame spread**.

surface water drain Any pipe for rainwater in the ground or elsewhere. *See* **field drain** (C).

surface waterproofer *See* **water-repellent treatment**.

surfacing materials For wall *coverings see* **wallboards**; for floor surfacings, *see* **flooring tiles, jointless floors**.

surround Material placed around something to protect or decorate it, e.g. the concrete round a drain, the bricks round a fireplace, the frame around glass.

surveyor A *building surveyor, quantity surveyor*, planning and development surveyor, land surveyor, minerals surveyor, etc.

suspended ceiling *See* **false ceiling**.

suspended floor Any floor which is supported only at its ends.

suspended scaffold A *cradle* or a *projecting scaffold*. *See* B S C P 97.

suspension [pai.] (1) Small particles of solid, distributed through a liquid. Most paints are suspensions of this sort.

(2) An *emulsion* (C). One liquid carries another liquid suspended within it in small separate drops. *See* **emulsion paint**.

Sussex garden-wall bond *Flemish garden-wall bond*.

swage [mech.] A smith's tool for shaping hot or cold metal, particularly rivet heads. Swages are made in pairs, one male and one female, of which one acts as the hammer and the other, the swaging block (usually hollow), as the anvil. *See below.*

swage-setting [tim.] A method of *setting* circular saws for ripping (not for cross cutting). Such saws are often very thin, e.g. 1 mm (0·040 in.). No sideways set is given, but the point of each tooth is spread by a hammer in such a way that it looks fishtailed. The point is symmetrical; each side projects an equal amount beyond the blade. An average set is 0·25 mm (0·01 in.) each side, so that the swage-set saw makes a cut of about 1·5 mm (0·06 in.) thickness. Swage-set saws take a faster feed than other saws. More even than other saw setting, swage-setting is highly skilled.

swan-neck (1) An S-bend, particularly a junction between a *downpipe* and an *eaves gutter* under overhanging eaves. *See* **offset.**

(2) A combination of *ramp* and knee in a handrail.

swan-neck chisel [carp.] A strong *socket chisel* curved so as to extract the chippings of a *mortise*. *Compare* **corner chisel.**

swatch [tim.] A pile of samples of *veneers*, each sheet being taken from the centre of its *flitch*. The term is also used for a pile of samples of *linoleum* hinged into book shape.

sway A 2 cm (¾ in.) dia. hazel or willow sapling 2·7 m (9 ft) long used for holding *thatch* down. It is laid horizontally across the *rafters* under the thatch and fixed to them by iron hooks or tarred cord.

sweat [plu.] To unite metal parts by holding them together while molten solder flows between them. *See* **capillary joint.**

sweating (1) [plu.] *See* **sweat.**

(2) [pai.] The defect of separation of the liquids in a paint; one of them appears at the surface of the film.

(3) [pai.] A *gloss* developing in a dry paint or varnish film after *standing*.

(4) *See* **condensation.**

sweat out [pla.] Plaster which, after it has set, appears damp and mushy. It may be caused by cold weather, by imperviousness of the backing brick, or by dirty sand which needs an excessive amount of mixing water.

sweep tee [plu.] A *tee* for copper or screwed pipe, in which the branch is not, as in the normal tee, sharply perpendicular to the run, but curves gently away from it.

swept valley A *valley* formed of *shingles*, *slates* or *plain tiles*, cut or made to a taper so as to eliminate the need for a *flexible-metal* gutter. *Tile-and-a-half* tiles are cut to make their *tails* narrower than their heads. The laborious cutting is compensated by a fine appearance. *Compare* **laced valley**, *see* **strip soaker, valley tile**, B S ⁴ , 534.

S W G [mech.] *Standard wire gauge.*

swing door [joi.] A door which can open in both directions and therefore has no *stop* in the frame. It may be hinged on a *floor spring* or a *helical hinge*, or be a *revolving door*.

swinging post The *hanging post* of a gate.

swirl [tim.] The irregular *grain* round knots or *crotches*.

switch and fuse [elec.] A switch usually built into a cast-iron fitting containing *fuses*. The fuses are not built into the switch.

switchboard [elec.] Any group of switches which is hand-operated and with or without instruments.

switch fuse [elec.] A switch containing a *fuse*.

synthetic paint A vague term which sometimes means paints containing *synthetic resin* in the *medium*.

synthetic resin *Urea-* and *melamine-* and *phenol-formaldehyde* glues and casting *resins* (and other synthetic resins) have been in commercial use since the 1930s. They are immune from attack by moulds or bacteria and are all highly water resistant. Although more expensive they are replacing the older *glues* for exterior work in *plywood* for aircraft, houses, or bridges. *See* **accelerator, alkyd, epoxide, film glue, glassfibre, plastics, separate application,** *also* B S 1755.

synthetic-resin-bonded paper sheet *See* **laminated plastics.**

synthetic-resin cement [tim.] (1) A *synthetic resin* used as a *glue*.

(2) The synthetic resin without its *accelerator*.

(3) *See* **Perspex.**

synthetic stone (Scotland) *Cast stone*.

system building *Industrialized building methods*.

T

tack (1) A sharp, short nail for fixing *linoleum*.

(2) *See* **tingle**.

(3) [pai.] Stickiness of a paint film which is *drying*.

tack rag [pai.] Cheese cloth or other cotton fabric damped with slow-drying varnish to remove dust from a surface after *rubbing* down and before putting on the next coat. Tack rags should be kept in an airtight tin so that they do not harden.

tacky [pai.] Sticky, a stage in *drying*.

taft joint [plu.] A joint between two lead pipes made by conically reducing the end of one, enlarging the end of the other, and filling the gap between with *plumber's solder*, smoothing it with a *wiping cloth*. It is smaller, therefore uses less solder than the *wiped joint* (BS 4118).

tag A strip of copper folded in several thicknesses and used as a wedge for holding copper sheet into a masonry joint. *See* **lead wedge**.

tail (1) The lower edge of a *slate* or *tile*. *Compare* **head**.

(2) The built-in end of a stone step. *See* **tailing in**.

tailing in, t. down Fixing the end of a member which is cantilevered from a wall by laying stones or bricks or any heavy weight on it.

tailing iron A steel section built into a wall to hold down the end of a member which is *cantilevered* (C) out below it.

tailpiece [carp.] (USA) A *trimmed joist*.

tail trimmer [carp.] A *trimmer joist* close to, and parallel to, a wall on which it is undesirable to carry the floor *joists*.

taker-off [q.s.] An experienced *quantity surveyor* who specializes in reading drawings, taking dimensions from them, and writing them on *dimensions paper*. *See* **taking off**.

taking off [q.s.] Taking off quantities is the first step in working out *quantities* from a drawing when compiling a *bill of quantities*. It involves writing down the dimensions of each *item* systematically on sheets of *dimensions paper* so that the next operation (squaring up or working up) can be done without misunderstanding by someone else. *See* **dotting on, measurement, timesing column**.

takspan Swedish pine roof *shingles* 43–51 cm (17–20 in.) long, 10–25 cm (4–10 in.) wide, 3 mm ($\frac{1}{8}$ in.) thick, made like *sliced veneer*.

tall boy A hood about 1·5 m (5 ft) high, made of steel sheet 0·56 mm ($\frac{1}{64}$ in.) thick or more, galvanized after it is made, fixed over a chimney to prevent downdraughts.

tally slates *Slates* sold by number, not by weight. *Compare* **ton slates**.

talus wall A wall to hold back an earth slope, therefore built at a *batter*.

tamarack [tim.] (USA) *Larch*.

tambour (1) A circular wall carrying a dome.

(2) **vestibule** A ceiled, circular, wooden lobby enclosing *revolving doors* to prevent draughts through them.

(3) Any drum shape such as a stone in a circular column.

tampin, turning pin [plu.] *See* **boxwood tampin**.

tang The pointed part of a steel tool such as a file, knife-blade, or *chisel* which is driven into the wooden handle. (In the *socket chisel* the handle is simultaneously driven into the socket.)

tangential shrinkage [tim.] The *shrinkage* of timber parallel to the *growth rings*. *See* **flat-sawn** (illus. p. 140).

tank [plu.] *See* **cistern**.

tanking A waterproof skin, usually of 19 mm (¾ in.) asphalt laid beneath a *basement* floor and up the basement walls. The wall skin is protected outside by a half-brick (or thicker) wall from stones which might pierce it during *back filling*. On the inner face it is in contact with the basement *retaining wall* (*C*). The floor skin is also laid between two slabs, the upper being the *loading coat*. *See* **damp course, watertight basements**.

tap [plu.] A screwed plug, accurately threaded, made of hard steel and used for cutting internal *threads*. *Compare* **die**.

tape [tim.] *See* **joint tape**.

tapeless splicer, t. jointer [tim.] A machine for gluing sheets of *veneer* together at their edges without *joint tape*.

tapered-edge plasterboard *Gypsum plasterboards* with their long edges reduced to half their normal thickness on the face side by sloping the face towards the edges at about 1 in 5, useful in *dry lining*. An invisible joint can be made with the maker's *joint cement*, etc., but construction is not completely dry.

tapered parapet gutter A *box gutter*, behind a *parapet*. Its bottom becomes narrower towards the lower end because it is laid at a slope.

taper ground [joi.] *See* **setting of saws** (illus. p. 298).

taper pipe, diminishing p. [plu.] An *increaser* or *reducer*.

taper thread [plu.] A standard *screw thread* used on pipes and their *fittings* to ensure a gastight joint. Taper threads are used on all usual pipes and fittings except *connectors*, on which the thread is too long to be tapered. The amount of the taper is 1 in 16, that is, if continued to a point, the taper would form a cone 1 unit dia., 16 units long. *Compare* **parallel thread**. *See* **fittings** (p. 138).

taping strip A strip of *bitumen felt* laid over the joints between precast slabs in a roof before it is covered with felt and *bonding* or *sealing compound*.

tar–gravel roofing (USA) A low-cost roof covering of *bitumen felt* mopped with hot tar or pitch and covered with gravel or sand.

teak [tim.] (Tectona grandis) A *hardwood* from Burma, India, Siam and (of less good quality) Java, and Indo-China. Because of its fire- and acid-resistance, it is used for making laboratory sinks and benches, but also for outdoor *carpentry* and good *joinery*. In *workability* it is about equal to *oak* or higher.

tear [pai.] *See* **run**.

technical assistant [q.s.] A *quantity surveyor's* assistant. He may be described as a worker-up or as a *taker-off* according to the work he is doing.

tee [plu.] A short *fitting* with three openings of which one is a *branch* at right

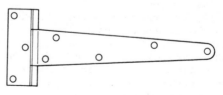

Tee hinge.

angles to the other two and half way between them. The *run* is the length which carries the two openings in line. *See* (illus. p. 138) **sweep tee**.

tee hinge [joi.] A *hinge* resembling the *cross garnet*.

Teflon *See* ptfe.

tegula The under-tile of *Italian tiling*.

telescopic centering, collapsible pans, self-centering formwork Floor *formwork* (*C*) made of *pressed-steel* sections which fit into each other telescopically. The end sections are laid on the wall or beam which carries the floor. Generally no posts are placed under the formwork.

telltale A glass slip, fixed across a crack in a wall with cement mortar, with the date of setting written in the mortar, will indicate by its breakage or movement whether the crack is getting worse. Other types of telltale exist.

temper To toughen *steels* (*C*) by reducing their hardness (and brittleness) in a heating process followed by controlled cooling. Copper is softened by heat alone – *annealing* (*C*) to *dead-soft temper*.

tempera [pai.] A mural painting method practised in the Middle Ages, using a *medium* of gum, egg, and water on *gesso*.

temperature movement, thermal m. Most cement products, *ceramics*, rocks, steel and iron increase in length by an amount varying between 8 and 13 mm per 10 m (1 and 1⅝ in. per 100 ft) length per 100° C. temperature rise, and shorten correspondingly when the temperature drops, often with resulting cracking. This is in addition to or subtracted from any *moisture movement*. A temperature range of 40° C. is used in the UK for calculating the total possible movement, or at most 45° C. for dark surfaces exposed to the sun. Even so, brick walls are often built with joints at intervals of 4 m to 6 m (13 to 20 ft), when designed by careful detailers. Exceptions to the figure of 8 to 13 mm given above are mainly higher, but asbestos board is as low as 2·5 mm (⅛ in.), dense plasters reach 20 (2½ in.), stainless steel 18 (2¼ in.), aluminium alloys 24 (2¾ in.), zinc 33 (4 in.), while wood across the grain is up to 70 (8 in.) but only 4 to 6 (½ to ¾ in.) with the grain. Some plastics expand and contract ten times as much as other materials with change in temperature. Consequently *plastics pipes* laid in hot weather need to be provided with a considerable loose length or they will break during frost (BRE Digests 227, 228, 229).

tempered hardboard [tim.] *Hardboard* that has been made specially strong and water resistant.

template, templet, profile (1) A full size pattern of wood or metal used for testing or forming the shapes of building stone, plaster, concrete, etc.

(2) A *pad* to spread a concentrated load.

templating [tim.] Cutting *veneers* to shape e.g. for *flexible-bag moulding* work in which very difficult compound curves are used.

templet A *template*, illus. p. 308.

tender (USA **bid**) [q.s] An offer from a *contractor* to do certain work for a price which he names, usually in the *priced bill*.

tendering [q.s.] The procedure of sending out drawings and a *bill of quantities* to *contractors* for them to state their prices for all the *items* of one contract. Tendering may be open, in which case the contract is advertised and every contractor who wishes may tender, or it may be 'restricted', by inviting only a few contractors of known ability for the work.

tenon [joi.] An end of a *rail* or similar member, reduced in area, to enter a *mortise* in another member, often a *stile*. The width of a tenon should be about four times its thickness. The word, like mortise, is from the French, but tenons were also used by the ancient Egyptians on their wooden beds. *See* **plywood**, *also* **abutting, haunched, lapped, stub, tusk tenons**.

tenon saw, mitre s. [joi.] A saw, up to 30 cm (12 in.) long, with about 14 points per 25 mm (1 in.), stiffened like the *dovetail saw* with a fold of steel or brass along its back.

terminal (1) A *finial* or similar decorative ending.

    (2) The end of a lightning conductor, gas flue, etc.

    (3) [elec.] The end of a power line, or the connection for leading power into, or out of, a piece of electrical plant.

termite An insect which lives in colonies, does very much more damage than an ant and eats most sorts of wood (*see* **termite shield**). It is found in tropical countries and in some temperate parts of USA.

termite shield (USA) A metal sheet resembling a *damp course* with overhanging lip to throw off water. It prevents termites climbing into the house and eating the woodwork. It must be placed below any wood in the building and must also be fixed round any pipes entering the house.

terne plate Steel sheet for roofing, coated with an alloy of lead containing up to 20% tin, that enables the sheet to hold paint firmly. *See* **tin roofing**.

terrace A raised, level, earth platform with at least one upright or battered side.

terrace house One of a row of houses touching each other. *Compare* **semi-detached**.

terra cotta Italian for burnt clay, a finer-grained *ceramic* than *brick* or *tile*, for making *cornices*, vases, statuettes or *building blocks*, fired in moulds. In Britain the limits of size of terra cotta are 150 litres (5 ft^3) total volume and a maximum face area of 0·19 m^2 (2 ft^2). Terra cotta may be unglazed but is more usually covered with a clear glaze or an opaque *colour* and should then be called *faience*. About twenty colours are obtainable. Most terra cotta, even unglazed, is very durable. It was used about 1500, and revived in Victorian times. *See* **ceramic veneer**.

terrazzo, Venetian mosaic [pla.] Coloured stones, laid in cement mortar, in a layer about 2 cm ($\frac{3}{4}$ in.) thick over level concrete or a screed. When the mortar has set, the stones are abraded to smooth them and improve their colour. The finish can be pleasingly bright in colour, easily cleaned, and in plain geometrical patterns. *See* **monolithic screed, Roman mosaic**.

terrazzo layer [pla.] A *tradesman* who lays *terrazzo*, fixes expansion joints, polishes the terrazzo with a stone or by machine, and on small jobs prepares the stones. He sometimes fixes precast terrazzo.

terrazzo tiles Concrete floor tiles with a *terrazzo* facing, often 300 mm (12 in.) or more square (BS 4357, 4131).

tessellated pavement *Roman mosaic*.

tessera (plural, **tesserae**) A small cube or square of marble, glass, stone, or pottery used in *Roman mosaic*.

texture [tim.] The distribution and relative size of the cells of wood. It may be *coarse, even, uneven*, or *fine*.

texture brick A *rustic brick*.

textured finish [pai.] The great thickness and rough texture of some *masonry paints* seems to give them durability, reducing rain penetration into the wall and making expensive *cement rendering* unnecessary. Outside plaster with a textured surface also resists the weather well. *Compare* **plastic paint**.

thatch A roof covering of *reed, straw* (or heather), laced with *withies*. A *reed* roof can last sixty or seventy years but the life of a good straw roof is not more than twenty years and it needs cleaning and patching every seven years. It has a high insulating value but its main disadvantage (apart from its short life, the unpleasantness of thatching work, and the difficulty of finding thatchers) is the fire risk. This can now be lessened by soaking the reed or straw in a fire-resisting solution instead of in water before laying. *See* **liggers, sways, spar, yelm**.

thatcher A *tradesman* who prepares and bundles *reed, straw*, or heather, soaks it in fireproofing solution, and fixes it while damp with tarred string, wire, straw rope, or osier strips over *sways*. He combs and trims the surface, cuts the eaves square with shears, and can thatch strawstacks or haystacks. The craft is dying out because the work of handling wet thatch is unpleasant for the hands.

thatcher's labourer, t. server A helper to a thatcher who usually soaks the *reed* or *straw* and hands it up to him.

thermal bridge *See* **cold bridge**.

thermal conductance, conductivity *See* **conductance, conductivity**.

thermal movement *See* **temperature movement**.

thermal transmittance, air-to-air heat-transmission coefficient. The *U-value*.

thermal wallboard [pla.] A *gypsum plasterboard* glued to a backing sheet of *expanded polystyrene* or other foam. It can be used in dry conditions only and may be up to 65 mm (2½ in.) thick. Vapour-check thermal wallboard has a *vapour check* at the junction between plaster and insulation. The foam should not be too much compressed or its insulation value will drop.

thermal wheel *See* **heat-recovery wheel**.

thermofusion welding (formerly **fusion welding**) Joining polythene tubes with heated tools that melt the contact surfaces. Polythene tube can be bent hot at temperatures between 105° and 132° C. depending on the type of tube (BSCP 312).

thermoplastic Description of a *synthetic resin* or other material which softens on heating and hardens again on cooling. *Plywoods* made with thermoplastic glue must cool before the pressure is released from them. Thermoplastic roof lights soften at 75° to 150° C., which may help the early venting of gases from a fire, though this may not always be desirable, especially if the fire is outside the building. *See below, also* **thermo-setting resin**.

thermoplastic putty *Glazier's putty* which is made plastic by adding tallow, enabling it to move with the glass.

thermoplastic tiles *Flooring tiles* made from asphalt, *asbestos* fibre, thermoplastic *resins* and similar materials. They are about 3 mm (⅛ in.) thick, are glued down, and should be fixed only to a *sub-floor* which is as rigid as *concrete*. They are brittle when cold, therefore, however smooth the base is, they need heating to about 70° C. before laying, so as to soften them enough to enable them to mould themselves to the floor.

thermo-setting resin A *resin* such as *film glue* which hardens on heating and does not soften when reheated. *Plywoods* made with thermo-setting glue do not need to be cooled before they are released from pressure. *See* **caul, cold-setting, thermoplastic**.

thermo-siphon *Gravity circulation.*

thermostat A device for maintaining temperature between limits. It often incorporates a *bi-metal strip* (*C*) which bends on heating (or cooling) and breaks (or makes) a circuit or turns off (or on) a gas supply. Automatically controlled *central heating* always includes a thermostat. *See* **froststat**.

thickening [pai.]. *See* **fattening**.

thicknessing machine, thicknesser, panel planer [tim.] A *planing machine* which reduces, to the desired thickness, wood which may have already had the face made true on the *surface planer*. The two faces can be made parallel and planed to the correct thickness by the setting of two feed rollers at a certain level above the table.

thimble [plu.] A *sleeve piece.*

T-hinge [joi.] A *hinge* resembling the *cross-garnet.*

thinner [pai.] *Solvents* (*white spirit, turpentine*, toluol) added to paint, varnish or lacquer to make it flow easily. Like a solvent it should have complete compatibility with the *medium* but may contain non-*volatile* liquid. It dries by *evaporation.*

thinning ratio [pai.] The proportion of *thinner* recommended for a particular *paint* in a particular use.

thin-wall plaster, thin-coat p., Scandinavian p. *Pre-mixed plaster* that may be used in plastering machines or applied by hand. One type, sold wet in steel drums, hardens by the drying of its organic binder and keeps indefinitely in the unopened drum.

third fixings, second f. [joi.] The final *joinery* fixings such as door hanging and *door furniture*, which follow the first painting.

thousand slates, 1000 actual Now 1000 slates, though previous to 1940 a thousand slates were 1200.

thread A spiral or helical ridge formed on the surface of a metal cylinder or cone (the *screw*). Screws into wood are spiral (conical) with a *gimlet point*, those through metal being helical (cylindrical) and blunt ended.

thread rolling [mech.] Forming a *screw thread* on copper or similarly ductile metal tube or rod by pressure, without cutting metal away.

three-coat work (1) **render, float, and set** (on walls), **lath, plaster, float, and set** (on lathing) [pla.] The best quality plastering, in which the first coat (*rendering coat* on walls or pricking-up coat on lathing) fills the rough places, and the second forms a smooth surface for the third. The total thickness is about 2 cm ($\frac{3}{4}$ in.), of which the *finishing coat* is 3 mm ($\frac{1}{8}$ in.) or less.

(2) Paint or mastic asphalt applied in three layers. *See* **priming coat**.

three-foot rule A three-feet-long *fourfold rule.*

three-pipe system A water-circulation system with two flow pipes, one for *central heating* and one for water heating, with a common *return* (B S 5643).

three-ply (1) [tim.] The commonest sort of *plywood*, built of a core *veneer* and *cross bands* each side, i.e. *balanced construction.*

(2) *Built-up roofing* or a *damp-proof* membrane formed of three layers of felt lapping over and bonded to each other.

three-prong plug [elec.] A plug with three prongs for insertion into a *socket-outlet*. Two plugs provide power, the third is an earth connection for safety reasons. *See* **shuttered socket**.

three-quarter bat A *brick* cut straight across to reduce its length by one quarter. *Compare* **king closer**.

three-quarter header A *header* of length equal to three quarters of the wall thickness.

three-way strap [carp.] A steel tee-plate with its three arms shaped so as to anchor together at a node three members of a wooden *truss*. It is fixed to them by *coach screws* or through-bolts. This old fixing is being used again, with modifications.

threshold, sill (USA **saddle**) [joi.] A horizontal timber at the foot of an outside door.

throat (1) The undercut part of a *drip*.

(2) A narrowing of the bottom of a *flue* just above the fireplace, that improves the draught from an open fire. Sometimes it is fitted with an adjustable metal 'throat restrictor' to vary the draught.

(3) [carp.] The opening from which shavings come out of a *plane*.

through and through sawing *Flat sawing*.

through bonder A *bond stone*.

through lintel A *lintel* of the full thickness of the wall.

through stone A *bond stone* which is seen on both faces of the wall.

through tenon [carp.] A *tenon* which passes beyond the mortised member.

thumb latch, Canadian, Norfolk, Suffolk, Garden City latch (USA **lift 1.**) [joi.] A steel fall bar, under which a lifting lever, worked by the thumb, passes through a slot in the door. When raised, the lever lifts the fall bar and unfastens the door.

thumb screw (1) [mech.] A *wing nut*.

(2) [joi.] A metal screw which passes through the *meeting rail* of one *sash* and screws into the meeting rail of the outer sash to form a burglar-proof fastening.

tie (Scotland) A *tingle* for fixing *flexible-metal roofing* sheets.

tie-beam [carp.] The horizontal, lowest timber of a roof *truss*, equal in length to the full *span* (*C*) of the roof. It ties together the feet of the *rafters* and is held to them in large trusses by a *heel strap*.

tier (USA) A leaf of brickwork half a brick thick. *See* **withe**.

tight cesspool (USA) A cesspool which does not leak, as opposed to a *leaching cesspool*.

tight knot [tim.] A *knot* held firmly in the wood around it. *Compare* **loose knot**.

tight sheathing [carp.] Diagonal *matchboards* nailed to *studs* or *rafters*.

tight side [tim.] The side of a sheet of *sliced veneer* which was not in contact with the knife when it was cut off. *See* **loose side**.

tight size, full s., rebate s. The size of the rebated opening for glass, about 3 mm ($\frac{1}{8}$ in.) more than the *glazing size*, or about 6 mm ($\frac{1}{4}$ in.) more for double-glazing *sealed units*.

tile (1) A thin, burnt-clay, concrete, aluminium, plastics, or asbestos-cement plate for roofing (either a *plain tile* or a *single-lap tile*) or for flooring or wall covering. There is much more variety in the materials for *wall* or *flooring tiles* than for *roofing tiles*.

(2) *Field drains* (*C*).

(3) (USA) *See* **structural clay tile**.

tile-and-a-half tile A *plain tile* of width one and a half times that of the tiles with which it courses, used at *swept valleys, verges,* and *laced valleys*. It is normally 25 cm ($9\frac{3}{4}$ in.) wide. It avoids the use of half-tiles, which are difficult to fix and therefore hazardous.

tile batten A *slating-and-tiling batten*.

tile clip Corrosion-resistant spring wire or strip metal anchors of various types for fixing *single-lap tiles* especially at *eaves* and *verges* but also in the middle of the roof, as well as or instead of nails. They are either hooked over and under the *slating-and-tiling batten* or nailed to it. Tile makers stock clips suited to their tiles.

tile creasing *See* **creasing**.

tiled valley A *valley* covered with purpose-made *valley tiles*.

tile fillet, t. listing *Tiles* cut and set in mortar at an angle to a *parapet* instead of a *flashing* at the *abutment* with a sloping roof.

tile floors *See* **flooring tiles**.

tile hanging, weather tiling, vertical tiling Fixing *plain tiles* on a wall to keep out the rain.

tile listing *See* **tile fillet**.

tile pins *Oak* pegs used instead of *nails* for fixing *tiles*.

tile slabber [pla.] A *floor-and-wall-tiler*, who builds up hearths, curbs, and fire-places in the workshop by setting *tiles* in a mould to a design, and filling the mould with *concrete* or cement *mortar*, reinforced with steel.

tiling batten A *slating-and-tiling batten*.

tilt-and-turn window [joi.] A *casement window* which can be either side-hung or bottom-hung according to the position of its handle. Opening inwards, it is easily cleaned.

tilting fillet, t. piece, arris f., doubling piece, eaves board (USA **cant strip**) A thick horizontal board, sometimes triangular in cross-section, nailed across the rafters or roof boarding under the *double eaves course* to tilt it slightly less steeply than the rest of the roof and to ensure that the *tails* of the lowest tiles or slates bed tightly on each other. It may also be needed at a *verge* or the edges of a *valley gutter* made of *flexible metal*. A *fascia* at an *eave* may do the same job. (Illus. p. 305) *Compare* **cocking piece**.

timber (USA **lumber**) (1) Wood for building, generally large in cross-section and sawn to *baulks, battens, boards*, etc.

  (2) In USA a timber is *lumber* 4 × 6 in. (100 × 150 mm) or larger. *See below*.

timber connector [carp.] *See* **connectors**. (Illus. p. 83)

timber framing [carp.] A load-carrying frame of timber, used in the early medieval *cruck house* and in the *frame construction* of the present day. Nowadays in Britain timber walls have been largely superseded by brick but roofs are still of timber. *See* **Belfast truss, king post, queen post, scissors truss**.

timber in the round *Round timber*.

timbers [tim.] Out of the hundreds of timbers now in commercial use, the following are the best known in the United Kingdom:

alder	elm	oak
ash	Douglas fir	redwood
balsa	silver fir	Canadian spruce
beech	greenheart	Sitka spruce
birch	hickory	teak
boxwood	larch (tamarack)	walnut
western red cedar	mahoganies	whitewood
chestnut		

timber scaffolder A man who builds *scaffolds* by lashing wooden *standards, putlogs*, and *ledgers* with fibre rope or steel whips. *Tubular scaffolding* has superseded wood in industrial countries.

time limit, completion date The date specified in the *contract* for completion of the work. It may be postponed because of bad weather or other difficulties.

time-and-a-half The 50% additional payment usual in Britain for *overtime* worked less than three hours after normal finishing time or up to 4 pm on Saturdays. After this, *double time* is paid.

timesing column [q.s.] A column on a sheet of *dimensions paper* for the purpose of showing how many times the same quantity must be taken.

tin A silvery metal becoming increasingly valuable. Its main use is as a very thin, protective coating to sheet steel or copper. Steel which has been tinned is *tinplate* (colloquially 'tin'). *See* **solder, tin roofing**.

tingle (1) **cleat, ear, latchet, tab, tack, bale tack**, etc. A strip of *flexible metal* about 5 cm (2 in.) wide to tie down an edge of flexible metal, to fix a *pane* of glass in *patent glazing* or secure a *hollow roll* or *seam* or fix a replacement *slate*. One end is nailed to the roof and the other folded into the edge of the sheet to be secured. They are also used for holding pipes or electric cables.
(2) A support at the middle of a long *line* used by *bricklayers*.

tinker's dam A clay or *solder* dam which prevents solder overflowing.

tinning Coating steel, copper, or other metal with a film of tin or tin alloy to reduce corrosion.

tinman's solder [plu.] *See* **fine solder**.

tinplate Sheet steel about 0·12 mm (0·005 in.) thick coated with a thin film of tin both sides by dipping it in molten tin. It is used in *tin roofing*.

tin roofing Roofing with *tinplate* or *terne plate*. It must be kept painted to prevent rust and even then is not used in wet climates.

tin saw A *bricklayer*'s saw with which he cuts bricks.

tinsmith [mech.] *See* **sheet-metal worker**.

tin snips [mech.] Strong scissors used for cutting thin metal sheet. The smallest (jeweller's snips) are about 18 cm (7 in.) long. *See* **plumber's tools**, p. 250.

tint [pai.] A *colour* made by mixing much *white pigment* with a little coloured pigment.

tinters [pai.] *Stainers*.

tinting [pai.] The final adjustment of the *colour* of a *paint*.

tinting strength [pai.] *See* **staining power**.

tip The thin end of a tapered *shingle*, laid at the upper end.

titanium dioxide, t. white [pai.] The most widely used *white pigment*, outstandingly opaque and non-poisonous, it does not lose colour. Used in cosmetics.

title The right of ownership to a property, shown on legal documents called title deeds.

toe [joi.] The lower part of the *shutting stile* of a door. *See also* C.

toe board A *scaffold board* set on edge at the side of a scaffolding to prevent tools dropping off the *scaffold* and doing damage below.

toe nailing [carp.] *Skew nailing*.

toggle bolt [joi.] A proprietary device which enables a strong fixing to be made to thin board such as plasterboard or hardboard.

tolerance [mech.] The allowable range of dimensions of a part, whether hand- or machine-made. It is usually expressed as in the following example of common building bricks: 214·5 × 103 × 65 mm with tolerances on length of

±2·5 mm, on width and depth of ±2 mm; meaning that the length may be from 212 to 217 mm (also written 214·5±2·5 mm, the usual method). Concrete walls and floors can, with care, be built to within 3 mm of the dimensions shown on the drawings, but variations of 25 mm (1 in.) are often allowed.

tommy bar [mech.] A loose bar inserted into a hole in a box spanner to provide the leverage for turning it.

toner [pai.] A pure organic dye without *extender*, usually of strong *colour*.

tongue [carp.] *See* **cross tongue, straight tongue**.

tongue-and-groove joint [carp.] A joint between the edges of boards to form a smooth wall, floor, or roof surface which is relatively air-tight. The tongue in one board fits the groove of its neighbour. *See* **matchboard**.

Tonk strips [joi.] *Sherardized* steel strips housed into the inner faces of the sides of an adjustable book-case. These strips are slotted for small metal tongues which, inserted into the slots, carry the shelves.

ton slates *Random slates*.

tool [mech.] An object held in the hand, used for working metal, timber, earth, masonry, mortar, and so on, such as the file, saw, shovel, hammer and trowel. However, since lathes and other metal- and wood-working machines have come to be called *machine tools* (C) the first are called hand tools. For illustrations *see* **carpenter, house painter, mason, plasterer, plumber**.

tooled ashlar *Batted surface*.

tooling (1) *See* **batting**.

(2) The shaping and compressing of a mortar joint in *jointing* with any tool other than a trowel. *Concave* and *vee-joints* are both tooled in this sense.

tool pad, t. holder, pad [joi.] A combination tool consisting of a handle with a screw clamp for holding one of several small tools, such as gimlets, saws, awls, and screwdrivers of various sorts.

tooth [pai.] The surface roughness of a paint *film* which has coarse or abrasive *pigment*. Such a surface is very suitable for rubbing and gives good adhesion to paints put on to it, but is not a good top coat.

toothed plate, bulldog p [tim.] A *connector*. (Illus. p. 83)

toother A *stretcher* which projects in *toothing*.

toothing, indenting Leaving stretchers projecting 6 cm (2½ in.) at the end of a wall to bond with future work. Bricks project like teeth from alternate courses.

top beam [carp.] A *collar beam*.

top course tiles The *tiles* of the *course* next the *ridge*, shorter than those in lower courses to maintain the same *gauge*.

top cut [carp.] (USA) A *plumb cut* at the top of a *rafter*.

top-hung window [joi.] A window hinged at its top edge, opening outwards and held by a *casement stay*.

top lighting Lighting from overhead by *roof light*, *borrowed light*, or artificial light.

top log [tim.] The highest log from a tree trunk.

topman A *demolisher*.

topping, jointing, breasting [carp.] The first operation in putting a cutting edge on a handsaw or *circular saw*, making level the tips of all the teeth with a file. The later operations are *shaping*, *setting*, and sharpening. *See* **stoning**, also C.

torching, tiering, rendering Pointing the underside of *slates*, over the *heads*, to prevent the *tails lifting* (*shouldering* or half torching). Full torching includes, in addition, the plastering of the whole underside of the slate seen between battens. It has been common practice on unboarded, unfelted roofs, in spite of the fact that moisture is sucked on to the battens by capillary movement through the mortar. The battens therefore decay quickly and the practice is now condemned particularly for concrete tiles and asbestos-cement slates, unless the torching is between slates or tiles only and does not touch the battens.

torn grain [tim.] *Chipped grain.*

touch dry [pai.] A stage in *drying*, when very slight pressure with the fingers leaves no mark and does not show stickiness.

toughened glass, heat-treated g., tempered g., hardened g. Glass which has had its surface cooled quickly from near the melting point, leaving the surface compressed by the later cooling of the core. This strengthens it, enabling it to break as a *safety glass*.

tower bolt A massive, steel *barrel bolt*.

town gas The gas provided in the piped supply of a town or village, usually sold by the therm. *See* **manufactured gas**.

town planning The coordination by town planners, who are usually architects or municipal engineers, of the interests of the town, represented by the views of economists, doctors, sociologists, and so on. In USA town planning is a short-term process, city planning the long-term process of continuously developing the master plan. *See* **planning**.

trace heating, cable h. Heating of pipes with electrical cables wound round them. The cables are designed electrically to provide enough heat e.g. to enable the oil in a pipe to flow easily.

TRADA, Timber Research and Development Association A research association founded in 1934, half of whose income is earned from commercial testing and consultancy, 40% by subscription from timber importers, and 10% in payment for work done for government departments. TRADA is a recognized fire-test centre, and also tests timber units for mechanical strength. Other important parts of its work are window testing and consultancy on woodworking, sawmilling, and the use of timber in architecture and in domestic, industrial and farm structures. *See* **appraisal**.

trade A building trade is the same as a building *craft*. *See* **tradesman, sequence of trades**.

tradesman, craftsman, journeyman, mechanic, artisan A man who has been an *apprentice* for some years in a building trade and is therefore fully skilled in it. He may be a *bricklayer, carpenter, joiner, electrician, floor and wall tiler, glazier, hot-water fitter, house painter, mason, paperhanger, plasterer, plumber, slater-and-tiler, steeplejack*, etc. Before 1815, when Thomas Cubitt in London first employed tradesmen permanently, they frequently travelled long distances in search of work except when they were lucky enough to find semi-permanent building sites such as cathedrals, castles or abbeys. *See* **semi-skilled man**.

trade union Organization of people who work in the same trade, such as *carpenters, bricklayers*, or *plumbers* (craft union), or of people who work in the same industry, such as miners (industrial union).

translucent glass *Obscured glass.*

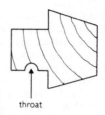

throat

Transom (horizontal).

transmittance *See* **U-value**.

transom, transome (1) A horizontal beam, particularly the stone or timber bar separating the *lights* of a window, or separating a door from a *fanlight* over it. (Illus. above)

(2) (USA) A *fanlight*.

trap (1) [plu.] A U-shaped bend in a *waste pipe* or *soil* pipe containing enough water to *seal* the air downstream of the U from that above it.

(2) A *scaffold board* which overhangs its support and is therefore dangerous to tread on.

traverse A *dressing iron. See also* C.

tray, lead safe, drip sink (USA **receptor**) A shallow lead, plastics or stoneware sink, under a shower or draw-off tap, drained and trapped like a basin.

tread The level part of a step, or its length. *See* **flight** (illus. pp. 142, 326).

treadmill The only source of power on building sites in the Middle Ages, introduced into British prisons in 1817 as a wooden wheel 5 m (17 ft) wide of 1·5 m (5 ft) dia., with twenty-four equidistant treads round the rim, on which the prisoners had to climb.

treenail, trenail [carp.] A hardwood pin driven into a hole bored across a *mortise-and-tenon joint* or other joints in *carpentry*. A treenail is sometimes called a *drawbore* pin, but this term is best reserved for the steel pin which pulls the holes into line before the treenail is inserted. The word *dowel* is used more for *joinery*, treenail for *carpentry*. *See also* C.

trees The National House-building Council recommends builders not to locate a house wall nearer to a live tree than 4 m (13 ft) or one third of its mature height, whichever is the lesser. The mature height of yews is about 14 m (40 ft); of oak and sycamore about 24 m (80 ft); of ash, beech, chestnut and elm about 27 m (90 ft); of larch and lime about 30 m (100 ft). *See also* **timbers, poplar**.

trellis window A *lattice window*.

trench [joi.] A groove across a member, a *housing*.

trestle A support for *scaffold boards*, used by *plasterers* or *painters* working on a ceiling.

trim (1) (USA **casing**) [joi.] *Architraves, skirtings, dado*, or picture rails, etc. made, if of wood, by linear machining. *See* **metal trim**.

(2) *See* **trimming**.

trimmed joist (USA **tailpiece**) [carp.] A *common joist* which has been cut short (trimmed) at an opening and is carried by a *trimmer joist*, illus. p. 354.

trimmer [carp.] (1) A *trimmer joist*.

(2) (USA) A *trimming joist*, illus. p. 354.

(3) *See* **joist trimmer** pp. 190, 354.

trimmer arch A brick arch carrying the concrete floor under the fireplace in an otherwise wooden floor, spanning from *chimney back* to *trimming joist*.

trimmer joist (U S A **header joist**) [carp.] A short *joist* which encloses one side of a rectangular hole in a wooden floor, carrying the *common joists* which are cut off by the hole. Another trimmer joist may form the side opposite and parallel to it, and trimming joists form the two sides parallel to the common joists. The trimmer joists were carried on the trimming joists by *tusk tenons* through them. *See* **joist trimmer**.

trimming Framing round or otherwise strengthening an opening through a floor, roof, or wall, whether of timber or other material. *See* p. 354.

trimming joist [carp.] A heavy joist parallel to the common joists. One is fixed each side of a hole in a wooden floor in place of a *common joist*. It carries one end of the *trimmer joists*, and thus the loads from the common joists carried by the trimmer joists.

trimming machine, mitring m., guillotine, bench trimmer [joi.] A lever- or pedal-operated machine with a heavy sharp blade for cutting the ends of *mouldings* or timbers at any desired angle. (For mitring a 90° bend, the angle is 45°.)

trimming piece A *camber slip*.

triple course Three rows of *shingles* laid together at eaves.

trough gutter A *box gutter*.

trowel Wooden-handled steel-bladed tools of many different shapes and sizes used by *bricklayers*, *masons*, and *plasterers*. *Compare* **float**.

trowelled face [pla.] A plaster or mortar surface finished with a trowel. Cement mortar must be trowelled with care, as over-trowelling brings cement to the surface and often leads to *crazing*.

trowelled stucco [pla.] *Stucco* which, after ruling off and *scouring*, is trowelled with a *brick trowel*.

trowel man A *finisher*.

trunk, trunking Large sheet-iron or wooden pipe, generally for ventilation.

trunk lift *See* **freight elevator**.

truss A frame, generally nowadays of steel (but also sometimes of timber, concrete, or *light alloy*) to carry a roof built up from members in tension and compression. Steel trusses generally weigh 10 to 15 kg/m^2 (2 to 3 lb/ft^2) of floor area for spans of 12 m (40 ft) or less. For every 3 m (10 ft) increase in span, another 2 to 5 kg/m^2 (0·5 to 1 lb/ft^2) should be added. Bracing against wind adds a further 2 to 5 kg/m^2. Roofing with *slates* instead of the usual *asbestos*, steel, or aluminium sheets increases the truss weight by 15%. Trusses are usually placed about 3 m apart, but their spacing is fixed by the design of the *purlin*. *See* **trussed rafter**.

trussed partition [carp.] A *framed partition* made of timber, strongly framed like a *truss*, so as to carry weight in addition to its own, for example, the floors above it. It was superseded by *building blocks* around 1915.

trussed purlin A *purlin* reinforced by a camber rod beneath it like a *trussed beam* (*C*).

trussed rafter [carp.] A lightweight, modern, prefabricated roof *truss* that is superseding the heavy rafters, *ridge*, purlins and ceiling joists of the traditional building that were separately hoisted up to roof level. Trussed rafters are made of light timbers joined with timber *connectors* or plywood gusset plates that are nailed and often also glued in the factory. The spans vary from

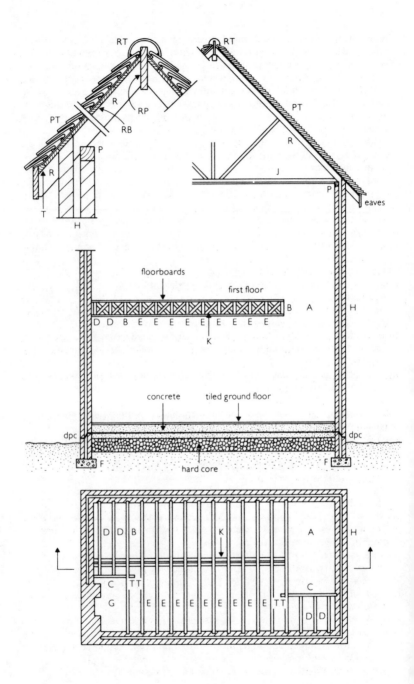

RT

RT

R

RP

RB

PT

PT

R

P

J

R

P

eaves

T

H

floorboards

first floor

B

A

D D B E E E E E E E E E

H

K

concrete

tiled ground floor

dpc

dpc

F

F

hard core

D D B

K

A

H

C

TT

G

E E E E E E E E E E TT

C

D D

354

5 m to 11 m (16 ft to 36 ft), slopes from 15° to 35° to the horizontal and truss spacings are about 0·6 m (2 ft). The different designs include *scissors trusses* and trusses sloping one way only. Roofs can be completed in a quarter of the time needed for a traditional roof. Because the traditional ridge cannot be inserted into the factory-made trusses, 'ridge binders' are used to hold the frames together. These are 100 × 25 mm (4 × 1 in.) boards placed under the rafters in as near a vertical position as possible and nailed to them or the nearest strut, usually both at 'ridge' and midspan, so three ridge binders may be used instead of one ridge (BSCP 112).

trying plane, try p., truing p. [carp.] A *bench plane* about 56 cm (22 in.) long used after the *jack plane*. It is usually 6·3 cm (2½ in.) wide with a 5·7 cm (2¼ in.) *cutting iron*.

try square [carp.] A *square. See* **mason's and bricklayer's tools** (illus. p. 211).

tubular [plu.] A steel screwed pipe *fitting* formed from pipe, for example, a *connector* or *bend*. Most other fittings are of *malleable cast iron* (C).

tubular saw [mech.] A *hole saw*.

tubular scaffolder A *skilled man* who erects steel or *light alloy* scaffolding, joined with clips, fish plates, nuts and bolts, and so on. If he also puts up suspended scaffolds he may be called a *rigger* (C).

tubular scaffolding *Scaffolds* of 5 cm (2 in.) outside dia. steel or *light-alloy* tube. Steel is much stronger, about three times as heavy, and half the cost of light alloy per metre. Both are made of tubes with wall thickness of 4·5 to 4·9 mm. Light alloy has the advantage that it does not rust. *See* BSCP 97.

tuck A recess in a horizontal mortar *joint* made in *tuck pointing*. It is filled with a line of *lime putty* which projects about 3 mm (⅛ in.), showing as an outstanding white line.

tuck in That part of a *bitumen felt* roofing, *skirting*, or *cover flashing* which is bent into a chase in the wall.

tuck pointing A decorative and protective method of *pointing* old brickwork. The joints are first filled flush and then grooved to form a *tuck* to emphasize the joint.

tumbler [joi.] The part of a *lock* which holds the bolt in place until the key is turned.

tumbler switch [elec.] A simple lever-operated switch.

tumbling bay [plu.] A *back drop*.

Plan and section of a house carcase, omitting doors, windows, and plaster; and floorboards in plan.

A = *opening trimmed for stair*	K = *herring-bone strutting*
B = *trimming joist*	P = *wall plate*
C = *trimmer joist*	PT = *plain tiles (resting on battens)*
D = *trimmed joists*	R = *rafter*
dpc = *damp-proof course*	RB = *roof boarding (covered with*
E = *common joists*	*sarking felt)*
F = *footing*	RP = *ridge piece (or ridge)*
G = *opening trimmed for fireplace*	RT = *ridge tile (set in mortar)*
H = *cavity wall*	T = *tilting fillet*
J = *ceiling joist*	TT = *tusk tenon*

tumbling in, t. courses Sloping *courses* of brickwork meeting horizontal courses as at the sloping top of a *buttress* (*C*) or as a *coping* to a *gable wall*.

tundish A saucer shape with a central drain hole, sometimes formed (among other places) in a *flue* below a *soot door*, with *Portland* or *aluminous cement* mortar, to collect *condensation in flues*.

tung oil, wood o., China wood o. [pai.] A water-resistant *drying oil* from the seeds of tropical trees (Aleurites) which grow also in China and Japan. It dries quickly but suffers *frosting* unless properly heat treated (BS 391).

tupper A *bricklayer's labourer* in the north of England.

turn button [joi.] A simple catch for a cupboard door consisting of a metal or wooden piece held pivoted on a screw.

turner A *tradesman* who works on wood or metal in a lathe. *See* **wood turner**.

turning [joi.] Making an object in a lathe.

turning bar A *chimney bar*.

turning piece, trimming p. A *camber slip*.

turnkey contract A *package deal*.

turnpin, turning pin [plu.] A *boxwood tampin*.

turnscrew [joi.] A screwdriver.

turpentine, spirits of t. [pai.] A valuable *solvent* obtained by distilling the *oleoresin* of the pine tree. Resin is leached from the living tree, as in the Landes of France, or given off when the wood is heated.

turpentine substitute [pai.] *White spirit*.

turret step A triangular stone step from which a *spiral stair* is built up. The central *solid newel* consists of the rounded ends of the turret steps laid on top of each other.

tusk nailing [carp.] *Skew nailing*.

tusks, tusses Stones projecting as *toothing*.

tusk tenon, keyed mortise and tenon joint [carp.] A small *tenon* usually formed at the end of a *trimmer joist* to fix it to a *trimming joist*. The tenon passes through a mortise in the trimming joist, and is itself mortised and clamped to the trimming joist by a wedge-shaped key.

twin cable [elec.], **duplex c.** Two insulated conductors laid in a common insulating covering.

twin-shaft paddle mixer (USA **twin pug**) A *pug mill* with two horizontal shafts turning in opposite directions.

twin tenon, divided t. [carp.] A *tenon* from which the central part has been cut away.

twist [tim.] *Helical warp*.

twist drill [mech.] A hardened steel *bit* with helical cutting edges, used in electric drills, *hand drills*, or *breast drills* for drilling metal or wood.

twisted fibres [tim.] *Interlocked grain*.

twist gimlet [joi.] A simple *gimlet* with a helical groove by which the wood cuttings are removed.

twitcher [pla.] An *angle trowel*.

two-bolt lock [joi.] A common combination of a lock turned by a key, with a *latch* operated by a knob on a spindle.

two-coat work (1) [pla.] Plastering with a *floating coat* and a *finishing coat*, now very common.

(2) Paint or asphalt applied in two layers. *See* **three-coat work**.

two-foot rule A *fourfold rule* 2 ft (61 cm) long.

two-handed saw [tim.] A long hand-operated saw worked by two men, one at each end, for example, a felling saw, or a saw for cross-cutting logs, superseded by the *chain saw*.

two-light frame [joi.] A window with one *mullion* dividing it into two *lights*.

two-part, two-pack [pai.] Description of *glue, sealing compound, paint*, etc. sold as two different materials in tins or tubes, to be mixed immediately before use. *Epoxy, polyurethane* or *neoprene* paints of this type are used for the severe service of lock gates or chemical plants. Two-pack materials are almost always of very high quality but awkward in use because of the meticulous cleaning needed for the *ground*.

two-pipe system [plu.] (1) An old system of house drainage in which *soil* and *sullage* flow through two independent pipes, a soil pipe and a *waste pipe*. The waste pipe discharges through a trapped gulley. *Anti-siphon pipes* may be needed (BS 4118). *See* **one-pipe system**.

(2) A *central heating* circuit with a flow pipe as well as a return connected to each radiator. The furthest radiator is therefore only slightly cooler than the one nearest the boiler. It is usually one half of a *four-pipe* system. (Illus. p. 64)

Tyrolean finish [pla.] Outside plaster with a rough *textured finish*, usually thrown on by a hand-operated machine. The plaster is porous, as is generally desirable for a rain-proof surface, and it sticks well to the backing.

U

UCATT Union of Construction, Allied Trades and Technicians. *See also* **Association of Building Technicians**.

U-duct A duct for ventilating gas heaters, resembling the *SE-duct* except that its air inlet is at roof level. Two ducts are therefore needed, one solely to bring fresh air down from the roof to the bottom of the intake duct. The minor complications with the SE-duct's air inlets at ground level are thus avoided.

U-gauge, water g. [plu.] A glass U-tube half filled with water, one end being connected by rubber flexible tube to a system of drains or gas pipes under test. It quickly shows whether they are gas-tight. (Illus. below) *See* **air test**.

ultramarine [pai.] A *pigment* that is *alkali-resistant*, a complex sulpho-silicate of aluminium and sodium obtained in the past from crushed *lapis lazuli*, first synthesized commercially in France in 1828.

ultraviolet radiation Radiation from the sun, often called ultraviolet light although it is not light, being beyond the visible part of the spectrum. This part of the sun's radiation inflicts the most damage on *plastics*.

umber [pai.] The pigment, raw umber is natural hydrated iron oxide with some oxide of manganese. When calcined it turns to a rich deep reddish brown (burnt umber). *See* **sienna**.

uncoursed rubble (USA **broken-range ashlar**) *Random* or *snecked rubble*, sometimes coursed.

undercloak (1) A course of *asbestos-cement* or natural slates or plain tiles or shingles laid under the upper ones at *eaves* or *verges*. At verges they give a slight slope towards the roof. *See* **double eaves course**.

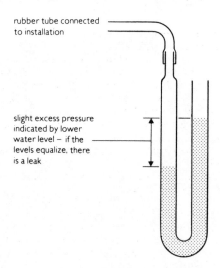

rubber tube connected to installation

slight excess pressure indicated by lower water level – if the levels equalize, there is a leak

U-gauge used in testing for leakage in a gas or drain installation, for indicating the gas pressure, etc.

Underfloor heating designed to reduce heat loss. Most of the heat from floors is lost at the edges, therefore these have extra insulation, both above in the form of quilt and below as air spaces in well drained hardcore or ballast. (After Peter Burberry, Environment and Services, *Mitchell's Building Series, B. T. Batsford, 1979.)*

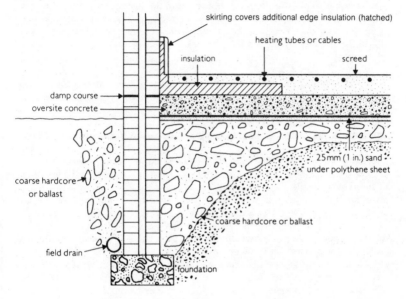

(2) In *flexible-metal roofing* the lower sheet of metal at a *roll, drip* or *seam,* which is covered by the *overcloak.*

undercoat (1) [pai.] Any coat applied to a surface after *priming* and before the finish coat. It is matt with a high content of *pigment* and *extender* and a *colour* approaching or helping that of the *finish* coat. It increases the thickness and therefore the protectiveness of a *paint system. Varnish* undercoats have less oil per unit of *resin* than varnish finishes.

(2) [pla.] A *floating coat* or *rendering* or *pricking-up coat,* in any case not a *finishing coat.*

undercuring [tim.] Insufficient hardening of a *glue* due to low temperature or too short a hardening period.

undercut tenon [carp.] A *tenon* with its shoulder cut slightly off square to ensure that it bears on the mortised piece.

under-eaves course A course of *eaves tiles* in the *eaves course.*

underfloor heating Electric heating cables or hot water pipes, sunk near the upper surface of a concrete floor slab or in the screed over it, provide a warm floor that heats the room without cumbersome radiators. Expert design and execution are essential. For example, if the floor temperature exceeds 27° C. (81° F.), failures with floor gluing may cause vinyl tiles to curl. The Romans warmed their floors and walls with flue gases passing through them.

underlay (1) **isolating membrane, separating layer** One or two layers of polythene sheet or *building paper* placed between two building components to ensure that slip (relative movement) can take place. A concrete beam cast on top of a brick partition needs to be separated from it because otherwise the partition would crack. A *damp course* may act as an underlay. Clay flooring tiles need an underlay below the screed they are bedded on, so that the slight expansion of the tiles does not result in the disastrous failures by arching or lifting that have happened in the past. There should also be an expansion joint at the skirting. The reasons for an underlay below asphalt or *flexible-metal roofing* are similar and below slates or tiles it ensures a water-tight roof.

(2) *See* **double-skin roof**.

(3) Hardboard or plywood placed over a rough floor to make a smooth surface suitable for laying lino, cork tiles, parquet flooring, etc.

underlayment A *levelling compound*.

underlining felt *Sarking felt*.

underpitch groin, Welsh g. An intersection of two cylindrical *vaults* of different *rise*. *See* **groin**.

under-ridge tiles, under-tiles Special *plain tiles* laid in the top *course* of a roof below the *ridge tiles*. They are 23 cm (9 in.) instead of 27 cm (10½ in.) long. *Compare* **eaves tile**.

under-tile (1) A short plain tile laid in the first course at the *eave* or the last course at the *ridge*, either an *under-ridge tile* or an *eaves tile*.

(2) **tegula** The lower tile of *Spanish* or *Italian tiling*.

undertone [pai.] (1) The *colour* obtained when a coloured *pigment* is reduced with a large proportion of *white pigment*.

(2) The colour seen when a coloured pigment is spread on glass and viewed with light passing through it.

undressed timber, unwrought t. Sawn but not planed timber.

uneven grain, u. texture [tim.] A texture with considerable contrast between *springwood* and *summerwood*.

unfixed materials [q.s.] Building materials on site but not fixed represent a large outlay for a *contractor*, especially at an early stage of the job. For his prudence in making this outlay, the contractor usually is paid a percentage of their value in the monthly *certificate*.

unframed door [joi.] A *batten door* or *ledged and braced* door.

ungauged lime plaster [pla.] *Plaster* made with *lime*, sand, and water only, sometimes with neat lime. Only those limes which have a compressive strength of at least 689 kN/m² (100 psi) at twenty-eight days are recommended. Otherwise *Portland cement* or *gypsum plaster* should be *gauged* with it to give early strength.

unified thread [mech.] A screw *thread* accepted by the *BSI* and by Canadian and US authorities, intended before metrication to replace the Whitworth thread in Britain.

union [plu.] A pipe joint originally used for threaded steam pipe but adapted to many other types of tube. A conical male surface of one pipe end meets a conical female surface of the other pipe end to make a gastight joint that is easily unscrewed or re-connected. *Compare* **plumber's union**, p. 138.

union bend, u. cock, etc. [plu.] A bend, cock, etc., with a *union* at one end.

unit air conditioner Usually a steel box (the unit) measuring about 60 × 30 × 30 cm (2 × 1 × 1 ft) containing an electrically driven fan, a compressor, an evaporator and a condenser, through which air is blown, filtered and cooled. The box can be placed in a window or in a hole through an outside wall. Sometimes the unit is 'split' with the evaporator (the cooler), the air fan and filter in one box and the noisier parts, the compressor, condenser, and condenser fan elsewhere. Often used in hot countries, these units have the advantage that they can be installed very quickly in any room that has an electrical supply and an outside wall or roof, but they are noisy and a central *air conditioning* system is preferable because the machines are away from living rooms.

unit heater (1) A fixed space heater used in large rooms or workshops, hung about 2·5 m (8 ft) above floor level. Air is blown over its heated tubes by an electric fan. It may receive heat from hot water or steam through pipes like a *fan convector* or be gas-fired. Because of the forced air flow over its surface, it supplies several times as much heat as a radiator of the same size. Although it is a true warm-air heater, this description is usually reserved for heaters that are ducted, at least for the supply into the room.

(2) A *fan convector*.

unit of bond The smallest length of a brick *course* which repeats itself. In *Flemish bond* it is 1½ bricks long; in *English bond* 1½ bricks thick, it is 1 brick long.

universal plane, combination p. [joi.] A hand-operated metal *plane* with many *cutting irons*, often about fifty, each of different shape, to cut different *mouldings*, *tongues* or grooves, *rebates*, *beads*, etc.

unsound [pla.] A description of slaked *limes*, *cements*, *plasters*, and *mortars* that contain particles which may expand (*blowing*).

unsound knot, rotten k. [tim.] A *knot* which is softer in any part than the wood round it.

untrimmed floor [carp.] A floor carried on *common joists* only.

unwrought timber Sawn, unplaned timber.

upset [tim.] A tear across the fibres of wood caused by a shock, often during felling. *See also C*.

upside-down roof An *inverted roof*.

upstand (1) **upturn** That part of a felt or *flexible-metal* flashing, or roof covering which turns up beside a wall without being tucked into it, and is covered usually with a *stepped flashing*.

(2) **u. beam** A beam in a concrete floor which rises out of the floor like a wall, instead of, as usual, projecting below it.

UPVC, unplasticized polyvinyl chloride A relatively stiff material, sometimes brittle in cold weather, of which sewer pipes or water pipes are made.

urea-formaldehyde glue [tim.] A *synthetic resin* glue made by chemically condensing urea with formalin. An *accelerator* must be added to the liquid *resin* to make the *glue* harden. The two can be mixed in a pot or applied to each face of the joint in *separate application*. With some slight chemical modification these glues are used in baking enamels. Urea glues can be used cold, but if heated they harden more quickly.

urethane [pai.] *See* **polyurethanes**.

usable life The *pot life* of a glue.

U-tie A *wall tie* used in USA, made of heavy wire bent into a top-hat shape.

utility A *service* such as water, gas, electricity, telephone, sewage disposal, etc., which is available to all (USA).

U-value, thermal transmittance, air-to-air heat-transmission coefficient A figure determined by experiment for a certain wall, roof or floor in a certain situation, which tells how many watts (Btu/hour) will pass through one m^2 (ft^2) of the structure when the temperature of the air is 1° C. (1° F.) higher on one side than the other. An exposed wall has a higher U-value than a sheltered one. The U-value in good Continental practice for the outer wall or roof-plus-ceiling of housing is 0·5 watt/m^2 deg. C. (0·09 Btu/ft^{2}h deg. F.). British values imposed by the Building Regulations for dwelling roofs and outer walls respectively are 0·6 and 1 watt/m^2 deg. C. (0·1 and 0·17 Btu/ft^2 h deg. F.) but these values are expected to be lowered to improve energy conservation. Lower values imply better insulation.

V

vacuum-cleaning plant, centralized v.-c.p. Vacuum-cleaning plant, permanently installed in a building, consists of an exhauster fan and filter, usually in the *basement*, connected to all floors through a network of smooth-bore pipe (usually cold-drawn, hard-steel tube). The pipe diameter is fixed by the air velocity (15 to 24 m/sec (50 to 80 ft/sec)) and by the quantity ($2 \cdot 2$ m³ (80 ft³)) per minute for each operator cleaning bare floor. Such a performance can be achieved only by a fan working to the considerable suction of 17 kN/m² ($2\frac{1}{2}$ psi or 127 mm of mercury). For carpet cleaning, the air consumption is about $1 \cdot 1$ m³ (40 ft³) per minute. Hose outlets are so spaced that hoses from 6 to 12 m long (20 to 40 ft) can reach all the floor.

vacuum heating A steam-heating system for buildings in which a vacuum pump is connected to the return main. It removes condensate and air from the radiators and returns the water to the boiler feed tank (USA).

valley An intersection between two sloping surfaces of a roof, towards which water flows, the opposite of a *hip*. With *thatch, plain tiles* or *slates*, the valley can be continuous with the slopes, that is, there need be no sharp angle and no *valley gutter*. Valleys are vulnerable because they slope at an angle appreciably less than the main roof, yet carry water from two roof slopes. *See* **laced valley, swept valley, valley tile**.

valley board [carp.] A board about 28 × 2·5 cm (11 × 1 in.) fixed on and parallel to the *valley rafter*. It supports a *valley gutter* or slates or tiles in a *laced valley* or *swept valley*.

valley gutter A *gutter* lined with *flexible metal* in a *valley*, for example, a *secret gutter*. It may also be of concrete, precast, or cast in place.

valley jack (USA) A *jack rafter* which fits on to a *valley rafter* or *valley board*.

valley rafter The *rafter* which lies along the line of a *valley*, carrying a *valley board*. The *jack rafters* meet on it.

valley shingle A *shingle* laid next to the *valley*, cut so that its *grain* is parallel to the valley.

valley tile A specially large *tile*, concave upwards, shaped to form a *valley*

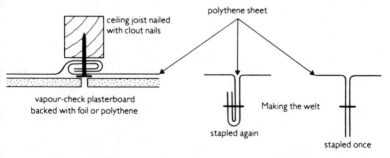

Vapour check of polythene sheet at ceiling level applied before fixing ceiling plasterboard. Many other methods exist, including the application of non-staining sealant to the underside of the ceiling joist, or painting the underside of the plasterboard with polyvinyl chloride emulsion paints, etc.

without *flexible metal* and without lacing or sweeping the tiles. They are not holed for nailing. Burnt clay valley tiles may be less well burnt than the *plain tiles* which course with them owing to the maker's fear of the tile warping when it is hard burnt. They may therefore not weather well.

value-added tax, VAT Under the Finance Act 1972, new buildings are zero-rated, and demolition work does not pay any VAT. Maintenance, repairs or improvements, however, pay VAT at the full rate. Details are obtainable from HM Customs and Excise.

value–cost contract [q.s.] A *cost-reimbursement contract* in which the *contractor* receives a larger fee when his final costs are low than when his final costs are high.

valve [mech.] A device to open or close a flow (stop valve or stopcock) or to regulate a flow (discharge valve).

vapour barrier An airtight skin, consisting of rubber-like paint, metal, roofing felt sheets, etc., bonded together to prevent *interstitial condensation*. A vapour barrier or *vapour check* placed on the inner, warm face of the plaster or other *insulator* should prevent all condensation but this should not be attempted until the structure is completely dry, one or two years after the completion of a brick and plaster wall.

vapour check An imperfect *vapour barrier*, sometimes intentionally so, e.g. foil-backed plasterboard without edge seals (p. 363). *See* **thermal wallboard, breather membrane**.

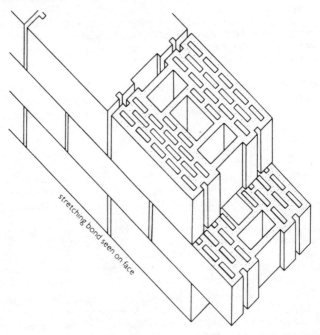

V-brick showing stretching bond.

vapour heating A steam heating system in which the condensate returns to the boiler by gravity. The pipes are at a pressure near atmospheric (USA). *Compare* **vacuum heating**.

variation order A written order from the *building owner* (represented by the consulting *architect* or engineer) authorizing an increase of the work above the amount shown in the *contract*.

varnish [pai.] A *resin*, asphalt, or pitch dissolved in oil or spirit, which dries in air to a brilliant, transparent, protective film. Varnishes are either oil varnishes that dry by oxidation of *drying oil*, or *spirit varnishes*. Varnish may be mixed with paint, put on over it to increase its *gloss*, or put on unpainted wood. *See* **lacquer**.

vault (1) A room or passage with a, usually, smooth, arched masonry roof, or the roof itself.

(2) A room below ground, of massive construction, for keeping valuables safe from fire and thieves.

vault light A *pavement light*.

V-brick A *perforated brick* 215 × 215 mm (8½ × 8½ in.) in plan and 65 mm (2½ in.) deep, with vertical cavities to make a one-brick wall equivalent in dryness and warmth to the 28 cm (11 in.) *cavity wall*. It was designed by the Building Research Station in 1958 but did not become popular although it is easier to build than a cavity wall. (Illus. p. 364)

vee joint (1) [joi.] A small chamfer on the face edge of *matchboards* made so that the two boards, when put together, form a V at their junction which masks shrinkage.

(2) A slight concave horizontal < formed in a mortar joint by *tooling*.

vee roof The shape formed by two *lean-to roofs* which meet at a *valley*.

vee tool [joi.] A *parting tool*.

vegetable glue [tim.] Glue made from starch or *cassava* or ground nuts or rape seed or a protein like *soya glue*.

vehicle The liquid in *paint*. *See* **medium**.

veneer (1) [tim.] A thin layer of wood of uniform thickness which may have been *sliced*, *rotary cut*, cut *half-round*, or *sawn*. It is used either as a facing, for its beauty of *figure*, to stronger, less beautiful wood or for its strength.

(2) (mainly USA) A layer of brick or marble or other facing outside a wall. The veneer looks well and resists the weather. *See* **brick veneer**, *and below*.

veneer cutter [tim.] A *tradesman*, who may decide on the method of cutting *veneer* from a log, whether by *slicing* or *rotary cutting*, but who in any case can set a knife and operate the machine. If he works a slicing machine, he is called a veneer slicer.

veneered stock [tim.] An early name for *plywood*.

veneered wall A wall having a *facing* attached to the backing that, not being bonded to it, cannot resist load equally with the facing. A veneered *brick* facing is attached to the backing across the cavity by *wall ties*, which may be of wire only 2·5 mm (0·1 in.) dia. If it is desired to count the strength of the facing with the backing, the two must be bonded without a cavity, by bricks. *See* **bonding brick, brick veneer, faced wall, veneer tie**.

veneering [tim.] Fixing a decorative *veneer* to a structural backing of wood, *plywood*, *hardboard*, etc.

veneer tie (USA) A *wall tie* for holding a *veneered wall* to its wood backing.

Venetian mosaic [plu.] *Terrazzo.*

Venetian red [pai.] Red iron oxide (Fe_2O_3), a *pigment* from Italy.

vent (1) An outlet for air and water vapour through a ventilating duct, *expansion pipe*, etc. In particular, roof screeds covered by a *damp course* need vents to allow the screed to dry out, with at least one vent pipe to every 20 m^2 (National Housebuilding Council). Roof insulation has failed because this precaution has been overlooked. *See below, also* **smoke outlet**.

(2) Glazier's term for a crack in a pane.

ventilating bead [joi.] A *deep bead.*

ventilating brick An *air brick.*

ventilation *See* **air change**.

ventilation pipe, vent stack, vent p. (USA **continuous vent**) A *soil drain* must be ventilated at its upper end by a pipe of at least 7·6 cm (3 in.) dia., which is often a continuation of the *soil stack. Waste pipes* also may need ventilating. *See* **anti-siphon pipe, fresh-air inlet, loop vent.**

ventilator, ventlight Any means of ventilating a room, such as a *night vent.*

vent pipe [plu.] An open-topped pipe to allow air and steam to escape from a *boiler* (BS 4118), often called the *expansion pipe.*

vent stack A vertical *ventilation pipe.*

verdigris Green basic acetate of copper formed as a protective *patina* over copper exposed to the air. It may be of any colour from brown to black in cities.

verge The edge of a sloping roof which overhangs a *gable*, sometimes including the bricks which cope the gable wall. The overhang of a slate or tile should not exceed 50 mm (2 in.) (BS 5534). *See also C and* **pitched roofs** (p. 279).

verge board, v. rafter A *barge board.*

verge fillet A *batten* fixed on a *gable* wall to the ends of the roof battens, as a neat finish beyond which roofing *shingles* overhang.

verge tile A *tile-and-a-half tile* used at the *verge* of a roof in alternate *courses.*

vermiculite A highly insulating, lightweight material made by heating a mica found in USA and South Africa. It is used in floor and roof screeds for its insulation and fire resistance. *See* **exfoliated vermiculite.**

vermiculite–gypsum plaster [pla.] For a 4-hour *fire grading* which ordinarily necessitates a 15 cm (6 in.) concrete slab with simple plaster ceiling, a 10 cm (4 in.) slab can be substituted, having a vermiculite–gypsum plaster ceiling 19 mm ($\frac{3}{4}$ in.) thick. This also greatly reduces the slab-and-plaster weight. The *pre-mixed plaster* is usually a 1·5 to 1 mix which weighs only 670 kg/m^3 (42 lb/ft^3).

vermilion [pai.] A brilliant red, slightly orange-coloured *pigment* composed of mercuric sulphide (HgS), the mineral cinnabar, which was used first in ancient China, but is now too expensive except in very small quantities.

vertical grain [tim.] The *edge grain* of *quarter-sawn* wood.

vertical shingling, weather s., hanging s. *Shingles* hung on a wall, like *tile hanging.*

vertical spindle moulder [tim.] A *spindle moulder.*

vertical tiling *See* **tile hanging**.

vestibule An important *lobby.*

vice (USA **vise**) A screwed metal or timber clamp fixed to a workbench and used for holding material being worked. *See* **chop.**

vinyl flooring Vinyl polymers are many but this usually means PVC, either vinyl asbestos tiles to BS 3260 or flexible vinyl tiles or sheet to BS 3261.

vision-proof glass *See* **obscured glass**.

vitreous enamel *See* **enamel**.

vitrified brick Bricks which have been surface glazed by beginning to melt in the kiln. *Hard-burnt* bricks may be vitrified.

vitrified clayware Drain pipes and fittings fired at about 1100° C, consequently vitrified right through. No surface glaze is needed on this hard *ceramic* (BS 65).

void former *See* C.

volatile [pai.] Literally that which flies away. It therefore describes *thinners* well.

volt [elec.] The unit of electrical pressure, related to the units of flow (amperes) and power (watts) in the following way: watts = volts × amperes.

voltage [elec.] Electrical pressure expressed in volts. The conventional descriptions are: high voltage, more than 650 volts; medium voltage, from 250 to 650 volts; low voltage, from 50 volts DC or 30 volts AC to 250 volts; extra low voltage, below 50 volts DC or 30 volts AC.

volume yield (1) The volume of *lime putty* of a stated consistency obtained from a stated weight of *quicklime*.

(2) The volume of *concrete* of a certain mix obtained from unit weight of *cement*.

voussoir An *arch-stone* in a stone arch or an *arch-brick* in a brick arch.

W

waffle floor *See C.*

wagtail [joi.] A *parting slip*.

wainscot, wainscoting [joi.] Wood panelling on boards up to *dado* height in a room.

wainscot oak [tim.] *Quarter-sawn* oak used for panelling. That used in Britain is usually imported from central Europe.

waist The narrow part of an object, in particular the least thickness of a reinforced-concrete *stair* slab. *See* **flight** (illus. p. 142).

walking line A setting-out line at 45 cm (18 in.) from the centre line of the handrail of a stair. Along this line the *going* of the *winders* is the same as that of the *fliers*.

walk-up apartment house (USA) A block of *flats* of four storeys or less, without a lift.

wall *See* **bond, loadbearing wall** (*C*), **panel wall, partition, party wall**.

wall anchor, joist a. [carp.] A steel strap screwed to the end of every second or third *common joist* and built into the brickwork to ensure that the joists give lateral support to the wall. It is fixed to the same joists as those to which the *strap anchors* are fixed.

wallboard *Building boards* made for surfacing, rather than for insulating ceilings and walls. Wallboards include *plywood*, *tapered-edge* and other *plasterboard*, and glossy *laminated plastics* glued to a backing of *hardboard* or plywood. Hardboards give some insulation, are fairly cheap, and much quicker to put up than matchboard, but most of them cannot be installed in a damp place such as a bathroom. *See also* **compressed straw slab, woodwool slab**.

wall box, beam b. A cast-iron box built into brickwork to provide a bearing for a timber beam or joist. *See* **wall hanger**.

wall column A steel stanchion or reinforced-concrete column partly within the thickness of a wall.

wall hanger A *joist hanger* built into a wall. *See* p. 189.

wall hook A spike or heavy nail driven into the mortar joint of a wall to carry a pipe or timber. Its head is specially shaped for the purpose. *See* **wall plate, fasteners** (illus. p. 130).

wall-hung boiler [plu.] A gas boiler mounted on a wall, of very light weight because of its low water content. Many are provided with *balanced flue*.

walling mason, waller A *mason* who sets stones in walls and bridges, cutting them to shape with a *scutch*.

wall joint A mortar *joint* parallel to the face of the wall.

wall panel *See* **panel wall**.

wallpaper Decorated printed paper sold in rolls for sticking on the plaster of walls. At least a *sealer* or *lining paper* should be put on new plaster to prevent it discolouring paper. A roll (or piece) of paper in Britain is 10 m × 53 cm (33 ft × 21 in.), in France 8·2 m × 46 cm (27 ft × 18 in.), in USA 7·3 m × 46 cm (24 ft × 18 in.).

wall plate (1) A horizontal timber along the top of a wall at *eaves* level. It carries the *rafters* or *joists*.

(2) **w. piece** A vertical timber in *raking shoring* held on to the shored wall by *wall hooks* and by short *needles* which pass through it into the wall. The shores bear on it under the needles (illus. p. 268).

UK rigid wall tie made of galvanized steel strip 19 × 5 mm (¾ × 3/16 in.) and 150–200 mm (6–8 in.) long.

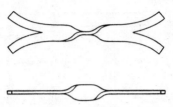

wall plug *See* **plug**.

wall string [joi.] The *string* on the side of a *stair* next the wall, as opposed to the *outer string*.

wall tie (1) **t. iron** A piece of twisted bronze or galvanized steel plate or wire built into the *bed joints*, across the cavity of a *cavity wall*, to hold the two leaves together. In USA wall ties are less carefully designed for their function of keeping water from the inner leaf than in Britain, and often consist of a straight bar which would not be acceptable in the British climate. *See also* **bonding brick, butterfly wall tie** (p. 53), **prefabricated tie, rectangular tie, veneer tie**, *also* BS 1243.

(2) (USA) Reinforcement placed in the bed joint of a brick or glass block wall parallel to its length.

wall tile [pla.] A tile of burnt clay, glazed or unglazed, *faience*, glass, concrete, *asbestos-cement, plastics*. which gives a decorative or smooth face to a wall when stuck to it. For internal walls the joints are filled with Keene's or similar *gypsum plasters*. Clay tiles are usually 15 or 10 cm (6 or 4 in.) square and about 1 cm (⅜ in.) thick. Plastics or glass tiles are thinner. The best background is a smooth *rendering* of cement mortar to which the tiles can be glued. It must be dry, therefore at least four weeks old, before glueing starts, unless the tiles are applied direct to the fresh rendering. Organic, cement-based and many other glues can be used. Cement beds are normally used only on mature concrete or brickwork (BS 5385).

walnut (Juglans regia), **European w.** [tim.] A decorative hardwood, mainly from southern Europe. The English variety has a finer *figure* and colour but is rare. Walnut is a wood with a grey background and dark, sometimes ruddy streaks, used for carving, turnery, and *veneers*, in which its *burrs* and *crotches* are valued.

wane, waney edge [tim.] Bark or the rounded surface under the bark, on sawn timber.

ware pipes Pipes of *vitrified clayware*.

warm air heating [plu.] A *central heating* method introduced in Britain in the 1950s with small so-called selective heaters of about 6 kilowatts capacity. They are now made as large as any other unit and are heated by any fuel. All types use a *heat exchanger* and an electric fan.

warm roof (illus. p. 370). *See* **cold roof**.

warning pipe [plu.] An overflow pipe from a *cistern*, which discharges overflow water into the open so as to show up this plumbing fault. *See* **expansion pipe**.

warp [tim.] Any distortion of timber during seasoning such as *cup, bow, spring*, and *twist*, always caused by changing *moisture content*.

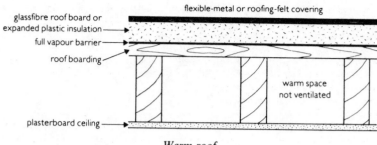

Warm roof.

Warrington hammer A *joiner's hammer*.

wash (USA) A weathered slope or *weathering*.

washability [pai.] The ability of a coat of *paint* to withstand washing without damage, including the ease of removal of dirt.

washboard (USA) A *skirting board*.

washer (1) [plu.] A flat ring made of rubber or plastics or leather or fibre, which is held by a nut to the underside of the *jumper* of a water tap to make it watertight.

(2) *See C.*

(3) *See* **diamond w., limpet w.**

washleather glazing Bedding of glass in washleather instead of putty, commonly used for swing doors; the fixing is by *glazing fillet*.

waste (1) (USA) Building rubbish.

(2) All dirty water except rainwater, and *soil*. It usually means *sullage*, but includes industrial wastes.

(3) [q.s.] The space in the description column of *dimensions paper*, in which *collections* and calculations are entered.

waste-disposal unit [plu.] A small electrically driven (0·5 hp) rubbish grinder placed near a kitchen sink, into which all garbage can be disposed of down the drain, as in the *Garchey sink*.

waste mould [pla.] A mould for fibrous plaster used once only and then destroyed.

waste pipe [plu.] A pipe to carry water away from a basin, bath, or sink. It is trapped at its exit from the basin. An *access eye* at the *trap* enables blockages to be cleared.

waste preventer, w. water p. [plu.] A flushing *cistern*.

waster (1) A *facing brick* with minor defects which allow it to be used as a backing brick.

(2) A *mason*'s chisel, either one with claw cutting edge for removing waste stone or a 19 mm (¾ in.) wide chisel. *See* **mason's tools and bricklayer's tools** (illus. p. 211).

waste table A *water table*.

wasting Removing excess stone with a *waster* before dressing a stone block. *See* **picking**.

water bar A galvanized steel bar 25 × 6 mm (1 × ¼ in.), bedded on edge in a groove filled with white lead, on the stone or concrete *sill* of an opening. It fits a corresponding groove under the sill of the fixed wooden frame. It prevents draughts and water passing into the gap between sills during storms. Modern *sealing compounds* are superseding water bars.

water channel A *condensation groove* in a *patent glazing* bar.

water check A kerb standing above a *flat roof*.

water-checked casement [joi.] A *casement* having *sill* and *meeting stile* grooved to break any possible *capillary* path for water.

water content *See* **moisture content**.

water gauge [plu.] A *U-gauge*.

water joint A *saddle joint*.

water level An instrument for setting out levels on a building site. It is a rubber hose filled with water, connecting two vertical glass tubes. If there are no air bubbles or other blockages in the hose, the level of the water surface in the two tubes will be the same.

water paint Paints that can be thinned by water. Some types were bound by an emulsified oil. They are being superseded by *emulsion paints*.

water pipe Water supply pipes are usually of dead mild steel or cast iron, or, for small diameters, also copper or plastics. Large iron or steel mains are lined internally with 3 to 6 mm ($\frac{1}{8}$ to $\frac{1}{4}$ in.) of bitumen or with up to 25 mm (1 in.) of cement mortar for protection against corrosion. Buried pipes are covered outside with asphalt. *See* **fittings, light-gauge copper tube**.

waterproofing Asphalt *tanking* or other waterproof skins of bituminous material over a wall are the only certain methods of waterproofing walls and floors, apart from the provision of an air gap between the wall and the source of damp. *Integral waterproofers* are occasionally effective, but most concretes can be made waterproof by careful grading, mixing, and placing without any admixture. *See* **watertight basements**.

waterproof paper *Building paper*.

water-reducing admixture A *plasticizer*.

water-repellent treatment, surface waterproofer A paint, cement slurry or other liquid brushed or sprayed over a wall to reduce its absorption of rain. The effect is to increase the flow of water over the wall since less is absorbed. This increases the chances of water entering large cracks and these should therefore be carefully pointed before the treatment. Modern water repellents are often silicone resins dissolved in paraffin or similar solvents, or silicone emulsions or siliconates in water. Ten years is their expected life but the surface effect dies off quickly. They cannot be used as tanking below ground, nor in any other way to resist water under pressure. They should never be applied to indoor wall surfaces of stone which is flaking because they might aggravate the defect. Outside application might help. *See* **injection of a damp course, waterproofing**, *also* B S 3826 *and* B R E Digest 125.

water retentivity A property of *mortar* which prevents it losing water rapidly to bricks with high *absorption rate*. It also prevents water coming to the surface when the mortar touches *vitrified* or other bricks with low absorption. It thus allows mortar to develop good bond and high strength with every sort of brick. *See* **masonry cement**.

water seal [plu.] The *seal* in a *trap*.

water seasoning [tim.] Soaking timber for fourteen days and then air-drying it.

watershot walling *Dry walling* with stones laid sloping so that water falling on them pours to the outside of the wall. Walling is often built like this in the English Lake District where the rainfall is about 3·7 m (150 in.) per year.

water softener [plu.] A chemical unit that treats water in such a way that soap lathers easily in it. It removes the calcium and magnesium salts called hardness, which produce *furring* in pipes, kettles, and boilers. The best known types are *base exchange* softeners. For domestic use, some chemical manufacturers now produce a low-cost water softener consisting merely of a metal basket that hangs in the cold water tank, and contains crystals of low solubility. The crystals have to be replaced every six months. They discourage furring but cannot remove scale that is already deposited.

water spotting [pai.] Pale spots on a paint film caused by drops of water on the surface. They may or may not be permanent.

water stain [tim.] (1) A discoloration (which may improve the *figure* of the wood) caused by *converted timber* getting wet.

(2) Colouring matter dissolved in water and applied to wood to accentuate the grain. *See* **spirit stain**.

water table, earth t., watershed, offshoot, canting strip A board or masonry projection fixed to the foot of a wall (particularly if it is weather-boarded) to shoot water away from it.

water test [plu.] The *hydraulic test* (*C*).

watertight basements Concrete basements of many government buildings have been made watertight on the basis of designs by structural engineers of the Department of the Environment, especially since the 1950s. Any basement built of good concrete can be made watertight. Leaks can be blocked by drilling the concrete near them and pressure grouting it with *epoxy* or cement grouts. This is surer and cheaper than tanking but it is not vapour-proof. Consequently lino laid on the floor may become damp underneath.

water-waste preventer [plu.] The *cistern* which flushes a W C.

wavy grain [tim.] A curly attractive *grain* often seen in *birch, mahogany*, and sycamore.

wayleave A permission to pass over land, which may sometimes include leave to lay cables, pipes, etc.

weather The amount measured along the slope, by which a *shingle* overlaps the next shingle but one below it. It is the same as the *lap* of a *centre-nailed* slate.

weather bar (1) A term occasionally used for *water bar*.

(2) A water and draught excluder for an inward-opening *casement*. *See* **weather strip**.

weather-board [joi.] A *weather moulding*, but *see below*.

weather-boarding, weather boards (U S A **siding**) [tim.] Horizontal boards on edge, nailed over the outside of light buildings. The boards overlap, often with a rebate at the lower edge of each board, to help keep out rain and wind. *See* **clapboard, shiplap boards**.

weathercock, weathervane A pivoted ornamental *finial* which turns with the wind to show which way it is blowing.

weathered *See* **weathering**.

weathered pointing *Weather-struck joints*.

weather fillet A *cement fillet*.

weathering (1) (U S A **wash**) A slight slope to throw off rainwater.

(2) A change in colour of the surface of a building material after exposure to rain and sun.

(3) [tim.] The mechanical and chemical break-up of a wood surface exposed to rain and sun. It is not *decay*.

(4) *See* **double-skin roof**.

weather joint A *weather-struck joint*.

weather moulding, w. board [joi.] A moulding housed into the bottom *rail* of an outside door to throw water off the *threshold*. It includes a *drip*.

weather-proof glues These include phenolic, resorcinol and perhaps melamine resins. Other *synthetic resins* are, however, at least weather resistant, even if not quite weather-proof.

weather shingling *Vertical shingling*.

weather slating *Slate hanging* (vertical slating).

weather strip, wind stop (USA **air lock**) A piece of metal, wood, rubber, or other material which stops the draught passing the joints of a closed door or window.

weather-struck joint, struck j., struck-j. pointing A mortar *joint* smoothed off by pressing the trowel in at the upper edge so as to throw rain out to the face of the *brick*. This work can be done as the walls go up and is therefore more durable than *pointing*.

weather tiling *Tile hanging* (vertical tiling).

weathervane A *weathercock*.

weaving (USA **Boston hip**) Laying *shingles* on adjoining surfaces of a wall or roof so that shingles on each face lap each other alternately. This provides a weathered angle at a *ridge*, *hip*, or corner of a wall.

webbing [pai.] The wrinkling in *gas-checking*, sometimes desirable.

wedge A tapered piece of wood, used in timbering or centering, e.g. a *folding wedge*. *See also* C.

wedge coping A *feather-edged coping*.

weephole A small drain hole for water. One is drilled through a wooden window sill to allow *condensation* water to escape; *cross joints* in the outer leaf of a cavity wall are left without mortar at intervals, etc. *See area* (p. 23), *also* C.

weight box [joi.] The space for the sash weights in a *cased frame*.

weighting out [q.s.] Multiplying out to obtain quantities in tons or other weight unit, for the *extended prices*.

well (1) The space (horizontal distance) between the *flights* of a *stair*. Some stairs have no well in this sense.

(2) **wellhole, liftshaft** The open space passing through one or more floors for a lift or stair.

Welsh arch (USA **jack arch**) A small opening, less than about 30 cm (12 in.) span, bridged by a *stretcher* cut to a wedge shape, resting on two *corbelled* bricks or stones of matching shape.

Welsh groin An *underpitch groin*.

welt A *seam* in *flexible-metal roofing*.

welted drip *Roofing felt* turned down at an *eave* or *verge* to make a *drip*, folded back on the roof and continuously sealed.

welted nosing A junction of *flexible-metal roofing* between a vertical sheet and a horizontal sheet. They are folded together and dressed down at the top of the vertical surface.

welting strip A *tingle*.

western framing [carp.] *Platform framing*.

western method (USA) Bricklaying by *buttering*.

western red cedar [tim.] (Thuja plicata) Also called British Columbia cedar, giant cedar, and Pacific red cedar. A straight-grained, coarse, soft, weak *soft-*

wood, very useful for making *shingles* and cheap *joinery*. Shingles made of it have a reddish-brown colour which weathers to grey. The wood contains an aromatic oil which repels insects and rot. It splits easily and shingles were originally made from it by splitting, but are now usually sawn. The least yearly treatment outside is a coat of a linseed oil-paraffin wax solution containing a fungicide.

Westmorland slates Thick heavy random slates which can be walked on without breaking. They are from 6 to 16 mm ($\frac{1}{4}$ to $\frac{5}{8}$ in.) thick, of a pleasing green colour, with a chipped edge that gives a satisfactory rough texture to a roof.

wet-and-dry paper [pai.] Emery cloth. *See* **glasspaper**.

wet on wet [pai.] Painting with special paints in which one coat is sprayed on to another before the first has dried.

wet rot [tim.] Decay of timber in alternate wet and dry conditions, caused by fungi such as Coniophora cerebella, Poria vaillantii or other Poria. Unlike *dry rot* it does not spread into neighbouring timber. Certain hardwoods (oak, teak, utile, gurjun, agba) and the *heartwood* of softwoods resist wet rot but it is usually impossible to buy softwood that is heartwood only. *See* **moisture content**.

wet sanding [pai.] Where dry sanding produces harmful dust, wet sanding produces none and is just as effective.

wet sprinkler *See* **sprinkler system**.

wet time The smaller-than-usual payment which men receive when they report for work on a site where work is stopped because of bad weather.

wet trades *Trades* that use concrete, mortar or plaster, excluded from *dry construction* except for the concrete base for the house and the drains beneath it.

wheelbarrow A wooden, steel, or *light-alloy* container with a single steel or rubber-tyred wheel in front and two hand-holds behind, by which it is lifted and pushed forward. It carries 60 to 70 litres (2 to $2\frac{1}{2}$ ft^3) of material, of which the man lifts about a quarter.

wheeling step, wheel s. Scots for *winder*.

whetstone A stone used for sharpening cutting tools. It is sometimes a gritty slate containing garnet or a quartz rock with cavities which are abrasive.

whip A steel-wire *bond* (*C*) for use as a crane *sling* (*C*) or lashing.

white cement *Portland cement* which has been selected and ground without contamination by iron (the green colour of ordinary cement) or to which *white pigment* has been added. It can be used as cheap, durable but dirty white paint for masonry.

white coat [pla.] A *finishing coat.*

white lead [pai.] An opaque but not very brilliant *white pigment* in the best *undercoats* for exterior work. Although poisonous, it was used as a cosmetic in ancient Greece. It consists of basic lead carbonate ($2PbCO_3 \cdot Pb(OH)_2$), sometimes basic lead sulphate. *See* **lead paint, titanium dioxide**.

white lime *See* **high-calcium lime**.

whitening in the grain [pai.] A streaky white unpleasant appearance which is sometimes seen in varnished or polished woods with *coarse texture*, whether filled or not.

white pigments [pai.] The commonest white *pigments* are *antimony oxide, basic lead sulphate, leaded zinc oxide, titanium white, white lead, whiting, zinc oxide.*

white spirit, turpentine substitute [pai.] A thinner for *oil paint*, distilled from petroleum at about 150° to 200° C.

whitewash [pai.] *See* **limewash, whiting**.

whitewood [tim.] (Picea abies and Abies alba) **White deal, yellow pine, white pine, common spruce, Norway spruce**. A soft, light, general purpose timber described under *silver fir*.

whiting, Paris white [pai.] Crushed chalk, the cheapest *white pigment*, used as an *extender* or for making *glazier's putty*.

Whitworth screw thread [mech.] A British *screw thread*, used in building but being superseded by metric threads.

whole-brick wall A wall whose thickness is the length of one *brick*, about 23 cm (9 in.) in Britain.

whole timber [tim.] A square *baulk*, usually about 30 × 30 cm (12 × 12 in.).

wide-ringed timber, coarse- or **open-grained t.** Timber with *annual rings* which are far apart. It has grown quickly and is known as coarse growth. In *softwoods, narrow-ringed timber* is stronger, but not always in *hardwoods*.

wiggle nail [carp.] A *corrugated fastener*.

Winchester cutting The intersection between *tile hanging* and a *verge*. The two tiles at the ends of each course are splay cut so that each cut tile has one nail hole left for fixing.

wind, winding [tim.] The twist of converted timber. *See* **warp**.

wind beam A *collar beam. See also C*.

winder, wheel step A *tread* of triangular or wedge shape, changing the direction of a *stair. See* **balanced step**.

wind filling *See* **beam filling**.

winding [tim.] *See* **wind**.

winding stair (1) A *spiral stair*.

(2) A circular or elliptical *geometric stair*.

winding strips, w. sticks Two short straight edges about 45 cm (18 in.) long and 5 cm (2 in.) wide, tapering in thickness from 8 to 3 mm ($\frac{5}{16}$ to $\frac{1}{8}$ in.). They are used for setting out a plane surface on wood or stone by *boning* (*C*).

window, sash Windows are usually either side-hinged on vertical hinges (*casements*) or they slide up and down (*sash windows*). Other less usual windows are *sliding sashes*, pivoted sashes, *night vents, hopper windows. See also* **dead light, opening light, roof light**.

window back [joi.] The vertical panelling, *matchboarding*, or other *joinery* between the floor and the *window*.

window bar [joi.] A *glazing bar*.

window bead A *sash stop*.

window board, w. sill, elbow b. (USA **stool**) [joi.] A horizontal board fixed like a shelf at sill level inside a window. It was always wooden, but now may be of pressed steel.

window efficiency ratio The *daylight factor*.

window frame [joi.] The part of a *window* surrounding the *casements* or *sashes*, in which they hinge or slide as the case may be.

window glass *See* **sheet glass**.

window lock [joi.] A *sash fastener*.

window sill, w. ledge A flat stone that extends for the full width outside the window opening and often wider. It should be firmly bedded on mortar only at its ends, otherwise the inevitable settlement of the building may break it.

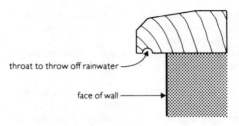

Window sill.

Its outer edge slopes down and overlaps the wall about 7 cm (2¾ in.), enabling a throat cut under it to throw the water clear of the wall. Sills can also be made of brick, tile, timber, precast concrete or pressed steel. (Illus. above)

window stile [joi.] A *pulley stile*.

window stool [joi.] (USA) A *window board*.

wind shake [tim.] *Ring shake*.

wind stop A *weather strip*.

wing (1) Part of a building projecting from one side of the body of the building.
   (2) Heavy slates each side of a *slate ridge* covered by a slate roll.

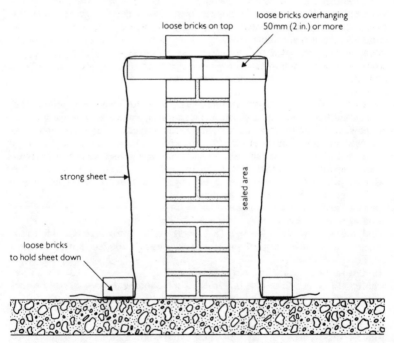

Protection of newly laid brickwork against frost by the warm air space created under a polythene sheet.

(3) In *patent glazing*, a leaden or aluminium part of the sides of a *glazing bar*, that bears on the glass to exclude water. Aluminium wings also restrain the glass.

wing compasses [joi.] *Quadrant dividers* adjusted by a *wing nut* on the quadrant stay.

winglight [joi.] A *flanking window*.

wing nut, thumb screw [mech.] A nut which can be turned by hand without a spanner. Wings outside it can be gripped with the fingers.

winter working For safe concreting at air temperatures below +2° C., aggregates may be heated up to 50° C. and water to 80° C. Cement should not be heated. Placed concrete should be kept warm, between +2° and +27° C. until it has hardened appreciably. Precautions for bricklaying are similar but for walls even more care is needed because they are usually more exposed to cold winds than slabs. Plastering on frozen backgrounds is forbidden but work during frost is possible subject to precautions like those for concreting. (Illus. p. 376)

wiped joint [plu.] A joint made with *plumber's solder* between lead pipes of which one is widened with a *boxwood tampin* and the other tapered down to be inserted in it. The *solder* is poured on molten and moulded round the pipes as it cools, with a cotton (moleskin) wiping cloth, so that as the more-fluid solder drops out of the bottom of the joint it is wiped back to the top. The *blow lamp* was not available in ancient times and the joints wiped 2000 years ago were heated over an open fire, the solder being held in a ladle.

wiping cloth *See* **plumber's tools** (illus. p. 250) and **wiped joint**.

wiping seal A seal against cold draughts, usually a flexible strip of rubber along the edge of a door, that presses against the door frame or threshold. Other types exist, e.g. those made by a long brush with short bristles, fixed to the door edge.

wire comb [pla.] A *drag*.

wirecut bricks Bricks which are shaped by *extrusion* (*C*). A long bar of clay is thus formed which is cut into bricks by a set of wires 23 cm (9 in.) apart attached to a frame. They are cheaper and less dense than *pressed bricks*, and have no *frog*. (Illus. below)

wired glass *Safety glass* in which wire mesh is used as reinforcement to hold the pieces together if it breaks. It is used for *roof lights* or for glass screens in gardens.

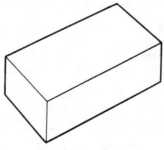

Wirecut brick.

wire gauge [mech.] A method of defining wire diameter by a number which stated originally the number of passes through different, increasingly smaller dies, to make the wire. The number for large wire is therefore smaller than that for thin wire. The commonest gauge used in Britain is the *Standard Wire Gauge* or SWG but many other gauges exist in Britain and USA. The Paris wire gauge increases with the wire diameter, unlike English-speaking countries. *See* **cold drawing** (*C*).

wire nail A *nail* made by cutting and shaping a piece of round or elliptical steel wire. (Brass wire is used for escutcheon pins, and other expensive metals for *roofing nails*.) Steel nails in exposed places are galvanized or *sherardized*. The commonest are round wire nails stocked in sizes from 25×1.6 mm to 150×5.9 mm, oval wire brads from 19 to 100 mm long, and clout nails, usually galvanized, from 19×2.6 mm to 50×3.7 mm.

wire scratcher [pla.] A *devil float*.

wiring regulations [elec.] In Britain wiring regulations are issued mainly by the Institution of Electrical Engineers in consultation with the Department of Industry but also by the Factory Inspectorate. Many electrical codes and standards are issued by the *BSI*.

withdrawal load [carp.] *Wire nails* driven across the grain are considered to have a safe pulling resistance of about 4.3 kg per cm length per 2.5 mm dia.

withe (1) **mid feather** (Britain) A half-brick wall such as a *partition* between chimney *flues*.

(2) **wythe, tier** (USA) One leaf of a *cavity wall* or *hollow wall* or a half-brick thickness of a wall bonded into solid brickwork.

withies or **osiers** Flexible sticks like those used for basket-making, cut every two years from willow trees. Several are twisted into a cable for tying *reed* on to rafters in thatching. *See* **runner**.

wobble saw [tim.] A *drunken saw*.

wood [tim.] *Blockboard, laminated wood, plywood, timbers*, etc.

wood-block floor, w.-b. paving Wooden flooring blocks are usually tongued and grooved, vary from 19 to 38 mm ($\frac{3}{4}$ to 1.5 in.) thick, up to 90 mm (3.5 in.) wide, and in length from 150 to 380 mm (6 to 15 in.) They should not be brought into the building until glazing, plastering and the heating plant are completed, so as to enable the blocks to acquire the moisture content they will have in the floor, before they are laid. Gluing down to the concrete originally was with hot tar, which formed a good *damp course*, but other glues are now also used. Many types exist, from the smallest of only 25 mm (1 in.) cube, to *parquet floor, plywood parquet*, and *mosaic parquet*. *See* **parquet-floor layer**.

wood borer [joi.] A slow reversible power tool which drills a hole with an *auger bit*.

wood-casing system, casing or **moulding s.** [elec.] An old method of interior wiring in grooves in wood strips which are later covered by strips called capping.

wood-cement particle board [tim.] A particle board bonded with cement, that is consequently more fire-resistant than resin-bonded *wood chipboard*. It also loses less strength on alternate wetting and drying than other UK types bonded with urea-formaldehyde glue.

wood chipboard, resin-bonded c. Artificial boards 1.2 m (4 ft) wide and of any length, made by compressing wood waste with *synthetic resin* glues. The longest stocked are 3·7 m (12 ft) long. They have been used more for making furniture than for *carpentry* because of their low strength and stiffness, the *modulus of elasticity* (*C*) being only one third that of wood. The *moisture movement* is as high as wood and not always 100% recoverable. Because of their good fire resistance and airtightness with tongued and grooved edges all round they have superseded wood in some applications for flooring but not in damp places. U K consumption increased twentyfold between 1960 and 1980 (B R E Digest 239, B S 5669).

wood-cutting machinist [tim.] A craftsman who sets and operates every type of *circular saw* and *band saw*.

wood element [tim.] A wood cell, botanically called xylem.

wood flour [tim.] Fine sawdust, sometimes used as an *extender* for glues. It is also used in explosives, *plastic wood*, and so on.

wood lath [pla.] *See* **lath**.

wood mosaic *See* **mosaic parquet panels**.

wood ray [tim.] *Ray*.

wood roll A piece of wood, usually round-topped, fixed on to roof boarding to enable *flexible-metal roofing* sheets to be lapped over it.

wood screw [joi.] An ordinary *screw* for fixing into wood.

wood slip A *fixing fillet*.

wood turner [tim.] A *tradesman* who works to drawings, setting the wood in a lathe, and marking the parts to be cut. He works the lathe, cutting the wood with *gouges* and *chisels*.

woodwool nailing slab A *woodwool slab* with a 6 × 2 cm (2½ × ¾ in.) timber let into the face along the centre of the slab.

woodwool slab Slabs 2·5 to 10 cm (1 to 4 in.) thick, of long-fibre wood shavings compressed and bound together with cement. This cheap, lightweight, fire-resisting insulating material was first made in Austria in 1914. Most boards are 60 cm (2 ft) wide and lengths can be up to 3·8 m (12 ft). *See* **reinforced woodwool**.

woodworking machinist [tim.] In Britain, a *tradesman* with considerable experience, capable of setting and operating every woodworking machine except, possibly, a *spindle moulder*, which is a specialist's machine. For woodworking machines see B S 3997, 4361.

workability (1) [tim.] The labour of working hard dense timber with twisted grain may be five times as much as for soft, light timber with straight grain. The following table gives the rough order of workability of some well-known timbers, the least workable first.

6. Lignum vitae
5. Ebony, greenheart
4. English oak
3. Ash, beech, makore, Japanese oak
2. Pitchpine, larch, redwood
1. Spruce, poplar

    (2) For the workability of concrete *see* *C*.

    (3) [pla.] The *plasticity* of a mix, its cohesiveness, and its *water retentivity* against the *suction* of the background.

work or **working edge** [joi.] (U S A) The *face edge* of timber.

work or **working face** [joi.] (USA) The *face side* of timber.

working [tim.] Swelling and shrinkage of timber as the relative humidity of the air becomes higher (in winter) or lower (in summer).

working life [tim.] The *pot life* of a glue.

working up [q.s.] *Squaring* quantities and adding them.

worm hole [tim.] Any hole bored by insects such as *beetles* in timber, whether *shot hole, powder-post* damage, or *pinhole*.

wreath [joi.] That part of a handrail which is curved both in plan and in elevation. It occurs in every *geometric stair*.

wreath piece, wreathed string [joi.] The curved part of the *outer string* below a *wreath*.

wrecking (USA) Demolition.

wrecking bar A *pinch bar*.

wrench [mech.] A spanner, usually adjustable. *See also* **pipe wrench**.

wrinkle [tim.] An unglued area caused by failure of a *veneer* to slip into place.

wrinkle finish, wrinkling [pai.] A *finish* with intentional wrinkles made during drying, usually by *stoving*. *See* **webbing**.

writer (1) **signwriter, glass painter, letterer, advertisement painter** [pai.] A *tradesman* who paints signs for shop fronts either in the workshop or on the site. He uses a palette, *sable pencils*, and other artists' tools, sketching the outline first in chalk. He can make his own stencils and may also do gilding and silvering.

(2) *See* **sable writer**.

writing short [q.s.] Placing *items* out of their proper category in a *bill of quantities*; they are often small items, for example *shoes* (1) (priced each) with *downpipes* (priced per metre length).

wrot [joi.] Abbreviation for *wrought timber*, common in British *bills of quantities*.

wrought nail A wrought iron *nail* with a head forged to a rounded 'rose' shape. It can be bent over and clenched like a wire nail but is now less used than *wire nails*.

wrought timber, wrot t., surfaced t. [joi.] Timber which has been planed on one or more surfaces.

wye, Y (USA **yoke**) [plu.] A branch pipe leading off a straight main *run* usually at 45° to the run.

wythe *See* **withe**.

X

X-mark [joi.] *See* **face mark**.
xylem [tim.] The botanical name for wood.
xylol [pai.] A *solvent* for *synthetic resins* and gums. distilled from coal tar.

Y

Y *See* **wye**.

Yale lock [joi.] A common *cylinder lock*.

Yankee gutter, g. strip (USA) [carp.] A wooden *gutter*, lined with *flexible metal* and built directly on the *boarding* of a *pitched roof* near the *eaves*. The metal is held in place by an upright board near the edge of the roof.

Yankee screwdriver A quick-action screwdriver with a steep thread cut on the shaft. This thread causes the screw to be turned when the handle is pushed home. For wood screws, this tool acts better screwing in than out. *See* **carpenter's tools** (illus. p. 59).

yard An *area*.

yardage [q.s] A volume of earth excavated or filled, measured in cubic yards, or an area in square yards or a length in yards.

yard lumber [tim.] (USA) *Lumber* graded according to its size, length, and intended use, stocked in a lumber yard. *See* **dimension lumber**.

year ring [tim.] An *annual ring*.

yellow pine [tim.] *See* **whitewood**.

yelm, yelven A double handful of *reeds* or *straw* laid on the roof as *thatch*.

yield *See* **volume yield**.

yoke (1) *See* **pulley head**.

(2) [plu.] *See* **wye**.

Yorkshire bond *See* **monk bond**.

yorky A *slate* with a curved cleavage.

Z

zax, sax, slater's axe, slate knife, chopper, whittle A straight blade like a butcher's chopper with a point projecting from the back for punching holes in *slates*. *See* **plasterer's tools** (illus. p. 246).

Z-bar, zee-bar (USA) A Z-shaped bar used as a *wall tie*.

zee American pronunciation of Z, pronounced 'zed' in Britain and Australia.

zein [pai.] A protein from maize. When dissolved in alcohol it gives a tough *film* which has partly replaced *shellac* in USA.

zeolites Minerals used in *water softeners* that function by *base exchange*.

zig-zag rule, folding r. A rule made of wood or metal pieces 15 cm (6 in.) long, pivoted together at each end, not hinged like the *fourfold rule. Compare* **push-pull rule**.

zinc A metal used in *flexible-metal roofing*, also as a protective coating to corrugated steel sheet in *galvanized iron* (C) and to smaller articles in *sherardizing*. Zinc is attacked by tar or by copper, iron, or steel in contact with it and it is therefore in roofing fixed direct to wood. British sizes of zinc sheet are up to 2·4 by 0·9 m (8 by 3 ft), in thicknesses from 0·6 to 1·0 mm. Zinc gauge thicknesses are not the same as *standard wire gauge. See also* **metal coating**.

zinc chromes [pai.] Bright yellow *pigments* which may contain alkali chromates (potassium chromate) but are mostly zinc chromate ($ZnCrO_4$) combined with some zinc hydroxide. *Lead chromes* are affected by hydrogen sulphide (H_2S).

zinc drier [pai.] The most important zinc *drier* is zinc naphthenate, which is used to prevent *wrinkling* in *stoving*. It is also a preservative for wood.

zinc dust [pai.] Powdered zinc, used in *priming* paints on galvanized iron.

zinc oxide, z. white, Chinese white [pai.] (ZnO) A permanent *white pigment* which prevents *chalking* in other pigments but may cause *feeding* in an unsuitable medium. It is not poisonous. *See* **leaded zinc oxides**.

zipper strip A stiff rubber strip inserted into a glazing *gasket* after the glass has been placed in it, so as to tighten its hold on the glass.

zoning The reservation under the master plan of certain areas of land for certain uses and the enforcement of these uses by restrictions on building types, heights, and sizes. In this way some areas can be kept for light industry, others for heavy industry, dwellings, offices, shops, and so on, each area being called a zone. *See* **local authority, noise**.